THE HISTORY OF THE FALLSCHIRMPANZERKORPS HERMANN GÖRING

SOLDIERS OF THE REICHSMARSCHALL

by

Franz Kurowski

Cover Art
by
Brian Molloy

Translated
by
David Johnston

THE HISTORY OF THE FALLSCHIRMPANZERKORPS HERMANN GÖRING
SOLDIERS OF THE REICHSMARSCHALL

by Franz Kurowski

Translated by David Johnston

Published by
J.J. Fedorowicz Publishing Inc.
106 Browning Blvd.
Winnipeg, Manitoba
Canada R3K 0L7
(204) 837-6080

Copyright 1995

Printed in Canada
ISBN 0-921991-25-8

Typesetting by George Bradford Type & Design
Printed by FRIESEN PRINTERS

J.J. Fedorowicz Publishing Inc.

PUBLISHER'S ACKNOWLEDGEMENTS

We wish to thank the following friends who have contributed to the publishing of this book.

David Johnston – Translation
George Rugenius – Proof Reading
Shawn Biettner – Proof Reading
Brian Molloy – Cover Art
Brian Molloy – Signing Box Art

We also wish to thank you the reader for purchasing this book, and all those of you who have purchased our other books, and have written us with your kind words of praise and encouragement. It gives us impetus to continue to publish translations of the best German books and specially commissioned books, as you can see by the additional books which are in preparation for publication in the near future. Other titles are either being negotiated or seriously contemplated, many as a result of your helpful proposals. Such proposals have also motivated us to pursue the start of a serious military art print series, focusing on the Waffen-SS and German armor. More on these in the near future, further suggestions are always welcome.

John Fedorowicz & Michael Olive

Books published by J.J. Fedorowicz Publishing
    THE LEIBSTANDARTE (1 SS Panzer Division) volumes I, II, III and IV/1
    EUROPEAN VOLUNTEERS (5 SS Panzer Division)
    DAS REICH I (2 SS Panzer Division)
    THE HISTORY OF PANZERKORPS GROSSDEUTSCHLAND I
    OTTO WEIDINGER
    OTTO KUMM
    MANHAY, THE ARDENNES; CHRISTMAS 1944
    TIGER; THE HISTORY OF A LEGENDARY WEAPON 1942-45
    HITLER MOVES EAST
    TIGERS IN THE MUD
    PANZER ACES
    FOOTSTEPS OF THE HUNTER
    HISTORY OF THE 12 SS PANZERDIVISION HITLERJUGEND
    GRENADIERS (Kurt Meyer)
    FIELD UNIFORMS OF THE GERMAN ARMY PANZER FORCES IN WW2
    TIGERS IN COMBAT 1
    INFANTERIE ACES
    FREINEUX AND LAMORMENIL – THE ARDENNES
    THE CAUCASUS AND THE OIL
    DAS REICH II
    THE HISTORY OF THE FALLSCHIRMPANZERKORPS HERMANN GÖRING

In preparation for publication
    EAST FRONT DRAMA 1944
    LUFTWAFFE ACES
    THE HISTORY OF PANZERKORPS GROSSDEUTSCHLAND II
    HISTORY OF 7 SS MOUNTAIN DIVISION PRINZ EUGEN
    WESTERN FRONT 1944: MEMOIRS OF A PANZER LEHR OFFICER

Table of Contents

INDEX

I. PEACETIME 1
The Origins of the Hermann Göring Units 1
From Guard Company to Guard Battalion –Further New Formations 5
List of Command Positions as of 1 October 1937 6
The Southern Cross 10
The Regiment's Guard Duties in Berlin and at Karinhall 10
The Outpost Positions 14
The General Göring Regiment and the German Parachute Troops 15
Operation "Otto" – The German March into Austria 17
The Occupation of Bohemia and Moravia 19

II. THE GENERAL GÖRING REGIMENT AT WAR
Final Preparations 37
War Zone Germany 38
The 14th Railway Flak Battalion 39
The "Führer" Flak Train in the Polish Campaign 40
The General Göring Regiment 1939-1940 41
Operation "Weserübung" 44
Action in Norway 46
Advances from Oppdal to Sunndalsöra and Kristiansund 52
In Support of the Dietl Group at Narvik 52
The General Göring Regiment in France 54
The General Göring Regiment in the Air Defense of Berlin 66
Action in the Balkans 66
The General Göring Regiment in Action
   from 22 June to 25 November, 1941 73
The General Göring Regiment in Action against Russian Tank Forces 76
Operations by 16th Company, RGG in the Sverdlinko Area
   on 2 August, 1941 77
In Action – 6th Battery, General Göring Regiment 79
The Luftwaffe's II Special-Purpose Rifle Battalion
   (Neubauer Battalion) in the East 80

III. THE INTERVENING PERIOD
Reorganization and Reformation 86
The Flak Regiment of the Hermann Göring Division 90
The Evolution of the Hermann Göring Rifle Regiment 91
The Reichsmarschall's Special Train Guard Detachment –
   The Führer Flak Battalion 92

IV. THE AFRICAN THEATER

A Brief Overview 101
The Allied Landings – The Western, Central & Eastern Task Forces 102
The 5th Parachute Regiment in the First Actions in Tunisia 104
The Hermann Göring Division in Africa – Initial Overview 105
Actions Preceding Operation "Lilac Blossom" 110
The Armored Reconnaissance Battalion HG –
    Command Positions and First Action 113
Kampfgruppe Kiefer in Action 114
The End in Tunisia 117
Command Positions of the Hermann Göring Division in Africa
    in early 1943 119
After Capture in Africa 120
I Battalion of the Hermann Göring Panzer Regiment after
    the Collapse in Africa 125
False Alarms – Equipment and Organization 127
The Führer Flak Battalion 127
The Flak Regiment HG from June 1943 132

V. THE GATE TO FORTRESS EUROPE

The Attacker's Plan 136
The Defenders: Italian and German Forces 138
The Hermann Göring Panzer Division in Sicily 139
The Allied Landing Operations 143
The American Landing 147
The German Side on the First Day: The Schmalz Brigade 148
With the Hermann Göring Panzer Division 153
2nd Company, 504th Heavy Panzer Battalion in the Attack on Gela 157
The Schmalz Brigade in Sicily:
    An Account by Generalleutnant Wilhelm Schmalz 160
General Montgomery: "The 13th Corps Has Broken Through
    on the Catania Plain." 167
Retreat to the Catania Position 171
The Second Phase of the Battle and the Retreat 173
The Final Battle – Withdrawal and Crossing of the Strait of Messina 175
The Ferry Flotillas in the Strait of Messina 177
Commanders of German Forces in Sicily 179
Strength and Organization of the Divisions in Sicily................................180
The Hermann Göring Panzer Division in Sicily as of July 1943................181
The Assault Gun Battalion of the Hermann Göring Parachute-
    Panzer Division – Beginnings, Technology, Tactics 188
Unteroffizer Hans Bethke's Account of the Fighting in Sicily 193
The Odyssey of Unteroffizier Kanert...195

The Retreat 200
The Hermann Göring Panzer Regiment – Formation & Employment 202

VI. BATTLE ZONE ITALY
I Battalion, Hermann Göring Panzer Regiment
    Following Its Return to the Mainland 206
The Rebuilding of the Hermann Göring Reconnaissance Battalion 206
Prelude: Allied Landings on the Italian Mainland 207
The Hermann Göring Panzer Regiment in the Combat Zone 208
Further Operations – Developments in the Overall Situation 212
II Battalion, 1st Panzer-Grenadier Regiment HG in Italy 213
The Monastery at Monte Casino 217
III (Assault Gun) Battalion, Hermann Göring Panzer Regiment
    in the Italian Battle Zone, November 1943-July 1944 220
The Battle of Castelforte: Leutnant Ringel's Account 221
The Road to the Hermann Göring Parachute Division 224
The 1st and 7th Panzer Companies of the Hermann Göring
    Parachute Panzer Regiment in Action...225
Operation "Shingle": The Landing at Anzio-Nettuno –
    The Invasion Forces 231
The German Countermeasures 231
The Other Units at Anzio-Nettuno 233
The 10th (Anti-tank) Company, 1st HG Parachute-Panzer-Grenadier
    Regiment at Anzio-Nettuno 234
The Assault Guns in the Anzio-Nettuno Battle Zone 237
The Allied Breakout from the Beachhead...239
With the Hermann Göring Parachute-Panzer-Grenadier Division –
    The Battles of 26 May - 5 June 1944 243
The Battle of Chuisi 252
The Hermann Göring Parachute-Panzer Armored Reconnaissance
    Battalion from the Garigliano to the Vistula 255
In the Gustav Line 258
The Defense of Cisterna 261
The Battle of Rome 267
The Herman Göring Assault Gun Battalion Heads South 267
Oberleutnant Heinz Göring: Service and Death 276
The Hermann Göring Assault Gun Battalion in Action in Poland 278
Accounts by Fw. Fleischmann, Uffz. Kanert and Karl Kattum 283
The Battle of Warsaw – The Kanert Crew in the City 284

VII. THE WESTERN THEATRE
The Training Elements of the Hermann Göring Units 287
The Training Units (by Alfred Otte) 287

The Hermann Göring Parachute-Panzer Replacement and
    Training Regiment in Action on the Western Front 290
The Two Hermann Göring Parachute-Panzer Replacement
    and Training Brigades 291
The Hermann Göring Replacement and Training Regiment
    in Action in Holland 292

VIII. THE WAR IN THE EAST – A GENERAL SUMMARY
Soviet Preparations 298
Russian Distribution of Forces before "Bagration", June 1944 303
The Hermann Göring Division Moves East 303
Battles in Siedice-Warsaw Area 306
The Encirclement of the Soviet 3rd Tank Corps 307
Battle for the Warka-Magnuszew Bridgehead 310

IX. FORMATION OF THE HERMANN GÖRING PARACHUTE-PANZER CORPS
The Battle for East Prussia 314
The Soviet Offensive and German Countermeasures 316
The 13th Battery, Hermann Göring Parachute Flak Regiment
    at Gumbinnen 321
A Brief Account of the Assault Gun Battalion, Later the
    Hermann Göring Parachute Tank Destroyer Battalion 322
1st Company, Hermann Göring Parachute-Panzer Regiment
    from October to December 1944 324
1st Company, Hermann Göring Parachute-Panzer-Grenadier Regiment
    in Action 329

X. THE HERMANN GÖRING PARACHUTE-PANZER-REPLACEMENT AND TRAINING BRIGADE (September 1944 until March 1945)
Formation Sites – Formation and Purpose 332
Personnel 332
Quarters 333
Organization of the Brigade 334
Equipment and Armament 347

XI. DECISION IN THE EAST
The Lull before the Storm 348
The Defenseive Battles 350
The Graudenz Bridgehead – The General Situation 356
German Defensive Measures 357
The Final Battle for Fortress Graudenz 362

XII. THE HERMANN GÖRING PARACHUTE-PANZER CORPS
The Frontier Battles in East Prussia 369
Positional Warfare in the Winter of 1944-45 372
In the Heiligenbeil Pocket 377
Oberst Bern von Baer: Portrait of a Soldier 380
The Hermann Göring 1st Parachute-Panzer Division
    in the Final Battles 381
Oberfähnrich Hartelt in Action 382
Battles of Retreat – The Attack on Steinau 385
The Battles from 13 March to 11 April 1945 387
The Hermann Göring Parachute-Panzer Division from
    13 March to 11 April 1945 388
The Hermann Göring Parachute-Panzer Corps Is Coming 397

XIII. APPENDICES
I. Evolution of the Hermann Göring Parachute-Panzer Corps....................413
II. The Commanders 414
III. Winners of the German Cross in Gold 415
IV. Winners of the Knight's Cross 419
V. Sources..474

Generalleutnant Wilhelm Schmalz (left), Commanding General of the Hermann Göring Parachute-Panzer Corps, and (right) Reichsmarschall Herman Göring, the initiator and namesake of all the Hermann Göring units.

I. PEACETIME

Origins of the Hermann Göring Units

"Polizeiabteilung Wecke" was created on 23 February 1933 as the result of a proclamation by the Prussian Ministry of the Interior at the urging of the Minister of the Interior, Hermann Göring. The unit was organized as follows:

Police Detachment Headquarters with
    3 police squads
    1 police motorcycle platoon
    1 police signals platoon
    2 special vehicles

Each of the police squads had on strength 4 officers and 106 sergeants. The motorcycle platoon had a strength of 1 officer and 38 sergeants. The signals platoon consisted of 1 officer and 25 sergeants. The Detachment Headquarters was formed with a strength of 6 officers, 3 administration officials and 12 sergeants.

With a few exceptions all of the detachment's officers and men came from the Greater Berlin City Police. Commander of the detachment was Police Major Wecke.

The battalion's personnel were assembled in the Augustaner Barracks on Friesenstraße in Berlin-Kreuzberg. There they began special training intended to enable them to "Engage and wipe out all communist cells and sanctuaries which still remained."

In addition to its primary role the unit, which very soon earned a reputation for its outstanding bearing and discipline, was used to provide honor guards at public events and receptions. In the course of these duties it was revealed that the police training alone was inadequate. It was obvious that this would have to be changed to a purely military syllabus.

Additional units were formed, as the Police Detachment's personnel strength was inadequate for the multiplicity of roles it was now being called upon to perform: a second police squad was added in late March 1933, followed in April by a mortar and a machine-gun detachment. From this point on the unit's role was changed to guard and ceremonial duties exclusively. Nevertheless a larger framework was necessary for such an expanded unit; consequently the Police Detachment was redesignated as a Police Group and was enlarged to two detachments.

The unit's new organization was as follows: A group headquarters, two detachment headquarters and eight police squads. Each squad consisted of one mounted and one motorcycle platoon, a motorized detachment and a signals platoon. The group also included a band. Following this reorganization, on 17 July 1933 the Police Group was withdrawn from police service and placed under the direct control of the Prussian Ministry of the Interior. At the same time it received its ultimate title: *"Landespolizeigruppe Wecke z.b.V."* (Special Purpose State Police Group Wecke). The unit thus became Germany's first state police unit. All officers were trained riders; the group's mounted platoon had a complement of 25 horses.

In the period that followed, the Prussian Minister of the Interior, Hermann Göring, increased his influence to the point where, on the one hand, he knew every one of the group's officers personally, and on the other, demanded that the unit be at his disposal at all times. At Göring's direction the unit was transferred to the barracks of the former main cadet institute in Berlin-Lichterfelde on 2 May 1933.

At this point, also on Göring's order, the police group began receiving purely military training. As part of this training the unit's officers and sergeants were temporarily detached to every type of army unit. Hermann Göring visited his special unit often to see for himself the state of their training.

On 13 September the Wecke Group received its first flag, which was presented with the "Blood Flag of the Movement" and the flag of the Guards Rifle Battalion. In his address Hermann Göring declared:

"It is my goal to make the Prussian State Police a keen weapon of Germany and, if the day should come when we are called against an outside enemy, to hand it over to the Reichswehr and our Führer."

At that point Göring had already informed his intimate circle that he intended to use the unit to build up his own armed forces. It was with this in mind that the expansion of the following years took place. General training followed the principles of an infantry regiment. On 22 December 1933, in a letter to the unit's commanding officer, *Oberst* Wecke, Göring decreed that all of the group's soldiers were to wear a cuff band on the left sleeve. The title was to read:

LANDESPOLIZEI GENERAL GÖRING

From this point on the blue police uniform was replaced by the "green cloth" of the State Police, and on 15 May 1934 the unit was placed under the command of Headquarters, Chief of State Police. The former detachments were retitled light infantry (*Jäger*) battalions. The men now served with the rank of *Jäger*, *Oberjäger*, etc.

On 22 June 1934 *Oberst* Wecke left to take up other duties and Hermann Göring's former adjutant, *Oberstleutnant* Jakoby, became the new commander of the State Police Group HG. The group was placed under the command of the State Police Inspectorate Brandenburg. The enabling directive received Hermann Göring's special endorsement, to the effect that he reserved the personal right to direct the employment of the unit. A change of barracks followed on 1 October 1934. The group's three battalions (the third had been added on 1 October 1934) moved into the barracks in Berlin-Spandau, Berlin-Charlottenburg and Berlin- Reinickendorf.

On 16 March 1935 the law for the expansion of the German Wehrmacht was promulgated. The General Göring State Police Group became an independent unit once again; on Hitler's order it was placed under the personal command of the Prussian Minister-President, Hermann Göring. This was Göring's special request of his comrade-in-arms Hitler and the latter granted it immediately.

The group quickly became fully motorized and its training manuals were brought into line with those of the army's motorized infantry units. In addition to the revised training program, an anti-tank squad and a special-purpose squad, consisting of a dispatch rider platoon and a newly-formed pioneer platoon, were added to the group. From this point on, the General Göring State Police Group provided the personal guards at the seat of the Prussian Minister-President in Berlin and at Göring's representative seat in Schorfheide (more about this later). By now the officers and men of the group were already referring to their unit as the General Göring Regiment.

In mid-1935 the General Göring State Police Group adopted an organization—including unit designations—that corresponded to that of an army infantry regiment. The first inspection of the police regiment by Adolf Hitler took place on 5 June 1935, during which the unit's officers were introduced to the Führer by Minister-President Göring. A major autumn exercise which began on 8 September 1935 took the regiment from Berlin to Nuremberg and then back to Berlin via the province of Saxony.

In Nuremberg on 11 September 1935 the regiment underwent a close inspection by the current Chief-of-Staff of the Luftwaffe, *Generalleutnant* Walther Wever. For insiders this was an unmistakable sign that the unit was soon to be "taken home" into the bosom of the Luftwaffe. This in fact took place on 23 September, when Hermann Göring announced that his police regiment was being placed under the command of the Luftwaffe. The official Reich Air Ministry decree for the assignment of the unit to the Luftwaffe followed on 19 October 1935. A Luftwaffe General Staff close to Göring was given the task of determining how the regiment was to be used in case of war.

"Defence against enemy operations in the Luftwaffe's own war zone (home war zone) and guarding of the headquarters of the Reich Minister of Aviation and the Commander-in-Chief of the Luftwaffe."

"Competence in the defence against low-level air raids by the enemy."

"In peacetime: Use in police role and provision of guards for the Commander-in-Chief of the Luftwaffe as required."

Integration of the regiment into the Luftwaffe resulted in the following changes:

General Göring State Police Regiment	Reorganization (as of 1.11.1935)	**General Göring Regiment**
Regiment HQ	became	*Regiment HQ*
Music Corps	became	Music Corps
Signals Platoon –	became	Signals Platoon
I Battalion	became	*I Light Infantry Bn.*
		(cover designation for parachute rifle)

Signals Platoon –	became	Signals Platoon (parachute rifle)
New formation on 1.10.1936		Pioneer Platoon (parachute rifle)
1st-3rd Rifle	became	1st-3rd Light Infantry Companies (parachute rifle)
4th Machinegun Company	became	4th Machinegun Company (parachute rifle)
II Battalion	became	*II Light Infantry Battalion*
Signals Platoon –	became	Signals Platoon
New formation on 1.10.1936		Pioneer Platoon
5th-7th Rifle Companies	became	5th-7th Light Infantry Companies
8th Machinegun Company	became	8th Machinegun Company
III Battalion (former "Derfflinger" LP-Bn.)	became	*III Light Flak Battalion*
New formation		HQ Battery
New formation on 1.10.1936		10th Battery (12 - 20mm Flak)
13th MW Battery (6 MW)	became	11th Battery (9 - 37mm Flak)
14th Anti-tank Co. (9 - 37mm Pak)	became	9th Battery (12 - 20mm Flak)
15th Special Purpose with: 3 armored cars –	became	13th Motorcycle Infantry Co. with 3 armored cars
Pioneer Platoon	became	14th Pioneer Company (parachute rifle)
Cavalry Platoon	became	Cavalry Platoon (regimental unit)
New formation 11.7.1936		15th Guard Company
New formation 1.4.1937		16th Guard Company

Formation of the 12th Searchlight Battery (12 - 600mm) was to follow later. (Source: BA-MA, RL 2 III/334)

Following a brief transitional phase, during which the old uniforms were retained, the General Göring Regiment received Luftwaffe uniforms with white collar patches and a cuff band bearing the legend GENERAL GÖRING. The collar patches of the *Jäger* Battalions were green and those of the Flak Battalion red.

On 1 December 1935 the regiment's organization was as follows:

Regimental Headquarters with regimental signals platoon.

Regimental formations:

1 motorcycle rifle company

1 pioneer company

1 cavalry platoon

Regimental Units:

1 Jäger battalion (paratroop) with headquarters and signals platoon, 3 rifle companies and one machine-gun company.

1 Jäger battalion with headquarters and signals platoon, with 3 rifle companies and a machine-gun company.

1 flak battalion with headquarters and signals platoon, 3 flak batteries (two with 20mm and one with 37mm guns).

The next move saw the special formation of guard units within the regiment. On 11 July 1936 another company was formed as the Guard Company of the General Göring Regiment and incorporated into the regiment. With the expansion of the regiment's guard duties, a second Guard Company had to be formed on 1 April 1937, followed soon afterward by a third.

From Guard Company to Guard Battalion – Further New Formations

On 21 August 1936 *Oberstleutnant* Jakoby was made Reich Air Ministry Special Duties Officer. His successor as commander of the General Göring Regiment was *Major* von Axthelm, who was promoted to *Oberstleutnant* immediately after assuming command.

On 1 October 1937 the new commanding officer ordered II *Jäger* Battalion expanded to a heavy flak battalion. The same day saw the formation of the Hermann Göring Guard Battalion within the regiment. 1937 had witnessed a considerable expansion and reorganization of the regiment:

In addition to the previous headquarters positions it now had a Heavy Flak Battalion with three batteries of 88mm guns and one battery of 37mm guns. As well there was a Light Flak Battalion with three batteries of 20mm automatic weapons, and the Guard Battalion with headquarters and cavalry platoons, a motorcycle company, a machine-gun company and a pioneer company. The Parachute Rifle Battalion was removed from the General Göring Regiment on 1 April 1938 and transferred to Stendal as I Battalion, 1st Parachute Regiment.

A further company was formed for the ever-expanding guard role and assigned to the Guard Battalion. On 1 July 1938 followed the formation of a special formation with a 20mm flak battery for the personal protection of Adolf Hitler and the Commander-in-Chief of the Luftwaffe, Hermann Göring. This unit's personnel were selected from the various flak regiments. Every member of one light flak battery applied to join this special unit.

Following this latest addition the General Göring Regiment consisted of the Regimental Headquarters, three flak battalions, a heavy searchlight battalion, and a guard battalion. Finally the regiment was moved into the newly-constructed barracks in Berlin-Reinickendorf and the Velten barracks camp, which was erected at the edge of the regiment's training grounds.

The barracks installation was occupied in September 1937. Its functional style was to become an example for all later Luftwaffe barracks. It was acknowledged by soldiers and officers alike as: "a real soldier's home." It included more than 120 buildings, with gymnasiums, an indoor swimming pool, a public bath, a sports field, a post office, and many other installations.

List of Command Positions as of 1 October 1937

By the beginning of October 1937 the General Göring Regiment had developed into a homogenous regimental unit. The following is a list of the unit's command positions as of 1 October 1937:

GENERAL GÖRING REGIMENT

Commanding Officer:	Oberstleutnant von Axthelm
Staff Major:	Hptm. von Oppeln-Bronikowski
Adjutant:	Hptm. Bertram
Machine-gun Officer:	Hptm. Götzel
Company Officer:	Hptm. Meyer
Special Duties Officer	Oblt. Kluge

HQ Battery

Commander:	Hptm. Lüdecke
Signals Officer:	an Oberfähnrich

I (Heavy) Flak Battalion

Commanding Officer:	Hptm. Hullmann
Staff Hauptmann:	Oblt. Schmudlach
Adjutant:	Lt. Oetting
Office Officer:	Hptm. (E) Lorenz
Weapons Officer:	Oblt. Bobrowski (from 1938)

HQ Battery

Commander:	Oblt. von Jablonski
Signals Officer:	Oblt. Münchenhagen

1st Battery

Commander:	Hptm. Rösner
Battery Officer:	Oblt. Seewald
Battery Officer:	Lt. Brandenburg
Battery Officer:	Oberfähnrich Arnold

2nd Battery

Commander:	Oblt. Geicke
Battery Officer:	Oblt. Stauch (at same time adjutant with Commander-in-Chief Luftwaffe)

Battery Officer:	Lt. Gustmann
Battery Officer:	Lt. Becker (Karl-Heinz)

3rd Battery

Commander:	Oblt. Schröder
Battery Officer:	Lt. Wildhagen
Battery Officer:	Oberfähnrich Graf

4th Battery

Commander:	Hptm. Thimm
Battery Officer:	Oblt. Funck
Battery Officer:	Oblt. Schreiber
Battery Officer:	an Oberfähnrich

II (Light) Flak Battalion

Commanding Officer:	Major Conrath
Adjutant:	Lt. Götte (Richard)
Staff Hauptmann:	position vacant
Office Officer:	Hptm. (E) Kuhl
Weapons and Equipment:	Oblt. (WE) Komorowski (at same time delegated to Rgt. HQ)

HQ Battery

Commander:	Oblt. Schulz (Robert)
Signals Officer:	Oblt. Walther (Erwin)

5th Battery

Commander:	Hptm. Barg
Battery Officer:	Oblt. Jacobi
Battery Officer:	Lt. Oehme at times: Oberfähnrich Roßmann

6th Battery

Commander:	Hptm. Müller
Battery Officer:	Oblt. Weidemann
Battery Officer:	Oblt. Hoffmann

7th Battery

Commander:	Oblt. Neubauer

Battery Officer:	Oblt. Wittke
Battery Officer:	an Oberfähnrich (Uxküll?)

III (Guard) Battalion

Commanding Officer:	Major Sydow
Adjutant:	Oblt. Morawetz
Cannon Officer:	position vacant
Leader:	Oblt. Preuß

8th Company (Motorcycle)

Commander:	Hptm. Weber
Company Officer:	Oblt. Schmidt
Company Officer:	Oberfähnrich Specht

9th Company

Commander:	Hptm. Seeger
Company Officer:	Oblt. Klosinsky
Company Officer:	Lt. Plate
Company Officer:	Lt. Behrendt
Company Officer:	Lt. Geßner

10th Company

Commander:	Oblt. Zorn
Company Officer:	Lt. Illgner
Company Officer:	Lt. Baranowski
Company Officer:	Lt. Bergmann
Company Officer:	Lt. Lübke

IV (Parachute Rifle) Battalion

Commanding Officer:	Major Bräuer
Adjutant:	Lt. Herrmann
Staff Hauptmann:	Hptm. Walther
I/F Parachute:	Oblt. Koch
Company Officer:	position vacant
Signals Officer:	position vacant
Pioneer Officer:	position vacant

11th Company

Commander:	Oblt. Gericke
Company Officer:	Lt. Paul
Company Officer:	Lt. Jung
Company Officer:	Lt. Kieß

12th Company

Commander:	Oblt. Vogel
Company Officer:	Oblt. Gröschke
Company Officer:	an Oberfähnrich

13th Company

Commander:	Oblt. Merten
Company Officer:	Lt. Götte (Wilhelm)
Company Officer:	an Oberfähnrich

14th Company

Commander:	Oblt. Noster
Company Officer:	Lt. Schmidt (Herbert)
Company Officer:	an Oberfähnrich

15th Company

Commander:	Hptm. Schulz (Karl-Lothar)
Company Officer:	Oblt. Dunz
Company Officer:	Lt. Specht

It is obvious from a perusal of this list of positions that there were still large gaps in officer personnel which had to be filled by NCOs selected for officer training (ranks of *Fähnrich* and *Oberfähnrich*). This was to change in the coming months, at least for the 1st Parachute Regiment.

(The commander of 10th Company, *Oberleutnant* Heinz Bernhard Zorn, was to enjoy a meteoric career. An *Oberst* and Luftwaffe staff officer at the end of the war, on his return from Soviet captivity Zorn became Chief-of-Staff of the Air Force units in the East German *Volkspolizei*. In 1956 he was promoted to *Generalmajor* of the East German Air Forces and later taught as acting commander of the Friedrich Engels Military Academy in Dresden. In 1977 he officially retired, but was active as an agent for the East German secret service in Paris until his arrest in September 1980. Following his arrest in Lille he was sentenced to several years imprisonment by a French court. (At the time of his arrest Zorn had in his possession secret French documents concerning tanks and anti-tank rockets.)

The General Göring Regiment was reorganized once again on 1 November 1938, which resulted in a considerable increase in its anti-aircraft capabilities. I Battalion formed III Searchlight Battalion, while II Battalion formed IV Light Battalion, as a result of which the General Göring Regiment was structured as follows:

I Heavy Battalion	Hptm. Hullmann
II Light Battalion	Major Rüdel
III Searchlight Battalion	Major von Oppeln-Bronikowski
IV Light Battalion	Oberstleutnant von Hippel
Guard Battalion	Major Weber

The Southern Cross

It was during the formation of the General Göring State Police Group that the Southern Cross first appeared, an emblem worn by the group's first *Hundertschaft* on the sleeve of the left forearm. The same heraldic figure was included in the unit flag beneath a wreath of laurel.

The Southern Cross had earlier been the badge of the police units in German-East Africa (not the German colonial forces, as has often been claimed incorrectly). With the integration of this coat of arms into the group flag the tradition of the first *Hundertschaft* was passed on to the entire group. Even after I Battalion, General Göring Regiment was renamed IV Parachute Rifle Battalion, the Southern Cross remained the unit's emblem.

Not until the unit was redesignated I Battalion, 1st Parachute Regiment was this coat of arms removed from the new unit flag and passed on to the General Göring Regiment's cavalry platoon as an interim measure pending a new ruling. This took the form of a decree by the Reich Minister of the Interior on 8 November 1938:

"The mounted echelon of the Berlin Municipal Police is entrusted with the maintenance of tradition."

The formal handing over of the flag took place at the General Göring Regiment's training grounds in Berlin-Reinickendorf. A delegation from the General Göring Regiment was drawn up on one side of the parade ground and a party from the municipal police mounted echelon on the other. *Oberstleutnant* von Axthelm took the flag from his cavalry platoon's color bearer and handed it over to *Generalmajor der Schutzpolizei* von Kamptz, the commander of the Berlin Municipal Police. Kamptz then passed the flag to the party from the Berlin Municipal Police's mounted echelon.

For the General Göring Regiment the Southern Cross was now only a reminder of the police units who had kept peace and order in the former colony of German East Africa.

The Regiment's Guard Duties in Berlin and at Karinhall

The General Göring Regiment provided guards in the following locations:

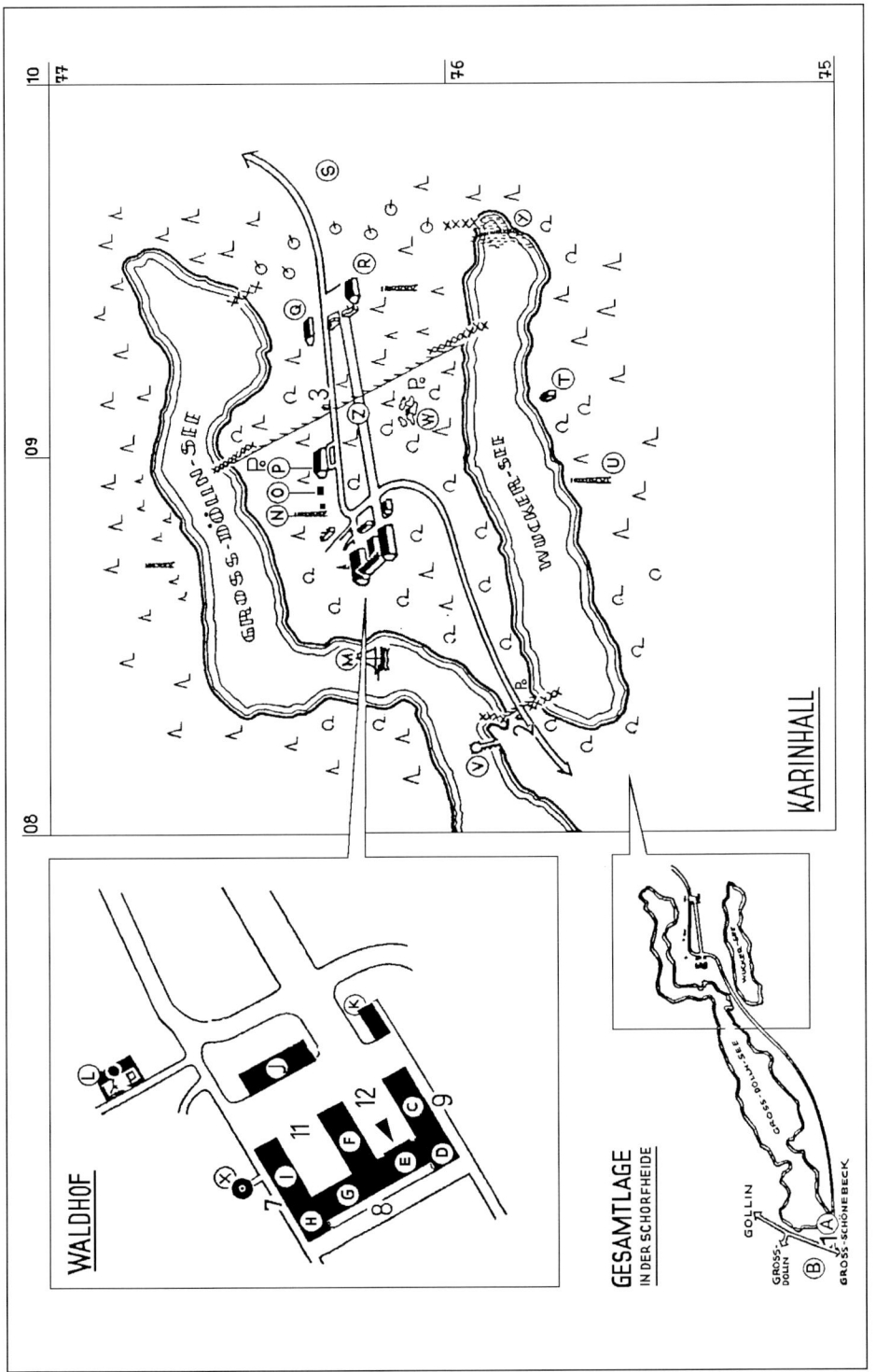

The Karinhall installation – seat of the Reichsmarschall with forest lodge.

1. The barracks in Reinickendorf. A military guard stood to the left of the main entrance in front of a small building which housed the military guardhouse.

2. A guard was always positioned in front of Gate 7 leading to the Tegeler Exercise Grounds.

3. The parading of the guard in front of the headquarters office and in front of the residence of the Minister of the Interior, Hermann Göring—a villa situated between the Prussian Diet and the Prussian House of Lords—was always an exciting event for onlookers. Incidentally, there was a direct structural link between the villa and the Reich Air Ministry on the corner of Leipziger Straße and Prinz Albrecht-Straß. The Prussian House of Lords later became the *Haus der Flieger*.

The guard was driven by truck from the barracks to the Hofjägerallee. From there it marched through the Brandenburg Gate – led by the mounted commander of the guard and followed by the band – up Leipzigerstraße and Prinz Albrecht Straße to the villa of the future *Reichsmarschall*.

The large guard parade held each Wednesday in front of the National War Memorial was also the responsibility of the General Göring Regiment. The troops were trucked as far as the police barracks on Universitätstraße, where a horse waited for the commander of the guard. From there the guard marched to the Straße unter den Linden and then to the memorial, where the mounting of the guard took place. On completion of its duties the guard was marched down the Unter den Linden and Prinz Albrecht Straße to its starting point.

Every Thursday the *Leibstandarte-SS Adolf Hitler* mounted a guard in front of the memorial. On the remaining days the guard was provided by the Army's Guard Regiment (which later became the *Großdeutschland* Guard Regiment). On the other hand Skagerrak Day always saw a Navy guard in front of the memorial.

On March 1, Air Force Day, and on 21 April, the date of Manfred von Richthofen's death, there was a march-past at the Air Ministry in front of Hermann Göring, who took the review. Together with the Luftwaffe's guard battalion, a company of the General Göring Guard Regiment always occupied a prominent place at the head of the march-past.

One of the most important, and for the soldiers most impressive, guards was that in front of Karinhall, Göring's forest estate. Named after his deceased first wife, Karin, it was located about 50 kilometers north of Berlin in the Schorfheide. As well as being an official government building, the forest estate also contained living quarters for the family and friends of the Reich Minister. The entire property was situated somewhat to one side of Reichsstraße 109, which ran between Berlin and Prenzlau.

Guarding Karinhall was also the responsibility of the General Göring Regiment. In peacetime a platoon from one of the regiment's guard companies was always stationed there with 40 to 80 men. Initially the guard was

The First Order for the Formation of the German Parachute Troops

The Reich Minister of Aviation   Berlin, 29 January 1936
    and
Commander-in-Chief of the Luftwaffe   Secret

To:
              Air Force Area Headquarters II, Berlin

In preparation for training of the "General Göring" Regiment in parachute jumping, I order the following:

15 volunteer officers, NCOs and junior leaders from the regiment are to be readied and traned as future instructors. Consideration will only be given to persons with a weight of less than 85 kg. (clothed) who are in good physical condition and able to pass an aviation medical examination.

Projected commencement of training: 1. 4. 1936.

Duration 8 weeks, of which 4 weeks involves training as a parachute technician with Luftwaffe equipment inspectors, subsequent 4 weeks of practical training in parachute jumping from an aircraft. The airport at Neubrabdenburg is being considered as the training site.

One Ju 52 will be provided by the RLM (LC). Suitable instructors will be provided by the RLM (LA III).

Training guidelines will be provided on a timely basis by the RLM (LA III). The LKK II will report the following by 15. 3. 1936.

1. Rank and names of volunteers.
2. Results of aviation medical examinations.
3. Suitability of selected airfield. If necessary another is to be suggested.

Any extra costs are to be claimed under Chapter A 2 Title 34 Subsection 4b, they will receive special priority.

Flight pay as per Ordnance D. R. d. L. L. P. 4010/35 1 A g.v. 3. 5. 35 Line IV b (front-line) is authorized for the duration of the four-week practical training in parachute jumping.

                                           draft
                                           signed for
                                           Milch

relieved daily under the command of two officers who came by truck from Berlin to Karinhall. On several occasions during the first winter, precarious road conditions prevented the guard from being relieved. As a result the guard platoon had to take up quarters in a guard barracks. This was later replaced by the *Haus der Wache*, which consisted of three buildings containing living quarters and a main building, as well as stables and supply buildings. This entire installation was located at the spot where the road from Groß-Schönebeck to Gollin branched off to Karinhall.

Also situated there was Outpost I. Inside the stone building were the guard room, the officers' rooms with showers, the kitchen, and the company orderly room with the office of the senior NCO. Next to this was a single-story stone structure with stalls for the horses of the cavalry platoon. Off to one side were the four wooden barracks which housed the Guard Company. The weekly routine for the men on detached duty with the Karinhall guard was as follows: three days barracks duty, three days guard duty, one day off.

Guard duty, which was conducted in short shifts, began with a brief drive by car to the Karinhall guard house. If the *Reichsmarschall* was not at Karinhall the guard wore standard uniforms. Dress uniforms were reserved for when the *Reichsmarschall* was visiting Karinhall.

The Red Passes

The only people allowed entrance to the Karinhall and free movement within the entire installation were those possessing one of six red passes. Such a pass also entitled the bearer to enter all of the *Reichsmarschall*'s other estates and residences, such as the one in Rominten in East Prussia, his castle near Nuremberg, his house in Berchtesgaden, and his apartments in Munich and Berlin. As well there were twelve green bound passes which gave the bearer unrestricted access to Karinhall only.

All other persons required a pass card on which was printed the dates of its validity. Even the officers of the General Göring Regiment required such a pass if they were not on duty as officers of the guard.

The Outpost Positions

The Karinhall installation was bordered on two sides by Great Dölln Lake and Lake Wucker. A single road led into the complex, dividing into two lanes between the two main buildings and then continuing on as a single-lane road again. It was the job of the sentries at the barbed wire barricade to maintain a watch on these roads and the bordering wire mesh fences.

Sentry 1 was responsible for watching over the entrance to the Karinhall complex on the Gross-Schönebeck – Gollin road, south of Great Dölln Lake. The guard house was situated in the stone house of the barracks. Passes were checked and pass cards issued there.

Sentry 2 stood at the entrance to the Karinhall in front of a small sentry box and was armed with a pistol. It was his job to check visitors coming from the area of Sentry 1, who reported their arrival by telephone. Next to the sentry box was a bushy tree, which concealed the second sentry standing behind the guard house. This man was armed with an MPi 38 submachine-gun and was known as the "listening sentry."

Sentry 3 stood at Karinhall's rear exit/entrance, where visitors coming from the fake Karinhall and the airfield arrived; his duties were similar to those of Sentry 2.

Sentry 7 was responsible for watching over the area from the household wing to the hunting wing. The household wing also included the officers mess. Opposite this building was the turret- like entrance to the bunker. It was in this climate-controlled bunker that all of the *Reichmarschall*'s art treasures were kept during the war. From here the sentries could scan Karinhall's park as far as the pier where the *Reichsmarschall*'s yacht was tied up. By night two sentries patrolled the park on foot in order to keep the entire area under scrutiny.

Sentry 8 was responsible for watching over the area from the hunting wing past the private rooms and the reception hall to Göring's office. This watch was also doubled at night. Since Göring always slept with the windows open, a strip of carpet was laid out for Sentry 8a, who had to watch over this area, in order to muffle the sound of his footsteps on the gravel path.

Sentry 9 had to walk from Göring's office along the guest wing. On the ground floor of the guest wing was the library, which was also used as a map room. His sentry area continued to the guard room. There, too, two sentries were employed at night. A mounted guard patrolled outside Karinhall, while the sentries of the light flak batteries stationed around the lakes carried out foot patrols there.

Ten to twelve plainclothes police were quartered on the upper floor of the fire station. The firemen were kept at readiness day and night. Practice drills showed that they could be ready for action within a minute of the sounding of the alarm.

The General Göring Regiment and the German Parachute Troops

The Hermann Göring Regiment was also the birthplace of the German parachute troops. Acting on instructions from Göring, the Luftwaffe began parachute trials after it was learned that parachute units were being formed in the USSR, where the Red Army had begun experiments in dropping troops from aircraft by parachute in 1928. Soviet parachute troops made their first public appearance in the Red Army's All-Union maneuvers of 1930. The General Göring Regiment received the necessary orders from the Reich Minister for Aviation and the Commander-in-Chief of the Luftwaffe on 29 January 1936.

The formation order named Neubrandenburg airfield as the practice site; nevertheless, the first training courses took place at Stendal airfield. The graduates of these first parachute courses formed the German Parachute School. This was the first *official* formation of a parachute unit in Germany. Earlier, however, at the time of the transfer of the General Göring Regiment from the State Police to the Luftwaffe on 1 October 1935, plans were made for the formation a battalion of parachute troops from volunteers drawn from the regiment.

The General Göring Regiment was subsequently transferred to the Altengrabow Troop Training Grounds near Magdeburg in October 1935. Its orders: "Development of the German parachute troops." The first parachute jump was conducted at the Döberitz Troop Training Grounds following the unit's return to its garrison in Berlin. Although this was somewhat less than successful – the jumper was injured – more than 600 members of the regiment subsequently volunteered for jump training.

The formation order of 29 January 1936 led to the selection of the first fifteen volunteers, who were destined to become instructors for later courses. The first parachute jump by a soldier of the new parachute troops took place on 11 May 1936 during the first jump course. It was the commanding officer of the General Göring Regiment's I Battalion, *Major* Bruno Bräuer, who jumped from the wing of a Klemm Kl 35 light aircraft that day. As a result of his successful jump Bräuer received Parachute Certificate Number 1 and was later known to his soldiers as "*Fallschirmjäger* Number One!."

On 5 November 1936 Hermann Göring created the Parachutist-Rifleman Badge (*Fallschirmschützenabzeichen*), which was presented only to possessors of the Parachute Certificate. Sixty men of the General Göring Regiment took part in the second course, which, on orders from the then Luftwaffe Chief-of-Staff, *Generalleutnant* Albert Kesselring, was held at Stendal airfield.

Among those instructing the course were *Hauptmann* Immans of the Quedlinburg-Lübeck Aircrew Replacement Battalion (course director), *Hauptmann* Reinberger of the General Göring Regiment (special duties officer), and *Oberlteutnant* Walther Koch of the General Göring Regiment (adjutant).

Numbered among the officers who participated in the first jump courses were soldiers who not only achieved high positions during the course of the war but who also gained great honor. Here are several names which call to mind to every student of military history the most difficult battles and operations of the German parachute troops:

Major Bräuer, *Hptm.* Reinberger, *Oberleutnante* Vogel, Walther, Kroh, Schulz, Herrmann, Gröschke and Gericke. *Leutnante* Paul, Koch, Merten, Noster and Dunz. It was they earned the German parachute troops as the sobriquet "the Green Devils", and later on many of them returned to their parent unit, Hermann Göring.

At a somewhat later date than the Luftwaffe, the Army High Command initiated planning for the creation of an army parachute corps. On 1 April 1937 a parachute infantry company was formed in Stendal, initially as a trials unit. In the following months this trials unit evolved into the Parachute Infantry Battalion under *Major* Richard Heidrich. This unit also produced several well-known parachute soldiers, names such as Heidrich, Prager and Böhmler.

On 1 July 1938 *Generalmajor* Kurt Student was given the job of continuing the development of the *Fallschirmtruppe*. He formed the existing unit into the 7th Aviation Division, a name which was retained for some time so as to camouflage the unit's true purpose. Both parachute battalions, – Army and Air Force – were displayed during the Wehrmacht maneuvers of 1937. This served as the public unveiling of the German parachute troops, whose development had until then been internal and secret, for almost every military attache of the western countries took part in the maneuvers as did the one from the Soviet Union.

As part of the reorganization of the Hermann Göring Regiment on 1 October 1937, I (*Jäger*) Battalion was renamed IV Parachute Rifle Battalion, General Göring Regiment. Not until its incorporation into the 1st Parachute Regiment was the term parachutist rifleman (*Fallschirmschütze*) replaced by paratrooper (*Fallschirmjäger*).

On 1 October 1937 the parachutist riflemen of the General Göring Regiment began wearing white collar patches with gold-yellow piping. This was meant to indicate that they were part of the *Fliegertruppe* (aviation troops), whose members wore gold-yellow collar patches but with similar piping. The remaining units of the regiment wore white collar patches with green, or in the case of the Flak Battalion, red piping.

In July 1938 the General Göring Regiment, whose development and war service up to the formation of the Hermann Göring Panzer Corps forms the basis of this work, formed another air-landing battalion as a training unit. Its commanding officer was *Major* von Sydow. The site of the unit's formation was Berlin-Reinickendorf. The battalion was assembled from two companies of the Hermann Göring Regiment's guard battalion and two companies from the Luftwaffe's guard battalion. It also included an howitzer battery under *Leutnant* Schramm, initially equipped with 75mm Skoda 16 guns designed for the alpine troops.

This formation was part of the preparations for Operation "Green" (the occupation of the Sudetenland). The battalion was placed under the command of the 7th *Fliegerdivision* commanded by *Generalmajor* Student. On 1 January 1939 the battalion was incorporated into the 1st Parachute Regiment as III Battalion and later saw action in the Polish Campaign.

Having outlined the close association between the creation of the German parachute troops and the General Göring Regiment, we will now turn exclusively to the further development and operational service of the General Göring Regiment.

Operation "Otto" (The German March into Austria)

On 11 March 1938 at four thirty in the morning the alarm horns sounded in the quarters of the General Göring Regiment's barracks in Berlin-Reinickendorf and ended a half hour before the official waking of the soldiers. Everyone thought it must be another of the early alerts, but this time it was different. The officers returning from a briefing held by the battalion's commanders informed their soldiers that the regiment had to come to battle and march readiness within 12 hours.

At 0800 hours the advance detachment set out for Passau, which made it clear that this could only be the entry into Austria, details of which had come to light as rumors. By 1630 hours all units had assembled on the assigned roads and squares within the barracks complex, ready to depart. But it wasn't until 1800 that the regiment, led by its commanding officer, *Oberstleutnant* von Axthelm, moved out.

Early on the morning of 12 March the regiment arrived at the autobahn access at Schleudnitz and stopped there to rest and refuel. The subsequent drive to Nuremberg was uneventful. From there, however, secondary Reichsstraßen had to be used, and in the early evening we arrived in Straubing. During refuelling in a large field beside the Danube, flying sparks from a starting motorcycle caused a truck of I (Heavy) Flak Battalion, which was loaded with 200-liter containers of fuel, to catch fire. By the time the first gasoline container exploded, all vehicles had left the danger area.

The drive to Passau was resumed at dawn. The columns became backed up in front of the Schärding border crossing. From then on we were in Austria, passing Linz and Anstetten, Melk and St. Pölten. Hermann Göring's soldiers received an enthusiastic welcome everywhere, especially from the young. The march into Vienna turned into a triumphant drive. We were showered with flowers and refreshments. It was our unanimous opinion that this was no staged reception. Further proof of this was the tears of joy we saw in many people's eyes.

That night, after passing through Vienna, a halt was ordered in Bruck an der Leitha, which is located between Lake Neusiedler and Preßburg (Bratislava), and quarters were occupied. Several days later the unit was moved to Wiener Neustadt and the surrounding area. I (Heavy) Flak Battalion took up quarters in the tradition-rich Maria Theresia Military Academy. Soon afterward it became a German Army Officer Candidate School. The school's first commander was Erwin Rommel, at that time an *Oberst*.

On 1 May 1938 Adolf Hitler created a commemorative medal to mark the entry into Austria. The personnel of the General Göring Regiment, which returned to Berlin from Vienna in mid-April, were among those who received the medal.

This first great event had been preceded by the "Day of the Luftwaffe" on 1 March 1938. A parade was held in Berlin in which all branches of the Luftwaffe took part. The Hermann Göring Regiment was represented by the 10th (Guard) Company under the command of *Hauptmann* Kluge; it took part in the march-past which was reviewed by Göring. Flank man was *Unteroffizier* Scheid. (Scheid was awarded the Knight's Cross for actions in Tunisia. More of this later.)

Following its return from Austria, there was another event of great significance to the General Göring Regiment, when the Commander-in-Chief of the Luftwaffe inspected his regiment's Guard Battalion, which was drawn up in front of the Reich Aviation Ministry in the Wilhelmstraße. Walking behind him were Luftwaffe Generals Kesselring, Stumpff and Weise. Accompanying Göring, behind and to one side, was his close friend and adviser *Oberst* Bodenschatz, and, behind him and to the left was the

Commanding Officer of the General Göring Regiment, *Oberstleutnant* von Axthelm. Hermann Göring had earlier been promoted to the rank of *Generalfeldmarschall* on 4 February 1938. The band played the parade march of the General Göring Regiment: *Ein Jäger aus Kurpfalz*.

The Occupation of Bohemia and Moravia

The General Göring Regiment participated in the March 1939 occupation of Bohemia and Moravia with its march to Prague. The regiment's IV Flak Battalion accompanied the 2nd Light Infantry Division (later to become 2nd Panzer), its role being to guard the division's assembly areas. The battalion travelled overland through Grafenwöhr and Weiden, crossing the Böhmerwald into the Pilsen area. There it was given the mission of guarding the Skoda works.

The war diary kept by General Staff *Oberst* Walter von Hippel, the battalion's commanding officer, reveals that the headquarters of IV Flak Battalion was quartered in Dobris and Zamek – in the Hotel Heintz in the latter location – while the 15th Battery was quartered in Minisek, the 16th Battery in Novy Knin (later Hostomice), and the 17th Battery in Dobris. Also quartered in Dobris were the signals platoon and the motor vehicle transport column. The headquarters and main body of the 2nd Light Infantry Division occupied quarters in Beneschau before moving later to Konopiste Castle.

The move by HQ, IV Flak Battalion to Prague followed on 18 March 1939. On 5 April the battalion set out for home, driving to Meissen via Teplitz, Altenberg and Dresden. The following day the battalion completed the journey to Berlin via Großenhain, Jüterbog and Luckenwalde.

On 16 March Adolf Hitler addressed an order of the day to all who had participated in this occupation action:

"To the Commander-in-Chief of the Army

On 15 March 1939, through its rapid occupation of the most important cities of Bohemia and Moravia, the Army placed this former region of the Reich under the sovereignty of Greater Germany. In spite of the inclement winter weather that day and the difficult winter conditions, the units of the Army and the attached Luftwaffe units crossed the frontier and reached their objectives within a few hours of the order being issued.

The troops I encountered during the drive to Prague made an outstanding impression, in spite of the exertions which lay behind them.

I wish to express my special appreciation to each officer and man for his effort and conduct."

Adolf Hitler

The "Führer" addressed another decree to commander of the Luftwaffe *Generalfeldmarschall* Hermann Göring. In it Hitler stressed that the Luftwaffe had demonstrated a high degree of readiness, personal courage and skill in the decisive days of 15 and 16 March, for which he, Adolf Hitler, expressed his "special appreciation."

The Commander-in-Chief of the Luftwaffe concluded these mutual reassurances with an order of the day to his men:

"We thank fate that this objective was achieved in a peaceful manner. The powerful German Armed Forces were the guarantors of the maintenance of peace in the decisive days of the past week."

Göring's thanks were directed in particular to his "flying and signals units", as well as to the flak artillery for the work they had done in the past months of securing the Reich. His closing words were:

"In recent days our German brothers and sisters in Bohemia and Moravia and the whole Czechoslovak people have seen the imposing strength of our proud Luftwaffe. They shall all be protected forever by the strength of our arm. – Hermann Göring."

In August 1939 the General Göring Regiment completed its reorganization in preparation for war. Joining the elements which existed in peacetime were:

The 14th (Heavy) Railway Flak Battery (105mm) under *Leutnant* Arnold.

The Reserve Searchlight Battalion.

The Replacement Battalion under *Major* von Ludwig.

On 16 August the General Göring Regiment received the order to mobilize. This was carried out without any official announcement and was completed within a few days, almost unnoticed by the population. At this time the following units were assigned to the Replacement Battalion:

HQ Battery, 1st and 2nd Batteries with 88mm Flak.

The 3rd Battery, which was equipped with 37mm and 20mm weapons, and the 4th Battery, which was equipped with Scheinwerfer 150 searchlights.

The unit's commanding officer, who had transferred from the Army to the Luftwaffe only weeks before, was known fondly by his soldiers as "Old Fritz." The Replacement Battalion was quartered in the barracks in Berlin-Reinickendorf. These were now largely empty, as the main body of the regiment had left for the areas designated in the event of war.

As part of the mobilization the entire regiment was inoculated. The first man to be inoculated by *Stabsarzt* Dr. Siebert was the regimental commander, *Oberst* von Axthelm, after which Siebert and his assistants set about injecting every member of the unit.

Peacetime, and with it the formation and equipping of the General Göring Regiment in preparation for the real thing, was over. What followed was a years-long struggle on all fronts and the steady expansion of this unit first to a division and finally to a parachute panzer corps.

Tables of Establishment for Flak Units, 15 July, 1939.

KStN	Einheit	Personen				Geschütze (cm)				Scheinwerfer (cm)		Kraftfahrzeuge							Bahn-wagen	Fahr-räder
		Offz.	Beamte	Uffz. u. Mannsch.	Gesamt	2	3,7	8,8		60	150	Krad (u. Beiw.)	Pkw	Lkw	Anh.	Kom.	Sdr. Kfz.	Kfz+Anh. ges.		
2101 (L)	Stb. Flak-Rgt.[1]) }	5			76							6 (1)	1	3			13	23		
2181 (L)	Nachr.Zug		71																	
2111 (L)	Stb. le.Flak-Abt. (mot.) }	7	4	75	86							11 (4)	3	6			10	30		
2184 (L)	Nachr.Zug																			
2401 (L)	Flak-Bttr. 3,7 cm (mot. Z)	5		197	202		9			4		15 (3)	6	18	14		13	66		
2202 (L)	Flak-Bttr. 2 cm (mot. S)	6		169	175	12						17 (3)	2	9			30	58		
2462 (L)	Flak-Kolonne (20 t) (mot.)	2		54	56							5	1	15				21		
2131 (L)	Stb. Flak-Abt. (mot.) }	7	5	101	113					4		11 (3)	3	7			15	36		
2185 (L)	Nachr.Zug																			
2447 (L)	Flak-Meßzug (mot.)	1		27	28							1		2			1	4		
2451 (L)	Flak-Wetterzug (mot.)			9	9							1					1	2		
2331 (L)	Flak-Bttr. 8,8 cm (mot. Z)	4		152	156	2		4				8 (2)	4	9	9		12	42		
2201 (L)	Flak-Bttr. 2 cm (mot. Z)	6		215	221	12						18 (3)	7	9	17		28	79		
2464 (L)	Flak-Kanone (42 t) (mot.)	2		57	59	2		2				5	1	16				22		
2353 (L)	Flak-Bttr. 8,8 cm (Eisb.)	3		74	77	2									3			3	13	3
2253 (L)	Flak-Zug 2 cm (Eisb.)	2		40	42	4										2		2	2	
2151 (L)	Stb. Flak-Scheinw. Abt. (mot.) }	7	4	82	93							10 (4)	3	6			12	31		
2186 (L)	Nachr.Zug																			
2531 (L)	Flak-Schw.Bttr. (mot.)	5		225	230						9	13 (5)	5	35	28		10	91		
2157 (L)	Stb.Res.Flak-Schw.Abt.	4	1	54	59							4 (2)	5	6			4	19		3
2537 (L)	Res.Flak-Schw.Bttr.	4		149	153						9			34				34		10

[1]) Without Band

A grenadier unit on the march.

The first members of Police Battalion Wecke.

The men of Special-Purpose Police Battalion Wecke assembled for a group photo.

Heiligendamm 1936. From left: Göring, his servant Kropp and adjutant Conrath.

Special armored car of the Wecke Special-Purpose State Police Group. The vehicle was armed with two machine-guns in a revolving turret.

Charlottenburg 1934: General der Infanterie Göring inspects the Special-Purpose State Police Group Wecke. Left, Major Wecke.

The "General Göring" State Police Group in parade formation at the Lichterfelde Cadet Training Institute on 19 May, 1934.

Göring, now Luftwaffe Commander-in-Chief, on hand to see the police group presented its colors on 29 May, 1934.

Fall 1935. I Battalion "General Göring" Regiment's honor company. In the middle with drawn sword is Lt. Schlichting.

The funeral of Chief of Air Armaments Ernest Udet.

Göring and the honor guard at Udet's grave side.

The Ju 52 "Wilhelm Cuno", one of the aircraft assigned to carry the Führer.

Budapest 1935: Wreath-laying ceremony at the memorial on Margaretha Island. From right: State Secretary Milch, Göring. On the far left is Göring's adjutant Major Conrath.

Göring salutes at the memorial in Budapest.

The new barracks in Berlin-Reinickendorf; here the regimental headquarters building.

Göring at the ceremony opening the barracks. Behind him is Oberstleutnant von Axthelm.

The flag of I Battalion, General Göring Regiment.
Left: Leutnant Hubert, middle: Oberfeldwebel Büttner

Flugkapitän Hans Bauer, Hitler's chief pilot and a veteran of the First World War, photographed in 1938 in the uniform of an SS-Gruppenführer.

Hitler and Göring in conversation.

The Reichsjägerhof (Reich Hunting Lodge) in the Rominten Heath. Göring in conversation with an officer; on the far right is Oberst Conrath.

Leutnant Lübke at Karinhall with the duty watch, 1937.

Adolf Hitler visits Karinhall. On the right is Emmy Göring with daughter Emma.

At the evening reception. Hermann Göring tries his luck.

The 10th Guard Company, RGG on Air Force Day 1938.

Oberst von Axthelm photographed in November 1938.

The "Flak Eighty-eight", a thoroughly effective weapon against air and ground targets.

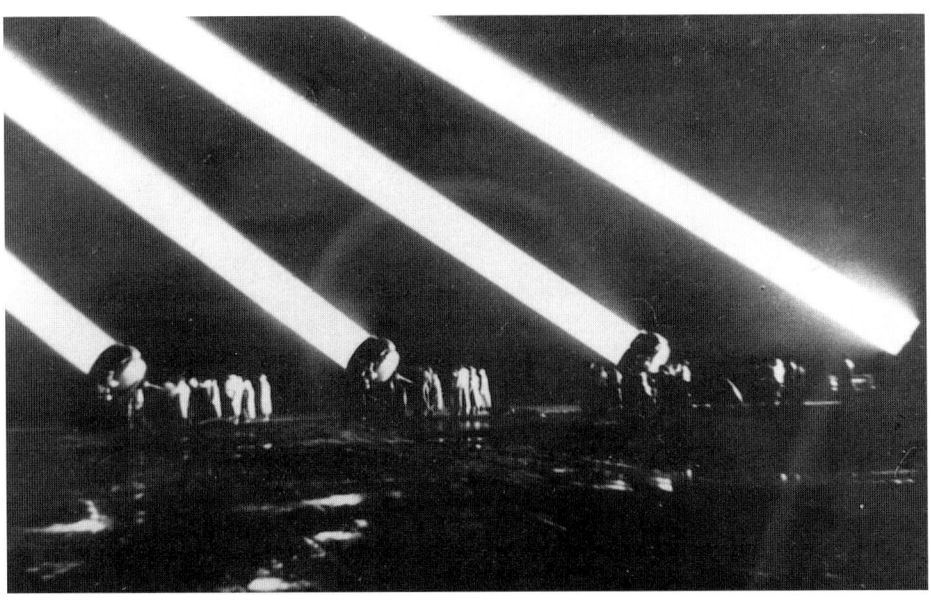
Night exercise by a searchlight battalion of the General Göring Regiment.

II. THE GENERAL GÖRING REGIMENT AT WAR

Final Preparations

On Friday, the 25th of August 1939, the Commanding Officer of III Battalion, *Major* von Oppeln-Bronikowski, called all the officers of his battalion together and informed them that he had just come from a command briefing, where the Commanding General of *Luftgaukommando* III, *Generalleutnant* Weise, had informed those present that:

"The Reich government considers a war with Poland unavoidable, if the unbearable threat in the east of the Reich is to be brought to an end. Poland must be eliminated as a military power. An entry into the war by the western powers must be reckoned upon, as these will fulfill their obligations to assist Poland. In this event the ground forces will go into battle under French command and the air and sea forces under British command."

On the following Saturday the regiment received a teletype from *Luftgaukommando* III stating that effective immediately the Wehrmacht Allowance Law was in effect. As a result the entire unit supply organization had to be converted from peacetime to wartime economy and the men paid active service pay and, if warranted, a front-line allowance.

On 1 September every member of the regiment who could listened to the radio broadcast from the Kroll Opera House, where the hastily-convened *Reichstag* was sitting. When the words "Have been returning fire since 0545" rang out, everyone knew that the decision had been made. The following evening it was announced over the radio that the rationing of foodstuffs would begin on Monday, 3 September 1939, and that all rations cards, including tobacco and clothing cards, would be distributed on Sunday.

On 3 September hopes that the Western Allies would not intervene in the war were dashed. In their declarations of war, France and England observed that they now "found themselves at war with Germany."

One of the first wartime "accomplishments" of III Light Flak Battalion was the near shooting down of an unidentified aircraft in early October 1939. A "light and fire ban" was in effect, nevertheless III Battalion was given the order to turn on its searchlights to identify the aircraft. The cluster of searchlight beams illuminated the aircraft, which turned out to be a Ju 52. The pilot of the Junkers was so blinded by the beams that he lost control of his aircraft and crashed. As fate would have it the Junkers crashed almost at the feet of the Commander-in-Chief of the Luftwaffe Hermann Göring.

That same night the battalion commander was summoned to report directly to "Hermann." Although completely innocent of any blame in the disaster, *Major* von Oppeln-Bronikowski was immediately relieved as commanding officer and transferred to the "red" (Army) flak. III Flak Battalion had brought down its first aircraft (albeit with searchlights); however, it was a pity that it was one of their own. (The relief of cavalry officer Hermann von

Oppeln-Bronikowski was a stroke of luck for the panzer arm, for the Olympic champion of 1936 found a new home there, rising to the rank of General and earning the Knight's Cross with Oak Leaves and Swords.

At the end of October the persistent rumors became a reality and the General Göring Regiment was transferred to the West. At the outbreak of war the command positions of the General Göring Regiment were occupied as follows:

General Göring Regiment:	Oberstleutnant von Axthelm
I (Heavy) Battalion:	Hauptmann Hullmann
II (Light) Battalion:	Hauptmann Rüdel
III (Searchlight) Battalion:	Major von Oppeln-Bronikowski (after mid-October Hauptmann Lindenberg)
IV (Light) Battalion:	Oberstleutnant von Hippel
Guard Battalion:	Major Weber (formed in course of mobilization from 16 August 1939:)
Reserve Searchlight Battalion:	Reserve Major ...
Reserve Battalion:	Major von Ludwig

War Zone Germany 1939

One of the regiment's most vital missions was the protection of the Commander-in-Chief of the Luftwaffe's headquarters in Potsdam, Wildpark-Werder and in the Karinhall. It also provided the escort units for the Führer train and for other headquarters, especially at the front in Poland. Beginning in October 1939 elements of the regiment were transferred to the *Westwall* (known to the Allies as the Siegfried Line).

During the Polish Campaign the flak units of the General Göring Regiment, which made up the bulk of the unit, were primarily deployed around Berlin to protect the Reich capital. At the end of October 1939 Headquarters, General Göring Regiment was given the cover designation 103rd Flak Regiment. The regimental headquarters and I and IV Battalions were placed under the command of the newly-formed II Flak Corps. III Battalion came under the command of the likewise recently-created I Flak Corps. It was the latter battalion that was transferred to the *Westwall* in the area of Trier and Aachen in October.

In September 1939 the Guard Company's cavalry squadron under *Hauptmann* Kluge was transferred, partly by air, into the Warsaw area, in order to protect and defend the airfields and installations of the Polish aviation industry located there. Other elements of the Guard Battalion were transported to their operational area around Warsaw by truck.

Located in the Rominten Heath, the *Reichsjägerhof*, the HQ of the Commander-in-Chief of the Luftwaffe during the Polish Campaign, was guarded by the 8th Battery. On their way there the soldiers of the battery passed by time-honored Marienburg. Göring was in his element among the circle of his officers and faithful followers there. *Oberstleutnant* Conrath, who was to lead the General Göring Regiment during the French Campaign, was among the guests.

The 14th Railway Flak Battery

The path of this battery of the General Göring Regiment, which was equipped with 105mm anti-aircraft guns, led from mobilization in Reinickendorf to Hollersleben near Magdeburg. The battery stayed in Hollersleben and Satzkorn, ready for action, from September until 25 November, 1939 when it was transferred to Stolpmünde. Later the battery was moved back to Satzkorn. In the first ten days of December the 14th Battery was transferred by rail 854 kilometers to Krozingen. Thus in the period which ended on 10 December this single battery had travelled 2,140 kilometers. Even this record performance was soon topped, however, for on 10 December the battery set out on a journey that took it to Offenburg, Lahr, Riegel-Ort, Königsschaffhausen, Breisach, Rastatt, Lahr, Iffezheim, and back through Breisach to Krozingen again, which meant an additional 839 kilometers.

The battery spent a great deal of time riding the rails, with the result that the gunners got to know the lovely Black Forest very well. On the other side of the coin, the Commander-in-Chief of the Luftwaffe gained new insights into the use of this potent weapon. This shuttling about affected almost every one of the regiment's units. The Army made no exceptions in this regard. This illustrates one of the most time-consuming and senseless caprices of the home command, about which nothing has ever before been said. It is worth noting that by 22 June 1941, the day of the beginning of the Russian Campaign, the 14th Battery had travelled a total of 12,377 kilometers.

Concerning the operation of the battery, which was the first one to carry out trials with the 105mm Flak, the battery commander, *Oberleutnant* Arnold, has stated that it was initially placed under the direct command of the Commander-in-Chief of the Luftwaffe on account of its special status. The battery was also equipped with two 20mm light Flak. The entire battery was loaded onto railway cars. Only the battery commander was provided with an automobile.

In addition to the previous general information, Dr. Arnold also provided details concerning actions involving the battery. Action in the *Westwall*, in particular the engaging of bunkers in the Maginot Line, were highly successful. The penetrative power of the 105mm Flak was phenomenal. However, its secondary effects were considerable as well; the tremendous shock waves produced by the firing of this battery in German positions stripped the shingles from the roofs of all the houses in the vicinity, which did not contribute to the battery's popularity.

Oberleutnant Arnold commanded the battery from 30 September 1939 until 20 October 1941, a period of more than two years. His battery officers were *Leutnante* von Goetze, Jahr, and Haacke. The crews servicing the four guns consisted of four officers and 161 men.

The overall makeup of the battery was: battery HQ detail, ranging section, signals section, support section, command sections I and II, and a light flak squad. Other battery equipment consisted of four cars, twelve trucks, and eight motorcycles.

On 20 October 1941 this successful battery left the General Göring Brigade and became the 321st (Railroad) Reserve Flak Battalion.

The "Führer" Flak Train in the Polish Campaign

When Adolf Hitler travelled to Poland with his staff, he made use of the "Führer" Flak Train, which has often been mentioned but never described in detail. It was a special train which was made up as follows:

>First and second locomotives.
>
>Flak car, baggage wagon.
>
>Hitler's salon car
>
>Command car with storeroom and switchboard.
>
>Escort detachment car with 11 compartments and 22 man escort detachment, consisting of SS soldiers and police officials.
>
>First dining car.
>
>First guest car with 10 compartments.
>
>Second guest car with 10 compartments.
>
>Second dining car.
>
>First and second sleeping cars, both first class.
>
>Press car, baggage car.
>
>Second flak car.

A third locomotive was added on routes that included long uphill grades, installed at the end of the train. Each flak car accommodated a section leader and two crews of eight men; the entire flak crew consisted of 34 soldiers. Additional cars included a bathing car, a car with an electrical generator, and a railroad personnel car.

The flak cars each had a crew of 16 men and a section leader. The soldiers were accommodated in four similar compartments; the fifth compartment, whose door could be locked, was used by the section leader. Each of the four compartments was occupied by four soldiers. The section leader's compartment was equipped with a wash basin, a small locking closet and a couch. In 1939 the commander of the flak platoon was *Oberleutnant* Aetting. He was later relieved by *Leutnant* Sehmsdorf. The two guest cars were reserved for Hitler's high-ranking guests. They were used by Mussolini, as well as by Ribbentrop and Himmler.

The functions of the flak car personnel were as follows: K1 = gunner, K2 = range finder, K3 and K4 = ammunition carriers, K5 and K6 = loaders. Until mid-1940, on Führer trains the crews were quartered in the middle of the train. Ammunition was stored near the guns. It should be noted that changes were frequent, however this description is accurate for the period 1939.

The General Göring Regiment 1939-1940

On completion of its guard duties in Wildpark-Werder, which mainly concerned securing the wooded area surrounding the headquarters there, the cavalry squadron was reorganized as a motorcycle rifle company. The reorganized company consisted of a cavalry section (which was taken over from the former cavalry squadron and which assumed the previous role of the squadron) and three platoons. In addition to two rifle platoons, there was an armored reconnaissance platoon equipped with three eight-wheeled armored scout cars. This motorcycle company was one of the first units of the General Göring Regiment to see combat, as will be described in the chapter concerning the Norwegian Campaign.

On 1 September 1939 the four flak battalions which were later to form the Hermann Göring Flak Regiment were:

I (Heavy) Flak Battalion with 1st-3rd Batteries armed with 88mm Flak and 4th and 5th Batteries with 20mm FlaMW as well as a heavy (48-tonne capacity) flak transport column.

II (Light) Flak Battalion with 6th Battery armed with 37mm and 7th-9th Batteries armed with 20mm FlaMW, as well as a light (28-tonne capacity) flak transport column.

III Searchlight Battalion with 11th-13th Batteries equipped with 1500mm searchlights.

14th Railway Flak Battery with 105mm railway Flak.

IV (Light) Flak Battalion with 15th Battery with 37mm and 16th and 17th Batteries with 20mm FlaMW, as well as a light (28-tonne capacity) flak transport column.

RGG Replacement Battalion with HQ Battery, the 1st and 2nd Replacement Batteries with 88mm Flak, the 4th Replacement Battery with 1500mm searchlights, and 5th Convalescent Battery.

Reserve Searchlight Battery. Its cadre personnel came in part from III Searchlight Battalion, 32nd Flak Regiment, Berlin-Heiligensee.

As described earlier, a replacement battalion was formed within the General Göring Regiment in the course of mobilization, this unit consisting of an HQ Battery, the 1st and 2nd Replacement Batteries with 88mm Flak, the 3rd Replacement Battery with 37mm light flak, the 4th Replacement Battery with 1500mm Searchlights, and the 5th Convalescent Battery.

Assigned to the General Göring Regiment were: a 48-tonne flak transport column for I Battalion, General Göring Regiment, and the 14th Company, General Göring Regiment equipped with 105mm Flak which was described earlier.

II Battalion, General Göring Regiment established a 28-tonne transport column, which was responsible for the transport of its equipment and material, while III Battalion, General Göring Regiment formed the reserve searchlight battalion. The necessary personnel, as far as "specialists" were concerned, came from the neighboring 32nd Flak Regiment's III (Searchlight) Battalion.

IV Battalion, General Göring Regiment likewise formed a 28-tonne flak transport column, which was responsible for this battalion's transport requirements.

All of the named flak battalions of the General Göring Regiment, with the exception of the Flak Replacement Battalion, were at first deployed to defend the Reich capital against air attack. They moved into their prepared mobilization positions in the Wildpark-Werder – Wustermark – Bötzow – Velten area, in the western and northern sectors of the anti-aircraft ring around Berlin.

The 7th Battery, together with the 2nd Guard Company, was delegated to protect Führer Headquarters. The 8th Battery was selected for special missions, for example with the Kluge Detachment in the Norwegian Campaign. The 9th Battery, the so-called "escort battery," provided crews for the railway flak platoons designated "Führer Platoon," "Foreign Minister Platoon", and "Reichsmarschall Platoon." These platoons were equipped with 20mm guns in quadruple mounts. Headquarters, II Battalion, General Göring Regiment served as the headquarters of the Potsdam Flak-Subgroup within the framework of the Berlin Air Defense.

After the end of the Polish Campaign a number of active flak battalions were concentrated in two newly-formed Flak Corps and readied for the Western Campaign. Among the units so detached were I (Heavy), III (Searchlight), and IV (Light) Battalions of the General Göring Regiment. The Regimental HQ was also forced to accept detached service. For the next twelve months it used the cover designation of the 103rd Flak Regiment; together with the three named battalions, it was withdrawn from Berlin's air defences and transferred to the *Westwall*.

During the fighting Western Europe these units served in the Army's I Flak Corps – III Battalion temporarily with II Flak Corps – and after the conclusion of hostilities as part of the air defenses on the Atlantic Coast. The end of September 1940 saw them transferred back to Berlin, where the Regimental HQ received its old designation once again and, with its battalions, took over the duties of the newly-formed 1st Air Defence Command.

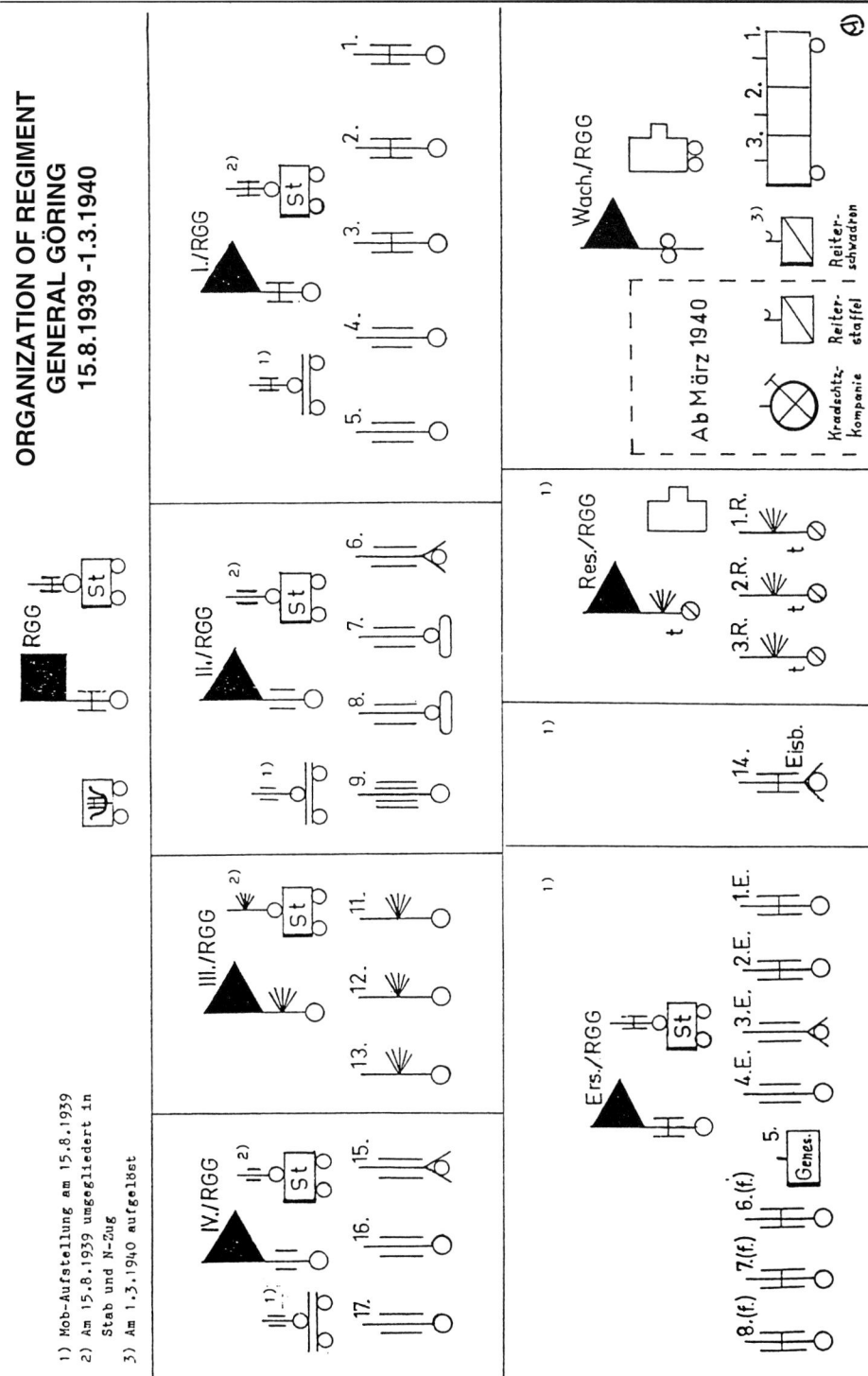

Operation "Weserübung"

The formation and training of the Motorcycle Company had just reached the stage where the company was combat-ready when Operation "Weserübung" – the march through Denmark and the occupation of Norway to safeguard German shipments of iron ore – began. Elements of the General Göring Guard Battalion and the Motorcycle Company took part in the operations in Scandinavia as the "Kluge Detachment" under the command of *Hauptmann* Kluge.

The battle group was formed as a security unit and placed under the command of X *Fliegerkorps*. The unit's special mission was the safeguarding of forward Luftwaffe airfields. As a security battalion the unit was fully motorized. It was to be the first unit of the General Göring Regiment to see action. *Hauptmann* Kluge, commander of 2nd Guard Company, was given this special command on 5 April 1940. His instructions were to form a battalion-size formation, but initially he was not told what the unit's equipment and role would be. At first the unit was known only as the Kluge Battalion. The formation was then given the title General Göring Regiment Motorcycle Battalion, before, on orders from above, it was designated the "Kluge Detachment."

The unit's composition was as follows:

HQ with signals platoon: Formed from Headquarters, Watch Battalion RGG:	Hptm. Kluge
Motorcycle Company RGG:	Hptm. Preuß
1st Guard Company RGG:	Hptm. Funck
8th Battery RGG:	Hptm. Seewald

Planned as an escort detachment for the Commander-in-Chief of the Luftwaffe and organized especially for this role, the Motorcycle Company consisted of three light and one heavy platoons, as well as an armored reconnaissance platoon with three eight-wheeled armored cars and a radio platoon with five 100-watt stations.

1st Guard Company was a motorized rifle company of three platoons. The 8th Flak Battery RGG consisted of four platoons each with three 20mm light anti-aircraft guns on self-propelled carriages. According to the directive issued by the OKW on 1 March, all three components of the *Wehrmacht* – Army, Navy and Air Force – were to participate in a joint issuance of orders during *Fall Weserübung*. This was the first triphibious operation of the Second World War. As plans for the campaign in Western Europe had already been finalized, forces for Norway and Denmark had to be kept as limited as possible. "Numerical weakness was to be compensated for by bold action and surprise operations."

On 5 April 1940 *Hauptmann* Kluge brought his unit to alert march readiness. At 0220 hours the next morning it left the barracks in Berlin-Reinickendorf and set out for its initial destination, Borstel, near Winsen/Luhe. During the Norwegian Campaign all Luftwaffe units and formations operated under the command of *Luftflottenkommando* 5 or X

Fliegerkorps, on the understanding that in the course of the action it might be necessary to place them under the command of Army units, which in fact happened.

On 6 April the Kluge Detachment was placed under the command of the 6th Panzer Division's 11th Rifle Brigade commanded by *Oberst* Angern. From brigade headquarters in Lüneburg *Hauptmann* Kluge received news that his unit had been selected for action in Denmark.

On 7 April the detachment resumed its march from Borstel. The march was halted again in Koldenbüttel near Friedrichstadt. At 2300 hours the detachment set out from Koldenbüttel for its assembly area. Not until this was reached was Kluge permitted to inform his unit leaders of their objective, which bore the cover designation "Exercise Weser-South." As part of March Group B of the reinforced 11th Rifle Brigade, the detachment moved up into its jumping-off positions. The last stage of the drive through Husum and Bredstedt to Holt was made in the dark without lights. In spite of these measures, at times the vehicles had to travel at speeds of 60 kph in order not to lose contact.

Holm-Medelby was reached at four o'clock in the morning on 9 April. There XXXI Special Corps' Corps Order No. 3 was issued. In it the Commanding General, *General der Flieger* Kaupisch, charged the Kluge Detachment with the "surprise occupation of Denmark." It was to take possession of the city of Ejsberg, with its harbour, airfield and cable station, as quickly as possible. On reaching Ejsberg the detachment was to be placed under the command of the 170th Infantry Division. Following the issuing of all weapons, including hand grenades, the march was continued to the border.

As per orders, the first patrols of the von Hassel reconnaissance squadron were sent across the Danish border at 0515. At the same time other German forces were crossing the frontier on its entire width. Meeting no resistance, the leading patrol, which consisted of four armored cars, rolled through the first Danish villages. After several kilometers of unhindered progress on Danish soil the patrol came under fire from anti-tank guns. Casualties were three dead and four wounded. All four armored cars were put out of action. The Danes lost two killed and 39 men surrendered.

At 1200 hours the Kluge Detachment, which was still in its jumping-off positions, received orders to drive on and crossed the border near Pepersmark. Passing through Rends, Bredevad, Lögumkloster, Rödding, Holsted and Tarp, the detachment arrived in Ejsberg. The airfield north of the city was reached at about 1800. Both the sea and land airfield and the telegraph office were seized without bloodshed. Soon afterward the first air base company and a ground echelon went to work on the airfield. The signals company occupied the telegraph office. Contact was established with elements of the Navy and Army arriving by sea.

On 9 April the Danish War Ministry and the Naval Ministry issued a joint order to the Danish forces, instructing them "to cease all resistance and dispatch liaison detachments to the units of the Wehrmacht." The Danish armed forces were to retain their arms. It was agreed that German and Danish soldiers would be required to salute one another. The attitude of the population was a cooperative one. Any intimidation of the Danish population or soldiers by German troops was a punishable offence. *Oberst* Angern, Commanding Officer of the 11th Rifle Brigade, expressed his appreciation to all participants in this action.

Action in Norway

Once arriving Luftwaffe units took over the job of guarding Ejsberg airfield, naval units secured the harbour, and the Army occupied the most important points in the city, the Kluge Detachment was free for new duties. On 11 April it received orders from the 170th Infantry Division to move into the area east of Aalborg and guard the coastline against attempted enemy landings, while at the same time assuming responsibility for the air defence of the area.

The Lökken-Fjerritslev-Ellidsbök security area, a strip of coastline along the Jammer Bight, formed the detachment's new area of responsibility. The companies and batteries quickly moved into positions there which had been scouted ahead of time. On 13 April, the Flak Battery was placed under the command of the 300th Special-Purpose *Luftgau* Headquarters and incorporated into the air defenses of Frederikshavn. All of the remaining units of the detachment continued their security duties. The idea of transferring all available troops from Denmark to Norway was raised on 11 April at a situation briefing in the OKW. This notion became reality on 13 April with the order to transfer to Norway machine-gun battalions and panzer units, as well as the "air battalion" – as the Kluge Detachment was referred to. *Hauptmann* Kluge handed over his positions to I Battalion, 110th Rifle Battalion. The detachment made ready for sea transport and on the evening of 17 April 1940 embarked on the troopship *Campinas*; however only the vehicles and 96 drivers remained on board the transport ship.

The next afternoon the main body of the detachment was taken by rail to Frederikshavn. From there the unit embarked on the torpedo boats *Falke* and *Jaguar* on 20 April – the Führer's birthday. At 0500 hours both vessels left Frederikshavn and set course for Norway. At this point the Flak Battery was released from the detachment and returned to Berlin.

The weather was fair as the two torpedo boats sailed through the Skagerrak. An enemy submarine was spotted and forced to submerge. Oslo was reached at 1800 hours, and after disembarking the troops marched into the city and occupied quarters in the Ila-Skole. A German convoy, which included the troopship *Campinas* with the detachment's vehicles and heavy equipment, arrived in Oslo the next day. The vehicles were unloaded and driven to the Ila-Skole. The detachment was thus fully operational again.

By now the *Kriegsmarine* and units of the Army had occupied the most important ports in Norway. Further troops landed and began the advance into the interior of the country. Among these units was I Battalion, 1st Parachute Regiment under *Hauptmann* Walther, who later became commanding officer of the 2nd Parachute Panzer-Grenadier Division Hermann Göring. The situation of the German forces in Norway became precarious when the Western Allies landed powerful units at Harstad (60 km east of Narvik), Namsos, and Andalsnes on 13 and 14 April. This was one of the reasons why the Wehrmacht sent additional units, such as the Kluge Detachment, to Norway.

The main Allied objectives were the seizure of Narvik, held by the 3rd Mountain Infantry Division under *Generalleutnant* Dietl, and Trondheim, which was also occupied by German troops.

The allied command decided not to take Trondheim by sea through the 40-kilometer-long fiord, rather via the land route, outflanking the German positions from Namsos and Andalsnes. The German command soon became aware of this move, which it countered by attempting to quickly establish an overland link between Oslo and Trondheim.

After disarming the 2nd Norwegian Division positioned around Oslo, the German 196th Infantry Division under *Generalleutnant* Pellengahr, which had landed in the Norwegian capital, was given this assignment. The division had lost approximately 1,000 men during the voyage to Oslo, when the transports *Wigbert* and *Friedenau* were sunk, as a result of which it had to be divided into individual battle groups. To provide the division with the firepower necessary to allow it to advance to Andalsnes, the 13th Machine-gun Battalion, the 40th Panzer Battalion, and the Kluge Detachment were all placed under its command. As the detachment was fully motorized, it represented a worthwhile reinforcement for the 196th Infantry Division.

The difficult nature of the terrain compelled the German forces to confine their advance to the precipitous valleys. The two selected were the Österdal and the Gutbrandsdal. Also advancing on the left was *Kampfgruppe* (Battle Group) Adlhoch of the 163rd Infantry Division. Resistance by Norwegian forces and the 148th British Brigade was smashed in bitter fighting on both sides of Mjös Lake and west of Rand Fiord. The enemy suffered heavy losses.

On the evening of the 22nd *Hauptmann* Kluge received orders from the commanding general of XXI Group, *General der Infanterie* von Falkenhorst, to immediately leave Oslo for Rena via Hamar-Elverum; on arrival there he was to report to the commander of *Kampfgruppe* Fischer, the reinforced 340th Infantry Regiment. Rena was reached. A motorized advance battalion was formed in the village of Aamot. The unit was called the "von Burstin Motorized Detachment" after its commander, *Hauptmann* von Burstin of the 40th Special Purpose Panzer Battalion from Wünsdorf.

The battalion consisted of:

> 1st Company, 40th Special Purpose Panzer Battalion (equipped with Panzer I and II tanks),
>
> 2nd Company, 82nd Mountain Pioneer Battalion (Motorized),
>
> two platoons of the 14th (Anti-tank) Company, 340th Infantry Regiment,
>
> the Kluge Detachment.

This potent battle group was supposed to reconnoiter the advance roads and open them for *Kampfgruppe* Fischer. Its primary tasks were to remove the roadblocks set up by Norwegian troops, render ineffective other blocking measures, secure all bridges, find alternate routes where bridges had been destroyed, scout the enemy, and guard the battle group's flanks to the greatest extent possible. In this way the advance battalion was to ensure that *Kampfgruppe* Fischer reached Trondheim quickly and that British troops which had landed were prevented from reinforcing the Norwegians, who were putting up a fight.

A series of raids were planned into the enemy's rear by the fast unit to keep the advance road open in front of *Kampfgruppe* Fischer. The situation was completely unclear, the road conditions were unknown, the weather was unfavorable, and the supply situation, especially deliveries of fuel, was doubtful. On the day of its formation, the motorized von Burstin Battalion was sent forward in the direction of Stor Lake. At the same time part of the motorized battalion under *Hauptmann* Preuß was sent along the shore to Koppang, west of Stor Lake. Parts of the Kluge Detachment accompanied both elements of the battle group.

All units were under orders to immediately clear any disabled vehicles from the road and if necessary to push them into the gorges. Nothing was to be permitted to impede a rapid advance. The following account of the events of the first days by Rolf Gerhardt of the Motorcycle Company says more than all the war diary entries could:

"When we stopped near the infantry sentries at the exit from Rhena on the afternoon of 23 April, we were met by a terrible scene. The bodies of German soldiers killed the previous day were still lying on the road about 400 meters in front of us. The infantry there greeted us with tears of relief on account of our armored vehicles. Never in all my later actions in Norway, Russia, Tunisia, and elsewhere did I see such a demoralized unit and such a helpless infantry command. The sight of the unburied dead in particular went through and through us. Here we became acquainted with the fury of war and many of the young soldiers were unable to deal with it."

This was never mentioned in any report on Norway, especially not in the reports of success by the OKW and the units, from division up to army. Gerhardt's report continues:

"The demoralization of the troops there had been inevitable. It was a completely inexperienced unit, facing an invisible enemy well capable of inflicting lethal blows on the German troops. When our troops approached the roadblock the Norwegians had shot them down like wild animals, with bullets to the head, heart and lungs. Following their military service, every Norwegian was allowed to take his rifle and telescopic sight home for use in hunting. They were the best marksmen I ever saw.

Oberst Fischer, the unit's commander, was dismayed. The old *Reichswehr* officer didn't have a very high opinion of the alien art of inter-service cooperation. Not until *Hauptmann* Kluge threatened to contact the *Reichsmarschall* if he didn't request air support, did we receive support from the air near Naverdalen." This concludes Gerhardt's account.

After motorcycle troops and infantry had removed several roadblocks and the nests of Norwegian resistance had been outflanked, attacked from the rear and eliminated, the advance was much quicker. In Aasheim the motorized von Burstin Battalion turned southward in the direction of Koppang. One objective was the securing of the important bridges near Koppang and Stai for the following main body. This was successfully accomplished. In addition to this, contact had to be established with the second attacking spearhead, the motorized battalion advancing west of Stor Lake. This battle group captured a Norwegian corps headquarters with five officers and 60 members of the headquarters staff.

The next morning the advance was continued from Aasheim north to Tynset. This time the bridges in Tynset were the objective. In Tynset the west road had to be barricaded to stop enemy forces approaching from that direction. Near Rendal, 20 kilometers north of Aasheim, there was an engagement with Norwegian ski troops. The Kluge Detachment suffered no casualties. Tynset was taken on the morning of 25 April and cleared of enemy forces. *Hauptmann* Funck was installed as local commandant.

Thirty Norwegians with horse-drawn vehicles were captured when they failed to escape in time. A fuel dump and an explosives dump were captured, together with a loaded munitions train standing in the station. A goods train was also seized. The rapid German advance was beginning to have an effect, taking away much of the aggressiveness of the retreating Norwegians.

From Tynset the battle group advanced to Stören and Berkaak. The advance battalion received orders to reconnoiter to the front and sides as quickly as possible, so as to ensure the main body a rapid advance and prevent the enemy from settling down again. Near Ulsberg and Berkaak the roads from the south and northwest had to be secured against advancing British forces. For this purpose the von Burstin Battalion once again formed two groups and sent them towards Stören and Röros, as well as through Kvikne towards Berkaak.

Elements of the Kluge Detachment's fast and armored units as well as those of the panzer and mountain pioneer companies were assigned to both groups. Their orders were: "conduct reconnaissance to assess enemy resistance, determine whether units on the road to the north should reckon on contact with British units, and locate and if possible remove road barricades. Also block the side roads from Ulsberg to Oppendal and from Berkaak to Renebu, from where British units are expected."

The battle group deployed towards Stören set out early on the morning of 25 April, reached the garrison city of Röros without interference from the enemy, and seized it. Residents reported that their soldiers had fled toward the border with Sweden the previous evening. Norwegian reservists picked up during the advance to Röros stated that they had been released and sent home.

Continuing the advance, the battle group came upon a blown bridge 4 kilometers north of Röros. Bypassing the bridge in the narrow Gaul Valley with motorized units was impossible and the group returned to Tynset. An aerial reconnaissance report that day stated that British forces were advancing on Tynset. The group which returned from Röros was ordered to reconnoiter from Tynset to Alvdal, advance into the valleys which branched off to the west, and bring in a number of prisoners in order to discover the strength and nature of the enemy. After driving 25 kilometers there was an half-hour battle with Norwegian troops. The group suffered several casualties before the enemy fell back. Pursuit of the enemy forces was impossible as they blew a bridge behind them as they retreated. The group returned to Tynset.

On that same 26 April the 3rd Platoon of the Motorcycle Company under *Leutnant* Gerhardt came under heavy fire from three sides after driving around a blind curve 10 kilometers west of Foldal. The platoon had been spotted by a light ski-equipped sport aircraft and its position reported to the enemy. The men of the platoon jumped from their still rolling motorcycles and took cover in a shallow ditch at the side of the road. A German armored car spotted muzzle flashes and opened fire, inflicting casualties on the invisible enemy. Fortunately the following tanks arrived on the scene, which decided the battle in favor of the Germans. The enemy was blasted out of his mountain positions, which would have been impervious to attacks by the motorcycle troops.

At the same time the battle group under *Hauptmann* Preuß was moving towards Berkaak. It had set out on the morning of 25 April, however at 1700 hours the advance was halted in front of a destroyed bridge over the Orkla, 4 kilometers south of Kvikne. Not until three hours later was the group able to cross the frozen river with the help of the pioneers. The advance was halted again an hour later near Lillefossen, 12 kilometers north of Kvikne. The bridge there had been blown too. Lengthy repairs by the pioneers were necessary before the bridge was passable again. The Preuß Battle Group found shelter for the night near Lillefossen.

On the morning of 26 April a squad from the motorcycle company set out on foot along a road high above the Orkla to scout the next bridge, located 500 meters south of Naaverdalen. It was halted by Norwegian ski troops after advancing two kilometers. The Norwegians fell back following a heavy exchange of fire; however, when the squad resumed its advance it was stopped again, not just by the knee-deep snow but by fire from the Norwegian rear guard as well. In spite of these difficulties, the squad reached the village of Naaverdalen, where to its disappointment it found that the bridge had been blown. Bypassing the wrecked bridge was impossible on account of the Norwegian positions in the rocks. An attack towards Naaverdalen by elements of the 340th Infantry Regiment was likewise halted in front of well-camouflaged and entrenched Norwegian positions.

Oberst Fischer now deployed the bulk of his battle group to open the Naaverdalen Valley; air support was requested as well. The attack planned for 0000 on 28 April was delayed by two hours on account of the narrow roads. Supported by two tanks and two 105mm guns, *Hauptmann* Funck's motorized rifle company dashed into Naaverdalen. Elements of the company occupied all the houses and established a bridgehead around the blown bridge just beyond the village to give the pioneers freedom of movement as they carried out repairs on the bridge.

It was the company's 1st Platoon, led by *Oberleutnant* Tobias, that left the houses on the left and advanced through the village to the bridge. The 2nd Platoon under *Oberleutnant* Budig and the 3rd Platoon under *Oberfeldwebel* Todzi combed the houses from which they had been fired upon the previous day. The 3rd Platoon occupied the houses while 2nd Platoon moved up to the bridge and reinforced *Oberleutnant* Tobias and his platoon.

1st Platoon, which was accompanied by *Hauptmann* Funck, was fired on by the Norwegians when it crossed the bridge; the enemy also rolled stones down the steep slopes. The enemy fire, especially from automatic weapons, intensified as the day grew lighter. 1st Platoon and elements of 2nd Platoon, as well as the two accompanying tanks, were forced to withdraw to the entrance to the village, from where the tanks fired upon identified enemy positions. The bridge lay under concentrated enemy fire. 1st Platoon sustained casualties of two dead and eight badly wounded. Eventually the bulk of the battle group was forced to pull back into the village houses. *Hauptmann* Funck was wounded during the retreat. As well, two men were killed and another 11 wounded seriously. *Oberleutnant* Budig assumed command. The requested air support arrived in the shape of one He 111 and one Bf 109 (!). They made several passes, dropping bombs and strafing, but without significantly disturbing the Norwegians, who were in good cover.

At 2335 an aircraft dropped a report signed by *Oberleutnant* Groschupf of the 222nd Bicycle Squadron (of the 181st Infantry Division). It stated that the Trondheim Group was advancing without meeting any resistance; at 1320 the infantry spearhead was near Soknedalen. *Oberleutnant* Paulus immediately formed an assault group made up of motorcycle troops, tank crews, and pioneers, and with this marched through Berkaak in order to establish contact with the approaching unit of the 181st Infantry Division. *Oberleutnant* Paulus and *Oberleutnant* Groschupf shook hands the next day, April 30, at 1145. Overland contact between Oslo and Trondheim had been established.

In spite of this success, the threat from Norwegian and British forces had yet to be eliminated. On 1 May the von Burstin Battalion was ordered to block the retreat of enemy forces withdrawing along the Oppdal – Hjerkinn road. The tanks and motorcycle troops of the Kluge Detachment were selected for this mission. The first 25 kilometers of the march was made by rail, as the roads were impassable on account of the blown bridges. An attempt was made to leave the train at a bridge five kilometers south of Ulsberg and continue by road, however the bridge collapsed beneath the weight of the leading tank. The operation was abandoned and the force withdrew towards Inset. On the evening of that 1 May it was learned that the Pellengahr Group – which had also been formed from the 196th Infantry Division and led by its commanding officer, *Generalleutnant* Richard Pellengahr – had occupied Oppdal and Hjerkinn. Furthermore, making use of four locomotives and fifty rail cars that had fallen into German hands, the group had captured the Hjerkinn – Oppdal – Ulsberg rail line intact. It was therefore now possible to transport the motorized von Burstin Battalion to Oppdal by rail.

Advances from Oppdal to Sunndalsöra and Kristiansund

The motorcycle riflemen were instructed to reconnoiter toward Sunndalsöra and Kristiansund, the next objectives. The result was a series of critical situations, but pleasing successes as well. For example, a British supply dump was seized near Thamshavn, while in Kvisvik motorcycle riflemen captured the war chest of the 2nd Norwegian Division. The latter unit ceased resistance on 3 May and was disbanded.

Following the hasty evacuation of Norway from Andalsnes and Namsos by the British on the night of 30 April/May 1, on 5 May two platoons of motorcycle riflemen advanced to Kvistvik, from where they crossed over to Kristiansund by ferry. As the main site of Norwegian resistance, the city had been destroyed by German bombers. A Norwegian garrison of one sergeant and fifty soldiers was taken prisoner in an undamaged school in Kristiansund. The sergeant was placed in charge and instructed to use his men, who were allowed to keep their weapons, to prevent looting. A platoon of motorcycle riflemen was left behind in Kristiansund as an occupation force. 200,000 liters of gasoline, 2.5 million liters of heavy oil, and 2 million liters of petroleum were secured in the harbour.

When the men of the Kluge Detachment in Kristiansund learned that there was an intact, but unoccupied, direction-finding station near the city and that a Norwegian camp with German prisoners was located on Kristvik, an island west of Kristiansund, they acted quickly. A ferry was requisitioned and a platoon of motorcycle riflemen sent to Kristvik. The Norwegian sergeant showed them a concealed route to the POW camp, allowing the Germans to rush and overpower the machine-gun crews and sentries of the camp guard. Moving quickly, they reached the camp itself at 1200 and called upon the commandant to release the prisoners. The Norwegian agreed. Three officers and 130 men of 1st Company, 1st Parachute Regiment, two naval aviators from the cruiser *Hipper*, and an interned German salesman were released.

Kampfgruppe Fischer now returned to its division. The von Burstin Battalion was disbanded on 5 May and the Kluge Detachment was released. Both *Oberst* Fischer and *Hauptmann* von Burstin issued orders of the day in which they lauded the efforts of the men of the General Göring Regiment who, together with their Army comrades, had covered approximately 600 kilometers in fourteen days of fighting. The detachment suffered casualties of 5 killed and 23 wounded in the course of these operations. During the night of 6/7 May the detachment moved to Trondheim and took up quarters in a school. After several days of quiet it was given a new assignment.

In Support of the Dietl Group at Narvik

The first few quiet days were spent cleaning and repairing weapons and equipment. It was in Trondheim that the men of the detachment first learned that in the far north, in and around Narvik, the alpine infantry under *Generalleutnant* Eduard Dietl were engaged in heavy fighting and that the situation there was very serious. Dietl's force – alpine infantry, together with the crews of ten German destroyers sunk in battle, Luftwaffe personnel, and the paratroopers of I Battalion, 1st Parachute Regiment under *Hauptmann* Walther (formerly of IV Parachute Rifle Battalion of the General Göring Regiment) – was fighting for its very survival.

It was imperative that help be sent to Dietl via the overland route. To this end a battle group was formed in Trondheim under the command of the commanding officer of the 2nd Mountain Infantry Division, *Generalleutnant* Feurstein. Included in the battle group were all the elements of the 3rd Mountain Infantry Division left behind in Trondheim, and the bulk of the 2nd Mountain Infantry Division, which had been transported to Oslo by sea and air and subsequently moved to Trondheim. Attached to the battle group for supply purposes were the 1st and 2nd Batteries of the 730th Heavy Artillery Battalion, the 1st Company of the 40th Panzer Battalion, and vehicles of the machine-gun battalion. From 17 May 1940, elements of the Kluge Detachment, which by now was fully combat-ready again, were attached to *Kampfgruppe* Feurstein in order to take part in Operation *Büffel* (Buffalo).

It was no surprise that the British command quickly realized the purpose of this operation. They committed strong forces to halt this advance aimed at relieving the 3rd Mountain Infantry Division under *Generalleutnant* Dietl. In several places the result was bitter fighting. The enemy landed fresh forces near Mo i Rana and Bodö. General Auchinleck, commander of British and French forces at Narvik, finally withdrew forces from this area when the mountain infantry under *Generalleutnant* Dietl continued to hold. This brought a noticeable easing of the pressure on Dietl's forces.

Progress by *Kampfgruppe* Feurstein slowed as its supply lines lengthened. Supplies from the air could only make good the most urgent shortfalls. Finally even the Kfz 70s of the machine-gun battalions and the motorcycles of the Kluge Detachment had to be used to transport ammunition. The motorcycles were shipped across the fiord on home-made ferries. *Generalleutnant* Feurstein said of the improvised transport:

"For once something different for our motorcycle drivers!"

Generalleutnant Feurstein thought highly of the motorcycle troops, whom he called the "white patch boys" (in reference to the color of their collar patches), a fact reflected in his lavish praise of their efforts and the number of decorations he handed out.

Between the 18th and 20th of May there was bitter fighting near Stien and Mo i Rana. The latter city was not taken until 20 May. There were further battles near Saltdal, Rognan and Djupvik in the period 25 to 27 May. Nevertheless, by 1 June the battle group succeeded in occupying and securing the entire Soersfold – Evjen – Fauske – Straumen – Bodö – Valvik area. The battle group had by now covered about 700 kilometers since it left Trondheim. The Kluge Detachment crossed the Arctic Circle approximately 70 kilometers north of Mo i Rana. They were the only soldiers of the General Göring Regiment to advance so far north.

When the ice began to melt at the beginning of May, the frozen lake surfaces which had served as "airfields" were no longer usable. The Kluge Detachment's armored reconnaissance car section, which had been left behind, was sent to search for a suitable landing field near the Swedish border. One such field was found near Hattfjelldal. It seemed an ideal jumping-off base for Stuka missions against Narvik. The site was prepared for its new role as an airfield by the Kluge Detachment on orders from Luftwaffe Command Norway.

First, however, it was necessary to break Norwegian resistance 10 kilometers west of Hattfjelldal. Assisted by the 14th Machine-gun Battalion and construction squads of the Reich Labor Service, a 700-meter runway was built and an approach path cut out of the woods. On 2 June work on the runway had progressed to the point where the Stukagruppe under *Hauptmann* Nolz was able to take off from Hattfjelldal for Narvik. Three aircraft failed to return from this first mission.

On 28 May *Generalleutnant* Dietl found himself forced to abandon Narvik to the enemy. His battle group, about 6,000 men strong, withdrew eastward along the ore railway before the 20,000 troops of the enemy. On 7 June the Supreme Allied War Council ordered the evacuation of Narvik. The city was abandoned the following day. Dietl's troops moved back into Narvik.

On 10 June the Kluge Detachment received orders to return to its base in Germany immediately. The troops departed on the evening of 11 June and reached Trondheim after a journey of 18 hours. Several hours later everything was loaded aboard a train which soon left for Oslo, arriving there on the afternoon of 14 June. In Oslo the Commander-in-Chief of *Luftflotte* 5, *General der Flieger* Stumpff, personally bade farewell to the Kluge Detachment. He thanked the soldiers for their courageous actions and excellent composure in all situations.

The commander of XXI Group, *General* von Falkenhorst, also said goodbye to the unit before it embarked on the steamer *Bahia*. Immediately after the *General* reviewed the RGG soldiers assembled on the pier, the detachment went on board. The steamer made the 13-hour journey to Aalborg in convoy with four other transports. From Aalborg the detachment continued its journey by train to Wittenberge via Arhus, Flensburg and Oldeslohe. Berlin was reached after a 40-hour train ride and the detachment moved back into the barracks in Reinickendorf. There all the "Norwegian fighters" received ten days special leave.

The General Göring Regiment in France

After the completion of the "103rd Flak Regiment's" tour of duty at the *Westwall*, from 10 May 1940 the General Göring Regiment took part in the Western Campaign with I Flak Corps. III Battalion, General Göring Regiment was attached to the 101st Flak Regiment. The Regimental Headquarters with I and IV Battalions, General Göring Regiment served with the flak corps and were assigned the above-mentioned cover name. The individual flak units advanced with the army divisions. In this way they were able to soften up the heavy French fortress works for the Sixth and Fourth

Armies and demonstrate their capabilities in the anti-tank role against attacks by enemy armor.

Enemy aircraft also experienced the accuracy and striking power of the heavy flak batteries. The soldiers of the *Reichsmarschall* took part in the piercing of the Dyle position, the capture of Löwen, and the occupation of Brussels. In the tank battle near Bembloux and the struggle for the Mormal Forest they demonstrated that the prejudice shown against the unit as "Göring's parade unit" was misplaced. The men of the General Göring Regiment kept pace with the Army troops and were always to be found at the forefront of the advance.

The following is a brief account of actions by the regiment's 3rd and 5th Batteries in the Mormal Forest, in which gun "Cäsar" engaged French Renault D 2 tanks. These 18-tonne tanks, armed with a 47mm cannon and two machine-guns, were formidable opponents.

On 17 May the 3rd Battery of the General Göring Regiment rolled through the shell-blasted town of Gembloux. The streets were pitted with shell holes and the retreating French troops had placed mines. Like the rest of the German troops, the men of the battery had to find their way around the town on secondary roads. They drove through parts of the Dyle Position and went into positions again between Sombreffe and Ligny. The next day saw a march of only three kilometers to Velaine.

The next change of position took place on the evening of 19 May, with the battery moving through Tamiens to Vosses. There the battery was attacked by a Fairey Battle light bomber of the RAF. Having been spotted, the battery continued across the Belgian-French border, which it crossed on 20 May near Solre-le-Chateau, not far from Cambrai. As the battery advanced through the Mormal Forest near Locquignol, the order suddenly rang out from the front: "Gun section forward!"

The platoon leader arrived: "In front of us in the forest, about three to five kilometers away, the French are attempting to break through with armored forces. We must stop this attempt." The engines of four prime movers roared as they towed their 88mm guns forward into the Mormal Forest. When they reached the shot-up forest village of Locquignol, the four eighty-eights found themselves trapped in the middle of a column of vehicles. Trees at the sides of the road prevented them from passing. A motorcycle dispatch rider came roaring up to the guns. The man stopped long enough to report: "Tanks in front of us!" then drove on immediately.

Fortunately the traffic jam of vehicles cleared at that moment. The road was open, the four eighty-eights could drive on. The first gun went into position farther up the road to prevent a surprise by fast-approaching enemy tanks. Several 37mm anti-tank guns, the so-called "Army door-knockers", were seen in the cover of the trees as the eighty-eights rolled forward. French and German machine-gun fire rang out from the forest. Gun "Bruno" likewise went into position, but there were still no enemy tanks to be seen. Guns "Cäsar" and "Dora" rolled onwards. At a crossroad a *Hauptmann* waved to "Cäsar".

"We had almost reached the *Hauptmann*," reported *Wachtmeister* Kubaschk, "when we saw a two-centimeter sitting some distance in front of us. The gun commander was an *Unteroffizier* of our battalion's 5th Battery. At that instant a French tank rolled onto the road from our ten o'clock position. Flames spurted from both of its machine-guns. Then it halted briefly. There was a flash of flame from its 47mm gun. The next salvo of machine-gun fire was on target. Bullets spattered against the steel parts of our prime mover and cannon."

Hein Lübberstedt continues the account: "We jumped down and sought cover behind the tracks. Suddenly our prime mover rolled on with the gun towards the nearest steel giant. The gun commander's voice rang out: 'Unlimber!'."

"This maneuver was carried out while the prime mover was still rolling. The first gunner jumped onto the gun and brought the eighty-eight to a halt after it was unlimbered. Because of the heavy machine-gun fire it was impossible to move the gun into position. We acted quickly; we'd have to fire from the carriage. About 15 meters now separated us from the tank, which was still firing with all weapons. I jumped to the breech and tore it open. The third and fourth gunners lowered the side trails. We took aim at the tank over the barrel cradle. But the ammunition was still in the prime mover! The *Hauptmann* at the crossroad jumped onto the tractor, tore open the box, and dragged a basket of ammunition to the gun. Our first gunner ran towards him and took the basket. *Leutnant* Koschwitz passed me the first round. Seconds later there was a roar as the gun fired. The tank disappeared in smoke and dust.

We fired three rounds one after another in the direction of the tank. The second gunner was now in the seat, and he aimed precisely at the spot from which machine-gun fire was still coming toward us. The next shot silenced the machine-gun, but only for a matter of seconds. Hans Braschwitz, our second gunner, now placed the fourth round directly between the tank's turret and tracks. There was a mighty blast as the enemy tank was blown to pieces by the explosion of its reserve ammunition. The remaining tanks turned away and disappeared. We turned the gun and drove back to the other guns of our battery. We had survived our baptism of fire."

The General Göring Regiment further distinguished itself in the subsequent battles at the Somme and the Aisne, in the crossing of the Marne, and in the pursuit to the Loire. The Honor Company of the Führer Escort Battalion was formed for the signing of the cease fire in Compiegne Forest on 21 June 1940. The company consisted of two army platoons and a platoon from the 7th Battery, General Göring Regiment, which was employed as a flak battery at the Führer Headquarters, under the command of *Oberleutnant* Dieke.

After the 26th of June the regiment was employed on security duties in occupied France and to protect Paris and other locations. This included the Channel Coast, in particular the Boulogne area. In the Paris area special protection was given the airfields of Orly and Villacoublay.

September 1939 at the headquarters of the Luftwaffe Commander-in-Chief.

The Kluge Detachment under steam.

One of the deep valleys in Norway near Stahlheim, where Norwegian defenders mounted stubborn resistance.

The German hospital ship "Wilhelm Gustloff" in Oslo harbor in April 1940.

This obstacle failed to stop the soldiers of the Kluge Detachment.

The grave of Obergefreiter Bruno Mann, killed in action in Norway on 26 April, 1940.

German troops advance through the fjords in the far north of the country.

This blown bridge proved to be a major obstacle.

The men of the Kluge Detachment at the Arctic Circle.

OberLeutnant Kleinmann (army) and Oberleutnant Dieke of the General Göring Regiment salute Hitler during his visit to the front-line units in France.

Hitler inspects the General Göring Regiment.

1940. Two panzer soldiers sitting on top of their armored car (possibly an Sd Kfz 222). Note the first style, and now extremely rare, Panzer berets.

Knocked-out Renault B1 bis tank.

Sitting in a prime mover, members of the General Göring Regiment study the paper for the first special bulletins during the campaign in France.

A forest of German signs in Paris.

A Renault Bis 1 bis tank, knocked out by "Cäsar" gun during the fighting in France.

A truck-mounted anti-aircraft gun of the Kluge Detachment during the campaign in Norway.

The General Göring Regiment in the Air Defence of Berlin

In September 1940 the General Göring Regiment returned to Germany, where it was committed to the air defence role as Flak Group Berlin-West with I, III and IV Battalions. Their commander, *Oberst* Conrath, became commander of Flak Group West. The transfer of the regiment back to the Reich capital was on account of the increased activity of the enemy air force in the Berlin area. The first British air raid on Berlin took place on the night of 30/31 August 1940. Subsequently the anti-aircraft defenses of the capital were greatly strengthened in order to make further such attacks impossible. Part of the flak defenses in the West were withdrawn as part of this strengthening of Berlin's defenses, especially the Reich's searchlight batteries.

Generaloberst Weise, Commanding General of I Flak Corps, took command of the air defenses in *Luftgau* III-IV. After several light raids, in the course of which the guns of the General Göring Regiment participated in the defence, on the night of 8 October there followed the heaviest attack on the Berlin metropolitan area so far. By this time the defensive forces in the Berlin flak zone had been increased from 29 heavy and 14 medium batteries with 11 searchlight batteries to 45 heavy, 24 medium and 18 searchlight batteries.

Commander-in-Chief of the air defenses in *Luftgau* III-IV and air defence commander was now *Oberst* Schilffarth. When the General Göring Regiment returned to Berlin from France in September 1940 it was placed under *Oberst* Schilffarth's command. Headquarters, General Göring Regiment under *Oberst* Conrath assumed command of Flak Group Berlin-West.

Action in the Balkans

The winter of 1940-41 saw the General Göring Regiment deployed around Berlin with other flak units to protect the Reich capital against enemy air attacks. On 27 March 1941 a new government took power in Belgrade as a result of a military coup. The Serbian Lieutenant General Dusan Simovic, Commander of the Serbian Air Forces and leading member of the influential secret league "The Black Hand", toppled the government and installed himself as Minister President of Yugoslavia and Commander-in-Chief of the Serbian Army. He revoked the non-aggression pact with Germany concluded two days earlier in Vienna with the slogan: "Better war than pact, better death than slavery." (Belvedere)

Hitler, who saw his Russian plans acutely upset as a result, was furious at what he called those "bomb throwers" and the "nest of conspirators in Belgrade." Prior to that day he had harbored no thoughts of an attack on Yugoslavia, but now he decided "to smash Yugoslavia militarily and as a state." He ordered the Second and Twelfth Armies to attack Yugoslavia. *Luftflotte* 4 under *General der Flieger* Löhr received orders "to destroy Belgrade through continuous air attack."

6 April 1941 was chosen as the day of the attack. *General der Flieger* Löhr, veteran Austrian flying officer and creator of the Austrian Air Force, ordered only the following targets to be attacked: the seat of the government, the buildings of the military command, the traffic and communications net, and purely military installations. *Luftflotte* 4 launched its attack early on the

morning of 6 April, sending horizontal and dive-bombers with a powerful fighter escort to strike Belgrade. For the first time in the history of World War II Bf 109 fought Bf 109 in aerial duels. A year earlier Yugoslavia had ordered and received from Germany Messerschmitt fighters for its fighter units.

A total of 468 aircraft were sent against Belgrade (this high total was achieved by each aircraft flying multiple sorties). By late morning on 6 April all military targets had been bombed. General Simovic and his government had fled. The Serbian Council of Ministers did not meet again. The Yugoslavian command apparatus was completely shattered. This was the reason why all Serbian units laid down their arms after only twelve days of the fighting. The tale that Serbia-Yugoslavia was "nearly defenseless in the face of the German war machine" has no basis in fact. The Serbian Army mobilized 1.8 million men – what it lacked was leaders, all of whom had fled.

The strike against Yugoslavia ordered by Hitler was also the reason for the deployment of the General Göring Regiment to the Balkans. Among the precautionary military measures taken by the Reich government was the rapid transfer of the General Göring Regiment to Romania to protect the oil fields near Ploesti. Without the Romanian oil any further prosecution of the war would have been impossible.

Thus the Regimental Headquarters, I and IV Battalions and elements of II Battalion were transferred to Romania. The Guard Battalion formed a rifle battalion under the command of *Hauptmann* Funck. His adjutant was *Oberleutnant* Rebholz. On its arrival in the Balkans the regiment was placed under the command of the Twelfth Army's XXXXI Army Corps. This army corps was the army reserve and saw no action during the Balkan Campaign, consequently action by the General Göring Regiment was limited to defending the Ploesti area against air attack. Both searchlight battalions remained in the Berlin area. There now follows a brief account of the rifle battalion.

The new rifle battalion was formed from elements of the General Göring Guard Battalion. The flak battery assigned to the unit was the 8th Battery RGG with 20mm light anti-aircraft guns, which had previously been attached to IV Battalion. The rifle battalion's march south took it through Pirna/Elbe to Stockerau near Vienna and from there to Hainburg near Preßburg (Bratislava).

On 3 April the battalion continued its journey through Budapest and Arad to Tinusoara. There *Oberst* Conrath informed his unit commanders of their future role. The rifle battalion subsequently left the General Göring Regiment for the duration of its stay in Romania and was placed under the direct command of the German Air Force Mission in Romania. The battalion marched through Sibui, Braso and the Predal Pass to Ploesti and from there directly to Bucharest. The 8th Battery was deployed to defend Otopeni airfield located north of the city and went into position there with twelve 20mm guns on self-propelled carriages. In this role the battery was placed under the command of Flak Sub-group Bucharest.

Following several days of rest the rifle battalion resumed training with route marches, live firing, and night and day exercises lasting several days. Most of the battalion's time was spent training for "attacks within the framework of an army battalion" and "opening a bottleneck through surprise attack".

In mid-May the battalion received orders to transfer to the East with the rest of the regiment. Thus the battalion was once again placed under the regiment's command. It set out during the night of 17/18 May, reaching Sibiu on 18 May, Klausenburg the following day, and Kaschau on 22 May. A five-day rest was laid on in Kaschau. Two more days on the march saw the battalion arrive in Cracow on 29 May.

In the meantime a teletype order had reached the General Göring Guard Battalion in Berlin on 5 May, instructing it dispatch its 1st Company to Cracow so as to arrive no later than 27 May. The company arrived on time and was incorporated into the rifle battalion. The rifle battalion's organization prior the start of the Eastern Campaign was as follows:

    Headquarters and Signals Platoon
    1st and 3rd Rifle Companies
    Motorcycle Company
    6th (light) Flak Battery (motorized)
    Light transport column.

The following two weeks in Cracow were used to complete training and to integrate the newly-arrived company from the guard battalion into the unit. On 13 June the battalion moved farther east and took up quarters in the towns of Strochcice and Kaczorki. A few days later it moved up to Wasylow and Rusin. On 21 June the battalion's officers received the operational order from the commanding officer. B-Day was 22 June, Y-Hour 0315. Shortly before the midnight of 22 June a Führer Order was read out "to all the soldiers of the Eastern Front". Now everyone in the General Göring Regiment knew for sure.

"It was a warm summer night. Sleep was out of the question. Everyone sensed that difficult weeks and months lay ahead. No one could suspect, however, that it was to become years. Having heard the Führer Order, many soldiers may perhaps have suspected that their fate was now sealed."

As a Luftwaffe unit the General Göring Regiment – including the rifle battalion – was under the command of II Flak Corps, which employed its units in cooperation with units of the Army and in some cases assigned these to them. This was the case with the entire General Göring Regiment. The rifle battalion was placed under the command of XXXXVIII Panzer Corps in the Sokol area. Its battles were fought primarily in the Radziechow, Dubno, Kiev, Briansk, Cherkassy, Kremenchug and Dniepropetrovsk areas and lasted until November 1941. The eighty-eights engaged the bunkers of the Sokal Heights with devastating effect.

At the end of November the General Göring Regiment Rifle Battalion returned to Berlin and in early 1942 was transferred to Brittany, where several months later it was incorporated into the Hermann Göring Rifle Regiment, part of the newly-created Hermann Göring Brigade. The table of organization of the General Göring Regiment on 15 June 1941 follows this account.

ORGANIZATION OF THE GENERAL GÖRING REGIMENT

(as of 15 June 1941 (Ia-53/41 Secret Command Matter)

Commanding Officer:	Oberst Conrath
Adjutant:	Hptm. Stauch
Regimental Units:	
Headquarters:	8 officers, 28 NCOs, 74 men
Transport Group:	Hptm. Kumacsek with 5 NCOs and 26 men
Signals Platoon:	Oblt. Schirmer with 12 NCOs and 64 men
Workshop Platoon:	Amtmann Gmelch, 6 NCOs and 47 men
I Battalion RGG:	Major Hullmann
Adjutant:	Lt. Jahr, 7 officers, 28 NCOs and 129 men
1st Battery 88mm:	Oblt. Graf with 4 guns
2nd Battery 88mm:	Hptm. Schulz with 4 guns
3rd Battery 88mm:	Hptm. Schröder with 4 guns
4th Battery 20mm:	Hptm. Neubauer with 12 FlaMW
IV Battalion RGG:	Hptm. Geicke
Adjutant:	Oblt. Bock
6th Battery 37mm:	Oblt. Behrens with 9 guns
15th Battery 20mm and 37mm:	Hptm. Beinhofer with 6 + 6 guns
16th Battery (motorized/heavy tracked):	Oblt. Roßmann, 12 - 20mm FlaMW
Rifle Battalion RGG:	Hptm. Funck
Adjutant:	Oblt. Rebholz
8th Battery (motorized/heavy wheeled)	Hptm. Seewald with 12 20mm FlaMW
1st Rifle Company:	Oblt. Kroh, 4 officers, 32 NCOs & 160 men
3rd Rifle Company:	Hptm. Brandenburg with 4 officers, 31 NCOs and 155 men
Motorcycle Company:	Hptm. Preuß with 6 officers, 59 NCOs and 180 men
II Battalion, 43rd Flak Rgt.:	Major Karlhuber
Adjutant:	Oblt. Grothe
6th Battery 88mm:	Oblt. Rengermann with 4 guns
7th Battery 88mm:	Oblt. Wittkowsky with 4 guns
8th Battery 88mm:	Oblt. Hagel with 4 guns
9th Battery 20mm:	Oblt. Belau with 12 FlaMW
10th Battery 20mm:	Hptm. Schlechtweg with 12 FlaMW

Units under the direct command of the battalions were:

I./RGG:	Lt. von Lochow with 1 officer, 9 NCOs and 45 men
IV./RGG:	Oblt. Fischer, 1 officer, 9 NCOs & 43 men
Rifle Battalion/RGG:	Hptm. Wendt, 1 officer, 16 NCOs & 40 men
II./43rd Flak Rgt.:	Hptm. Petri with 2 officers, 8 NCOs and 47 men

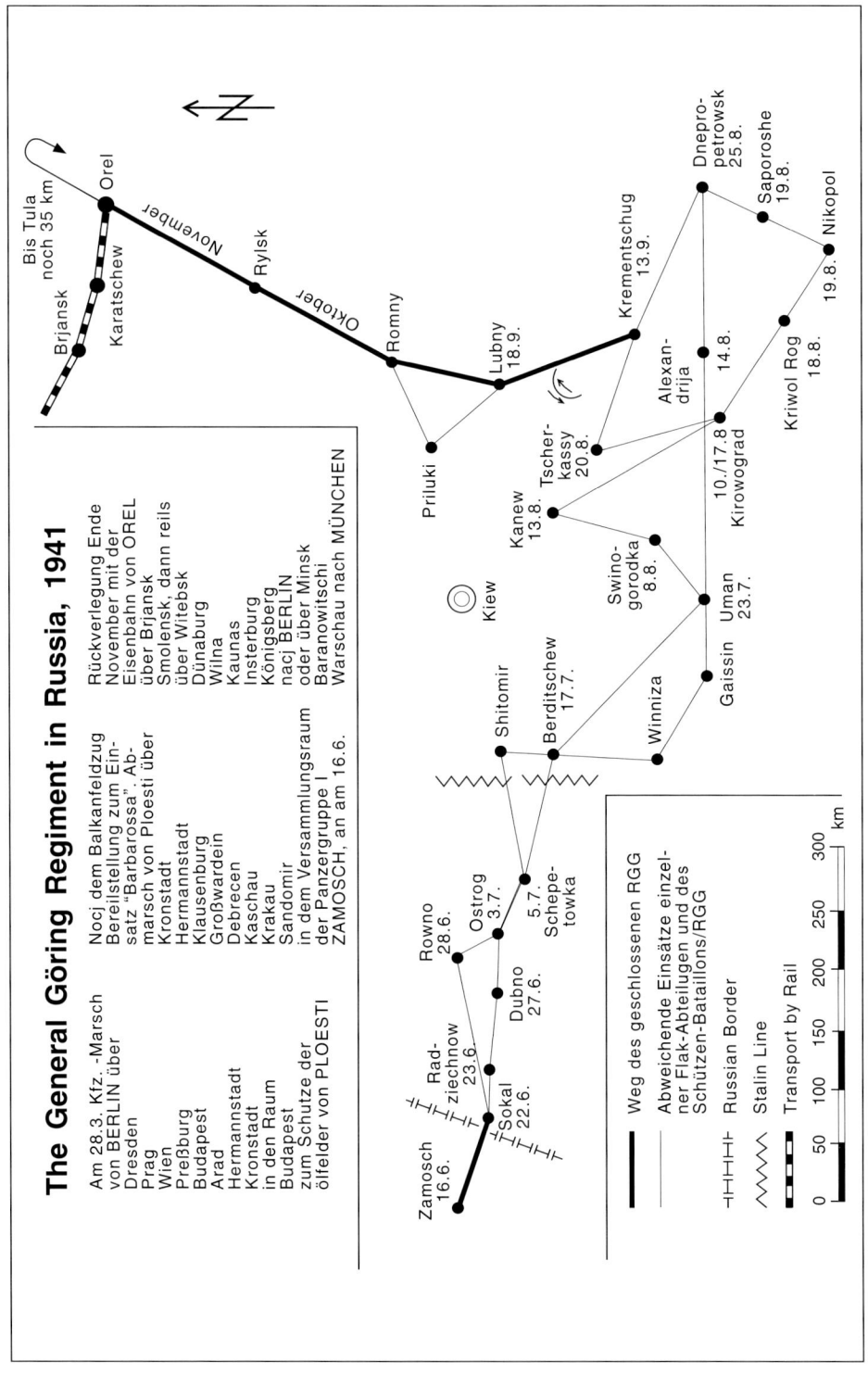

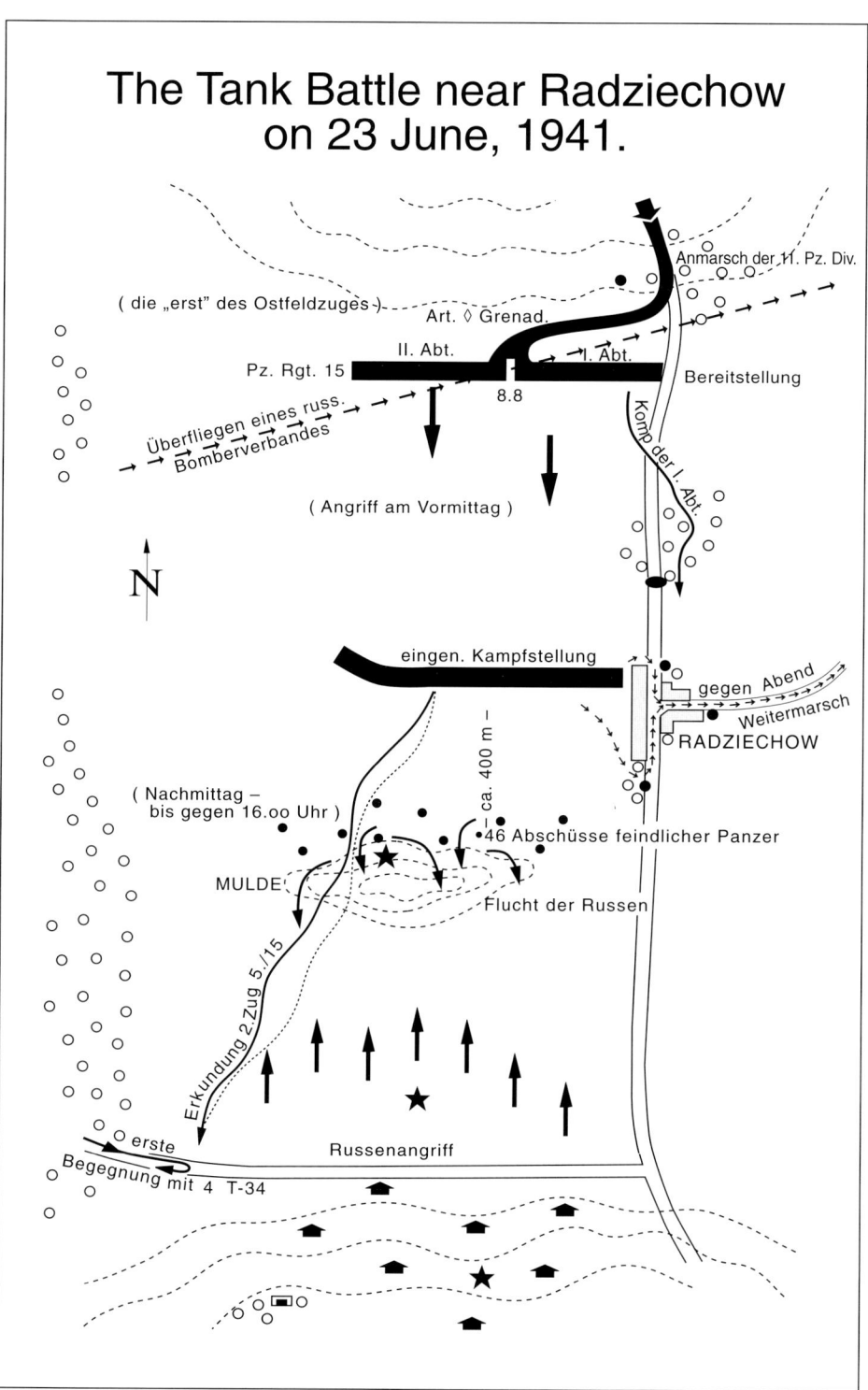

In the March Group of the 11th Panzer Division

The regiment, which now bore the title "HG" for the first time, received its first major combat assignment in the tank battle near Radziechow, where a bitter struggle developed on 23 June. The CO of the regiment's 3rd Battery, *Hauptmann* Schröder, was killed in action there. *Leutnant* Dirk Itzen, the battery's reconnaissance officer, offered the final respects to his dead commander. Itzen, who already wore the Iron Cross, further distinguished himself near Ostrog and Zhitomir. While pressing forward far ahead of his company in the Berdichev area Dirk Itzen was badly wounded by artillery fire. He died of his wounds on 12 July 1941. The same month his regimental commander submitted a recommendation for the Knight's Cross, which was awarded posthumously on 13 November 1941. Itzen thus became the first member of the Motorcycle Company to win the decoration.

On 29 June there was a furious tank battle near Dubno. Enemy forces surrounded by the 11th Panzer Division threw everything they had at the German encircling ring in an effort to break out. In the first days of this bitter battle against enemy tanks near Radziechow, Beresteczki, and Lescniow, the Hermann Göring Regiment destroyed 30 heavy tanks and shot down 18 enemy aircraft.

In the tank battle near Dubno on 29 June the surrounded enemy made desperate attempts to break out. Heavy losses were inflicted on the Russian forces by 2nd Battery under *Hauptmann* Schulz with platoon leader *Leutnant* Wilmskötter. The Wehrmacht communique of 7 July 1941 declared:

"A battery of the General Göring Flak Regiment under the command of Hauptmann Schulz and Leutnant Wilmskötter distinguished itself in the tank battle near Dubno." Several of the tanks put out of action by 2nd Battery that day were super-heavy KV-IIs.

Once Dubno had been secured by the panzers and flak the motorcycle company resumed its advance. The heavy anti-aircraft guns of the General Göring Regiment drove with the armored spearhead on the road to Ostrov. A Russian tank was knocked out while the advance was under way and finally Berdichev was reached. On 19 August the regiment reached the Dniepr River near Zaporozhye. This was the site of the *Hydrostanzia* power plant, the third largest hydroelectric plant in the world; *Oberst* Conrath and his officers passed by the huge dam, whose mid-portion had been destroyed by the Red Army before it withdrew.

In the Dniepropetrovsk bridgehead the RGG's rifle battalion was placed under the command of the 59th Motorcycle Battalion, which belonged to the 9th Rifle Brigade. Commander of the battalion was Knight's Cross wearer *Major* Wilhelm Schmalz. This was the first time Schmalz commanded men wearing the white tabs of the RGG. Later he was to command the *Reichsmarschall*'s soldiers as an *Oberst* and regimental commander, then as divisional commander and finally as commanding general.

After six months of heavy fighting the General Göring Regiment reached Orel. Elements even advanced to within 35 kilometers of Tula, but that was as far as the regiment could go. Completely exhausted, in November it was withdrawn from the fight and sent back to Germany by train. The first stop for the flak battalions and the Regimental HQ was Munich. The rifle battalion remained behind in Russia until February 1942, before it was transferred to Brittany to rest and reequip.

In December 1941 the rifle battalion was joined by a sister unit. II Rifle Battalion, RGG had been formed in France in October- November 1941. In command of the new battalion was *Hauptmann* Neubauer.

The General Göring Regiment in Action from 22 June to 25 Nov. 1941

The following account is based on information provided by the then *Leutnant* Rolf Gerhardt. According to Gerhardt, on 23 June the company marched through Sokal to Zubkov and 24 hours later took up quarters in a barn. The company's armored reconnaissance platoon went on a patrol and returned with two Russian prisoners.

At 0900 on 25 June the company was placed on alert for departure to Tartakov-Kopytov. The Russian positions there were placed under heavy fire. At an hour past midnight a strong Russian patrol was repulsed. In the afternoon, following preparatory artillery fire, the armored reconnaissance platoon and the 2nd Platoon under *Leutnant* Gerhardt undertook an advance toward Bobiatyn- Luczyce. Four kilometers southwest of Luczyce they came under heavy fire from anti-tank guns and then artillery. At 1730 hours the armored reconnaissance platoon carried out a reconnaissance in force toward Jazefka-Scarponca. The advance was halted by Russian forces about 1,500 meters north of Jazefka, after which the platoon withdrew.

On 27 June Soviet close-support aircraft dropped bombs on the advance road and the Kopytov area. On 26 and 27 June the motorcycle company captured one 105mm and one 175mm guns and three 35mm anti-tank guns.

On 28 June there was an inspection by *General* Dessloch in Zubkov, where the company had taken up quarters. The General presented the Iron Cross, Second Class to ten soldiers, eight of them from 8th Battery, which had repulsed vastly superior Russian forces on the advance road. The other two went to members of the armored reconnaissance platoon. Dubno was reached on 30 June following a march of 154 kilometers. Two light tanks were captured there.

At 2200 hours on 1 July the company occupied a position at the Dubno-Rovno road fork. Reinforcements arrived in the shape of a Flak 88. 2nd Platoon reconnoitred toward Rovno, but this was broken off when contact was made with enemy forces. A second attempt was made the following day, but once again it was halted by strong enemy fire. The company set out for Astrog at 0900 hours on 3 July and moved into a bridgehead position there at 1500. When enemy armored units fleeing the battle for Dubno appeared in front of the bridgehead the anti-aircraft and anti-tank guns were able to destroy 6 scout cars as well as 3 medium and 21 light tanks.

The advance resumed on 5 July in the direction of Shepetovka. The 50 kilometer drive was made in three hours. Three of the company's platoons took up positions on the road to Zaslavl on Hill 300. There, too, the Russians attempted to break through, which cost them 21 medium and 13 heavy tanks. After temporarily securing a large Russian barracks area, the 2nd Platoon returned to the company.

The company set out along the advance road again on the afternoon of 6 July, however all movement was halted 90 minutes later as the road was completely blocked with traffic. While returning to its starting position the company was attacked by about ten Rata fighters and nine bombers. The first German fighters appeared minutes later and shot down four bombers in short order while the rest fled.

By 12 July the motorcycle company was approaching Zhitomir. The advance was held up for two days by heavy rain. Not until the afternoon of 15 July did the advance continue to Berdichev. The rains returned however and the advance was held up for another 36 hours. On 18 July the company reached Skivra, where 2nd Platoon stood field guard.

The advance resumed on 21 July. On orders from the regimental commander, *Oberst* Conrath, *Leutnant* Gerhard led three motorcycles through retreating Russian forces to Taracha and established contact there with the 5th SS-Division *Wiking*, which had been surrounded. Gerhardt delivered orders for the SS division to hold out until the next day when two panzer divisions would relieve them. The patrol returned at 0130 on 22 July without having been fired upon.

23 July saw the RGG involved in the defence of the bottleneck at Buzovka. From there 2nd Platoon carried out a reconnaissance patrol to Konela, which was found to be occupied by enemy forces. When German fighters attacked Konela on the basis of this report, their first target was 2nd Platoon's fuel truck, which was set on fire. Later ten Stukas arrived, but these dropped their bombs accurately on Konela. Ten minutes after the Stuka attack *Leutnant* Gerhardt and his men once again drove towards Konela, which was now burning in several places, but again they were met by fire from the Russian defenders.

The subsequent attack by the motorcycle company supported by six 20mm light flak on self-propelled carriages of the 8th Battery succeeded after heavy street fighting. The defenders had to be blasted out of every house. Three tanks were captured and several others destroyed. The General Göring Regiment then marched off to Shaskov for several days of rest. *Generalleutnant* Crüwell, commander of the 11th Panzer Division, to which the RGG was attached, visited the unit there and expressed his appreciation to *Oberst* Conrath for the accomplishments of his men.

The regiment remained at rest until 31 July, when it marched to a point just short of Manshurov. At 0100 hours on 1 August the alarm was sounded. The advancing armored reconnaissance platoon had discovered that the enemy had occupied the village. Russian heavy artillery opened fire from the area northwest of Manshurov and *Oberst* Conrath ordered the rifle battalion to go into positions northwest and northeast of the village. The attack on Manshurov took place on 2 August after a ten-minute artillery bombardment. Advancing with the men of the RGG's motorcycle battalion were the motorcycle troops of the 11th Panzer Division. They found that Manshurov had been abandoned by the enemy the night before. In the days that followed the RGG moved through Talnoye to Svenigorodka to Smietshensi. The subsequent advance led through Medvin and Moskalenki to Peshky. Advancing and fighting where resistance was offered, the regiment reached Statopol and finally Krivoy Rog. Not until 20 August was there another rest day.

The 23rd of August saw the beginning of the RGG's attack on the Russian bridgehead on the southwest side of the Dniepr near Dniepropetrovsk. This time the advance was made in concert with the 9th Panzer Division in the face of uninterrupted Russian artillery fire and air attacks. By 2000 hours on 23 August the objective had been reached and the Russian bridgehead eliminated. The next day the regiment combed Starye Koidaki and occupied the southwest bank of the Dniepr. There the armored reconnaissance platoon came upon several enemy ships on the Dniepr. These were fired upon and two were sunk by hits below the water line. On 23 and 24 August the RGG's rifle battalion alone took 2,000 prisoners and captured 10 heavy mortars and 44 heavy machine-guns.

On 2 September five light and one heavy artillery batteries began placing barrage fire on the Soviet's northeastern Dniepropetrovsk bridgehead. At 0900 hours the RGG launched a feint attack across the Dniepr, after which the enemy intensified his artillery fire. The motorcycle troops were subsequently pulled back. All was quiet for the next eight days, before the advance resumed on 11 September. Kremenchug was reached on the 13th. The RGG set up a bivouac there and was placed under the command of XXXXVIII Panzer Corps as corps reserve. Further days of quiet followed. 18 September saw the unit set out in the direction of Lubny. Positions were occupied in Tyorny in support of XXXXVIII Panzer Corps.

The next day a patrol from 3rd Platoon under *Leutnant* Rennmayer was ambushed while driving towards Vyazivok and was pinned down by direct artillery fire. *Leutnant* Gerhardt led elements of 2nd Platoon, reinforced by a tank-destroyer, forward, attacked the artillery position and freed the Rennmeier Platoon. *Obergefreiten* Platte and Heinrich were brought back badly wounded. 26 prisoners were taken and one heavy machine-gun and one gun captured.

The daily routine alternated between security duties and patrols. On 22 September *Hauptmann* Preuß returned from hospital. The following day saw the unit leave for Romny via Lokhvitsa, where five more rest days saw to it that the RGG was well rested. The unit moved out on 29 September. The next objectives were Putivl, Linov and Sofrontiyevski Monastery. The first snow fell on the night of 6/7 October. The snow melted straight away, resulting in muddy and slippery roads, over which the regiment made its way to Dmitryev. There the individual companies occupied their positions, holding these until 4 November while mounting patrols into the surrounding area.

The march to Orel began on 5 November. Passing through Orel on the morning of the 9th, the advance continued to Karachev. The next objectives of the day were Roslavl, Borisov, and Vilna. The regiment's units rested there from the 17th to the 22nd of November, before heading for home by train. Berlin was reached via Kovno, Insterburg, Posen, Frankfurt/Oder and Fürstenwalde. When the General Göring Regiment arrived in Berlin-Tempelhof at 2350 hours on 24 November it was greeted by the regiment's band playing lively military marches. The regiment arrived at its barracks in Berlin-Reinickendorf at 0230 hours on 25 November.

This outline of a company's daily activities in Russia cannot be concluded without mentioning casualties. The Motorcycle Company alone lost 10 killed and 26 seriously wounded in this first phase of the Russian Campaign. A tough and privation-filled operation had ended in the icy cold.

I Battalion,
General Göring Regiment in Action against Russian Tank Forces

On 23 July the 9th Panzer Division initiated the encirclement that was to become the Uman Pocket with its deep thrust into the Russian withdrawal; the division also severed a rail line north of Uman vital to the Red Army. Attached to the 9th Panzer Division, the General Göring Regiment was placed on alert on the evening of 23 July. The Soviets were trying to cut "Panzer Road Center" with strong armored forces.

As the tanks of the 9th Panzer Division were already in combat, heavy anti-tank guns were requested. *Leutnant* Str. drove to the threatened spot with an eighty-eight, but was unable to intervene on his arrival due to the onset of darkness. The rattle of tank tracks and the roar of engines were heard during the night, indicating that the enemy tank unit was assembling in a nearby wood.

Meanwhile the 9th Panzer Division's tank battalion arrived and made ready to go on the defensive. Placed in the center of the German position, the Flak 88 was ready as well. The first enemy heavy tank emerged from the wood at first light; it was immediately targeted by the Flak 88. The first shot, from a range 1,800 meters, passed over the Russian tank. Then something surprising took place. The entire Russian tank unit dropped smoke shells about 700 meters in front of the German positions; the tanks quickly disappeared behind the drifting smoke.

When the first tank appeared from out of the smoke the panzers opened fire. They diverted the enemy from the anti-aircraft gun, and *Leutnant* Str. succeeded in knocking out two heavy tanks before the Flak 88 was spotted and fired upon from a range of 600 meters. The first shells landed in front of and behind the anti-aircraft gun. The next one must be a direct hit.

"Faster, fire!" roared the *Leutnant*. The Flak fired fractions of a second before the enemy and silenced the tank with a direct hit. Several German tanks had meanwhile been hit. Individual enemy tanks had approached to within 500 meters of the anti-aircraft gun. *Leutnant* Str. now had nine rounds of ammunition left.

"Fire!" ordered the *Leutnant*. The subsequent hit caused the Soviet crew to abandon their vehicle, the next tore it apart. The rest of the enemy tanks turned away.

Meanwhile a second eighty-eight had gone into position on the flank of the attack and from there destroyed two more Soviet tanks as they withdrew. The attack had been beaten off, but now the Russian artillery opened fire. Before the German front lay five smoldering enemy tanks. A dispatch rider came roaring up with new orders: "Flak change position immediately. 12 enemy tanks reported by battalion."

The anti-aircraft gun was driven to the village entrance to pick up ammunition. As it moved out, escorted by four panzers, it was spotted by the enemy. The commander of I Battalion, RGG briefed *Leutnant* Str. on the situation. The anti-aircraft gun left the road and rolled through a fruit grove to the most forward infantry positions so as to be able to catch the enemy as soon as possible. The call went from man to man: "Hermann's men are here!"

The eighty-eight had just been moved into position when the three leading enemy tanks halted. One of them obviously had transmission trouble. The order to fire was given. The immobilized tank was fired on first, resulting in a direct hit. The remaining two tried to escape over a shallow rise. The second tank was hit and, after a slight correction, the third as well. This ended the Russian attack as their other tanks gave up the fight on seeing the fate met by their comrades.

Another change of position brought the gun back into its old sector with I Battalion. *Leutnant* Str. completed a written report, the key sentence of which read:

"Today the gun destroyed eight tanks in two engagements with enemy armor."

This brought *Leutnant* Str.'s total of tanks destroyed since the beginning of the Russian Campaign to 11. The Army Commander sent a letter of appreciation to the commander of I Battalion, RGG for his men.

Operations by 16th Company, RGG in the Sverdlikovo Area on 2 August 1941

When the battle of encirclement of Uman was nearing its climax there were only weak German security forces between Uman and Slatopol in the area around Sverdlikovo. Sverdlikovo itself was also occupied only by weak German forces. During the night of 1-2 August, Russian forces struck Sverdlikovo with an eighty-fold superiority. Attacking with fanatical determination they tried to break through the German encircling ring at its weakest point, in an effort to escape to freedom.

Facing this onslaught were the men of the 16th Company, RGG under *Oberleutnant* Roßmann (IV Battalion RGG) with their battery of 20mm guns on self-propelled carriages, a handful of men of the Waffen-SS Division *Wiking* and infantry. This small group of forces fought a fourteen-hour defensive battle against the numerically-superior enemy and ensured the complete capture of the elements of the 6th, 12th, and 18th Soviet Armies in the Uman Pocket. It was midnight, the 2nd of September; a patrol under the command of *Leutnant* Bock was under way. It had been raining steadily for three hours. Suddenly rifle and machine-gun fire whipped through the darkness. Then tank noises were heard. The patrol leader, who was at the front, reported to *Leutnant* Bock that the Russians had already reached the southwest outskirts of Sverdlikovo and were continuing to advance from there with tank support. *Leutnant* Bock drove to a small bridge over a stream with his three 20mm light flak.

Heavy artillery fire was falling on the village. Then Russian hand grenades detonated nearby. By then the three guns had reached the hill above the bridge. It wasn't a moment too soon, because at that moment the Soviets attacked, shouting loudly. Soon afterward an enemy tank began to fire as well. It was silenced by three short bursts of fire. Russian artillery began pounding the German positions. The barrage went on for three and a half hours. At daybreak Russian infantry attacked across the stream. The Red Army soldiers who made it across fell in the concentrated fire of the light flak and the handful of machine-guns. Enemy anti-tank guns and mortars were located, fired upon, and eliminated. Fresh waves of brown-clad Russians continued to attack. The first German casualties were reported. Then the defenders also began taking heavy rifle and machine-gun fire from the north end of Sverdlikovo. They were surrounded.

Suddenly the enemy rifle fire in the rear ceased. The first German steel helmets came into view. It was a company of the Waffen-SS, which had arrived to relieve the defenders. They worked their way toward the enemy-held bridge, clearing the village's main street left and right. Quickly the light flak rolled forward, followed by the infantry and the SS men. The bridge was reached. One machine-gun nest after another was silenced. Bitter close-quarters fighting broke out among the houses.

At the end of the four-hour battle Sverdlikovo had been cleared of the enemy, but the Red Army still surrounded the entire village. Two-hundred Russians stormed across an open field toward the village, but they were mown down by the fire of the German defenders. The situation was saved at the last minute when, at about 0800 hours, *Oberleutnant* Roßmann, who earlier that morning had repulsed a powerful Soviet armored attack, broke through to the surrounded defenders. Supported by another company of the Waffen-SS, Roßmann's relief force fought its way through in bitter close-quarters combat, bringing the hard-pressed defenders six light flak and a large quantity of ammunition.

Oberleutnant Roßmann now assumed command of all the forces defending Sverdlikovo. Not only had he thought to bring ammunition, but an ambulance as well and a supply truck, which brought hot tea. The wounded were cared for and evacuated in the ambulance. *Oberleutnant* Roßmann personally relieved the driver of one truck who had held out for some hours, though wounded and in great pain. The defending forces now set about combing Sverdlikovo from one end to the other. This resulted in hand grenade duels and bursts of machine-gun fire; by 1200 hours the village was firmly in German hands.

The relieving force of German infantry arrived after its forced march. *Oberleutnant* Roßmann suddenly found a flask of cognac in his hand. Two officers of the RGG and two of the Waffen-SS toasted one another. One of the Waffen-SS officers expressed what everyone felt: "We won't forget this true comradeship in arms!"

The enemy breakout had been stopped and on 8 August the Uman Pocket was cleared. 103,000 Russian soldiers went into captivity. Among them were the commanding officers of the 6th Army (Lieutenant-General Musytshenko) and the 12th Army (Major-General Kyrilov). 317 tanks, 858 guns and 242 anti-tank or anti-aircraft guns were destroyed or captured. For this outstanding defensive success *Oberleutnant* Karl Roßmann was recommended for the Knight's Cross, which he received on 12 November 1941.

In Action – 6th Battery, RGG

The 3rd Platoon of the 6th Battery, General Göring Regiment was assigned to the 60th Motorized Infantry Regiment of the Westphalian 16th Infantry Division. The platoon's 37mm anti-aircraft guns advanced with the battalion. As soon as the enemy was sighted the guns went into position and opened fire. A village near the advance road was occupied while still under enemy mortar fire. Suddenly about 20 tanks rolled down from the heights east of the village.

Shouts of "Tank alarm!" rang out through the village. The 37mm anti-aircraft guns rolled forward to meet the threat. As a precaution *Leutnant* Söhnken fired a signal flare. It was answered by the tanks; they were German. The 37mm guns moved into position at the edge of the village. Armor-piercing ammunition was loaded, as the panzers had reported enemy tanks approaching.

During the next few days the enemy did not come, however. But then an Hs 126 reconnaissance aircraft dropped a smoke cartridge. It contained a message to the effect that an assembly of Russian tanks had been spotted in a wood to the right of the road, approximately 800 meters from the village. Soon afterward track and engine noises were heard. The first three tanks rolled out of the wood and headed straight toward the village. Gun commander *Unteroffizier* Schlüter waited until the tanks were in range before giving the order to fire. The first rounds bounced off the enemy's sloped frontal amour. Not until it was 50 meters away was the leading enemy tank halted by a hit in the tracks, but even so it continued to fire its machine-gun.

A lone He 111 dropped its bombs on the wood. Then an assault gun approached, followed by an eighty-eight of the RGG. Both went into position in front of the 37mm guns. The bombing attack brought on the Russian tank attack. One after another tanks rolled out of the wood and headed toward the German positions. Altogether there were at least 20 enemy tanks. One after another the advancing tanks were hit from a range of about 800 meters. Only a few escaped back into the wood. The advance by the 16th Infantry Division went on. Russian close- support aircraft attacked repeatedly. They swooped down to release their bombs and strafe. All of the 37mm anti-aircraft guns opened fire. One Il 2 was shot down. Suddenly one of the attackers dove steeply at one of the anti-aircraft guns and straddled it with bombs. One scored a direct hit, killing the gun commander and range finder operator and wounding the rest of the gun crew.

Oberleutnant Behrens ordered the guns to change positions to concentrate their fire, for he was certain that the close- support aircraft would repeat their attack. The guns were ready when twelve Il 2s attacked. The massed fire from the eight 37mm guns caused the formation to turn away. Two of the Il 2s trailed dense banners of black smoke as they flew away.

The 6th Battery under *Oberleutnant* Behrens spent long months protecting the 60th Motorized Infantry Regiment. Orders came to defend Kuznotsevka. The icy cold of the winter of 1941-42 had set in. Like other German units in Russia, the RGG lacked warm winter clothing. The only possibility of obtaining such clothing was from the enemy, whose troops were outfitted with lined boots, fur hats, and padded pants and jackets.

After long weeks in the biting cold orders came for a change of position. When rumors spread that the unit was going home everyone secretly breathed a sigh of relief. The first stop on the journey home was Smolensk. From there the unit marched to Vilna where it was loaded aboard trains. The long train ride ended in Munich. From there the men of 6th Battery were allowed to take a well-earned leave in February.

The Luftwaffe's II Special Purpose Rifle Battalion (Neubauer Battalion) in the East

The last unit formed from the RGG and sent to Russia was the Special Purpose Luftwaffe Battalion, which was later renamed "II Rifle Battalion of the Luftwaffe".

The unit was created to meet a need to quickly deploy capable combat units into Army Group Center's area near Rzhev, Vyazma and Briansk, in order to halt the Russian counteroffensive which had begun in early December. *Generalmajor* Eugen Meindl received instructions from *Reichsmarschall* Göring "To form Luftwaffe combat units and insert them into the gaps in the German front."

The Special Purpose Rifle Battalion was the first such unit ready to see action and it began its journey to Russia from Berlin on 30 December 1941. The battalion's commanding officer was *Major* Neubauer. On 9 January 1942 the unit was flown from Orsha to the front-line airfield of Yukhnov-South, which already lay under Russian fire. The battalion received orders to secure the Yukhnov – Medyn – Moscow section of the highway, in order to hold the road open for elements of XXXXII Army Corps withdrawing from the Medyn position.

On the morning of 10 January the villages of Pogorelka, Nikitina and Dubrovka, which lay south of the highway, were occupied. The following night the Red Army attacked Nikitina and Pogorelka. The Nikitina strongpoint was captured by the enemy; the platoon under *Leutnant* Ritter which was defending the strongpoint was completely wiped out. Nikitina had fallen, but Pogorelka held. A counterattack retook Nikitina. The enemy withdrew back across the Ugra; the Russian advance south across the highway had been halted.

The battalion was transferred into the area northwest of Yukhnov and committed against the units of the 43rd Soviet Army advancing from the direction of Moscow. The days that followed saw heavy fighting for possession of the villages of Alonyi-Gori, Kholm and Karamasovo. Losses were heavy but some breathing space was gained for the German forces defending Yukhnov.

On 18 January the Soviets threw the fresh 9th Moscow Guards Division into the battle. The division's orders were to link up with airborne troops dropped at the same time between Vyazma and Yukhnov. On the German side it was vital that the corridor running north from Yukhnov to *Panzergruppe* 4, which was blocking the escape of enemy forces stuck in the Vyazma pocket, be reinforced and held against reserve units of the Russian 33rd and 43rd Armies attacking from the direction of Moscow. Committed at the focal point of the battle near Morosovo and Penyazi, on 24 January the Neubauer Battalion, together with a company of the SS-Regiment *Langemarck*, was given the mission of taking the village of Khmylovka and cutting the Russian supply line which ran behind it.

The first attack on the morning of 25 January was halted by heavy Russian fire. The platoon under *Leutnant* Kühn got to within a few meters of the enemy positions, but then bogged down in the deep snow and had to be withdrawn in the evening after sustaining heavy casualties. Russian counterattacks were repulsed in the days that followed. On 29 January another advance had the desired result: the enemy supply line behind Khmylovka was cut.

After the focal point of the enemy offensive had shifted farther north the battalion was once again thrown into the defensive battles near Morosovo – Morosovskaya Komuna. On 11 February it was given the assignment of securing one of the key Soviet positions north of Yukhnov – Zacharova with the crossing over the Ugra. Reconnaissance had discovered the Russian intentions in this area, namely to breach the German front and open the Vyazma pocket.

The Soviet attack began on the night of 13 February 1942 along the Ugra. The enemy units, which had strong tank support, broke into Zacharovo. By evening the village was cleared of the enemy again in bloody close-quarters fighting. The following night the badly-battered enemy forces withdrew. When deployed near Zacharovo on 12 February, the 3rd Company had a strength of 5 officers, 18 NCOs and 197 men; by the evening of 13 February all that was fit for duty was 1 officer, 6 NCOs and 52 men.

Major Neubauer was wounded seriously on the morning of 13 February. His adjutant, *Oberleutnant* Kiefer, took over the battalion. He was wounded at about midday while repelling an attack by enemy armor and handed over command to the commander of the heavy machine-gun company, *Oberleutnant* Rebholz. That evening Rebholz, too, was wounded and put out of action. During this period the company under *Hauptmann* Bergmann, which was assigned to Parachute Battle Group Koch, defended the airfield at Anisovo-Gorodishche with the paratroops. On 8 March it was placed under the direct command of the Luftwaffe Combat Group under *Generalmajor* Schlemm and in a bitter night attack took the village of Anisovo and on 18

An extremely successful Flak 88 of the Hermann Göring Regiment.

The sIG 33/1 (Sf.), a 150mm heavy infantry gun mounted on the chassis of a Panzer 38(t).

Officers of the General Göring Regiment discuss the situation, Russia 1941.

A Flak 88 fires at approaching enemy tanks.

A Flak 88 bogged down in the mud on the Eastern Front, winter 1941.

The "highway" in the central sector of the Eastern Front in the winter of 1941.

This KV II self-propelled howitzer was knocked out by the General Göring Regiment's 2nd Company near Dubno on June 29, 1941.

Soviet Polikarpov I-16 fighter shot down by the General Göring Regiment near Dubno-Ostrog.

March, Hill 238 near Anisovo. *Hauptmann* Bergmann was killed during this operation.

At the beginning of 1942 the remnants of the battalion, in total 42 men, were withdrawn from the front near Yukhnov and sent back to the parent unit in Berlin. This battalion suffered appalling losses in one of the toughest battles fought by the men of the General Göring Regiment in Russia. In three months of uninterrupted action it lost 132 dead, 258 wounded, 65 casualties through freezing and 37 to sickness from an original strength of 14 officers, 66 NCOs and 488 men.

A member of the battalion's 4th Company was *Unteroffizier* Gottfried Freiherr von Cramm, the Wimbeldon champion of the thirties. He, too, was wounded and suffered frostbite in both legs, as a result of which he had to be evacuated to hospital. He was returned to Germany on account of his injuries. The commander of VIII *Fliegerkorps*, *Generaloberst* von Richthofen, and *Generalmajore* Schlemm and Meindl expressed their appreciation to the battalion for its unparalleled exploits. *Generalmajor* Schlemm said of these in an order of the day from 8 April 1942:

"Mindful of the great responsibility which the name of the regiment places on every one of its members, the battalion has always fearlessly fulfilled its duty in attack and defence and has not been reluctant to sacrifice to the last officer and man. In farewell I express to the battalion my appreciation and admiration for its heroic actions."

III. THE INTERVENING PERIOD

Reorganization and Reformation

When the individual units returned from Russia they were given several weeks of rest and then transferred into the Gascogne area in the south of France. It was there that the planned expansion of the General Göring Regiment into the Hermann Göring Brigade and later the Hermann Göring Division was to take place. Among the units transferred to France was the Rifle Battalion RGG under *Hauptmann* Funck.

At the same time the cavalry squadron was enlarged to become a cavalry platoon and was transferred to East Prussia to take over security for the headquarters of the Commander-in-Chief of the Luftwaffe in the *Reichsmarschall*'s hunting lodge in the Rominten Heath. The cavalry platoon remained in east Prussia until the loss of the Rominten Heath in late autumn 1944, when it was destroyed in the fighting there.

After a series of great successes – which had won *Oberst* Conrath the Knight's Cross on 4 September 1941 –, exhausted and suffering from heavy losses, lacking heavy weapons and equipment which it had been forced to leave behind with the infantry, the General Göring Regiment returned to the Reich.

On its arrival in Munich, orders reached *Oberst* Conrath to reorganize and reequip the regiment as the "Reinforced Regiment Hermann Göring (motorized)". The regiment's flak battalions were reorganized as mixed battalions and reequipped. Each of the mixed battalions received three batteries of 88mm flak and two batteries of 20mm light flak. The former II Battalion, RGG was disbanded, in the course of which the battalion headquarters was integrated into the Berlin flak defenses as "Flak Sub-group Center".

The new regiment received the title Reinforced Regiment "Hermann Göring (HG)". At the same time new "Hermann Göring" cuff bands were introduced. In March 1942 the regiment was organized as follows:

I Battalion: 1st-3rd Batteries (88mm), 4th Battery (former 8th Battery, 20mm), 5th Battery (20mm).

II Battalion: (former IV Battalion) 6th Battery (88mm), 7th and 8th Batteries (new formations), 9th Battery (former 15th Battery, 20mm), 10th Battery (20mm).

III Battalion: 11th-13th Searchlight Batteries (employed with Flak Group Northwest in Berlin area, this battalion left the HG Rgt. in summer 1942 and received the designation 528th Searchlight Battalion).

Flak Replacement Battalion:
Transferred to Utrecht, Holland in May 1940, organization remained unchanged.

Guard Battalion:
1st-3rd Guard Companies and Cavalry Platoon. Employed to guard the headquarters of the Commander-in-Chief Luftwaffe.

The Reserve Searchlight Battalion, RGG, with the 1st-3rd Reserve Searchlight Batteries, continued to be employed in the northwest sector of the Berlin flak defenses. It left the RGG in early 1942 and received the new designation of III (Searchlight) Battalion, 32nd Flak Regiment. It remained in its previous positions. The 14th (Railway Flak) Battery (105mm) had previously left the RGG in 1941, when it was integrated into the 321st (Railway) Reserve Flak Battalion.

Following a brief period of rest and refitting, both of the flak battalions which returned from Russia joined the flak defenses of metropolitan Munich. At the end of 1942 the Renault factory in Paris, which was an important part of the German armaments industry, was attacked by the Allied air force. The Regimental HQ, which was still in Munich, and the two flak battalions positioned there, were transferred to Paris to guard the Renault factory.

Several months later these units were withdrawn from Paris and transferred to Brittany, where the formation of the Hermann Göring Brigade had begun in the meantime. Formed in July, the HG Brigade consisted of two regiments, a rifle regiment, and a flak regiment. The HG Rifle Regiment was formed on 15 July 1942. Its makeup was as follows:

Commanding Officer:	Oberst Heydemeier
I Battalion:	Major Funck
1st Company:	Oberleutnant Grüne
2nd Company:	Hauptmann Weber
3rd Company:	Hauptmann Stauch
4th (Machine-gun) Company:	Hauptmann Spieler
II Battalion:	Hauptmann Schreiber
5th Company:	Hauptmann Nagorny
6th Company:	Hauptmann Rebholz
7th Company:	Hauptmann Oehme
8th (Machine-gun) Company:	Hauptmann Dingelstedt
9th (Heavy Infantry Gun) Company:	Oberleutnant Wilmskötter
III (heavy) Battalion:	Major Preuß
10th (Motorcycle) Company:	Hauptmann Kiefer
11th (Armored Pioneer) Company:	Oberleutnant Musil
12th (Anti-tank) Company:	Oberleutnant Stiller
13th (Panzer) Company:	Hauptmann Lübke
Tank Repair Shop Platoon:	Oberleutnant Zacher
Motor Transport Column:	Hauptfeldwebel Franke

The senior officer complement of the new Brigade Headquarters, which was formed in Pontivi in Brittany, ultimately looked as follows:

Brigade Commander:	GenMaj. Conrath
Ia:	Major Bobrowski
IIa:	Hptm. Beinhofer
Signals Officer:	Hptm. Vogel
Senior Technical Inspector:	Funk
Senior Regimental Inspector:	Große
Brigade Medical Officer:	Stabsarzt Dr. von Ondarza

On 15 October 1942 the rifle regiment was renamed the Grenadier Regiment HG. The individual battalions were renamed as follows:

I Battalion, Rifle Rgt. HG became III Battalion, Grenadier Rgt. HG
II Battalion, Rifle Rgt. HG became II Battalion, Grenadier Rgt. HG

As well several new units were formed: elements of III (Heavy) Battalion were used to form the 13th (Infantry Gun) and 14th (Anti-tank) Companies. The remaining elements of this now discarded battalion formed the basis of I Battalion, Panzer Regiment HG. The 10th (Motorcycle) Company formed the core of the new Armored Reconnaissance Battalion HG.

During the period from autumn 1942 to early 1943 preparations were made in the Mont de Marsan area of southern France to form two grenadier regiments from the "New Formations Group Division HG" under *Oberst* Wilhelm Schmalz. Their anticipated designations were 1st Grenadier Regiment HG and 2nd Grenadier Regiment HG. The following units were ready for action at the beginning of March 1943:

(a) I (Armored) Battalion, 1st Grenadier Regiment HG under *Major* Neubauer. (On 1 April 1943 it received the designation 1st Panzer-Grenadier Regiment HG. In Africa it was for the most part still referred to as 1st Grenadier Regiment HG.)

(b) II (Motorized) Battalion, 2nd Grenadier Regiment under *Hauptmann* Pfeiffer.

(c) Regimental Units: 13th (Infantry Gun) Company and 14th (Anti-tank) Company, 2nd Grenadier Regiment HG.

These new units were loaded aboard Italian destroyers and the captured Greek destroyer *Hermes* on 22 and 27 April 1943 and shipped to Tunisia. They saw action as part of the HG Division under *Generalmajor* "Beppo" Schmid, only to begin many years of American captivity three weeks later.

On 19 February 1943 an order was sent to the 5th Parachute Regiment under *Oberstleutnant* Walter Koch, which had been in action since the first days of the Allied invasion of Northwest Africa, stating that effective immediately it was being integrated into the HG Division as the 5th Jäger Regiment HG. The official transfer of the unit did not take place until 14 March 1943, however. Even after this the troops of the former parachute assault regiment (*Fallschirmjäger-Sturmregiment*), whose number included veterans of Eben Emael and Crete, considered themselves an independent unit.

Following its renaming as I Battalion, Panzer Regiment HG, the former III (Heavy) Battalion, Rifle Regiment HG was organized as follows:

Base:	Camp de Meucon
Battalion Command Post:	Grand Champ near Locimine (Brittany)
Organization:	HQ with signals platoon, 13th Panzer Company with Panzer III tanks armed with 50mm long and 75mm short guns.

Command Positions List:

Battalion Commander:	Hptm. Preuß
Adjutant:	Oblt. Stronk
Operations Officer:	Lt. Moegling
Battalion Medical Officer:	Stabsarzt Dr. Sporer
Administrative Officer:	Oberzahlmeister Klingbeil
Commander Signals Platoon:	Lt. Groll
Commander 13th (Panzer) Company:	Hptm. Lübke
Commander 10th (Motorcycle) Company:	Hptm. Paulus

Commander 11th (Armored Pioneer) Company: Oblt. Musil

On 9 and 10 November 1942 this unit departed by train for Caserte, arriving on the 15th. The unit remained in Caserte until 20 November before moving by road to Santa Maria, where it took up quarters in new barracks. There the battalion was issued tropical equipment. Furthermore a headquarters company was formed with the following units:

The HQ Signals Platoon joined the HQ Company, which was itself expanded through the formation of:

a panzer platoon under *Fahnenjunker-Feldwebel* Richtberg,

a pioneer platoon under Lt. Mohr,

a reconnaissance platoon under Lt. Lenz, and

a flak platoon under Lt. Walter.

At this time *Hauptmann* Preuß was promoted to the rank of *Major*. At the same time he was named garrison commander of Santa Maria. At the end of January 1943 the Headquarters Company was transferred to the seaside town of Castel Volturno, where it remained until mid-February 1943. The shipment of the battalion to Africa and its action there without tanks will be recounted later.

The Flak Division of the HG Division

At the end of 1942 elements of the former 211th Flak Battery – the 11th-13th Batteries (88mm) and the 14th and 15th Batteries (20mm) – joined the flak regiment of the Hermann Göring Brigade as its new III Battalion. Following the expansion of the brigade into a division, however, the battalion was re-equipped as a light field howitzer battalion, retaining the 11th to 13th Heavy Batteries. Finally, the unit received the designation I Battalion, 1st Armored Artillery Regiment HG.

IV Battalion, Flak Regiment HG, which had been newly formed in the meantime, consisted of the 14th Battery with 37mm Flak (the former 4th Battery RGG) and the 15th (Railway) Escort Battery with 20mm light anti-aircraft guns (the former 9th Battery RGG) with the flak platoons "Führer Train", "Foreign Minister Train" and "Reichsmarschall Train", as well as the 16th Battery (the former 17th Battery RGG) and a 17th Battery, likewise equipped with 20mm light flak.

In january 1943 the regimental headquarters of the Hermann Göring Flak Regiment together with the Ist and IInd Battalions were sent to Africa for use in the Tunisian battle zone. In the course of the heavy fighting there all the personnel of these units were killed or captured.

The examples of redesignations of units and the formation of new units through the dividing of existing formations depicted in the previous chapter are good examples of how the German Armed Forces created and enlarged units during the war. This was especially true of the formation of units which bore the titles Hermann Göring (HG) or General Göring (GG). Not unexpectedly, during the formation process the division was provided with a more capable supply regiment under the command of *Oberst* Ritter. The regiment was organized into two supply battalions and a maintenance battalion. Due to the shortage of transport space for Africa it saw no action in Northwest Africa and instead remained with the division during its formation period.

The staff of the "New Formation Group HG Division", which was based in Mont de Marsan under *Oberst* Wilhelm Schmalz, brought the risky venture of forming a division to a successful conclusion. This was due to the efforts of this capable officer, who went on to command the Hermann Göring Regiment, Division and finally Parachute Panzer Corps, and who led his units not only with great bravado, but with concern and circumspection as well. It was Schmalz who developed the parachute panzer corps into the powerful weapon which gained great honor for the name Hermann Göring in the Eastern Reich.

Further building up of the division took place in the Gascogne area of southern France. The Hermann Göring Reconnaissance Battalion (AA HG), which was established in the course of the expansion, included the following units at the end of 1942:

HQ, Reconnaissance Battalion HG with signals platoon.

1st Motorcycle Company with armored scout car platoon.

2nd Grenadier Company (motorized).

By early 1943 this battalion had once again been reorganized and expanded, as a result of which its composition was as follows:

HQ, Reconnaissance Battalion HG with:

1st Armored Scout Car Company.

2nd Motorcycle Company.

3rd Grenadier Company (motorized).

4th (Heavy) Company with pioneer platoon, mortar platoon and signals platoon.

5th Light Reconnaissance Column.

After being forced to transfer its 2nd Company to Tunisia in January 1943, the entire Reconnaissance Battalion HG was transferred to Caserta in April 1943 and then in June to Sicily, where it took part in the fighting on the island from 10 July to 16 August, as will be described later.

The Evolution of the Hermann Göring Rifle Regiment

Following the second major expansion from brigade to division, the organization of the Hermann Göring Rifle Regiment (which escaped transfer to Africa and thus was available for the formation of the division after the disaster in Tunisia) was as follows:

I Battalion with 1st-3rd Companies and 4th (Heavy) Company.

II Battalion with 5th-7th Companies and 8th (Heavy) Company.

III Battalion with: 9th Infantry Gun Company,

10th Motorcycle Company,

11th Pioneer Company,

12th Anti-tank Company,

13th Panzer Company.

As well the regiment had an armored force repair shop platoon and a horse-drawn transport column. With the formation of the Hermann Göring Division the following additional changes took place:

HQ Rifle Regiment HG became HQ 1st Grenadier Regiment HG,

I Battalion, Rifle Regiment HG became I Battalion, 1st Grenadier Regiment HG,

II Battalion, Rifle Regiment HG became II Battalion, 1st Rifle Regiment HG,

13th Panzer Company (less armored recon. platoon) became I Battalion, Panzer Regiment HG,

Armored Reconnaissance Platoon (of the 13th Company) became 3rd Company, Armored Reconnaissance Battalion HG,

10th Motorcycle Company became 1st (Motorcycle) Company, Armored Reconnaissance Battalion HG,

2nd (VW) Company became 2nd (VW) Company, Armored Reconnaissance Battalion HG,

11th Armored Pioneer Company became 1st Company, Armored Pioneer Battalion HG.

That the formation of the Hermann Göring Division took some months was due to the nature of the process and to the fact that, in the fourth year of the war, the intake of new recruits was not unlimited. The formation of the new unit, or at least of its key elements, thus represented a major accomplishment for the new formation group of the HG Division. However the entire progress was seriously hindered by the need to send individual units to Tunisia. The Hermann Göring Panzer Regiment did not see action in Tunisia, although its I Battalion later proved itself in combat in Sicily, where it was sent on its own.

The "Reichsmarschall" Special Train Guard Detachment – The Führer Flak Battalion

In addition to the trains of the early war years in which Hitler travelled to Poland – among other places – from time to time new escort trains were assembled and were likewise equipped with flak defenses. The Commander-in-Chief of the Luftwaffe, *Reichsmarschall* Hermann Göring, eventually came to possess two such trains, "Asia" and "Robinson". As previously described, "Asia" included flak cars at the front and end of the train, each with two 20mm light flak. The adjacent large cargo spaces were used to carry ammunition, weapons and replacement parts.

The General Göring Regiment and its successor units supplied the guard

Hermann Göring with the troops on 12 January 1942, his birthday.

Anti-aircraft guns arrayed in front of the Reich War Flag for the swearing-in of the newly-formed HG units at the Kromhout Barracks.

Swearing in members of the new HG units in Utrecht.

The swearing-in of the 3rd Replacement Battery, Replacement and Training Battalion RGG. The battalion commander, Major Grauert, inspects the troops.

The swearing-in ceremony.

A 20mm Flak on a self-propelled chassis on the Atlantic Coast.

Another 20mm Flak position on the Atlantic Coast.

Troops cross a river in inflatable boats.

Crossing by a pioneer assault boat.

20mm light anti-aircraft gun in a camouflaged position.

The 10th Motorcycle Company of the HG Rifle Regiment at Camp de Meucon, Brittany in October 1942.

Unteroffizier Kanert's Sturmgeschütz III at Camp de Meucon. At the time Kanert was a member of 10th Company, Panzer Regiment HG.

A panzer company of the HG Brigade in the field. The tanks are Panzer IIIs.

A heavy infantry gun is manhandled into position.

detachments for the trains *Reichsmarschall* I and II, "Reich Foreign Minister", "Mussolini" and all the others that came later. A brief description of these detachments has already been given. Not mentioned however were the units which eventually developed into the Führer Flak Battalion.

At the beginning of the war the guard for Führer Headquarters was provided by the *Großdeutschland* Infantry Regiment and was called the Führer Escort Detachment and later Guard Company Führer Headquarters. The increasing demands on the unit resulted in it being expanded to become the Führer Escort Battalion. The 7th Battery of the General Göring Regiment, which was equipped with 20mm light flak on self-propelled carriages, was chosen to provide protection against low-level air attack. When mobilization came in August 1939 the unit was moved to Führer HQ as "7th Battery RGG – Flak Battery with the Führer Headquarters"; it was deployed wherever Führer Headquarters was located.

I Battalion, 604th Flak Regiment was initially used to defend the *Wolfsschanze*, a permanent installation which was often home to Führer Headquarters. In 1942 this unit was renamed the Führer Flak Battalion and absorbed the RGG's 7th Battery. A short time later it was designated IV Flak Battalion of the Flak Regiment HG. Coincident with this move the battalion's personnel were issued white collar tabs, thus confirming their membership in the Hermann Göring units.

When Führer Headquarters was not at the *Wolfsschanze*, the units stationed there to defend the installation had to be ready at short notice to take on other roles. One such occasion saw the unit participate in the winter battle at the Donets River as "Battle Group Führer Flak Battalion" from December 1942 to March 1943. The main scene of action was the Millerovo area, where the battalion suffered heavy losses. It was thus the second unit wearing the HG cuff band to see action in the East.

With the formation of the Führer Flak Regiment in October 1944 as part of the Führer Escort Division—then in the formation process – the Führer Flak Battalion left the Parachute Panzer Division HG and was incorporated into the Führer Flak Regiment.

IV. THE AFRICAN THEATRE

A Brief Overview

On his arrival in London on 23 June 1942, Lieutenant General Dwight D. Eisenhower assumed command of all US forces in Europe. In his luggage was an order from American President Roosevelt to undertake an offensive operation in the European Theater in 1942. However, by 24 June the Allied leaders in London had agreed that the objective of their next action would be the occupation of Northwest Africa. To this end a striking force comprising all Allied services would be assembled. The operation's code-name was "Torch".

The occupation of Tunisia would mean that the Axis pressure on Malta would finally be relieved. The island could then be used as base from which the land, sea, and air supply lines to Panzer Army Africa could be paralysed and the latter forced to withdraw westward. The forces of the Western Allies were assembled into three large groups, which were to occupy Casablanca, Oran, and Algiers and from there advance in the direction of Tunis. Casablanca was chosen because of the rail line from there to Tunisia via Oran and Algiers. Oran and Algiers, on the other hand, were major seaports, and Allied bomber units could be employed against the Axis forces from Oran's airfield.

The troops for the landing near Casablanca were to come directly from the USA. In command of this battle group was Major General George S. Patton. The central landing group, the 2nd US Corps under Major General Fredenhall, went into action near Oran. The Algiers Group was led by Major General Ryder. Immediately after the capture of Algiers General Anderson, the Commander-in-Chief of the British First Army, was to assume command of this most important group.

Advance convoys began sailing from England to Gibraltar in early October. These were followed by four large convoys from England carrying the main attack forces in the period from 22 October to 1 November. The warships, a total of 160 units ranging from battleships to patrol boats, did not leave Scapa Flow until late October.

On the German side, by 4 November Axis military leaders in Rome had agreed that the operation discovered by radio intelligence might be a landing attempt in North Africa. By 6 November Mussolini was firmly convinced: "This operation is aimed at North Africa!"

Force 34 –the US naval group under the command of Admiral Hewitt – consisted of a total of 104 units. It left Casco Bay, Maine on the morning of 23 October 1942. A second convoy set sail the next morning. The warship group rendezvoused with the first convoy on 26th October and on the 28th the air cover group, led by the aircraft carrier *Ranger* with the escort carriers *Suwannee*, *Sangamon*, *Santee*, and *Chenango*, left port.

The forces destined for the landings near Casablanca were divided into four landing groups. Escorting them were the battleships *Massachusetts*, *New York* and *Texas*, the five named carriers, seven cruisers, and a series of destroyers and minelayers. General Eisenhower and his entire staff flew to Gibraltar in five Flying Fortresses on 5th November; there they were greeted by the local governor, Lieutenant General Sir F.N. Mason-MacFarlane.

The commander of U-Boats Italy, KAdm. Leo Kreisch, received the first reports of the approach of the extensive Allied operation in the late morning of 6 November. Two hours later he received a radio message from Führer Headquarters:

"The fate of the Africa Army rests on the smashing of the Gibraltar convoy. Expect ruthless and victorious action – Adolf Hitler."

That same evening KAdm. Kreisch committed all available U-boats against the convoy heading for the Northwest-African coast. At the same time *Generalfeldmarschall* Albert Kesselring, the Commander-in-Chief South, initiated his first countermeasures from his headquarters in Frascati near Rome. One of his first actions was to strengthen *Luftflotte* 2. Reconnaissance activity was doubled. In addition Führer Headquarters called for at least one division to be readied immediately in Sicily to throw against an enemy landing wherever it might take place. This proposal was rejected by the OKW.

The Allied Landings –
The Western, Central and Eastern Task Forces

At 0400 hours on the 8th of November 1942 the southern attack group of Western Task Force 34 transmitted the message "Play Ball". The landings near Safi had begun. The French batteries there offered resistance but were crushed by naval gunfire. The US troops came ashore on Safi's commercial pier.

In the case of the northern group, which was to take possession of the port of Mehadia and the surrounding area, intervention was delayed, and when the special ships carrying the landing troops approached the harbour they were met with shellfire from the French batteries. Vice-Admiral Michelier, the Naval Commander Casablanca, had ordered "resistance to the last round". The batteries fought until they were destroyed. One coastal battery, near Lyautey airfield, fought on until the morning of 10 November; as a result the scheduled landing by US Rangers near Sebou was delayed until later that day.

The central attack group of Western Task Force 34 was supposed to land 34,000 American troops near Fedala. A number of heavy French coastal batteries were located there and these opened fire. The destroyer *Murphy* was badly damaged by the "Blondin" battery. Locally-based French naval forces attempted to ambush the landing fleet at 0815 hours. The cruiser *Primauguet* under Captain Mercier set out from Casablanca with two light cruisers and four destroyers. The result was an hour-long naval engagement. The French light cruiser *Milan* damaged the US destroyer *Wilkes* so badly that it was left rudderless and drifting on the sea. The destroyer *Boulonnais* was engaged by the battleship *Massachusetts*. Salvoes from the American vessel pounded and finally sank the French ship. The destroyer *Fougeuex* also sank after taking hits from the US battleship. The French cruiser *Primaguet* and its escorting destroyers *Brestois* and *Frondeur* were also hit. The destroyers were sunk and the cruiser had to be beached.

The French battleship *Jean Bart*, which was not seaworthy and only partially combat-ready, exchanged fire with American warships until its guns were silenced. Subsequently the French ship was heavily bombed by carrier-based aircraft. Vice-Admiral Michelier still refused to give up. On 11 November he rejected an offer from General Patton for a cease-fire with the remark:

"The French fleet stands here to defend Morocco against any enemy and is doing its duty."

In spite of French resistance Patton was able to put a total of 37,000 soldiers and 250 tanks ashore. Algiers was handed over to the Allies on the basis of political events.

There was French opposition to the Allied landings near Oran. Vice-Admiral Roult, Naval Commander of Oran, had his forces open fire. His coastal artillery sank the first two transports. Here again the French Navy saw action. The light cruiser *Epervier* was sunk in action against enemy destroyers, cruisers, and battleships. Captain Laurin remained on board. The French also lost three destroyers and six submarines. The submarine *Fresnel* escaped to Toulon.

France's losses were 803 killed and more than 1,000 wounded in this unequal battle – but it had saved its honor. The Western Allies lost 700 dead and about 800 wounded. Twenty-nine Allied ships were lost. In a radio broadcast to the French people Marshall Pétain affirmed the stance of his navy with the words:

"I have always said that we would defend our colonial empire against any attacker no matter who it is. We were attacked, so we defended ourselves. I gave the order."

But secret Anglo-American diplomacy succeeded in "putting out the fire", as Ambassador Murphy and his aides termed it. It was they who persuaded Admiral Darlan – who had initially obeyed Pétain – to issue an order to all the troops in North Africa "to cease fire in the name of Marshall Pétain".

General Charles de Gaulle, leader of the Free French, was not informed of this lightning occupation of French territory overseas. Not until 8 November was he brusquely informed by Winston Churchill at 10 Downing Street that the Allies had landed in Northwest Africa. In de Gaulle's opinion – which no one wanted to hear, but which he did his best to get across – the landings had taken place much too far from harm's way and this would mean their failure.

But back to the German side, where during the night of 8 November the first reaction was being shown (Hitler was on his way from the *Wolfsschanze* to Munich for his traditional speech in the Bürgerbräkeller that evening). Hitler called the Commander-in-Chief South, *Generalfeldmarschall* Kesselring, and ordered him "to send everything we have to Africa". Hitler told Kesselring:

"We will not give up Africa, for to give up Africa would mean giving up the Mediterranean and in doing so we would lose the entire Mediterranean Theater by the end of the year. But this, Kesselring, would mean an unimaginable loss of prestige and would strike the Italians to the core." More than that, however, it would have given the Allies the freedom of initiative. Kesselring's job was to prevent the loss of Africa.

On the morning of 9 November *Generalfeldmarschall* Kesselring named *Oberst* Martin Harlinghausen, who knew his way around Africa, Commander of Aviation Forces in Tunisia and enjoined the latter:

"You are to take possession of the Tunis and Bizerte bridgeheads with your aviation units and secure them until the arrival of German combat troops." The first German aircraft landed at El Aouina airfield near Tunis the same day. The French soldiers at the edge of the airfield stood at attention and Admiral Esteva, Governor-General of Tunis, greeted the German airmen. On 10 November the first sorties were flown from there against the Anglo-American landing forces.

Command of the German units being sent to the Tunisian bridgehead was given to *General der Panzertruppe* Walther K. Nehring. He received a quick briefing on the situation from GFM Kesselring in Frascati. Nehring learned that all he had under his command at the moment was a very few battalions, but that capable units would be sent as quickly as possible to allow him to form the headquarters of the XC Army Corps, which he was to command. This was the situation which made necessary the deployment of the parachute troops.

The 5th Parachute Regiment in the First Actions in Tunisia

The more than 100,000-man-strong Allied landing force assembled in the landing areas near Casablanca, Oran, and Algiers and a few miles to the east before beginning their advance on Tunis. This gave *Generalfeldmarschall* Kesselring time to send two battalions of the 5th Parachute Regiment and his own guard battalion to Tunis. He outlined the tactics which *General der Panzertruppe* Nehring was to employ:

"Delay enemy operations and secure Tunis. Push own forces to the west and south to establish a strong Tunisian bridgehead."

When *Generalfeldmarschall* Kesselring landed in Tunis on 19 November, *General* Nehring was able to inform him that the enemy had been stopped, but that their own front was 500 kilometers long and desperately needed heavy weapons and tanks.

Soon the first elements of the 10th Panzer Division arrived in Tunis, followed by the 1st Company of the 501st Heavy Panzer (Tiger) Battalion. These forces, together with the Italian *Superga* Armored Division, which had also been hastily sent to Tunisia, succeeded in halting the advance by the enemy units. *General* Nehring had meanwhile been forced to give way to *Generaloberst* von Arnim, who had formed the Fifth Panzer Army on 5 December. The latter force consolidated the situation in the bridgehead by the end of December and held the battle zone with its 100 Panzer IIIs and IVs and eleven Tigers.

But what of the Hermann Göring Division?

The Hermann Göring Division in Africa: Initial Overview

The first elements of the Hermann Göring Division were sent to Africa in December 1942. In January 1943 the fully-equipped I and II Battalions of the Flak Regiment HG under *Oberstleutnant* Hullmann were shipped to Africa. The regimental headquarters initially remained in southern France to organize further shipments.

Until the end of December the flak regiment had been deployed in the Naples area, where it was used against the fighter-bombers and bombers of the American 12th Air Force and the aircraft of the British Western Desert Force, which had begun the sustained bombing of targets in southern Italy in addition to those in North Africa. The HG Regiment's flak batteries that were sent to Tunisia were unable to significantly improve the situation in the air as they were used mainly in a ground role to combat enemy armor.

Elements of the division bound for Africa from southern France, the replacement battalion in Holland, or Germany were first transported into the Naples, Caserta, Averso Santa Maria, Capua Vetere, or Castel Volturno areas. The second stage of the journey led to Trapani in Sicily. From there the personnel were generally flown to Tunisia, while the vehicles, heavy equipment, and weapons were sent by ship.

The transport ships sailed from the ports of Naples or Livorno. Many of the ships arrived late and several not at all because they had been sunk at sea by aircraft or submarines of the famous 10th Submarine Flotilla based at Malta.

The newly-formed I Battalion, Panzer-Grenadier Regiment HG under its commander *Major* Neubauer was transported from Gaeta to Tunisia aboard two Italian and one Greek destroyers (the latter was the *Hermes* which had been put back into service under the German flag). The three ships were unable to approach an harbour, however, being turned away once by mines and another time by British air attacks. Near Cape Bon the ships succeeded in disembarking their troops by lighter craft but they were unable to unload the heavy weapons. Consequently the unit was unable to go into action straight away.

I Battalion, Panzer Regiment HG was transferred from southern France to Italy in January 1943. It established a bivouac near Castel Volturno and not until the end of February did it move to Villa San Giovanni on the Strait of Messina, which was only six kilometers wide at that point. Travelling the northern coastal road it reached the Marsala area via Cefala and Palermo. There it established another bivouac.

The wait for air transport lasted until 4 April. The battalion was driven to the airfield by companies and assigned Ju 52 transports. The tanks remained behind in the Castel Volturno bivouac area and received orders to drive to Livorno, where they were to be loaded aboard ships and taken to Africa.

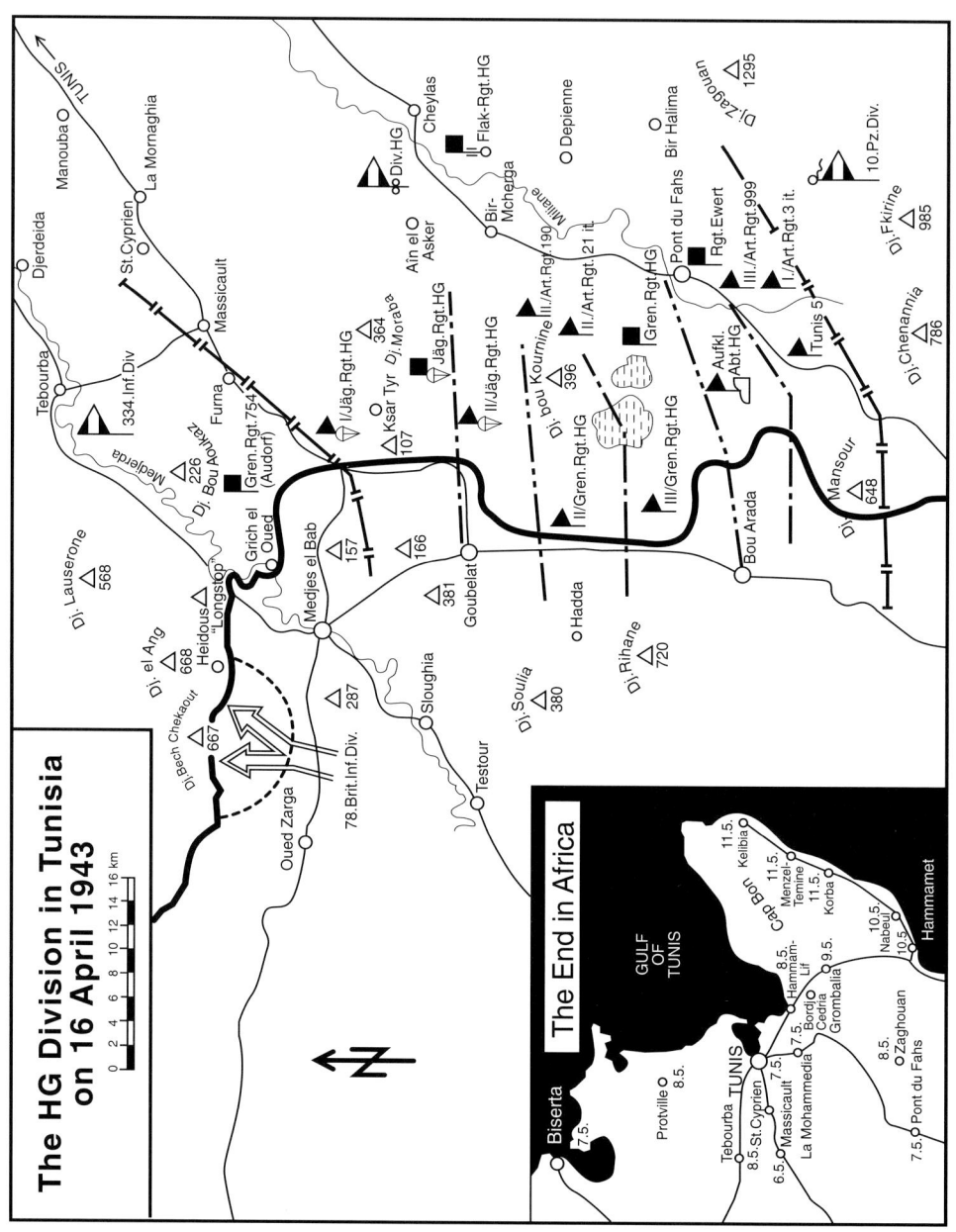

These plans came to nothing, however. On 5 April, following the departure of the first personnel elements of the battalion, Trapani airfield was heavily bombed by Allied aircraft, destroying many of the Ju 52s parked there. No replacements were available (large numbers of Ju 52s had been committed to the attempt to supply surrounded Stalingrad from the air).

Command of the division elements in Africa lay in the hands of *Oberst* (soon to be promoted to *Generalmajor*) Josef "Beppo" Schmid. *Oberst* Schmid had arrived in Tunis with the advance detachment of the division at the beginning of 1943; initially the force under his command was designated *Kampfgruppe* Schmid, later it was referred to by its actual name, the HG Division.

The actions by the division elements required the utmost of every man. Their mission was to stop an enemy superior in numbers and weapons under difficult conditions and without heavy weapons. The men with the white collar patches performed magnificently, especially in the Kairouan, Goubella, Medjez el Bab, Pont du Fahs, and Zaghouan areas as well as in the area surrounding Tunis.

Oberst Schmid initially had to do without the bulk of I Battalion, Panzer Regiment HG and its tanks. They remained behind on Sicily and were assigned to an Army panzer battalion under *Major* Kurt Gierga as a mixed company. The personnel of the panzer battalion who arrived in Tunis, on the other hand, had neither vehicles nor tanks. They were employed as infantry, a role in which their valuable training as tank men was wasted.

The Commander-in-Chief of the Luftwaffe issued a report concerning losses suffered by the transport units ferrying men and equipment to North Africa:

"In April 14 Me 323 *Giganten* and 76 Ju 52s with 275 flight personnel and 212 tonnes of materiel were shot down over the Mediterranean and the African Front."

"The transport units nevertheless succeeded in flying into Tunisia 8,388 soldiers and 5,040 tonnes of materiel in a first-rate effort. These operations resulted in the destruction of *Transportgeschwader* 5 (large-capacity transport unit equipped with the Me 323 *Gigant*)."

On 19 February 1943 the 5th Parachute Regiment under the command of *Oberstleutnant* Walter Koch was renamed the 5th Light Infantry (Jäger) Regiment and incorporated into the Hermann Göring Division. Prior to this the regiment – the first combat unit to arrive in Tunisia – had performed magnificently. Its ranks included a number of the first German parachute troops and early members of the Hermann Göring units. The regiment's soldiers opposed this move; although they were officially a part of the Hermann Göring Division, within the unit the soldiers still referred to themselves as the 5th Parachute Regiment.

After their independent actions, which were conducted completely on their own and led by the commanders of the two battalions, their subordination to another unit was a heavy blow. In spite of this the paratroopers continued to fight with the same elan as before. The 5th Light Infantry Regiment distinguished itself in many battles in Tunisia, as will be shown.

The Ist and IIIrd Light Infantry Battalions now saw action under their new designations. The regiment's command positions list during its period in Africa is presented below. Some of the battalion and company commanders listed had already been killed or wounded by the time the regiment was absorbed by the HG Division.

The 5th Parachute Regiment

Regimental Commander:	Oberstleutnant Walter Koch
	Major Gerhard Schirmer
	Hptm. Horst Zimmermann
I Battalion:	Hptm. (Major) Hans Jungwirt (until 20 April)
	Hptm. Christian Spieler
1st Company:	Lt. Erich Schuster (KIA)
	Oblt. Werner Kleinfeld
2nd Company:	Oblt. Gerhard Maier
	Lt. Richard Palm
	Oblt. Helmut Schütz
3rd Company:	Hptm. Otto Langbein (KIA)
	Oblt. Dewet Klar (died)
	Oblt. Hübner
	Oblt. Rolf Winkler
4th Company:	Hptm. Hugo Paul
	Hptm. Christian Spieler
	Hptm. Robert Hoefeld
III Battalion:	Hauptmann Wilhelm Knocke
	Hptm. Gerhard Schirmer
	Hptm. Horst Zimmermann
	Hptm. Robert Hoefeld
9th Company:	Hptm. Rudolf Becker
	Hptm. Fritz Quednow (KIA)
10th Company:	Oblt. Ullrich Jahn (KIA)
	Lt. Werner Kempa (KIA)
	Oblt. Walter Gasteier
11th Company:	Oblt. Arthur Schneider
	Oblt. Wilhelm Kristufek
12th Company:	Oblt. Hans Hoge
	Hptm. Werner Wöhler

Battalion Medical Officer:	Stabsarzt Dr. Kurt Scheiffle (I Battalion)
Battalion Medical Officer:	Stabsarzt Dr. Fritz Nödl (III Battalion)
Other doctors:	Stabsarzt Dr. Werner Hasenfuß
	Stabsarzt Dr. Renner
	Assistenzarzt Karl Reuter
	Stabsarzt Rudolf Weitzel
Other:	Regimental Inspector Ernst Freiburg (KIA)
	Regimental Inspector Hans Hahn
	Regimental Inspector Kurt Klopfer
	Regimental Inspector Richter

A Look Back

When *General der Panzertruppe* Walther K. Nehring arrived in Tunisia as the new commanding general of XC Corps he had the following units at his disposal, in addition to the air units under *Oberst* Harlinghausen:

I Battalion, 5th Parachute Regiment under Hptm. Jungwirt

III Battalion, 5th Parachute Regiment under Hptm. Knocke

The regiment's II Battalion under *Hauptmann* Hübner had been assigned to Parachute Brigade Ramcke, which was in action in the area in front of El Alamein. The parachute troops had initially been transported to Caserta by train, arriving on the evening of 10 November. *Hauptmann* Knocke formed an advance detachment from 10th Company under the command of *Leutnant* Baitinger. This advance detachment became the first German unit to land at El Aouina airfield near Tunis, arriving on the morning of 11 November shortly after an Allied air raid.

Acting on orders from *Oberst* Harlinghausen, the highest ranking officer in the new Tunisian bridgehead, *Leutnant* Baitinger and his unit drove south through the city to the intersection where the main road to the west branched off. Knocke secured the crossing and with it the arterial road to the west. Sent back as a messenger, First-aid *Gefreiter* Fink from Vienna took a street car for want of other transportation. The trip went off without a hitch. "I didn't even have to buy a ticket," he assured the author during a trip to Medjez el Bab by former members of the 5th Parachute Regiment 25 years later.

Personnel of III Battalion, 5th Parachute Regiment were flown into La Marsa airfield. Still residing there were the Bey of Tunis and the French General Resident Admiral Estevan. On 11 November *Generalfeldmarschall* von Rundstedt had conveyed from Vichy Marshall Pétain's approval for the entry of German troops into Tunisia. On 14 November *General der Panzertruppe* Nehring landed in La Marsa. He took command and, employing the troops that had arrived, neutralized the political leadership of the country. On 16 November 1942 the Wehrmacht communique stated:

"German and Italian troops have landed in Tunisia with the full approval of the French president and military command."

On 16 November 1942 Headquarters, XC Army Corps had at its disposal the following units:

    5th Parachute Regiment: Oberstleutnant Koch,

    Parachute Pioneer Battalion: Major Witzig,

    5th Personnel Replacement Transfer Battalion,

    An 88mm flak battery with four guns,

    An armored scout car company: Oblt. Kahle,

    An Italian General with two battalions of Marine Infantry in Bizerte,

    Two battalions of the *Superga* Division in the area of Pont du Fahs.

The battle for Medjez el Bab, which began on 19 November 1942, was decided in the favor of the Germans by a night attack carried out by the paratroops several days after the start of the battle. *Hauptmann* Schirmer led the subsequent advance as far as Oued Zarga. He was then ordered back by the regiment and took up positions in Medjez el Bab.

During the battle for Tebourba, in which *General* Nehring won the race to Tunis against the numerically far superior enemy, the parachute troops were once again the difference. Operation "Ox Head" in the Blue Mountains of Bou Arada saw the regiment in action alongside the soldiers of the newly created Manteuffel Division, *Kampfgruppe* Witzig, the Barenthin Parachute Regiment, and others. The main objective of the operation was the capture of the principal line of hills in the Tunis area. The subsequent incorporation of the 5th Parachute Regiment into the HG Division was a logical solution to the need to find a headquarters for the regiment. And what made more sense than to look for this in the Hermann Göring Division?

Further elements of the Hermann Göring Division were transported to Africa in the period from January to April 1943. On 19 April, when it became obvious that the end was near in the Tunis area, the Armored Pioneer Battalion under *Hauptmann* Schiffner, which had also been scheduled for departure, was held back. Additional units were sent to Tunis as late as 18 April, when two grenadier battalions and II Battalion, Artillery Regiment HG were dispatched to Africa only to go into captivity less than a month later.

Actions Preceding Operation "Lilac Blossom"

From February 1943 the Hermann Göring Division defended a sector fifty kilometers wide, running from Medjez el Bab through Bou Arada to Rooba. The 5th Parachute Regiment – now the HG Division's 5th Light Infantry Regiment – had been in action there since 19 November 1942. Deployed on the right of the Hermann Göring Division was the 334th Infantry Division, on the left the 10th Panzer Division. Of its own units, all that were available to the HG Division were the fully-equipped and battle-tested soldiers of the 5th Light Infantry Regiment now under the command of *Hauptmann* Schirmer, two battalions of the 1st Grenadier Regiment HG, the Flak Regiment HG with two battalions, elements of the Armored Reconnaissance Battalion HG, and 1st Company, Armored Pioneer Battalion HG.

Permanently attached to the division was the 5th Tunisian Battalion (formerly the 5th Personnel Replacement Transfer Battalion).

As yet none of its own artillery forces were available to the division. This was reason for the command of the newly-formed Fifth Panzer Army to assign an artillery commander to the division. Under his command were: Headquarters, II Battalion and II Battalion of the 190th Artillery Regiment, together with I Battalion, 90th Armored Artillery Regiment. From mid-April these units were joined by I Battalion, 999th Artillery Regiment and two Italian artillery battalions.

The division's positions were fortified to the maximum extent possible with the means at hand. This was problematical, especially considering the difficult-to-defend terrain in the southern sector where 1st Grenadier Regiment HG was deployed.

Following the withdrawal of the German southern front to a line Enfidaville Position – Enfidaville – Djebel Mansour, the enemy had launched an offensive on the western Tunisian front; it was directed against the front held by the 334th Infantry Division under *Generalmajor* (later *Generalleutnant*) Weber. The enemy advanced quickly out of the area northeast of Oued Zarga, which posed a threat to the right flank of the Hermann Göring Division.

On 16 April division reconnaissance discovered another Allied assembly area in front of the northern sector. *Generalmajor* Schmid decided to strike out at the enemy assembly areas, smash them, and after completing this task to withdraw the front line back to the original main line of resistance. This pinning down of enemy forces in front of the division's northern wing was primarily intended to reduce the serious threat to the 334th Infantry Division and bring relief to the division.

This operation was code-named *Fliederblüte* (Lilac Blossom). *Generalmajor* Schmid was summoned by the Commander-in-Chief of the Fifth Panzer Army, *General der Panzertruppe* von Vaerst, to explain his plan. The latter endorsed the plan and it was subsequently approved by *Generaloberst* von Arnim, Commander-in-Chief of Army Group Africa.

The command briefing for the attack took place on 17 and 18 April. The following forces were available to *Generalmajor* Schmid:

    5th Light Infantry Regiment HG: Major Schirmer
    II Battalion, 1st Grenadier Regiment HG: Hptm. Schreiber
    Elements of the Flak Regiment HG
    14th Company, 1st Grenadier Regiment HG
    18th Battery, Flak Regiment HG
    1st Company, Armored Pioneer Battalion HG
    2/3 of the 4th Company, Armored Reconnaissance Battalion HG
    (anti-tank guns)

Also participating in *Fliederblüte* were two battalions of the 7th Panzer Regiment (10th Pz. Div). The attack force was divided into three groups:

(a) Group Audorf: flanking cover north.
(b) Group Schirmer: attack groups north and south.
(c) Group Funck: flanking cover.

On the evening of 20 April 1943 the order went out to all three groups: "Execute Lilac Blossom!" The division headquarters moved into its forward command post. the attack groups set out at 2300 hours. After six hours of fighting they had reached the following positions:

Group Audorf: Hill 157, 6 km east-southeast of Medjez el Bab.
Group Schirmer (North): Hill 166, 800 meters east of the road 5.5 km southeast of Medjez el Bab.
Group Schirmer (South): Hill 381, 4.5 km northwest of Goubel
Group Funck: Narrows south of Djebel Soulia, Si Naceur Raghet, Lalla Hadda, northern arterial road from Djebel Rihane.

The Schirmer Group, consisting of the 5th Light Infantry Regiment, ran into a reinforced defensive sector and was halted. The Audorf Group likewise failed to reach its attack objective, as a result of which the Schirmer Group's flank was threatened from Medjez el Bab.

This was the reason why at 0330 on 21 April, *Generalmajor* Schmid issued an order for the attack groups to conduct local withdrawals and establish hedgehog positions for the day. Now that it was daylight, a direct withdrawal of the units to their jumping-off positions was impossible without heavy losses. At 1400 hours Panzer Battalion Burk had to go to the aid of Schirmer Group North, which was under attack, until finally it was withdrawn to its starting position.

Schirmer Group South held on to the positions it had reached and there repulsed several tank attacks which should have been followed by infantry. Under the command of *Major* Funck, II Battalion, 1st Grenadier Regiment HG held its newly-won positions against every attack launched by the enemy, thus eliminating a threat from the south against the flank of the Schirmer Group.

At 1800 hours division ordered all battle groups to disengage from the enemy. Operation "Lilac Blossom" had ended. The German units returned to their starting positions and once again took up position there. In spite of losses of 34 killed, 92 wounded, and 201 missing (the majority of which were captured), the strike had been a success, for the enemy halted his preparations for a major offensive. His assembly areas had been smashed and the Allies had suffered heavy losses in men and materiel. Nevertheless, while the other side received replacements almost daily to fill the gaps in their lines, any losses in personnel or materiel suffered by the weak German forces meant a further weakening, for they could not be replaced.

The anticipated attack on the 5th Light Infantry Regiment also failed to materialize. Only in the sector held by the 1st Grenadier Regiment HG did the enemy launch an attack with limited objectives – and was repulsed.

According to their own figures the enemy had lost 400 men killed. About the same number had been wounded and 318 were brought in as prisoners by the German battle group.

The booty taken by the German troops was great. Especially important were two munitions dumps from which captured guns could be supplied with ammunition; 8,000 shells were found there. Also captured were a tank truck with 15,000 liters of fuel, three artillery batteries, individual artillery pieces, seven anti-tank guns, seven tanks, ten armored vehicles, 67 loaded ammunition trucks, and a large quantity of small arms.

The Wehrmacht communique of 26 April 1943 announced:

"Committed at the focal point of the Tunisian western front, the Hermann Göring Division and its neighboring units distinguished themselves through exemplary fighting spirit and unshakable bravery and frustrated the enemy's hopes for a breakthrough."

Oberfeldwebel Johannes Scheid, who participated in these actions as a member of 11th Company, 1st Grenadier Regiment HG, was awarded the Knight's Cross for bravery in action in Tunisia. The decoration was presented to him in captivity on 21 June 1943 by the International Red Cross, which transported the decoration into the camp where he was being held as a POW. *Generalfeldmarschall* Albert Kesselring assessed the role played by the troops of the Hermann Göring Division in his book *Soldat bis zum letzten Tag*:

"During my frequent visits to Tunisia I always found a mood of confidence. What I saw of the troops, whether panzer-grenadiers, light infantry, paratroopers, or men of the Hermann Göring Division, was beyond all praise."

Now let us turn to a unit which first arrived in Africa in March 1943 but which held out until the final day.

The Armored Reconnaissance Battalion HG: Command Positions and First Action

Under the command of *Hauptmann* Otto Brandenburg, the Armored Reconnaissance Battalion HG was organized as follows at the time of its initial formation:

Commanding Officer:	Hptm. Brandenburg
Adjutant:	Oblt. Renmayer
1st Company (Motorcycle):	Hptm. Kiefer
2nd Company (VW Company):	Oblt. Gerhardt
3rd (Armored Personnel Carrier) Company:	Hptm. Rebholz
4th (Armored Scout Car) Company:	Hptm Karras (Karlas?)
5th (Pioneer) Company:	Hptm. Ringelstedt
6th (Flak) Company:	Hptm. Rieke

Once established, in January 1943 the battalion was transferred into the

Naples-Volturno area. Some of the units were quartered in the Santa Maria barracks in Capua Vetere. Training continued there, with unit exercises and live firing carried out in the Volturno area.

At the beginning of March 1943 the 1st, 5th and 6th Companies moved overland to Reggio. From there they were shipped by ferry through Palermo to Trapani, where the companies camped in an olive grove. The 6th (Flak) Company guarded the local airspace and a few days later shot down a Vickers Wellington of the Royal Air Force.

The battalion headquarters and 1st Company had flown directly to Tunis. There they occupied positions along a *wadi* in front of Pont du Fahs. To the left were the grenadiers of the Grenadier Regiment HG and to the right the former 5th Parachute Regiment, now the 5th Light Infantry Regiment.

The latter regiment secured the area as far south as Medjez el Bab. The Flak Regiment HG under *Oberstleutnant* Hullmann had likewise been incorporated into this large defensive zone. The reconnaissance battalion's 2nd Company arrived a few days later. It was sent directly from El Aouina airfield into the new area of operations to the left of the road from Bou Arada. The crossroads at Bou Arada was mined by the 5th (Pioneer) Company and covered by the few available anti-tank and infantry guns. Only the battalion's 3rd Company under *Hauptmann* Rebholz remained behind in Italy. Later it provided a cadre of personnel for the formation of a new reconnaissance battalion for the Hermann Göring Division.

In April the signals platoon and the train were flown to Tunis as an advance detachment. In command of the platoon was *Leutnant* Richard Mohn (later the head of the world-famous Bertelsmann Publishing House). *Leutnant* Mohn's orders were to set up a train position for the 6th Flak Company in front of Pont du Fahs, where there was a fresh water well. The 6th Company's 3rd Platoon flew in the next day aboard Me 232 *Gigant* transport aircraft. While landing, the aircraft carrying the platoon were caught by an enemy bombing attack on the airfield; the platoon lost *Unteroffizier* Kremme, *Gefreiter* Mack and *Gefreiter* Renz.

That evening the platoon went into position near 1st Company with three guns. The flak company's 2nd and 4th Platoons followed some time later and were likewise moved into position there. From these positions the 1st and 2nd Companies covered the withdrawal of Italian units and the 21st Panzer Division into the Pont du Fahs area.

Kampfgruppe Kiefer in Action

On 25 April 1943, after repulsing an enemy armored advance in the valley of Bou Arada, the 1st and 2nd Motorcycle and VW Companies of the Armored Reconnaissance Battalion HG were relieved in their former positions. The two companies had been withdrawn from the line to take up positions along the Pont du Fahs – Tebessa road in order to guard the flank of the Italian *Superga* Division, which was involved in heavy fighting. Late in the afternoon both companies ran into the 1st Battalion of the 1st Cadre Regiment of the French Foreign Legion. A surprise enveloping attack scattered the enemy. His point company was wiped out and more than eighty men were taken as prisoners.

Both companies received instructions to make their way as quickly as possible to the von Manteuffel Division, which was in the area of Mateur. They were thrown into the midst of this division's desperate defensive battles between the Sedjenane Valley and the Kef en Nsour massif, and on 2 May covered the von Manteuffel division's withdrawal into the Mateur area to a point close to Mateur.

On the evening of 3 May *Generalmajor* von Manteuffel's division command post was located seven to eight kilometers east of Mateur, as Mateur itself had been taken by the enemy. During the night of 4 May *Generalmajor* von Manteuffel personally gave the commander of the Armored Reconnaissance Battalion HG, *Major* Brandenburg, and the two company commanders, *Hauptmann* Kiefer and *Oberleutnant* Gerhardt, the order to take possession of the Djebel Achkel, already in enemy territory, and to hold it no matter what the cost. More than 500 meters high, this ridge commanded the entire plain as far as Tunis.

Since the approach to the two raised roadways which led through the swamp toward Djebel Achkel could not be taken from the enemy, after a brief firefight the troops had to be led through the swamp – which was chest deep in places – by native guides. The following account was provided by Eduard Kiefer:

"Our own troops still holding the hill, about 100 strong, had already been pushed back to the eastern end of the ridge by the enemy. A strong assault detachment of sixty men was assembled to attack the Americans of the 9th US Infantry Division through the mountain gorge the same day. This operation, carried out with the intention of deceiving the enemy as to our own weakness, was a success. Following several brief engagements, the enemy initially withdrew to the west side of the hill before finally surrendering during the night of 6 May."

From 6 May on, Djebel Achkel was bombarded from morning until night by American self-propelled artillery from the area on the far side of the swamp. As many as forty-eight guns were counted attempting to soften up Djebel Achkel. All of the infantry units which attacked behind the bombardments were repulsed. The ground assaults were preceded by attacks from the air by 25 to 30 fighter-bombers.

An attempt by the enemy to cross the muddy water of the Garaet d'Achkel in assault boats and to storm the hill from there also failed. Once again the excellent account by Eduard Kiefer:

"On the evening of 7 May – the Allies had already reached the Tunis area and continuing to hold onto Djebel Achkel had become pointless – we received instructions by radio to fight our way through in the direction of Target Point 83. This point was located near the coast between Bizerte and Tunis. As preparations for the break-out were being made a new order arrived: 'Djebel Achkel is to be held!' The next morning – it was 8 May

1943 – the Americans moved eight heavy howitzers into position in addition to their self- propelled guns and began an hour-long bombardment with all weapons. The subsequent infantry assault was beaten off."

"On 9 May a parlementaire appeared at the end of the raised roadway. He was accompanied by two other officers. We signalled the flag-waving officer that he might come. He identified himself as Major Green from the headquarters of the US 2nd Corps. His two officers also told us their names, but I can no longer remember them."

"The leader of the party explained to us that their corps headquarters expected our immediate surrender. He passed a note from the corps chaplain of the US 2nd Corps to *Hauptmann* Kiefer, who was representing the seriously ill Major Brandenburg (who subsequently died while a POW):"

"To the commandant of Djebel Achkel! In the name of God and your country: give up! Generals Bassenge, Neuffer (there followed two illegible names) have surrendered. We ask you: do the same!"

"As we still had radio communications with division, we sent the parlementaire on his way with our thanks. During the night of 10 May the Manteuffel Division's radio station sent the following message: Enemy tanks in front of the division command post. We are proud of you! Long live the Führer!"

"During the night we sent a message blind to the army:"

"The Reconnaissance Battalion HG on Hill 508, Djebel Achkel near Mateur, has repulsed heavy enemy attacks. We request an air drop of ammunition and food."

"The message was received by an army radio team and passed on to the Commander-in-Chief south in Italy. On the morning of 10 May we established radio contact with the headquarters of the Commander-in-Chief South in Frascati near Rome. Air drops of ammunition and food were promised. A little later we received a second message, which consisted of three words:"

"Hold! Hold! Hold!"

"In the afternoon Major Green appeared once again with a fresh request for our surrender. He brought with him a postcard on which General Vaerst had written:"

"To Major Brandenburg or his representative. Panzer Army Africa has ceased fighting. You are to do the same. Von Vaerst. As Major von Brandenburg's representative, *Hauptmann* Kiefer accepted the offer to go to the American headquarters and see the situation for himself. He drove with Major Green to the headquarters of the US 2nd Corps in Mateur, where he was briefed on the situation by Colonel Wilson, the corps Chief-of-Staff."

"Afterwards the Colonel had *Oberst* Barenthin, who had been captured earlier, brought in. The latter confirmed the unconventional postcard order from General von Vaerst and explained to *Hauptmann* Kiefer that the situation was hopeless."

"*Hauptmann* Kiefer worked out the terms of surrender before returning to the hill. When, during the night of 11 May, the last link with Italy was lost and Medical Officer Dr. Dahmen reported that he had neither medicines nor bandages left, the decision was made. *Hauptmann* Kiefer sent an officer to the American command with his terms of surrender. These were accepted immediately."

"The transport of prisoners from Djebel Achkel into American captivity began. There the unit, true to the agreements which had been reached, was allowed to remain together. On 12 May Colonel Wilson appeared on Hill 508. His amazement was obvious when he learned that only about 200 men had been holding out there."

This concludes former *Hauptmann* Eduard Kiefer's account.

The End in Tunisia

The "Cactus Farm", so named for the dense cactus hedges that surrounded Hill 107, was held by the men of the Schäfer Platoon of 4th Company, 5th Light Infantry Regiment HG. They were defending the important hill, which denied the enemy a direct thrust to Tunis, with everything they had. The enemy assembled his forces during the night of 29 April and attacked at dawn. The attack was repulsed. In the afternoon thirty bombers approached the hill and carpeted the "Cactus Farm" with heavy bombs. Then fighter-bombers came and strafed the defenders' positions. The last of 4th Company's vehicles were destroyed in these attacks.

The enemy tried again on the morning of 30 April. Artillery fire was called for, which destroyed three enemy tanks. The Allied infantry withdrew. A further bombing raid and subsequent tank attack with supporting infantry also failed. The first ten tanks were knocked out on the slopes of the hill, nevertheless several others managed to break into the defenders' positions. These were destroyed by Schäfer and the platoon headquarters squad using explosives and hollow charges. When evening came another fourteen enemy tanks lay smoldering on the plain and the slopes of the hill. After darkness fell *Leutnant* Endlich of I Battalion, Light Infantry Regiment HG arrived with word that the hill had to be held for another twenty-four hours.

The next attack was made in battalion strength. Tanks advanced on the hill from the west and south. Directed from the hill, German artillery laid down barrage fire. Shortly before midnight Ofw. Schäfer led what was left of his platoon - 48 soldiers, many of them wounded - back to the German lines. *Leutnant* Endlich counted 37 knocked-out enemy tanks on the hill and on the slopes.

Oberfeldwebel Heinrich Schäfer was recommended for the Knight's Cross. It was presented to him on 8 August 1944 at Camp Harne, a POW camp in Texas, by an American Colonel. The entire prisoner complement of the camp witnessed the presentation of the decoration.

On 6 May Allied armored units numbering about 1,000 tanks broke through the German defensive front west of Bizerte. The port facilities were blown up by the Manteuffel Division. Counting all the units under his command, including the last Tigers of the 501st and 504th Battalions and an Italian assault gun battalion, *Oberst* Franz J. Irkens, the new Panzer Commander Africa, had at his disposal a total of 70 tanks. With these he was supposed to stop the armada of enemy tanks rolling directly toward Tunis.

The enemy assault was halted for a short time. *Hauptmann* Schnelle lost ten tanks, *Oberst* Irkens eight. Ninety shot-up enemy tanks lay scattered about the battlefield. During the night of 7 May *Kampfgruppe* Irkens rolled back to El Alia airfield. The final battles were fought there, in the area west of Tunis. When the panzers had expended the last of their ammunition they were pushed into a steep ravine.

On that same 7 May the Allied armored units broke through the thin German defensive front west of Bizerte. Once again a heavy bombing raid struck Tunis and its environs. At 1740 hours the first Allied troops entered Tunis; but it was not until 9 May that the enemy was able to break through east of Lake Bizerte. The last order from Headquarters, Fifth Panzer Army arrived there at 1525 hours:

"Destroy documents and equipment! Farewell. Long live Germany!"

British armored divisions broke through near Hammanlif on 10 May. The Indian 10th Infantry Division turned toward Cap Bon and by 12 May had occupied the entire peninsula.

All of the German divisions signed off with Army Group Africa on 12 May. With his last two tanks *General* Hans Cramer fought his way through to the command post of Panzer Army Africa in St. Marie du Zit. From there at 1100 hours *Generaloberst* von Arnim signalled Rome: "Are surrounded on two sides."

Immediately afterward he offered to surrender to the Allies. *General* Cramer had the final message sent to the OKW:

"To the OKW: ammunition gone! As per orders, the German Africa Corps has battled the enemy until it is no longer able to fight."

The following morning General Sir Harold Alexander, the Allied Commander-in-Chief in Northwest Africa, sent the following message to the British Prime Minister, Winston Churchill:

"Sir, it is my duty to report that the Tunisian Campaign is over. All enemy resistance has ceased! All of Africa is ours!"

Caught up in the defeat of Army Group Africa were 130,000 German and 180,000 Italian soldiers, who became prisoners of war. The African Campaign cost a total of 100,000 dead on both sides. The elements of the Hermann Göring Division in Africa were also caught up in this maelstrom of defeat. About 1,000 soldiers succeeded in escaping from Africa, among them a handful of the *Reichmarschall* men.

For the Hermann Göring Division the loss in Africa of about 10,000 men was a heavy blow. A large proportion of these soldiers and almost all the officers originated from the State Police Group or were at least volunteers who had joined the old General Göring Regiment after 1935.

"It was the cream of the Hermann Göring troops who were lost in Africa. Their absence was keenly felt, especially in the reformation of the Hermann Göring Division."

Command Positions of the Hermann Göring Division in Africa in Early 1943

Division Commander:	Generalmajor Josef Schmid
Light Infantry Regiment HG:	Oberstleutnant Koch (later Major Schirmer)
I Battalion, Light Infantry Rgt HG:	Hptm. Jungwirt (until 20 April 1943) then Hptm. Spieler
III Battalion, Light Infantry Rgt HG:	Hptm. (Major) Schirmer later Hptm. Zimmermann

1st Panzer-Grenadier Regiment HG:

I Battalion, 1st Panzer-Grenadier Rgt HG:	Major Neubauer
II Battalion, 1st Panzer-Grenadier Rgt HG:	Hptm. Schreiber
III Battalion, 1st Panzer-Grenadier Rgt HG:	Major Funck

Flak Regiment HG:
Oberstleutnant Hullmann

I Battalion, Flak Regiment HG:	Major Schröter
II Battalion, Flak Regiment HG:	Major Gercke

Panzer Regiment HG:
Oberstleutnant Straub

I Battalion, Panzer Regiment HG
II Battalion, Panzer Regiment HG

Armored Artillery Regiment HG:

I Battalion, Armored Artillery Regiment HG:
II Battalion, Armored Artillery Regiment HG
III Battalion, Armored Artillery Regiment HG

Armored Reconnaissance Battalion HG:	Hptm. Brandenburg
Armored Pioneer Battalion HG:	
Armored Signals Battalion HG:	
Supply Regiment HG:	
Administration Unit:	Ob.Feld.Zm. Klöpfel
First-aid Battalion HG:	

Elements of other units attached to the HG Division:

9th Company, 69th Panzer-Grenadier Regiment
14th Company, 104th Panzer-Grenadier Regiment
2nd and 4th Companies, 90th Anti-tank Battalion
Africa Battalion T 4
Tunisia Battalion 5
I and II Battalions, 90th Artillery Regiment
2nd Company, 190th Artillery Regiment
von Bülow Rocket Battery
2nd Company, 1st Rocket Battalion

After Capture in Africa

For a large part of the Panzer Division HG as it then existed, the end of the fighting in North Africa marked the beginning of several years of captivity. The following account of one man's experiences in the final stages of the fighting and subsequent transport to a POW camp is representative of all the others; as well it serves to illuminate this dark episode in the life of each of these soldiers. A total of 130,000 German soldiers became prisoners of war after 12 May 1943.

"We reached the center of the Cap Bon peninsula and there destroyed our vehicles, which infuriated the British officers; but our group was too large for them to do anything about it, so they finally drove away. We stood around in groups, discussed the situation, and tried to sleep as night fell. Afterward we walked farther to the north and eventually reached the tip of Cap Bon.

In the caverns carved out of the rock, which had served as quarters for a naval unit, we found food and several large containers of water. I found it interesting to discover cans of meat and sauerkraut from Siekmanns Meat Packers in Lage, my home town. We had never seen anything like that at the front. We ate as much as we could and waited for what was to come. But the English were in no hurry. We were trapped and they could take their time rounding us up.

We found a Krauss-Maffei prime mover which had been used to tow the eighty-eight flak. We succeeded in getting it going and were able to drive off in it, towing an Opel Blitz truck and several other vehicles. This convoy made its way toward the nearest assembly point near Hammanlif. During the night we stopped and rested. The next morning we resumed our journey. Just short of our destination we met an English tank coming the other way, just at the moment when we were about to cross a half-destroyed bridge. We had to cross on the still-intact side, on which the tank was approaching. They gesticulated wildly that we should pull off to the side. This was impossible because of the vehicles we were towing, so I drove on with my comrades. The English tank backed up and let us pass. In this way we reached Hammanlif, our destination by the sea.

We all climbed down, drained the water from the prime mover's radiator then let it roll, engine screaming, into the trucks and cars which were sitting there. We remained in this camp for about 14 days. We had neither food nor toilet things. From time to time the British brought food from captured German stocks. Nevertheless we suffered from hunger, for there was never enough for the large number of prisoners there.

From time to time we were led down to the beach to bathe. No one knew what was going to happen. English engineers set up a barbed wire fence and right afterward further engineers came, who excavated large pits for a latrine installation with compressors and compressed air shovels. In doing this they did not make use of any prisoners of war, who could surely have done the job, but instead did it all themselves. Our officers divided the prisoners into groups of one hundred, so as to be able to distribute our meager portions fairly.

Fourteen days later we were told to get aboard trucks. We were driven away, destination unknown. The journey ended at the race track in Tunis. We spent only one night there, however. That evening we were given one loaf of German army bread for each 34 men. Those were our rations. A friend and I walked around the large camp looking for something edible. In a German field kitchen we found two rock-hard cubes of dried peas. Obtaining water in which to boil the cubes was not easy, but we finally succeeded.

From Tunis our journey continued to Bone, which took us through the Atlas Mountains. There the trucks were stopped by the Americans. This was our first contact with them. What struck us most was their olive-green fatigues and the plastic helmets which they wore most of the time. When the need arose they could simply put their steel helmets on over top of them. The Americans handled the drive through the various mountain passes and valleys very casually. A small single-axle trailer was hooked to each truck, and a sentry with a submachine-gun rode on the trailer to prevent the POWs from jumping off. We stopped for the night in Souk el Arba before reaching Bone.

In the transit camp there we found ourselves in a large open field surrounded by barbed wire. Here we once again formed groups of one hundred which were further subdivided into groups of ten. The food we received there consisted not of unpacked rations or food from a field kitchen, but of flour, butter, crackers, or fruit in sacks and boxes. Beans and peas were likewise given out in sacks. This meant that they also had to be distributed in large quantities. It was thus the responsibility of each leader of a group of one hundred to ensure that each man received his allotted portion.

We had a discussion with an American soldier, who said to us:

'The difference between us and you is that you want to die for your fatherland, while we want to live for America.'

This knowledge was of little use to us and it also changed our situation not in the least. In Bone we also saw the huge quantities of materiel, food, and weapons that the Americans possessed. From Bone we sailed in a French freighter to Oran. A French Sub-Lieutenant was commander of the guard detail. The freighter, small, filthy, without washing facilities and toilets, was a floating infection installation. The aim of the Senegalese guard detail was to obtain what we had left in the way of valuables in exchange for bread.

The French Sub-Lieutenant who stood on the bridge of this tub, a slender little fellow with embroidered pants, made a game of taking a bite from a bar of chocolate and then tossing it 'to the people'. He did the same thing with cigarettes, much to his own amusement.

Finally we reached Oran. Once again we were amazed by the huge quantities of war materiel and weapons. There we were handed back over to the Americans. We complained about our guards and their frisking. Afterwards they were made to line up and empty out their pockets and field bags onto a large tarpaulin. A tall American picked up the tarpaulin, walked across the pier and with one swing threw everything into the sea.

We ourselves were packed into the pitiful cars of a small train and taken on a rattling trip to a camp in Tizi. There we were packed in like sardines, four

Battle zone Tunisia. Oberleutnant Arnold of the Flak Regiment HG at Camel Hill.

VW Kübelwagen on the move with one man on the lookout for mines, January 1943.

12 May 1943: The end in Tunisia. German troops march into captivity.

each in one of the small four- man tents that had been pitched there. On a low rise there was a water tank with a line to the camp, which held 1,000 POWs. The frequent tornadoes and whirlwinds often blew away entire tents, which were irretrievably lost. The same went for our precious items of clothing. The American guards lounged about in their wooden watchtowers. We soon looked like redskins, for it was only on the rarest of occasions that we had an opportunity to wash off the red dust that coated us.

After several weeks we went back to Oran, where we were once again loaded aboard a ship. During the voyage we sighted a lone Condor aircraft. There were several U-Boat alarms. On board we received a type of square-shaped white bread. Breakfast consisted of two slices of this with jam. We suspected that we were going to Canada to cut trees, but instead our route took us to Glasgow in Scotland. There the British had set up a small camp of Nissen huts in the tiny village of Comrie.

For some unexplained reason in the Comrie camp they took away for good our spoons and Wehrmacht field knife and fork. Our breakfast there consisted of porridge, a type of thick oatmeal, which we could and had to eat with our hands. Anyone who still had an identity disk used this as a spoon replacement. Our uniforms literally fell apart. Many of the prisoners, me among them, suffered from purulent dermatitis. The medics rubbed on an unidentified blue salve, which was the extent of our treatment.

From Comrie we were eventually shipped to America. As we were marched up the gangway we passed a galley in which a huge, fat negro was at work. From him we received enough to eat. The small brown beans which were almost always given us as a 'vegetable' had a terrible effect on us at first. The few toilets could not cope with the onrush of soldiers.

At least we were given some tobacco and the trip, although boring, was not as bad as the one we had made earlier. Using home-made cards we played skat continually. Once I was assigned to a work detail. We had to cut up and sink empty tin cans. As well we had to toss overboard full containers of powdered milk, flour, and sugar. Later we learned that the stores had to be used up on the crossing, in order to ensure the firms supplying provisions further fat contracts. After several weeks we reached the New World – with very mixed feelings I must say."

I Battalion of the Hermann Göring Panzer Regiment
Following the Collapse of the Africa Front

The small component of I Battalion, Panzer Regiment HG which was not shipped to Africa remained behind in the quartering area in Sicily under the command of *Oberleutnant* Groll. It became a mixed company of the Army's 215th Panzer Battalion, which was commanded by *Hauptmann* Kurt Gierga (Knight's Cross on 30 June 1941 as commander of 5th Company, 5th Panzer Regiment in Africa).

Following the collapse and the surrender of Army Group Africa in the Tunis area on 12 May the remaining elements of the HG Division in Sicily and on the Italian mainland travelled overland back to Santa Maria/Capua

Vetere. There the division was reorganized as a panzer division. This was accomplished by transferring personnel from the replacement regiment in Holland and adding complete units. Commander of the panzer division was *Generalmajor* Paul Conrath. Following the initial conclusion of the formation process and the achievement of operational readiness, the Hermann Göring Panzer Division moved to the Italian troop training grounds at Castel Volturno. There *Hauptmann* Roßmann took command of I Battalion, Panzer Regiment HG. *Major* Preuß became commander of the newly-formed Armored Reconnaissance Battalion HG which was quartered in Sparanise. At this time I Battalion, Panzer Regiment HG was organized as follows:

Battalion Commander:	Hptm. Roßmann
Adjutant:	Lt. Schuster
Unit Medical Officer:	AssArzt Dr. Kullmann
Administration Group:	Oberzahlmeister Günther
Headquarters Company:	Oblt. Groll
1st Panzer Company:	Oblt. Nischelsky
2nd Panzer Company:	Lt. Tschierschwitz
3rd Panzer Company:	Oblt. Renz
4th Panzer Company:	(still in formation)

During this time further panzer companies were established at the Münsingen Troop Training Grounds and in southern France. After completing basic training these were successively incorporated into the Panzer Regiment HG.

A large-scale training exercise was held on the coast of the Tyrrhenian Sea in mid-June 1943. It was followed by an inspection of the entire unit by Italian Crown Prince Umberto. Immediately following this exercise the Hermann Göring Panzer Division moved to Sicily and occupied assembly areas in the area surrounding Caltagirone-Grammichele. The initial stage of the move, to Villa San Giovanni, was made by rail. From there the unit sailed to Sicily on ferries of the *Kriegsmarine*. The subsequent overland march was made over the main road which ran along the eastern coast of the island.

With the sea to the left and the lush green countryside to the right – which occasionally allowed a view of Mount Etna – movement of the units was at first unhindered. Very soon, however, they came under attack from the air. In the coming days and weeks the enemy air raids were directed at the German front-line airfields on the island. This suggested intensive attack preparations by the Western Allies.

Results of the exercises, which were held on an ever-increasing scale, were satisfactory. Following the main exercise involving the entire unit, which took place on 8 July, the division was inspected by *Generalfeldmarschall* Albert Kesselring. In a meaningful speech to the *Reichsmarschall*'s division, Kesselring talked of the imminent Allied invasion of the island. He spoke to the men of the important role the Hermann Göring Panzer Division was to play and urged them to fight bravely in the battle which was to come.

False Alarms — Equipment, and Organization

Level II and III alerts were ordered during the night of 9 July. The alert was subsequently cancelled at first light on the morning of 10 July. Nevertheless, everyone sensed that an Allied attempt to invade Sicily was imminent. A level III alert was once again ordered during the night of 10 July. This time it was serious: US airborne troops came down in the immediate vicinity of the bivouac site at Grammichele airfield. The battle for Fortress Europe – through the gateway of Sicily – had begun.

The Hermann Göring Panzer Division's armored units consisted of two panzer battalions and an assault gun battalion, which were equipped with Panzer III and IV tanks and Sturmgeschütz III assault guns. Both types of tank weighed about 23 tonnes and could reach speeds of 40 kph. Their range over roads was 160 kilometers, which was reduced significantly when operated cross-country. The panzer battalions were initially equipped with Panzer IIIs mounting the long-barrelled 50mm L/60 *Kampfwagenkanone*, while later versions were armed with a short-barrelled 75mm L/24 gun. The Panzer IV was armed with either an L/43 or L/48 long- barrelled 75mm gun. As well there were a few Panzer IVs with the short 75mm L/24 *Kampfwagenkanone*. All of these tanks also carried two machine-guns.

The Sturmgeschütz III weighed about 25 tonnes. It could reach a speed of 35 kph and its range was 105 kilometers on roads. It was armed with a 75mm *Sturmkanone* L/24. The StuG III was unfortunately not equipped with a machine-gun, which was always a disadvantage in close-in fighting. Not until the autumn of 1943 did I Battalion, Parachute Panzer Regiment HG convert to the Panzer V (Panther). This tank was far superior in all areas of design to the tanks which had preceded it. With a weight of about 50 tonnes and a speed of 54 kph, it was the fastest tank used by the Wehrmacht. Armed with a long- barrelled 75mm L/70 gun and two MG 34 (later MG 42) machine-guns, and with a range on roads of 180 kilometers, it was one of the fastest and best all-round tanks on either side of the front.

The Führer Flak Battalion

According to the Luftwaffe's pre-war mobilization plan, in the event of war a 20mm motorized flak battery of the RGG was to guard Führer Headquarters against air attack as the so-called Führer Escort Battery, while two railway flak platoons were to protect the "Führer" command train. It was anticipated that the Führer Escort Battery would be assigned to the Führer Escort Detachment. This was to be formed on mobilization by the Army, primarily from the *Großdeutschland* Infantry Regiment (until April 1939 still the Berlin Guard Regiment).

The Führer Escort Battery was to be provided by II Light Flak Battalion of the RGG, which in 1939 was organized as follows:

HQ II Battalion	CO Major Rüdel
HQ Battery	Oblt. Robert Schulz
6th Battery (37mm motorized)	Hptm. Timm

7th Battery (20mm motorized, self-propelled) Hptm. Barg
8th Battery (20mm motorized, self-propelled) Hptm. Seeger
9th (Railway Escort) Battery Oblt. Tilcher
   (20mm quadruple)

Since the escort battery had to be a self-propelled unit, only the 7th and 8th batteries came into consideration. The better of the two units was to be chosen. In order to determine which of the two was the better unit, several live firing competitions were held in the summer of 1939 at the Deep Flak Artillery Range, located on the Pomeranian Baltic coast south of Kolberg. The decisive comparison shoot between the 7th and 8th Batteries was carried out under the personal supervision of *Generalleutnant* Weise, the commander of Air District III Berlin. 7th Battery emerged as the victor.

Battery commander was *Hauptmann* Barg, battery officers were *Leutnant* Rossmann – who later commanded the Hermann Göring Panzer Regiment – and *Leutnant* Faber, who went on to become a fighter pilot. The battery was initially equipped with the 20mm Flak 30 on self-propelled carriages, but this was later replaced by the 20mm Flak 38 on 1-tonne prime movers with amour plates. The 7th Battery of the General Göring Regiment was assigned to the Führer Escort Detachment at the outbreak of war and saw action in Poland.

After returning from Poland, on 1 October 1939 the Führer Escort Detachment was expanded to become the Führer Escort Battalion. The battalion was subordinate to the commander of officers quarters in Führer Headquarters, at that time one *Oberst* Erwin Rommel, who went on to become the legendary "Desert Fox". In October 1939 the Führer Escort Battalion was quartered in the barracks of the RGG in Berlin-Reinickendorf. A ceremony took place there involving the RGG band with a parade formation and subsequent march-past in front of *Oberst* Rommel, in which the battalion presented a standard to replace its unit flag. 7th Battery RGG was the sole Luftwaffe unit to take part. In 1939 the Führer Escort Battalion was organized as follows:

HQ Führer Escort Battalion CO Rittmeister von Blomberg
Führer Operations Company Hptm. Leithäuser
1st Rifle Company Oblt. Gruß
2nd Fast Company Rittmeister von Blomberg
3rd Heavy Company Hptm. Nehring
Führer Escort Battery (7/RGG) Hptm. Barg
assigned:
Railway Flak Platoon I (from 9/RGG) Oblt. Tilcher
Railway Flak Platoon II (from 9/RGG) Oblt. Kiefer

The functions of the Führer Operations Company were similar to those of a headquarters company, but with special emphasis on supply and guard duties; the operations company included a guard platoon.

The Fast Company had three motorcycle platoons and an armored scout platoon (4th Platoon), which was commanded by Lt. Guderian, son of the panzer general "fast Heinz" Guderian. (The then *Leutnant* Guderian subsequently rose to the rank of general in the post-war West German *Bundeswehr*.) The heavy company was equipped with 37mm anti-tank and 20mm anti-aircraft guns.

The two railway flak platoons consisted of two half-platoons each with two 20mm quadruple flak. As soon as the train halted, the gun crews immediately assumed an all-round defensive posture. The flak platoon's rail cars accommodated the guns and gun crews and served as quarters for the crews during operational journeys. *Leutnant* Student, one of the sons of *Generaloberst* Student, was a member of Railway Flak Platoon I in 1939/40.

From November 1939 the soldiers of the Führer Escort Battalion wore a black cuff band on their tunics, service coats, and greatcoats bearing the legend *Führer-Hauptquartier* in gold. The soldiers of the RGG also wore their blue "General Göring" cuff bands, but only on their tunics. In October 1940 those members of the Führer Escort Battalion who were members of the Army received permission to wear the black "Großdeutschland" cuff band on their right sleeve. In August 1942 the "*Führer-Hauptquartier*" cuff band was replaced by one bearing the legend "*Führer-Begleitbataillon*".

Following the Western Campaign the Führer Escort Battalion initially remained in Paris. 7/RGG took up quarters in the City Universitaire, the international university quarter. The 7th Battery RGG received a special honor at the end of the Western Campaign: it was chosen to represent the Luftwaffe in the honor company which stood in front of the railway car in Compiègne Forest on 21 June 1940, when the cease-fire conditions were presented to the leader of the French delegation, General Huntzinger.

In late summer there was a change of command in 7th Battery RGG. *Hauptmann* Timm handed over command of the battery to *Hauptmann* Gasda. There were changes among the battery officers as well: Oblt. Dieke, Oblt. Reimers, Lt. Karass, Lt. Gerdes, and Lt. Pein. The latter officer suffered a tragic fate: he was shot at a checkpoint in Führer Headquarters in East Prussia as the result of an unfortunate error by a sentry.

With the beginning of the Eastern Campaign, another Führer Headquarters installation was set up east of Rastenburg in East Prussia. The new installation was given the cover designation *Wolfsschanze* (Wolf's Lair). The Führer Escort battalion moved there in June 1941. Also deployed there, to protect Führer Headquarters against air attack, was Heavy Flak Battalion I/604, commanded by *Hauptmann* Lauterbacher. At the end of 1942 the battalion received the designation "Führer Flak Battalion". In conjunction with this, the flak battery of the Führer Escort Battalion, the former 7/RGG, was removed from the Führer Escort Battalion and incorporated into the Führer Flak Battalion as its 7th Battery. In addition the 2nd Company of the Guard Battalion HG joined the Führer Flak Battalion as 8th (Guard) Company.

In 1943 the Führer Flak Battalion was attached to the Flak Regiment HG as IV Battalion. In the process the 6th and 7th Batteries exchanged their battery numbers. Now, in addition to the former 7th Battery and 8th (Guard) Company, all the other soldiers of the Führer Flak Battalion wore the white collar patch and the "Hermann Göring" cuff band on their right sleeve. It is noteworthy that the batteries of the new IV Battalion did not receive consecutive numbers following those of the Flak Regiment HG, rather they started over, beginning with the number one.

In 1944 the four units of the Führer Flak Battalion were reformed as firefighting units with the unit numbers 11 to 14. As IV Battalion, Flak Regiment HG, the Führer Flak Battalion continued to be under the operational control of Führer Headquarters, however where personnel were concerned it was responsible to the Liaison Staff of the Hermann Göring Panzer Division (Parachute Panzer Division from February 1944).

The following table provides an overview of the creation of the Führer Flak Battalion from Flak Battalion I/604 and its incorporation as IV Battalion, Flak Regiment HG:

Incorporated at end of 1942:	In Führer Flak Battalion as:	To IV Battalion, Flak Regiment HG 1943 as:	Type of unit
1./604 Flak Bn.	1./Führer Flak Bn.	1./IV Btl./Flak Rgt. HG	88mm Battery
2./604 Flak Bn.	2./Führer Flak Bn.	2./IV Btl./Flak Rgt. HG	88mm Battery
3./604 Flak Bn.	3./Führer Flak Bn.	3./IV Btl./Flak Rgt. HG	88mm Battery
6./604 Flak Bn. (former 1/407)	4./Führer Flak Bn.	4./IV Btl./Flak Rgt. HG	88mm Battery
4./604 Flak Bn.	5./Führer Flak Bn.	5./IV Btl./Flak Rgt. HG	88mm Battery
7./RGG	7./Führer Flak Bn.	6./IV Btl./Flak Rgt. HG	20mm Battery
5./604 Flak Bn.	6./Führer Flak Bn.	7./IV Btl./Flak Rgt. HG	88mm Battery
2./Guard Bn. HG	8./Führer Flak Bn.	8./IV Btl./Flak Rgt. HG	Guard Company
7./604 Flak Bn. (former 4/321)	9./Führer Flak Bn.	9./IV Btl./Flak Rgt. HG	20mm Battery
8./604 Flak Bn. (former 5/321)	10./Führer Flak Bn.	10./IV Btl./Flak Rgt.HG	20mm Battery
New Formation	11./Führer Flak Bn.	11./IV Btl./Flak Rgt.HG	Fire-fighting Sqd.
New Formation	12./Führer Flak Bn.	12./IV Btl./Flak Rgt.HG	Fire-fighting Sqd.
New Formation	13./Führer Flak Bn.	13./IV Btl./Flak Rgt.HG	Fire-fighting Sqd.
New Formation	14./Führer Flak Bn.	14./IV Btl./Flak Rgt.HG	Fire-fighting Sqd.

Not incorporated into the Führer Flak Battalion were the two railway flak platoons of 9/RGG, which since 1942 had been redesignated 15th (Railway) Battery, Flak Regiment HG. The two railway flak platoons remained under the operational control of Führer Headquarters.

When the Führer Headquarters were unoccupied, elements of the Führer Escort Battalion were employed elsewhere as front-line units, such as on the Volkhov in the winter of 1941/42 as Battle Group Nehring, and in the winter battle on the Donets in the triangle formed by the cities of Kharkov-Rostov-Kalach in the winter of 1942/43. 7th Battery, formerly 7/RGG, took part in these battles and like all the other units suffered heavily there. There was especially heavy fighting in mid-January 1943 when a battle group under the command of General Kreysing defended a strongpoint around a front-line airfield near Millerovo. The battle group was encircled for 22 days and had to repulse more than fifty determined enemy assaults before it was able to break out of the pocket. The following is an extract from a contemporary report:

"The battle group moved out during the evening. The infantry fanned out and the light flak circled the column like watchful sheep dogs. When four Soviet tanks appeared on the scene they were immediately fired on by the heavy weapons. Two were destroyed, one disabled, the fourth turned around and fled. At about midday three waves of Russian aircraft attacked our column. Our anti-aircraft guns brought down two. The following night was bitterly cold. The enemy laid down a lethal wall of fire in front of the nearest village, which lay 25 kilometers in front of us. We had to go through. The anti-aircraft guns stalked towards the village from the sides; the anti-tank guns positioned themselves behind a railway embankment and poured a hail of fire onto the Soviet positions. Meanwhile the main body of the column, with the supply train and wagons, raced through the fire zone at high speed. There were repeated similar engagements, in the course of which seven more enemy tanks were knocked out. Finally, the infantry and the light flak were the last to disengage from the enemy. After another five kilometers we reached our own lines. We had been on the march for three days and nights and had broken out of three Soviet pockets, nevertheless the breakthrough had succeeded.

One picture will long remain in my memory: the grotesque and horrible sight of a horse in a field to the side of the road; it had frozen into a statue while still standing."

On 1 June 1944 the Führer Escort Battalion was expanded into a regiment, the Führer Escort Regiment. At the end of 1944 the unit was increased in size again to a brigade, the Führer Escort Brigade, and simultaneously shipped from the Eastern Front to the West in preparation for the Ardennes offensive. In autumn 1944 the Führer Flak Battalion was increased to regiment size, becoming the Führer Flak Regiment; it was then reorganized and deployed within the Führer Escort Brigade.

At this time the Führer Flak Regiment was organized as follows:

Führer Flak Regiment	Major Roth
I Battalion	Hptm. Lücke (or Lücken)
1st Battery (88mm)	Oblt. Kropf
2nd Battery (88mm)	Oblt. Pachmeyer
3rd Battery (88mm)	Oblt. Springstein
4th Battery (88mm)	Oblt. Günther
II Battalion	Hptm. Dentzer
5th Battery (20mm self-propelled)	Oblt. Wilk
6th Battery (20mm self-propelled)	Oblt. Mittag (the former 7/RGG)
7th Battery (37mm self-propelled)	Oblt. La Grange

Towards the end of 1944 an expansion of the Führer Flak Regiment to 14 batteries was undertaken, whereby the former 7th battery received the battery number 12.

Following the Ardennes offensive, in January-February 1945, the Führer Flak Regiment and other units were deployed in Lower Pomerania within Corps Group Munzel, while elements of the regiment, namely the 1st, 2nd, 4th, 5th, 8th and 9th Batteries saw action in Silesia (according to the records of the tracing service).

The Flak Regiment HG from June 1943

In May 1943 work was begun to reform the two battalions of the Flak Regiment HG, both of which had been lost in the heavy fighting in Africa. These efforts intensified in June of that year. The rebuilding process began in Naples with the disbandment of the Flak Regiment HG's IV Battalion and the use of its 16th and 17th Batteries (20mm light flak) to form the new 4th and 5th Batteries.

A new IV Battalion was formed in mid-1943. It became IV Führer Flak Battalion, Flak Regiment HG (See chapter: The Führer Flak Battalion). With the incorporation of the Panzer Division HG into the First Parachute Army in 1944 and the redesignation of all units of the Panzer Division HG as "Parachute Panzer Division units", the designation Flak Regiment HG was changed to Parachute Flak Regiment HG.

On 24 February 1944 I Battalion of the 49th Flak Regiment was incorporated into the HG Division, where it received the designation III Battalion, Parachute Flak Regiment HG. With the transfer of the Parachute Panzer Division HG from Italy to the Eastern Front in July 1944, the Parachute Flak Regiment HG was reorganized and partially reequipped. The heavy batteries, for example, received six guns each and larger numbers of 20mm light flak, while the light batteries were issued larger numbers of quadruple flak.

With the formation of the Parachute Panzer Corps HG, IV Führer Flak Battalion of the Parachute Flak Regiment HG left the Parachute Panzer Division HG and became the Führer Flak Regiment within the newly-formed Führer Escort Division. The new IV Battalion, Parachute Flak Regiment HG took over the former II Flak Battalion, Escort Regiment HG. At the same time the Parachute Flak Regiment HG became a corps unit of the Parachute Panzer Corps HG.

The following is the organization of the Parachute Flak Regiment HG:

I (mixed) Battalion: 1st-3rd Batteries (88mm),
4th-5th Batteries (20mm and 20mm quad.),
6th Battery (20mm quad.)

II (mixed) Battalion: 7th-9th Batteries (88mm),
10th Battery (37mm),
11th Battery (20mm and 20mm quad.),
12th Battery (20mm quad.)

III (mixed) Battalion: 13th-15th Batteries (88mm),
16th Battery (37mm and 20mm),
17th Battery (20mm),
18th Battery (20mm quad.)
IV (mixed) Battalion: 19th-21st Batteries (88mm),
22nd Battery (37mm),
23rd and 24th Batteries (20mm).

Each of the heavy batteries had six guns, the medium and light batteries twelve guns. As well each battalion possessed a flak transport column with a capacity of 78 tonnes.

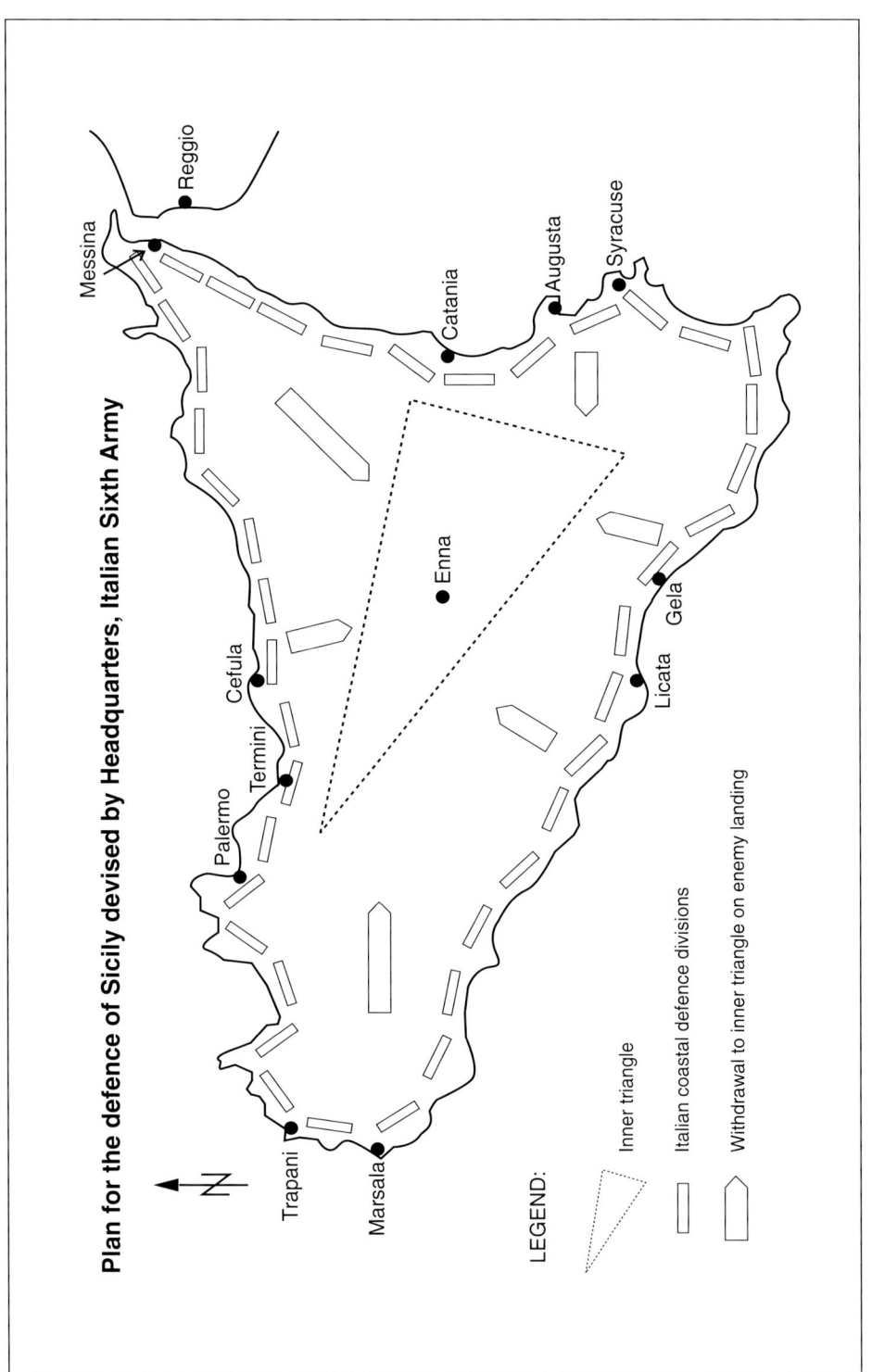

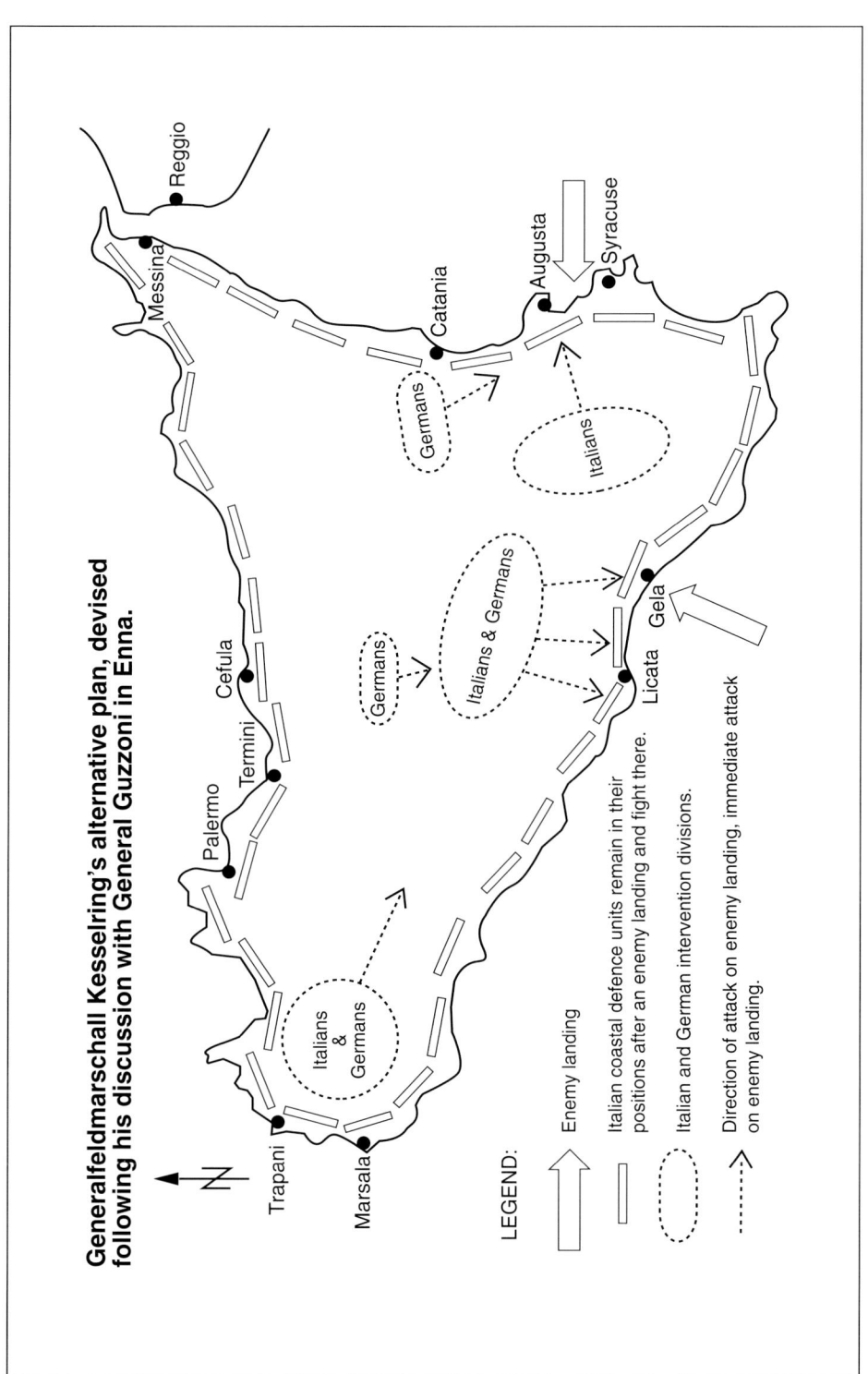

V. THE GATE TO FORTRESS EUROPE

The Attackers' Plans

The first Allied plan for the conquest of Sicily was developed in 1940 at the recommendation of Winston Churchill and received the code name INFLUX. This plan became the basis for all subsequent Sicily plans.

The next plan – WHIPCORD – was developed by the Liaison Planning Staff in October 1941. Like INFLUX, it was later shelved. Once again it was Winston Churchill who, on 28 September 1942, asked the planning staff to devise a new attack operation aimed against Sicily. It received the code name HUSKY and became the plan which was ultimately carried out.

The Allied conference at Casablanca also concerned itself with the conquest of Sicily. There, on 19 January 1943, it was decided that an offensive would be directed against Sicily in the summer. Sardinia and Corsica were also mentioned as possible targets, however General Eisenhower advanced the view that Sicily had to be the next operational objective if the Mediterranean was to be made safe for Allied shipping. Sicily divided the Mediterranean into two halves; the capture of the island must reduce the threat to Allied shipping traffic.

It was General Marshall who restored the consensus of all the participants when he observed that the planned operation in the Mediterranean could only be seen as a secondary supporting operation. The main task remained the landing on the French Atlantic coast planned for early 1944, Operation OVERLORD.

On 22 January 1943 the Allied Chiefs-of-Staff agreed that the operation should begin in July. British General Harold Alexander was to be the operation's overall commander. Alexander had the following units at his disposal:

15th Army Group	General Alexander
7th US Army	Lieutenant General Patton
45th Infantry Division	Major General Middleton
1st Infantry Division	Major General Allen
3rd Infantry Division	Major General Truscott
2nd US Corps	Lieutenant General Bradley
505th Parachute Combat Team	Colonel Gavin
Eighth British Army	General Montgomery
13th Army Corps	Lieutenant General Dempsey
5th Infantry Division	Major General Bucknall
50th Infantry Division	Major General Kirkman

1st Airborne Brigade	Brigadier "Pips" Hicks
30th Army Corps	Lieutenant General Leese
231st Independent Brigade	Lieutenant General Urquhart (Malta)
51st Highland Division	Major General Wimberley
1st Canadian InfantryDiv.	Major General Simmonds
40th and 41st Royal Marine Commandos	Brigadier Laycock and Lieutenant Colonel Slater

Just prior to the invasion, the G2 of the 7th US Army reported that the Hermann Göring Panzer Division was located near Caltagirone, only 20 miles north of Gela, directly in the path of Major General Allen's 1st Infantry Division. Admiral Cunningham, the British Commander-in-Chief of Mediterranean naval forces, sent the available boats of the 8th and 10th Submarine Flotillas from Malta and Algiers to reconnoiter the bays containing the selected landing sites on the south and southeast coasts of the island.

Embarkation, transport, and disembarkation of the British forces was under the control of Vice-Admiral Ramsay – the man who had brought back the British expeditionary forces from the beaches of Dunkirk in 1940 – and thus in the best of hands. Providing the main cover for the landings was H Squadron under the command of Vice-Admiral Willis, with four battleships, two aircraft carriers, four cruisers, and eighteen destroyers. The squadron was to assemble on 9 July in the Ionian Sea and, together with the submarines, screen the invasion area against the Italian Fleet as well as carry out diversionary attacks against the Greek coast.

In reserve was Z Squadron of the U.S. Navy under Vice-Admiral Hewitt. This force consisted of two battleships, an aircraft carrier, two cruisers, and six destroyers. The 12th and 15th Cruiser Squadrons of the Royal navy were to bombard coastal targets during the landings, their primary objectives being coastal batteries. The two squadrons were led by Commodore Agnew and Admiral Harcourt.

The US fleet, designated the Western Task Force, was likewise under the command of Vice-Admiral Hewitt. It consisted of 1,700 vessels – primarily transports, landing craft, and small escort ships. Vice-Admiral Hewitt had to land his troops at three different points on the island:

Licate ("Joss"): Attack Force 86: Adm. Conolly with the 13th Destroyer Squadron.

Scoglitti ("Cent"): Attack Group One: Adm. Kirk with the flagship *Ancon*, with Omar N. Bradley on board, and several warships.

Gela ("Dime"): Attack Force 81: Adm. Hall with the flagship *Monrovia*, with Admiral Hewitt on board, two cruisers and eleven destroyers.

A total of 2,500 transports and 400 landing craft, escorted by a total of 750 warships, were to deliver 160,000 Allied troops with 600 tanks and 1,800 guns to the island of Sicily to kick in the gate to Fortress Europe.

At about 1900 hours on 9 July the glider-tug combinations of the British 1st Airborne Brigade began taking off. 137 gliders took 1,600 men to their landing sites on the island. Close behind them followed 226 C-47 transports of the American Air Transport Command with 2,700 paratroops of the regimental battle group of the 82nd US Airborne Division.

The C-47s, which had taken off from airfields in and around Kairouan in Tunisia, homed in on the Cap Passero beacon in southern Italy. Ahead of them flew Hurricane night-fighters, whose task it was to eliminate the searchlight batteries on the island. At the same time Mosquito bombers attacked targets near Catania.

The Defenders: Italian and German Forces

After the struggle in North Africa had ended with the surrender of Army Group Africa and all Italian forces there, the German side feared an immediate follow-up attack by the Allies against the islands off the coast of Italy. Most of all they feared an invasion of Sicily. Commanding in Sicily was Headquarters, Sixth Army, at first under General Roatta, then General Guzzoni. Under its command were two army corps with five coastal divisions, two coastal brigades, and an autonomous coastal regiment. Mobile forces totalled four divisions. As well there were harbour detachments, artillery units, and militia. (See the order of battle at the conclusion of Sicily chapter.)

In the event of an Allied landing on the island the Italian coastal divisions were supposed to defend their coastal sectors and counterattack immediately with prepared local reserves. The army reserves, which consisted of German and Italian divisions stationed farther inland, were not to intervene in the fighting until the enemy had made a successful landing. Once this had taken place the reserves would contain and reduce the enemy bridgehead.

These reserves were:

Western Intervention Group:
15th Panzer-Grenadier Division, Generalmajor Rodt
26th Italian Division *Assieta*, General Papini
28th Italian Division *Aosta*, General Giacomo

Eastern Intervention Group:
Hermann Göring Panzer Division, Generalmajor Conrath
4th Italian Division *Livorno*, General Chirieleison
54th Italian Division *Napoli*, General Porcinari

The 15th Panzer-Grenadier Division was stationed in the area of Salemi and to the southeast. Its I Battalion was moved to Piazza Armerina, south of Enna, as special army reserve.

Ten days before the invasion *Generalfeldmarschall* Kesselring visited General Guzzoni's army command post in Enna. The two men discussed the command measures to be taken in the event of a landing, the probable landing sites, and the resulting allocation of army reserves. General Guzzoni considered a landing on the southeast part of the island as most likely, specifically in the Catania – Gela areas. *Generalfeldmarschall* Kesselring, however, felt that the landing would come in the western part of the island; he had Headquarters, Sixth Army transfer the 15th Panzer-Grenadier Division to the west and assemble the Hermann Göring Panzer Division in battle groups west of Catania and north of Gela. This move was intended to allow the units to drive the enemy back into the sea during the initial phase of the landings.

The Hermann Göring Panzer Division in Sicily

The main body of the Hermann Göring Panzer Division was located in the Caltagirone area. The division's Schmalz Brigade was in the Catania area. Four possible landing sites had been identified in the area of Eastern Intervention Group:

(1) Near or east of Gela – the most likely location as the terrain there was the most favorable for a beachhead.

(2) South of Comiso

(3) In the Syracuse—Augusta area.

(4) The area around Catania.

For operational reasons *Generalmajor* Conrath separated the Schmalz Special Purpose Brigade from the division and made it responsible for potential landing sites 3 and 4. Division headquarters, with the main body of the division, assumed responsibility for sites 1 and 2. In early July the division headquarters had been moved from Catania into the Caltagirone area.

In addition to the measures already described, since early July the Hermann Göring Panzer Division had positioned armored scout cars at several points along the coast between Gela and Augusta. In the event of an enemy landing the scout cars were to report this direct to division headquarters by radio. In view of the catastrophic state of Italian signals communications, this precautionary measure proved to be completely justified. One of the most important questions which the German command had to ask itself, was what were the chances of keeping the Strait of Messina open as a lifeline to the German forces in Sicily. Only by keeping the strait open could they ensure the supply of the troops on the island and – later – their evacuation to the mainland.

The then *Oberst* Ernst Günther Baade, a regimental commander in Africa and later commander of the newly-formed 90th Panzer-Grenadier Division, was named "Commander Messina Strait". He was responsible for the strict organization and execution of all security measures such as active and passive air defence, use of artillery and heavy flak against naval targets, traffic across the strait, alerts, and the regulation of traffic. To this end he was given full powers of command in the areas of the beachheads on the island and in Villa San Giovanni on the mainland.

Oberst Baade removed both heavy batteries from the 15th Panzer-Grenadier Division. He sent them and their 170mm guns across to the mainland and positioned them on both sides of Villa San Giovanni to protect the main crossing site. As well, thanks to the cooperation of *Luftflotte* 2, flak cover over the Strait of Messina was greatly extended. All of the airfields

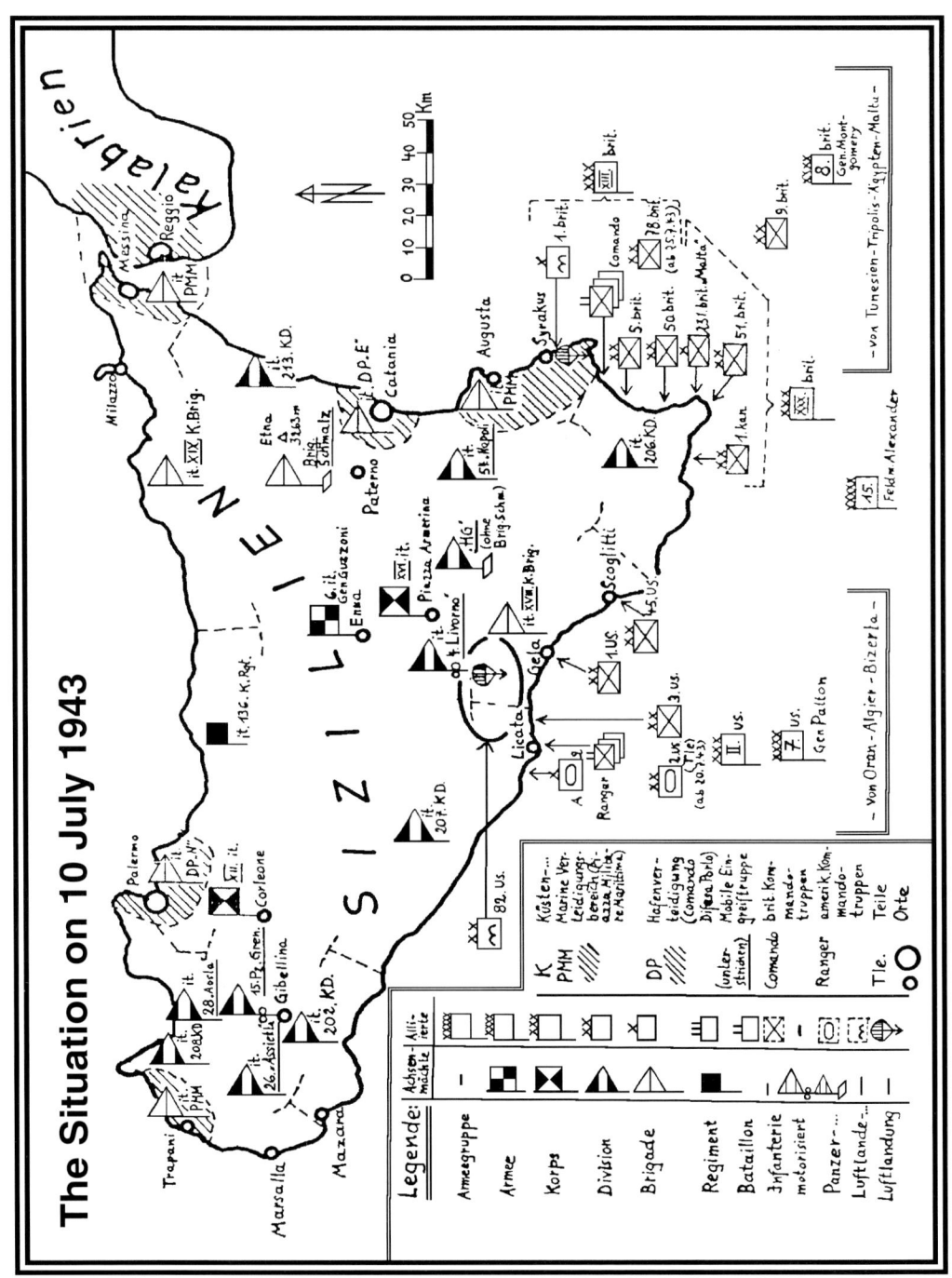

Overall study of the Battle of Sicily and the units committed

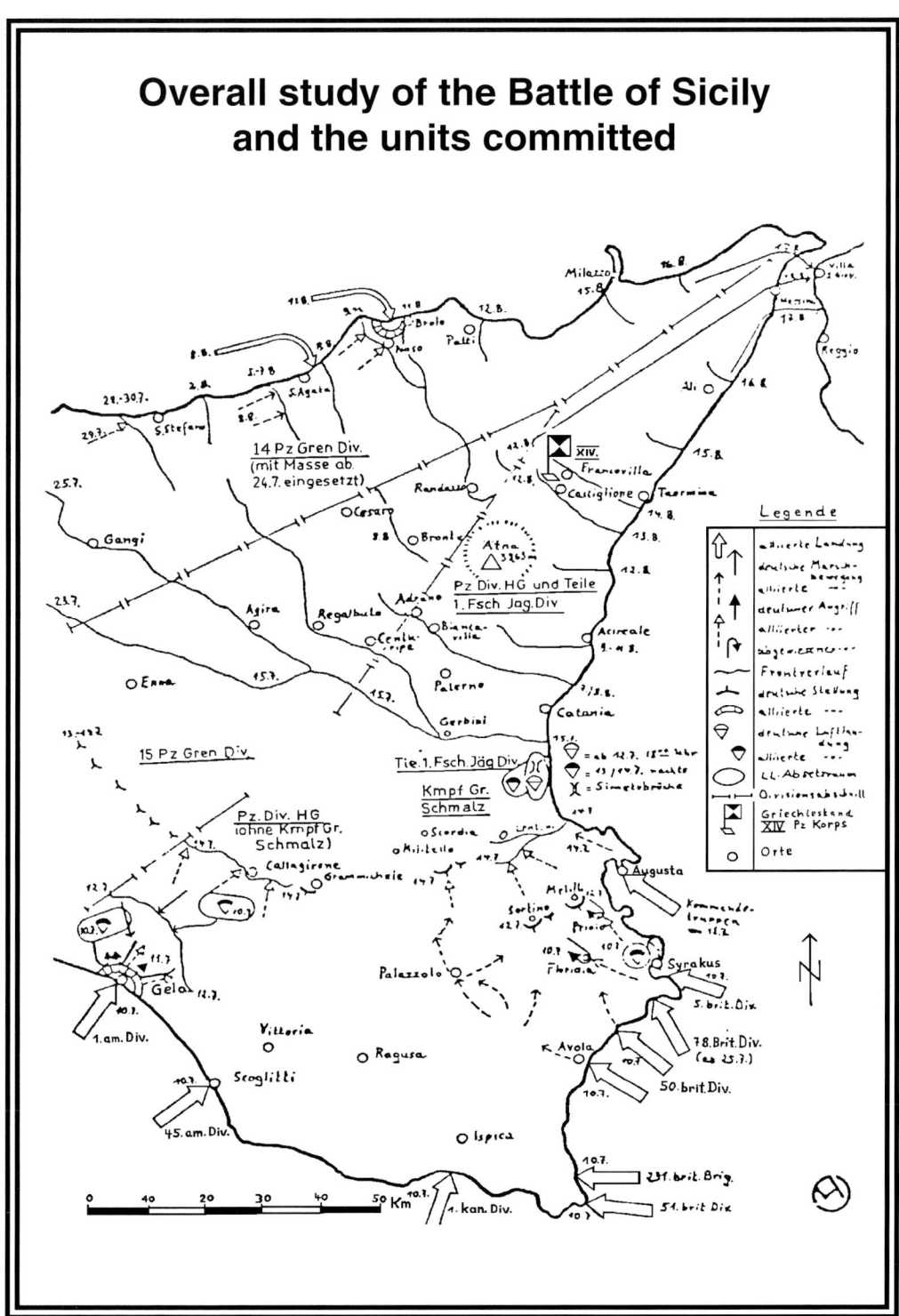

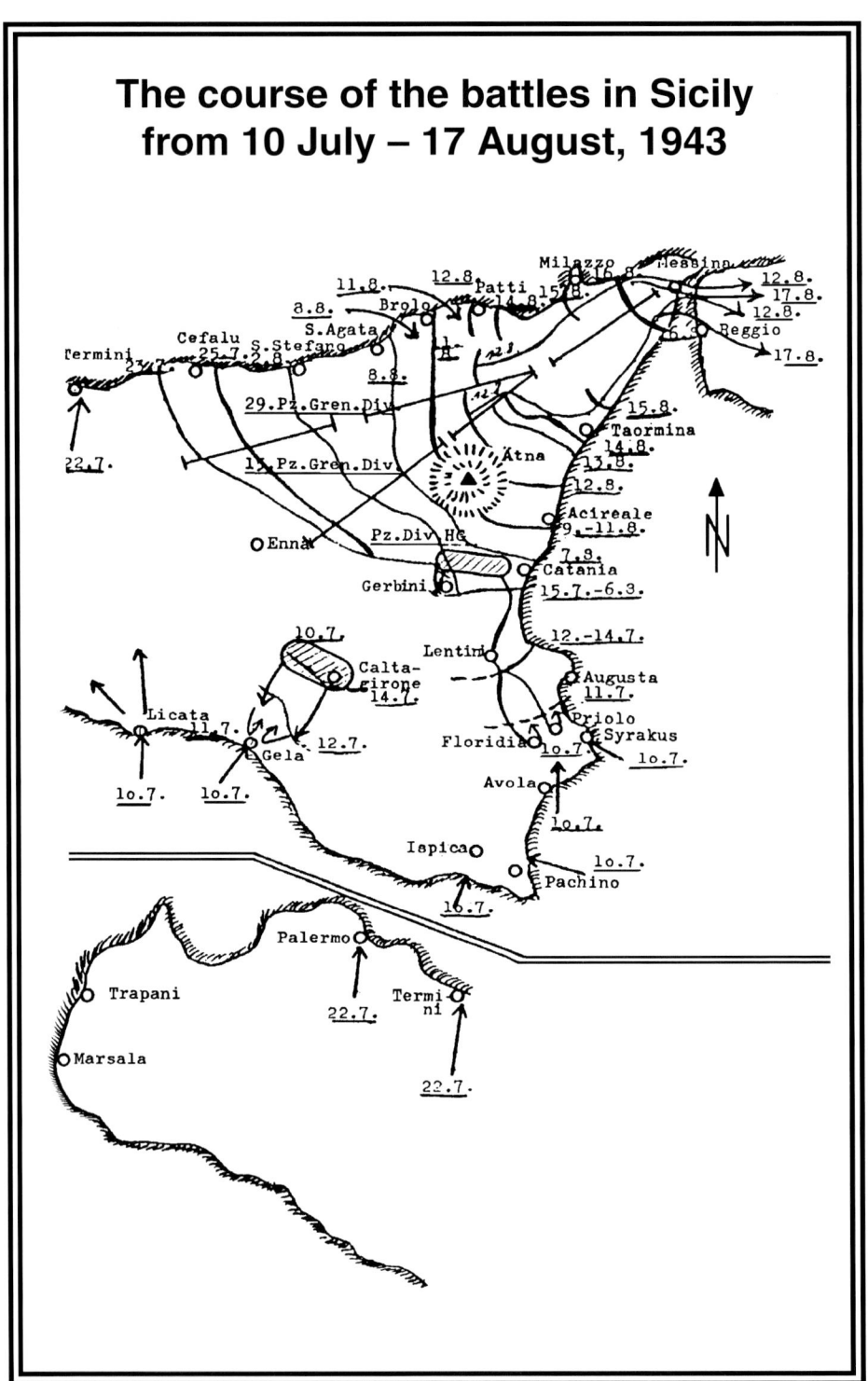

and industrial facilities on the mainland had to give up most of their anti-aircraft protection. It was thus possible to build up a force of about 400 (!) anti-aircraft guns, enough to stop every enemy air attack.

Generalleutnant Richard Heidrich, commander of the 1st Parachute Division, was given the job of organizing the troops on the mainland. He had previously received instructions to organize the defense of the coastline in South-Calabria by using remnants of units, supply troops and other units.

The Allied Landing Operations

On 9 July 1943 the airborne troops of the British 1st Airborne Division and the American 82nd Airborne Division took off from the 13 airfields around Kairouan. The first to take off, at about 1900 hours, were the men of the British 1st Airborne Brigade under Brigadier Hicks. The airborne force consisted of 109 Dakotas, 9 Halifax bombers, and 12 Albemarles towing 120 American Waco gliders and 8 British Horsa gliders. The Horsas, designed to carry freight, had weapons and jeeps on board. The other gliders carried a total of 1,600 paratroopers. Pilots of the American 51st Wing, Troop Transport Command, carried out the flight. Before takeoff they had received instructions to release the Wacos at a height of 600 meters and the Horsas at 1,200 meters, just as soon as the formation was 2,800 meters off the coast.

The battle group's combat orders were:

"Jump between 2210 and 2230 hours west of Syracuse at the important bridge over the Anapo: the Ponte Grande. Further: put out of action the heavy coastal batteries located by aerial reconnaissance and occupy the nearby base of the Italian Naval Air Force."

Brigadier Hicks and Colonel Chatterton, the latter the CO of the glider regiment, wanted the first wave to land west of the Maddalena Peninsula and the second north of the channel bridge (on the west side of Syracuse harbour). Both officers led their units from one of the leading Horsas. The two units initially homed in on the Delimara radio beacon in southeastern Malta. From there they turned toward Cape Passero on the south coast of Sicily.

The airborne force came under fire as soon as it flew into range of the German coastal artillery. One of the first salvoes struck a Horsa loaded with Bangalore torpedoes. The machine exploded in a brilliant fireball. Some of the pilots had become confused by the many course changes and the explosion of the Horsa and released their gliders too soon. A total of 47 gliders were driven by the wind into the open sea. Almost all those on board drowned. Only a few survived to be picked up hours later by the following landing craft.

Of the remaining gliders a total of 12 reached the general target area. Only one came down right at the bridge. It was glider 133 piloted by Staff-Sergeant Galpin; on board were men of the South Staffordshire Regiment under Lieutenant L. Withers. This officer gained renown for taking the Ponte Grande with only a handful of men. Lieutenant Withers had one section swim to the other bank, in order to launch a simultaneous attack from both sides of the river. The gamble paid off. The Italian troops defending the bridge were overcome after a thirty-minute firefight; the explosive charges were removed and tossed into the river and a small bridgehead was established directly north of the bridge.

At daybreak seven members of the brigade staff, led by Lieutenant-Colonel Walsh, arrived at the bridge. With them were eight more paratroopers, whom Walsh had "collected" along the way. In the end there were eight officers and 65 soldiers assembled at the bridge. These held the bridgehead, initially against attacks by the Italians, but later against attacks by the leading unit of Battle Group Schmalz as well. This small group of British troops held the bridgehead until the arrival of the 5th British Infantry Division, by which time their numbers had been reduced to four officers and 15 men.

The reinforced 505th Airborne Regiment of the 82nd Airborne Division under Colonel Gavin received the designation 505th Parachute Combat Team for this operation. The regiment was flown to the target by the 52nd Troop Carrier Wing. The battle group consisted of 3,405 soldiers. It had earlier carried out several takeoff and landing exercises in the Kairouan area. Its combat orders were:

"Take possession of the plateau and crossroads four miles north of Gela and block same. Support the US 1st Infantry Division in the capture of the airfield at Ponte Olivio."

This regimental battle group took off in 227 C-47 transports. Just before takeoff it was reinforced by the division's anti-tank battalion. The battle group was supposed to capture a large bridgehead and hold it until the amphibious landing by the US 1st Infantry Division.

Colonel Gavin flew in the leading aircraft of the 316th Troop Carrier Group under Colonel McCanley. The C-47s reached the Sicilian coast after a three-hour flight. There they were caught by the massed fire of the German anti-aircraft guns. Hardest hit was the group bringing the anti-tank battalion to the island. Its pilots lost their nerve when the time came to fly through the curtain of German flak. Six of the aircraft were shot down. The glider tugs blindly released their 118 gliders, while the paratroopers were dropped wherever the transports happened to be – and that was not over the target.

1st Company, 3rd Battalion of the 505th Parachute Combat Team was the only unit to reach its designated target area. Most of the transports carrying the 3rd Battalion turned away and headed back in the direction of the sea. Then the aircraft turned again and at approximately 0025 hours dropped their paratroops, scattering them over a seven kilometer area southeast of the Acate River.

Eighty-five men of G Company seized and held a crossroads and the river crossing. Others were later able to link up with the advancing US 45th Infantry Division. Colonel Gavin, together with his staff and several small groups, came down about 15 kilometers south of Vittoria, which placed him approximately 50 kilometers away from the designated combat zone.

Lieutenant Harris of 3rd Battalion was captured by the Italians near Vittoria. He was held for seven hours, but following a brief exchange of fire with US troops the Italians raised the white flag and surrendered. The largest group of the reinforced regiment – 320 men – came down in the British attack zone near Avola. They were able to deal with the half-hearted attacks by the Italians and soon afterward were picked up by the British 50th Infantry Division.

3rd Battalion, 504th Airborne Regiment was also scattered, coming down from the Castel Nocera area to south of Nicemi. A small number of the unit's soldiers found themselves 80 kilometers east of Gela. They attacked Noto, took the city away from the Italians and held it until they were relieved. Lieutenant Thomas of 1st Company, 3rd Battalion, 504th Airborne Regiment and several of his men were taken prisoner by outposts of the Schmalz Brigade.

The main body of 3rd Battalion, 504th Airborne Regiment under Major Alexander came down some 50 kilometers from its target. Alexander nevertheless threw what there was of his battalion against a major Italian strongpoint near Santa Croce-Camerina and succeeded in entering and occupying the city. 45 Italian soldiers surrendered to him.

In spite of the dispersed manner in which they were dropped, the American airborne forces reached their objective. The American war diary had this to say:

"The actions of both battle groups may be looked upon as successful—on the one hand because at least one objective was reached, and on the other because this dispersed drop created the impression that a huge group of forces had been deployed over a large area. As well, they succeeded in blocking forces of the Hermann Göring Panzer Division." (See war diary of the 505th and 504th Airborne Regiments.)

With the operational use of these airborne units, Sicily became the birthplace of the American airborne landing technique. The British parachute troops had received their baptism of fire in Tunisia. It was there that their nickname, the "Red Devils", was born.

At Nuremberg *Generaloberst* Kurt Student, who was there as a witness, said of the use of Allied parachute troops:

"The Allied airborne landing operations in Sicily were decisive. Even with their completely scattered jumps they met the expectations of a night landing. I am convinced that had the Allied forces not succeeded in blocking the Hermann Göring Division and preventing it from reaching the beach quickly, the Reichmarschall's division would have driven the initial landing troops back into the sea."

In the British sector of the amphibious landing, the 13th Corps under General Dempsey, with the 5th and 50th Infantry Divisions, had as its objective Avola and Cassibile, while General Montgomery's 30th Corps under General Leese was to take and secure the Pacchino Peninsula with its airfield and the city of Pacchino.

It was the 15th Brigade of the 50th Infantry Division "Tyne and Tees" which was the first to step on Sicilian soil, even though it was not until 0415 hours, ninety minutes after the planned landing time. B Company, 6th Battalion of the Durham Light Infantry landed due north of Punta Giorgio. A

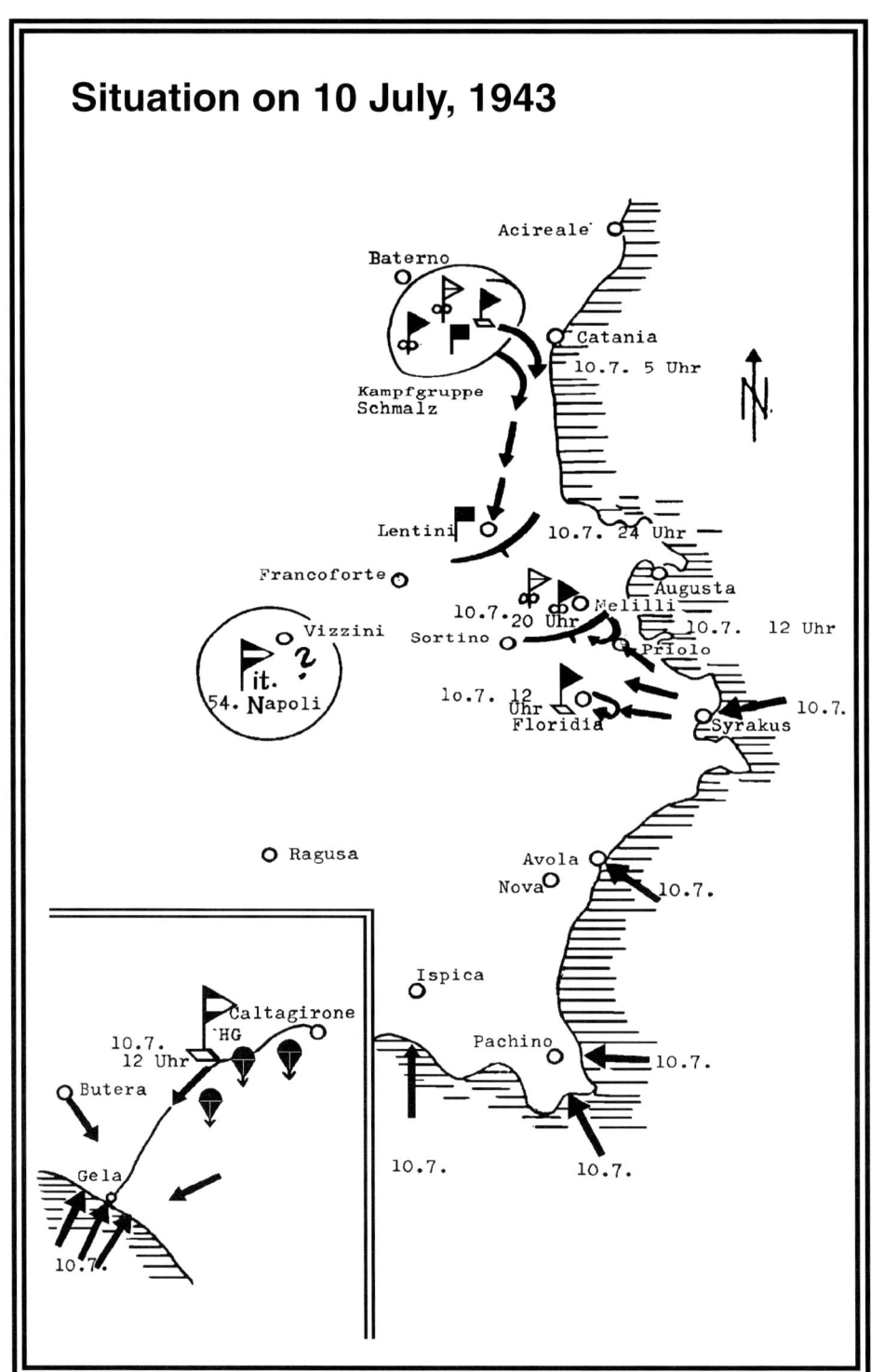

Company under Captain Richard Golloway went ashore near Calabernardo, where minefields caused the first casualties. C Company suffered heavy casualties while still at sea. Captain Walton was killed as was the battalion commander, Lieutenant Colonel Watson. 8th Battalion, Durham Light Infantry landed in the bay near Avola. On the Lido di Avola it was met by artillery fire. Both Italian strongpoints, at Avola and Santa Venerina, fought bravely. The 30th Corps, directed against the Pacchino Peninsula, likewise landed shortly after 0415 hours, coming ashore between Marzamemi and Porto Ulysse on a front of 30 kilometers. With the 154th Brigade under Brigadier Rennie on the left and the 231st Malta Brigade under Brigadier Urquhart on the right, the corps first attacked the port of Portopalo, which quickly fell into its hands.

The 1st Canadian Infantry Division under General Simmonds, which was scheduled to land south of Modica, followed close behind two commando units: the Royal Marines under Brigadier Laycock and the 3rd Commando under Lieutenant Colonel Slater. Pachino airfield was reached at 0645 hours and after 45 minutes of fighting was firmly in the hands of the attackers; however, the city of Pachino itself did not fall until about midday. In the rear several Italian strongpoints held out until after noon. Nevertheless the first Allied aircraft were able to land and take off from Pachino airfield at noon. The British units had thus reached their objective for the day. Apart from several skirmishes, German units had not opposed the British on this day. There was a special reason for this, as will be explained later.

The Eighth Army's next objective, Syracuse, lay completely open before the attackers, for the "Napoli" Division which was stationed there had apparently disappeared into thin air. This, too, will be explained in the chapter dealing with the Schmalz Brigade.

The American Landings

The three landing groups, "Joss", "Dime" and "Cent", reached their attack positions and areas at about 0000 hours on 10 July. The cruisers and destroyers began laying down preparatory fire. H-Hour was 0245. On board the flagship of the "Cent" group was the American Commander-in-Chief, General Omar N. Bradley. The 3rd US Infantry Division under General Truscott, which went ashore near Licata with the support of a tank battalion of the 2nd Armored Division, charged into the city and fought its way through to the airfield. At 1505 hours General Truscott reported the captured airfield as operational.

The troops of the 1st Infantry Division under General Allen, which landed near Gela, had received two battalions of US Rangers to lead the assault. Gela was taken and the Ponte Olivio airfield reached. General Middleton's 45th Infantry Division was supposed to come ashore east and west of Scoglitti. Its assignment was to take possession of the territory from Punta Bracchetto to the area due east of Gela, capture the airfields at Comiso and Biscari, and prepare them for use by the Allied air forces. The division arrived at the departure point on time. At 0345 hours naval artillery opened fire on the Italian coastal fortifications and strongpoints, which in return began firing on the assembled ships off the coast. The coastal guns were soon silenced and, as there was no Axis unit defending the shoreline there, the landings were successful.

The first reports from the landing forces reached General Bradley aboard the *Ancon* at daybreak. He learned, for example, that the Rangers under Lieutenant Colonel Darby had sailed straight into the harbour jetty and wharves and had "woken from its sleep" an Italian armored company.

At 0458 hours, in the midst of the landing operation, a lone He 111 attacked the Allied ships. The Heinkel's bombs struck the destroyer *Maddox* commanded by Lieutenant Commander Sarsfield. The destroyer's stern exploded in a cloud of flame and smoke. The bow rose steeply from the sea and then the ship went down, taking 202 seamen and eight officers with it to the bottom. Only 74 survivors were rescued.

Several other He 111s which attacked at about the same time managed to sink several landing craft. However the number of available machines was too small for the Luftwaffe to achieve a decisive success.

The German Side on the First Day: The Schmalz Brigade

At the beginning of July 1943 the Hermann Göring Division received orders to depart for Sicily. Representing the division commander, *Oberst* Wilhelm Schmalz reported to Headquarters, Sixth Army in Enna. His purpose for being there was to discuss questions concerning accommodations for the division as well as the battle plan in the event of an enemy landing.

"The Italian High Command intended to conduct the battle as follows: In view of the weak coastal fortifications and their inadequate garrisons, they planned to withdraw all units to an inner triangle immediately after the first enemy landings and then mount a successful defence of this triangle, an extremely rugged mountainous area. This meant abandoning the coast without fighting.

I then made the following alternative proposal: Position the two German divisions (the 15th Panzer-Grenadier and the Hermann Göring Panzer) at the likely landing sites near Catania and Gela, ready to attack, so that they might intervene immediately at the beginning of an enemy landing. The artillery of both divisions should go into position at these two points straight away, with the troops themselves quartered nearby. Then, in case the enemy should land elsewhere, the divisions could be sent straight to the counterattack there.

I considered it a mistake to position the divisions in the interior of the country and wait. However, my proposal was rejected and we were ordered to follow the Italian battle plan: That meant fighting from the inner triangle, with the concession that we could attack from the interior as soon as the opportunity presented itself. When I brought up the subject of strengthening the island's defenses by adding another German division (as was intended), I received the impression that reinforcing the island garrison by a further German division would not be looked upon favorably (by the Italians).

What struck me most of all, however, was the feeling that the Italian command lacked the serious will to prevent a landing at all costs. I returned to my headquarters and after careful consideration reported the proceedings to *Generalfeldmarschall* Kesselring, with the request that he go to the island personally to discuss conduct of the battle in the event of an enemy landing with Headquarters, Sixth Army, as I considered their plan to wait to be wrong."

Generalfeldmarschall Kesselring went to Enna at the end of June. *Oberst* Schmalz was also there.

"We were received by elegantly-dressed officers and sat in lovely air-conditioned rooms. Coming as we did from the extremely hot tent city on the lava masses of Mount Etna, we were dressed in our tropical uniforms, which did not at all fit this peaceful scene. Instead we brought a firm determination to fight into this idyll of peace. There was no trace of a comradely feeling among brothers in arms. It was solely due to the amiability and eloquence of *Generalfeldmarschall* Kesselring that the discussion finally turned to its true purpose. Our proposal was received very coolly and without enthusiasm. The following result was achieved:

The five Italian reserve divisions and the two German divisions will be positioned near the expected landing sites for an immediate counterattack.

At first General Guzzoni stubbornly defended his defensive plan, convinced that we couldn't fight on the coast and that only in the interior of the country would we have a chance. I did not have the impression that he was convinced himself of the correctness of his views. When we left the conference room I told Generalfeldmarschall Kesselring of my doubts as to the readiness of the Italians to fight and said:

I believe that General Guzzoni only said yes to our proposal in order to get rid of us as quickly as possible. In my opinion he is going to carry out his plan to evacuate the coast.

The *Generalfeldmarschall* stated emphatically that he did not share my opinion. Naturally I had no way of knowing whether he felt differently inside. In all of his discussions with us commanders he gave us the solid impression that he trusted our Italian allies. Not until 25 July 1943 was the *Generalfeldmarschall*'s confidence shaken by Badoglio. I, on the other hand, was not convinced that the Italian Sixth Army would stick to the plan we had discussed. I informed the commander of the 15th Panzer-Grenadier Division, *Generalmajor* Rodt, and my own commanding officer, *Generalmajor* Conrath, of this following their arrival on the island."

As a result of the new agreements between General Guzzoni and *Generalfeldmarschall* Kesselring, Headquarters, Sixth Army had to issue completely new orders in order to make all units aware of the new state of affairs. This was only done very slowly and then incompletely or in some cases not at all. Proof of this is the fact that the Italian units in the Syracuse – Augusta area did not fight when the Allied landings came, rather they withdrew to the previously mentioned "inner triangle" as specified in the first order. Furthermore the Italian units blew up their heavy weapons as they did so. Once again *Generalleutnant* Schmalz:

"Italian officers, for example an Admiral and a Colonel from Syracuse whom I met fleeing down the Syracuse – Lentini road near Malleoli on 10 July, both told me that they were under orders to evacuate the coast in the event of enemy landings. Other Italian officers and soldiers made statements to the same effect."

"Believing that the Italian and German divisions would attack simultaneously and immediately, as agreed in the discussions at Enna, the behavior of the coastal garrisons presented the German command with a totally unexpected situation – especially as the Italian divisions did not participate at all, or at least only halfheartedly, in the counterattack."

The following intervention groups had been formed on the basis of the discussions in Enna:

In the Marsala area: elements of the 15th Panzer-Grenadier Division and two Italian divisions.

In the Gela – Agrigent area: the bulk of the Hermann Göring Panzer Division and an Italian division.

In the Syracuse – Augusta – Catania area: the Schmalz Brigade and an Italian division.

The artillery of the German units was positioned near the coast, in order to be able to place the anticipated landing sites under fire immediately. The Schmalz Brigade, commanded by *Oberst* Wilhelm Schmalz, consisted of the following units:

Brigade Headquarters of the Hermann Göring Panzer Division,

- Infantry Regiment: Oberst Maucke (made up of soldiers on leave, convalescents, and members of the former Africa Corps who escaped from Africa),

- Armored Personnel Carrier Battalion of the Hermann Göring Panzer Division,

- Assault Gun Battalion of the Hermann Göring Panzer Division,

- Flak Battalion of the Hermann Göring Panzer Division,

- an Italian armored battalion.

The brigade's quartering area was Catania-Misterbianco-Paterno-Belpasso. Positions had been prepared on the northern edge of the Catania plain, front facing south, in the event of an invasion alert. Near Catania the front faced south, towards the sea. Since the beginning of July there had been heavy Allied air attacks on lines of communication, roads, and rail lines, as well as on all the airfields on the island.

On 9 July the brigade received an aerial reconnaissance report indicating that the Allied invasion fleet had sailed from African ports. Further reports revealed the splitting in two of the invasion fleet and suggested landings on the south and southeast coasts. The brigade occupied its prepared positions on the north slope of the Catania plain between Paterno-Gerbini-Catania. These movements were completed during the night of 10 July. All reports were passed on from the brigade to division. This was done by way of armored radio trucks positioned on the south and southeast coasts, which ensured direct transmission of all reports.

On the morning of 10 July 1943 German scout car patrols reported:

"Enemy landing near Syracuse-Ispica-Noto."

As per the agreement with Headquarters, Sixth Army, the brigade immediately launched a counterattack toward Syracuse. The Hermann Göring Panzer Division, which was in the Gela area, was informed of this. Because of the disruptions in communications caused by the subsequent fighting and aerial bombardments, this was the brigade's last communication with a German command unit for several days.

"As soon as I left Catania to launch the attack near Syracuse I left Catania undefended. I had my doubts whether this was the right thing to do, for a subsequent landing by Allied troops against Catania – in order to advance to Messina as quickly as possible and thus achieve a quick success – could come at any time. It was therefore a leap into the unknown, which later was to prove correct. But I considered it better to do something than to wait until the enemy forced me to react.

I knew that the *Napoli* Division, which was assigned to my brigade, was in the Vizzini area and that we should meet in the Floridiana area in the attack toward Syracuse. Early that morning the following units went to the attack behind a thin screen of armored reconnaissance vehicles: the armored personnel carrier battalion, the assault gun battalion, and the flak battalion. The march route led through Catania and Lentini in the direction of Syracuse. The Italian light armored battalion and several German armored radio squads were supposed to set out through Catania, Lentini, and Floridiana towards Syracuse. The German radio squads led the advance and near Floridiana became involved in fighting with advancing Allied elements. They remained in contact with the enemy and passed a stream of reports to brigade. Nothing more was seen of the Italian armored battalion which was supposedly following. It remained missing."

As determined later, and mentioned here to preserve the honor of the unit, this Italian armored battalion fought very bravely. Under the command of the energetic *Tenente Colonel* (Lieutenant Colonel) Maximini, the battalion fought with exemplary bravery in Floridiana. Whether it fought with the *Napoli* Division is questionable. In any case, on 13 July 1943 the commander of the *Napoli* Division and his entire staff surrendered to British forces under the command of Brigadier R.M.P. Cavet (4th Armored Brigade). The Italian commander showed a white flag to the British, who were advancing along the Palazzuolo – Solarino road.

The Schmalz Brigade's armored group encountered the enemy near Priolo. The two battalions of the Maucke Infantry Regiment, which had been motorized through improvisation, were sent to Lentini via Catania. The regiment's III Battalion, which was not yet fully equipped, remained in its previous positions at the northern edge of the Catania Plain.

On the evening of 10 July the situation in front of Battle Group Schmalz was as follows: the Italian tanks and the armored patrols were in combat near Floridiana; the armored personnel carrier battalion was in action near Priolo.

Italian coastal garrisons blew up their weapons and fled between Augusta and Syracuse. Supported by naval artillery, the enemy pressure was so great that any further advance in the direction of Syracuse was impossible. The Schmalz Brigade therefore went over to the defensive near Malleoli.

The necessary conditions for a joint conduct of the battle with the *Napoli* Division – which was confirmed by an operations officer of a senior Italian commander who arrived at the brigade command post on 10 July, even though he was unable able to say where the *Napoli* Division was – no longer existed on the evening of 10 July 1943.

The Italian troops had, as far as the Schmalz Brigade could determine, left their positions in the coastal area, even where they weren't being attacked. As a result the entire coast was denuded of troops and left open to seizure by the enemy. The Schmalz Brigade was left alone on a broad stage, its rear and flanks completely unprotected. It was obvious that it was the enemy's intention to overrun this fighting unit, which meant that his objective was Catania and subsequently Messina. If the attack succeeded, all German-Italian units on the island would be cut off from their lifeline across the Strait of Messina.

As attempts to establish contact with other German units failed, *Oberst* Schmalz was forced to make his decisions on his own. The completely open Catania Plain remained his main concern. If the plain was lost, a defence of Malleoli and Lentini would be pointless. Wilhelm Schmalz personally ordered *Oberst* Maucke to go into position near Lentini and dig in there. The three artillery battalions were fighting with the armored personnel carrier battalion. The units fighting near Floridiana suffered losses and were forced to withdraw under heavy fire toward Sortino during the night.

Had these soldiers not fought so courageously, the British forces would have reached Lentini via Sortino easily, dislodging the most forward elements of the Schmalz Brigade and drawing the Maucke Regiment into the battle prematurely. Allied preparations for a landing near Augusta were recognized. The Schmalz Brigade's artillery shifted its artillery fire there, which delayed these landings.

After the war Wilhelm Schmalz said of this situation:

"It was clear to me that the position near Lentini could also only be a temporary one. If the counterattack by the Hermann Göring Panzer Division and the 15th Panzer-Grenadier Division did not lead to success, a combination of forces at the northern edge of the Catania Plain would have to be effected in order to continue the battle."

Schmalz continued his account:

"Near Melilli a dashing Italian officer, a Major, turned up. Still in command of a battalion, he assembled all the Italian soldiers retreating from Syracuse in order to form these into fighting units. During the night of 11 July he brought his troops into position and fought shoulder to shoulder with my men. I witnessed several instances of this type of behavior, where the middle and lower levels of Italian command were ready to fight, while the higher command harbored other intentions (because they obviously knew that an Italian withdrawal from the Axis pact was only a matter of a few weeks)."

With the Hermann Göring Panzer Division

In the early morning hours of 10 July 1943 the Hermann Göring Panzer Division, the bulk of which was in the Caltagirone area, received orders from *Generalfeldmarschall* Kesselring to immediately launch a counterattack. Although Kesselring had no power of command in Sicily, he saw himself forced to act. Of this the *Feldmarschall* said:

"When I nevertheless intervened with a radio order to the Hermann Göring Panzer Division in the early morning hours of 10 July, the day of the invasion, it was only to make good an omission."

As the division (less the Schmalz Brigade) was responsible for defending against any enemy landings near or east of Gela and south of Comiso, since the beginning of July it had deployed radio-equipped armored scout cars at several points in the coastal area between Gela and Augusta. If an enemy landing came the division wished to know immediately, so as to be able to initiate planned countermeasures without delay. Not until the late morning of 10 July was the division – which had received no orders from Headquarters, Sixth Army – placed on alert by *Generalfeldmarschall* Kesselring's order. On receipt of the order *Generalmajor* Conrath initiated the prearranged measures. The reconnaissance scout cars had already reported the landings near Gela and Syracuse. *Generalmajor* Conrath had both battle groups of the Caltagirone Group (Hermann Göring Panzer Division less the Schmalz Brigade) move out as soon as he received Kesselring's order. He gave both battle groups the following mission:

"Break through to the sea and destroy the enemy forces which have landed near Gela by enveloping them from both sides."

The right battle group set out from the area east of the Gela Plain and the left from the area southeast of Caltagirone. Composition of the two battle groups was as follows:

Right Battle Group: Panzer Regiment with the companies of the Reconnaissance Battalion, Artillery Regiment with two heavy battalions, Armored Pioneer Battalion less one company.

Left Battle Group: Panzer-Grenadier Regiment with two battalions, 1 artillery battalion with two batteries, 1 Tiger company (2nd Company, 504th Heavy Panzer Battalion).

Late on the afternoon of 10 July *Generalmajor* Conrath was ordered to Sixth Army headquarters in Enna. There he learned that the Italians wanted to examine the possibility of an attack in the direction of Gela. To this end the Hermann Göring Division and the *Livorno* Division were to attack simultaneously. The army planned to issue the attack order that evening.

Instead of the order to attack toward Gela, late that evening the division received a radio message from Headquarters, Sixth Army instructing it to establish a defensive front near Gela and to advance east with the bulk of its forces – passing to the south of Comiso. The division did not carry out this order because it was not in keeping with the situation on the battlefield or the fighting strength of the division.

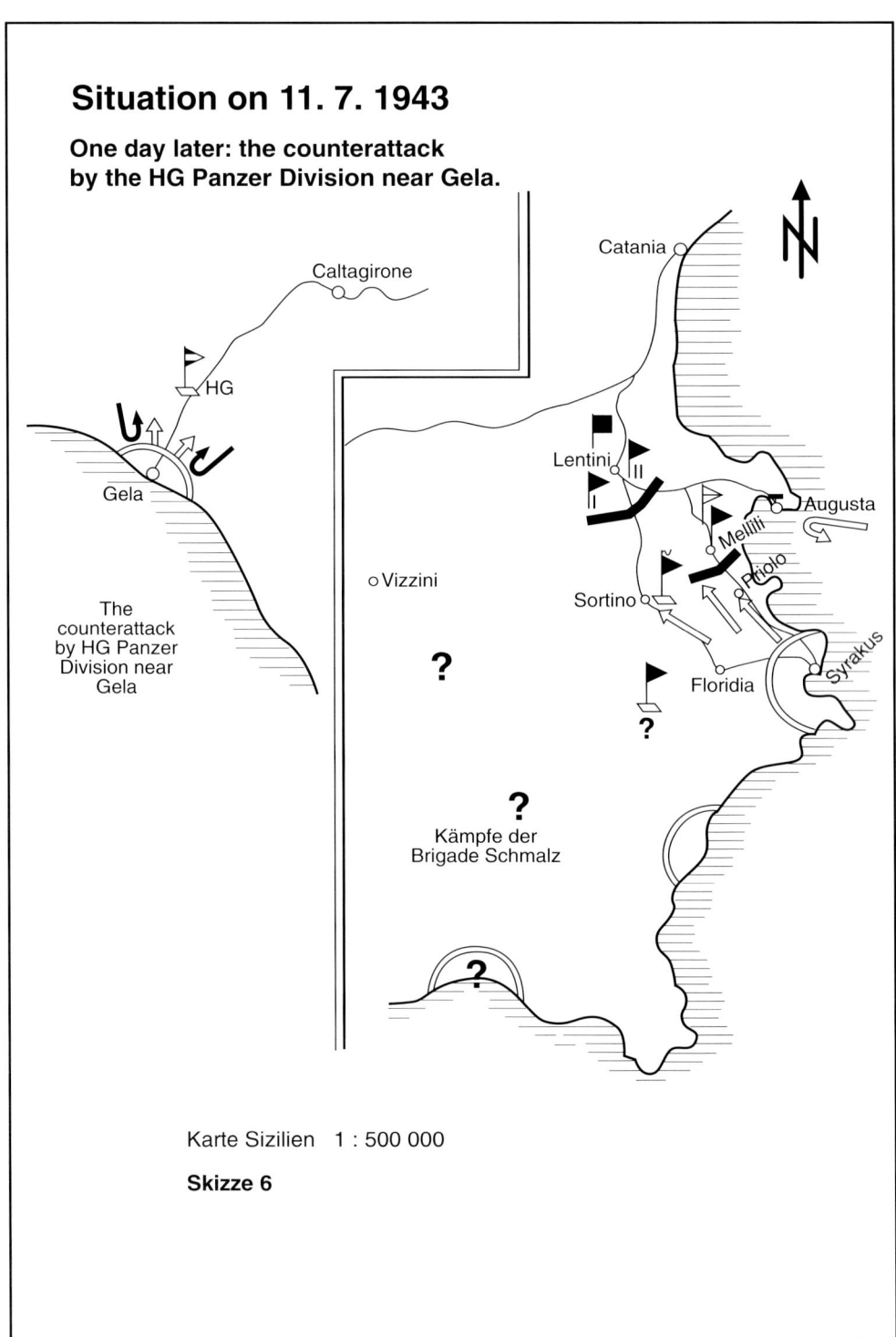

On the morning of 10 July the Hermann Göring Panzer Division's advance stalled repeatedly on the narrow mountain roads. As well the division was further held up by the Allied paratroops. The terraced terrain, traversed by olive groves, continually presented fresh obstacles to the progress of the division's heavy elements. The Tiger company in particular had to deal with numerous difficulties. Several times the tanks became stuck in the narrow village streets. Nevertheless, by the late evening of 10 July the division reached a good jumping-off position for the attack planned the next morning.

When *General* von Senger, head of the German liaison staff at Headquarters, Sixth Army in Enna, arrived at *Generalmajor* Conrath's command post at about 1800 hours, he learned that the division had already reached the Gela – Vittoria road late that morning. The right group with its tanks was already south of Niscemi, while the left group with the panzergrenadier regiment had reached a point southwest of Biscari. *General* von Senger wrote that night:

"HG Division will, after clearing the intermediate terrain, attack with both groups in a southwesterly direction early on 11 July at the latest, in order to retake Gela and the coastal area."

Generalmajor Conrath summarized the situation at midnight on 11 July as follows:

"The enemy is holding all the hills around Gela within a radius of five to six kilometers. In the Licata area he has advanced about 10 kilometers along the north road."

Paul Conrath had assembled all his units and was confident that his attack on 11 July must break through and lead to success. The following is I Battalion, Hermann Göring Regiment's battle report, written by the regiment's Ia:

"An order from division reached the battalion at about 2230 hours on 10 July, according to which it was to attack south along the road to Priolo on the morning of the following day, in order to link up with the Heinrici Group at the coast. On the basis of our own reconnaissance the attack was carried out, not through the complex terrain along the road, but 500 meters farther west on the Gela Plain. A reinforced armored pioneer company was assigned to reinforce the battalion. The battalion assembled for the attack, however it remained where it was, awaiting the arrival of the panzer regiment's II Battalion, which was to take over the positions. As the latter did not arrive until 1400, I Battalion, which had to drive forward through Niscemi, was unable to reach the assembly area in time. The beginning of the attack was delayed by 90 minutes as a result.

Several hundreds meters beyond the road 2nd Company, which was advancing on the right, was blanketed by naval artillery fire. An attempt to drive under the fire failed, because the company encountered a ditch dug at right angles to the direction of the attack for which there was no crossing on the plain. On receiving news of this the battalion decided to reorganize and cross the ditch in greater depth at another point, close to the ridge running along the eastern side of the plain, using a crossing discovered by the left company, and to reassemble in an olive grove behind the edge of the ridge facing the enemy. When this had taken place the unit, with 3rd Company leading the way, launched an attack into the undulating terrain in the direction of the coast, staying close to the ridge.

From this point on the battalion was constantly under mounting naval gun fire, which was splendidly directed by six captive balloons. The Armored Pioneer Company was separated from the battalion by this fire and pinned down. Only the elements of the assault company equipped with rocket launchers and flamethrowers were able to accompany the subsequent attack.

The 3rd and 4th Companies received instructions to advance left of the road in an eastward direction, in order to link up with the Urban Battalion coming from the north and Battle Group Heinrici, which was advancing from the east. The 1st and 2nd Companies were to follow the road. The subsequent advance by 3rd and 4th Companies was halted by anti-tank, artillery, and tank fire. About fifteen enemy tanks rolled down the hill from the direction in which the Urban Battalion was expected and went into position in a wood at the foot of this hill in order to fire on 3rd and 4th Companies. The advance by the two companies was stopped.

The 1st and 2nd Companies were now ordered to establish a fire front with 4th Company in order to give 3rd Company an opportunity to attack the 'tank wood' from the left flank. The fire front came under heavy naval gunfire and was only able to escape destruction by changing positions. The Armored Pioneer Assault Company played a major role in silencing the enemy tanks, firing two salvoes of rockets into the wood. In the midst of this situation the battalion received an order from division to resume the advance at once together with the Urban Battalion. When asked the location of this unit, the division named Hills 132 and 123, however these were in enemy hands. A patrol was sent out under the command of an officer and this finally located the Urban Battalion on Hill 172. Near Point 55, it was in the process of assembling for an attack.

The battalion withdrew two kilometers into a position on the right of the Urban Battalion."

Supplementing this account is a description by *Oberleutnant* Stronk, who was at the head of the battalion and whose 1st Company carried out the attack. The company succeeded in blasting open a path for the following units and rolled up the American 26th Infantry Regiment under Colonel Roosevelt. *Oberleutnant* Stronk destroyed two enemy tanks in the course of the attack. At this point the battalion, led by the 1st Company, was within 1,000 meters of the beach.

The units of the American 1st Infantry Division, which were still on the beach, fired smoke shells and began re-embarking under cover of the curtain of smoke. The panzers had pushed forward without regard to the lack of cover and escorting infantry. The division didn't have enough troops to eliminate the enemy infantry which it had overrun. It thus happened that American radio teams turned up behind the panzers and directed the fire of the naval artillery onto the unit.

The attack ground to a halt in the fire of the ships' guns. The German unit was forced to withdraw, leaving 1st Company as rear guard. The battalion lost seven tanks totally destroyed. A large number were disabled with battle damage, while others were lost through track and engine damage. Altogether the Hermann Göring Panzer Division lost 43 tanks on this day, including several Tigers.

The decisive factor in the attack's failure was not the naval gunfire – heavy as it was – but the failure to arrive of the escorting infantry from two Italian divisions which had been designated to fulfill the support role. An assessment of the situation on the morning of 12 July led *Generalmajor* Conrath to call off the counterattack and, while leaving behind strong rear guards, withdraw toward a line Catenanuova – rail line to Catania – Catania. There he planned to move into position beside the Schmalz Brigade to establish and defend a continuous front. Conrath had to take this decision on his own, as he had received no orders from his superiors.

Only the Schmalz Brigade could be reached; however the unit command had already drawn the same conclusions on its own. Once in the planned positions it was to be placed under the command of the Hermann Göring Panzer Division once again. This was reported to Headquarters, Sixth Army by way of *General* von Senger. The 15th Panzer-Grenadier Division also received word of the Hermann Göring Panzer Division's intentions.

2nd Company, 504th Heavy Panzer Battalion in the Attack on Gela

"On 11 July our company received the order to advance in a southwesterly direction toward the US landing site at Gela. *Oberleutnant* Hummel, commander of the 504th Heavy Panzer Battalion's 2nd Company, went ahead alone with *Leutnant* Heim and his platoon, in order to first gain a picture of the situation. The rest of the combat echelon under *Leutnant* Goldschmidt followed two hours later. It was there that the unit got its first taste of the enemy's air superiority. The smoke dischargers of *Leutnant* Goldschmidt's Tiger were holed.

We were almost overwhelmed, but with the arrival of the rest of the combat echelon our attack gained momentum and we gained ground quickly. However, we were without infantry protection on the left. *Oberleutnant* Hummel called a halt to refuel and rearm. He himself went on a scouting mission with the Company Headquarters Squad on the right flank in the direction of Gela. Soon afterward an anti-tank shell penetrated his tank's emergency escape hatch. *Leutnant* Heim assumed command of the company as the command Tiger had been disabled. Recovery proved impossible.

At this time a report was received of an enemy attack on Vittoria. *Leutnant* Heim ordered me to guard the three damaged tanks with my platoon. He himself attacked in the direction of the enemy threat with the combat echelon. While combing the area we took several American soldiers prisoner. In the evening *Hauptmann* Weber, a battalion commander with the HG, and several grenadiers who had become separated from their units arrived. Weber brought an order from the HG Division to advance in a westerly direction parallel to the coast as far as the road junction at Niscemi at 0400 hours the next day. The HG Panzer Division would attack from the north. I was then to take the point and advance with the division to Gela, roll to the beach, and drive the enemy landing force into the sea. Effective immediately I and my six Tigers were placed under the command of *Hauptmann* Weber.

During the night of 11 July I collected several infantry guns with limbers and about 100 men. The damaged tanks were repaired during the night. The command tank could not be repaired, however and had to be blown up. The attack began the following morning. After only a few meters we came under fire from bunkers and anti-tank guns. The grenadiers riding on our tanks jumped down. *Hauptmann* Weber stood on my tank. His company commanders were posted on the nearest tank to enable them to pass orders to the grenadiers.

We rolled on along an asphalt road and, halting several times to fire, silenced the anti-tank and machine-gun nests and the bunkers. Suddenly enemy tanks rolled toward us. I gave firing orders to the first and then the second Tiger, but both failed to open fire. To this day I don't know why. My tank opened fire. Our first shot hit the leading Sherman, which burst into flames. For us this was a demonstration of the penetrative capabilities of our Tiger's gun at a range of 2,600 meters. The second Sherman rolled past the first. It too caught fire after the first shot. The remaining enemy tanks withdrew and we were able to knock out a third from a range of 2,800 meters and then a fourth. The fifth enemy tank was also hit but managed to reach cover.

The advance continued. We reached the point where the north road from Niscemi joined the main road. This was where the tanks of I Battalion, Hermann Göring Panzer Division were supposed to meet us. Our two leading tanks turned onto this road. They came upon a tank, fired, and knocked it out. It was a German Panzer IV, which displayed a large hole in its side. Although I reproached both tank commanders, they didn't respond.

Heavy artillery fire now began. Anti-tank guns cracked. Contact was lost with the Weber Battalion. I fired signal flares and my radio operator, Köhler, tried to contact *Hauptmann* Weber, but in vain. We fired signal flares and even displayed orange recognition panels, but the firing intensified. We were still convinced that it was German firing on German, unaware that the German front had been pulled back 50 kilometers the previous night.

Now we had to seek contact with the HG Panzer Regiment to the north. However both leading tanks were disabled, and the crews bailed out and took cover beside their vehicles at the steep slope. While trying to establish contact I was hit on the left side of the turret. Fortunately it didn't penetrate, but rivets flew about our ears. Fred Güther, our only tank commander who was 'only' an NCO, called a warning to me: 'Sherman tanks at nine o'clock!'

That meant from the left. That was also the direction from which we had taken the hit. We turned and fired. One of the enemy tanks caught fire, a second was disabled with track damage. We were unable to reach the tanks in the valley below, because even our tremendous gun had its limitations. After traversing very steep terrain – and risking a backward somersault – we reached the road again. Günther's Tiger and mine rolled on until the radiator of Günther's Tiger began to boil. We drove into cover near a farm. An inspection of my Tiger revealed 110 hits. Pieces had been shot out of the tracks. The gearshift would only go into 2nd and 5th gears. The first pair of roadwheels on the right side were gone. The left side running gear had similar damage.

Our armour-piercing ammunition was almost gone and we had to select our reserve fuel tank. We had been 36 hours without sleep. The men sent into the farm to fetch water didn't return. I set out with my submachine-gun at the ready, and when I reached the farm I was met by a mixed group. It was our two soldiers and twelve Americans, led by a Lieutenant Thomas. Inside lay several wounded GIs and other American paratroopers. The Lieutenant asked me if he might use his radio to call one of his own doctors. He gave his word not to reveal the situation there.

We consented, but moved our two Tigers into a good firing position in case things didn't go as planned. The Americans, by now about 40 men, camouflaged our Tigers and brought food, cigarettes, and water. After an hour a doctor with the rank of Colonel arrived. He was a Texan, about six feet tall. *Gefreiter* Hahn brought him to me. He declared that we had done a good job of keeping them (the Americans) busy, but now we were 'at the end of the line' and had better give up, as we would never be able to reach our own forces. The German front had been pulled back a further 50 kilometers during the previous night.

We concluded a six-hour cease-fire and blew up both of our Tigers. When the ammunition detonated, the enemy answered with blind mortar and artillery fire. Taking nothing with us, we sneaked northwest in the direction of our main line of resistance, which the doctor had shown us on his map. Our own troops mistook us for a commando squad and we were almost shot. But then we landed at the HG Division Headquarters. *Leutnant* Heim, commander of what was left of the 504th Battalion, which was just then in the midst of a counterattack, was amazed to see us again.

The withdrawal into the Paterno area was already under way when we arrived at what was left of the company. There the front stabilized. Several soldiers contracted malaria in the valley of the Simeto River near Costatina, which was infested with mosquitoes. Our sector of the front was later withdrawn to the Paterno hills. No one got through there; however, when British units drove into our left flank from the direction of Catania, we were pulled back. *Leutnant* Heim, who had been wounded in Paterno, continued to lead the company. In Belpasso he was wounded again, this time severely, by a hand grenade, and he handed over command of the company to me. Two other officers had meanwhile arrived from Germany; *Leutnant* Steuber, who commanded the infantry platoon, and *Oberleutnant* Dietrich, who took over the train.

As we withdrew we were followed by the heavy bombardments of the enemy artillery and by fighter-bomber attacks as well. Only once did we get the chance to fire on enemy tanks, which subsequently remained at a respectful distance. In the Nicolosi – Trecastagni area we established a triangular defensive position facing east, south, and west. In my opinion the Etna position could have been held for some time; however, superior authorities with a better insight into matters decided that it had to be given up because of fears of an Allied landing on the mainland.

I carried out one more counterattack with four Tigers, in the course of which we came under heavy artillery fire. *Feldwebel* Uhlig's Tiger was hit and caught fire. We put out the fire and started back to the repair echelon with the Tiger, but there was an explosion and the blast reached the driver's compartment. Then the ammunition detonated. By the time the shells exploded I had already pulled the severely-burned driver out through his jammed hatch. The tank was sitting astride the road and could not move. A traffic jam of ambulances and communications vehicles began forming. The street was lined by walls a meter thick, and there was no way to go around the disabled tank. But then the Tiger, which by now was ablaze, did us a favor. The starter howled and the tank, which was empty, jerked forward. It reached the wall, drove into it, and then stood motionless on the left side of the street. The insulation had melted from the electrical cables as the tank burned; the starter wires made contact and, since a forward gear was engaged, the battery power set the tank in motion. The street was clear.

Two hours later I reported to *General* Hube. He ordered me to immediately ferry the last four Tigers to the mainland. When I arrived back at the assembly area that evening the crews of three badly damaged Tigers had already blown up their vehicles. As a result only one of our company's Tigers could be shipped to the mainland. (It later broke down with transmission damage in the serpentine mountain roads of Calabria and was blown up.)

The next morning I set off across the Strait of Messina with the crews. The remnants of our 2./sPzAbt. 504 consisted of 65 men. We were now supposed to be incorporated into the HG Panzer Division, however our wounded commander was able to prevent this by making a petition to *Generaloberst* Guderian. We were transferred to Pontecorvo near Sassino, where gradually there assembled about 180 men of sPzAbt. 504. These formed the basis of the new battalion, which was formed in Wezep, Holland under *Major* Otto (replaced a short time later by *Major* Kühn)."

The Schmalz Brigade in Sicily:
An Account by *Generalleutnant* Wilhelm Schmalz

"I expected the English to attack on a broad front with all forces for 12 July. Our battle plan was for the forward troops to take the brunt of the attack and not withdraw to the defensive line near Lentini until the situation became extremely serious. But what was happening farther to the west, where I expected the *Napoli* Division to be? Patrols had sighted British troops marching in the direction of Francofonte. I had no more troops with which to close this gap which gaped from Lentini to Gela.

If the enemy continued to advance on 12 July, which was to be expected, then he might push on unhindered through Francofonte- Scordia into the

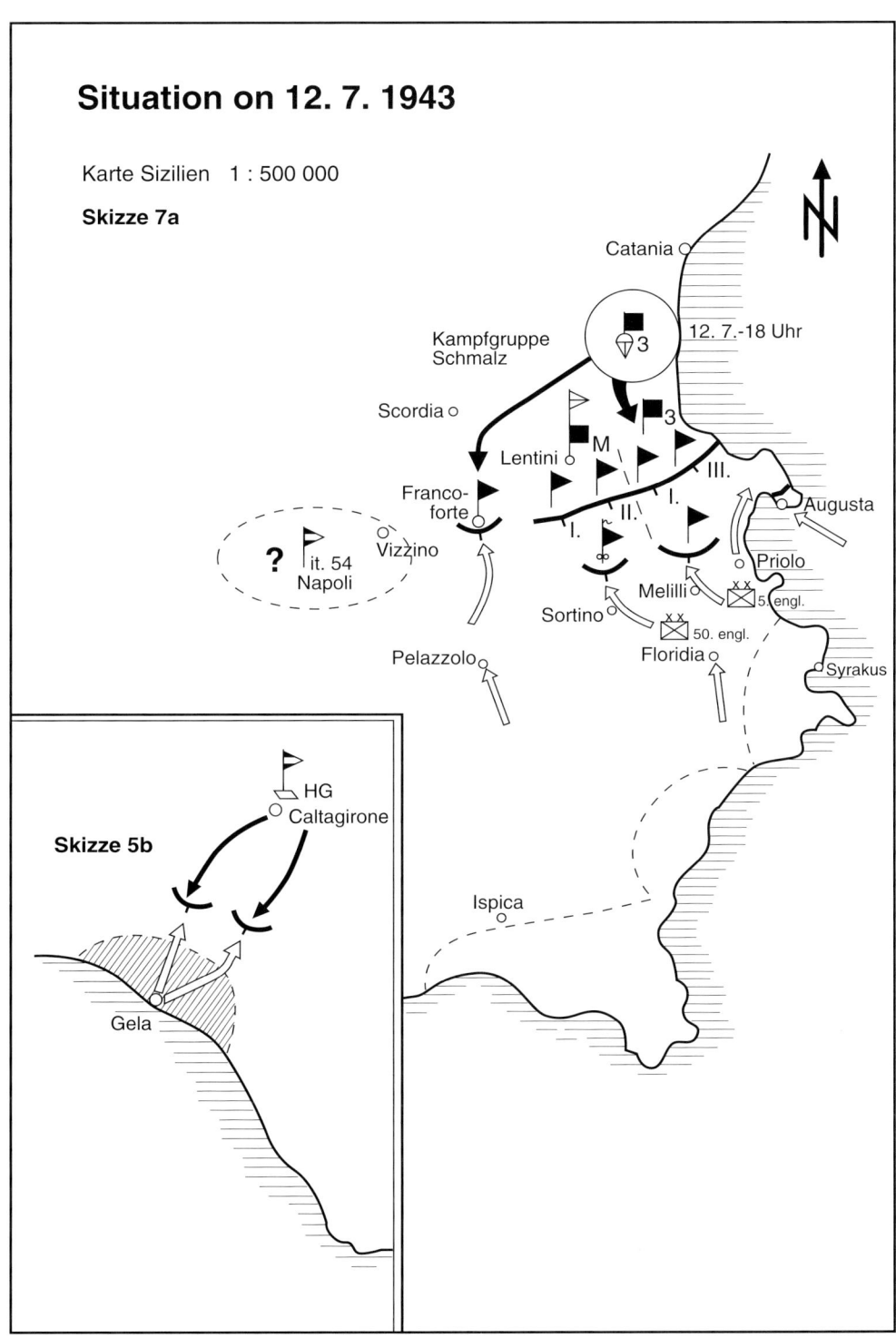

Catania plain, which was vital to our defence. I sent an operations officer to report this state of affairs to the HG Division. What was actually going on near Gela? Where was the 15th Panzer-Grenadier Division, elements of which had been in the Trapani area and near Enna? How would my troops halt the attack to come the next morning? That was my main worry. Would we succeed in stopping the enemy near Lentini? I had no tanks, only a few assault guns, and the three flak batteries which had been in action since the first day.

What would – and this was actually the greatest concern – happen in my rear near Catania?"

When dawn broke on 12 July the men of the Schmalz Brigade were awakened by the thunder of numerous guns and the rattle of machine-gun and rifle fire. The brigade commander called for his car. He wanted to drive forward and see the situation for himself and in this way confirm the reports coming in. His driver, *Feldwebel* Schumacher, reported the car ready.

Wilhelm Schmalz said of his comrade: "Schumacher had been with me for five years. The two of us had already travelled more than 80,000 kilometers in times of peace and war. Attached to each kilometer are unforgettably bitter and happy memories. Germany, Poland, France, the Balkans, and Russia, with their cities, villages, plains, and mountains, in heat, ice and snow, through air and mortar attacks, we were a team and we experienced everything together, he with his unshakably calmness and sure reliability. And no matter what I said to him his reply was always a drawn-out and imperturbable '*jawohl*'."

My escorting NCO, *Feldwebel* Busch, always attentive, always on the spot, was like Schumacher. And then there was my staff officer, *Leutnant* Kleine-Sextro – who was called Sextro Energen by his men – temperamental, always ready with open ears to take in something new, often talking at the wrong time when I was just about to come up with a 'brilliant idea'. Always concerned about me, he was a splendid, considerate comrade. Just as I was about to drive off, the fourth member of the group, my faithful orderly Karl Widham, came running up to the car. He had been with me as long as Schumacher, and both voluntarily went along to wherever I was ordered. He just wanted to ask what he should make for lunch."

There were few commanders with the rank of a Wilhelm Schmalz who readily acknowledged all the men who took care of them and saw to it that they were always ready for action. But that was the way of Wilhelm Schmalz, *Generalleutnant* of the German Wehrmacht and last commander of all the soldiers of the Hermann Göring Parachute Panzer Corps. It was small wonder that these men stayed with him, even in captivity, remaining at his side until they were separated from their commander by force.

The drive to the front began. Everywhere smoke drifted among the hills. The first active battery was reached. The battery chief came up and made his report. Schmalz saw the first stretcher bearers there. They had just brought back the first wounded and were preparing to head back to the front to continue their work. Schmalz also placed a lasting memorial to them in his report on the fighting in Sicily:

"Wearing the Red Cross arm band, they ran across the battlefield as if every bullet had to respect the Geneva Convention. Tirelessly they fulfilled their most difficult duty: caring for their comrades and the helpless. Wherever possible I made a special effort to laud their bravery."

Schmalz arrived at the battalion command post. Comfort packages for the soldiers were passed out from the car. *Major* Kluge reported to the brigade commander. He too was one of the *Reichsmarschall*'s men from the early days. *Major* Kluge drove the brigade commander forward to a lookout point. There was a heavy barrage of naval gunfire and everyone had to take cover.

"We climbed and crawled up the small hill; there a fantastic panorama unfolded before us. Behind us lay Malleoli, before us Priolo, to the right rose the rock plateau and to the left a sparsely covered plain which fell away toward the sea. Then there was the sea and far away the ships, their broadsides toward us. Flashes of fire rose from them long before the shells impacted on the island. Farther below I saw three assault guns by the road. They had driven into cover beneath a dense stand of olive trees. In front of them machine-gun fire flashed from a group of foxholes. British shells were falling everywhere in our front, throwing up fountains of rock and dirt. The impacts increased in number, the smoke and dust grew thicker. Two soldiers dashed through the fire to a wounded man. They saw to his wounds, placed him in a tent square, and carried him back.

Farther to the rear, on the road and in the fields to the left and right, were enemy tanks, their guns flashing in rapid succession. Something special seemed to be going on far to the left. The flashes were more numerous there. I could see enemy infantry. They crawled and ran forward, then took cover again before getting up and gaining a few more meters of ground. This was the attack we had been expecting!"

When *Oberst* Schmalz returned to the command post a report was waiting for him: "Enemy attack repulsed!"

The command car drove the brigade commander back to Lentini at high speed. *Oberst* Schmalz wanted to inspect the positions which were being built there. Satisfied with the state of the work he was generous with his praise and with the cigarettes and chocolate which he always took with him to the front.

Several warships approached the entrance to Augusta harbour. The heavy flak battery there received the order to fire. It took only seconds for the battery to open fire, an indication that the battery chief there had recognized the opportunity. Shots rang out from four eighty-eights. The first salvo fell short of one of the ships but the second scored a hit. The enemy ships made smoke.

Oberst Schmalz called to his driver: "To the flakbattery, Schumacher!" The battery chief made his report to the *Oberst*. One of the gunners reported:

"We got it, *Herr Oberst*! I saw it settle deeply, then the damned smoke obscured my view."

Seconds later there was an alert. The guns were trained toward the sky, in the direction from which the bombers would come. The brigade commander

13 July, 1943: Allied airborne landings at the Simeto bridge. The 5th and 50th British Divisions fight to force a breakthrough.

drove toward the bombers, so as to drive away from their target. On the road was a slow-moving column.

"Looking up, I saw the bombers release their deadly cargo. 'Stop, we're going into the ditch!' I called to Schumacher. He didn't listen, selected a lower gear, gave it the gas and drove under the bombs. Before I could reprimand him I saw that the falling bombs had blasted several craters in the ditch precisely where I had wanted to go. 'Well done Schumacher!'

'Jaaawohl!' he replied dryly. Then he smiled softly, selected a higher gear and drove on."

When *Oberst* Schmalz returned to the brigade command post at noon on that day, the adjutant placed new reports in front of him while orderly Widhahn served up the delicacies he had bought: potatoes, artichokes in hollandaise sauce, and a glass of juice.

The order for the forward elements to disengage themselves from the enemy was given following receipt of reports of growing enemy strength and increasing losses. A short time later a dispatch rider arrived:

"Feldmarschall Kesselring is here!"

Oberst Schmalz reported to the *Feldmarschall*, whose arrival had been delayed by a blocked road near Carlentini. Schmalz described the situation and the outlook. Kesselring told him the details of the Allied landing near Gela and that the counterattack carried out there by the HG Panzer Division alone had failed. Then Kesselring informed the *Oberst* of the arrival of elements of the 1st Parachute Division. The 3rd Parachute Regiment would land from the air in the Catania Plain. The focus of this discussion was the necessity of immediately regrouping the HG Panzer Division. The *Feldmarschall* agreed, but it did not happen until the following day. However, *Oberst* Schmalz at least learned that the division had decided to go over to the defensive with a shortened front along the line of the Catania Plain.

The first elements of the 1st Parachute Division landed in Battle Group Schmalz's battle zone at about 1800 hours on 12 July. Waiting columns of vehicles took the paratroopers to the front. The force consisted of three battalions of the 3rd Parachute Regiment, without their heavy weapons however. *Oberst* Schmalz positioned two battalions east of the Maucke Regiment. The third battalion and a flak battery had to be sent immediately to Francofonte, as the enemy was the point of breaking through there. It was important to hold this town, as its loss would threaten the entire front with collapse.

13 July saw the battle for the new defensive line. Holding onto Francofonte was vital, for after taking possession of this area the enemy could have broken through the entire front and prevented the German units from linking up. On the evening of the 13th a parachute machine-gun battalion was dropped; it was positioned in the area of the mouth of the Simeto and the threat seemed to have been averted. On the evening of that day the enemy directed powerful new attacks against Pancaldo. Pressure on the Malleoli – Lentini road and that from Augusta to Castelluzzo became stronger. Two batteries of artillery were engaged near Lentini, one near Francofonte. All available

artillery forces were thus committed. The anti-aircraft guns were positioned near Lentini and to the east, down to the sea.

Oberst Schmalz committed the infantry as follows: one battalion near Francofonte, and four near Lentini and to the east to the sea. The armored personnel carrier battalion remained at readiness northwest of Lentini as a mobile reserve. It had suffered considerable losses in the first days of the invasion through its delaying defensive tactics. The parachute machine-gun battalion guarded the bridge over the Simeto. During the course of 13 July the reserve infantry battalion south of Paterno was assigned to the Maucke Infantry Regiment to make good losses suffered by the unit. Due to a shortage in available transport space the men of the 1st Parachute Division were slow in arriving. Their greatest handicap was a lack of heavy weapons. West of the battle group's right wing a large gap still separated it from the HG Panzer Division.

Kampfgruppe Schmalz continued to receive orders from Headquarters, Italian Sixth Army. All were impossible to carry out, as the orders involved Italian units which were nowhere near where their supreme command suspected them to be. Late on the afternoon of 13 July telephone communications were established with division command. In this way *Oberst* Schmalz learned of the following directive: "All elements of the division are to meet in the prepared positions at the northern edge of the Catania Plain on the morning of 15 July 1943. Establishment there of a main line of resistance on a line Leonforte-Catania Nuova-Gerbini-Catania. Rear guards will remain in contact with the enemy, employing delaying tactics."

For reinforced *Kampfgruppe* Schmalz, this meant fighting a delaying action on 13 and 14 July to prevent the enemy from getting past the unit's positions. An enemy air attack on the evening of 13 July destroyed the sole bridge on the south side of the city. Luckily for the brigade, its heavy weapons were already north of the bridge.

During the course of 13 July this weak main line of resistance was pushed back by powerful enemy attacks, roughly in a line southern edge of Lentini-Minella-Castelluzzo. This was the last possible position before the Catania position and was to be held at all costs. The next day would thus be decisive. When the commander of the 1st Parachute Machine-gun Battalion, *Major* Werner Schmidt, reported to the brigade commander on the evening of 13 July, *Oberst* Schmalz was in high spirits. He said to the *Major*:

"Watch out! In the coming night there will be a surprise from the enemy side in the Catania Plain, which will find us not unprepared. Either the enemy will land from the sea or drop troops from the air, with the object of cutting us off and taking possession of the Catania Plain. You and your battalion stay at the Simeto bridge at the highest alert readiness."

This foresight on the part of *Oberst* Schmalz was to be confirmed. During the night of 14 July English paratroops were dropped near the Simeto bridge at the Catania – Lentini road.

General Montgomery: "13th Corps Has Broken Through on the Catania Plain"

By 13 July the advance by the British Eighth Army had slowed, and the units of the American Seventh Army, including the 45th Infantry Division – which had advanced to a point just south of Caltagirone – received orders to turn back toward the coast road. On the morning of 14 July the 45th Infantry Division was still advancing along the Vizzini – Caltagirone road in order to open the way to Enna, site of the Italian headquarters. Faced with this situation General Patton, Commander-in-Chief of the Seventh Army, had the commander of the US 2nd Corps, Omar N. Bradley, summoned to his headquarters in Gela. Patton informed Bradley that the 45th Infantry Division was to suspend its attack toward the north and instead drive west along the south coast road. This would require General Bradley to withdraw the 45th Infantry Division to the beach and redeploy it on the left flank of the 1st Infantry Division. General Bradley protested, but without success. General Alexander, the Allied Commander-in-Chief, had resolved the situation to the advantage of the Eighth Army. Montgomery now prepared to launch an attack in the Catania Plain near Lentini with the British 30th Corps.

As the first step he committed the 1st Airborne Brigade under Brigadier Lathbury and a commando unit to seize two bridges: the Ponte dei Malati, north of the Lentini hills, and the bridge over the Simeto near Primasole. The 1st Airborne Brigade received orders to take the Simeto bridge and establish a bridgehead on the north side, while the commando detachment, after landing west of Agnone, was to seize the Ponte dei Malati and secure the bridge. Lathbury's soldiers and the commandoes were then to link up and establish contact with the 50th Infantry Division.

At about sundown on 13 July 105 Dakotas loaded with paratroops took off from six airfields around Kairouan. Thirty Horsa gliders also took part in the operation, towed by nineteen Halifax and Stirling bombers and eleven Albemarle glider tugs. The Horsas carried anti-tank guns, jeeps and light artillery to the landing zone. Three aircraft carrying paratroops aborted their takeoffs, as did three gliders. The loss of the latter was more important.

When the formations passed over the Allied fleet, the ships mistook them for German bomber units and opened fire. A few minutes earlier several Ju 88s had attacked the port of Augusta, and the defenders suspected that this was the main force. Several machines were hit by the ships' anti-aircraft fire. Then the German flak joined in. A number of aircraft and gliders went down in flames. The pilots released their paratroops immediately and randomly, so as to be able to turn around as quickly as possible and escape the joint fire from friend and foe.

The machines flying directly toward Primasole were met by heavy machine-gun fire. It was the Parachute Machine-gun Battalion under *Major* Schmidt which had assembled there "to greet the paratroops from the other side". A single machine-gun platoon shot down three gliders, the rest were forced to turn away by the curtain of fire. Another machine-gun platoon succeeded in shooting down three troop transports. The operation had begun

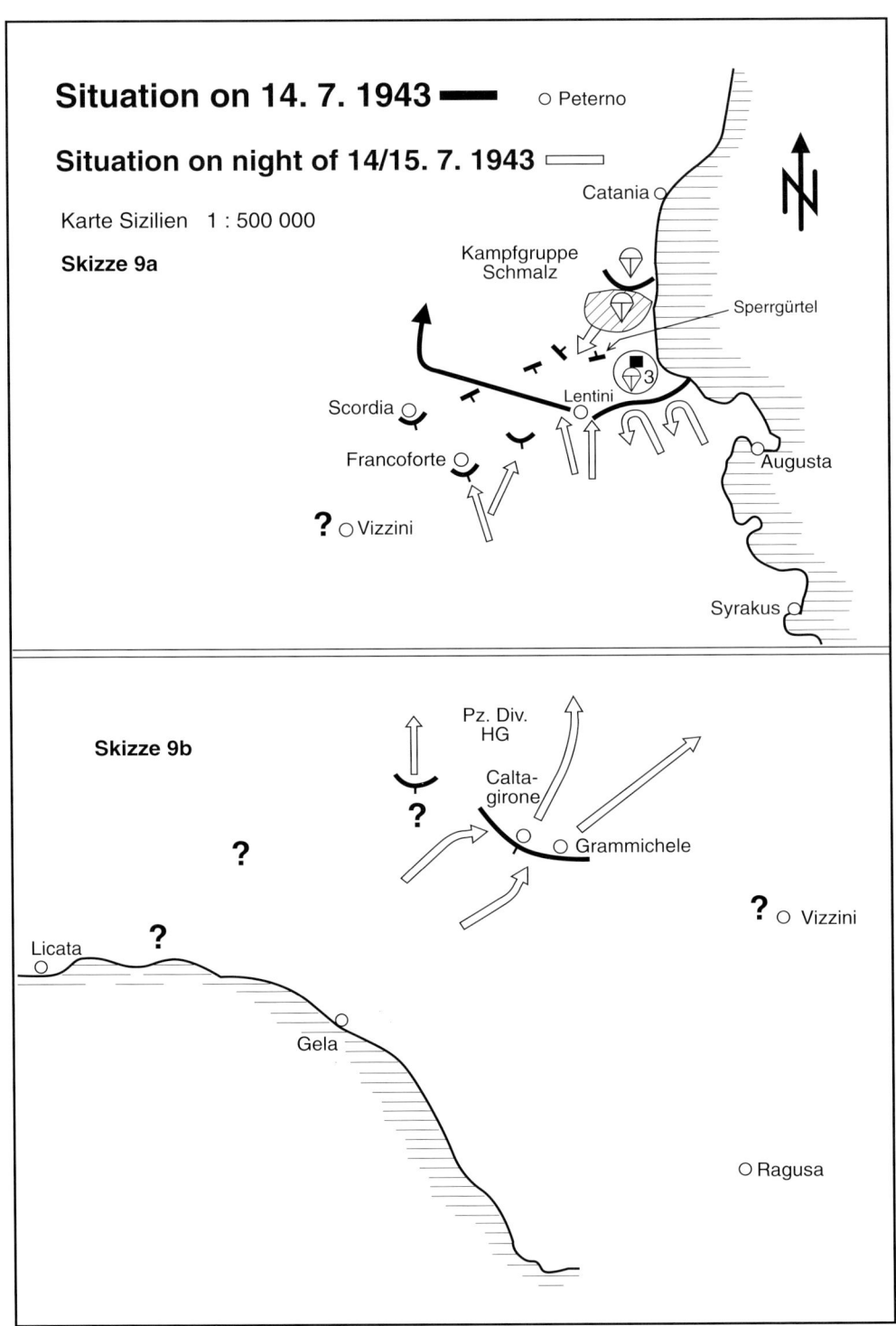

with the loss of more than twenty aircraft. A further large number had been hit and turned away. Lathbury's 1st Airborne Brigade alone had lost 300 men in this way. Eighty-two British soldiers were taken prisoner by the Parachute Machine-gun Battalion. Nevertheless, 22% of the paratroops came down in the general area of the Primasole bridge. Brigadier Lathbury still had available a fifth of his intended combat strength. The leading group of paratroopers reached the south end of the bridge unmolested. At that moment firing flared up at the north end. There, elements of the brigade's I Battalion had fired on and set on fire four German supply trucks which had just crossed the bridge. The British engineers removed the wires and explosives from the supports of the Simeto bridge. The elements of I and III Battalions which had reached the bridge dug in in a semi-circle around it. The Italian soldiers guarding the bridge had run away.

At about 1000 hours on 14 July several German Bf 109s appeared and fired on the troops defending the bridge. They also strafed with their cannon the hill south of the bridge, where the British 2nd Battalion had gone into position. The paratroopers opened fire on the Messerschmitts with machine-guns. Soon afterward German heavy anti-aircraft guns opened fire on the bridge from Catania. Then a lone German soldier on a motorcycle approached the bridge. It was *Hauptmann* Stangenberg from the HQ of the 1st Parachute Division, who was on his way to 3rd Regiment. Stangenberg was fired on by the enemy; he turned back and alerted the division that British paratroops were holding the Simeto bridge, blocking the only route to Battle Group Schmalz and the 3rd Parachute Regiment. *Hauptmann* Stangenberg sealed off the area north of the bridge with a heavy flak battery and several dozen men. Then he drove back to Catania and got in touch with *Generalleutnant* Heidrich, his division commander who was still in Rome, and informed him of the enemy seizure of the bridge. He requested the release of the division's radio company, which was in Catania. This was approved, and at 1500 hours the unit arrived near the bridge under the command of *Oberleutnant* Fassel.

The 3rd Commando under Lieutenant Colonel Slater landed near Agnone in assault boats at the same time as the parachute drops. While still at sea they came under fire from 2nd Company, 3rd Parachute Regiment and a still-functioning coastal battery. Near Stazione Agnone the commandoes came upon the command post of 3rd Company, 3rd Parachute Regiment. *Oberleutnant* of the Reserve Veth, the company commander, fought off the attackers, who turned away toward the north. Nevertheless, advancing through the Lentini Valley, Major Young and his battle group reached the Ponte dei Malati at about 0300 hours on 14 July and removed the explosive charges which had been installed there. He and his men established a bridgehead facing north. The commando was about to cross over the bridge to the southwest bank, but it was stopped by a single Tiger tank. The Tiger had driven forward from Battle Group Schmalz and it now placed the bridge under fire. Efforts to silence the tank with light weapons were fruitless.

By late morning there was still no sign of the 50th Infantry Division. German pressure was becoming too strong, and Lieutenant Colonel Slater

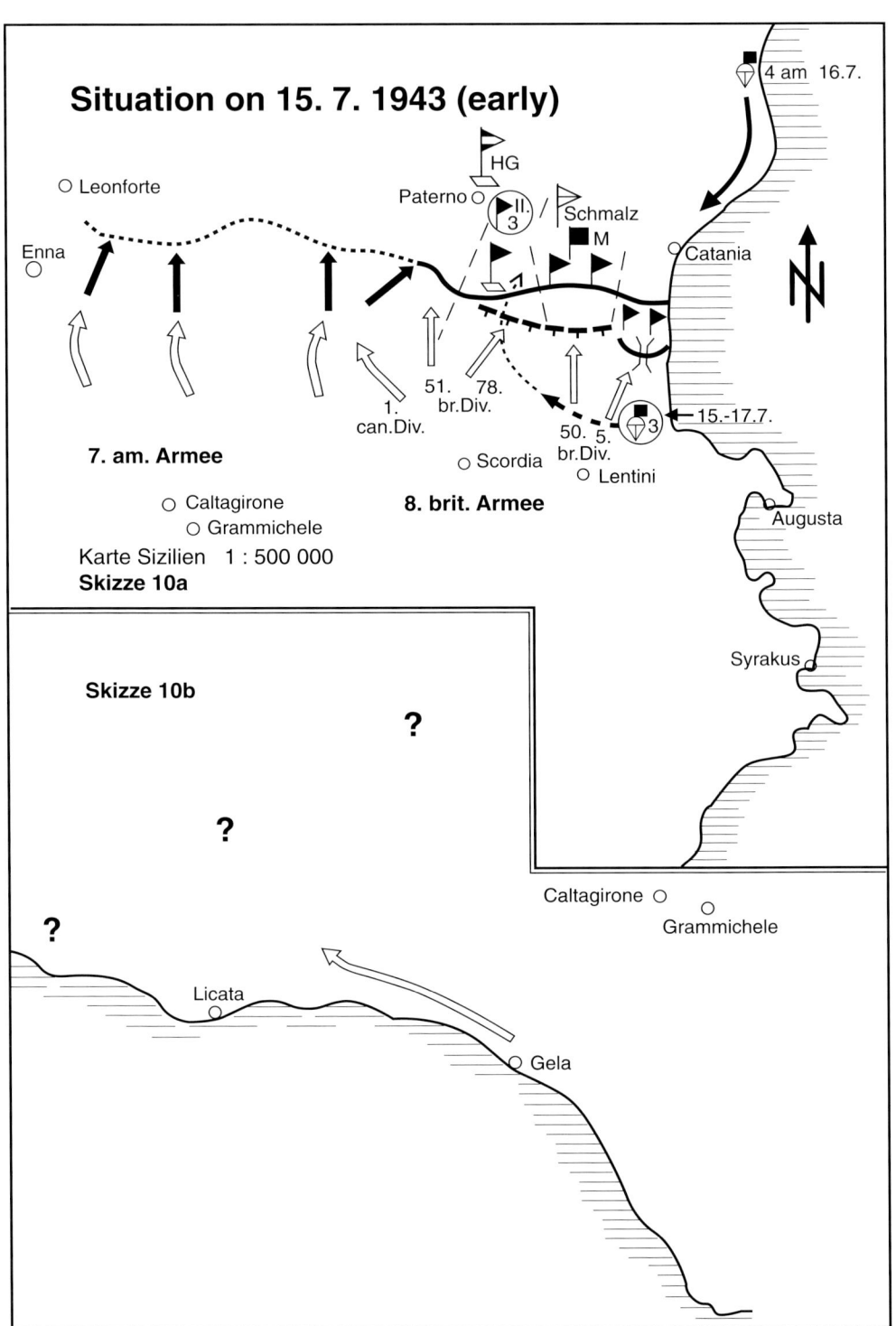

divided his men into small groups and ordered them to find a crossing east of the bridge and to make their way to their own lines. The individual groups of commandoes ran into the paratroopers of the 3rd Regiment and were captured. Nevertheless, the commando detachment's mission had been a success, because it had succeeded in removing the explosive charges from the Lentini bridge.

The British 50th Infantry Division now made a vigorous advance. Supported by tanks, late on the afternoon of 14 July the division succeeded in outflanking the eastern wing of the German defence and drove through Lentini. On the morning of 15 July the armored spearheads reached the Primasole bridge. This had been abandoned a few hours earlier by the 1st Parachute Brigade, because it had no more ammunition. The few German defenders had tried to reach the bridge from the north bank and blow it up with anti-tank mines, but the attempt failed.

Retreat to the Catania Position

The Parachute Pioneer Battalion, which had dropped near Catania, and a light parachute artillery battalion received orders to remain in the landing area and to occupy the prepared positions at the northern edge of the plain, establish contact with the machine-gun battalion at the Simeto, and support this unit in its battle for the bridge position. The troops of the Schmalz Brigade withdrew across the bridge near Favotto beginning in the late afternoon of the 14th; by the early morning of 15 July the entire brigade had crossed. This nocturnal withdrawal was a great test of nerve, for there was only one road and one bridge. If the enemy spotted these withdrawal movements too early and pursued hard with strong forces, everything would be at risk.

Weak groups remained in the front while the main body got aboard its vehicles and departed. The APC Battalion, reinforced by assault guns and artillery, formed a thin blocking line at all the inbound roads, in order to deal with any surprises which might come from there. Had the enemy approached along the Raitano – Scordia road, he would be stopped by these units which, though small in number, possessed considerable firepower. The elements of the brigade departed according to a predetermined sequence, avoiding all unnecessary noise. There was a brief exchange of fire south of Raitano. The troops which had been forced to evacuate Francofonte in the face of overpowering enemy pressure also had contact with the enemy near Scordia.

The sending of dispatches to the individual units had worked well; all units confirmed that they would withdraw in the specified order. A dispatch rider from 3rd Parachute Regiment arrived at the brigade command post during the night of 15 July and reported that his CO, *Oberstleutnant* Ludwig Heilmann, had said:

"Where German paratroopers stand, there is no retreat."

This was a *faux pas*. Not only was Heilmann's attitude not in keeping with the situation at the front, but he was committing an act of military disobedience as well. As *Oberst* Schmalz couldn't drive there, he radioed Heilmann and instructed him to move out immediately. However, by the time Heilmann did move, he was already surrounded and had to fight his way out with his regiment. (II Battalion was surrounded in Francofonte but managed to fight its way out under the command of *Hauptmann* Günther. Günther was captured during the breakout, as was *Oberleutnant* Magold, commander of the regiment's 13th Company.) For the remaining two battalions capture seemed a certainty. That *Oberstleutnant* Heilmann nevertheless succeeded in bringing them back through enemy lines was a major achievement. Nevertheless, in the process he lost 200 of his best men. *Generalleutnant* Schmalz said of this after the war:

"One can imagine my concern on the morning of 15 July, when Heilmann and his 800 men had still not yet arrived. I was forced to report that I had arrived in the new position, but without the 3rd Parachute Regiment. This was extremely embarrassing and questions rained down from the high command. As I did not wish to report that the regiment's commander had not carried out my orders, blame for its failure to arrive was placed on me.

When, on the afternoon of 16 July, a 3rd Parachute Regiment dispatch rider arrived and reported that the regimental commander and all his people were just beyond the English lines and would break through to us during the night of the 16th, a great weight fell from my shoulders. The entire front was informed that friendly troops would be coming from the enemy side of the line in the coming night.

On the morning of 17 July the paratroops had still not yet arrived. Instead *Generalfeldmarschall* Kesselring appeared at my command post. He agreed with all of my orders, but informed me that Führer Headquarters was highly displeased. My only reply was that I still expected the regiment to turn up that day. *Feldmarschall* Kesselring's astonishment culminated in his admonition that he very much hoped so for my sake. A little later the news reached me: "The 3rd Parachute Regiment is through and is behind our lines!"

The regimental commander appeared at the brigade command post a short time later. He made his report to *Feldmarschall* Kesselring, who had waited. With pure sunshine on all our faces, Kesselring drove off and I fortified myself with a good breakfast.

Until today (the writing of his Sicilian report) I have never said why the regiment did not arrive when it should have. That could have had severe consequences for *Oberst* Heilmann. That is why the *Feldmarschall* took no action against the commander of the 3rd Parachute Regiment. Now years have passed and all is forgiven."

Following an inspection drive through the new positions on the northern edge of the plain, *Oberst* Schmalz received a report from the Gerbini area on the right wing that contact had been made there with elements of the HG Division coming from Gela. Before the defenders lay the great Catania Plain. To the left front was the city of Catania and the sea with the English warships. To the south, at the end of the huge plain, lay the Lentini Hills. Militarily this combat zone could be observed down to the last detail. The Hermann Göring Division assumed command in this new Leonforte –

Catania sector. The 3rd and 4th Parachute Regiments were placed under the command of the Schmalz Brigade. The 4th Parachute Regiment commanded by *Oberst* Erich Walther had arrived on 16 July. It was deployed at Catania airfield. The Parachute Pioneer Battalion fought a sacrificial battle at the Simeto bridge near Raitano. Its commander, *Hauptmann* Paul Adolff, tried personally to blow up the bridge several times. Adolff was killed on 17 July while attempting to take aerial bombs onto the bridge in a truck and arm them there. (The actions of this brave soldier and his battalion were acknowledged in the posthumous awarding of the Knight's Cross on 26 March 1944.)

An Italian artillery battalion linked up with the APC Battalion near Totondella. Its commander, *Tenente-Colonel* Guglieri, led this battalion, which was well-supplied with ammunition, well and provided very useful assistance. His battalion's performance was outstanding. It had courageous observers for target spotting and the conduct of its officers was exemplary. *Tenente-Colonel* Guglieri received the Iron Cross, First Class from the hand of *Oberst* Schmalz. A short time later a second Italian artillery battalion, a heavy coastal battery near Misterbianco, joined the firefight. It, too, fought to the last shell, before blowing up its guns.

The Second Phase of the Battle and the Retreat

The commanding general of XIV Panzer Corps, *General der Panzertruppe* Hans Hube, had arrived on Sicily with his closest staff on 12 July. On 14 July overall command was passed to this panzer corps. The orders, reports and directives from Headquarters, Italian Sixth Army had become irrelevant, for there were scarcely any Italian units still fighting on the island. Nevertheless, at first the Italian headquarters continued to lead a shadowy existence.

On 15 July *General* von Senger of the German Liaison Staff transferred his command post into the area north of Catania. From there he had a direct wire link to *Generalfeldmarschall* Kesselring and could also contact the Hermann Göring Panzer Division and the Schmalz Brigade directly. *General* Hube soon gained a firm grip on the reins and established an orderly conduct of battle, thus ending the crisis in the Italian-German command that had existed since 10 July. All forces could now be concentrated toward carrying out a step-by-step withdrawal.

On 17 July *General* Hube officially took command of Axis forces on the island. The main concern of XIV Corps Headquarters had to be the keeping open of the Strait of Messina for marine traffic, in order to assure the delivery of supplies to the troops on the island and to enable them to be conveyed to the mainland at a later date. The order to remove unnecessary services and installations to the mainland was issued by *General* Hube without the approval of the OKW. Everything was arranged. *Oberst* Ernst-Günther Baade became Commandant Messina Strait. Command of the Calabria area on the opposite side of the strait was given to *Generalleutnant* Heidrich as his 1st Parachute Regiment was attached to the HG Panzer Division and he was available. However back to the front.

The enemy continued to attack the sector held by the reinforced Hermann Göring Panzer Division in an effort to gain further ground. Heavy fighting broke out for possession of the Primasole bridge. Strong attacks near Gerbini were beaten off and enemy penetrations cleared.

On 17 July *Generalfeldmarschall* Kesselring once again made his way to the command post of *Oberst* Schmalz. It was his opinion that the main line of resistance at the Simeto should be held; *Oberst* Schmalz made reference to the special difficulties which the open plain presented the enemy. As he told the Field Marshall, he was convinced that the enemy would have to advance across the open plain, that all of his supplies would have to be brought up under the eyes of the Germans, and that he would also have to bring his artillery into position on the open plain. These were advantages that the defence should not surrender voluntarily. Albert Kesselring accepted *Oberst* Schmalz's proposal. As a result of this decision the enemy, in spite of all his efforts, failed to break into the German positions. Not until the night of 6 August were the positions abandoned voluntarily by the defenders as part of a general withdrawal.

Catania lay under almost continuous bombardment by the Allied bomber squadrons. Intercepted radio messages revealed that the enemy was preparing for a new attack. The German tactics in this battle were of a delaying nature, with the final objective of conveying all troops to the mainland for the expected fight there. This decision raised morale. For the subsequent conduct of the battle the corps specified lines to which the troops were to withdraw when enemy pressure became too great. In each case strong rear guards were to maintain contact with the enemy.

On 16 July General Montgomery ordered the 51st Infantry Division to advance toward Paterno, in order to support operations by the 30th Corps there. That evening the division crossed the Simeto; the bridge had been abandoned the night before. During the night of 20 July the 129th Panzer-Grenadier Regiment, which was still under the command of the HG Panzer Division, withdrew north through Alimena. Not until 21 July did the enemy follow, and then only cautiously. That same day the 15th Panzer-Grenadier Division under *Generalmajor* Rodt became involved in heavy fighting in the Leonforte area. The division held.

On 21 July the Hermann Göring Panzer Division had under its command the following units:

Division CO: Generalmajor Paul Conrath
Division Headquarters:

Battle Group von Carnap: Oberstleutnant von Carnap
I Battalion, 3rd Parachute Regiment
IV Battalion, Armored Artillery Regiment HG
923rd Fortress Battery
5 reconnaissance squads

Battle Group Schmalz: Oberst Wilhelm Schmalz
115th Panzer-Grenadier Regiment (formerly Battle Group Körner)
III Battalion, HG Armored Artillery Regiment
III Battalion, HG Panzer Regiment
Schachtleben Battalion
4th Parachute Regiment   Oberst Walther
2 batteries of the Catania Flak Group
2 battalions of the 382nd Infantry Regiment
904th Fortress Battalion
I Battalion, HG Flak Regiment

Battle Group Preuss: Major Joachim Preuß
II Battalion, HG Panzer Regiment
One Flak unit

Battle Group Kluge: Major Waldemar Kluge
I Battalion, HG Panzer-Grenadier Regiment
I Battalion, HG Armored Artillery Regiment
Oria Tank Battalion
10 reconnaissance squads
I Battalion, HG Panzer Regiment (from Div. Reserve)

Battle Group Rebholz: Hauptmann Robert Rebholz
HG Armored Reconnaissance Battalion
II Battalion, HG Armored Artillery Regiment
Reggio Fortress Battalion
9 armored reconnaissance patrols
II Battalion, HG Panzer-Grenadier Regiment

Division Reserve: I Battalion, HG Panzer Regiment
3rd Parachute
Regiment (less one battalion)

The Final Battle – Withdrawal & the Crossing of the Strait of Messina

XIV Panzer Corps set itself the task of at least getting the German troops and all the weapons they could carry back to the mainland. In addition everything possible was to be done to also save the heavy weapons, vehicles, and equipment. Given the available ships and Siebel ferries, five nights would be required to transport the troops – about 50,000 men in total. *General* Hube and his XIV Corps Headquarters based their plans on this minimum requirement.

On 7 August *General* Hube called together the commanders of the three

German divisions (the first third of the 29th Panzer-Grenadier Division had arrived on the island by 25 July and was steadily reinforced, so that it was able to participate in the final phase of the battle in the northern part of the island, halting an advance by American troops on the north road) at the corps command post, located due north of Enna. Also in attendance were *Generalmajor* Stahel, commander of all anti-aircraft units in Sicily and on the mainland side of the Strait of Messina; the naval officer in charge of ferry traffic in the strait; *Generalleutnant* Heidrich, commander of the 1st Parachute Regiment, who had been made responsible for coastal defence in Calabria; and *General* von Senger.

General Hube gave all the officers the verbal order for the evacuation of the island five nights from a yet to be named X-Day. All of the commanders prepared these movements carefully. The "starting shot" for the withdrawal was fired when elements of the American 3rd Infantry Division landed in the rear of the 29th Panzer-Grenadier Division near Agata on 8 August and at Brolo on the 11th. 11 August was designated as X-Day.

On the night of 11 August the divisions were assigned specified nights, loading sites, and assembly areas. The corps command post was moved to the Barcellona area and finally into the area southwest of Messina. The corps headquarters' plan ran smoothly and without interruption. The divisions were allowed an additional night and an entire day in an intermediate defensive line to enable all the heavy weapons to be shipped to the mainland. Thanks to this masterfully-organized, smooth-functioning system, it was possible to ship the last man and the last vehicle to the mainland as programmed.

By the afternoon of 16 August it was apparent that the daring evacuation plan was going to be a complete success. Only then did the command and corps staff cross over to the mainland, where they established a new corps headquarters in the Reggio area. *General* Hube remained on the island with several operations officers. He left Sicily on the morning of 17 August 1943 – in the best German tradition – on the last boat. The German command and combat forces – abandoned by their Italian brothers in arms – had held out against far superior forces on the island for 38 days before conducting an orderly withdrawal. *General der Panzertruppe* Hube had been a rock amid the waves. *Oberst* von Bonin, XIV Panzer Corps Chief-of-Staff, had this to say of Hube:

"General Hube took no unnecessary risks, instead he merely added twenty-four hours to the original timetable without making a great fuss, although it was absolutely possible to gain even more time. His reward was the complete success of the mission given the corps. Brave and ever ready for action, always calm, deliberate, never fickle, and always ready to take full responsibility for a measure he recognized as necessary, even when it was dangerous and might at least have cost him his position."

Thanks to the efficiency of their command, on 17 August 1943 the three German divisions were back on the Italian mainland and fully operational. They had defied the four-fold superiority of the enemy, whose air and sea forces were unopposed, and reached the safety of the Italian mainland.

Nevertheless the German forces left behind 10,000 soldiers – dead, wounded and missing. Seen objectively, the highest levels of German command – the OKW and Führer Headquarters – also played a decisive role in the success in that neither interfered with the measures taken by *General* Hube. They obviously wanted to avoid another disaster like Stalingrad and Tunis and had no wish to precipitate a further catastrophe through their interference. Nonetheless, Hitler was dissatisfied with the outcome; he therefore denied *General* Hube any decorations or official recognition for the command of his forces on the island and their subsequent withdrawal, even though *Generalfeldmarschall* Kesselring proposed just that.

Consequently, the presentation to Hube of the Order of the Italians, one of the highest decorations that country had to offer, by the Italian Crown Prince Umberto on 30 August was in effect a slap in the face to the German Supreme Command. However, the conferring of this award on Hube confirmed a phenomenon seen and noted several times before, namely that in the Italian theater of war the Italian command had a better feeling for outstanding feats than did the German. This cannot, however, conceal the fact that *Generalfeldmarschall* Rommel's accomplishments were never acknowledged by the Italians, especially by Mussolini. After these marginal notes back to Sicily and to a necessary final observation which has not or only partially been dealt with in publications relating to Sicily.

The fact that the German troops succeeded in returning to the Italian mainland, not just with their hand-held weapons but with all their materiel and heavy weapons as well, was due in large part to one special unit.

The Ferry Flotillas in the Strait of Messina

The final phase of the battle in Sicily saw the HG Panzer Division, the 15th and 29th Panzer-Grenadier Divisions, elements of the 1st Parachute Division, and a few Italian units shipped across the Strait of Messina to the Italian mainland. For six days and nights the men of the 771st Pioneer Landing Unit under *Hauptmann* Paul were in the focus of events. The ferry flotillas of the Luftwaffe also took part in the evacuation. Each of the Luftwaffe flotillas consisted of four armed ferries and four transport ferries, as well as a repair boat. The ferries were Siebel ferries, so named for their designer, a Luftwaffe *Oberst* named Siebel. With a length of 24 meters, a width of 16 meters and a draught of only 0.6 meters, they were pioneer pontoons joined together catamaran fashion. Two rows of pontoons, spaced ten meters apart, and bridged by sturdy, impregnated planks produced a wide, sturdy platform. The two forward pontoons were slanted downward like a ship's bow to better cut through the water, while the two aft pontoons were rounded off. This gave the monstrosity the approximate appearance of a wide boat. Power was provided by two BMW 6 engines.

In the center of each ferry was the 2.5-meter-high anti-aircraft platform with four 20mm quadruple light flak and one 20mm or 37mm weapon. This applied to the armed ferries; the transport ferries had only a single 20mm or 37mm weapon on the flak platform. Landing craft were modified to serve as repair boats. They were also employed to transport important goods. The crew of each ferry crews consisted of the commander, two radio operators, two signalmen, two motor mechanics, and the gun crews. The gun crew of an armed ferry consisted of a *Feldwebel* and 29 NCOs and men. An NCO and five men made up the gun crew of a transport ferry.

Ferry Flotilla II was under the command of *Major* Karl Pruss, former captain of the airship LZ 129 *Hindenburg*. Until the beginning of 1943 he and his flotilla were employed on security duties on the Gironde between Bordeaux and the Atlantic. His main mission was combatting enemy aircraft attacking German merchant shipping and U-boats and the U-Boat support base at Bordeaux. In early 1943 *Hauptmann* Schönherr assumed command of the flotilla. Under his command the ferries were disassembled and shipped overland to Portici on the Bay of Naples, where they were reassembled in preparation for use in the transport role, carrying supplies to Africa. However the ferries saw no action there. They were instead employed in the anti- aircraft role along the coast of southern Italy. Following their great success there, they were transferred to the Strait of Messina just in time to take part in the withdrawal of German troops from Sicily to the mainland. Ferry Flotilla II began operations in the Strait of Messina on 10 August 1943.

Pioneers had erected landing bridges at the ferry landings on both shores of the Strait of Messina. Invisible from the air, the soldiers with their weapons waited in the ravines for the signal to board the ferries. There was little notice when the call came to move up. The entire embarkation was carried out with extreme discipline. During the evacuation every bit of available space on the ferries was used. Not a single ferry was lost in the course of the entire evacuation operation. Each ferry was loaded with two trucks carrying munitions or equipment, two APCs carrying munitions, or two guns with prime movers. As additional cargo came 40 soldiers with their personal weapons and packs. Each repair boat, which was loaded with minor replacement parts, also took on 50 soldiers.

The armed ferries sailed in line astern, with 800 to 1,000 meters between vessels, in full battle readiness. Positioned between them were the transport ferries and the repair boat. Crossings went on without interruption, twenty-four hours a day. The flotilla commander and the flak officer were always aboard one of the armed ferries. Transmission of orders from boat to boat was by signal-lamp and radio. Flag signals were used by day. II Flotilla had available three landing sites on each side of the strait. The flak defenses were kept manned and ready during all phases of embarkation and disembarkation.

When the air attack alarm was sounded the entire ferry crew and all members of the gun crew came on deck. The numerous low-level attacks were stopped by concentrated anti-aircraft fire. None of the low-flying aircraft got through the curtain of flak. Aerial torpedoes simply passed beneath the shallow-draught ferries. All repairs and maintenance work had to be carried out while the ferries were under way.

During the six days of the evacuation Ferry Flotilla II was able to transport to the mainland: 13,120 soldiers with weapons and packs, 256 trucks and APCs each with equipment and ammunition, 256 guns with prime movers.

Also participating in the evacuation, from 1 to 18 August 1943, was the 771st Pioneer Landing Unit under *Hauptmann* Paul. Its eighteen landing boats were in continuous use and shipped many wounded to the mainland. During these actions, which began before the general evacuation of the island, eleven landing boats were lost, including four which were clearly marked as hospital ships.

In the period 1 - 18 August this unit transferred from Sicily to the mainland: 3,305 trucks, 1,255 cars, 488 motorcycles, 37 prime movers, 6 Panzer IV tanks, 35 guns, 27,814 men (including 13,532 wounded to Scilla), 9,936 tonnes of materiel.

On the last night of the evacuation four ferries transported to the mainland: 413 men, 35 trucks, 34 88mm Flak, 8 prime movers, 1 trailer, one Panzer IV. In total 626.2 tonnes. (Source: Bundesarchiv/Militärarchiv, Freiburg: III M (F) 129/14 and KTB 1./Skl, page 419)

On 22 August 1943 the Sea Transport Chief Italy reported to the Commander-in-Chief of the *Kriegsmarine*:

"Total deliveries by the Kriegsmarine in crossing traffic between Sicily and the mainland have increased to: 38,836 men, 5,069 wounded, 10,356 vehicles. 110 guns, 47 tanks, 1,122 tonnes of ammunition. 970 tonnes of fuel, 15,736 tonnes of equipment."

Any commentary on this unique accomplishment would be superfluous – the numbers speak for themselves.

At this point a depiction of the strength and organization of all the units deployed in Sicily. From 10 July until 17 August 1943 they and their commanders had to take on an enemy possessing a four-fold superiority in forces in a wild country beneath a blazing sun. Alternating between delaying tactics and static defence, the German defenders succeeded in repeatedly stopping or delaying the enemy's advance in spite of the latter's total air superiority and unimpeded support by naval gunfire. The cost to the Hermann Göring Panzer Division was a heavy toll in dead, wounded and sick.

Commanders of the German Forces in Sicily
Headquarters, XIV Panzer Corps

Commanding General	General der Panzertruppe Hube
Chief of Staff	General Staff Oberst von Bonin (as of 16 July 1943) (previously Gen. Staff Oberst G. Thunert)
1st General Staff Officer	General Staff Oberst Birck

29th Panzer-Grenadier Division

Commanding Officer	Generalmajor Fries
1st General Staff Officer	General Staff Oberstleutnant Stünzner

15th Panzer-Grenadier Division

Commanding Officer	Generalmajor Rodt
1st General Staff Officer	General Staff Oberst Heckel

Hermann Göring Panzer Division

Commanding Officer	Generalmajor Conrath
1st General Staff Officer	General Staff Oberstleutnant Bergengruen
Commandant Messina Strait	Oberst Baade
Naval Commandant Messina	Fregattenkapitän von Liebenstein
Commander Calabria Base	Generalleutnant Heidrich (Commander 1st Parachute Division)

Leader of the German Liaison Staff with Headquarters, Italian 6th Army
                                Generalmajor von Senger und Etterlin

Strength and Organization of the Divisions in Sicily

(1) 29th Panzer-Grenadier Division

Division headquarters with dispatch rider platoon, map section, military police squad
2 Panzer-grenadier regiments (each with 3 battalions)
Armored reconnaissance battalion (5 companies)
Panzer battalion (3 companies each with 10 assault guns)
Artillery regiment with 2 light (one self-propelled) and 1 heavy battalion
Pioneer battalion
Army flak battalion (2 heavy, 1 light batteries)
Signals battalion
Supply service with columns and 2 repair-shop companies
2 First-aid companies
1 Ambulance platoon
Ration supply office
1 Bakery company
1 Butchery company
Army post office

Notes:

(a) At the beginning of its deployment to Sicily the division was up to authorized strength in personnel and weapons. Vehicle complement was below authorized strength but adequate to ensure the division's mobility.

(b) Armored reconnaissance battalion, panzer battalion (less one company) and rear-echelon services were not deployed to Sicily but remained on the mainland.

(2) 15th Panzer-Grenadier Division

(information supplied by Generalleutnant Rodt)

2 Panzer-grenadier regiments (each with 3 battalions)

Armored reconnaissance battalion (3 companies)

Panzer battalion (3 companies with a total of about 60 Panzer III and IV tanks) artillery regiment with 2 light (1 on self-propelled carriages) and 1 heavy battalion.

Pioneer battalion

Army flak battalion

Signals battalion

Rear-echelon services as 29th Panzer-Grenadier Division

The Hermann Göring Panzer Division in Sicily as of 10 July 1943

(A) Command List

Division Commander Generalmajor Conrath

Ia	General Staff Oberstleutnant Bergengrün
Ib	Oberstleutnant (W) Bobrowski
II	Major Beinhofer
III	Oberkriegsgerichtsrat Jagow (?)
IVa	Oberfeldzahlmeister Klöpfel
IVb	Oberfeldarzt Dr. ?
V	Major Schmudlach

(B) Organization of Forces

1. On 10 July 1943 at the beginning of the invasion

(a) HG Division Units

Headquarters Hermann Göring Division

HG Division Map Section

HG Military Band

HG Special Purpose Panzer-Grenadier Brigade

1st Panzer-Grenadier Regiment HG

Regimental Headquarters

I Battalion (APC)

Battalion Headquarters

1st-3rd Panzer-Grenadier Companies (armored)

4th Heavy Company (armored)

II Battalion (motorized)

5th-7th Panzer-Grenadier Companies (motorized)

8th (heavy) Company (motorized)

III (Assault Gun) Battalion
9th-11th Panzer-Grenadier Companies (motorized)
12th (heavy) Company (motorized)

Hermann Göring Panzer Regiment about 35 Panzer III and IV
Regimental Headquarters
Tank Repair Shop Company
I Battalion
Battalion Headquarters
1st-4th Panzer Companies
II Battalion
Battalion Headquarters
5th-8th Panzer Companies
Assault Gun Company HG

Armored Reconnaissance Battalion HG
Battalion Headquarters
1st (armored reconnaissance company)
2nd (motorcycle) Company
3rd (grenadier) Company (APC)

Hermann Göring Armored Artillery Regiment
Regimental Headquarters
I Battalion
Battalion Headquarters
1st-2nd Batteries (each with 4 105mm field howitzers)
II Battalion
Battalion Headquarters
4th-5th Batteries (each with 4 150mm field howitzers)
6th Battery (4 100mm long-barrelled cannon)
III Battalion
Battalion Headquarters
7th-8th Batteries (each with 4 150mm field howitzers)
9th Battery (4 100mm long-barrelled cannon)

Hermann Göring Flak Regiment
Regimental Headquarters
I Battalion
Battalion Headquarters
1st-3rd Batteries (each with 4 88mm Flak)
4th-5th Batteries (each with 12 20mm Flak)

Hermann Göring Armored Pioneer Battalion

Battalion Headquarters
1st-3rd Pioneer Companies
Hermann Göring Armored Signals Battalion
Battalion Headquarters
Supply Echelon
1st (field telephone) Company
2nd (radio) Company

Hermann Göring Supply Battalion

Battalion Headquarters
1st-3rd Motor Transport Companies
Supply Company

Hermann Göring Maintenance Battalion

Battalion Headquarters
1st-2nd Repair Shop Companies
Equipment Distributing Point
Replacement Part Echelon

First-Aid Units HG

1st-2nd First-Aid Squads
1st-3rd Ambulance Platoons

Administrative Units HG

Administration Company (formerly Division Rations Supply Office)
Bakery Company
Butchery Company

Military Police Squad HG

Military Post Office HG

(b) Attached Units: Maucke Grenadier Regiment, 3 battalions, non-mobile, limited motorization provided by vehicle columns of HG Panzer Div. It was planned to use the regiment to later bring the 15th Panzer-Grenadier Division up to strength.

Messina Construction Battalion

Reggio Grenadier battalion (non-mobile personnel replacement transfer battalion)

1 Tiger company, 1 heavy army artillery battalion with 3 batteries, each with 4 150mm field howitzers

(c) Status of HG Division Units

All units not at authorized strength but fully motorized and mobile. Units still missing from order of battle were still in the midst of formation in the area north of Naples (Santa Maria Capua Vetere) and were shipped to Sicily after the beginning of the invasion.

2. Units Shipped to Sicily after 10 July 1943 (until about 30 July)

(a) HG Division Units

  3 heavy flak batteries 88mm

  4 light flak batteries 20mm, several tanks, transport columns

(b) Other Units

About 2/3 of the 1st Parachute Division with elements listed below, which were air-dropped south of Catania on 12 July at about 1800 hours and on the two subsequent days:

3rd Parachute Regiment (Oberstleutnant Heilmann)

Regimental Headquarters

Signals Platoon

Pioneer Platoon

Bicycle Platoon

13th Mortar Company

14th Anti-tank Company

I Battalion

Battalion Headquarters

Signals Platoon

1st-3rd Light Infantry Companies

4th (machine-gun) Company

II Battalion

Battalion Headquarters

Signals Platoon

5th-7th Light Infantry Companies

8th (machine-gun) Company

III Battalion

Battalion Headquarters

Signals Platoon

9th-11th Light Infantry Companies

12th (machine-gun) Company

4th Parachute Regiment (Oberst Walther)

as 3rd Parachute Regiment

1st Parachute Machine-gun Battalion

Battalion Headquarters

Signals Platoon

1st-3rd Machine-gun Companies

1st Parachute Pioneer Battalion
Battalion Headquarters
Signals Platoon
1st-3rd Pioneer Companies
4th (machine-gun) Company

I Battalion, 1st Parachute Artillery Regiment
Battalion Headquarters
1st-3rd batteries – each with 4 75mm mountain artillery pieces

1st Parachute Anti-tank Battalion
Battalion Headquarters
Signals Platoon
1st-3rd Companies – each with 12 75mm anti-tank guns
1 replacement transfer battalion
1 battery with 2 170mm cannon
Luftwaffe flak in the area north of Catania

3. Disposition of Combat Units on 10 July 1943

(a) **Caltagirone Group**
   Hermann Göring Division Headquarters
   HG Armored Signals Battalion
   1st Panzer-Grenadier Regiment HG – less APC Battalion
   Armored Pioneer Battalion – less one company
   HG Armored Reconnaissance Battalion – less one company
   HG Armored Artillery Regiment
   HG Panzer Regiment
   HG Flak Battalion
   Tiger company (2nd Company, 504th Heavy Tank Battalion)
   Messina Construction Battalion

(b) **Catania Group (Battle Group Schmalz)**
   HG Special Purpose Panzer-Grenadier Brigade
   Headquarters
   Maucke Grenadier Regiment
   heavy artillery battalion
   1st Pioneer Company HG
   Reggio Grenadier Battalion
   I Battalion, 1st Panzer-Grenadier Regiment HG (APC battalion)
   1st Armored Reconnaissance Company HG

The divisional command post near Cave dei Tirreni, 22 September 1943.

From left: Brigade commander Oberst Schmalz, division commander Generalmajor Conrath and Ia General Staff Oberstleutnant von Bergengruen. The back of the original print bears Conrath's signature from November 1943.

An unidentified Leutnant of the Parachute-Panzer Division HG.

Oberleutnant Rebholz (left, beside him an unidentified Oberwachtmeister).

The Assault Gun Battalion of the Hermann Göring Parachute-Panzer Division:
The Beginning – Technology and Tactics

The following individual accounts are intended to supplement the previous descriptions of the action in Sicily and provide a more detailed account of the crossing to the mainland.

In March 1942, during the transformation of the HG Regiment into the HG Panzer Division, the first soldiers were chosen to form a cadre of personnel for an assault gun company. Under the command of *Major* von Preuß and the *Oberleutnante* Paulus and Lübke, young soldiers were trained to operate this support weapon within the Hermann Göring Division. Training took place in Berlin-Reinickendorf, with courses for tank drivers, gunner NCOs, radio operators, and loaders.

Initially the following armored vehicles were available: 3 Panzer III tanks with the short 50mm KwK and 2 assault guns on the Panzer III chassis with the short 75mm KwK. Preparations for the formation of 13th Company, Hermann Göring Regiment were begun under Oblt. Lübke. Official formation of the company took place on 3 May 1942. Training continued with field and battle exercises. The entire company had 78 authorized NCO positions. The individual platoon leaders were:

Oblt. Heidrich (assault gun)

Lt. Stronk (assault gun)

Lt. Lahousen (tank)

Lt. Block (tank)

Formation of the platoons took place at this time. Each platoon possessed five Panzer III tanks armed with the 50mm KwK, as well as a command tank and one replacement tank. Following initial formation the company was transferred into the Pontivy area, Loudéac and Camp de Meucon. There the 13th Company, HG Rifle Regiment was officially called into being under *Hauptmann* Preuß. Strength was about 150 men. Other officers included Oblt. Paulus and later Oblt. Lübke, as well as platoon leaders *Leutnante* Lahousen, Stronk and Siegetz.

This 13th Company, Hermann Göring Panzer Regiment was the first training company for all the future armored units of the HG Division. All of the initial volunteers for assault gun training came from the HG Regiment. They were soldiers of every rank who had already seen action in Russia. They also included soldiers from the Army and the Luftwaffe, among them *Leutnant* Block. The attitude of the men was casual but not sloppy. All were willing to work and did their jobs responsibly. The majority of those who found a new home in the assault gun unit were soldiers of the motorcycle company and armored reconnaissance platoon.

Camp le Meucon lay in gently-sloping wooded terrain, about 800 meters from the village of the same name. Towering above the camp was the observation hill, a feature known to all who served there. The hilly terrain was well suited to training purposes. Improvements were made to an old field road which ran through the camp. To the right and left of the road were the camp's eight wooden barracks. At the end was a stone building which served as the officers' quarters, and beside it an adjoining building in which were located the kitchen, washrooms and guard house. In the first barracks were the canteen and the classroom for "*Oberleutnant* Lübke's tactical sand-table games". All of the other barracks were occupied by the crews of the assault guns. There was a series of night alerts at Meucon, in which all the crews had to be in their vehicles within three minutes.

Not far to the right of the camp, extending to the forest, was a large rectangular latrine facility with a "twelve cylinder" thunder beam (spaces for twelve to sit). To the left of the road which bypassed the camp was a training area which consisted of a field surrounded by old chestnut trees. Beyond it was a country road with an adjoining acreage bordered by Breton stone walls. The assault guns, the repair echelon, and some of the tanks were parked on this road. The camp itself had a narrow-gauge railway link to Vannes. It had previously been used by French troops and from the summer of 1940 had been used as an assembly camp for French POWs. Cross-country drives, firing exercises, advancing in battle order, and other training ploys (including the previously mentioned night alerts) were part of the daily routine at Camp le Meucon.

One of the most important exercises was the function drill, whose purpose was to produce assault gun crews capable of functioning smoothly in battle. The following is a brief overview, which in slightly modified form also applied to tank crews, outlining the roles and responsibilities of each crew member of an assault gun:

Gun Commander: Target designation, issuing of orders after assessing enemy situation.

Gun commander: As to direction, cover, observation, firing driver: halt and vehicle speed.

From driver: Acknowledgement to gun commander.

From gun commander : Range to target, recognition points to gunner; terrain, target designation. Type and number of shells. "Fire" command.

Gunner: Periscope, other target information. Recognition of target. Telescopic sight. Targeting of enemy. Range, elevation and traverse mechanisms. Report to commander when ready to fire. Firing of gun.

Gun commander to Loader: Has already heard what type of shell is to be used, taken specified round from rack above the open breech mechanism, pushed round into breech and activated the safety switch. Order to man the machine-gun with target designation, order to leave vehicle for purpose of checking the tracks.

From loader: Response to gun commander.

The daily technical routine also saw each member of the crew carry out his specialized service drills. All preparations for a gun inspection were reported to the supervising officer:

Gun Commander: Status of weapons and ammunition.

Gunner: Serviceability of the optics, the gun and breech mechanism, the electrical firing system and the elevating and traversing mechanisms.

Driver: Serviceability of the engine, brakes and clutch and the presence of a complete tool kit.

Loader: Serviceability of radio, presence of specified ammunition, the submachine-gun, spare track parts and split pins.

All together: Inspection of the fighting compartment and running gear, and maintenance and cleaning of the vehicle. The vehicle inspection was the crowning conclusion for everyone.

The announcement of a visit by the designated division commander, *Generalmajor* Conrath, was met with a certain amount of apprehension. The reason for this lay in this commander's style. He had stamped the General Göring Regiment with toughness and strictness. Thanks to his reputation, only volunteers came to the regiment and to the division. Wearers of glasses and Saxons were rejected. The fact that he was equally strict with the officers improved his standing with the men somewhat; nevertheless, his behavior toward the officers was biting and caustic. As a result of this he became more and more alienated from the officers as well as the men.

In addition to the types of weapons already described, the 13th Panzer Company Hermann Göring Regiment also received the following equipment:

Two armored scout cars, *Seydlitz* and *Derfflinger*, which were armed with 20mm cannon. As well, 3 tank-destroyers armed with the 76.2mm long-barrelled gun, and two assault guns with the short 75mm StuK 37 L/24, Model SdKfz 142, numbers two and four. A recovery platoon with two 8-tonne prime movers each with a 30-tonne flatbed trailer, with the loading surface for assault guns or tanks.

Two maintenance echelons, seven trucks for the kitchen, rations, postal exchange, canteen, fuel, weapons, and ammunition. One Steyr Kfz 15 radio vehicle, one VW Kübelwagen for the company commander, one BMW motorcycle-sidecar combination for the mobile radio NCO with portable radio set. The 13th Panzer Company had ten authorized officer positions. *Oberleutnant* Paulus became company commander. His deputy was *Oberleutnant* Lübke. Platoon leaders were: *Leutnante* Sieger, Lahousen, Stronk and Münster. *Oberleutnant* Heidrich commanded the assault gun platoon; his deputy was *Leutnant* Block.

The assault gun commanders were: *Unteroffiziere* Heinemann, Behm, and Kanert. Gunner-NCOs: *Unteroffiziere* Schulte, Pers, Männel, Reim, Reis, Bark and Hausmann. Drivers: Schubauer, Jäger, Ahwe, Wittmann and Eichhorn. Maintenance echelon: Rodel. Mobile radio NCOs: Löschenkohl and Rödel.

1 November saw the formation of the Hermann Göring Panzer Regiment, which included an assault gun battalion and an anti-tank battalion. V (Assault Gun) Battalion, HG Artillery Regiment was officially formed on 8 November with the 13th, 14th, and 15th Batteries (which were to exist until 25 May 1943). The battalion was transferred to the Bordeaux area the same day, for after the Allied landings in North Africa there was the danger of a landing on the coast of Southern France. The operational alert was sounded from the new quarters of V Assault Gun Battalion in St. Jean Brevelac, which the assault guns had not yet reached.

On 11 November new Panzer IIIs with the long-barrelled 50mm gun and 22 Sturmgeschütz IIIs with the long-barrelled 75mm gun arrived by rail from Magdeburg for the battalion. Each of the three batteries received seven assault guns. The 22nd assault gun became *Hauptmann* Schmock's command vehicle. The now fully-equipped battalion was shipped by fast train into the Bordeaux – Cognac – Ruffec area of France. The days that followed saw the battalion transported by rail to Italy. At that time the battalion was organized as follows:

Battalion Commander:	Hptm. Schmock
Adjutant:	Oblt. Jekosch
Staff Officer:	Lt. Möhring
Battalion Medical Officer:	Stabsarzt Dr. Becker Oberarzt Schliep
Dentist:	Elverfeld

Gun Commanders: Hinsch, Löschenkohl, Bethke, Nienaber, Beihoff, Beyer, Tack, Grethe, König, Groß, Zart, Schulze-Ostwald, Last, Schulze, Rückert, Männel, Zwanzig, Schlössinger, Raschendorfer, Kanert.

From January until May of 1943, V Assault Gun Battalion of the Artillery Regiment HG was stationed around Santa Maria Vetere. There personnel joined the unit from army tank and assault gun units in Russia and from the assault gun replacement battalions at Schweinfurt and Neisse. At the end of the training period the command personnel of the three batteries was as follows:

13th Battery:		Oblt. Wilmskötter
	1st Platoon:	Lt. Schaper
	2nd Platoon:	Lt. König
	3rd Platoon:	Lt. Poetter
14th Battery:		Oblt. Heidrich
	1st Platoon:	Lt. Block
	2nd Platoon:	Lt. Stronk
	3rd Platoon:	Ofw. Sturm
15th Battery:		Oblt. Hagemann
	1st Platoon:	Lt. Wibbelt
	2nd Platoon:	Lt. Wittschonke
	3rd Platoon:	Lt. Wallhäuser

Further training took place in the Santa Maria Vetere, Capua, and Caserta areas. On 4 May the unit was ordered to alert readiness, and two days later the assault guns entrained for the transfer to North Africa, where there were already signs of the coming defeat of Army Group Africa. Shipment of the unit to Sicily by rail was halted at Battipaglia in southern Italy, and the battalion was immediately transported back to Caserta. There it detrained and returned overland to its former barracks in Santa Maria Vetere. Some of the assault guns stopped at the depot in Capua.

On 9 May the battalion's soldiers were in a tent camp bivouac on the Volturno. Gun commanders Grethe, Kanert, and several others were ordered to travel by train to the replacement regiment in Utrecht to select needed gunners and loaders. From there they and their chosen comrades went on to the training company in Berlin-Reinickendorf, where further trained personnel were picked up. This now rather large party continued on to the army tank depot in Magdeburg-Königsborn to pick up ten assault guns armed with the long-barrelled 105mm KwK. The assault gun howitzers were taken to Italy, from where they were shipped to the Belpasso area near Catania, Sicily.

In the meantime the battalion had been redesignated. Its new name was: III (Assault Gun) Battalion, Hermann Göring Panzer Regiment. The battalion comprised the 9th, 10th, and 11th Batteries (in place of the 13th through 15th Batteries). The assault howitzers were assigned to three heavy platoons, each with three vehicles. They were to advance in the second line, firing over the other platoons of the battery, intervene in the fighting in a support role, and fire on enemy assembly areas from ranges of up to 3,000 meters (their primary role). Unfortunately, these ten heavy weapons were never used in concentration within their companies. Following the Allied landings on Sicily in the early hours of 10 July 1943, the assault gun battalion saw action in the defensive battles near Augusta, Lentini, Carlentini, Agnone, in the Simeto Plain, near Gerbini, and Catania.

More than combat against the invading Allied forces, an epidemic of malaria caused casualties among the unit's personnel to swell to 30%. The assault gun units fought magnificently within the panzer regiment's battle group. The battalion suffered casualties of 15% to 20% in killed and wounded. Assault gun crews, grenadiers and artillerymen stood shoulder to shoulder in the division's battle group in front of Augusta. The 9th, 10th, and 11th Batteries, which started the battle with 22 assault guns and 10 assault howitzers, lost about 35 percent of their vehicles through enemy action, breakdowns, and destruction by their own crews. The assault howitzers fully lived up to expectations, often achieving success from the second rank. They successfully engaged not only enemy assembly areas, but truck columns, machine-gun nests, and anti-tank gun positions as well. Only one assault howitzer was lost in action, the result of a burst barrel.

The enemy's numerical superiority led to losses, but so did the lack of experience. Among those wounded were *Hauptmann* Schmock, *Oberleutnant* Heidrich and *Leutnant* Block. Individual scenes of action and dates were as follows:

From 10 to 14 July the 9th-11th Batteries were engaged in heavy defensive fighting at the landing sites near Augusta and in the Syracuse area. The situation was complicated and confused. Enemy airborne units were wiped out near Agnone and Lentini on 14 and 15 July. The British forces, which had landed by parachute and by glider, formed hedgehog positions by day and attempted to reach their objectives in surprise night attacks. On 17 July the defenders, including the assault guns, began a gradual withdrawal across the Cornalunga and Dittaino Rivers toward the Simeto. The latter position was held and the enemy prevented from crossing the river. German parachute troops also participated in this action. Their attempt to blow up the bridge over the river failed, however.

The assault guns held their positions at the Simeto in the Motta and Santa Anastasia areas and in the Catania Plain until 24 July. The enemy attacked repeatedly and on several occasions penetrated the German lines. In most cases the enemy was driven back again in close combat. On 28 July Gerbini airfield was reached and positions were held there until 2 August.

The primary role of the assault guns in this defensive role was to support the infantry and parachute troops in repulsing the repeated enemy attacks. For the assault guns, the meticulously planned withdrawal to the Strait of Messina and across it to the mainland began with their withdrawal toward Misterbianco, Belpasso, and Trecastagni on 6 August. As part of the withdrawal plan the assault guns formed a protective ring around the departure point, before moving on through Trecastagni, Fiume Freddo, and Taormina to Messina, the crossing point. Battalion members Langheiz and Wilmskötter were killed during the withdrawal and the associated battles with the pursuing enemy.

At noon on 8 August 1943 the assault guns, with their crews and weapons, crossed the Strait of Messina on Siebel ferries to Reggio di Calabria on the Italian mainland. The deadly curtain of flak over the Strait of Messina, directed by *Oberst* Nieper, kept marauding enemy aircraft at bay. *Hauptmann* Sandrock had assumed command of the battalion in place of the wounded *Hauptmann* Schmock.

On the 9th and 10th of July the battalion headquarters and the train moved through Paterno, Adrano, Bronte, and Fiume Freddo to Messina. The assault gun battalion moved into the Calabrian mountains on 9 and 10 August to rest and refit. Beginning on the 15th it drove along the east coast to Catanzaro; from there it turned onto the connecting road to the west coast and proceeded in the direction of Naples. At the end of August the battalion occupied a rest position in the Pozzuoli area. But what were the actions on the island like from the point of view of the assault gun crews?

Unteroffizier Hans Bethke's Account of the Fighting in Sicily

The following account is from *Unteroffizier* Hans Bethke, commander of an assault gun, and is intended to supplement the general account of the fighting in Sicily.

"Our assault gun battalion under *Hauptmann* Schmock comprised the IIIrd Battalion of the HG Panzer Regiment. The 9th, 10th, and 11th Companies were commanded by *Oberleutnante* Wilmskötter, Heidrich, and Hagemann. I belonged to the 10th Battery and *Leutnant* Block's platoon, which consisted of three 105mm assault howitzers.

When we crossed the Strait of Messina by Siebel ferry on 11 July, elements of our division were already engaged in defensive fighting against Anglo-American troops on the south and southeast coasts of Sicily. Our battalion assembled at the foot of Mount Etna. *Leutnant* Block's battery occupied an assembly area near Lentini for two days. So far there had been no contact with the enemy. Numerous Italian foot columns passed by us as they moved north from the Augusta area in the direction of Catania and Messina. Early on the morning of 14 July we moved into a new position three kilometers south of Carlentini on the road to Melilli. From there we could see the enemy ships at sea at a distance of about 8 kilometers.

Early in the afternoon British advance forces reached the area of our positions. We opened up with our 105s, firing high-explosive shells at the masses of infantry. The advancing British halted and took cover behind the many stone walls that divided up the countryside. In opening fire we revealed our position and toward evening the enemy's naval guns opened fire on us; we were able to avoid harm only by zigzagging. In spite of the heavy fire our losses in personnel and materiel were nil. We moved to Carlentini under cover of darkness. Several hours later enemy cargo gliders and aircraft carrying airborne troops flew over our positions. Soon afterward the gliders landed in the level terrain nearby while the parachute troops jumped over the outskirts of Carlentini.

Unteroffizier Körber, the commander of an assault howitzer, was killed in fighting with the landing force. Early on the morning of 15 July we occupied a new prepared position north of Lentini. That evening we withdrew from the position – we had not been attacked – and rolled back into the Pinadi Plain. There I was ordered to guard the Lentini – Scordia road fork with my assault howitzer and then follow as rear guard. The situation was as follows:

We were unfamiliar with the area, had no usable maps, and far and wide there were no more German soldiers. The entire Lentini area had been evacuated. It was fortunate that the enemy followed up very slowly, because the day before he had suffered heavy losses. Shortly before midnight we withdrew as ordered and drove through Palagonia and Ramacca to Gerbini. We rejoined our battery in a wooded area there at about noon on 16 July. We were given a rest break to rearm and refuel. 57 shells and 400 liters of fuel richer, we were once again combat ready and went into position in the Catania Plain behind a wall of earth left over from the digging of an anti-tank ditch.

The parachute troops of the 3rd Regiment were dug in there and for the first time we were installed in a continuous front line. Our three batteries constituted a welcome reinforcement for the paratroopers. Shortly after occupying this position we were blanketed by enemy artillery fire. Even this barrage fire was unable to break our position line. Not until late in the afternoon of 17 July did the firing abate. Soon afterward we spotted tanks moving on the other side, and our platoon went into position behind a shallow embankment. I passed instructions to the driver and told the loader to load an HL round (special amour-piercing ammunition). To the right of us was the assault gun of *Stabswachtmeister* Schulze-Oswald, a platoon leader with the 11th Battery. We were all concentrating on the same target, five British tanks which were rolling towards us.

When the command was given, all four guns fired at the same time. The four tanks we had targeted burst into flames. Veering right, the fifth tried to escape into cover at full speed. It was targeted. Just as I gave the order to fire, there was a terrible crash. Dense smoke filled the fighting compartment. I gave the order to bail out. Two members of my crew suffered burns and fragment wounds, my gunner in the head and my loader in the left arm. All that was left of our howitzer was the breech. Everything else had been ripped away when the shell exploded in the barrel. The reason for the accident was that the gun barrel – which was in a horizontal position, originally just above the lip of the embankment – ended up pointing into the wall of earth as a result of the hull sinking into the ground.

Just as my driver, *Obergefreiter* Wolgemuth, and I were about to climb back into the vehicle to take the two wounded to safety, a shell fell in front of us. Fragments crushed my lower jaw on the right side. My driver brought three wounded back to the train in our assault howitzer, which was no longer fit for combat. From there I was taken to the main dressing station, before being put aboard an Italian hospital ship in Messina with many other wounded comrades. The ship then sailed to Livorno. For me the action in Sicily was over."

The Odyssey of *Unteroffizier* Kanert

"We crossed the Strait of Messina on the morning of 9 July. A tremendous defensive barrage from the heavy flak kept the enemy aircraft at a respectful distance and forced them to release their bombs prematurely. During the march across the island, near Catania we ran into a bombing raid on the harbour. At night we took shelter in a wood with large baobab trees, where *Leutnant* Wallhäußer briefed the assault gun crews. The morning of 10 July saw the 11th Battery of III Battalion, Panzer Regiment HG, with the three assault howitzers of the heavy platoon under *Stabswachtmeister* Grethe, under way along side roads through the mountainous terrain from the Belpasso area in the direction of Lentini. The unit was attacked by individual fighter-bombers and reconnaissance aircraft, without suffering any losses. Arrival in the Augusta area was at 0400 hours on 11 July. We halted in the small town of Villasmundo – 18 kilometers from Augusta – and waited for operational orders.

Stabswachtmeister Grethe and *Unteroffizier* Kanert positioned their guns on a hill with a view of the port of Augusta. Grethe, a veteran assault gun commander from the army, who already wore the German Cross in Gold, was one of the most experienced men in the whole battalion. Nothing could be seen of the port of Augusta, which lay about 8 kilometers away, on account of dense morning fog. In the course of our 'inspection of the terrain' we found an Italian clothing stores, where we outfitted ourselves with black shirts and field jackets. Also there were sea bags with combination locks.

The two howitzers remained in position throughout the 17th of July. Then *Stabswachtmeister* Grethe decided to fire on the enemy ships, which were now clearly visible. After the second salvo the ships began returning our fire. Guided by an airborne observer, the impacting shells came ever nearer. We sneaked back across a rickety bridge over a deep gorge, which had already been hit by bombers. Once on the other side we breathed a sigh of relief. We then occupied a new position beyond the gorge.

Our howitzers moved up again after the enemy landed near Augusta – unopposed by the heavy Italian coastal artillery – and advanced inland. The first enemy tanks to appear were turned back with several shots, as were the infantry. A 75mm Pak was surrounded in the sector in front of us, which had been overrun by the enemy landing forces. The gun crew called for help. The Grethe and Kanert assault guns and a truckload of grenadiers rolled forward at top speed to relieve the surrounded anti-tank gunners. Grethe roared past the startled enemy, firing at them with his machine-gun. The infantry jumped down from the truck, stormed through to the surrounded men, and overcame the enemy in close-quarters combat. The crew of the anti-tank gun, which had spiked its weapon, climbed aboard our vehicles and we rolled back to our positions."

On 12 July *Generalfeldmarschall* Kesselring visited the assault guns of the HG Panzer Regiment and announced that parachute units would soon be arriving from France.

"Later that evening the assault gun battalion was moved farther to the rear, and it established a night camp in a gully between Lentini and Carlentini. *Leutnant* Wallhäuser woke the men early on the morning of 13 July. An Allied reconnaissance aircraft was circling above the battalion. The engines were fired up and the assault guns were driven forward to the road. Moments later a salvo from British naval artillery fell on the Carlentini hillsides. The houses in the town were hit hard.

The warmed-up assault guns drove away from the camp area to avoid being caught by the next salvo. The guns dodged the huge shell craters which were three meters across and two meters deep. The Kanert assault gun picked up three more men. On reaching the road it was stopped by *Oberleutnant* Hagemann. He ordered the crew to look for wounded and recover them. An Italian fighter shot down the enemy observation aircraft. The ships' guns fell silent.

Late on the morning of that 13 July the paratroops of the 3rd Parachute Regiment, who had come down in a wheat field, occupied a new position between Lentini and Carlentini. During this time the assault guns, under *Leutnant* Wallhäuser, drove into the Agnone area, another of the enemy's landing sites. There was a furious firefight in which *Leutnant* Wallhäuser destroyed four enemy tanks. Heinz Wallhäuser was already displaying his special abilities as a platoon and assault gun commander.

At about midday the Grethe and Kanert assault howitzers took up position at the slopes in front of Lentini, facing toward Agnone. *Stabswachtmeister* Grethe was wounded in the arm and had to abandon his howitzer, which was retrieved forty-eight hours later by *Unteroffizier* Kanert. At about 2200 an enemy 150mm battery drove up near the position of the two assault howitzers and began firing on Agnone. A flare was fired from the town, the agreed-upon signal that it was to be abandoned. At 0200 hours on the 14th *Oberleutnant* Hagemann appeared at the two assault howitzers. His comment: 'You're dozing here peacefully while paratroops are landing all around.' *Oberleutnant* Hagemann took a submachine-gun from Uffz. Kanert as well as his belt with its two ammunition pouches and together with his driver drove on in the direction of the enemy. He was never to return. It was later learned that he had been wounded and captured in an encounter with the enemy.

On 14 July *Unteroffizier* Kanert, who was now in command of two assault guns, ordered us to drive ahead to Lentini. Arriving at the city limits, he reached a roundabout where several roads came together in the shape of a star. Kanert positioned his assault gun there with its direction of fire toward the road from Agnone. The second assault gun was posted 150 meters to the rear at the arterial road to Catania. At about 1530 hours an armored vehicle appeared on the road from Agnone. It was an Italian assault gun under the command of a Captain. He informed the Germans that the English were advancing from Agnone toward Lentini. The Italian refused to comply with our request that he also take up position there, even though Kanert had drawn his pistol. He simply drove on, and they weren't about to shoot him.

Hours passed. Suddenly the engine of the second assault gun, positioned 150 meters behind us, roared. The gunner appeared in the hatch of the assault gun and waved to Kanert to follow, which he did.

We turned and followed, catching up after about three kilometers. The gunner had seen British troops entering the city. We were still discussing what to do next when two of our 75mm anti-tank guns appeared from Lentini. The platoon leader asked us to accompany them in the direction of Catania. We didn't have enough fuel, however, and the two canisters with a total of 40 liters which the anti-tank people gave us wasn't very much. We remembered a store of fuel in Lentini. My loader and I set out to see if the fuel was still there. We reached the premises with the fuel, went in through the entrance, and searched high and low for the drums. In doing so we determined that there was an observer in the bushes. We went on as far as the roundabout, where we were met by enemy machine-gun fire.

We zigzagged beneath the orange and olive trees, trying to evade the fire. When we had finally clambered up a slope which climbed away to the left, we were found by the fighter-bombers and showered with incendiary bullets. The machines made several passes, but each time we were able to take cover behind some boulders. Then we saw a line of tanks with small pennants on their antennas on our approach road. They were English! Behind the tanks was a line of infantry-carrying trucks. We still had about 900 meters to cover to our vehicles. Moving along the slope, we tried to get there ahead of the tanks and warn our two guns, however we were unsuccessful. When the first tanks came round a corner our gun opened fire and set the leading tank on fire. The rest stopped and our two assault guns withdrew. We continued on and that evening reached the Stazione di Valsavoia. There, too, there was no sign of German troops.

During the night of 15 July we encountered a German scout car, but it drove away before we could identify ourselves. From some Italians camped there we learned that enemy troops had landed in gliders. In spite of the darkness we saw them as we slipped past and crept away in the opposite direction beyond the road. We carried on in the late morning of 15 July following a brief rest in a dried-up river bed. We came upon a village, in front of which lay a glider. But the 'liberators' were there too and we slipped away into a low-lying plantation. We kept moving, following the boundary line of the plantation.

At noon we came to a road. Before crossing we waited and had a look around. We heard the sound of tank tracks, took cover, and watched as a group of armored vehicles rolled past us. They were German armored personnel carriers. We identified ourselves by waving and they stopped. We ran up to our comrades and reported to the officer in charge of this rear guard from our division. The detachment, which had disengaged from the enemy, had received orders to blow up each bridge behind it. We sat on boxes containing explosives and anti-tank mines, but we didn't mind. We had found our way back to our own people. It was afternoon when they roused us – we had fallen asleep from exhaustion. 'There are your assault guns!' one of our comrades said to us. We climbed down and walked toward one of our 105mm assault howitzers which was camouflaged behind some bushes. It was the vehicle of *Unteroffizier* Bethke of our 11th Battery.

There we learned that our battery chief, *Oberleutnant* Hagemann, and his driver had been overpowered by enemy troops after a brief struggle while attempting to free the surrounded 75mm assault gun platoon of *Wachtmeister* Strüßmann. This had happened on 14 July, the same day that he borrowed my belt with the ammunition pouches before going out to scout ahead armed with a submachine-gun. *Unteroffizier* Schulte and another member of the battery, *Gefreiter* Hagert, escaped and reported the incident. *Unteroffizier* Schulte was assigned to our assault howitzer as gunner-NCO."

The 11th Battery was now led by *Oberleutnant* Jekosch, who until the loss of *Oberleutnant* Hagemann had been battalion adjutant. *Hauptmann* Schmock still commanded the battalion, but soon afterward he fell ill with malaria. In the days that followed the battalion moved into a new assembly area; it was important that the advancing British tanks be stopped. On the evening of 15 July there was a duel between these and the assault guns. Several tanks were destroyed without any losses on the German side. Commanders Nienaber and Kanert were sent forward into no-man's- land with their assault howitzers. Their instructions were to advance until they could fire on all enemy tanks approaching on the road. Explosions and the glow of fires were observed during the night.

While the defenders fought a delaying action, on 16 July the assault guns were transferred to the open flank to establish a continuous defensive line. Contact was made with the neighboring units. With temperatures of 50 degrees it was boiling hot inside the steel hulls of the assault guns. Wearing only short tropical pants, the drivers squatted in their seats, repeatedly powdered with the small particles of the steering brake scrapings. Since the unit's days on the mainland there had been no mail and only rarely was hot food issued.

From the 16th to the 24th of July the entire battalion, its guns widely spread out, stood shoulder to shoulder with the men of the 3rd Parachute Regiment in the Catania Plain. The advancing enemy forces there were repulsed decisively. By night the enemy dropped leaflets which stressed the futility of our struggle against the numerically far-superior allied troops and called upon us to desert. None of the men on Sicily complied with this request. (Not until later were suspicions raised that two men who went missing under nebulous circumstances may have deserted.) The enemy now found himself facing a flexible defensive front. The 9th and 10th Batteries had fixed positions at the "anti- tank ditch", a natural obstacle in the Catania Plain, which was defended stubbornly. Several attacks with tanks and supporting infantry were repelled with losses to the enemy.

The fighting was bitter and naturally the defenders suffered losses as well. On 16 July the commander of the 9th Battery, *Oberleutnant* Wilmskötter, drove into one of our own minefields during an advance in spite of being warned. His assault gun was destroyed. He and his crew lost their lives."

The leader of 10th Battery, *Oberleutnant* Heidrich, and one of the battery's platoon leaders, *Leutnant* Block, were wounded by artillery fire. In 11th Battery the very popular dispatch rider Loewe was wounded. However the greatest losses to be suffered by the battalion in Sicily still lay ahead: the cause was malaria. The focal point of assault gun operations moved inland, along the Simeto River in the direction of the front-line airfield at Gerbini. There *Oberleutnant* Jekosch found himself forced to do more for order and discipline; he scheduled weapons cleaning and inspections during the quiet times, which did little to improve his popularity.

The men of the assault gun battalion made the acquaintance of the Canadians in the plain in front of Gerbini. A Canadian infantry detachment worked its way along the northern edge of the airfield and infiltrated as far as the German assembly area. There it was turned back. All flying activities at the airfield were halted and the enemy continued to push hard. Battle Group Conrath had already pulled back from Gela to the Catania Plain. Parts of the division withdrew through Caltagirone and across the Cornalunga and Dittaino Rivers in the direction of Gerbini. Elements of the 15th Panzer-Grenadier Division, a constant neighbor of the HG Division, occupied positions in front of Gerbini. These included an anti-tank unit.

The Nienaber and Kanert assault howitzers were sent to Gerbini airfield to scout the situation there. Both vehicles drove at high speed along a road that followed a tributary of the Simeto. The assault howitzers were stopped by a sentry at a wooden bridge with a span of only ten meters. He warned them that there might be enemy troops beyond the bridge in no-man's-land. The first gun crossed the bridge, the second followed. Once across, the pair halted to observe the area. A look through the binocular telescope revealed signs with German tactical symbols and a road sign pointing to the road which branched off to the left to Gerbini. Also visible were barracks at the edge of the airfield. Once again Bruno Kanert:

"Widely spaced, we drove toward the airfield. We slowed down as we approached the landing field. Located there were the hangars for the Me 109s. We rolled toward the barracks, which had been partly destroyed by bombing. On reaching a position between the barracks, two men got out of our vehicle to look around. The barracks were empty. We drove on to the hangars while Nienhaber provided cover. A look inside revealed several aircraft destroyed by the bombing.

We stopped at the bridge on our way back and informed the sentry of our observations. While still in sight of the bridge we met the transport truck which was to supply us with ammunition and fuel. Behind the truck to one side of the road I spotted a Kfz 15 with a command pennant. I stopped beside the truck. 'That's Oberst Schmalz!' the driver of the truck whispered to me, gesturing furtively behind him. 'He's waited for you here to learn the results of your reconnaissance'. I jumped from the assault gun and walked over to the command car dressed as I was in short tropical pants, a black Italian shirt, and sneakers. I came to attention in front of the car and reported to Oberst Schmalz:

'The guns of *Unteroffiziere* Kanert and Nienaber of the 11th Battery of the HG Assault Gun Battalion reporting back from reconnaissance to the airfield at Gerbini. The airfield is deserted.' Oberst Schmalz nodded gratefully. He asked several questions and then said affably: 'Go back to the truck. I've left cigarettes and chocolates for you with the driver. He will give them to you. And thank you Kanert!'

He said not a word about my sloppy and non-regulation attire. What would have happened if *Generalmajor* Conrath had seen us like that? He would have ordered us relieved and punished immediately. We took on ammunition and fuel from the truck. Suddenly the sentry shouted a warning: 'Look out, tank!'

Soon afterward a shot rang out from a wheeled armored scout car from the other side; it had approached the bridge almost unnoticed and taken us by surprise. It disappeared immediately, before we could turn our assault howitzers around. Oberst Schmalz drove ahead to the sentry and asked him in which direction the armored car had fled. After studying his map for a moment he drove on after the enemy. All due respect! How many other commanders would have done this?"

This concludes Kanert's account. We now return to the general story of the assault gun battalion in the days that followed.

The Retreat

The defensive battles at the Simeto River in the burning heat were difficult for all the men to bear. The enemy moved more and more infantry into the area and these movements were watched closely by the defenders. The assault howitzers opened fire from a range of 2,000 meters at a group of trucks discharging troops. The mass of vehicles, which had ventured too far forward, was smashed to pieces. Most of the fighting during the withdrawal to Motta – Santa Anastasia – Misterbianco took place at night. In the course of the withdrawal one of the assault guns became stuck in a bomb crater and was initially left there. The heavy platoon of the 11th Battery stopped on a road next to a convent. Everyone received a medal of the Holy Virgin from an elderly nun, who also brought food. Each man put his medal away in a safe place of his choosing. Plans were made to recover the abandoned assault gun during the coming night. The assault guns driven by *Unteroffiziere* Jäger and Hopp were selected. One of the guns was commanded by *Unteroffizier* Beihoff.

On reaching the assault gun it was discovered that the radio equipment had been removed by an enemy patrol. The enemy noticed the approach of the two assault guns and began firing on the recovery effort with his artillery. Jäger and Beinhoff were both wounded, nevertheless the assault gun was recovered and towed back to the German lines. August 7 saw a further retreat from Belpasso to Trecastagni. All the arriving units assembled there. That evening the battalion set out in the direction of the embarkation port of Messina, leaving the two assault howitzers of 11th Battery with commanders Mölzer and Kanert to cover the withdrawal. The two assault howitzers followed during the night. They drove along the coast road to Fiume Freddo. Near Giardini they were fired on from the sea, causing both vehicles to seek cover behind the houses of a small village.

Early on the morning of 8 August the two guns passed an ancient castle dating from the Hohenstaufen period. As they drove down into the valley the danger posed by enemy fighter-bombers was underlined by the wrecked vehicles that had been pushed to the side of the road. Both vehicles came through unscathed. While still some distance from Messina they were stopped and directed into the assigned rest area by a member of the military police. Bruno Kanert again takes up the narrative:

"It wasn't an hour before we were called out and led up to the crossing point. The organization was tremendous: without any fuss or shouting tanks and infantry vehicles were directed to the tied-up Siebel ferries and driven on board within a few minutes. Each ferry took on two armored vehicles and a truck loaded with infantry. During the crossing, which took a good thirty minutes, our anti-aircraft guns opened fire from both sides of the strait. A bomber formation was approaching. The exploding flak shells in the sky above us formed a dense screen into which the enemy dared not fly. The bomber unit dropped its bombs into the sea and thus disturbed only the fish. Undamaged, we reached solid ground again near Reggio di Calabria, and in the afternoon drove a good distance inland in order to leave sufficient room for all the other units to follow."

On 9 August the battalion drove into the mountains of Calabria and passed through Gambarini at an elevation of about 1,200 meters. During morning roll call the loader from the Kanert assault howitzer collapsed. Kanert himself felt the first symptoms of an attack of malaria and at noon of 10 August, following a second attack, he and four other assault gun crewmen had to taken by ambulance to the 610th Motorized Field Hospital in Gambari. From this reception hospital all malaria cases were sent to the hospital in Cosenza. From Cosenza they travelled in rail cars, often open flat cars, via Sibari to Tarent. From there the sick were transported via Sette Bagni (near Rome), Florence, and Bologna to the 2nd Reserve Hospital in Munich and the Aigolfinger School, and from there to the reserve hospital in Gars am Inn.

The assault gun battalion was transferred once again, this time into the formed 4th Company, HG Panzer Regiment. As there were no tanks available at first, the men were kept busy with drill and barracks duties. On 10 February 1943 the men were put aboard a train once again. This time their destination was France; they arrived in Mont de Marsan on 15 February.

The next day the 4th Company was assigned quarters in Garlin. I Battalion headquarters under *Hauptmann* Rossmann took up quarters in Aire sur l'Adour. Tank and infantry field training was conducted there until 25 May 1943. In command of the 4th Company was *Hauptmann* Schmidt. The company's officers were *Leutnant* Staab, *Leutnant* Zotter (KIA in Sicily) and *Leutnant* Peschke (KIA in East Prussia). Tropical uniforms were issued, an indication that they were bound for the "sunny" south instead of Russia. On 26 May the company entrained for Berlin. On the 29th it took up quarters in the General Göring Regiment barracks in Berlin- Reinickendorf, the ancestral home of the Hermann Göring unit, so to speak. The troops were issued black panzer uniforms with white collar patches, and further tank training was conducted with the small number of available vehicles until 7 June. New Panzer IV tanks armed with the long-barrelled 75mm gun were taken on strength. They were already finished in a tropical color scheme. When the panzer troops were instructed once again to put on tropical uniforms, the situation became clear. The train journey which began on 8 June confirmed that they were going to Italy.

The initial destination, Cancello e Arnone near Naples, was reached on 11 June. From there the unit travelled overland to Castel Volturno, at the mouth of the Volturno River. The tanks were dug in as fixed "batteries" and the company was employed in a coastal defense role. On 21 June it was back to Cancello e Arnone, where the unit entrained again. The next day the company was transported south, arriving in Reggio, Calabria on 26 June. On the following day the unit drove to Villa di San Giovanni, the narrowest point in the Strait of Messina. The company was transported to Sicily the same day, and after assembling in Messina it drove to Catania, taking the coast road through Letoianni, Giardini, and Acireale. From there the company took the southwest road into the Caltagirone area; it was now not far from the island's south coast. The period until 10 July was spent building positions. Once again the tanks were dug in.

When the alert was sounded on the morning of 10 July the combat echelon set out toward the coast in the direction of Gela. 1st Company, HG Panzer Regiment had already seen action in North Africa, where it went down to defeat with the other elements of the division which had been deployed there. All that remained of it was a detachment in Sicily, which was bolstered through the return of men from leave and detachments from other units. The 4th Company suffered its first casualties on 10 July. It was committed near Gela with other elements of the division; they were supposed to drive the invaders back into the sea but suffered heavy losses. On 13 July the combat echelon and the surplus personnel, which included the crews of knocked-out tanks who were now without vehicles, were separated. The 4th Company suffered heavy losses in the subsequent fighting in Sicily. On 18 July a special purpose company, consisting of members of I Battalion, was formed by

Oberleutnant Estel at Bronte. On 19 July the company withdrew to Paterno.

The special purpose company was committed in an infantry role near Gerbini. Near Regalbuto the men of this ad hoc company were able to inflict heavy losses on enemy infantry and repel their attack. The company fought a rearguard action, and coastal patrols were maintained near Giarre-Riposto until 9 August. The same evening the special purpose company boarded vessels in preparation for transport to the mainland. The men were placed in a reception camp high in the mountains. From the 12th to the 16th of August an inflatable boat detachment made up of volunteers from the special purpose company made several trips back to the island. Towed behind assault boats, the inflatable boats brought as many as possible of the division's men still on the island to the mainland.

In the last battle on the island, the surviving panzers of 4th Company destroyed the enemy forces which landed near Brolo. At 0400 hours on 17 August 1943 the last German troops in Sicily crossed over to the mainland in a Siebel ferry and in inflatable boats towed by assault boats. The special purpose company was disbanded on 18 August.

A day later a new 1st Company, HG Panzer Regiment was formed from the remnants of the old 1st Company and those elements of the 4th Company which returned from the island. The company commander was *Oberleutnant* Frey. Seven to eight panzers had returned from Sicily. These survivors and the wheeled element withdrew north into the Naples area. Travelling through Locri, Catanzaro, Cosenza, Crotone, Lagonegro, and Padula, the company arrived in the Salerno-Pompeii area on 4 September. Necessary maintenance was carried out on the unit's vehicles. While there the soldiers were caught by surprise by the surrender of the Italians and were obliged to take part in the disarming of Italian troops.

The battle fought by the division at the Salerno beachhead also saw the new 1st Company, HG Panzer Regiment in action. Following the defensive battles and the subsequent withdrawal to Caserta and Capua, on 9 October 1943 I Battalion was given an opportunity to rest. The remaining tanks of 1st Company were now placed under the command of II Battalion. They participated in the defensive battles at the Volturno River until 20 October and withdrew as far as the Teano area. There I Battalion's remaining vehicles were handed over to II Battalion and the tank crews of 1st Company returned to I Battalion, which was located in a former seminary of the Holy See near Cantalupo, northeast of Rome.

The recovery interval from 22 October to 7 November saw the 1st Company rest and reequip; it took delivery of ten Panzer III tanks armed with the short-barrelled 75mm gun (which the troops referred to as the *Stummel* or "stump"). Hitler had sent these ten vehicles to his friend Mussolini several years earlier. Repairs had to be carried out before they could be used. On 8 November the unit was transferred to Torrice, south of Frosinone. Coastal defence actions took place in the area between Gaeta and Formia from 12 December until 18 January 1944. One platoon of tanks was dug in, while the rest stayed in readiness in a tent camp near Itri. Also there was the train. 1st Company's senior NCO at that time was *Hauptfeldwebel* Lasczeny.

Hauptmann Frey left the company on 19 January, having been appointed regimental adjutant; *Leutnant* Pentschke became interim commanding officer. There was an alert that evening. The tanks were moved up into the area south of Formia. The company's mission was to repel an attack on the Minturno cemetery and undertake a counterattack south of the cemetery. III (Assault Gun) Battalion, HG Panzer Regiment also participated in the fighting in this area. Its story will be told in a subsequent chapter, but first the actions of the Hermann Göring Panzer Division on the Italian mainland.

VI. BATTLE ZONE ITALY

I Battalion, HG Panzer Regiment Following Its Return to the Mainland

After the end of the Battle of Sicily and the successful retreat of the German forces from the island, there was no rest for the surviving elements of the Hermann Göring Panzer Division after 38 days of combat. The panzer regiment's I Battalion was involved in continuous rearguard actions against pursuing enemy forces. Its mission: "Cover the withdrawal of the 29th Panzer-Grenadier Division and the 16th Panzer Division." The division was forced to take up the fight once again without first being given an opportunity to make good the heavy losses in personnel and equipment it suffered in Sicily.

On 9 September 1943 the Allies landed strong forces near Salerno (Operation Avalanche). The terrific summer heat, the overwhelming air superiority of the Allies, and the murderous naval gunfire demanded extraordinary efforts of the troops in the seven-day Battle of Salerno. Adding to German difficulties was the revolt by their Italian partner in the Axis Pact and his defection to the enemy camp. The Germans had been watching the attitude of the Italians with great concern for weeks. Their behavior on Sicily allowed no other conclusion but that they were about to "capsize."

The Hermann Göring Panzer Division, still part of XIV Panzer Corps under the command of the newly-formed Tenth Army under *General* von Vietinghoff, fought in the battles at the Volturno River, near Mignano, and at the Garigliano River. Not until the beginning of October could the first elements of the division be withdrawn from the battle. After four months of uninterrupted combat operations they moved into a rest position at the foot of the Lepiner Mountains in the province of Frosinone. Several units, such as the HG Flak Regiment and the HG Armored Artillery Regiment, were assigned to other divisions and took part in heavy defensive fighting until January 1944.

The Rebuilding of the HG Reconnaissance Battalion

Following the conclusion of the fighting in Sicily and the escape of the majority of the German troops across the Strait of Messina to the mainland, the HG Reconnaissance Battalion was reorganized once again in the course of the rebuilding and reequipping of the HG Division as the Hermann Göring Panzer Division. At the end of August 1943 the reconnaissance battalion consisted of the following units:

Headquarters HG Armored Reconnaissance Battalion

Signals Platoon

1st Armored Reconnaissance Company (2nd company was still absent)

3rd Grenadier Company (motorized, with troop-carrying trucks. Preparations under way for reequipping with armored personnel carriers).

4th Grenadier Company (motorized, with VW Schwimmwagen, still under delivery).

Organized in this way, on 9 September the battalion went into action with the division in the Battle of Salerno; it also saw action in the subsequent battles in the Naples area and at the Volturno River.

When, in November 1943, the HG Panzer Division was incorporated into the First Parachute Army, the organization and designation of the reconnaissance unit changed. The HG Armored Reconnaissance Battalion (PzAA HG) became the HG Parachute-Panzer Armored Reconnaissance Battalion (FschPzAA) and was enlarged by a pioneer company and a motorcycle company. The latter came as a new formation from the HG Replacement and Training Regiment in Utrecht and was considered a replacement for the motorcycle company lost in Tunisia. The HG Parachute-Panzer Armored Reconnaissance Battalion of November 1943 was organized as follows:

Headquarters and Signals Platoon

1st Armored Reconnaissance Company

2nd Motorcycle Company

3rd Panzer-Grenadier Company (armored)

4th Panzer-Grenadier Company (motorized, with VW Schwimmwagen)

5th Armored Pioneer Company

Supply Company

The unit was organized in this way when it was committed to the battle for the Anzio-Nettuno beachhead. It also participated in the battles in the Rome – Florence area. At the end of July 1944 the battalion was transferred to the Eastern Front with the HG Parachute-Panzer Division. There it saw action in the furious fighting in the Warka bridgehead and at the Vistula north of Warsaw. More of this in the main section on the HG Parachute-Panzer Corps. We now return to the chronological account of the events on the Italian mainland.

Prelude: Allied Landings on the Italian Mainland

After the fall of Mussolini on 25 July 1943, the new Italian government under Marshall Pietro Badoglio opened secret talks with the Allies, whose goal was to conclude a separate cease-fire with Italy. Hitler knew nothing of this, but recent events – especially the reluctance to fight of the Italian command in Sicily – had made him mistrustful.

The Commander-in-Chief South, *Generalfeldmarschall* Kesselring, recognized the danger of a new landing after the successful retreat from Sicily and predicted that it would come between Gaeta and Salerno. The Allied cease-fire with the Italians took place – secretly at first – on 3 September 1943 and officially took effect with its public announcement by General Eisenhower on 8 September. The German reaction was to issue the code-word "Axis," which resulted in the disarming of all Italian troops.

The first Allied landing on the Italian mainland took place near Reggio di

Calabria on 3 September. This was a diversionary landing aimed at drawing German troops away from the main landing area near Salerno. *Generalfeldmarschall* Kesselring saw through this trick and sent only limited forces to Reggio di Calabria to delay the Allied advance, while the main body of forces remained in the area north of Gaeta – Salerno. The main Allied landing did in fact take place in the Bay of Salerno. American General Mark Clark had under his command the troops of the 10th British and 6th US Corps, which formed the Fifth Army. This substantial force only managed to capture four small bridgeheads near Salerno. Farther south, however, near Reggio di Calabria, Montgomery's troops pushed north through Calabria. Farther east a British division landed near Tarent in the northeastern part of the Bay of Tarent.

The Hermann Göring Panzer Division in the Combat Zone

In concert with the 16th Armored Reconnaissance Battalion and the 16th Panzer Division, the Hermann Göring Panzer Division formed radio squads to guard the coastline and provide early warning of Allied landings. These squads were positioned near Salerno, on Capri, near Naples and Cuena, and at the mouth of the Volturno and were placed at alert readiness. On 7 September 1943 the division received aerial reconnaissance reports that a large invasion fleet had sailed from North African ports. The fleet's northeast course suggested the possibility of a landing on the west coast of the south-Italian peninsula. Exactly where these landings would take place was not yet clear, therefore the German command could not move up troops to defend against the landing operation.

As well there was the uncertainty as to what Germany's Italian ally had in mind. This state of affairs ended on 8 September and the code-word "Case Axis" – the disarming of all Italian troops – was issued. The landing point became known at about the same time, for early on 8 September the 231st Malta Brigade became the first Allied unit to land on the Italian mainland when it went ashore near Pizzo in the Gulf of Santa Rufemia (on the west coast of Calabria). During the night and early morning of 9 September the British fleet landed the 5th British Corps near Tarent. This force consisted of the 1st Airborne Division, the 78th Infantry Division, and the 8th Indian Infantry Division.

As the troops came ashore they very soon met resistance from elements of the 1st Parachute Division under *Generalleutnant* Heidrich. The main body of the invasion fleet arrived in the Gulf of Salerno, the site of the main landing, on the night of 9 September. Landing craft delivered the troops of the 10th British and 6th US Corps to the beach. Both units were included within the Fifth US Army under General Mark Clark. The HG Panzer Division received orders from XIV Panzer Corps to launch a determined attack to destroy the enemy landing force. In his account of the battle *Generalleutnant* Wilhelm Schmalz stated:

"Because of the losses suffered in Sicily, at that time the division had only two panzer-grenadier battalions, a pioneer battalion, a reconnaissance battalion, and about 30 tanks. It also had available an assault gun company, three battalions of artillery and three flak battalions."

The first blow from the Allied landing force struck the 16th Panzer Division, which was forced to endure a 40,000-round bombardment from the guns of three aircraft carriers and approximately thirty cruisers and thirty destroyers. By first light of 9 September the Allies had put ashore:

From the 6th US Corps: the 36th Infantry Division near Paestum.

From the 10th British Corps: the 46th and 56th Infantry Divisions south of Salerno.

US Rangers and British commandos landed near Amalfi-Maiori and Vietri-Salerno.

By the evening of the first day there were already 25,000 US and 30,000 British troops ashore. Further divisions were put ashore in the days which followed. Once again the account by Wilhelm Schmalz:

"On 9 September the division left its quarters near Caserta and drove through Nocera-Vietri to Salerno. Near Nocera contact was made with patrols from the 16th Reconnaissance Battalion (16th Panzer Division) which were being forced back by the enemy. The two Italian divisions employed as coastal defence units had been lost as a result of the Italian defection. The situation was described to me as follows:

"Salerno-Vietri occupied by the enemy. Strong enemy units and warships in the Bay of Salerno. The main body of the 16th Reconnaissance Battalion in battle at the northern edge of Salerno. The headquarters of the 16th Reconnaissance Battalion near Pellezzano."

Following the arrival of its units, the HG Division was deployed at the Nocera-Vietri road to stop the enemy and prepare for a later attack. On the evening of 9 September the attack spearhead, which was under heavy naval gunfire, reached the area north of Cava and the hills to the left and right of the road. One company was deployed from Camerelle toward the Monte San Angelo and elements of the HG Armored Reconnaissance Battalion at the Pagani-Maiore road. The division made contact with the enemy north of Cava as well as at the Monte San Angelo and near Camilola. The fighting, especially on the road to Vietri, was heavy and costly.

The 16th Reconnaissance Battalion was involved in heavy fighting several kilometers north of Salerno. It had been pushed back to that position during the day."

The landing appeared to have achieved its operational objectives by the evening of 9 September. The port of Salerno, as well as Montevornino airport and the important traffic junction of Battipaglia, were in enemy hands. The real objective of the American 5th Army – to reach Naples as quickly as possible – seemed almost within its grasp. However on 10 September began the German counterattack. Once again *Generalleutnant* Schmalz:

"The attack by the HG Panzer Division launched on 10 September got as far as the southern limits of Cava, but bogged down there. The panzers were unable to deploy in the narrow, difficult valley and thus failed to achieve their full effect. Heavy fighting broke out on the hills on both sides of the valley. Possession of these hills was important for the artillery observers to direct fire. The rugged mountain terrain seemed to literally absorb the individual companies. There were gaps in the front everywhere. The enemy infiltrated through these and attacked from the flanks and rear. The assault-team-style operations by the individual weak companies made the maintenance of even a loosely cohesive front extremely difficult. A unified battle and attack command was made extraordinarily difficult. The gunfire from the warships, which was well observed and directed, inflicted heavy losses on our units. North of Salerno the 16th Reconnaissance Battalion was relieved by the 3rd Panzer- Grenadier Division's 103rd Reconnaissance Battalion during the night of 11 September.

The 11th and 12th of September brought no improvement of any kind or any further success in our planned conduct of the attack. On 13 September all commanders were invited to the command post of XIV Corps for a discussion on the further conduct of the attack. This attack was to be carried out toward Salerno by the reinforced HG Panzer Division on 16 September. The main attack, which would take place in the Paestum area, 30 kilometers south of Salerno, was to be made by the 16th Panzer Division, the 29th Panzer-Grenadier Division, and elements of the 15th Panzer- Grenadier Division.

For this purpose, during the course of 13 and 14 September the 3rd Panzer-Grenadier Division's 64th Panzer-Grenadier Regiment, with three battalions, two artillery battalions, and a rocket brigade, was dispatched to the HG Division at the Avellino – Salerno road. The 64th Panzer-Grenadier Regiment was deployed northeast of Salerno near Sordina, where it immediately made contact with the enemy. On 15 September the HG Panzer Division's tanks were pulled out of the Cava area and sent to San Mango via San Saverino and Baronissi-Ogliara. The division's attack plan was as follows:

'Defence near Cava. Attack near Salerno. Attacking by night without preparatory artillery fire (taking advantage of the element of surprise), on the 15th and 16th of September the infantry will take the high ground south of Sordina and drive through to the sea. At daybreak on 16 September the panzer group will attack from San Mango and, advancing through Alfani, reach the coast and link up at the beach with the panzer-grenadier regiment. Both groups will subsequently launch a joint attack to take Salerno.'

"By early morning on 16 September the panzer-grenadiers, having taken the enemy completely by surprise, had taken the heights without heavy losses and advanced to a point abeam I. Monta to the west. There they ran into heavy enemy artillery fire as well as a British counterattack. Still in the midst of an energetic advance, both battalion headquarters were abruptly put out of action in close-quarters fighting. The resulting temporary confusion among the two leaderless units brought the attack to a standstill.

The panzer-grenadiers were committed too early through the unforseen intervention of a senior officer. As a result the supporting attack did not take place as planned. The latter attack also bogged down, in the Alfani area."

The limited success achieved by the German attack resulted in a reduction in the size of the bridgehead. However this did not lead to the planned cutting in two of the enemy landing front and to the capture of Salerno. The newly-won positions were unfavorable inasmuch as they suffered under heavy artillery fire, so much so that it was only with great difficulty that they were held until 18 September. On that day the Tenth Army ordered a withdrawal to the new front line.

The HG Panzer Division was withdrawn in stages in order to reach these new positions of the Tenth Army. The Volturno was foreseen as the new main line of resistance. The units were to stage a fighting withdrawal to this line in order to allow the forces in the rear to ready the front line as best as possible. Previously scouted fixed intermediate defensive lines were chosen, then reconnoitred by patrols, occupied by advance detachments and lightly fortified. The main body of the unit moved into these positions by night, leaving strong rear guards in contact with the enemy to prevent a rapid pursuit. In each case the rear guards were only permitted to withdraw to the new defensive lines at the last second.

This delaying tactic using rear guards was always enough to allow all the artillery to be in the new position and ready to fire by evening. The artillery was then used to keep the enemy at a distance. That this tactic worked at all was due to the cautiousness of the enemy, who was slow in following the withdrawing Germans. Moving up his artillery over the narrow mountain roads required the same amount of time as the German defenders needed to make their preparations to meet the next assault. Pioneer battalions blew up roads and bridges. These demolitions went smoothly after all the troops had passed. Once, however, a lightning strike on an explosive charge during a severe storm caused a bridge to be blown prematurely. The pioneers then had to carry out makeshift repairs as quickly as possible.

All efforts on the German side were focused on the withdrawing to new positions. A vigorous pursuit at that moment could have had unforeseen consequences, however all went well. The unit leaders, down to company commanders, had their men well in hand. Once again we turn to Wilhelm Schmalz for a summary of subsequent events:

"Looking back, I should like to summarize my views and conclusions about Salerno, including my battle experiences from the landings in Sicily and five river crossings, as follows: Every well-prepared river crossing and landing from the sea, which in a certain sense is comparable to a river crossing, must succeed if it is carried out using the element of surprise and if air superiority has been achieved. The possibility of the defender successfully repelling such an operation thus exists only when he has well-prepared fortifications or can bring in powerful land and air forces for a counterattack.

These conditions did not exist for the defenders in Sicily or at Salerno. Beyond that, the coastal fortifications were makeshift and inadequate. In Sicily the Italian troops positioned at the coast abandoned their positions and fled at the moment of the landing. In the case of Salerno the Italian units had just recently deserted their German allies. The only replacements in the entire critical coastal area were German observation patrols. In Salerno itself there was a German company and a battery with six guns at rest. The

German countermeasures could therefore not get under way until troops were moved up to the enemy landing sites. Due to the urgency of the situation, these movements had to be made by day, which exposed them to the strong enemy air forces. There was no sign of our own air force.

Only two narrow mountain roads were available for an immediate counterattack by the HG Panzer Division and these were watched by the enemy's air force and kept under fire from naval artillery. In order to set up our own artillery observation posts, hills first had to be taken in battle. The time lost in this way was used by the enemy to land further troops and bring up reinforcements.

Especially unpleasant was the fire from the heavy naval guns. In the infantry battle the German soldier felt himself to be at least the equal of any enemy, but against the gunfire of the untouchable enemy warships far out to sea he was powerless. In Sicily we had used an available 170mm battery against the Allied warships with good results. There was nothing comparable at Salerno. The enemy air force did not play a significant role in the ground war in the mountainous country near Salerno; however, its effects on our supply lines was considerable."

Further Operations – Developments in the Overall Situation

By 18 September the beachhead was firmly in Allied hands. Two days earlier the British Eighth Army had linked up with the American Fifth Army. Between the 8th and 13th of September General Montgomery successfully landed the US 5th Corps under Lieutenant General Allfrey near Tarent and Brindisi and established a foothold in the Gulf of St. Eufemia. This success was due in part to the fact that he met no resistance on account of the Italian collapse. The left flank of Montgomery's army very quickly reached Cosenza, while the right attack group took possession of Altamira.

When "Monty" received a call for help from the US Fifth Army, which found itself in great danger from the German attack, he immediately sent ahead the 5th Infantry Division and the 231st Malta Brigade; this fast battle group set out from Reggio in the direction of Naples. On the evening of 15 September it reached Scalea. Twenty-four hours later it rolled through Sapri and was thus only five kilometers from the Salerno combat zone. The two armies linked up near Agropoli on 17 September. The situation on the German side was now critical. *Generalfeldmarschall* Kesselring saw his troops threatened from the left flank and in the rear by the British Eighth Army. At the same time his signals service reported the landing of the US 3rd Infantry Division and the 82nd Airborne Division in the Salerno area. *Generalfeldmarschall* Kesselring drew the following conclusion from these events: "Fighting withdrawal to the north and northeast."

With the German troops went 4,000 prisoners taken in the Salerno area. 192 enemy tanks lay knocked out on the battlefield. The Tenth Army disengaged from the enemy during the night of 17 September. As one of its main units, on the 18th the HG Panzer Division began a step-by-step withdrawal. About 2,500 men from the divisions of the Tenth Army had to be left behind to cover the withdrawal. The HG Division showed its tactical skill by saving almost all the rear guards.

"After the follow-up landings by the Allies on the beaches at Salerno the German inferiority had become so marked that *Generalfeldmarschall* Kesselring dared not fight an open battle with the enemy in the open plains of Campagna or Apulia. The Commander-in-Chief South now endeavoured to reach an area of terrain which offered the prospect of a successful defence. As there was no such position south of Naples, Kesselring had to abandon the port city to the enemy."

On 1 October 1943 all of the installations in the port of Naples were blown up before the Germans withdrew from the city. The British Commander-in-Chief, General Alexander, wanted to prevent this withdrawal. On the morning of 4 October he landed a battle group of the Eight Army behind the German troops near Termoli in an effort to block their avenue of retreat. The 1st Parachute Division, which was attacked frontally by the British 78th Infantry Division, had already been outflanked by commando units, but it was successfully relieved by the 26th Panzer Division. In spite of all the efforts of the British command, it was unable to encircle the German units.

Ten days later the armored units of the Tenth Army were already in Abruzzi. There they met the 3rd and 90th Panzer-Grenadier Divisions and the 95th and 305th Infantry Divisions, which had installed themselves there to defend against the enemy attack. At any rate this masterfully-engineered withdrawal by Kesselring led to the first serious conflict between him and the commander in northern Italy, *Generalfeldmarschall* Rommel. Rommel wanted to abandon all of southern Italy and withdraw in one go to a line Rimini – La Spezia. Not as pessimistic as Rommel, Kesselring was convinced that the most economical way to employ his forces was to dig in for the winter in the defensible positions they now held. Subsequent events proved him correct.

"The OKW recalled Rommel from Italy, although a short time before it had looked as if he was to assume sole command of all German troops in Italy. Kesselring's strategy appealed more to Hitler than that of Rommel."

Regarding his appointment as the sole Commander-in-Chief Southwest – of Army Group C – Albert Kesselring observed: "My persistent request, which was finally presented at Führer Headquarters, to create in Italy a unified head of command, without respect to my person, was answered on 21 November 1943 by my being named Commander-in-Chief Southwest – Army Group C. Too late I set out with an even stronger will to make good the omissions and the resulting military disadvantages. The fortifications program of in-depth expansion behind the Gustav Line with its center at Monte Casino and the construction measures ordered by *Feldmarschall* Rommel were now adapted to fit my views, but not without my first acquainting myself on the spot with the terrain, state of construction and construction possibilities."

II Battalion, 1st Panzer-Grenadier Regiment HG in Italy

On 17 June 1943 *Leutnant* Klaus Arnheiter arrived in Utrecht and was welcomed by *Hauptmann* Reichel, the provisional commander of the new battalion, which was just then being formed. Arnheiter was made a platoon leader in 5th Company. The existing units at that time and their commanders were:

5th Company:	Hauptmann Langer
6th Company:	Hauptmann Fuchs
7th Company:	Oberleutnant Flemming

Battalion Adjutant: Oberleutnant Ötterer

Leutnant Arnheiter's roommate was *Leutnant* Fritz Alf, who came from a Luftwaffe construction battalion. The Krumhout Barracks in Utrecht was the fixed quarters of the new formation. The following account is based on the diary of Klaus Arnheiter:

Transfer of the trained battalion to Berlin-Reinickendorf was announced on 23 July. Preparations began the next day and the transport arrived in Berlin at ten o'clock on the evening of 26 July. Weapons and equipment were issued there. Training continued, with live firing at the training grounds in Döberitz. The new commander was *Hauptmann* Josef-August Fitz, an experienced officer who had already received the Knight's Cross on 11 December 1942 as commander of I Battalion, 74th Panzer-Grenadier Regiment.

Fitz very soon became well known in Berlin, such as when he made one of his fantastic flying leaps from the ten-meter board in his bathing trunks. Once he even did it while wearing his bathing trunks and Knight's Cross. (Whether or not this example may have inspired Brandtsohn to wear the Knight's Cross on his bathing trunks is unknown. But when he did, it wasn't something new, as this account proves.) *Leutnant* Arnheiter took command of the 5th Company in place of *Oberleutnant* Langer.

After further training at the Döberitz training grounds and a live-firing exercise, in the evening II Battalion, which was fully motorized, drove from Döberitz to Berlin-Reinickendorf via Dallgow, Heerstraße, Kaiserdamm, Großer Stern, Tiergarten, Unter den Linden, through Wedding and Müllerstraße. At ten after eleven in the evening on 13 August, the battalion left Moabit Station by train and travelled via Frankfurt-Worms and Kaiserslautern to Chalon sur Soane, where it arrived at midnight on 16 August. From there, already outfitted with tropical uniforms with short pants, at nine o'clock on the morning of 19 August the journey continued to the Italian frontier near Mondane. The subsequent trip through Turin, Asti, Alessandria and Genoa took place on 21 August. On the morning of 24 August it was continued as far as Nervi, a few kilometers east of Genoa. On 25 August the battalion travelled a further forty kilometers to Rapallo and from there via Pisa and Livorno to Civitavecchia.

On 27 August the transport train sat for twenty-four hours in a Rome station. Resumption of the journey was further delayed by a mysterious "loss of locomotives." Capua was reached on 31 August and from there the unit drove to a bivouac in Caiazzo. On 9 September the codeword 'Ballnacht', the signal for the commitment of II Battalion, 1st Panzer-Grenadier Regiment HG, was issued. The battalion drove through Maddaloni, Camelle, and Marigliano to Nocera, which was reached during the night of 10 September.

A point group was formed there and it was sent ahead with the mission of capturing intact a bridge near Cave de Tireni. Cave de Tireni had been destroyed by Allied bombers but was found to be free of the enemy. While on its way to the bridge, the assault detachment came under fire from machine-guns and 20mm weapons from the far side of the bridge and from the cliff. The bridge led across a deep gorge. At the south end of same the road bent in a sharp curve around a house. Behind this cover was an enemy armored car, which now and then rolled forward and fired several shots from its weapons. The enemy machine-gun nest was in the opposite steep bank, from where it kept the bridge and road under fire. While under continuous fire from these weapons, the pioneer *Leutnant* Paulus and the commander of 5th Company, which had been driving in the lead position, ran onto the bridge and removed an explosive charge that had been placed on the road surface in the center of the bridge.

The enemy was now placed under fire and after a brief exchange he withdrew. *Leutnant* Arnheiter led his 5th Company across the bridge and the 2nd Platoon reached La Molina. The battalion command post was set up in a protected hollow in the steep bank. An observation squad was installed in a hut made of quarry stone, from which it had a good view beyond La Molina as far as Marina on the sea. In positions to the left was the 7th Company under *Oberleutnant* Fleming. Its front faced the Liberatore, which the soldiers dubbed "Piz Palü". On the right was the 6th Company under Lt. Niemeyer. Its direction of fire was toward Dragonea. Niemeyer had replaced Oblt. Fuchs in the meantime. These positions were to be held against all enemy attacks.

In the days that followed, English artillery and mortars attempted to destroy the German positions. Commando squads attacked by night, but all were repelled. Between attacks the Allied naval guns fired on Cave de Tirena. Now and then enemy aircraft attacked the town. Among these were formations of Lightnings which flew over the front at low altitude, firing their guns as they went. During the night of 23 September the enemy made a surprise thrust which pushed its way between two platoons of 5th Company, cutting one of them off. The platoon was later rescued. A new blocking position was occupied at three hours past midnight on 24 September. The 5th Company established itself on the 662-meter- high Monte Arenella. This area, too, was covered by heavy naval artillery fire.

Withdrawing through a new position on Monte Cocu, and across the hills of the same, the battalion reached Roccapiemonte. From there the 5th Company, which had so far gone the entire way on foot, was able to travel to Lauro by motor transport. There the company left the vehicles and proceeded on foot to Beato and Quindici. The subsequent march led back through Nola to Cancello, where new positions were occupied. While passing through Nola the commander of 8th Company, *Oberleutnant* Drotbohm, was wounded by a hand grenade tossed from a rooftop by partisans. Drotbohm's left leg had to be amputated at the knee.

II Battalion, 1st Panzer-Grenadier Regiment HG had thus covered a considerable distance in its retreat northwest from the Salerno area. The subsequent withdrawal led the regiment through Caserta into a reserve position. Following the death of *Oberleutnant* Fleming, Arnheiter also temporarily took command of 7th Company. On 12 October *Major* Dedekind appeared in the battalion's positions. His battalion of the 15th Panzer-Grenadier Division was II Battalion's neighbor on the right.

On the afternoon of 13 October the battalion moved out in the direction of Tiflisco. Near Bellona it occupied a reserve position of the HG Panzer Division. In a rapid pursuit the enemy had crossed the Volturno near Ponte Annibale and reached the top of the monastery mountain there with his leading elements. Following an artillery bombardment which began at 1600, at 1830 hours German troops began climbing the hill in preparation for a counterattack. The attackers opened up with submachine-guns precisely at 2000. The enemy was driven back, eliminating the threat from that direction. The withdrawal to the old Bellona defensive line and the subsequent march from there as rear guard on the evening of 15 October required each man to call on his last reserves of strength. The withdrawal was made across the bare peak. Before descending to the south the 5th Company was caught by machine-gun fire which rose up from both sides. The former command post was reached. Further orders for the withdrawal were issued there on the evening of 16 October. At 0300 hours on 17 October the 5th Company withdrew as far as the area beyond Vitulazzi.

Early on the morning of that same day the withdrawal continued from Vitulazzi to Pietra Melara, where the company became the regimental reserve. The enemy pressed into this area from both sides with substantial forces. Finally they stormed down from the top of the mountain, on which there was also a monastery. The "Fifth" was fired on by artillery from the left flank. On 23 October the company command post was located at the western edge of Pietra Melara. Two six-barrelled *Nebelwerfer* went into position on the road to Riardo. These attempted to smoke out the enemy artillery observers on the Monte Maria-Madama.

On 26 October the enemy stepped up his efforts: 29 fighter-bomber attacks in ten hours and heavy artillery fire supported his slow advance. At midday on the 27th enemy infantry and 26 tanks reached Teano. The city had been identified as the site of a hospital, but it was attacked by enemy bombers all the same. The enemy tanks broke through on 5th Company's left. With its right wing on the Via Casilina, the 5th Company fought its way back as rear guard. The Post Platoon was surrounded at noon on the 29th. The enemy, who the day before had attacked the sector on the right held by the 15th Panzer Division's 115th Panzer-Grenadier Regiment, now turned to II Battalion, 1st Panzer-Grenadier Regiment HG. The Post Platoon was able to fight its way out in an heroic effort.

During the afternoon of that day the 5th Company, with one final effort, was able to escape the threat of being outflanked and rolled back along the Via Casilina. The enemy remained stationary during the night. Two Tiger tanks accompanied the withdrawal. 1 November once again saw the entire battalion in action. The enemy's attempt to break through on the right flank at the fork in the road from the Via Casilina to Pietravairano had to be repulsed, in order to secure the passage of the units which were still lagging behind, including the 15th Panzer-Grenadier Division. The panzer-grenadiers stood up to their knees in water in the deep ditches at the sides of the road in the pouring rain. Whenever a vehicle rolled past, the enemy poured heavy artillery fire onto the road fork. Point 240 was only 1,000 meters farther to the rear. It was reached and held the following night and witnessed yet another dramatic action. It was early on the morning of 5 November when 23 enemy tanks rolled past on the right and attacked the 5th Company command post for an hour. This attack was repulsed by 5th Company with the assistance of the artillery.

Afterward the armored unit attempted to outflank this position. The attempt succeeded: advancing four kilometers on the left flank and six kilometers on the right, the armored formation had deeply outflanked 5th Company. The order was given to withdraw during the night. On 7 November the division assembly area, 80 kilometers farther to the rear, was reached. Luckily part of the company was able to ride on the two Tigers, which rolled down the serpentine around Monte Rotondo under heavy artillery fire. At the bottom, the men of the "Fifth" were able to board vehicles of their own motor transport column and in this way reached the assigned rest area, 80 kilometers behind the front.

The battalion was placed on alert on the afternoon of 8 November. That evening *Leutnant* Arnheiter was transferred to the regimental HQ. Thus ended his diary, which illustrated far better than many combat reports written by larger units the abundance of guerilla-type warfare a company or battalion in Italy had to deal with. *Oberleutnant* Dratwa assumed command of the 5th Company. So far the battalion had not seen the face of regimental commander *Oberst* Haas. The latter, still occupied with the continued formation of his unit, remained in Utrecht.

On 18 November II Battalion, 1st Panzer-Grenadier Regiment HG began its return to Utrecht. The unit's rail journey took it through Rome and Chiusi to Innsbruck and from there to Cologne and back to Utrecht. Utrecht witnessed the reformation of the 1st Panzer-Grenadier Regiment HG, now under the command of *Oberstleutnant* Kluge. *Leutnant* Arnheiter became regimental adjutant.

The Monastery at Monte Cassino

While walking along the Pokornygasse in Vienna's District XIX, one comes upon a memorial tablet on house number 5 which would be unthinkable in Germany: "In this house lived and died the deserving Austrian Oberstleutnant JULIUS SCHLEGEL. Through his personal actions in autumn 1943 he saved the art treasures of the MONTE CASSINO monastery Dedicated by his comrades 31 October 1969."

In an age when German soldiery is dragged through the mud and everything to do with soldiering is made to sound evil, this memorial tablet proves that there were once also people who were grateful for the help of German soldiers and that there were men who were brave enough to act on their own initiative to save the cultural treasures of the monastery of the Holy Benedict. This is very much in contrast to the New Zealand General who insisted on a repeated bombardment of the Monte Cassino monastery even though there was no cause to, for the German defenders had declared the monastery mountain an unoccupied neutral zone in order to prevent the destruction of this time-honored monastery. Christianity and the entire world has Austrian *Oberstleutnant* Julius Schlegel to thank for the saving of the monastery's treasures from the Allied bomber forces.

The Gustav Line was established by *Generalfeldmarschall* Kesselring in October 1943. This barrier, which ran across the entire width of the Apennine Peninsula, was supposed to halt the enemy's northward advance. Near Casino this defensive line cut the strategically important Naples-Rome road, the Via Casilina. As a result the city of Cassino was incorporated within the defensive zone. When *Oberstleutnant* Julius Schlegel, at that time the commander of the HG Maintenance Battalion, learned that the Monte Cassino monastery – the very first Benedictine monastery founded in 529 – and the art treasures of the main monastery of occidental monasticism as well were in great danger, he immediately began planning countermeasures.

At the time *Oberstleutnant* Schlegel wasn't yet thinking of a bombardment of the monastery, rather only that it might be hit accidentally. An art historian and librarian by profession, he knew of Monte Cassino's unique treasures.

The devout Christian Schlegel went to the monastery to see the 80-year-old Bishop Gregorius on 14 October 1943 and suggested to him that, with his help, the treasures of the monastery, at least those which were transportable, should be taken to safety. At first Abbot Gregorius Delmare refused. He was firmly convinced that the Allies would spare the holy relics and the monastery. After all, they had set out on their crusade as "liberators and fighters against barbarism".

"I am certain," said the abbot to the *Oberstleutnant*, "that the Allies will show the same consideration as *Generalfeldmarschall* Kesselring, who has had a 300 meter neutral zone drawn around the monastery and who insists on the maintenance of the order. As you know, German soldiers may only enter the abbey for divine service if unarmed. They may also inspect the monastery only under the supervision of a monk."

In the end, *Oberstleutnant* Schlegel was able to obtain a guarantee of support from a German monk living on Monte Cassino, Father Emanuel Mundig. Together they succeeded in persuading the abbot to agree to transfer the treasures to the Vatican in Rome. *Oberstleutnant* Schlegel undertook this rescue effort on his own initiative and without the knowledge of his local superiors, and in doing so set in motion a cultural act of unique significance.

When the Allies crossed the Volturno and began their pitiless bombing of the city, Abbot Gregorius asked *Oberstleutnant* Schlegel to begin moving the treasures and relics to safety. Schlegel agreed immediately, but he soon found himself faced with a multitude of treasures, among them 80,000 volumes of the most priceless library there was, with original writings by Horaz, Ovid, Vergil, and Seneca, countless original scrolls and other records, many priceless artifacts, paintings, articles of worship and other irreplaceable assets.

One of the first things he discovered during the initial work was the closely-guarded secret that the monastery had taken charge of a number of world-famous paintings by Italian masters. These had been destined for a large art exhibition in Naples in early 1939. When the war began they were not sent back, because museums asked that their paintings be left in the protection of the monastery. It was 140 kilometers from Monte Cassino to Rome. 120 trucks were required for the goods removed from the monastery. These trucks were sent up to the monastery and loaded. Each transport was accompanied by two fathers, who ensured that the entire load was handed over at its destination.

The paintings removed from the monastery were placed in a castle near Spoleto, 150 kilometers north of Rome. (Not until later were they transferred to the Vatican in Rome.) Among the rescued paintings were three by Titian, two by Rafael, originals by Tintoretto, Ghirlandajo, Pieter Breughel, and many other world-famous artists. All remaining articles were taken immediately to Rome. The fathers who escorted the shipments remained in Rome, from where they reported the safe hand-over of the treasures to the church.

In the course of the first shipment it turned out that crates had to be made to safeguard certain important parchments and codices. The joiners and cabinet-makers of Schlegel's maintenance battalion voluntarily worked day and night to meet this requirement. When Schlegel's divisional commander, *Generalleutnant* Conrath, learned of his unauthorized activities, he covered up the independent action of his subordinate and lent his support to the rescue effort in the form of additional manpower. The matter had to be reported to *Generalfeldmarschall* Kesselring, who called the action a good one and gave his authorization.

One particularly ceremonious act was the transfer of the mortal remains of the Holy Benedict. They represented the greatest treasure held by the monastery, for they were one of the most significant sacred relics of Catholic Christianity. The relics were carefully packed in a suitcase. Deeply moved, monks and soldiers watched as the abbot blessed the bones before they were delivered safely to Rome. Most of the monks, except for the abbot and his closest circle, had already been evacuated to Rome. Likewise evacuated were the many nuns and the orphan children entrusted to their care. The rescue effort ended on 1 November 1943. At the close of a holy service for all the soldiers involved in the rescue effort, *Oberstleutnant* Schlegel received from the hand of the Abbey-Bishop Gregorius a certificate of gratitude written on expensive parchment. A translation of the Latin text reads:

"In the name of our father Jesus Christ! The people of Cassino thank with all their hearts the noble and beloved military tribune Julius Schlegel, who with much work and zeal has saved the monks and treasures of Monte Casino, and they ask of God that he prosper. Monte Casino, on the 1st of November 1943. Gregorius Diamare. O.S.B. Bishop and Abbot of Monte Cassino."

In front of the Mount of Angels in Rome, on the occasion of the hand-over of the last shipment, *Oberstleutnant* Schlegel met with the head abbot of the San Anselmo Abbey, Fidelis von Stotzingen, and informed him of the successful conclusion of the rescue operation. This marked the end of an action, whose scale was not matched by another in the Second World War.

On 15 February something happened that no one actually thought would take place: 229 Allied bombers dropped 453 tonnes of bombs on the monastery of Monte Cassino. The edifice of Holy Saint Benedict, which had stood on this hill since 529 AD, sank into rubble and ash.

The dedication of the memorial tablet to *Oberstleutnant* Julius Schlegel, who had died on 8 August 1958, took place in front of his home in Vienna. Participants included the Papal Nuncio in Austria, Archbishop Dr. Rossi, the Italian Councillor of Embassy d'Aragona, Defence Minister Dr. Prader, *General der Panzertruppe* Rülling and many former comrades as well as personalities from public and cultural life. Military Chaplain Tritz blessed the memorial tablet, while the widow of the deceased unveiled the tablet. Two sentries of the Guard Battalion of the Austrian *Bundeswehr* presented arms.

It should not go unmentioned that in Austria, too, there were forces at work which tried to defame this deserving soldier, who several months after his rescue effort lost a leg in a fighter-bomber attack. Even in his native land of Austria Schlegel had to endure humiliation (like so many upstanding German soldiers did in Germany). On the basis of false statements he was sentenced to jail. His discharge was achieved thanks to the help of the monks of the Monte Cassino monastery. Schlegel became a member of the city parliament of Vienna and a member of a regional diet.

III (Assault Gun) Battalion, Hermann Göring Panzer Regiment in the Italian Battle Zone November 1943 – July 1944

In October 1943 the assault gun battalion with its 9th, 10th, and 11th Companies was in its assembly position in the area of Cajanello – Teano – Mignano. Although identified as a hospital city, Teano was repeatedly bombed. The battalion stood ready for action under the following commanders:

Commanding Officer:	Hptm. (later Major) Sandrock
9th Company:	Oblt. Jekosch
10th Company:	Lt. Wallhäußer
11th Company:	Oblt. Olfermann

From 3 November until 6 December the units occupied quarters in Castrocielo and San Francesca and held courses for drivers and carried out training. On 6 December 1943 the Saint Angelo bridge collapsed under the weight of an assault gun and fell into the Liri River. From November until 13 January the assault guns occupied various alternate firing positions and in the process suffered several losses to artillery fire from Teano. The roads from the city of Cassino were choked with soldiers, including those of an Austrian unit.

The transfer to the new readiness area of Roccasecca and Pontecorvo began on 13 January 1944. The battalion remained in this area until 24 January, before moving on to Castelforte where it saw action against attacking British armor. The battle for the hill positions on both sides of Castelforte and San

Lorenzo developed into serious struggles, which led to losses among the assault guns. Among those killed was *Leutnant* König. The retreat to Roccasecca took place on 29 January. The battalion remained in this readiness position until 1 February 1944. The following is a report by the commander of an assault howitzer platoon, *Leutnant* Werner Ringel, describing his view of the assault guns in action. Ringel's company, commanded by Oblt. Bellinger, was supposed to be sent to the battalion, but did not make contact with it until the battle was already in progress.

The Battle for Castelforte: Lt. Ringel's Account

"The Allies crossed the Garigliano on the right wing of the HG Division's front and, advancing rapidly, broke into the German positions. On the evening of 17 January, *Oberleutnant* Bellinger received orders to counterattack with his assault gun company the next day.

The advance at first led over the narrow, choked streets and roads to Pontecorvo. There, too, traffic was snarled. The bridge over the broad, swift-flowing Liri River had been the target of several enemy air raids. Everything within a wide radius of the bridge lay in ruins. The bridge itself had also been hit several times. A single lane of traffic continued to cross the bridge at a snail's pace; it was the only passable bridge for a distance of 40 kilometers. Once the unit had crossed, it rolled on into the mountains. Santa Oliva was reached. The width of the assault guns made it almost impossible for them to make any forward progress on the ever-steepening roads. The unit rolled on past Monte d'Oro, which was visible from Arce to Cassino, and reached Esperia. There, once again, the assault guns had to negotiate several hairpin turns, and at about 2300 hours a halt was called in the middle of the village.

On 19 January the skies grew overcast. It became dark and the drive became a nightmare for everyone. The drive to Castelforte will long be remembered by all who were there. Our objective was still 15 kilometers away. Up to this point the unit had taken eight hours to cover every thirty kilometers and the most difficult part of the journey still lay before it. We continued up the mountain; Ausonio came into sight. When we came to the first dwellings, *Oberleutnant* Bellinger stopped at a half-collapsed house, where he held a situation briefing in the light of a kerosene lamp. He informed us that our objective was Castelforte. The enemy had the same objective and was already in San Lorenzo, from where two roads led to Castelforte. 'We attack enemy-occupied San Lorenzo at dawn', said Bellinger.

The last stragglers had meanwhile arrived. We resumed the drive to Coreno and from there in the direction of Montosa, a small village only a few kilometers from Castelforte. The first shells from long-range artillery crashed into the cliffs and caused the first casualties. Travelling as fast as possible, the unit rolled into Montosa. In the middle of the village it became stuck in a narrowing lane. There was nothing else to do but back up to the edge of the village and find good cover there. The attack scheduled for 0700 hours the next morning came to nothing as a result of this setback. When it became light, the men saw before them the city of Castelforte, strung out very high on a mountain slope, flanked left and right by projecting ridges. The valley opened up to the southeast and the view from the village extended to Garigliano and beyond to the slopes of Monte San Croce and Monte Massimo.

The road in front of the river was in enemy hands. Our main line of resistance had earlier run between the river and road. The enemy could be easily seen with binoculars. The first day in front of Castelforte we were targeted by enemy artillery fire from several batteries of every caliber. *Oberleutnant* Bellinger was wounded as were three veteran platoon leaders and assault gun commanders. Command was passed to me (Lt. Ringel). On the morning of 20 January I was visited by the commander of the grenadiers, who spoke vaguely about a counterattack toward San Lorenzo.

We set out soon afterward in order to take advantage of the morning twilight, the grenadier *Leutnant* and I with my two assault guns. We rolled down the mountain toward San Lorenzo. Everywhere there were dense olive groves which severely limited our field of fire. Several Tommies were nabbed by the grenadiers. We approached to within 300 meters of the village without a shot being fired. A Sherman suddenly drove out of the village; it slid into a bomb crater and was abandoned by its crew. Heavy small-arms fire flared up. We put a few shells into the houses to the right and left of the road, from which the fire was coming. *Feldwebel* Fuhr, who was commanding our number two gun, drove into the village. He spotted a Sherman and destroyed it with the first shot. The Sherman went up with a roar as its ammunition exploded. I covered Fuhr's advance, all the while remaining in contact with the grenadiers. We reached the spot where our path met the main road to Minturno.

Fuhr drove round a corner; he was hit by a concealed anti-tank gun positioned there, but without being seriously damaged. Fuhr quickly turned around and disappeared into safety behind the corner of the nearest house. San Lorenzo was now wide awake and the scene of hectic activity. Shots rang out from every corner and from the houses. Our grenadiers took cover. We drove back to the village entrance and fired our KwK at everything suspicious. Things quickly quieted down and we tried once again to move forward. At the crossroads we saw further enemy groups moving in from Minturno. San Lorenzo wasn't about to be taken by a surprise attack and we were too weak for combat in the town.

Since there were still several of our wounded grenadiers in the village, we dashed forward three times and recovered them. In doing so we were not fired on by the Americans. Heavily laden, we rolled back to our departure position, having failed to reach our objective. We arrived in Castelforte and were fired upon heavily. In the afternoon *Oberleutnant* Tobis arrived, and we learned from battalion command that he was to assume command of our gun.

We attacked San Lorenzo again on 21 January. It was an unfortunate repetition of the first attack and was equally unsuccessful. The number two gun was knocked out by a heavy anti-tank gun. The bow plates flew into the air following a direct hit from an American 91mm anti-tank gun, and further hits followed in rapid succession. I was able to locate the anti-tank gun, but was unable to engage it. I had to withdraw with my assault gun to avoid the same fate. Under good cover this was successful. San Lorenzo had been significantly reinforced during the night. We returned to Castelforte. At noon the battalion commander, *Hauptmann* Sandrock, appeared, bringing with him the order for another advance. I outlined my objections to *Hauptmann* Sandrock, but he informed me that the attack was to go ahead anyway. My assault guns were to lead the way, followed by a battle group under the command of an army *Hauptmann* and finally Hptm. Sandrock with several more assault guns.

I rolled past the Sherman lying in the bomb crater and reached our knocked-out assault gun. I searched for the enemy anti-tank gun and finally discovered it in a row of dense olive groves behind several trees. The gun was targeted and several shots put it out of action. As we were backing up a short distance, something struck the rim of the hatch and bounced off the helmet of the gun commander; it tumbled to the floor and lay there hissing ominously. 'Everyone out!' I ordered. We raced to the nearby bomb crater and took cover. But nothing happened. Our assault gun sat there with its engine running, unreachable by us in the by now heavy firing. The enemy defensive fire grew heavier; tracer flitted through the olive grove.

Everyone pressed themselves against the wall of the crater; but the enemy seemed to have no lust for an infantry attack. When it became quieter, I raced back to Castelforte during a pause in the firing. The assault gun was recovered that evening. Beneath the seat lay an intact 50mm anti-tank shell. Nothing special happened on the 22nd. Preparations were made to repel an enemy attack. On 23 January I led the command vehicle and two other assault guns to the east end of Castelforte. The San Lorenzo – Suio road came into view; Sherman tanks were rolling down the road. Sitting at the exit from the village was an assault gun from an army assault gun battalion; it had been hit in the vision slit by an anti-tank gun. We later learned that all four members of the crew had been found dead.

The next evening I was given a special mission. Between Castelforte and San Lorenzo there was a 75mm anti-tank gun belonging to the grenadiers, which on orders of the commander of the grenadiers was to be towed away by us. Accompanied by two assault guns, we drove our 105mm assault howitzer there, dragged the anti-tank gun out of its position, and brought it back to Castelforte. On our arrival I was berated by the regimental commander of the grenadiers for not also having brought the ammunition for the anti-tank gun. Castelforte was increasingly battered by gunfire in the days that followed. There was a series of casualties. This fortress at the gate to the mountains was important to the enemy. Had he kicked open this door, there would have been no stopping him, for the road to Casino would have been open. The battalion command post was located in a narrow mountain gorge halfway to Coreno.

On 26 January the last assault guns fell back toward the north, pursued by artillery fire."

Before we return to the history of the assault gun battalion, a description of the event which had long been feared by senior German commanders: the landing of Allied troops near Anzio-Nettuno, far in the rear of the defending German units.

The Road to the Hermann Göring Parachute-Panzer Division

Following the end of the seven-day Battle of Salerno the HG Panzer Division continued fighting a delaying action against the American forces. The division still belonged to XIV Panzer Corps, which was under the command of the newly-formed Tenth Army commanded by *General* von Vietinghoff. The division saw action at the Volturno, Lignano, and Garigliano Rivers. On 1 November 1943 it was incorporated into the First Parachute Army commanded by *Generaloberst* Student. This resulted in another change in the division's organization and designation. From that day on it was called the "HG Parachute- Panzer Division". Accordingly the HG Armored Reconnaissance Battalion became the HG Parachute-Panzer Armored Reconnaissance Battalion and was enlarged by a pioneer company and a motorcycle company.

The motorcycle company came to the division as a new formation from the HG Replacement and Training Regiment in Utrecht, Holland as a replacement for the motorcycle company lost in Africa. Following these additions the HG Parachute-Panzer Armored Reconnaissance Battalion consisted of the following units:

1st Armored Reconnaissance Company

2nd Motorcycle Company

3rd Panzer-Grenadier Company (armored)

4th Panzer-Grenadier Company (motorized) on VW Schwimmwagen

5th Armored Pioneer Company

Supply Company

In late autumn the fighting intensified at the Garigliano and Sangro Rivers. The front had become almost stationary; nevertheless, local battles and engagements, which were fought with great bitterness, frayed the nerves and used up the strength of the division. The American Fifth Army, which was fighting at the Garigliano, and the British Eighth Army, which was operating in the east of the peninsula, tried in vain to break through the German front and gain ground to the north and northwest. The Anglo-Americans were highly surprised to find such strong resistance there. The Allied command assumed that the grinding battles on Sicily, and later those at Salerno and at the Volturno, had worn down the German forces and that the survivors of those battles of attrition had lost their will to fight. It was assumed that they would not be able to withstand a determined attack by strong forces.

This assumption – and at the same time hope – on the part of the Allies proved to be wishful thinking. The persistent, determined resistance they met produced in the Allied command a desire for a landing in the defenders' rear in order to destroy their will to defend. The result would be the collapse of the German front. The Allied hopes went so far as to assign such a long-range effect to a successful breakthrough, that they might be able to avoid the much more dangerous invasion of France.

Given the nature of the extended Italian coastline, which due to the shortage of German infantry forces could not be adequately kept under surveillance or guarded, such an operation offered good prospects of success. Should a landing still be necessary in Western France, the experience gained in the Italian landing would prove invaluable in its planning and execution. These considerations very quickly developed into the plans for Operation "Shingle".

At the beginning of November the HG Parachute-Panzer Division was able to withdraw its first elements from the front lines and move them to resting and refitting areas which had been established at the foot of the Lepiner Mountains in the Frosinone area. However several units, in particular the HG Flak Regiment and the HG Armored Artillery Regiment, were assigned to other divisions and remained in the battle. Some of them remained at the front until January 1944, suffering heavy losses in the process.

Replacements were sent to the division between Frosinone and Gaeta and later there were changes in the division command. The division command post with the command staff was located in a small mountain retreat called Priverno in the Lepiner Mountains, about 20 kilometers from the most famous of Italian roads, the Via Appia. The division had been stripped of all its infantry units and the Tenth Army had no intention of granting requests for their return. These elements of the HG Division were too badly needed for defense. The most important requirement was to plug the gaps which kept reappearing in the front. Only the newly-formed division reserve under *Hauptmann* Fuchs, which at this point was only battalion strength, was available for important missions, for example guarding the division command post. It was not yet completely equipped with vehicles, and the weapons complement also left something to be desired.

Beyond that all that was available was the division combat school under *Oberleutnant* Lehmann, which for several months had been providing all the men coming to the division with close-combat training. It was a small, but first-class fighting unit. The unit's weapons and vehicles situation was also deplorable. A transfer of either of these two reserve units with the required speed was impossible because of the shortage of vehicles, even though the situation, which was becoming increasingly serious almost day by day, made the rapid movement of all forces of vital importance.

At this point let us turn to the operations of the small splinter groups of the HG Parachute-Panzer Division which saw action with foreign units.

The 1st and 7th Panzer Companies of the Hermann Göring Parachute-Panzer Regiment in Action

On 13 November 1943, the 1st Company of the Hermann Göring Parachute-Panzer Regiment was placed under the command of the 94th Infantry Division. Its mission was to maintain surveillance of the coast between Gaeta and Formia together with the division's 267th Grenadier Regiment. For six days from 10 January 1944 it also had to detach a platoon to the sector held by III Battalion, 274th Grenadier Regiment near Scauri, for security duties. During the night of 20 January 1944 the company received orders to go into readiness positions at the Formia – Spigno road fork for a further mission. 7th Company, HG Parachute-Panzer Regiment had been directed to work with the 274th Grenadier Regiment and was already in combat near Minturno.

"At 0800 hours on 10 January 1st Company was given the job of guarding the Santa Infante – Minturno road. The most forward line held by the infantry was in line with the Minturno cemetery. Since 7th Company's most forward vehicles were already 500 meters north of the cemetery on Hill 150 on the Santa Maria Infante – Formia road, I ordered 1st Platoon under *Leutnant* Lenz to move up to the most forward infantry position.

Continuous infantry attacks on the cemetery and the forward infantry lines were repulsed by the Lenz Platoon and the tanks of 1st Company, which were deployed farther north along the road and on Hill 163, using high-explosive and hollow charge shells. The enemy laid down heavy artillery fire – which at times increased to a heavy barrage – on our positions. Panzer 123 under *Feldwebel* Ruppert succeeded in destroying the enemy artillery observation post on Hill 167 north of Minturno. In the afternoon hours there was a low-level air attack, which caused no losses, however. Because of the weak infantry forces the point platoon remained in position during the night.

An attack by a battalion of the 200th Grenadier Regiment and 1st and 7th Panzer Companies of the HG Parachute-Panzer Regiment was ordered for 21 January to retake the hills east and west of the cemetery. In order to assure unified control of the tanks, command was handed over to *Leutnant* Karsch of the 7th Company. I sent two 75mm (long) tanks of 7th Company to my forward platoon under *Leutnant* Lenz. This increased Lenz's force to four tanks armed with long-barrelled 75mm guns. He received instructions to advance with the grenadier company under Oblt. Wenzel. The remaining tanks of 1st and 7th Companies were to provide covering fire and in particular keep Hills 131, 167, 146, and 156, as well as Monte Natale – all of which were held by the enemy – under fire.

The grenadiers moved out at 1710 hours. Both panzer companies provided effective covering fire, while at the same time the four tanks under *Leutnant* Lenz moved forward. The enemy was shaken by this attack with tank support. When our leading tank under *Feldwebel* Lübke of 1st Company turned the corner at the cemetery, Lübke found himself facing a Sherman. The enemy tank was put out of action with the first shot. Continuing to advance, *Leutnant* Lenz destroyed a heavy anti-tank gun and a Churchill tank. In the meantime twilight had begun to settle. The tanks then withdrew to the cemetery for the night. At dawn the grenadiers, who had dug in, launched a surprise attack and successfully stormed and occupied the enemy-held white house, 100 meters farther down the road to the southwest.

On 22 January the enemy began the fighting with heavy artillery and rocket fire. Nevertheless, the grenadiers, supported by the panzers, succeeded in taking possession of the specified hills. *Leutnant* Lenz was wounded in both hands by a burst of machine-gun fire while opening the turret hatch. The accompanying first-aid NCO begged Lenz to go at once to the dressing station. But the *Leutnant* merely had his wounds bandaged and then returned to his tank. While doing so he sustained severe head injuries from an exploding artillery shell and died on the spot.

I immediately assumed overall command and deployed the tanks to guard against an attack from Minturno. The most forward panzer was 150 meters in front of the white house, and the second, which I commanded, was positioned 50 meters behind it. The other three were positioned to the left and right to provide cover. Peering through the 'scissors' I spotted targets on Monte del Duca and on Hill 141. The enemy tanks were rolling cautiously in the direction of Minturno. When we opened fire on them they withdrew.

The enemy's response was heavy artillery fire; the forward tank was hit and had to withdraw with a damaged gun. I moved my vehicle up to take its place. The enemy fired smoke shells and obscured my view. At this point tanks and infantry attacked Hills 156 and 131. At the same time I was hit by a round from an anti-tank rifle fired by a tank-killing squad. The tank-killing squad and anti-tank rifle were put out of action. We succeeded in stopping the enemy attack at the white house, however Hills 156 and 133 fell into enemy hands. This forced me to withdraw to the cemetery.

During the night my tanks placed heavy fire on Hill 131, which was subsequently recaptured by the grenadiers. The tanks of both companies were once again moved up to the first curve in the road at the cemetery and just behind it. Throughout the 23rd of January the tanks' positions lay under well-directed artillery fire. Individual anti-tank guns fired at the panzers from the hills 1,600 meters to the east. A heavy barrage began at 1600 hours, and after 45 minutes enemy tanks broke through, driving under their own artillery fire. Our point tank drove back at maximum speed, followed by the number two vehicle. Both rolled past me at high speed. Then I saw the reason why: a Sherman was following them. I turned my gun toward this foe and knocked it out. The tank's momentum carried it past me. It grazed my fender and stopped a few meters behind my tank, blazing fiercely. This forced me to back up 50 meters. A second Sherman became visible in the glare of the fire from the first tank. I fired immediately and it turned around. It was hit again, but this failed to stop the enemy tank.

The enemy opened fire once again; my point tank suffered damage to an idler wheel and lost a track as a result. I had my panzer tow the damaged tank to safety. Climbing into a vehicle of 1st Company, I took charge of the forces defending north of the cemetery with their front facing south. The grenadiers had also withstood the enemy infantry attack. Nevertheless, during the night the 274th Grenadier Regiment ordered a withdrawal to a new main line of resistance. All that was left behind was 9th Company, 200th Grenadier Regiment, and to its right 3rd Company, 361st Grenadier Regiment. Two vehicles of 1st Company, HG Parachute-Panzer Regiment moved up to a position 150 meters north of the cemetery to provide cover for the outposts. The remaining tanks were in defensive positions on Hills 150 and 157. The left flank was open. On 25 January I instructed *Leutnant* Wladarz to take charge of the tanks protecting the grenadiers. While trying to establish contact with the grenadiers he was captured.

9th Company, 200th Grenadier regiment was withdrawn on 27 January. Only one squad was left in the area of the cemetery and the two tanks of 1st Company assumed responsibility for protecting this last rear guard near Hill 150 during the night of 28 January 1944.

On the night of 30 January 3rd Company, 361st Grenadier Regiment withdrew to Hills 131 and 160 as ordered. *Oberleutnant* Deckert ordered a change of position and occupied a position 150 meters northwest of Kilometer 5 on the Formia – Santa Maria Infante Road from which to protect I Battalion, 361st Grenadier Regiment. The tanks of 7th Company assumed the covering role in the direction of Minturno. This new position was placed under heavy fire by enemy artillery, which already had the range.

Since the situation was otherwise quiet, on 1 February 1944 I ordered the panzers to an assembly area two kilometers northeast of the Formia – Naples – Casino road fork on the road to Casino. Their orders were to withdraw to the positions of I Battalion, 367th Grenadier Regiment at the road fork to Spigno when enemy pressure became intense and then go into position there.

On 4 February, as per orders from the 267th Grenadier Regiment, 1st Company was once again placed under this regiment's command and was instructed to cooperate with its II Battalion. Its mission was:

"Drive forward to Solovorano and together with the grenadiers counterattack and drive the enemy back to his jumping-off positions."

The enemy did not attack, however, and the company saw no further action. The 1st and 7th Companies returned to their unit. Further elements of the division fought in other sectors of the front, such as the area south of Casino on Monte Maggiore and at the Rapido River. The fighting on Monte Samucro and Monte Troccio and finally near Castelforte in January 1944 was very heavy. On 6 January 1944 the division was officially redesignated as the Hermann Göring Parachute-Panzer Division. In spite of this change in name it continued to be employed as a panzer division within the army."

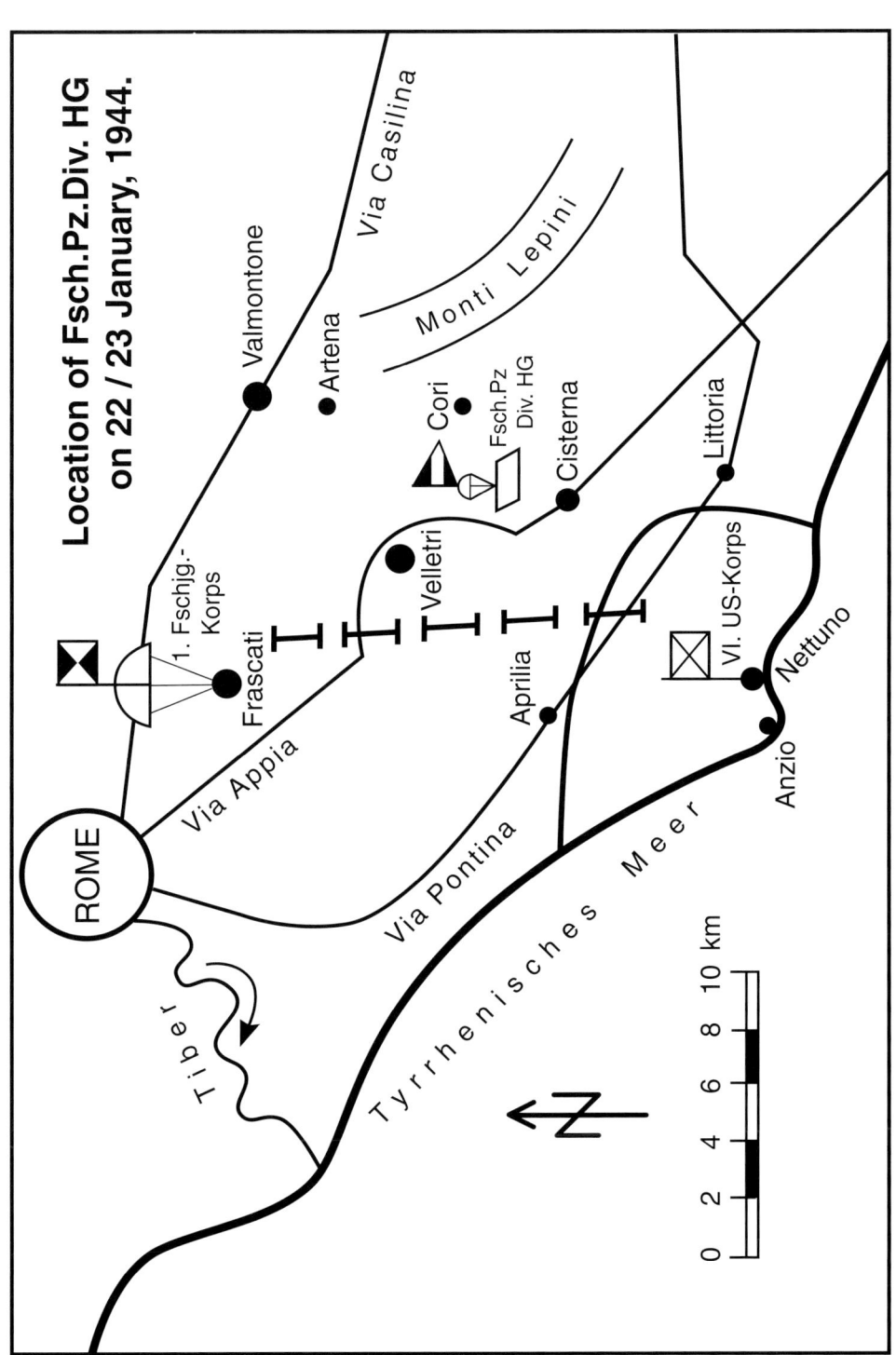

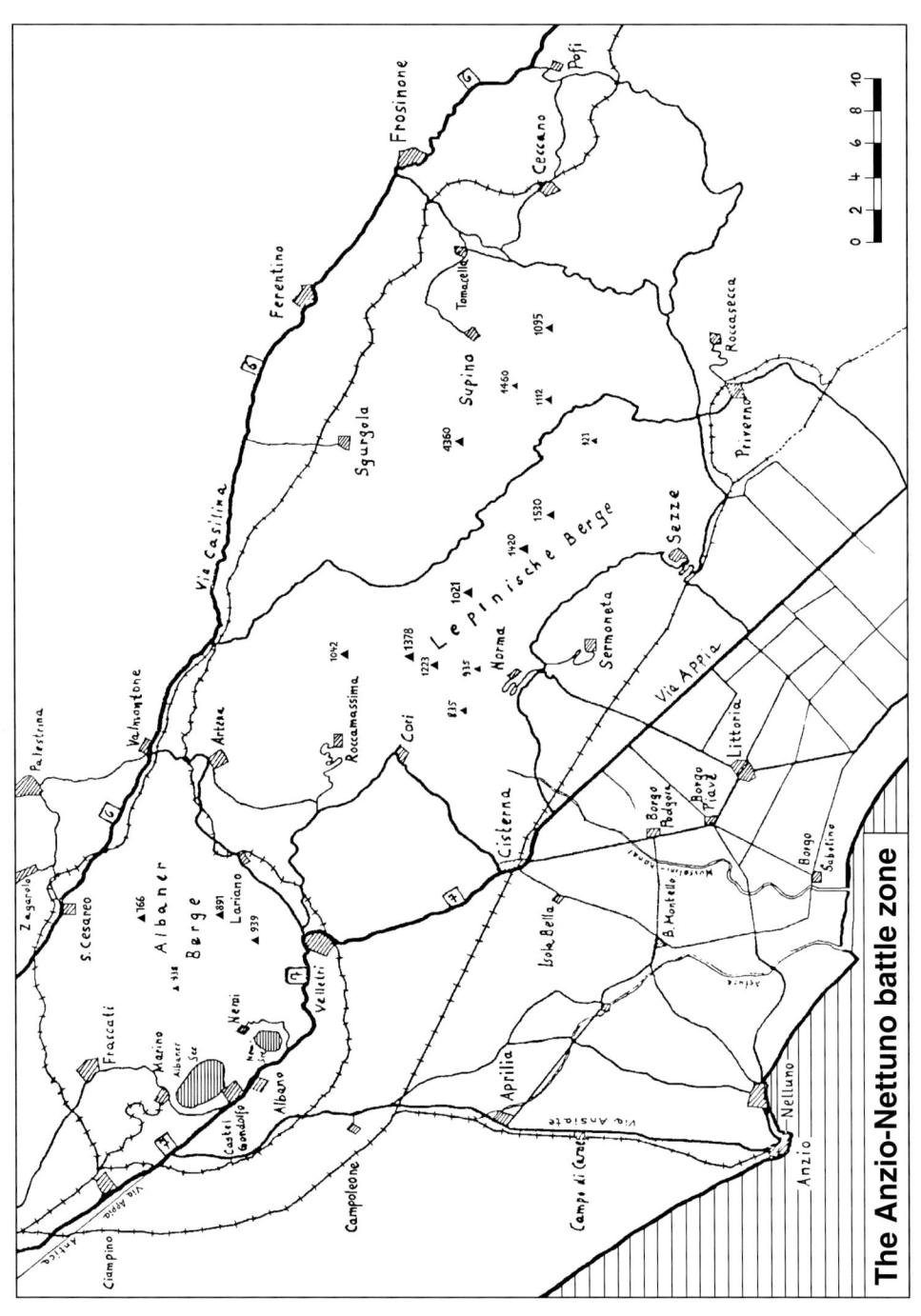

Operation "Shingle": The Landing at Anzio-Nettuno

The Invasion Forces

In spite of intensive attacks and an unprecedented superiority in materiel, the Allied forces had failed to break through the German front in southern Italy. Now a new landing was to strike at what Churchill called "the soft German underbelly" and "open the way to Rome". The operational planning for this operation foresaw the formation of three bridgeheads, which would soon be joined to create a single large bridgehead with a depth of seven kilometers and a width of twenty-five. The landing of the American 1st Armored and 45th Infantry Divisions and the British 1st Guards Division, which had sailed from Naples, would take place once this large bridgehead had been established.

This planned breaching of the German positions with all forces was supposed to lead directly to Rome. The Allies went so far as to set up a radio station on Corsica in order to deceive the German command; this simulated "corps headquarters" was to maintain a high volume of radio traffic with units supposedly preparing to land on the island. In order to distract the German units guarding the coast, commando units carried out a noisy raid on Civitavecchia.

On 21 January 1944, 243 ships with 40,000 men and supplies on board left Naples harbour. Ten cruisers and 20 destroyers guarded the landing fleet. At 0150 hours on the 22nd this large force reached the waters off Anzio. The first assault teams went ashore unopposed and found the entire coast free of the enemy. After a brief, massed bombardment the landing craft headed for the beach. They, too, were not fired upon. Six hours later Anzio was in the possession of the invasion forces. The first German reaction took place at 0850 hours, when a battery of 170mm guns engaged a group of landing craft. By just before midnight on this 22nd of January, 36,000 men and 3,250 vehicles had assembled in the bridgehead. Access to the fully intact port of Anzio simplified the landings significantly.

The initial phase of the operation had exceeded all the expectations of the Allies. German naval forces had not intervened, while the Luftwaffe was far too weak to counter the seaborne assault. In spite of this success and the fact that the road to Rome lay almost completely open before them, the landing force did not undertake to exploit this uniquely favorable situation for a direct drive across the peninsula to Rome. Had they done so they would have severed the supply routes to all the German units south of the landing site.

Instead the Allies brought more troops ashore and expanded the bridgehead even further. The Allied commanders were expecting a German counterattack at any hour. This hesitation on the part of the enemy allowed *Generalfeldmarschall* Kesselring to amass 24,000 men at the beachhead by 24 January 1944 and establish a weak but continuous defensive line.

The German Countermeasures

The first German troops to appear in the area of the bridgehead, several hours after the Allied landing, belonged to the 4th Parachute Division under *Oberst* Heinz Trettner. This unit, which was stationed in the Perugia area, was still in the midst of formation. Heinz Trettner had created the new division from elements of the 2nd and 6th Parachute Regiments. On 18 January 1944 he had been requested to form an alert battalion from each of the 10th, 11th and 12th Regiments; in the event of an Allied landing they were to be assembled behind the Cassino front and employed as a reserve unit under the command of *Major* Gericke.

Three days before the landings *Major* Gericke, CO of the 11th Parachute Regiment, reported to *General* Schlemm in Grottaferrata, where he received the following assignment for his task force:

"The battle group will remain in the Isola Farnese area and continue its training. Expect ammunition and fuel stocks to be filled by 22 January." *Major* Gericke drove to Isola Farnese. At 0530 hours on 22 January he received the following report there:

"Alert! Enemy has landed on both sides of Nettuno. One battalion to leave immediately by vehicle for Albano. Battle group commander to leave beforehand."

The Huber Battalion was equipped and sent to Albano at 0900. Gericke had earlier left for corps headquarters, arriving at 0730. There he received the following briefing on the situation:

"Enemy landed on both sides of Nettuno in the early morning hours. The coastal defence unit II/GR 71 could only meet the landing with very weak forces. It was thrown back. No information yet available as to the scope of the Allied landings."

During the course of 22 January all German units in the Rome area were placed on alert and, in order to assure a unified command, were placed under the command of Battle Group Gericke. By now the enemy had possession of the coastal strip between San Lorenza and Torre Astura, and his advance troops had advanced to the railway station at Campo di Carne and the village of Borgomontello.

As his units arrived, *Major* Gericke had them block all the major roads so as to eliminate a possible fast advance by the enemy's motorized or armored forces. The most threatened roads were Nettuno – Aprilla and la Fossa – Ardea. The entire battle group had arrived in the combat zone by noon on the 22nd of January. The last unit to arrive was *Major* Kleye's battalion from the 11th Parachute Regiment. Immediately thereafter *Generalleutnant* Gräser, commander of the 3rd Panzer-Grenadier Division, appeared at the command post in Albano. He set up his command post on the first floor. At 1905 hours an order arrived from corps:

"Weak enemy forces advancing on Ardea were repulsed by train units of II./GR 71. City of Ardea is still in our hands. Kampfgruppe Gericke is to occupy Ardea and la Fossa with one battalion and hold both towns."

Generaloberst Mackensen, the Commander-in-Chief of the Fourteenth Army, which was commanding there, initiated the German counterattack.

The Other Units at Anzio-Nettuno

Like the 4th Parachute Division, the Hermann Göring Panzer Division was placed on alert on 22 January 1944. Its headquarters and elements of the division were in the Priverno area in the Lepiner Mountains, about 20 kilometers from the Via Appia. The division was under the command of I Parachute Corps, commanded by *General* Schlemm. The corps also included the 29th Panzer- Grenadier Division and the 114th Light Infantry Division. Those individual units that were available were likewise thrown into the battle. These included:

    The guard platoon of the Commander-in-Chief South,

    The guard platoon of the city commandant of Rome,

    A battery of the 307th Army Flak Battalion,

    An assault gun battalion,

    A Tiger company,

    The flak platoon of 14th Company, 200th Panzer-Grenadier Regt.,

    A platoon of 13th Company, 191st Grenadier Regiment

Based in northern Italy, Headquarters, Fourteenth Army under *Generaloberst* Mackensen was placed in command of all troops surrounding the bridgehead. Von Mackensen arrived at the headquarters of *Generalfeldmarschall* Kesselring on Monte Soratte on the morning of 23 January 1944.

The HG Panzer Division, which had been placed on alert on Saturday the 22nd of January, set out with all available forces and reached its area of operations on the left wing of the beachhead, from Cisterna to the coast near Borgo Sabotino, and at the Mussolini Canal and Borgo Floro. The division and its individual units stayed there in the battle for the beachhead until the beginning of March 1944. The battle, which for several elements of the division lasted until the end of April, was greatly influenced by the poor weather conditions. Day-long rainfalls turned the former area of the Pontine Marshes into a sea of mud. As well there was the enemy's superiority in troops, materiel and weapons. Once more the fighting was constantly accompanied by heavy naval gunfire. Air superiority unquestionably lay in the hands of the Allies.

Only weak elements of the 1st and 2nd HG Panzer-Grenadier Regiments reached the landing area. The divisional and regimental units fought completely on their own during the first phase of the battle. This applied to the infantry gun company, as well as to the anti-tank company and the assault guns. The reason for this lay in the fact that almost all the infantry components of the HG Division were stripped away by the Tenth Army command, contrary to existing senior directives, and used to plug the gaps in the main front near Cassino. What infantry was left to the division consisted of exhausted and decimated units, the rebuilding of which was only in its initial stages.

The only available motorized reserve was a small division reserve force – roughly the size of a company – under *Hauptmann* Fuchs. Thus it was that this trunk of a division was sent from one stopgap position to another; nevertheless, it was able in each case to justify the trust which had been placed in it.

The Allies continued to reinforce the bridgehead without making any special effort to leave it and take the offensive. However, in spite of all the efforts to limit the size of the bridgehead it continued to grow. In fourteen days General Lucas brought 18,000 vehicles and 380 tanks into the bridgehead – all this for a force of 70,000 men. Such an aggregation of vehicles led Churchill to remark sarcastically:

"We must have a great superiority in chauffeurs. I am shocked that the enemy has more infantry than we."

After three weeks of inactivity General Lucas was relieved. His place was taken by General Lucien Truscott, who had previously commanded the US 3rd Infantry Division. New units flowed into the battle zone from all over Europe. The First Battle of Cassino broke out at about the same time. Only the weak elements of the HG Panzer Division mentioned earlier took part in the battle. They did not participate in the second Cassino battle, for their place was in the bridgehead front.

The various German attempts to crush the bridgehead failed. Pressured by several directives from the OKW and from Hitler personally, *Generalfeldmarschall* Kesselring was finally forced to transfer Headquarters, LXXVI Panzer Corps and the 362nd Infantry Division from the Adriatic Front into the Nettuno area.

At 0200 hours on the morning of 30 January 1944, the US 3rd Infantry Division, reinforced by the 504th Airborne Regiment, attacked between the Mussolini Canal and Fosse Carano. The Americans attempted to break through the German defensive line on an 18-mile front. German pioneers blew up the bridges over the canal. Fighting was bitter between the enemy and the 26th and HG Panzer Divisions. The attack gained about 2,000 meters before it was stopped. The enemy had failed to reach his declared objective of Cisterna. Only six soldiers from the two battalions of US Rangers survived the attack. Six out of 767! Let us now turn at this point to the individual units of the HG Panzer Division.

The 10th (Anti-tank) Company, 1st HG Parachute-Panzer-Grenadier Regiment at Anzio-Nettuno

The 1st HG Parachute-Panzer-Grenadier Regiment's 10th (Anti-tank) Company, consisting of three platoons each with three 75mm anti-tank guns (motorized), was stationed in the Supino area on the north slope of the Lepiner Mountains, about 14 kilometers west-southwest of Frosinone. The company was at full strength in personnel and weapons.

The following account by Ernst Hermann provides a striking depiction of the situation facing the individual units of the HG Division.

"We were placed on alert at about eleven o'clock in the morning on the Saturday in question, 22 January 1944. Within 45 minutes everything was loaded, the guns limbered and camouflaged to prevent them being seen from the air. The company was ready to move. Not until an hour later did the order arrive containing the departure time, our march route and the destination area. The supply train remained in Supino.

Our orders were such that we were to be in the march area at dusk. This had the advantage of allowing us to reconnoitre the area of operations and go into position during the last light of day. Experience had shown that air activity was at a minimum just before the arrival of darkness.

The disadvantage was that we had to drive in bright sunshine under the watchful eyes of the British fighter-bombers. Thus the company received several visits from the other side while driving through open country. When this happened only the speed and maneuverability of the drivers was a certain guarantee of escaping the bombing and strafing.

We often fired on the well-armored machines with machine-guns and cannon as they attacked from a very low altitude. The crew of one gun fired its rifles at one of the attackers; flames suddenly spurted from its engine, the machine rolled over on one wing, fell to earth like a blazing torch, and exploded as it hit the ground. Afterward it became quieter and we reached our objective without further trouble.

We drove from Supino through Tomacella over the large connecting road leading south from Frosinone to the Via Appia, and passed just south of barricaded Sezze, initially on a side road. Near Casale di Palme we reached the Via Appia, our initial objective. The platoons took cover and the company commander waited for our operational orders."

Everyone knew from previous Allied landings that the enemy could only be driven back into the sea if they drove quickly into the forming beachhead while there was still a state of confusion there. This was obviously not the case at Anzio, since there were no heavy weapons available – especially tanks – with which to carry out such an attack.

"Before the company received its orders I climbed onto the roof of a nearby villa. In the fading evening twilight I saw the sea. Along a considerable stretch of the coastline lay a huge convoy of freighters, which were busily unloading their cargos and delivering them ashore. Beyond I saw a heavy and a light cruiser as well as several destroyers. We thus found ourselves facing a considerable number of large-calibre naval guns."

The platoons received the following orders:

1st Platoon: Advance as quickly as possible via Cisterna in the direction of Isola Bella – Borgo – Montello – Nettuno.

2nd Platoon: Advance from Point 51 of the Via Appia (later to gain a certain notoriety) as far as the Podgora estate. From there move positions forward by night into the open terrain, according to the situation.

3rd Platoon: Advance as far as Borgo Piave. From there cross the large road to Aprilia (called the Avenue of Poplars). Go into position west of the road and move positions forward as far forward as possible. The company command post was set up in a small house a few meters to the side of a small communications road. The road led to the estate.

"After setting up the command post I went over to 3rd Platoon, because that was where the next enemy attack was likely to come. For protection against enemy infantry each platoon had two MG 42 machine-guns; on account of their unbelievably high rate of fire these weapons were called 'Hitler saws' by the enemy.

At 2130 hours we heard the sound of battle from the direction of Cisterna. An enemy advance was under way there; its objective was to take possession of Cisterna, where there was an important road junction. First contact with the enemy was near the Isola Bella farm on the Cisterna-Nettuno road. 1st Platoon opened fire and halted these movements. The enemy pulled back toward Borgo Montello. As ordered, 1st Platoon followed closely to gain more ground and advanced to a point just outside Borgo Montello. The enemy had moved into the town itself and now opened fire with machine-guns, anti-aircraft and anti-tank guns, and tanks. A further advance was out of the question, especially since none of our infantry was yet on the scene to provide protection. The platoon sought out the best gun positions and went over to the defensive. By this time it was midnight.

The 2nd Platoon had meanwhile reached the Podgora estate. When engine noises were heard from the direction of the enemy it opened fire. When peace returned it undertook an advance toward the enemy with a change of positions. There were no friendly units to the right or left and the sound of heavy fighting could be heard from the right flank, the Isola Bella area. As well track noises could be heard from the area directly in front of the platoon.

3rd Platoon had occupied provisional positions west of Borgo Piave, south of the Borgo – Piave – Aprilia road. Loud battle noise was heard from behind and to the right (1st Platoon's engagement). Since, apart from some tank noises, nothing was happening in front of our own positions, I had the platoon fire into the American concentration area, using the indirect fire method, and maintain harassing fire. As 2nd Platoon did the same, the enemy was uncertain as to the type of opponent and numbers he was facing and consequently operated in a cautious manner. The 3rd Platoon was once again able to move its positions forward several hundred meters. There, however, the tank noises were so intense and so close to the position that the platoon was unable to advance one meter farther. Enemy mortar and artillery rounds soon began falling.

The platoon nevertheless continued firing, using the method of salvoes fired at intervals associated with changes of position to the left and right, in order to give the appearance of a continuous front. Occasional explosions and the glare of fires indicated that we had hit a fuel or munitions dump, perhaps even a supply vehicle moving up to the front.

When the enemy fire grew too heavy and tank and anti-tank shells began landing near us, we went over to the defensive. The two MG 42s were positioned to the left and right, each about forty meters to the side, to protect the position. With this action we had brought the enemy advance to a halt and prevented an initial rapid expansion of the bridgehead. American accounts of this first night showed that we had been a great thorn in the enemy's side and that they must have sustained considerable losses. Shortly after midnight on 23 January further units arrived on the battlefield, but still no infantry. The light flak platoons of the HG Parachute-Panzer-Flak Regiment were a welcome reinforcement for the thin front line.

With the arrival of these reinforcements the attack on Borgo Montello was repeated, however the enemy's defenses had become significantly stronger. Shortly thereafter American troops launched a counterattack. They forced us to withdraw to Isola Bella, where we occupied new positions. In the days that followed we had to watch helplessly as the enemy further expanded his beachhead. On the morning of 23 January the first infantry forces arrived, several pitiful remnants of our panzer-grenadier battalions and alert units. Now we were supposed to advance again. However during the second half of the night the Americans landed considerable artillery forces, which had gone into position in the scrub-covered terrain due north and northeast of Nettuno. They opened fire, which was well directed by forward observers. Over the next few days the firing intensified into a hail of shells. Losses were heavy.

Following extremely heavy preparatory artillery fire, US forces went over to the attack in several places and succeeded in breaking through our thin front line at a number of points. Isola Bella changed hands several times. Following a heavy artillery bombardment, tank and infantry forces attacked in several sectors in which the Americans had initially planned their main assault after the direct route to Cisterna had been blocked. The anti-tank guns of 2nd Platoon became involved in a duel with these tanks. Two were knocked out, two others were hit and turned away. A wheel of one of the anti- tank guns was wrecked. When the enemy infantry attack began, the gun had to be blown up. The German strongpoints had to be withdrawn several hundred meters. 2nd Platoon went into position near the Podgora estate.

The men of 3rd Platoon discovered that they had moved into flat, open terrain during the night. The platoon hastily evacuated this death zone and established itself near the Borgo Piave – Aprilia road (near the Avenue of Poplars). Meanwhile Hptm. Radke, the commander of 10th Company, HG Parachute-Panzer-Grenadier Regiment, had been killed in a car accident. I took command of the company and made my way to the company command post in order to establish contact with my own regiment and the neighboring units. Next to our company was the command post of the 2nd Parachute-Panzer Regiment, under whose command we were, because our own regimental command was still in the reformation process.

Oblt. Olfermann and members of his assault gun company went into position in the critical sector in the Podgora area. The front stabilized in all sectors. Both sides tried to reorganize their forces. It may be said that the heavy weapons of the HG Panzer Division helped prevent the enemy from expanding any further and attacking. Had the American forces achieved a breakthrough in their first attempt during the night of 23 January 1944, then nothing could have stopped them. The entire main front on the Garigliano would have faced an extremely serious threat."

The Assault Guns in the Anzio-Nettuno Battle Zone

On 24 January 1944 the first units of the assault gun battalion under *Major* Sandrock were still in combat with British tanks near Castelforte, where they were involved in many individual engagements until 29 January. Not until then were they transferred to Roccasecca, where they received a hasty refitting; on 2 February the assault guns were thrown into the fighting at Anzio-Nettuno.

On 29 February the fighting near Porco Flora intensified into bitter duels. The Panzer III tanks taken over from the army, armed with the short 75mm gun, saw action in the main line of resistance at the Mussolini Canal. They fought in the Cisterna area where they came under extremely heavy artillery fire. 100 to 120 shells fell for each tank. Only by immediately making smoke and changing positions frequently did they succeed in escaping the barrage. Churchill II tanks also fired at them with solid armor-piercing shot.

Not until 5 March were the assault guns withdrawn from the battle zone and rested near Cori, Ninfa and Norma. Oblt. Bellinger and Oblt. Leininger, who had been wounded earlier, rejoined the unit there. On 7 March the battalion sent an advance detachment to Livorno, and the entire battalion followed on the 12th. Driving overland, the battalion reached the Pontina, Littoria area on the coast via Artena, Valmonone (Rome area), Orvieto, Ficulle, Florence, Capannoli and Viterbo. The battalion rested and refitted in this rest area. From 23 March until May 1944 it was stationed in the Monteccio, Bientina, Lucca, Santa Maria ai Monte and Pontedera areas.

Late on the evening of 3 March a sentry was fired on at the gate to the castle yard in Monteccio. This and a number of similar, but not so serious, occurrences led to the introduction of measures to counter these nocturnal snipers. Following a preliminary scouting of the area, on 9 April an action began against the partisan band's hiding place in the mountains near Arezzo in the area of Florence. This followed the murder and mutilation of a *Feldwebel* and an *Obergefreiter* in this area.

This was the decisive spark which set off the powder keg. If not dealt with immediately, the bands would become even more bold and the result would have been more casualties to snipers and murderers. The objective was to arrest or neutralize the "Red Star" band and likewise destroy the "Garibaldi" band. Both partisan groups conducted their operations from the Partina, Bardia-Pratallia, Frasinetta and Monte Morelli areas and from the St. Ermo-Camaldoli monastery. The infantry-style action in the Arezzo Mountains saw the soldiers deployed in squad-size groups, each equipped with two MG 42s, together with infantry units riding in trucks and self-propelled 20mm anti-aircraft guns. Command of the individual units lay in the hands of Hptm. Bellinger and Oblt. Karl-Heinz Göring (more about him later). The individual groups and platoons were led by Oblt. Schulz, Möhring and Wallhäuser.

From captured band members the operation's leaders learned that it was British officers who had reviewed or organized the band units. Individual groups consisted of from 15 to 40 men and were supposed to operate independently. Striking was the fact that no men were seen in the fields and in the villages. Priests, women and children were obviously insincere in their attitude toward the Germans, some even aggressive, while others were scared.

Above the Camaldoli monastery was found an abandoned resting place with a command book, shell casings and dirty washing. The day before the partisans had intimidated the monks of the monastery into giving them food and wine. Acting on information provided by civilians and prisoners, a British Lieutenant who had escaped from a prisoner-of-war camp in southern Germany was picked up in this area. The anti-partisan action, which lasted until 17 April, witnessed several engagements and skirmishes. On the eve of Easter Sunday the individual groups had to assemble in Partina monastery. Field positions were set up at the village limits and at the edge of the forest. Single shots from scattered partisans, some of whom crept forward as far as the field sentries, were answered. One morning, after driving out of a village, the Germans came under 20mm cannon and machine-gun fire from atop a hill. A house, from which one of the patrols had been fired on, was blown up with anti-tank mines after the inhabitants were moved out.

At night identification fires burned on mountain tops and at level spots in the mountain valleys, beacons for the aircraft that supplied the bands with clothing, munitions and cigarettes. These drop sites changed constantly and were extremely difficult to reach, so that it proved impossible to cut this supply line. Early one morning two workers from the Todt Organization, which was in the area to build firing positions, were seized and taken away as they walked to the construction site. On 25 April 1944 the assault gun battalion was transferred to Buriano. There Lt. Wallhäußer assumed command in place of Oblt. Leininger. Wallhäuser in turn handed over command to Lt. Witschonke on 1 May. Oblt. Karl-Heinz Göring became a company commander. His platoon leaders were *Leutnante* Schulz and Schulz-Ostwald. On 9 June Lt. Wallhäuser assumed command of 11th Company, while Lt. Lindau took over Wallhäuser's platoon.

On 24 May the 9th and 11th Companies of the HG Assault Gun Battalion transferred to Tivoli. 10th Company remained in its old quarters for coastal defence near Salina, south of Livorno and Cecina. There, too, the activities of the bandits were a problem. Uffz. Klein was shot and killed by partisans. The withdrawal to the Klara Line south of Chianciano and Macoiano il Bagno took place on 25 June. There was an engagement with enemy tanks on 27 May in which three of the enemy vehicles were knocked out, two by Grob and a third by another assault gun commander. Fw. Dahnke was killed in this action. There was a breakthrough by strong enemy armored units during the transfer into the threatened Torrita area on 30 June. This made necessary a further withdrawal to the Edith line on 1 July. Nusea was reached on 14 July and the battalion command post was set up there. The 10th Company was stationed in the San Marino area near Budrio, Florence.

The Allied Breakout from the Beachhead

The US 6th Corps, which was deployed in the Anzio beachhead, was not supposed to go to the attack until the major offensive began against the German Tenth Army. The objective was to achieve a degree of tactical cooperation between the two fronts during the course of the battle. By as early as February the strength of the 6th Corps within the beachhead was approaching that of an army. Nine Allied divisions were to be held by five German divisions which never had enough heavy weapons, to say nothing of air superiority, which was firmly in the hands of the Allies.

General Truscott had received orders to attack on 23 May and to cut the Via Casilina – the Tenth Army's most important avenue of retreat – near Valmontone. This was to be done at a time when the German Tenth Army was in the midst of a withdrawal after abandoning Cassino. These two operations were preceded by an air offensive code-named "Strangle", which lasted for weeks and caused heavy casualties among the German troops and the civilian population. At the end of April 1944 the German side was still convinced that any attack from the beachhead could be repulsed with the help of the army group reserve positioned behind the front, and that it could keep the Allied troops from leaving the bridgehead. Events surrounding the Tenth Army led to the withdrawal of several large units from this front and on 20 May the army's left border was moved to the east.

The Fourteenth Army under *Generaloberst* von Mackensen now reckoned on an imminent attack from the beachhead whose direction of advance would be along both sides of the Anzio-Albano road toward Rome. Army Group C disagreed; it predicted that the objective of the Allied attack would be the area around Valmontone. The Fourteenth Army had received orders from army group "to defend vigorously" at the beachhead, and the favorable terrain gave the defenders a good chance of doing so. But the terrain also offered a good chance of stopping the enemy in the event of a retreat.

The Allies continued to significantly reinforce their forces inside the beachhead until 22 May, the day before the breakout from the beachhead. The additional units were the American 1st Armored and 36th Infantry Divisions, which had been moved into the beachhead following the success against the Tenth Army. Thus, in addition to powerful corps units, General Truscott had at his disposal five full strength American divisions and two British divisions, all under the command of the US Fifth Army in the beachhead. The Commander-in-Chief of the US Fifth Army, General Clark, was determined that his Fifth Army should be the first to march into Rome. However, from the beginning General Alexander, Commander- in-Chief of the 15th Army Group (comprising the US Fifth and British Eighth Armies), had wanted the attack to be made in a northerly direction with the initial objective of Valmontone and the severing of the Via Casilina, the German supply line to the southern wing of the Tenth Army. Such a move would at the same time block this army's main avenue of retreat.

So on 20 May General Alexander ordered the attack to begin in the direction of Valmontone. General Mark Clark fixed the point of main effort for the piercing of the German lines south of Cisterna. The 34th Infantry Division was positioned in the very front line there. After passing through this division's lines, the American 2nd and 3rd Infantry Divisions were to attack toward Cisterna. Attacking on their left would be the US 1st Armored Division and on the right the reinforced 1st Special Service Force. The 45th Infantry Division was deployed on the left of this main group, while the newly-arrived 36th Infantry Division remained in reserve. The two British divisions deployed on the left wing of the beachhead, the 1st and 5th Infantry

Divisions, were to carry out attacks toward the east to deceive the Germans as to the focal point of the offensive. General Clark had ordered the division commanders to be prepared to alter their direction of attack as developments in the situation required.

The Allied attack began on 23 May 1944 after a heavy preparatory bombardment by artillery and naval guns. The Allied air attacks were so heavy that more than 700 aircraft were counted over the defensive front of the 362nd Infantry Division alone in the course of this first day. In addition to these support operations, the Allied air forces continued Operation "Strangle", with the objective of destroying all targets spotted on the roads.

By noon the German main line of resistance had been pierced near Cisterna. By evening the American 1st Infantry Division had advanced across the Cisterna – Campoleone rail line. When *Generaloberst* von Mackensen requested permission to withdraw the left wing, the army group command radioed that he was to hold. "The HG Panzer Division, the army group reserve located southeast of Pisa, is already on its way!" This, and why it wasn't true, will be described in the following chapters from the division's point of view.

The second and third days of the offensive brought the Allies further success. On 25 May the units from the beachhead linked up with 2nd Corps which was advancing from the southeast. The divisions from the beachhead now formed the left wing of the overall Allied attack.

On 26 May General Clark, with the authorization of the 15th Army Group, transferred the focus of his offensive into the area south of the Alban Mountains. Clark's dream of being the first to enter Rome was to become a reality, for his thrust was now aimed directly at the eternal city. A telegram from Churchill, which pointedly reminded the command in Italy that the encirclement and destruction of as many German divisions as possible was more important than the capture of Rome, which would fall to the Allies anyway, changed nothing.

The HG Panzer Division had been ordered by the Fourteenth Army to drive as quickly as possible, travelling by day as well as night, to the 362nd Infantry Division, which was engaged in extremely heavy defensive fighting. Racing toward the battle front, the HG Division was forced to take very heavy losses from the enemy air force and suffered serious delays as well. Nevertheless, the division's units arrived in the area in front of Artena on time. The first division elements to arrive, the reconnaissance battalion and a flak battalion, halted the enemy. A great threat to Army Group C had been averted; a breakthrough by the Allies had been headed off.

The HG Panzer Division should have arrived much earlier. What stopped it from doing so will be described in the following chapter. After the attack by the American 1st Armored Division bogged down in front of Velletri, on 27 May the division was withdrawn and the next morning deployed on the left wing of the new main group, whose objective was Rome. On 29 May it drove deep into the front held by the 3rd Panzer-Grenadier Division. East of Velletri, where the greatest danger faced the Fourteenth Army, LXXVI

Panzer Corps had ordered the HG Panzer Division to establish contact with *Generalleutnant* Greiner's 362nd Infantry Division, which was at the corps boundary on the left wing of I Parachute Corps. A battalion of the HG Panzer Division retook an enemy-occupied position near Lariano. No further advance was possible as the battalion already had to hold a 10 kilometer section of front. A patrol from the battalion reached the left wing of the 362nd Infantry Division due north of Velletri.

"Among the men of the 362nd Infantry Division hope grew for the establishment of contact, which was so important to survival. At that time we were not yet aware that the HG Division had suffered serious losses in men, vehicles and materiel to heavy enemy air attacks while approaching on the Via Casilina. We also did not know that it had been released twenty-four hours too late by army group, had been delayed considerably en route and that its point units had become involved in combat with superior enemy infantry and tank forces in the Artena area."

Heinz Greiner's important account of this battle zone continues:

"As feared, the enemy took advantage of the gap between the 362nd Infantry Division and the HG Panzer Division – which had widened to more than six kilometers as a result of the loss of Lariano – to begin an advance toward the ridges of Artemisio."

On 30 May the enemy attacked the HG Panzer Division, which had not yet fully arrived on the battlefield, in the direction of Valmontone and pushed it back to the rail line northwest of Artena. The division's losses were so high that it was not in a position to close this large gap by counterattacking. The enemy recognized his golden opportunity and that evening the US 36th Infantry Division pushed through the gap almost unopposed; both of the division's regiments reached Artemisio Ridge, north of Velletri.

The German C-Position had been breached. The 362nd Infantry Division received orders to pull a battalion out of its thinly- manned front and shortly thereafter a second in order to close the gap. The HG Panzer Division received orders to counterattack from the east to help close the gap in the German line. The attack by the US 2nd Corps on the morning of 1 June struck the weakened LXXVI Panzer Corps so hard that the remnants of the HG Panzer Division were overrun. Valmontone was lost. The British armed forces communique reported:

"Fighting heroically, the Hermann Göring Division has gone down for the third time near Valmontone."

What was left of the division continued to offer stubborn resistance. A unified command of the same was impossible, however, as a result of the destruction of communications by artillery bombardments and air attacks. Brigade commander *Oberst* Schmalz intervened personally and tried to direct the operations of these groups by means of radio and liaison officers; but like the elements of I Parachute Corps they were forced to pull back. At noon on 3 June the HG Parachute-Panzer Division received a corps order instructing it to withdraw beyond the Aniene into the sector Tivoli – eastern edge of Rome. The last combat unit still fighting at the eastern outskirts of

Rome was the 4th Parachute Division.

Army Group C intentionally avoided defending Rome and blowing the Tiber bridges in order to prevent the city from being destroyed, which would surely have happened, for none of the Allied commanders was so beguiled by the aura of Rome that he would not have ordered the bombing and destruction of the city – as they had at Cassino – if resistance was met. Let us now turn from this general description of the situation directly to the Hermann Göring Parachute-Panzer Division.

With the Hermann Göring Parachute-Panzer Division
The Battles of 26 May to 5 June 1944

In mid-March 1944 the Hermann Göring Panzer Division was withdrawn from the front around the Anzio-Nettuno bridgehead and transferred into the Toscana area (Livorno and Pisa, Castelfranco Pontedera, Vada and Cecina). The object of this move was to restore the division to full operational readiness. Its new assignment was coastal defence.

The division travelled more than 300 kilometers overland to reach the rest area. On 15 April the division's commanding officer, *Generalleutnant* Conrath, was appointed Commanding General of Training and Replacement Troops of the First Parachute Army. His successor as HG Division commander was *Oberst* Wilhelm Schmalz, who had previously commanded the HG Parachute-Panzer- Grenadier Brigade. With the appointment Schmalz was promoted to the rank of *Generalmajor*.

When the fighting in the Anzio-Nettuno bridgehead had ended, *Major* Josef-August Fitz, commander of I Battalion, HG Parachute-Panzer-Grenadier Regiment, became the 511th German soldier to receive the Knight's Cross with Oak Leaves. In the bitter fighting against an enemy vastly superior in numbers of men and weapons, Josef-August Fitz had led his grenadiers with indefatigable bravery, courage and skill. His style of commanding from the front was evidenced by the fact that he was wounded nine times. In the end, for all intents and purposes he commanded the entire regiment – if indeed one could speak of a regiment. This Tirolean soldier from Voralberg was an example to every man of the regiment.

After arriving in the billeting area southeast of Pisa in early May 1944, the division had to prepare for the following mobile operations as army group reserve:

1. Attack in the direction of Rome.
2. Direction of advance Ravenna for the Italian coastal theater.
3. Direction of attack Genoa in the event of a further landing in western Italy. Preparations were made to deal with possible enemy landings, which could be engaged from the billeting area itself:
 (a) An enemy landing north of Livorno.
 (b) An enemy landing near Cecina-Piombino-Elba.

To this end the two panzer-grenadier regiments were quartered so that they could immediately go to the attack from the areas near Pisa and Cecina. The artillery now occupied fixed positions; its preparations included scouting of march routes and the tactical evaluation of potential points of main effort throughout the entire coastal area for which the division was responsible.

Since early May *Generalmajor* Schmalz had been stressing to the Commander-in-Chief Southwest that the division's available fuel was only adequate for a range of about 200 kilometers and that consequently it could not cover the 300 kilometers to its designated area of operations. He pointed out that the division had no access to fuel reserves held by the Chief Quartermaster Southwest, which were stored near Florence.

This matter was pursued by the division with great concern, resulting in a series of requests for the release of fuel, all of which were turned down by the Chief Quartermaster Southwest. At about 1030 hours on 23 May 1944, the Commander-in-Chief Southwest's Chief of Staff, *Generalleutnant* Westphal, called the division commander and personally gave him the order for the division to move out at once. *Generalmajor* Schmalz asked what was the purpose of the movement. He was given to understand that the division was to see action in the area south of Rome. Wilhelm Schmalz informed Westphal that heavy losses to enemy air attacks were to be expected in the case of movement by day. Nevertheless, the request for a night departure was refused. Wilhelm Schmalz also pointed out that the available fuel would only allow the division to travel as far as Viterbo. *Generalleutnant* Westphal assured him that sufficient fuel would be delivered on a timely basis in the Viterbo area.

The first element of the division to move out, the HG Armored Reconnaissance Battalion, departed as planned at 1130 hours on 23 May. No rest stops were planned en route. Not until the unit stopped in Viterbo to take on fuel was there a scheduled rest. The HG Armored Reconnaissance Battalion came under low-level air attack as soon as it departed, resulting in the first delays. On arriving in Viterbo it was discovered that the promised fuel was not in place. Not until after a discussion between the Division Ia, *Oberstleutnant* von Bergengruen, and the Chief Quartermaster Southwest late on the morning of 24 May were improvised arrangements made for the delivery of fuel to the Viterbo area. *Generalmajor* Schmalz had sent liaison officers ahead by car to set up forward message centers in Viterbo, Oriolo and two other villages and plug into the existing postal telephone net. The division drove south on three advance roads:

(a) The right (coastal) road: through Cecina, Grosseto, Tarquinia, Vetralle, Bracciano, Rome perimeter road.

(b) The mountain road: Poggibonsi, Siena, Aquapendente, Viterbo, Rome perimeter road.

(c) The Florence – Arezzo – Orvieto – Rome road.

Road a: Bulk of the units with tracked vehicles: the Panzer Regiment, Armored Artillery Regiment, one flak battalion.

Road b: 1st Panzer-Grenadier Regiment, 2nd Panzer-Grenadier Regiment, Armored Pioneer Battalion, one flak battalion.

Road c: Division Headquarters, Armored Signals Battalion, Armored Reconnaissance Battalion, Light Flak Battalion.

The supply troops were assigned proportionately to all three roads. The division's operational orders did not arrive until late evening of 23 May. The unit's movements had been spotted by the enemy within several hours of departure, however, and they were bombed day and night almost without pause. First of all the losses: Initially only 11 of the panzer regiment's 60 tanks reached the area around Valmontone. Approximately 30% of the fighting units' motorized transport and about 20% of the heavy weapons were lost en route, as were 18 of the armored artillery regiment's guns.

Inadequate preparations for the supplying of fuel further delayed the division's march. The march columns became widely scattered; consequently the division arrived piecemeal and was unable to go into action in concentration. The batteries of three heavy flak battalions were positioned at intervals along each of the advance roads. The light batteries of these three battalions were incorporated into the march groups.

The division had to pay a heavy price for its superiors' refusal of its request to be allowed to travel exclusively by night. This refusal contributed, on the one hand, to its late arrival in the combat zone and, on the other, to the fact that not all elements of the division arrived. A night march would not have incurred such delays and would have avoided the shocking losses suffered by the division. After the war questions were often asked about two of the division's units: III Battalion, 1st Panzer-Grenadier Regiment and III Battalion, 2nd Panzer-Grenadier Regiment. Both battalions were not available, as they did not exist at that time.

Both the 1st and 2nd Panzer-Grenadier Regiments, each with two battalions, were late arriving in the battle zone. The regimental headquarters of the 2nd Panzer-Grenadier Regiment and elements of individual companies, equivalent to about one battalion, arrived during the course of 26 May. The remaining units were stranded on March Road B, their vehicles having been shot up. Empty vehicles went to collect the soldiers, not arriving until 27 and 28 May. Destruction by fire of the transport trucks resulted in the loss of their cargoes of machine-guns and mortars, and it was not until the 28th that the regiment reached full operational readiness, following the delivery of replacement weapons.

The 1st Panzer-Grenadier Regiment's experience was similar, but it did not arrive until a day later. The panzer regiment arrived in the battle zone on the evening of 26 May with eleven tanks and one battalion headquarters. The arrival of stragglers raised the number of tanks to 18, 11 of which were combat-ready. The division commander bore no blame whatsoever for the disaster that had befallen his division, which after this death march was only a shell of a division, but which nevertheless fought with great bravery.

Generalmajor Schmalz and his Ia, *Oberstleutnant* Bergengruen, had already reported to *Generalfeldmarschall* Kesselring on 24 May. Schmalz informed the Commander-in-Chief of Army Group C of the losses suffered in the daylight march and of the non-existence of the necessary fuel. *Generalleutnant* Westphal replied that he had instructed the Chief Quartermaster to provide the needed fuel. As to the division's future employment, *Generalfeldmarschall* Kesselring declared:

"It will assemble in the area northwest of Valmontone at the disposal of the army group, in order to then go into action in concentration. What is desired is an offensive action to clear up the point of penetration east of Velletri, whereby the opportunity may eventually present itself to drive through to Anzio.

Also possible is a blocking action by means of an attack with limited objectives. It remains for the army group to decide whether the division will receive the operational order directly from me, or will be placed under the command of Headquarters, Fourteenth Army or Headquarters, Tenth Army."

Generalfeldmarschall Kesselring asked *Generalmajor* Schmalz to go and see the situation for himself by driving to the command post of Headquarters, Fourteenth Army. *Generalmajor* Schmalz arrived at the command post at about 1500 hours on 24 May. *Generaloberst* Mackensen briefed him on the situation and informed him of the difference of opinion that existed between Headquarters, Fourteenth Army and the army group command.

Wilhelm Schmalz subsequently pointed out that his division was the army group reserve and drove to his command post near Oriolo. During the night of 25 May, *Generalmajor* Schmalz called Headquarters, Fourteenth Army on the radio while driving to the front and was informed of the worsening situation by the army's Chief-of-Staff, General Staff *Oberst* Hauser. The Chief-of-Staff considered the immediate commitment of the arriving elements of the division an absolute necessity. He said:

"The army command will obtain an appropriate order from the Commander-in-Chief Southwest." *Generalmajor* Schmalz could not close his mind to these compelling arguments and drove forward to the troops, with the intention of immediately committing those elements that were just arriving. On 26 May the division received an order from Headquarters, Fourteenth Army to attack at noon the following day. To be carried out toward the south in broad daylight, it seemed to offer little prospect of success. Moreover, II Battalion, 2nd Panzer-Grenadier Regiment, which had meanwhile moved closer, first had to be transported to the battlefield, while the few panzers which had arrived in the meantime had to be moved into optimal positions.

The attack, which did not get under way until 1930, initially achieved partial success. The attackers took possession of the Lariano-Artena road, but there the attack ran into extremely heavy fire from enemy artillery and other weapons and became bogged down. At this time the division was organized as follows:

Group 1st Panzer-Grenadier Rgt.:

    Commander: Oberstleutnant Kluge in assembly east of Rocca-Priora

Group 2nd Panzer-Grenadier Rgt.:

    Commander: Oberst von Necker with: elements of the panzer regiment, about 8 tanks, elements of the armored artillery regiment, as well as non-divisional artillery under the command of Oberst Heine. Elements of the armored pioneer battalion, one flak battalion with heavy flak batteries in a ground role.

Group Commander Panzer Rgt. :
> Commander: Oberst von Heydebreck, with: armored reconnaissance battalion, two battalions of the 29th PGD, one flak battalion, divisional and non-divisional artillery in the strength of two battalions under the commander of the HG Armored Artillery Regiment, Oberst Oehring.

After overcoming the previously-described fuel problem, the march group travelling on Road C (armored reconnaissance battalion, one flak battalion, Division HQ and signals battalion) arrived near Monte Ponio, east of Frascati, during the course of 25 May. That evening the armored reconnaissance battalion and the flak battalion received orders to drive ahead through Valmontone and capture and hold the high ground south of Artena.

On 26 May the reconnaissance battalion encountered American tanks at the southern edge of Artena, resulting in a firefight. The enemy advance was stopped. A German attack from Artena aimed at taking the high ground failed. No artillery support was available. On 26 May the division had no noteworthy forces available, apart from the reconnaissance battalion, the regimental headquarters of 2nd Panzer-Grenadier Regiment and scraped-together elements of this regiment, which were roughly the strength of a battalion. The division's artillery, half of which had been shot up by the enemy air force, was still en route. As the commanders of the individual artillery battalions reported in at the division's command post, *Generalmajor* Schmalz integrated them into the C-Line near Labico.

The division formed a second battle group in addition to the armored reconnaissance battalion. Of roughly battalion strength, it was put together under the command of the 2nd Panzer-Grenadier Regiment. The group received orders from division to advance to the Lariano-Artena road during the night of 27 May and there maintain contact with the armored reconnaissance battalion. It was the intention of the division command to initially block the valley between Cisterna and Valmontone, assemble the arriving elements of the division behind this barrier, then carry out a further attack in the direction of Giulianello.

This battle group reached the Lariano – Artena area but was pinned down there by enemy artillery fire. The army group command was obviously not in agreement with these measures and turned directly to *Reichsmarschall* Göring. On the morning of 27 May Göring sent a sharply-worded order to the division by radio, instructing it to cease all offensive activities and to assemble north of Valmontone.

In the opinion of *Generalmajor* Schmalz, only ignorance of the true situation could have led the high command of Army Group C to act this way. The armored reconnaissance battalion's action near Artena had stopped an enemy advance, and it was only as a result of this that the division was able to assemble in the assembly area for later offensive action. The operation by the battle group of the 2nd Panzer-Grenadier Regiment was conducted for the same reason.

The division did not carry out Göring's order, for this would have meant giving up the blocking position it had won, and might have induced the enemy to launch a further advance toward the north in the direction of Valmontone. In the course of 27 May the division was placed under the command of the Fourteenth Army. During the night of the 28th it received the following order from LXXVI Panzer Corps, under whose command it also was:

"On 28 May HG Panzer Division will continue the attack south of Valmontone and capture the line Giulianello – Roccamassima. The division's right wing is to establish contact with the left wing of I Parachute Corps."

This attack was carried out by the 1st Parachute Panzer Regiment, which had meanwhile arrived from the area north of Lariano, with the objective of reaching the C-Position with the point unit – II Battalion – and, without stopping, continuing the attack to the southwest through Lariano to the corps boundary.

The armored personnel carrier battalion, which was deployed on the left, was to set out toward the southeast, link up with the von Necker group and together with it attack in the direction of Giulianello. The Kluge group – the 1st Panzer-Grenadier Regiment – and the von Necker group with the 2nd Panzer-Grenadier Regiment were supported by the Heine artillery group. The Necker group's attack on 28 May bogged down in the face of extremely heavy enemy fire. The Kluge group, led by the APC battalion, reached the C-Position north of Lariano and advanced about 1,000 meters past it to the southeast. There it was halted by a German mine field and had to be withdrawn to the C-Position. The division's attack had failed.

The right battalion of the Kluge group (II Battalion of the 1st Panzer-Grenadier Regiment) succeeded in breaking into the C- Position near Lariano. Veering to the right and advancing along the Lariano – Velletri road, in the face of weak resistance but under heavy artillery fire, the battalion reached the corps boundary near Menta, where it dug in. Patrols advanced toward Velletri and found the wing of the 362nd Infantry Division at the road fork due north of Velletri. Information brought back by the patrols revealed that there was a gap between the two corps of three kilometers. The enemy sent forces into this gap during the course of 28 May, as *Generalmajor* Schmalz was able to see for himself through a binocular artillery telescope. He now committed the Kluge group's last reserve, the regiment's pioneer platoon, near Castello d'Ariano. By the evening of 28 May these attacks by elements of the division against a superior enemy had resulted in heavy losses. The division was able to repel the subsequent ceaseless attacks on 29 May, but carrying out the requested attack on Valmontone was out of the question. There were no reserves left whatsoever. Heavy and light flak units were employed to close the gaps near the von Necker and von Heydebreck groups. On 30 May the HG Division was reinforced by the 71st Nebelwerfer Regiment under *Oberst* Wolf Andrae, who was awarded the Knight's Cross on 24 June 1944.

In telephone conversations on the 28th, 29th and 30th of May, *Generalmajor* Schmalz requested Headquarters, Fourteenth Army to send an officer-led reconnaissance patrol from the neighboring corps (from the 362nd Infantry Division of same) to Menta, to where he had already sent a similar patrol the day before, in order to report the closing of the gap between the corps. This did not happen.

During the night of 30 May the division received an order from HQ, Fourteenth Army. Together with the northern wing of the 29th Panzer-Grenadier Division, it was to launch a concentric attack on the Allied area of penetration southeast, south and southwest of Valmontone and reduce it as quickly as possible. LXXVI Panzer Corps reported that the attack could not take place until the evening of 30 May at the earliest, since from Artena the enemy had a good view of the potential battlefield to the north and east and consequently a daylight attack must lead to heavy losses from enemy artillery and aircraft.

The enemy attacks of 30 May precluded this plan. They drove back the von Necker group to the railway line northwest of Artena and the von Heydebreck group to a point north of Kilometer Marker 16. Losses were heavy on both sides. *General der Panzertruppe* Herr discussed the new attack order with *Generalmajor* Schmalz personally. Following the discussion, *General* Herr explained that the HG Division had so far lost almost two-thirds of its infantry. He emphasized:

"The HG Division is no longer in a position to carry out the attack orders, in two directions no less. The only thing the division is still capable of would be an attack by the von Heydebreck group, supported by all available tanks, from the southern edge of Valmontone through N16 to Stazione d'Artena."

Both Generals were of the unanimous opinion that the Fourteenth Army should leave the Parachute Corps to close the gap between Velletri and Menta on its own. On 31 May *Generalmajor* Schmalz learned that strong US forces had infiltrated onto Artemisio ridge. The pioneer platoon, which was deployed at the northeast tip of the ridge, reported that it was in battle. The enemy force was equivalent in strength to two regiments. At about midnight on 1 June *Generaloberst* von Mackensen ordered LXXVI Panzer Corps to launch an attack with the HG Panzer Division employing all available tanks and infantry in at least company strength in the direction of Vigna Menta (northeast of Velletri)! At the same time the 362nd Infantry Division was to attack northwest toward Vigna Menta with at least one battalion of the 12th Parachute Regiment (assault regiment). This was the only way to close the gap in the front. Afterward the infiltrated US troops were to be smashed. The HG Division was promised a company from another division for the attack; it failed to arrive. The unit's five (!) operational tanks were involved in the fighting near Valmontone. The attack had to be conducted with the weak forces of II Battalion, 1st Panzer-Grenadier Regiment. The battalion did not break through and was forced to repel vigorous counterattacks, in the course of which the enemy further enlarged the gap.

This gap had been recognized and reported by the division command on 28 May. In Schmalz's opinion it "Must have a catastrophic effect on the overall command of Army Group C." This explains the stream of warning reports sent by the division commander to his superiors, urging them to close the gap at all costs.

The division had carried out attacks at diverse areas of the front almost daily. In spite of the intensive efforts of the repair shop companies the number of tanks was never more than company strength. The daily number of usable tanks never exceeded nine. On 1 May only four tanks were operational. In defending each foot of ground, the von Necker, Kluge and von Heydebreck groups were finally overrun in their positions by the superior forces of the enemy. The heavy losses suffered on 1 June also contributed to this collapse. By the evening of 1 June the von Necker group had ceased to exist. Only a few small groups managed to fight their way through to the division.

On 1 June the tireless *Oberst* von Heydebreck and two battalion commanders of the left battle group were badly wounded in the fighting. Near Valmontone the commander of the Armored Reconnaissance Battalion assumed command of what was left of the regiment. (*Oberst* Georg-Henning von Heydebreck subsequently received the Knight's Cross on 25 June 1944.) Since the telephone lines had been cut during the course of this day, the only way the division commander could only issue his orders was in person. On the evening of that day the division's fighting strength was as follows:

50% of the troops were still available, as well as 4 Panzer IVs, 12 motorized anti-tank guns, 8 self-propelled anti-tank guns. None of the young panzer-grenadiers surrendered on that decisive 1 June 1944. They held their positions and were killed there or were wounded and taken prisoner. This day saw the destruction of the HG Division's 2nd Panzer-Grenadier Regiment.

The regimental and battalion headquarters and the surviving units and groups which had been scraped together continued to resist on 2 and 3 June. The enemy broke through the Kluge group, which had suffered equally heavy losses, on 2 June. The next day it was wiped out in fighting on both sides of Colonna. *Kampfgruppe* von Heydebreck had four combat-ready panzers, a handful of units of the armored reconnaissance battalion and the 1066th Grenadier Regiment (attached), and a heavy battalion of the armored artillery regiment.

The division's narrow front had been pierced on both sides of Valmontone and it had been outflanked on both sides by other enemy units. The situation on 3 June was grim. Remnants of I Battalion, 1st Panzer-Grenadier Regiment under *Major* Fitz were fighting in Colonna, while the regiment's II Battalion was located southwest of Colonna. These remnants of the division were attacked on the morning of 3 June. Once again the enemy broke through and the battalions were outflanked. The division commander assigned targets on the spot to several batteries, which engaged the enemy with direct fire.

The command echelon transferred into the Cervaro area on the Amiene. At the front *Generalmajor* Schmalz gave orders for a withdrawal beyond the Amiene, where a new defensive front was to be established. The division commander arrived at his new command post at 1500 hours and discussed the situation with *Oberstleutnant* Bergengruen. When *General der Panzertruppe* Herr arrived he confirmed the division's decision and gave the general order to withdraw beyond the Amiene.

The transfer of the division command post to Mentana began at 1800 hours on 3 June 1944. By the evening of 4 June the situation had firmed up somewhat after the insertion of the 15th Panzer-Grenadier Division on the left wing of the division. That evening the division's positions lay along the following line: right wing on the Tiber in the area of the Rome airport – northern outskirts of Secro – Settecamini – Lunghezza. Point of main effort was on the right wing. The remaining tanks were directed there as well. A corps order issued on the afternoon of 4 June had the division withdraw to a defensive line running from the Tiber through Monte Rotondo, Mentana and San Angelo on the morning of 5 June.

The enemy's gathering in and near Rome and his hesitance to leave there gave the German command time to build a new defensive front north of the city. The combat strengths of the grenadier regiments, the armored reconnaissance battalion and the armored pioneer battalion sank rapidly. Only a ruthless combing of the rear-echelon units and headquarters and the merging of various units enabled the unit to increase its combat strength, which had fallen to only 977 men on 9 June 1944, to 3,124 men by 19 June. Nevertheless, on 18 June 1944 Army Group C protested to the division about its actions, in that it had sent more than the average number of personnel to the rear and even beyond the Apennines, "while acknowledging fully its accomplishments in battle."

On 22 June *Generalmajor* Schmalz reported that not all the required strength reports had been sent, and that only the third echelon supply train had been transferred into the Budria area near Bologna, and then only on the express order of LXXVI Panzer Corps. Obviously someone wanted to find fault with the HG Parachute-Panzer Division in order to conceal his own failings. Carried out in the tropical summer heat, the retreat from Rome through the Tiber Valley was extremely exhausting. The US Fifth Army pursued vigorously. Not until 15 June were the Americans halted in the Ciusi area. The HG Division remained on the defensive there for some time, likewise at Lake Trasimeno.

The German forces withdrew slowly. From its positions south of the Arno, on 15 July the division was pulled out of the fighting, assembled between Bologna and Ferrara and shipped to the Eastern Front on 72 transport trains. The Red Army had crushed Army Group Center with its June 22 offensive, code-named "Bagration", and had stormed through the several-hundred-kilometer gap toward the west. Divisions had to be withdrawn from other theaters as quickly as possible to stem the tide of the Soviet advance. One of these was the Hermann Göring Parachute-Panzer Division.

On 24 July 1944 the division set out for the Warsaw area via the Brenner Pass, Innsbruck, Munich, Dresden, Breslau, Ostrovo- Litzmannstadt and Skiernewice, arriving three days later. Before turning to this new chapter in the history of the division we will first deal with the action by 11th Company, 2nd Parachute-Panzer-Grenadier Regiment HG in the Chiusi area. Information concerning the action there has been provided by former officer candidate and company headquarters squad leader Walter Stiewing.

The Battle of Chiusi

On 21 June 1944 the South African Regiment of the Cape Town Highlanders received orders to take possession of the city of Chiusi. Reconnaissance had revealed that it was defended only by a weak rear guard consisting of several companies of a panzer-grenadier battalion of the Hermann Göring Division. On 21 June the regiment's A Company under the command of Major F. Bartlett received orders to clear Chiusi. The three remaining companies of the battalion were to provide support.

Leading the company was 1st Platoon under Lieutenant Wylie. At about 2300 hours, when the platoon had approached Chiusi, Allied artillery opened fire on the city. The platoon met the first German resistance soon afterward. A second platoon under Lieutenant E.P. Hardy was moved up, but enemy machine-gun and mortar fire pinned down both platoons. The two platoons nevertheless succeeded in entering the city during a pause in the firing and reached the Theatro Communale in the Piazza.

At 0200 hours the regimental commander, Brigadier Furstenberg, ordered the battalion to break through quickly. The Germans withdrew before A Company. However, D Company, which advanced on A Company's right, met heavy resistance and was unable to go any farther. When A Company reached the Theatro at 0300 it moved inside as well as into a nearby building, a wine shop. However C and D Companies were stopped by heavy German fire. Who were these German forces?

At about the same time as the South African battalion was advancing toward Chiusi, the 11th Company of III Battalion, 2nd Parachute-Panzer-Grenadier Regiment HG occupied the hills extending in front of Chiusi to the north and northwest. Early on the morning of 22 June an order reached the company command post, which was situated in a wine cellar, for the company to prepare for action at Chiusi. Battalion commander *Hauptmann* Briegel had just received the following order from regiment:

"The city of Chiusi, which the enemy has occupied during the night, is to be retaken by 1st Company, in order to free the rear of the German units still fighting south and southwest of the city."

After briefing the platoon leaders, company commander Oblt. Böcker and *Fähnrich* Stiewing set out to reconnoitre the situation in the city. One platoon followed at a distance, while the others sought out assembly areas.

"When we reached the first houses of Chiusi," reported Stiewing, "Oblt. Böcker ordered the following platoon to wait there for further instructions. We crept into the city, Oblt. Böcker with his zero-eight (9mm pistol) at the ready, I with my Karabiner 98 a few paces behind him, followed by a company runner who kept us in sight.

The town had been destroyed by a hail of bombs and shells. Shells were still whistling in from the south and southwest, blasting holes in the walls of houses. Bent low, we moved along the walls of houses on the right side of the street, away from the enemy fire. The noise in the town was deafening. The street led to a small square. Directly in front of us stood an old church, the cathedral of Chiusi. In the center of the Piazetta there were several trees, and on the left a rather large building, probably a movie theatre. As we left cover behind the church we heard the sound of exploding shells, but also the characteristic noise of rifle-calibre bullets hissing past and striking nearby.

The enemy had established himself in the buildings around the square. We took cover. The company runner fetched the platoon and squad leaders for a situation briefing, while the platoons moved up and went into cover by a wall above an embankment. The platoon now moved to the center of the city as ordered. As we left the cover of the church together, we were met by a hail of bullets from the surrounding houses. We took our first casualties. Our first-aid NCO tended to the wounded in the square under enemy fire.

There was no way to approach the enemy-occupied houses. Oblt. Böcker therefore requested tank support. It was with relief that we observed the arrival of two Panzer IVs a short time later. The two tanks appeared one after another at the north side of the square. A Leutnant clambered out of the turret hatch of the leading panzer and we discussed the subsequent advance."

The 2nd Platoon advanced behind one of the tanks to storm the theater. Two attempts, each by two squads, failed. Then the 3rd Squad under Obergefreiter Zideck tried its luck. Zideck provided the following account of the action:

"Cautiously we entered the building. I expected hand grenades to come down from above immediately. When nothing happened we climbed higher. It became ever more sinister. I begged my squad leader, who was walking just in front of me, not to go any farther. He just said, 'Don't worry, I'll make it!'

Almost unconcerned, because nothing had happened so far, we stepped onto the last landing. Suddenly a submachine-gun rattled to life above us. The burst struck the squad leader full in the chest. He fell to the floor and died in a rapidly-expanding pool of blood. The now leaderless 3rd Squad withdrew from the building and took cover behind the tank standing in front of the theater. The tank trained its 75mm gun on the upper story of the theater and opened fire. From up there the South Africans fired like mad at everything that moved in the square. The impacting shells ripped away part of the roof framework, shattered the walls, and blasted out the windows.

Suddenly the men saw an arm appear from an empty window opening and wave a white flag. We stopped firing and one of the South Africans shouted to us in German that they wanted to surrender."

Afterward Zideck and several comrades of 4th Squad went back into the theater and slowly climbed the stairs, holding their weapons in front of them at the ready. Zideck reached the theater hall. The thick dust and powder smoke made it almost impossible to see, but then he was able to make out the awful scene. Numerous dead and wounded lay side by side. Lt. Wylie surrendered to Zideck. Many years later he was to become his friend.

The first highlanders left the theatre unarmed, their hands raised. *Fähnrich* Stiewing, who spoke English well, took charge of the prisoners on behalf of Oblt. Böcker. The enemy artillery fell silent. Dead and wounded were recovered. A dressing station had been set up in a tavern. The first-aid NCO provided help to friend and foe alike. By about midday everyone was convinced that the mission against Chiusi had been completed and were hoping for the order to withdraw. But then, suddenly, the enemy opened up a heavy fire with artillery and infantry weapons. Explosive bullets from automatic rifles whipped into the square.

Shells fell on and around the square in the center of Chiusi. Then the sound of tanks was heard and, all of a sudden, infantry fire began coming from a building that housed a wine store. A group of highlanders had hidden out there. Lieutenant Colonel Flemmer had moved forward the Prince Albert Guards in order to rescue their comrades thought to still be in Chiusi. Three Sherman tanks also approached the town, but luckily for the company they got stuck in the impassable terrain.

The final phase of the Battle of Chiusi began. The wine shop was stormed by the panzer-grenadiers and Lieutenant Hardy, who was in command there, and his men were taken prisoner. The counterattack by the South Africans foundered in the face of concentrated machine-gun fire. They began to pull back. Only then was 11th Company's mission complete. Battalion commander *Hauptmann* Briegel congratulated the company on its success. During the course of the following night the men were withdrawn from Chiusi. Pressed hard by the enemy and repeatedly involved in brief, hard rearguard actions, the panzer-grenadiers withdrew northward with the other units of the Hermann Göring Parachute-Panzer Division. The retreat was further complicated by frequent ambushes carried out by Italian guerrilla bands and by rampant disease.

The HG Parachute-Panzer Division suffered the following losses in the period 1 May - 31 May 1944:

Killed:	11 officers	255 men	total: 266
Wounded:	19 officers,	402 men,	total: 421
Missing:	11 officers,	952 men,	total: 963
Sick:	10 officers,	629 men,	total: 639
Other:	11 officers,	247 men,	total: 258
Totals:	62 officers,	2485 men,	total: 2547

The division's losses in the period 1 June – 30 June were:

Killed:	19 officers,	411 men,	total: 430
Wounded:	43 officers,	1101 men,	total: 1144
Missing:	26 officers,	920 men,	total: 946
Sick:	14 officers,	841 men,	total: 855
Other:	17 officers,	245 men,	total: 262
Totals:	119 officers,	3518 men,	total: 3637

The division's personnel situation was examined in a report by the HG Parachute-Panzer Division to LXXVI Panzer Corps on 1 July 1944. We present it here to illustrate that the Hermann Göring Parachute-Panzer Division's strength was no longer equivalent to that of a division:

Officers: Authorized strength 655   shortfall 163
NCOs: Authorized strength 5,162   shortfall 1,877
Men: Authorized strength 15,368   shortfall 2,220
Auxiliary volunteers: Auth. strength 972   shortfall 852
Total: Authorized strength 22,157   shortfall 5,112

The division's status in armored vehicles on this day was:

Authorized strength:

Assault Guns	31	Pz 38 t	12
Pz II	3	Armored Cars & APCs	341
Pz IV	98	S/P Anti-tank Guns	28
Pz V	3		

Operational at that time were:

Assault Guns	0	Pz 38 t	?
Pz II	2	Armored Cars & APCs	118
Pz IV	12	S/P Anti-tank Guns	0
Pz V	0		

In his report to the Inspector of Armored Troops on the fighting worth of the HG Panzer Division, *General der Panzertruppe* Traugott Herr wrote:

"It is suitable for any offensive mission. The division has fully proved itself."

The HG Parachute-Panzer Reconnaissance Battalion From the Garigliano to the Vistula

On 12 November 1943 *Oberleutnant* Wolfgang Bach made his way to the command post of the HG Armored Reconnaissance Battalion at Castro dei Volsci. He was going there to report to the battalion commander before assuming command of one of the battalion's companies. Bach received a friendly reception from the battalion commander and after their initial general discussion he was newly outfitted from the clothing stores.

Bach was assigned to a small transport detachment, and at 2100 hours he left for Vitri aboard a Steyr multi-purpose vehicle. Travelling via Ceprano-Pico along the Via Appia, they arrived in Vitri at 0300 on 13 November. That morning Oblt. Bach was informed by Lt. Vetter, an operations officer in the battalion headquarters, that his transfer papers had arrived and that he should report to the commander of 5th (Heavy) Company for a briefing. *Hauptmann* Wenzel, the commander of 5th Company, had set up his command post in a *Casa Cantonieri* on the Itri- Formia road.

The hand-over of the company was carried out the next day by Hptm. Wenzel. What Oblt. Bach received in weapons and equipment was shocking. The company had been involved in heavy fighting since the beginning of July 1943 and only the heavy weapons that had survived these battles remained. After all, the battalion had taken part in the bitter battles in Sicily as well as in the Salerno bridgehead, north of Naples, at the Volturno, near Mignano and at the Garigliano.

The 5th Company's senior NCO informed Oblt. Bach that he was the unit's thirteenth commander since January 1943. The new commander of the 5th (Heavy) Company assumed command of a unit whose organization was as follows:

Company Commander:	Oblt. Bach
Leader Company HQ Squad:	Uffz. Becker with a total of 10 men, 2 vehicles and 2 motorcycles.
Wespe Platoon (SP):	with four "Wespen" (light armored howitzer 18/2, 105mm, on Pz II chassis, SdKfz. 124). Ammunition capacity 32 rounds, crew of 5.
Pioneer Platoon:	
Platoon Leader:	Fahnenjunker-Feldwebel /Lt. Osterhaus
Deputy Platoon Leader:	Ofw. Lochner
1st-3rd Pioneer Squads:	30 NCOs and men
Pioneer Equipment:	Land mines, power saws, rollers, inflatable boats, explosives and fuel, entrenching tools.
Vehicles:	4 trucks (Opel-Blitz) 3 tonne, all-wheel drive
Infantry Gun Platoon:	
Platoon Leader:	Fahnenjunker-Feldwebel Drews
Guns:	one light Infantry Gun 18 (75mm) Crew: 1 NCO and 6 men
Tractors:	2 light prime movers, 1 tonnne (SdKfz. 10) halftracks, 90H.P., 2 + 4 seating, 50/55 kph.
Anti-tank Platoon:	
Platoon Leader:	Lt. Wirth
Deputy Platoon Leader:	Uffz. Bauer
1st and 2nd Guns:	Uffz. Bauer, – 1 NCO, 5 men
Crew:	Uffz. Dittner – 1 NCO, 5 men
Reserve Crew:	Uffz. Mondro – 1 NCO, 5 men
Guns:	two 75mm Pak 40 L/48 with gun shields and split-trail gun carriages
Tractors:	3 light prime movers, 3 tonne (SdKfz. 11) half-tracks, 2 + 4 seating, 46/50 kph.
KWK Platoon:	(Heavy cannon platoon) not yet assigned.
Planned:	4 medium cannon-armed APCs with 75mm Stuk 37 L24 (SdKfz. 251/9)
Planned Platoon Leader:	Lt. Barthel

Combat Train:	3 trucks (Opel-Blitz 3-tonne, all-wheel drive) for the transport of munitions, equipment and fuel. Automotive oil, gasoline and diesel fuel in 20-liter drums.
Supply Train:	
Leader:	Hauptfeldwebel Uffz Popp
Personnel Strength:	3 NCOs, 10 men. Vehicles: three 3-tonne Ford all-wheel drive trucks, one 5-tonne Krupp truck.
Loaded:	repair echelon, field kitchen, weapons and equipment, office, clothing and repair installations. Ammunition, fuel in drums, field first-aid kits, etc.,

This list illustrates the numbers and types of weapons, materiel and equipment which belonged to a fully-equipped motorized company or a panzer company. General equipment, such as small arms of all types, clothing and so on, was mentioned only in passing.

What particularly struck *Oberleutnant* Bach was the poor condition of the trucks. The fighting worth of the company following the heavy fighting of the previous months was good, although the lack of or inadequate replacement of the lost heavy weapons, vehicles and equipment weighed heavily. During the night of 25 November there was a practice alert, with orders to engage a fictitious amphibious landing. Several accidents resulted. Two bombing raids on Formia emphasized the imminent Allied threat.

On a late November day in 1943 5th Company received a surprise visit from a senior officer. A command car stopped in front of the unit's quarters; it was *Oberst* Schmalz, commander of the HG Special Purpose Panzer-Grenadier Brigade. Schmalz had come to get a report from Oblt. Bach. Everything the company commander heard pointed to an action at the Garigliano. In his book, Wolfgang Bach wrote:

"From that hour on I knew what I had only previously heard second-hand, namely that Oberst Schmalz was a man for whom the well-being of the troops lay near to his heart. He radiated something engaging and fatherly which one couldn't escape. When I returned to the company the men confirmed my initial impression: 'The Oberst is always like that!'"

The battalion was placed on alert on the afternoon of 2 December 1943. Hptm. Lübke ordered: "Make preparations to leave for the area of operations. Load everything. Report when ready for departure."

It did not take long for the unit to come to march readiness, however the departure itself was delayed twenty-four hours. Not until darkness was falling on 3 December did the HG Armored Reconnaissance Battalion set out in the general direction of Cassino. The battalion drove through Itri and Pico to Pontecorvo and from there to Aquino and Cassino. The unit travelled by company, with lights dimmed and shielded. The march road, the Via Casilini, had to be cleared in the area of the western foothills of the Cassino Massif. Vehicles and guns were camouflaged. All company commanders were called forward.

In the morning twilight of 4 December the men could see the sustained fire from enemy artillery to the east, along the Via Casilini. Hptm. Lübke instructed the company commanders to reconnoitre positions for a fire-brigade action at the foot of Monte Cassino. In the evening they were to advance as far as Sant Angelo in Theodice, only about four kilometers south of Cassino on the Rapido River. The battalion resumed its march as darkness fell, to keep out of sight of enemy aircraft. Just short of Cassino on the Via Casilini, at an intersection within sight of the first houses, the troops found both sides of the road littered with burnt-out vehicles. They belonged to a German march column that had been caught by enemy fighter-bombers.

After reaching the village of Sant Angelo the company moved into a mixed forest through which ran a defile leading to the Rapido River. There the battalion's company commanders learned that they were the division reserve and would be sent into this action alone; the rest of the division had remained in rest positions in the Gaeta-Frosinone area to rest and refit.

Several other HG units took part in this action on the right wing of the Reinhard Line as part of *Kampfgruppe* Corvin: units of the flak artillery and the division's 2nd Panzer-Grenadier Regiment. The assignment given the HG Armored Reconnaissance Battalion was to occupy and further expand a prepared defensive sector in the Gustav Position, approximately 12 kilometers behind the Reinhard Line.

In the Gustav Line

On 2 December, following a heavy preparatory artillery barrage, troops of the US Fifth Army under General Mark Clark launched an offensive on the mountain massif east of Cassino. After piercing the Reinhard Line, the Fifth Army hoped to also break the Gustav Line along the Garigliano-Gari and Rapido Rivers and then storm through the Liri Valley toward Rome. The HG Armored Reconnaissance Battalion assembled near the village of Sant'Angelo and was attached to the division's battle group, which was commanded by *Oberst* Corvin-Wierbitzki. During the night of 6 December it was supposed to occupy a sector of the Gustav Line which lay opposite the confluence of the Rapido with the Cesa Martino. Beginning at midnight, the 1st, 2nd, 4th and 5th Companies moved into the planned positions. The companies remained in these positions until 11 December. The battalion commander was spending some time with 5th Company that day when he was suddenly summoned to the headquarters of *Kampfgruppe* Corvin, where he received new orders.

Once darkness had fallen, the battalion, minus 1st and 5th Companies, was to leave its positions and travel to its new area of operations in the northeast by motor vehicle. The 5th Company was placed under the command of *Kampfgruppe* Corvin. Oblt. Bach reported to *Oberst* von Corvin-Wierbitzki and also met his adjutant, Oblt. Werner. When Oblt. Bach returned to the company command post it was under heavy enemy fire; fortunately there were no casualties.

On 15 December *Oberleutnant* Bach, who had just made his way to Fw.

Drew's hedgehog position, received orders from Hptm. Lübke by field telephone for the company to withdraw from its positions after dark and assemble in Aquino, 10 kilometers west of Cassino. When 5th Company arrived there on 16 December, it found that the battalion had left for the Adria Front on the 12th to receive a new mission in the Chieti area with the Tenth Army. The 5th Company was to follow as quickly as possible.

Chieti was 200 kilometers away. The company reached its destination over the "fighter-bomber racetrack" without loss. On the morning of 17 December it took up quarters in a group of houses east of Chieti. There the company was to take up the fight in the rain and snow and other hindrances against the British Eighth Army. The latter had launched a major offensive under General Montgomery on 27 November; the attack's objective was the Pescara – Avezzano – Rome highway. With this operation Montgomery hoped to fall on the rear of the German defensive front in the Cassino area.

The battalion was instructed to establish defensive positions at the Arielli River below Cassino Vezzani, on both sides of the former boundary between the 90th Panzer-Grenadier Division on the right and the 1st Parachute Division on the left. The companies reached their assigned operational areas late on the afternoon of 18 December. The defensive sector in the main line of resistance was occupied in the following order:

    2nd Company (motorcycle), Oblt. Sailer

    4th VW Company, Hptm. Vogel

    5th (heavy) Company, Oblt. Bach

    1st Armored Recon. Company, Lt. Flechsig in reserve.

To the left of the battalion's positions, the men of the 3rd Parachute Regiment under *Oberst* Heilmann defended the village of Villa Grande against an attack by Indian troops with strong artillery support. The village lay in rubble and ashes.

On 20 December *Oberleutnant* Bach drove with the company headquarters squad to the battalion command post. While driving on the road to Villa Grande they were attacked by fighter-bombers about 1.5 kilometers from Tollo. Nine Hawker Hurricanes attacked one after another in low-level flight. The Kübelwagen (Kfz. 15) was hit several times but remained serviceable. Just before reaching the command post the squad was again attacked without success by nine fighter-bombers.

The next few days passed with night patrols and skirmishes. On 22 December the battalion commander ordered the 5th Company command post moved closer to his battalion command post. Oblt. Bach found a roomy cave on the slope's back side and set up shop there. While there was fighting near Villa Grande and Ortona all of Christmas Day, the reconnaissance battalion's sector remained quiet. Lt. Flechsig was ordered to take a platoon from the 1st Armored Reconnaissance Company and cross the Arielli in 2nd Company's sector on foot at 0200; then at 0630 he was to storm the enemy-occupied Casa Fusanio estate and the hill positions at the village of Casino Vezzani. The surprise attack was a success, losses were minimal. The patrol returned with 1 officer and 16 men of the Indian 8th Infantry Division.

The final days of 1943 passed quietly apart from increasing fighter-bomber attacks on Tollo. Battalion train units in Tollo suffered casualties of 2 killed and 6 buried alive, as well as several wounded. An immediate rescue effort managed to recover the buried men.

As the year turned the fighting increased. The daily steady rain changed to snow at night, so that the battalion medical officer, *Oberarzt* Dr. Erich Rader, had to tend to a growing number of sick as well as wounded, which he did tirelessly. On 8 January *Oberarzt* Dr. Rader had to send Oblt. Bach and the battalion signals officer, Lt. Geiger, to the 1st Parachute Division's field hospital on account of acute rheumatic fever. There was a row, because neither officer wished to leave the unit. The battalion commander was forced to intervene before the two left for Chieti. Wolfgang Bach wrote in his diary:

"In the midst of our hospital idyll we were shocked by the news that our commander and his aide had been killed. What had happened? During the night of 2 January our battalion had dispatched a combat patrol in platoon strength toward a group of Indian positions. Hptm. Lübke and Lt. Streller followed the patrol to observe the outcome of the operation. After successfully breaking into the system of positions and destroying weapons and equipment, the patrol withdrew, taking a number of prisoners. At this point our two officers set out to return to the passage in the defensive position.

The machine-gunner posted at this reception point, Obgefr. Abendroth, spotted two figures coming toward him from the direction of no-man's-land. He called out 'Halt! Who goes there?'

When there was no reaction to his challenge, he fired a single burst in the direction of the two unidentified persons. Both Hptm. Lübke and Lt. Streller were fatally hit. Our two well-loved comrades were buried at the German cemetery in Chieti on 14 January 1944. As the longest-serving company commander, I was given the task of placing wreaths on the coffins in the name of the Hermann Göring Parachute-Panzer Division and delivering the eulogy. All of those who knew Hptm. Martin Lübke and Lt. Albert Streller will never forget them."

The first rumors of an Allied landing operation on the coast of the Tyrrhenian Sea south of Rome began circulating on the evening of 22 January 1944. When the Wehrmacht communiqueé confirmed this on the 23rd, there was no keeping the two officers in the hospital any longer, especially when they learned that their battalion had been withdrawn from the Tollo sector and sent in the direction of Anzio-Nettuno.

Hptm. Rebholz, who had led the battalion before being wounded, had once again assumed command of the unit. On 25 January 1944 Oblt. Bach was released from the hospital to rejoin his unit. An ambulance took him to 5th Company's supply train in the Sezze area. From there he drove by VW to the battalion command post near Littoria. En route Oblt. Bach witnessed the effects of the enemy's air force and heard the distant rumble of ships' guns. Destroyed German war materiel littered both sides of the badly-battered road.

Bach reported his return to Hptm. Rebholz in a modern farm house at the edge of Littoria (the city was renamed Latina after the war). Rebholz was a wearer of the Knight's Cross, which he had received on 2 August 1943 as commander of the armored reconnaissance battalion. After being briefed on the situation by the battalion commander, Lt. Osterhaus, who had commanded the company in Bach's absence, drove him on a motorcycle to the positions of the anti-tank and light infantry gun platoons. The drive over the destroyed road, accompanied by artillery fire, smoke and fighter-bomber attacks, turned into a foot race. The two Germans were repeatedly forced to quickly leave the road and take cover. They had to cover the last few hundred meters bent low, on hands and knees, or at a running crouch. Finally they reached the positions, where the men had dug in "up to their collars".

The following details are taken from the diary of the former Oblt. Bach as a supplement to the general account of the fighting in this area:

"On 22/23 January 1944 the HG Parachute-Panzer Division took command of the eastern sector of the beachhead. (See sketched map) With the arrival of larger elements of the division by 24 January, a thin but continuous screening ring had been thrown around the beachhead position. Following my arrival in my battalion's defensive sector I got the impression that the situation on the German side had already firmed up."

The Defence of Cisterna

On 30 and 31 January 1944 the American 3rd Infantry Division attacked south of Cisterna with massed artillery and tank support. Its objective was to capture the town with the Via Appia and the railway station on the Rome – Naples line. The attack was repulsed on the first day. On the second day, however, the Americans attacked under cover of a heavy bombardment. The HG Parachute-Panzer Division led the defense in this sector. Among its units was the HG Armored Reconnaissance Battalion.

The enemy attack was repulsed and Cisterna remained in German hands. Counterattacks eliminated local penetrations. Afterward there was a brief pause. The attackers were unable to pierce the ring around the beachhead to the north toward Aprilia or to the northeast toward Cisterna. On 12 February the HG Parachute-Panzer Division was taken out of the line and transferred to an assembly area near the Via Appia.

On 14 February, while scouting positions in the sector manned by the Fallschirmjäger-Lehr Regiment's II Battalion, Oblt. Bach reported to the battalion commander, *Major* Herrmann. Referring to the situation map, the latter showed Bach where he wanted 5th Company deployed as reinforcement. In the afternoon Oblt. Bach encountered the division commander, *Generalleutnant* Conrath, while a parachute officer was describing the situation to him.

"I walked straight into the arms of the commanding officer. General Conrath was a commander who was more feared than loved by the troops. Often he went too far in a sudden rage and frequently imposed harsh disciplinary penalties for trifling, meaningless incidents, from which no rank was safe. As well he often 'lent his ear' to informants, which was often the subject of sarcastic comment in secure circles. The former commander of the parachute flak regiment, Oberst Meyer, declared that he wasn't surprised that General Conrath stayed away from division and corps reunions after the war.

I therefore went up to General Conrath and reported. When I had finished he dismissed me with a friendly gesture, something which no one would believe later."

Attached to the 4th Parachute Division (*Oberst* Trettner), on 14 and 15 February the HG Armored Reconnaissance Battalion was transferred into the Moletta sector. In spite of swampy terrain the battalion was able to deploy its guns and dig in and camouflage them and their crews so that they weren't spotted by the enemy straight away.

"It was there that the men learned of an incident which gave them cause to think. Two captured paratroopers had managed to escape their captors. During interrogation by US troops they had so badly beaten that they sustained serious head and facial injuries. We had heard of similar treatment of German prisoners by an Indian unit in the Arielli sector."

On the evening of 15 February Hptm. Rebholz briefed the company commanders on the situation at the beachhead and his own intentions. The battalion was to complete its move into the new assembly area near Sessano, about 8 kilometers southeast of Cisterna, by midnight. Beginning at 0100 hours on 16 February, the companies were to drive forward into their firing and jumping-off positions, which had yet to be scouted, followed at 0630 by the attack from Sessano west across the Mussolini Canal together with a battalion of the *Fallschirmjäger-Lehr* Regiment. The German bombardment began right on time at 0630 hours on 16 February. When the panzers drove forward and *Nebelwerfer* salvoes roared overhead, the infantry began to advance.

"We learned that our attack was seen as a diversionary maneuver to conceal the focal point of the attack along the Albano – Aprilia – Anzio road (the present-day National Highway No. 207)."

During a briefing of company commanders by the battalion commander, an artillery salvo fell near the officers. Hptm. Rebholz suffered a shrapnel wound in the calf. After a temporary dressing was applied he was driven to the first-aid cave where he was cared for by Oberarzt Dr. Rader. Hptm. Vogel, commander of 4th Company, assumed temporary command of the battalion.

The attack by the parachute and armored reconnaissance troops made good progress. The first assault broke into the forward American positions. In the afternoon the American artillery laid down heavy barrage fire and smoke. Naval artillery joined in. That evening the German attack was called off. The companies dug in. The *Fallschirmjäger-Lehr* Battalion was withdrawn under cover of darkness. The HG Armored Reconnaissance Battalion moved into the sector vacated by the paratroops.

This diversionary attack proved to be of little advantage to the main assault and resulted in a number of dead and wounded. Among the wounded was Oblt. Sailer, commander of 2nd Company, who died of his wounds on 31

March. On 17 February there was another change of position to the west into the "Middle" Sector. The units approached their new position under heavy fire. Some of the men marched onward over the ties of the rail line to Point 105. At least the men who had followed Oblt. Bach were able to find refuge there in a linesman's hut. The new battalion commander, *Rittmeister* von Loeben, who was from the Army's officer reserve, arrived and issued new orders for 0600 hours on 18 February. Army units familiarized the battalion's elements with the terrain. Following the failure of the previous attack, the German plan was now to break through the beachhead and drive through to the port of Anzio. "After a short drive I accompanied Dr. Brand and Hptm. von Loeben over a poor field road into the assigned operational area. The battalion commander fell into a deep water-filled hole and we had to pull him out again. The enemy fired phosphorous shells, which illuminated the terrain. Our own artillery opened up at 0400 hours. Fires and explosions deep in the landing area marked the successful engagement of enemy targets." In the neighboring sector there was an attack by another armored reconnaissance battalion under the command of *Rittmeister* von Perfall. Perfall, an outstanding soldier, was killed in this action.

The attack by the HG Armored Reconnaissance Battalion began at 0600 hours. Considerable ground was gained in the initial hours. Hill 62 was taken. Then the enemy artillery began laying down barrage fire. Everyone on Hill 62 took cover.

"On the way to Cisterna I passed the aid station, which was set up in a farm. A Red Cross flag clearly marked this first-aid center. Dr. Rader, heavily taxed by caring for the many wounded men, gave me a shot (for my rheumatism). Then I took leave of my friend. Several hours later I learned that Dr. Erich Rader had been badly wounded by shrapnel at the farm. He died of these wounds on 21 February 1944. A day earlier our battalion had been given the mission of carrying out an attack on a group of farms at Carano, together with an assault unit of the 715th Infantry Division, on 21 February. The entire operation foundered due to inadequate preparation. As it became light on 21 February the enemy so showered our jumping-off positions with shells of all calibers that it was impossible for us to advance. Not until this fire slackened did the 2nd, 3rd and 4th Companies gain ground. The units of the 715th Infantry Division remained behind however.

A barrier of Allied barrage fire ended our attack on Carano. The battalion had been forced to take bloody losses. Lt. Eichhorn was so badly wounded that he died at the main dressing station in Velletri. That evening Hptm. von Loeben expressed to the assembled company commanders his displeasure at the hesitant manner in which the companies had acted. The company commanders refused to accept this reproach. Hauptmann Vogel reacted spontaneously and emphatically rejected this general slight. This breach of trust could not be glued back together."

A second German offensive, planned this time south of Cisterna in the East Sector, and in which the HG Parachute-Panzer Division was finally to see action as a unit, began hesitantly. The battalion held an officers briefing on 26 February, at which the division's mission was explained. It was to attack on both sides of the Cisterna – Isola Bella – Montello road with all available operational elements and establish a bridgehead across the west branch of the Mussolini Canal (see map). As well, the "Conrath Group", as the assembled regiment-size unit was called, was to be reinforced by a Tiger unit and an assault howitzer unit.

It had been raining steadily for days, and this called forth bad memories of similar preparations earlier that winter in muddied terrain. The unit moved into its assembly areas during the night of 29 February. The attack began at 0500 hours with what was – at least by current German standards – a massive bombardment and subsequent harassing fire. At dawn an assault detachment of the Conrath Group took Isola Bella. This attack literally became stuck in the mud as a result of enemy barrage fire. Oblt. Bach was covered by dirt and mud from heavy naval artillery shells exploding nearby. He was unable to get free on his own and had to be literally dug out of the mud by the crew of a rocket launcher.

In the afternoon American troops attacked the Conrath Group. *Nebelwerfer* rocket launchers and heavy infantry weapons brought the attack to a halt. The attack in the Cisterna area was called off on the evening of 1 March. The HG Parachute-Panzer Division was pulled out of the line and withdrawn to the area surrounding Lucca, Pisa and Livorno – about 250 kilometers northwest of Rome on the Ligurian coast – to rest and refit. One of the last units to be withdrawn was the armored reconnaissance battalion, which was transferred to the Bologna area. The soldiers of the HG Division, notorious among the Americans as "those damned Göring boys", had got away once again.

Oblt. Bach was delivered to the division hospital in Fiuggi on 2 March. On the 8th he was sent to the division's hospital for minor cases in San Martino di Castrozza, making the trip there by bus and train. There were about 100 members of the division in the "Sass Major" Sport Hotel. Director of the rest home was Hptm. Keller. Hptm. Rebholz was also among the convalescents staying at the hotel. On 30 March 1944 Oblt. Bach was released to return to his unit. On 1 April he rejoined his company in the village of Zola Predosa west of Bologna.

Following a period when little was done, the restoration of 5th (Heavy) Company quite surprisingly began with the assignment of personnel – about 60 NCOs and men – and equipment. Within a few days the company had been brought up to strength and was able to commence unit exercises. It was there that Oblt. Bach was told the following dramatic story by the commander of I/JG 53, *Hauptmann* Harder. Harder, who had won the Knight's Cross on 5 December 1943, told his tale to Bach while the two were drinking in the battalion's officers' mess after a joint exercise:

At the beginning of December 1943 (on the night of 3 December) two *Gruppen* of a Ju 88 *Geschwader*, a total of 88 aircraft, bombed installations in Bari harbour and the American transport ships anchored at the roadstead and the pier there. Nineteen cargo ships, a combined total of 73,343 gross registered tons, were sunk and seven others badly damaged. The explosion of a fully-laden munitions ship caused further damage. Two direct hits caused one freighter to explode. Included in its cargo were containers of lethal poison gas. The ship was the 10,617-ton *John Harvey*. On board was poison gas specialist Lieutenant Colonel Beckström.

The escaping clouds of poison gas and smoke killed far in excess of 1,000 American soldiers and an unknown number of Italian civilians. Hptm. Harder drew the following conclusion:

"Don't ignore chemical defence training. The Allies could open the gas war tomorrow, even in our area of operations and in the rear, without worrying about losses to the civil population."

As a result of this report work on chemical defence was begun again with the note that

"The Allies could begin the gas war tomorrow, including in our area of operations and in the rear of same."

The Wehrmacht communiqueé of 3 December 1943 confirmed the attack by Ju 88 bombers on Bari's harbour installations and roadstead. Chemical defence training was restarted, even though the use of poison gas in war had been banned by the Geneva Treaty of 1925.

In mid-April the battalion was committed to an anti-partisan operation. This action was led by *Rittmeister* von Loeben. A platoon from each of the 2nd, 3rd and 4th Companies, as well as all of 5th (Heavy) Company minus the infantry gun platoon led by Lt. Drews, remained in the unit billets. These units were concentrated under the command of Oblt. Bach as "Battle Group Bologna", with the mission of guarding the country west of the city against enemy airborne landings and partisans. Oblt. Bach deployed motorized and bicycle patrols around the clock to watch over the countryside between Bologna and Modena. There were no incidents. However, there was no lessening of partisan activity following the April operation, indeed the first days of May witnessed several partisan ambushes and the harassment of German supply traffic – the result of an appeal by the Italian Commander-in-Chief Marshall Badoglio. As a result orders were issued for a second anti-partisan action.

It should be clearly stated that the treacherous, brutal nature of partisan warfare invalidated all the conditions of the Hague Rules of Land Warfare. Their ambush-style of warfare was criminal and in every way the equal of the worst acts committed by Soviet partisan bands. The partisans boasted about the most vile crimes, but when they were themselves attacked they considered it a crime. They felt, however, that they were entitled to commit murder. How were the Germans to defend themselves?

The alert was sounded on 3 May, and at 1400 hours the 5th (Heavy) Company formed up and drove into the Etruscan Apennines. The unit drove through Modena, La Spezia and Vezzano-Sasina to Collagna at the Passo de Cerreto. The partisans had blocked the German supply road there. The behavior of these bands was bestial. They took no prisoners, as evidenced by the mutilated bodies which were found. The partisans fought in civilian clothing and wore no identifying insignia, which often allowed them to get behind German soldiers and kill them. A larger unit was required for this new anti-partisan operation. It was commanded by an *Oberst* on the staff of the commander of the army rear area.

Soldiers from the army, air force and navy were brought together in the anti-partisan unit. In addition there were units of senior SS and police commanders and several dozen men from neo-fascist organizations. The latter had scouted the bandit area in cooperation with the SD, the fascist militia and the secret military police. The area was sealed off to ensure that all the bandits caught in the trap were destroyed. The HG Armored Reconnaissance Battalion received the following instructions:

"Attack across the extended plateau, staying in contact with neighboring units on the left and right. All prisoners are to be handed over to the battalion."

Of this Wolfgang Bach wrote:

"Since these bands showed no consideration for their own people, we soldiers were to try and move the civilians to a neutral position through correct behavior on our part. However, given the mutual distrust which existed, this was a difficult task. The imposition of reprisals was expressly reserved for the commander of the overall operation."

Advancing in their attack lanes, the soldiers saw the burnt-out wrecks of German military vehicles in the gorges in front of and beyond the 1,261-meter-high Passo di Cerreto. They had surely not plunged into the gorges by accident. The attack began on the morning of 4 May at 0600 hours. Very soon small arms fire flared up. As the Germans combed the villages the partisans fired on them from well-camouflaged positions. The 5th (Heavy) Company advanced toward the village of Vendaso with the pioneer platoon. The village was surrounded. Large quantities of American-made ammunition, fuses and explosives were found in a farmhouse located off to one side. A senior Italian police officer determined that this was a munitions depot for the bands. The household effects were removed from the dwelling. A senior officer ordered the house to be set afire by a flamethrower. When the flames reached the concealed stocks of fuses and explosives the house blew up with a tremendous explosion.

In the morning *Oberleutnant* Bach established contact with the commander of 3rd Company, Oblt. von Poschinger. Both came to the conclusion that a much larger area would have to be cordoned off in order to catch the partisans. The advance progressed slowly. Then a complete stop was ordered. Patrols had discovered a large bandit stronghold. It and the surrounding area were littered with colorful parachutes, proof that the partisans were being supplied by American aircraft. Infantry guns were moved up and these shot up the stronghold. About eight band members were taken prisoner. They were unshaven and dirty and wore torn clothing, which consisted of parts of old Italian Army uniforms supplemented by civilian clothes. One man even wore a German service coat.

The prisoners were brought to battalion headquarters at the Passo di Cerreto. 3rd Company, which had been sent to Mommio on 5 May, found ammunition and explosives in an apartment house and a barn there. Weapons were found in the organ of the local chapel. It turned out that in recent weeks the inhabitants of the village had been forced by the partisans to hide the weapons. After first removing the furniture, the apartment house and the barn were blown up. *Rittmeister* von Loeben received orders from the battle group commander to destroy the village. He rejected this and intervened energetically in further such attempts by the Italian police and fascist leaders. The action ended that afternoon. The units began their withdrawal and after a 150-kilometer drive arrived back in their cantonment area in Bologna.

The battalion's only casualties in the action were several men with minor wounds. Wolfgang Bach observed:

"The battalion had fortunately been spared the taking of hostages, the carrying out of reprisals and similar measures."

During the subsequent respite in the Bologna area, it became clear to every soldier that after the Italian cease-fire and the desertion to the enemy of a large number of Italian soldiers, the rear areas had become unoccupied enemy territory. Several areas of the country were in open revolt.

THE BATTLE OF ROME
The Hermann Göring Armored Reconnaissance Battalion Heads South

On 22 May 1944 the companies of the HG Parachute-Panzer Armored Reconnaissance Battalion left their cantonment area and headed south on National Highway 65 in the direction of Florence. Instead of *Rittmeister* von Loeben, the battalion was now commanded by *Major* Roßmann, the CO of I Battalion, HG Parachute-Panzer Regiment. (There were rumors about the quiet removal of *Rittmeister* von Loeben. Christian von Loeben was killed on the Eastern Front on 24 March 1945 and was posthumously promoted to *Major*. It is thus most unlikely that he had been arrested by the Gestapo as the rumors suggested.)

The battalion travelled by night on 22 and 23 May. This type of movement was made necessary by the Allied fighters and bombers which prowled the sky by day. Lago di Bolsena was reached during the night of 23 May. In the afternoon the senior NCO arrived with food and other supplies. He also brought news that the four battalions of the HG Parachute- Panzer Artillery Regiment and several grenadier companies of the 1st and 2nd Regiments had suffered heavy losses while travelling by day on the coast road from Pisa to Rome. The artillery regiment had been reduced to a shell.

Major Roßmann denounced the companies' poor march performances in an order of the day and voiced his "displeasure" to the battalion. These denunciations showed that he was under pressure from above and that the battalion was urgently needed. Shortly afterward it received the following order:

"The motorized march is to be resumed at dawn without regard to the enemy's control of the air. Rome is to be bypassed to the northwest. The preliminary march objective is 40 km east of Rome on the Via Casilina."

During the night of 24 May the battalion drove toward Rome on the Via Casilina past Lake Bolsena and Viterbo. This drive over the notorious "fighter-bomber race track" of the Via Casilina, in the face of refugee columns fleeing north from Rome and the surrounding areas, nevertheless went off fairly well. The Allied fighter-bombers had apparently taken a break. The northern outskirts of Rome were reached late on the afternoon of 24 May. There was a military police blocking detachment there to direct the unit around Rome. Not until dawn on 25 May did 5th (Heavy) Company, the point unit, reach the Via Casilina, which led to Valmontone. This followed a night drive over secondary roads and main roads pitted with bomb craters. Still unscathed, the unit arrived in the city of Artena on the Colleferro – Rome road.

Near Artena the men of the battalion encountered army soldiers who had become separated from their units. Victims of the air war lay at the side of the road. *Major* Roßmann briefed the company commanders on the defensive sector at the southern limits of the village of Artena. The 2nd Motorcycle, 3rd Panzer-Grenadier and 4th Schwimmwagen Companies, backed up by the 5th (Heavy) Company, first had to set up their positions before they could move in. The heavy weapons reported ready to fire. At about 1200 hours a mixed enemy unit was sighted approaching on a broad front. The troops were American. Seventy-five armored vehicles were counted, approaching on a front of 400 meters. The vehicles were organized in several waves, one behind the other.

Spearheading the American force were twelve Sherman tanks. These drove at a walking pace on both sides of the road from the south to Artena. 5th Company's anti-tank gun platoon opened fire and knocked out several Sherman tanks. The crews bailed out. After that the anti- tank gun platoon was shot up and overrun. Two of the anti-tank guns were lost. The third was manhandled out of the firing zone. All wounded were recovered. The American tanks broke through the grenadiers' weak lines in several places. Several more enemy tanks were destroyed from close range. After a brief pause, during which the Americans – unhindered by the Germans – recovered their wounded, the fight went on. At the last second the order was given to withdraw toward the outskirts of Artena, which is situated on a small hill. The heavy cannon and infantry gun platoons fired everything they had in to support these withdrawal movements.

The second line of resistance was established in the vineyards and olive groves and behind walls. Following orders, the pioneers mined the approach roads and blocked them with heavy obstacles. The American troops attacked as darkness fell. Two more Shermans were destroyed by the heavy cannon platoon in front of the Artena monastery. The GIs pulled back and there was a pause in the firing. Standing patrols guarded the flanks. Food and hot coffee were brought up to the troops.

On the morning of 26 May *Oberleutnant* Bach received orders to form a battle group from the remnants of the battalion's 2nd, 3rd, 4th and 5th Companies and hold the present positions as long as possible. Available were approximately 150 grenadiers, 2 heavy cannon, 1 light infantry gun and two squads of pioneers. During the night this line of resistance was outflanked to the west and east by American troops. The next morning the defenders were pinned down by tank and artillery fire. Sherman tanks systematically shot up all the buildings in the town. Heavy machine-guns opened fire from higher positions, already half in the rear of the defenders. Bach was forced to order a withdrawal to prevent being encircled and captured.

The German troops assembled in a wood northeast of Artena. Thanks to a covering pine grove the withdrawal went smoothly and without losses. After resting and reorganizing his forces, Bach led them on a "horizon crawl" across partly open terrain back into the area south of Valmontone, where the HG Parachute-Panzer Division had established a new defensive line. *Major* Roßmann acted immediately. While pacing off the terrain he revealed to *Oberleutnant* Bach that a new main line of resistance was to be created there. The necessary reinforcements were already on the way. The following units arrived in the course of the afternoon:

> one 20mm flak platoon of the HG Parachute Flak Regiment
>
> one platoon of assault guns of the HG Parachute-Panzer Regiment
>
> one platoon of Panzer IVs of the HG Parachute-Panzer Regiment

Soon afterward the forward observers of a light field howitzer battery and a 100mm *Nebelwerfer* battery arrived to take over the job of directing fire for their batteries. These troops now manned an approximately 500-meter-wide defensive sector between Valmontone and Artena. The grenadiers received orders to dig in. The daily American reconnaissance aircraft appeared over this sector and was soon relieved by an artillery spotter aircraft. It wasn't long before enemy artillery began firing on Valmontone. Opposite the weak German defensive line lay the entire American 3rd Infantry Division, ready to attack.

Towards evening, after the food had been delivered, the American attack began. At first it was a patrol in company strength, which was accompanied by several armored vehicles. This was obviously supposed to scout the German system of positions and find a weak spot. The American patrol had little time to do this, as it was quickly shot up from close range. The heavy cannon platoon knocked out two Sherman tanks. The 20mm flak platoon laid down direct fire. The enemy suffered heavy losses. Recovery of the American dead and wounded took until the early morning of the following day – again without German interference.

Surprisingly, the commander of II Battalion, HG Parachute-Flak Regiment, *Hauptmann* Rintelen, appeared early in the morning with a basket filled with bottles of champagne. He wanted to do something special for his 3rd Platoon. The enemy artillery opened fire in the morning, right after the collapse of the American attack. At about midnight a forward observer spotted and reported enemy troops assembling for another attack. Several salvoes from the 105mm battery smashed the attack force while it was still making preparations.

"There was a noticeable stabilization in the Valmontone sector with the arrival of the HG Parachute-Panzer Division in the Fourteenth Army's area of operations on 26 May. Units appeared on the right and behind us whose armament and striking power we knew. Even their commanders were familiar to us! Some of our division's units had suffered very heavy losses to air attack during their 350-kilometer drive from the Toscana to east of Rome to the forward armored reconnaissance battalion, and the fighting worth of many units had fallen. Since it was feared that the German front on the left wing of the Fourteenth Army, east of the Alban Mountains, might collapse, the Hermann Göring units had to go over to the counterattack straight from the march, from the Via Casilina in the direction of Velletri. A several-day battle began, which was fought between the Via Appia and the Via Casilina against an enemy superior in numbers and weapons."

On Whitsunday, 28 May 1944, the enemy attacked again. At first light one of the APCs destroyed an enemy armored vehicle with its 75mm gun. An assembly area was smashed by German artillery. The enemy countered with heavy artillery fire. At about 1500 hours Oblt. Bach was called to the battalion command post, where *Major* Roßmann explained the situation at the division level. The Valmontone bend had to be held at all costs, otherwise the neighboring sector would be in peril. In the midst of the briefing a tremendous artillery bombardment began in Bach's sector. *Major* Roßmann alerted the Panzer IV platoon. Bach drove toward the front in one of the tanks. After climbing out of the tank he and *Major* Roßmann, his submachine-gun at the ready, headed for the German line.

"We communicated using hand signals. 'Forward!' I ran forward into a group of bushes. As I forced my way through, armed only with a pistol, I suddenly found myself facing a group of English soldiers. They were squatting in a line, man beside man, in a heavily overgrown ditch, with slung rifles. They must have been so shocked by my appearance that they neither shot nor called to me. I threw myself into cover, ran back through the bushes and was met by a group of grenadiers. These informed me that the position south of the railway station had meanwhile been lost. That evening Major Roßmann and I selected new positions for the battle group. Many of my men were wounded. A number of others were missing and had probably been captured."

The battalion medical officer, *Oberarzt* Dr. Ernst Thomas, had set up the aid station in a rocky cave. A number of tank crewmen had been brought in with severe burns, and several of these screamed in pain. Throughout 29 May the enemy artillery continued to fire on recognized German positions. The enemy infantry did not attack on this day. At dawn on 30 May Oblt. Bach was ordered to lead a strong patrol to Artena to reconnoitre the village and – if possible – retake it in a surprise attack. The patrol, about 40 men including 5th Company's pioneer platoon, advanced about two kilometers to the east and found nothing. It then crossed the railway embankment and assembled in a deeply eroded stream bed which led in the direction of Artena. The patrol followed the stream bed until it veered off. Hidden by a wheat field, Bach and his men reached a position 400 meters north of the village.

Suddenly enemy artillery began laying down barrage fire in front of the patrol. This was soon joined by mortar fire. Finally, when American troops attacked with tank support, Oblt. Bach ordered the retreat. This proved a difficult undertaking, as the patrol was under constant fire from the enemy artillery. Back in Valmontone, Bach reported to the battalion commander.

Major Roßmann expressed his appreciation for the effort made by the patrol.

Early on the morning of 31 May enemy infantry, led by tanks, went to the attack. Bach's battle group, consisting of about 40 men, blocked the main road from the south to Valmontone. To a certain extent they fought as a rearguard, which deceived the enemy as to the real strength of the defenders. Oblt. Bach repeatedly ordered his men to dig in to escape the heavy artillery fire, even though they were almost all at the end of their endurance.

After the battalion headquarters had withdrawn – in the course of which *Major* Roßmann was wounded – the rearguard followed. Bach reported to the operations staff of the HG Panzer Regiment, where *Oberst* von Heydebreck said to him:

"Bach, without you we'd have never made it back here!"

Referring to the situation map, the regimental adjutant, Oblt. Sommer, explained to Bach the area of operation, mission and organization of the fighting units. The high point of this situation briefing was the realization that the HG Parachute- Panzer Division had prevented the collapse of the left wing of the Fourteenth Army in spite of the enemy's great superiority in troops and weapons. Oblt. Bach was now given command of the depleted battalion by *Oberst* von Heydebreck. The commanders of the 2nd and 4th Companies, Lt. Wesche (missing since 25 May) and Hptm. Heilmann (KIA on 29 May) had to be replaced. Oblt. Bach drove in the command car to Palestrina. On arriving at division HQ, Oblt. Bach was received by the 3rd Staff Officer, Lt. Kleine-Sextro, and taken to the division commander, who was in the midst of a conversation with *Oberst* von Necker, commander of the HG Parachute-Panzer Regiment. *Oberst* Schmalz, too, expressed his admiration of Bach and his battalion. As always, Schmalz radiated calm and confidence. Wolfgang Bach wrote:

"The most striking thing to me in this crisis situation was the friendly imperturbability of the division commander. No panic, no signs of nervous tension. Oberst Schmalz really stood out above the rest with the full authority of his person."

On the way to Valmontone and his battalion Oblt. Bach and his driver were stopped by a paratrooper officer, who warned them not to continue. They turned back and came upon the battalion radio station in Palestrina. Soon afterward they found the train as well. Its destination was Moricone, 25 kilometers northeast of Rome. The continued retreat led through Mentana in the direction of Rome. Halfway there what had been assembled of the battalion was halted by its own battalion headquarters.

On 2 June Oblt. Bach temporarily assumed command of the battalion in place of *Oberst* Roßmann. Staff officer was Lt. Dr. Brandt. The battalion's orders:

"Deceive and weaken the enemy through delaying action with remaining forces in the positions in the line of resistance. Gradual withdrawal only."

There was an exchange of fire with Italian civilians while the bridge over the Aniene in Monte Sacro was being destroyed. A counterattack rescued the pioneer platoon under Lt. Osterhaus from a difficult situation. During the night of 5 June the battalion, too, withdrew northward in the direction of Rieti. The Germans were on the retreat, the Allies entered Rome. From the 5th to the 7th of June the battalion held positions along the Via Nomentana to Monterotondo, and afterward along the Via Salaria in the direction of Rieti.

On 4 June the Wehrmacht communiqueé announced:

"The 'Hermann Göring' Parachute-Panzer Division has fought heroically in the difficult battles in the area northwest of Valmontone."

From Rieti the retreat continued to Lake Trasimeno. In spite of his vast superiority in armored forces and total air superiority, the enemy pursued only slowly. *Generalmajor* Schmalz led the division sensibly, taking no chances. A veteran commander, he succeeded in weakening and stopping the enemy while escaping with his skin basically intact, retaining the division's fighting capabilities as much as possible. During a briefing at the division command post, Oblt. Bach reported that the reconnaissance battalion had discovered an army weapons dump which had been prepared for demolition. The HG was supposed to obtain weapons there. Bach and *Major* Grün, the 2nd General Staff Officer, were instructed to short-circuit the demolition and to prepare measures to obtain as many weapons as possible.

They succeeded in acquiring four 120mm Granatwerfer 42 mortars and ammunition from the dump commandant "on receipt". These weapons were to subsequently prove very effective. *Oberst* Meyer, commander of the HG Parachute-Flak Regiment, was also able to "secure" a number of important weapons. The four heavy mortars were used by Lt. Drews to form a heavy mortar platoon under the command of Lt. Friedel. From Monte Buono the HG Armored Reconnaissance Battalion withdrew to the north shore of Lake Trasimeno near Ferretto during the night of 16 June. From there it moved into the Canciano Therme area, where it was to occupy a defensive position.

The Battle of Chiusi continued. On 20 June the reconnaissance battalion was transferred to Lake Chiusi, 4 kilometers north of the city, with the mission of guarding the division's left flank. Panzer-grenadiers of the von Necker Regiment took over the positions near Canciano. The unit had only just arrived and was being directed to its positions, when the next transfer order arrived, according to which the battalion was to occupy a system of positions northwest of the Lago di Montepulciano during the night of 22 June. While attached to the 334th Infantry Division, during the night of 28 June the battalion held a line from Stazione Montepulciano to the crossroads there. The HG Parachute-Flak Regiment placed several quadruple flak close behind the reconnaissance battalion. During the first fighter-bomber attack the anti-aircraft guns shot down four or five of these deadly foes.

Also in action there was a rocket battery equipped with 150mm *Nebelwerfer* launchers. On the evening of 28 June there was a move to Sinalunga. The enemy attacked on a broad front on the evening of 29 June. The battalion command post, located in a cellar, was hit twice by artillery fire. A further withdrawal into the area north of Lucignano took place under

From left: Generalmajor Conrath, Oberstleutnant Heydemeier and Major Jacobi, photographed on the occasion of the reformation of the Flak Regiment HG in March 1943 at the Deep Anti-aircraft Range in Holland.

Panzer III Ausf N armed with the short-barrelled 75mm KwK near Anzio. The vehicle is camouflaged to prevent it being spotted from the air. In the turret hatches are Gefreiter Wellner (left) and Gefreiter Rhade.

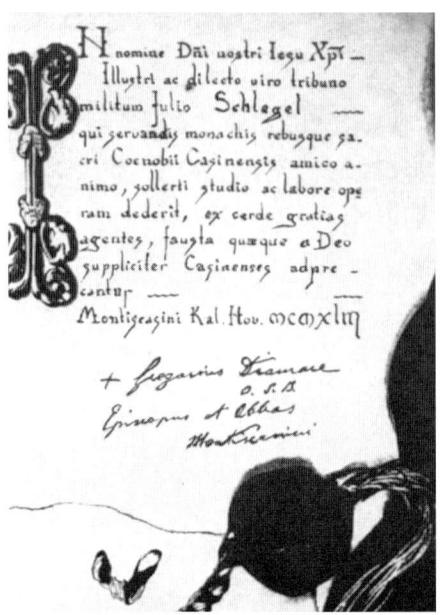

On 1 November 1943, Abbot Gregorius Diamare presented this hand-written document to the men who had saved the art treasures of Monte Cassino Monastery.

Oberstleutnant Julius Schlegel, the man responsible for saving the art treasures of Monte Cassino.

Abbot Gregorius Diamare, Pryor Fornari and Don Augusto bid farewell to one of the convoys transporting the monastery's art treasures to safety.

Livorno, March 1944. Generalfeldmarschall Kesselring visits the Fourteenth Army.

The Reichsmarschall on a visit. From the left: Generalmajor Schmalz, Oberst von Baer, Hauptmann of the Reserve Frevert (Senior Forest Superintendent) of the Volkssturm, and Oberfeldartz Dr. von Ondarza.

the cover of darkness. The rearguard company under Oblt. Poschinger became lost on the way to the new position. It was found in no-man's-land in front of Lucignano. It had fought its way through there in a running battle with the pursuing enemy.

The next eight kilometers to the new position near Monte San Savino were covered during the night of 3 July. This was the site of an important crossroads, and the enemy attacked with all available forces. All the division's heavy weapons participated in the engagement, allowing the important sector to be held until the evening of 4 July. The following day saw the arrival of *Rittmeister* Röther as new battalion commander. Following a series of outpost engagements in this area the enemy suddenly attacked with a group of Sherman tanks. Several salvoes from the heavy mortars and 150mm *Nebelwerfer* drove away the tanks.

On 16 July *Rittmeister* Röther was badly wounded in the back. Oblt. Bach once again assumed command. In a conversation with *Oberst* von Necker on 18 July he learned somewhat underhandedly that the entire division should begin preparing for a transfer to the Eastern Front. The transfer order arrived on 19 July. The march led to the Arno crossing near San Giovanni and from there to the suburb of Zola Predosa near Bologna. There the soldiers received a joyous welcome from the proprietors of their former quarters. The division was loaded aboard trains on 22 July. The HG Armored Reconnaissance Battalion entrained in two march groups. A total of 75 trains were required to transport the division. The trains passed through Bozen, Innsbruck, Munich, Eger and Aussig, which confirmed that the division was indeed headed east. The journey continued through Görlitz and Lauban to Litzmannstadt. The last stop was Warsaw-West, which was reached on 24 July. The division's battle in the south was over. What followed was the extremely costly struggle in Poland, before the Reich frontier and inside the Reich itself.

Oberleutnant Heinz Göring: Service and Death

Before beginning the final major section of this work, we will first turn to the subject of *Oberleutnant* Heinz Theodor Göring. In the summer of 1943 Göring was an instructor with the Hermann Göring Regiment in the Hojel Barracks in Utrecht, where he served as company commander. It was his ambition to receive training in the command of an assault gun unit and later obtain a transfer to a front-line unit and prove himself once again as his uncle, *Reichsmarschall* Hermann Göring, wished.

Heinz Göring was born on 4 September 1907 in Wiesbaden, the son of Heinrich Göring and his wife Dora, nee Barth. His father, a brother of Hermann Göring, was a professor in Wiesbaden. Heinz received a good education and on 20 July 1936 received his Doctor of Laws. Later he worked as a legal advisor at the Weserhütte in Bad Oeynhausen, where he went on to become a corporate lawyer. Several years later he and his wife Charlotte moved to Berlin.

From 1936 to 1937 Heinz Göring served in the 9th Flak Regiment's 11th Battery in Münster, Westphalia. In the years that followed he participated in several reserve exercises and at the end of 1938 was promoted to *Wachtmeister* in the 7th Flak Regiment's 3rd Battery. Following an officer training course in 1940 he was transferred to 1st Battery, 141st Reserve Flak Battalion on the Lower Rhine as an *Oberfeldwebel* and officer candidate. On 9 July 1940, at the request of his uncle, he was transferred to IV Battalion, General Göring Regiment, which after the victory in France had been deployed to defend Orly airport near Paris. There Heinz Göring was made a platoon leader and on 1 August 1940 was promoted to *Leutnant*.

That September IV Battalion transferred back to Germany and was stationed in the Oranienburg area to help defend the capital city of the Reich. From 8 to 27 April 1941, Lt. Göring and the rest of IV Battalion were stationed in the Ploesti area to guard the Romanian oil fields, which were of vital importance to the German war effort. 21 June 1941 found IV Battalion, General Göring Regiment in the strategic buildup area for the Russian Campaign; it was in the first wave, between the Bug and Styr, ready to attack. The General Göring Regiment distinguished itself in the Battle of Berdichev. Near Uman it destroyed a number of enemy tanks and helped close the pocket there.

On 8 July Göring received the Iron Cross, Second Class for acts of bravery. A month later he was awarded the Iron Cross, First Class. On 10 December 1941 he received the Flak Combat Badge for more than 25 days in combat. After much hard fighting the regiment reached the bank of the Dniepr in August. On 28 August the exhausted unit was withdrawn from the front for a rest, during which it was brought up to strength. Heinz Göring's new orders were to report for duty with the Railway Flak Battery deployed on the *Reichsmarschall* command train. There he took command of one of the 20mm battery's platoons. Göring left this privileged position at the end of April 1942 to serve with the regiment's 14th Battery guarding the airspace around Paris.

Heinz Göring began a new career as an instructor with his assignment to the HG Panzer Training and Replacement Regiment in Holland. His recruit company was in good hands. He spared it and himself nothing. On 1 July 1942 Göring was promoted to the rank of *Oberleutnant*. In the Hojel Barracks near Utrecht Göring became a well-known and valued officer. Among the well-known personalities who joined him in Utrecht for training and service were Under Secretary of State Dr. Paul Schmidt and the artist Gustav Gründgens. Under his command the regiment's 11th Company became one of its most proficient units.

When the *Reichsmarschall* introduced privileges for him, his nephew refused to accept them. He also did not hesitate to expose as a shirker a national-socialist command officer who suddenly "fell ill" several days before he was to see action and saw to it that he was sent to the front. On 17 October 1942 the HG Brigade received the order enlarging it to a division. As part of the expansion the unit received new weapons, especially artillery and armored forces. Part of the division was transferred, but Göring remained in Utrecht for ten more months as commander of 11th Company.

In October he and his assault gun platoon were transferred to Italy. Initially he took on the role of operations officer in the HG Panzer Regiment. This did not last long, however. It ended in mid-December with his transfer to the assault gun battalion's 9th Company as a platoon leader. His commanding officer there was Oblt. Hans-Joachim Bellinger, an officer who had already won his merits in Russia.

Göring continued to demonstrate his fondness for order and cleanliness. On one occasion he returned from a patrol with a bath tub, an action which did not entirely meet with Oblt. Bellinger's approval. In spite of all his efforts, it was no secret that Göring kept a certain distance from the other officers in the battalion. For one thing he was significantly older than others of his rank. Perhaps the other officers were also mistrustful because of his relationship to the *Reichsmarschall*. Nevertheless, Heinz Göring was an upright man, even though he had a somewhat introspective nature.

At the end of December Heinz Göring was slightly wounded; as he was watching the road from the window of a cellar a bomb fell nearby. On 28 January 1944 he was awarded the Wound Badge in Black. He refused to leave his unit and remained in action in the Anzio-Nettuno battle zone. Transferred into the Florence area, Heinz Göring led the assault gun battalion's 10th Company. After a period of rest and refitting in the Castel Monteccio area he led an infantry unit in the anti-partisan action described earlier. Göring was always at the head of his men, leading them on foot over the hills which ranged from 400 to 1000 meters high. He never asked more of his men than he could do himself.

With the Allied breakout from the Anzio-Nettuno bridgehead in May 1944 and their advance on Rome, the HG Parachute-Panzer Division saw heavy action. Fighting day and night, the division reached the front line south of Rome. It suffered heavy losses in the Caesar Line. Attacks alternated with counterattacks. US forces broke through near Valmontone at the cost of heavy losses. On 4 June the Allied service radio admitted that the HG Parachute-Panzer Division had fought bravely.

On 15 July the division was pulled out of the line in the midst of the retreat and in the next few days was shipped by train to the Eastern Front. Among the units headed east was the assault gun battalion (see Kanert account). On the night of 28 July 1944 *Leutnant* Wallhäuser was in command of 10th Company. The unit should have been under the command of Oblt. Göring, but he was not on the train. When the trains were leaving Göring was arriving by motorcycle at the regimental command post of the HG Panzer Regiment.

An account of the combat operations which followed is provided in the writings of Bruno Kanert.

The Hermann Göring Assault Gun Battalion in Action in Poland

On 15 July 1944 the HG Assault Gun Battalion was pulled out of the Budrio-Bologna-Florence area and sent over the Brenner Pass to the army ordnance depot in Breslau-Groß Masselwitz. There it was issued the Jagdpanzer IV (also called the Panzerjäger 39) which was based on the chassis of the Panzer IV and armed with a long-barrelled 75mm KwK. On 22 July the 13 tank-destroyers plus three additional tanks, each with a ferry crew of two, were loaded aboard trains at Herrnpotsch Station near Breslau. Gun commander Bethke was absent so Kanert took his place. Departure for Poland was not until 26 July. The trains rolled through Warsaw in the direction of Pilawa. The tank-destroyers detrained in Otwok, southeast of Warsaw, using the station's head ramps.

The unit drove on to Pogorzel, situated north of Siennice. The troops spent the night in the castle there. The first duels with Russian tanks took place on 28 July. By the afternoon four T 34s and two other tanks had been destroyed. Bruno Kanert wrote:

"It was 28 July, between one and two o'clock in the morning: 'Hold position in front of the village of Pogorzel.' At about four there was an alarm. The vehicles moved into firing position in front of the village. It was about 0900 when Oblt. Göring climbed aboard my tank destroyer. Together with two other vehicles, commanded by Uffz. Schlöffer and another comrade, we were about to start a reconnaissance patrol to the right to Siennice, bypassing the village of Pogorzel. We moved forward, alternately advancing and stopping to observe. The intervals between the vehicles became ever greater, because the spaced armor panels (Schürzen) of the individual tank destroyers were being torn from their mountings by the sheaves of wheat standing in the fields.

My vehicle caught up with the other two tank destroyers in front of a farm. They had stopped because the enemy had been sighted there. However the Russians fled the farm in panic. The patrol was resumed without meeting any resistance. We stopped at a wood. In the afternoon a dispatch rider arrived and ordered us back to Pogorzel. When we had approached to within a kilometer of the village, shells began striking the ground a short distance in front of and behind our vehicle. Acting quickly, Oblt. Göring ordered us to drive down from the road to the left into a field. We reached a plantation and opened fire on the estate's watchtower, which an enemy observer had obviously turned into an observation post.

We continued on our way and sighted a VW Kübelwagen just outside the village. It was the battalion commander, Major Sandrock. Standing in the ditch to the right of the car was battle group commander Bellinger. Oblt. Göring climbed out and went over to the two officers, leaving the vehicle to me. It was about 1700 hours on 28 July 1944. A short time later the commander pointed to the castle entrance and using hand signals ordered us to drive in and reconnoitre as far as the castle courtyard. Fw. Heinig's vehicle backed through the wall into the courtyard. He was instructed to remain on guard there.

At 1800 hours we received orders from the commander to drive into the village of Pogorzel and reconnoiter. It was free of the enemy. On the left side of the road directly in front of the village sat a burning anti-aircraft gun. We stopped to observe at the entrance to the village but saw nothing unusual."

On continuing into the village Kanert's tank destroyer was knocked out by a T 34 firing from close range from a camouflaged position on the left side of the street. The vehicle blew up after the third hit and began to burn fiercely. Three of Kanert's comrades, several of whom had been wounded, died in the blaze. Kanert himself was thrown through the tank destroyer's open hatch and escaped with minor burns.

We now return to the gun commander's own account, in which he explains how he drove so near to the T 34 without seeing it:

"We rolled slowly into the village. From my turret hatch I scanned the gardens and farm houses to the left and right and up the village street. Then, suddenly, a tree or a bush fell diagonally in front of me. I caught sight of a turret and a gun barrel and then everything was shrouded in fire and smoke. A lightning bolt shot over the vehicle about two meters above me, splitting the air sharply. The T 34 was so well-camouflaged that I didn't see it, especially since my view was severely limited by the fruit trees in the middle of the garden in front of the house.

The T 34 was sitting at the gable wall of the house, which was about six meters from the road. We had rolled right in front of the enemy's gun. The distance to the Russian tank was about six to eight meters. I roared, 'Halt! Pull to the left!' The driver had no chance to carry out this order for at this point, not three seconds after the first hit, we were hit a second time. The shot struck just beneath the deck abeam the gunner and bored its way into the interior of the vehicle. Cement fragments flew into my face and mouth. Repeating my order, I bent down to speak directly to the driver.

Gunner Buhlmann lay slumped over the sighting mechanism. The driver was sitting partially turned in his seat. Then our vehicle was shaken by a third hit. The tank glowed. This hit must have struck the fuel tank located behind the driver, which still contained about 300 liters of gasoline. As I tended to Buhlmann, who was sitting directly opposite me, I saw the floor of our vehicle being devoured by a multitude of small blue flames.

To my right, separated by the cannon's full recoil guard, Averbeck was busy with the hatch. He didn't appear to be wounded. He had obviously locked the hatch with the turn-lock, for he was trying to unscrew this. Had the hatch only been closed, he would only have needed to push it open before exiting the vehicle through it.

I called to Buhlmann, pulled him over the seat's back-rest and ordered him to get out, but he must have been badly wounded. Just as I was lifting Buhlmann over the seat to the hatch, there was a hard crash. Standing as I was in the hatch, I was ejected from the vehicle. I landed on the deck of the tank destroyer and jumped down to the right onto the road. Averbeck's hatch was still closed. There was no way I could save anyone there. As the ammunition might go up at any minute and the first shots from the escorting Russian infantry were already coming from the garden to my left, I dove headfirst over the garden fence and stopped to catch my breath behind the wooden house. The Russian followed. I ran into the wheat field and, dashing from one sheave to the next, disappeared in the deep furrows of a potato field. There I drew my pistol, fired several shots in the direction of my pursuers and crept back to report the destruction of my tank destroyer. I still had on my headset and the throat microphone with the torn-out cable."

The drama and tragedy of Kanert's account illustrates the type of situation faced by a tank crew at the moment their tank is hit. The commander, to whom Kanert reported, reproached him for not having reconnoitred farther, if need be on foot. When Kanert turned to go, he was called back and ordered to take charge of one of the two tank destroyers sitting in the rear, then drive up to a firing position to the right of the village and destroy the T 34. When Kanert climbed into the vehicle the crew, all NCOs, explained that the vehicle had been damaged and couldn't carry out the mission.

But Kanert had his way. They crept toward the T 34, halting several times along the way. The first shot was fired at 2000 hours, and after the third shot the T 34 was shrouded in flames. Kanert headed back. Two hours later Uffz. Heinig's tank destroyer was hit in combat with a Russian tank. Heinig, wounded in the arm, jaw and mouth, was evacuated. Afterward everyone withdrew behind a sand pit 800 meters from the village.

At midnight track noises were heard approaching the German position from the left of the village. The sound was also heard by the crew of the Wallhäußer tank-destroyer. The unidentified tracked vehicles stopped 600-800 meters in front of the German assault guns. If they were enemy vehicles, they were to be engaged and destroyed at first light on 29 July. Between 0400 and 0500 three assault guns moved out with engines throttled back. They rolled forward as far as the marks they had made when the tracked vehicle had first been detected, placing them in the correct firing direction. Gradually the vague outlines of three KV Is became visible; the German gunners made the appropriate range adjustments.

The first salvo struck all three enemy tanks. Two caught fire while the armor-piercing shot bounced off the third. Nevertheless the crew of the third tank also abandoned their vehicle and fled. Having been assigned a new assault gun with the crew of Schubauer, Hoffmann and Franzmann, on the morning of 29 July Kanert took up position to the right of the road between the sand pit and the edge of the forest, about 200 meters in front of the Panzer IV that had delivered him. Kanert resumes the narrative:

"At 1000 hours Oblt. Göring inspected the gun positions. When he came to me he took me with him across the road to search out a position for my assault gun which would allow me to provide flanking cover to the left. The ground conditions in the swampy depression, the crossing of the road and absence of visual contact with the assault guns on the right led us to decide that this was not the location we were seeking. I returned to my assault gun and remained there. Constant tank noises were audible from the village, suggesting that it was being used as a Russian assembly area. Tensely we waited for the enemy's attack.

At 1300 hours the motors of the enemy tanks roared to life all along the front facing the German assault guns. A wave of about a dozen T 34s drove out of the village. Soon afterward they appeared on the rise in front of us and, rolling toward our position, opened fire. The attackers were put out of action with one to three shots, one after another. Only two or three T 34s were able to turn and escape. The majority littered the ground to 200 meters in front of our position. The new Jagdpanzer IV had passed its baptism of fire.

Several T 34s had moved past us unnoticed and had moved into position to the side and partially in our rear. Two of our assault guns fell victim to these when the enemy opened fire from close range. One of the vehicles was commanded by Uffz. Schlöffel. For unexplained reasons these T 34s turned away after their ambush and disappeared again without exploiting the element of surprise to the fullest. Battle group commander Bellinger summoned the gun commanders in two groups for a situation briefing. The commanders exchanged experiences and rules of conduct. Then a monotone droning sound interrupted the briefing, which was being held in a grove of trees. A gun commander was sent in the direction of the noise to investigate. On his return he reported that two of the tank destroyers had sunk up to their roadwheels in the swamp behind the grove, and that the noise was coming from the running ventilators on the decks of the assault guns.

After becoming bogged down the vehicles had been abandoned by their crews. Under the prevailing conditions recovery was impossible. At this point the sound of multiple rocket launchers firing was heard from the right. The rockets exploded to the side and behind the assault gun position. A special unit which had moved up to join the assault guns suffered losses from the fragments whizzing horizontally over the ground. At 1400 the assault gun commanded by Fw. Weigand was able to knock out four T 34s from its concealed position. It took one hit, which damaged a track, and had to drive back to the road in order to change the track there. In the process the crew came under rifle and submachine-gun fire from Russians lying in the swamp.

The Weigand assault gun did not return to its former position in the sand pit, instead it withdrew to the edge of the forest. I therefore moved forward with my assault gun, which had given covering fire during the track change on the road, and moved into Weigand's position at the sand pit. At 1600 hours track noises were heard far behind the left flank. Soon afterward four T 34s drove over the rise from the wooded area in our rear and opened fire on the ferry tank parked on the road at the exit from the wood. The commander of the Panzer IV, a Feldwebel, died in the flames following a direct hit. After completing their ambush the T 34s disappeared.

A short time later we heard further tank noises from the village. A strong force of tanks approached. Commands were passed to the driver and gunner over the throat microphone. There was an exchange of ranges and target information then the command 'Open fire!' rang out. Shell after shell left the barrel. This Russian attack, too, was repulsed."

Why *Oberleutnant* Göring had not taken command of the panzer regiment's 10th Company as planned lay in the fact that he did not reach the battalion from Warsaw until the morning of 28 July. *Hauptmann* Bellinger, later promoted to battle group commander, took over the 10th Company and led it, while Oblt. Göring became a platoon leader on his arrival. Göring initially had to use the Kanert assault gun, because the vehicle reserved for him was now under the command of Hptm. Bellinger. Göring wasn't enthusiastic about this, especially since regimental headquarters considered his presence with 10th Company absolutely necessary. The then Hptm. Wolfram Stronk had received Göring, who arrived at the panzer regiment's command post on the motorcycle of ObGefr. Werner Könemann and not by train with the rest of the unit.

Accounts by Fw. Fleischmann, Uffz. Kanert, Hans-Dieter Ruf and Karl Kattum

"Several times on 29 July Oblt. Göring again assigned me positions. Apparently he still had no assault gun of his own. Late in the afternoon he was wounded by a Russian tank shell exploding in the branches of a tree to the right of the road. A little later he and several other wounded were placed aboard an assault gun and transported to the rear. On its way back to the aid station the assault gun was shot up by Russian tanks at a crossing. Only the assault gun's commander, Fw. Fleischmann, himself wounded, succeeded in escaping and making his way back to us. The Reichsmarschall must have been informed by teletype of the fate that had befallen his oldest nephew. Nothing is known of the subsequent fate of Oblt. Göring. Either he was wounded and captured by the Russians or was killed when the assault gun was hit." (Uffz. Kanert)

When *Oberleutnant* Göring was wounded outside the assault gun by an exploding shell, machine-gunner Hans-Dieter Ruf of III Battalion, HG 2nd Panzer-Grenadier Regiment, who was walking close behind the assault gun, ran over to the injured officer and turned him over. He saw that the *Oberleutnant* had been badly wounded and was bleeding heavily from a number of shrapnel wounds. He took him in his arms and the officer turned to him and, fighting for words and air, said:

"I'm Oberleutnant Göring, the Reichsmarschall's nephew." He wanted to say more but lost consciousness. Blood flowed from his mouth. At this point several more shells exploded simultaneously and Oblt. Göring was wounded again, in the right side of his face and arm. Ruf was also wounded, in the upper right arm. In spite of being wounded himself, a member of Ruf's machine-gun team dressed his wounds. Ruf tended to the *Oberleutnant*'s wounds. He applied his first packet dressing, but this was insufficient. Göring was severely wounded and lay unconscious. Several men called from the assault gun: "Göring has been killed." Nevertheless, the *Oberleutnant* and the two other wounded men were lifted onto the deck of the assault gun.

Gefreiter Karl Kattum, who had been Göring's orderly in Utrecht, provided the final clues to the subsequent fate of his commanding officer.

"This vehicle was commanded by Fw. Fleischmann. Fleischmann spotted three well-camouflaged T 34s while on the way to the rear; he turned, but it was already too late. The tank destroyer was hit hard, and the motor failed. When Fleischmann looked over to where the wounded were, he saw Kattum trying to maneuver Heinz Göring into the vehicle to protect him from the enemy fire. Immediately afterward the tank destroyer was hit again and Fleischmann and his gunner were wounded. In the following confusion they managed to exit the vehicle through the escape hatch. As there was nothing more they could do, they left the fire zone and tried to walk back to the departure point in Otwock. When they reached the assembly point, Fleischmann reported what had happened, that Göring and several other men, including Gefreiter Kattum, had been wounded and that they may subsequently have fallen into Russian hands or been killed."

Soon after the family and the Reichsmarschall received these reports, an obituary was placed in a Berlin newspaper by the Reichsmarschall's personal office, stating that *Oberleutnant* Dr. Jur. Heinz Göring had been killed.

"Like his two brothers, his life ended in the ultimate fulfillment of his duty as a soldier."

The last bereaved to sign was Hermann Göring, Reichsmarschall of the Greater German Reich. On 3 September 1944 Oblt. Heinz Göring was posthumously promoted to the rank of *Hauptmann* for bravery in the face of the enemy, retroactive to 1 July 1944. This is the story of a German officer whose photo was sold in a Berlin flea market after the war. (See also: Anderson, Paul: *The Unknown Göring*).

The Battle of Warsaw – The Kanert Crew in the City

On 31 July 1944 the Soviet 3rd Tank Corps drove into the German bridgehead on the east side of the Vistula and advanced as far as Wolomin. For the Commander-in-Chief of the Polish Home Army, General Bor-Komorowski, this was the signal for him to order the launching that same day of an uprising in Warsaw, which had been planned for some time. The insurgents opened fire at 1700 hours on 1 August; they blew up bridges and important installations in the city and fired on the few German troops in the city from concealed positions. General Bor-Komorowski, under the command of the Commander-in-Chief of the exile government in London, General Sikorski, struck with all the forces at his disposal. The Hermann Göring Parachute-Panzer Division did not participate in the Battle of Warsaw. Nevertheless one of the unit's tank destroyers was in the city, under the following circumstances. On 1 August 1944 the tank destroyer manned by Kanert and crew rolled toward the Warsaw suburb of Praga. Just beyond the bridge over the Vistula it was stopped by a Wehrmacht detachment, who informed Kanert that a revolt had broken out and that there was fighting raging in the city. Pointing out that the damaged tank destroyer had to reach the tank repair shop in Ursus because every armored vehicle was important, and due to the fact that he had a wounded man on board, Kanert was authorized to pass through Warsaw. Kanert now takes up the narrative:

"The glow of fires was visible at various points in the city. We first crossed the Vistula bridge. Several-hundred meters farther we were fired upon. The road, which curved to the right, had been barricaded. We drove on along the main street in the direction of the garrison headquarters as they had instructed us. We continued on past overturned autos, horse-drawn wagons, the bodies of men and horses and vehicles which had been squashed flat. There was sporadic gunfire. As commander of an armored vehicle I had obtained a Panzerfaust. In order to be ready for anything, my loader stood in his hatch with his submachine-gun in firing position. When we were fired on from a house, I ordered my loader to take cover inside the vehicle and I fired at the target with the Panzerfaust. There was a muffled boom as the projectile struck home and the entire wall came tumbling down. The firing from the house ceased.

When we reached the garrison headquarters we were able to hand over our wounded comrade Hoffmann. From there he was taken to hospital. For him, with his serious pelvic wound, the war was over. There was supper there for everyone. The following morning, 2 August 1944, the duty officer explained that we and our tank destroyer were required for an operation. For us the road to the tank workshop was therefore closed. That 2 August was quiet. The Polish resistance fighters flew the white-red-white flag in their positions. The old city had been barricaded by them. Obergefreiter Bendig, our gunner, obtained more rations. We were the only heavy weapon at garrison headquarters; consequently we were given the mission of driving to a nearby tower, which had been occupied by the Poles and from which a Polish flag was flying, and placing it under fire. However a shell had exploded in the barrel of our gun and we dared not fire our main weapon. We nevertheless drove to the tower and opened fire with our machine-gun. Rifle fire met us as we approached. We fired at the top of the tower and the windows and silenced the enemy guns.

Our next mission was to pick up a tank from the depot on the other side of Praga. We drove out of Warsaw on 3 August, passed unmolested through Praga and there picked up the ancient Panzer II with its tiny 20mm cannon. It was sitting there with no crew and there were only three of us in the tank destroyer. Gunner Bendig climbed into the tank and driver Schubauer familiarized him with the controls. We attached a tow cable to the Panzer II and set out on the return journey. On the Vistula bridge we came under machine-gun fire from the right bank. In our haste the Panzer II ran into the tank destroyer. The tow cable, which had become unattached, was put back in place and we continued slowly on our way. Bullets spattered against the armor. Rolling past barricades, we drove quickly back to the garrison headquarters, where we handed over the Panzer II.

The garrison headquarters had meanwhile received reinforcements and had been made a forward message center. Several more damaged tanks had arrived, including a number of *Hetzer* armored vehicles built by Skoda. Regional defence troops and grenadiers formed reconnaissance and combat patrols. The serviceable *Hetzers* attacked and shot up the enemy positions. German countermeasures were well under way on 4 August. Individual nests of resistance were blasted. But there was still fighting in the streets and the Poles had occupied the main post office. There was firing, too, in Pilsudski Park. Wounded soldiers there had to be recovered and evacuated. The first-aid soldiers with the Red Cross flag were fired on by snipers. One First-Aid Feldwebel was hit. All attempts to rescue the wounded failed in the face of fire from the insurgents, who gave no quarter.

Only by advancing behind a human shield of Poles – captured resistance fighters and civilians with Red Cross flags – was it possible to stop the firing by the resistance fighters and recover the wounded. Afterward the civilians were released.Kanert and his crew also took part in the fighting in their tank destroyer. Stukas supported the attack on the main post office. They circled above the target and then dove with their Jericho sirens howling. The post office was totally destroyed.

On 5 August the Kanert crew received orders to break out across the northern Vistula bridge with three other damaged tanks. Spaced laterally, the individual vehicles rolled through the streets to the bridge. At first they were unopposed apart from a few rifle shots. Then the four vehicles were stopped by an earthen barricade, about 200 meters ahead. People could be seen still digging. Several shots from the panzers' guns blasted a gap in the earth. The leading tank rolled through. The next two followed, all weapons firing left and right at trenches and houses. Molotov Cocktails were thrown onto the street from the right. Then the last tank passed through and all safely reached the bridge over the Vistula."

"On the drive to Modlin," continued Kanert, "We stopped to rest near a small village just as darkness was falling. Our tank destroyer was now all alone. We reached the tank repair shop in Ursus on 6 August. The Weigand tank destroyer was already there. The vehicle's main gun was removed and readjusted, while the hatch was repaired and other hits welded. With a lot of luck we had survived the five days in Warsaw in one piece."

VII. THE WESTERN THEATER

The Training Elements of the Hermann Göring Units

In previous chapters reference has been made to the fact that all Hermann Göring units had training and replacement battalions, not just in Germany, but particularly in Holland as well. From these reservoirs newly activated and equipped units were sent to the front and replacement personnel were sent to bring depleted units back up to strength. Other formations went to the front as independent units. The training facility near Utrecht saw many prominent names pass through its gates; some came for abbreviated training only, as it was never intended that they should actually see action against the enemy.

Nevertheless, such well known figures as Reinhard Mohn, the later head of the media giant Bertelsmann, and Gottfried von Cramm, the German tennis sensation of the nineteen-thirties, saw action at the front. Another was *Oberleutnant* Heinz Theodor Göring, who served as an instructor at Utrecht for some time before seeing action in Italy and on the Eastern Front. All of those who spent time at these training facilities and were trained as soldiers for their designated service specialties had one thing in common: they all spoke with great respect of their instructors and superiors and of the comradeship which existed there. It was this comradeship which molded them into a single, large blood brotherhood as soldiers of the *Reichsmarschall*.

The following is a brief history of the development of the training units:

The Training Units (by Alfred Otte)

Like all field units, the General Göring Regiment also had a replacement training unit, which provided the regiment with trained replacement personnel. The Replacement Battalion RGG was formed when the General Göring Regiment was mobilized on 15 August 1939 and went to a wartime organization, which included forming the planned mobilization units (including 14th Battery RGG, a 105mm railway flak battery, and a reserve searchlight battalion). The battalion's nominal parent unit was I (heavy) Flak Battalion, RGG. The replacement battalion was quartered in the Berlin-Reinickendorf-West barracks area which had become vacant following the departure of the regiment.

In June the Replacement Battalion RGG was transferred to Utrecht in occupied Holland. From then on Holland became familiar to all the soldiers who wore the white collar patches, for almost all the young volunteers received their basic training there. Later many soldiers attended courses there, were familiarized with new weapons or were sent there for retraining.

Just as the parent unit developed from a regiment to a brigade to a division and finally into a parachute-panzer corps, the training element evolved from the Replacement Battalion into the 2nd Replacement and Training Brigade

HG. The decisive factor in this evolution was the changed role necessitated by the war and the changing employment of the field units. The following list indicates the changes of designation on the dates specified:

16 August 1939:

Replacement Battalion, General Göring Regiment

25 September 1940:

Replacement Battalion, General Göring Flak Regiment

01 March 1942:

Replacement Battalion, General Göring Reinforced Regiment 21

July 1942:

Replacement Battalion, Hermann Göring Brigade

17 October 1942:

Hermann Göring Replacement Regiment

29 December 1943:

Hermann Göring Replacement and Training Regiment

06 January 1944:

Hermann Göring Parachute-Panzer Replacement and Training Regiment

24 September 1944: Hermann Göring Parachute-Panzer Replacement and Training Brigade in Rippin and Hermann Göring Parachute-Panzer Replacement and Training Regiment (Holland Detachment) in Utrecht

13 March 1945: Hermann Göring Parachute-Panzer 2nd Replacement and Training Brigade in Velten. Different dates for formation changes can be found in individual sources such as army post office records, unit records, service record books and pay books.

In some cases the designation "Training and Replacement..." is used instead of "Replacement and Training...", even in decrees, ordinances and orders from senior posts. Likewise from January 1944 the additional "Parachute-Panzer..." designation was dropped on occasion.

The organization of the individual units developed as follows:

August 1939:

Battalion CO Major von Ludwig, later Major Grauert.

HQ Replacement Battalion, RGG,

1st-5th Batteries, motor vehicle training company,

6th and 7th Advanced Batteries; the latter were temporary flak batteries, as the field units did not require replacements at first. These batteries, formed with surplus trained soldiers, were deployed within the Berlin air defenses for further front-line training in the "Berlin Flak Belt".

March 1942:

Battalion CO Major Grauert.

HQ Replacement Battalion,

HG Regiment, 1st-5th Companies, 6th-10th Batteries.

July 1943: Regimental CO Major Schulz (Robert)
HQ HG Replacement Regiment in Utrecht
I Battalion, HQ in Utrecht, 1st-5th Companies
II Battalion, HQ in Amersfoort, 6th-9th Companies
III Battalion, HQ in Hilversum, 10th-13th Batteries
IV Motor Vehicle Training Battalion in Velten near Berlin,
HQ 17th-19th Companies

December 1943:
Regimental CO Oberstleutnant Schulz (Robert)
HQ HG Replacement and Training Regiment in Utrecht
I Battalion, HQ in Utrecht, 1st-7th Companies
II Battalion, HQ in Amersfoort, 8th-12th Companies
III Battalion, HQ in Hilversum, 13th-16th Batteries
IV Motor Vehicle Training Battalion in Velten near Berlin,
HQ, 17th-19th Companies.

August 1944:
Regimental CO Oberst Fullriede Elements of the HG Parachute-Panzer Replacement and Training Battalion had already occupied defensive positions – especially in the coastal area.

I Battalion, HQ,
1st-5th Companies (grenadier)

II Battalion, HQ, 6th-11th Companies (panzer, panzer-grenadier, self-propelled artillery and self-propelled anti-tank guns)

III Battalion, HQ, 12th-16th Batteries (artillery and flak) Pioneer Battalion

29th NCO Candidate Company recruit Battalion. From 1940 there existed a convalescent company, in which soldiers released from hospital served until they were again ready for use in the field.

Apart from barracks at various locations in Holland, units were quartered elsewhere in barracks and temporary quarters, as well as at training grounds, sometimes in camp-type settings.

In the summer of 1944 a lack of aircraft and aviation fuel forced the Luftwaffe to severely curtail or even halt flying activities on the invasion front and disband many ground duty stations. The resulting excess personnel were sent – probably on Göring's personal order – to the Replacement and Training Regiment in Holland, which was scarcely in a position to accommodate, classify and redirect the incoming masses.

In August 1944, its ranks swelled in this way, the HG Parachute- Panzer Replacement and Training Regiment reached a strength of up to 12,000 men, equivalent to that of a division. Most of these soldiers lacked sufficient training for ground combat or for one of the available classes of weapons. Among their number were many highly-decorated soldiers – pilots for example – and highly-qualified specialists, such as aircraft mechanics. The officers and NCOs were retrained and the men trained in ground warfare, but the training was limited and very, very quick. It was impossible to equip the men properly. This explains why the resulting units, which were deployed in the northern area of the European invasion front (in Belgium and Holland), lacked the fighting worth of the other Hermann Göring units. It must be said, however, that the retrained soldiers demonstrated a great willingness to fight and a high level of personal bravery.

The Hermann Göring Parachute-Panzer Replacement and Training Regiment in Action on the Western Front

Following the collapse of the German invasion front in August 1944, the Allies quickly moved eastward and by the beginning of September had reached Belgium. Finally they also threatened Holland. The upshot of this was that the HG Parachute-Panzer Replacement and Training Regiment was incorporated into the ranks of the fighting units and employed at the front. In the process the regiment formed additional combat units, some of which were named for their commanding officers, for example Battle Group Schlutius and the Worrowski and Cherinow Battalions. To the dismay of the regimental commander, *Oberst* Fullriede, the regiment was not committed as a unit by the Wehrmacht Commander-in-Chief Netherlands, *General der Flieger* Christiansen, who was responsible for the defence of the Netherlands, rather it was employed in penny packets and the individual elements placed under the command of other units. Repeated protests to senior posts by the regimental commander changed nothing.

On 3 September 1944 the 1st Parachute Army under *Generaloberst* Student assumed command in the area, simultaneously concentrating all available units. This resulted in no changes for the HG Parachute-Panzer Replacement and Training Regiment.

The Allies planned to launch a pincer operation whose ultimate goal was to encircle the Ruhr region of Germany. The British Second Army would advance north across the Albert and Maas-Scheldt canals through Eindhoven, Son, Veghel, Grave, Nijmegen, Arnhem and Alpendorn, outflanking the east end of the Westwall, before linking up with the southeast arm of the pincer, the American First Army, which would be committed toward Aachen, Cologne and Münster. In the process all the supply lines to the German forces in western Holland would be severed and the V-2 launch sites, especially those in the Den Haag area, would be put out of action. A factor of prime importance in the fighting in Holland was the securing of the crossings over the many waterways, especially the Maas, the Waal and the Lower Rhine, as well as the many canals, some of which were very wide.

Throughout the month of September 1944 the I and, initially, II Battalions of the HG Parachute-Panzer Replacement and Training Regiment fought in the area of the Maas-Scheldt, Albert and Antwerp-Turnhout Canals near Hechtel, Geel, Ten Aart, Lichtaart, Kasterlee, Turnhout and Pomfort; elements of II Battalion later saw action at the Wilhelmina Canal near Son and

III Battalion at the South-Wilhelms Canal near Schijndel and Veghel. Losses suffered at the front were very high. In several cases what was left of the units was simply incorporated into the units to which they were attached.

An airborne landing operation by American, British and Polish parachute and airborne troops was supposed to shield the British northward advance from the bridgeheads at the Albert Canal near Geel and Neerpelt on 8 September 1944. One of the focal points of this airborne operation, the largest so far in the history of warfare, was the battle for the bridge near Arnhem ("Market Garden"), where the Worrowski Battalion of the HG Parachute-Panzer Replacement and Training Regiment was committed.

At the end of September 1944 the surviving elements of the HG Parachute-Panzer Replacement and Training Regiment were assembled and brought up to strength, part of them forming the HG Special Purpose Assault Regiment. Elements of the regiment and later the entire unit were first committed in the Rozendaal and Zevenaar area as well as at Elten and Kecken. Finally the regiment was shipped by rail via Krefeld, Mönchengladbach, Grevenbroich, Cologne, Bonn and Euskirchen into its new area of operations, the Zülpich – Ruhr Valley blocking position. The positions were held against vastly superior enemy forces from November 1944 until February 1945. After the Allies had succeeded in crossing the Rhine, the fight there had to be broken off and a retreat initiated through Euskirchen, Rheinbach, Meckenheim, Bad Godesberg and Bonn, where there was nothing left to do but surrender.

The Two Hermann Göring Parachute-Panzer Replacement and Training Brigades

When, at the end of September 1944 during its action on the Vistula, the Hermann Göring Parachute-Panzer Division was expanded to become the Hermann Göring Parachute-Panzer Corps, it received the HG Parachute-Panzer Replacement and Training Brigade as its replacement unit. The brigade's commanding officer was *Major* Ilius. When Ilius fell sick in November 1944 he was replaced by *Oberst* Friedrich August Meyer. The unit was first formed at the command level and it was not until 25 January 1945 that it actually came into being. Because Holland had by then become a front-line zone, using it as a quartering area for the new brigade was out of the question. Formation of the new unit therefore took place in Rippin, West Prussia. The HG Parachute-Panzer Replacement and Training Regiment in Holland, the majority of whose units were in combat, now received the supplementary designation "Remnant Detachment Holland". It detached elements to West Prussia as cadres for the new brigade. From then on the soldiers still streaming in from disbanded Luftwaffe units were directed to Rippin. The latest intake of young volunteers, most born in 1926 and 1927, was also ordered to report to Rippin.

After the beginning of the Soviet offensive in January 1945, on 15/16 January the HG Parachute-Panzer Replacement and Training Brigade was employed as a combat unit in West Prussia. It fought in the Skrwa and Drewen positions and battled its way back to Graudenz, where it fought a hopeless battle in the surrounded Courbiere fortress and suffered heavy losses. The surviving members of the brigade were forced to surrender on 6 March 1945 and were taken prisoner by the Soviets.

The remains of the HG Parachute-Panzer Replacement and Training Regiment (Remnant Detachment Holland) were used to form the 31st Parachute Regiment on 8 February 1945; organizationally, the unit was as good as disbanded.

On 28 January 1945 the HG 3rd Parachute-Panzer Replacement and Training Regiment was formed from a recruit training battalion which had been assembled in Berlin-Reinickendorf in the barracks of the former General Göring Regiment (CO Major Hahm). On 14 March 1945 a further regiment, the HG 4th Parachute-Panzer Replacement and Training Regiment, was formed in Velten near Berlin (CO Major Ilius). On 14 March 1945 the two regiments were combined to form the HG Parachute-Panzer 2nd Replacement and Training Brigade, which took the place of the brigade lost in Graudenz. *Oberst* Breuer, who came from the army, was the brigade's first commander. On 20 April 1945 *General der Fallschirmtruppe* Bräer, former CO of the 9th Parachute Division, assumed command of 2nd Brigade. Existing documentary evidence does not offer conclusive proof that this change of command in fact took place.

At the beginning of April 1945 the HG 2nd Parachute-Panzer Replacement and Training Brigade, together with another unit, the 1st Parachute-Panzer Replacement and Training Regiment, was employed as a combat unit on the Eastern Front. In the course of the costly fighting withdrawal to Mecklenburg the unit was wiped out. Survivors became prisoners of the Soviets. This marked the final destruction of the replacement and training units which had once borne the name Hermann Göring.

The Hermann Göring Replacement and Training Regiment in Action in Holland

On 26 August 1944 *Oberst* Fritz Fullriede assumed command of the replacement and training regiment stationed in northern Holland. Its history is a special one and will be presented here.*Generalmajor* Fritz Fullriede wrote this history, which exudes the atmosphere of the times, after the war.

In spite of the Allied invasion of Western France and the Russian advance from the East, in the summer of 1944 it still seemed rather unlikely that the regiment would become involved in dramatic combat operations. However as a result of the Allied airborne operation against Nijmegen and Arnheim it was drawn into the maelstrom of events.

From the writings of retired *Generalmajor* Fritz Fullriede (+13.11.1969), commanding officer Hermann Göring Parachute-Panzer Replacement and Training Regiment, Utrecht, Holland:

"After I was detached for a short time from the Army Personnel Office (HPA) to the HG Parachute-Panzer Division – where I commanded the 1st Regiment – on 26 August 1944, at the request of General Schmalz and with the permission of the HPA, I took command of the so-called HG Replacement and Training Regiment in Holland. Sadly all my relevant papers were lost during the Russian occupation of Silesia. I cannot therefore provide an exact description of the unit's organization. As far as I recall, the unit consisted of three battalions:"

I Battalion: 3 parachute-panzer-grenadier and anti-tank companies.

II Battalion: artillery, tank, self-propelled and anti-tank batteries.

III Battalion: artillery and flak batteries.

pioneer battalion: ?

29th NCO Training Company.

recruit depot

rations and equipment administration, etc.

"The regiment's headquarters was in Utrecht. The troops were distributed throughout northern Holland except for II and III Battalions, which were deployed near Bloemdal and Harten under Major Schlutius for coastal defence. Initially the unit was under the command of the Wehrmacht Commander-in-Chief Netherlands (WBN). At the beginning of September 1944 it was placed under the command of General Student, who placed it under Headquarters, First Parachute Army. In the course of the following months the unit was committed in penny packets to serve as "corset stays". It fought with exemplary bravery everywhere, but was often left completely in the lurch. My repeated protests to Headquarters, First Parachute Army achieved nothing. By the time I was recalled to Germany by the HPA the unit had been as good as wiped out. When I assumed command the unit had a personnel complement of about 12,000 men.

The following are entries from my notebook, which I still have:

02.09.44: II Battalion sent from Harderwijk to Eindhoven on order of HQ First Army.

10.09.44: II Battalion committed near Hechtel, took Hechtel, was left in lurch by its neighbor, surrounded by enemy and almost totally wiped out and scattered after three days of fighting. Only a few tanks and groups of soldiers came back. My personal request to HQ, First Army, to at least make an attempt to relieve the bravely-fighting unit, was not answered.

11.09.44: In spite of this, I and III Battalions also had to be dispatched to Eindhoven.

13.09.44: I drove to the NCO Training Company, which on order of the WBN had transferred to Grave and Nijmegen to guard the bridges. There I discovered that this force was totally inadequate to guard the bridges, and that the bridges had not been prepared for demolition; on the contrary, the primers had been removed a few days earlier on orders of the WBN Chief-of-Staff.

In the meantime I Battalion had arrived in Lon op Land and III Battalion in Udenhout. Both had already suffered considerable losses to air attack. Then I sought out the pitiful remnants of II Battalion, which I assembled near Son north of Eindhoven. That evening Oblt. Heider arrived with several men. They had escaped the pocket near Hechtel by swimming the canal. He told us that the remains of II Battalion still in the pocket had fought on until the evening of the 3rd day in hope of relief, which I had unfortunately had been unable to obtain from army headquarters. After the loss of almost all their officers, the few trained recruits had run into the concentrated fire of the enemy tanks. It was understandable that the few survivors were rather demoralized.

15.09.44: I Battalion under Major Wimmer counterattacked near Casterle, driving the English back and taking a number of prisoners, including 10 officers.

17.09.44: Drove to bridge guard near Salt-Bommel/Hede. A heavy bombing attack began on the scant blocking positions on both sides of the bridge. The bridge itself was spared. Since here too no preparations had been made to destroy the bridge, an understanding with the enemy was to be taken for granted. – Toward midday a broad, endless stream of transport aircraft and cargo gliders came into sight heading toward Nijmegen and Arnhem. They were escorted by a tremendous number of bombers and fighters which fired on any movement. – In Pomfort I reached the command post of III Battalion, behind which the 16th Flak Battery had gone into position. It shot down several enemy aircraft but then came under almost ceaseless fire from bombers and fighters. – During my subsequent drive to the front line near Casterle an artillery barrage dropped trees onto the road, making it impossible to go any farther. Back through Rethy-Arendonk-Bladet. – Enemy paratroops dropped in the area Best – Vechtel – Son, also near Grave, Nijmegen and Arnhem. Major Stark of HQ, First Army, whom I met in Eindhoven, informed me that all bridges had apparently fallen into enemy hands undamaged.

According to his statement the bridges near Salt-Bommel and Gorchen were also in enemy hands, which later turned out not to be true. On the basis of his statement I had to drive back to Helmond via Valkens. – There was mass confusion in Helmond; the troops there (construction battalion) were facing in the wrong direction. I oriented the commander as best I could. – After resuming my journey, in Bakel I came upon the remnants of II Battalion near Son. I got the impression that after the sudden fighter and bomber attacks and the dropping of enemy paratroops, these remnants had no longer been in a position to offer resistance, and, after all the officers apart from two young Leutnants had been put out of action, had run away. Furthermore, the last tanks had also been lost, supposedly having been hit by bombers.

What was left of II Battalion was once again assembled and used to guard the road. – According to a construction battalion, there was supposed to be a special duties General in Deurne; I found him after a long search in the rainy night. He had neither a staff nor any means of communication and had absolutely no idea of the situation. – I placed the Sommer Battalion under his command subject to recall, but I found the battalion on resuming my journey. I then ordered it to march via Germany to Utrecht. – In

Geldern I met the Ib of the parachute army headquarters, who told me that the headquarters of a division was in the barracks there and that it could surely bring me up to date on the situation. The division's Ia maintained that the division was advancing successfully against Nijmegen. The only way of reaching Holland at that time was via Wesel. In Soesterburg I met a dispatch rider from my HQ, who informed me that my staff had transferred from Utrecht to Schloß Hoevelaken. There was confusion everywhere. I then drove to the HQ of the WBN, which was less in the picture than I.

18.09.44: The enemy landed more troops near Ede/Arnhem and broke through the front to the left of I Battalion (Wimmer) near Eindhoven.

19.09.44: The enemy is now in possession of a wide strip of terrain from Lommel to Nijmegen and has all the bridges in his hands intact except the Arnhem bridge, which is once again in our possession. – As well my brave NCO Training Company, with the help of an SS company, has successfully retaken the bridges near Nijmegen. However these bridges had to be abandoned again following a courageous battle against the enemy's superior armored forces. As well the bridges could not be blown as there were no explosives in place and the pioneers who were responsible for destroying them ran away. Later, with the help of the Dutch Vatican Commission, I was able to debunk the fable that a Dutch youth had removed the explosives and in so doing lost his life.

20.09.44: The NCO Training Company and the SS company under Runge have withdrawn into the citadel of Nijmegen, but are still holding out in the bridgehead. Armed with a Panzerfaust, Gefreiter Casper took on the approaching enemy tanks on the bridge by himself. He destroyed the first tank but was simultaneously hit by a burst of machine-gun fire. – In the afternoon an order from parachute army HQ to withdraw the Worrowski Battalion from the sea front and commit it near Ede.

27.09.44: Survivors of the NCO Training Company surrounded on the coast who were able to save themselves by swimming the Maas report that the company fought on for days until it was almost completely wiped out. The Americans shot the few prisoners and threw the wounded into the river. They further report that the elements of the company deployed at the bridges near Grave were wiped out by bombers and fighter-bombers on 16.09.44. This important bridge could not be blown either, as the primer charges had been removed on 13.09.44 – allegedly on the order of the chief of the WBN. This chief later maintained that the charges had been destroyed by bombers.

(Note: If this had been the case the bridges should have been damaged by bombs, which in no way corresponded to the facts. Later, when I was delivered to Holland as a war criminal, I learned that this chief had been in constant contact with a relative who had gone over to the partisans. I personally met this relative, a Rittmeister, in the camp at Avegor, when he visited the former chief there. The chief later hanged himself at Avegor.)

21.09.44: I Battalion continues to fight near Casterle, driving the English back across the canal. The battalion's losses are very high. The commander,

Hauptmann Wimmer, 11 officers and two thirds of the men have already been killed. I learn that the Worrowski Battalion deployed near Osterbeck has lost all its officers, except for one Leutnant, and half its men. Together with the other hastily-assembled units the battalion has significantly reduced the English bridgehead. – The battalion's high losses are attributable to the fact that the Oberst in command forbade the heavy weapons to fire, allegedly to avoid endangering his own troops. What's the point, if our wretched command employs such people as commanders?

In the meantime the chief of the WBN informed me that the recruit depot is to be committed as well. I declared this to be "child murder" and requested rail transport to Germany. It was explained to me that, as per a Führer Order, no soldier may leave Holland. Afterward I sent the recruits with their officers on foot to General Student's depot in Emsland.

22.09.44: At my request the remains of I and III Battalions were finally withdrawn from the front, but on 24.09.44 they were sent into action again near Vechtel to destroy the bridge there, which had fallen into the enemy's hands intact. The remnants of the Worrowski Battalion fought in a hedgehog position in the Osterbeck gas plant so that the surrounded enemy could not retreat. – I now formed a new company in Utrecht from troops separated from their units, which I was able to equip relatively well with vehicles and weapons from the equipment dump. The existence of this company was not reported, so that in future I would have something at my disposal in addition to the pioneer company with which to help my units scattered all along the front, without having to wait for orders.

25.09.44: The Americans requested that I Battalion, which was fighting near Vechtel, surrender honorably. When this was rejected the American emissary explained that he couldn't understand such a thing. The Germans, who had been at war since 1939, would keep on fighting, and they, the Americans, had already had enough of the war after 6 days. Enquiry from the Worrowski Battalion as to whether the battalion was allowed to grant a request from an English medical officer to hand over to the English first-aid materials dropped in fields near the Rhine. In spite of orders to the contrary I gave my permission.

26.09.44: The rest of the English who had fought bravely near Osterbeck surrendered. A captured English Major whom I talked with spoke of the fair fight near Osterbeck. – The enemy landed further troops beyond the Rhine in 286 cargo gliders, which we could not engage on account of a lack of artillery.

Report that the commander of III Battalion had been killed near Schyndel, where the enemy had directed very heavy attacks against I and III Battalions.

28.09.44: Reports from I and III Battalions that the new commander, Hauptmann Westphal, has already been posted missing.

29.09.44: To Osterbeck to I Battalion, now commanded by Leutnant Niedermeyer. The enemy fires ceaselessly on Osterbeck. The battalion consists of 2 officers and a few men, who now join the infantry there.

01.10.44: Near Putten a car carrying Oblt. Eggert, Leutnant Sommer and two Obergefreiten is shot up by partisans led by an Englishman. Both officers were severely wounded. Leutnant Sommer dragged himself to a house about 2 kilometers away and died there. Oblt. Eggert was abducted but was returned weeks later. The two Obergefreiten escaped. On order of the WBN, Putten was surrounded by the pioneer company. The large village of Putten was to be burned down, women and children evacuated, the men between 17 and 50 deported for forced labor and the guilty parties shot. This seemed completely senseless to me, because by doing so they would achieve the opposite of what was intended. I forbade the SD who had arrived to take part and had a few less valuable buildings burned to avoid further reprisals.

The SD took away the prisoners. As was later determined at my trial in Arnhem, 5% of the houses were burned and 10% of the men taken away. Only because of these limited measures was Oblt. Eggert returned, and we avoided another Oradour or Lidice, which was also one of the findings at the trial.

04.10.44: Remonstrations were made against me by the WBN for not burning Putten to the ground, but these made little impression on me.

05.10.44: Order from HPA to go to Germany to take part in a course for division commanders. Nothing came of it, for a medical examination found me to be ill and I was sent to Genthin hospital. Soon afterward, with my consent, I was detached to the Eastern Front to take command of a division. I would undoubtedly have passed the course, for I had already led units of greater than division strength with success in Africa and Sicily."

VIII. THE WAR IN THE EAST – A GENERAL SUMMARY

Soviet Preparations

The worst defeat suffered by the German Armed Forces in the Second World War began on 22 June 1944 when the Red Army launched the Battle of White Russia. It was no coincidence that the start of this operation coincided with the third anniversary of "Barbarossa"; the Soviet High Command had purposely selected this date. Precisely a month before the beginning of the planned summer offensive, Stalin received the commanders-in-chief of the four army groups which were to take part in the attack on the second floor of the STAVKA building (Soviet headquarters) in the Kremlin. Among them was two-time Hero of the Soviet Union, Army General Rokossovski, a former stone mason and Master Sergeant in the Tsarist army. Also present were Marshal Vasilevski, Lieutenant General Chernyakovski and Marshall Zhukov. Representing the headquarters for aviation forces were Aviation Chief Marshall A.A. Novikov and Aviation Marshall F.J. Falaleyev. As well there was the Marshall of Strategic Aviation Forces A.J. Golovanov. Joining them were the members of the war councils.

The acting Chief-of-Staff of the Red Army, Army General A.L. Antonov, explained that the plan of operations – code-named "Bagration" – was complete and that the operation's objective was to eliminate the German salient in the Vitebsk-Minsk-Bobruisk area and reach a line Desna – Molodekhno – Stolpce – Starobin. Also present at this conference were Foreign Minister Molotov and Stalin's right hand man Malenkov.

It is your task," declared Stalin emphatically, "To liberate White Russia. This liberation will began on the third anniversary of the German invasion of our fatherland." This recollection of Russia's darkest hour was supposed to rekindle the passions of the soldiers of the Red Army and spur them on to give their utmost.

In the course of the discussion those present insisted to General Rokossovsky that he break out of his Dniepr bridgehead in a single thrust. Rokossovsky rejected this idea. He had other plans. It was clear to him that an attack with all forces from so narrow an area could not lead to success. Rokossovsky outlined how he planned to take possession of Bobruisk and tear apart the German front. He intended to launch two assault groups to break through the German positions north of Rogachev and another southeast of Parichi, encircle and capture Bobruisk, and subsequently attack Pukhovichi and Slutsk.

Three times the Commander-in-Chief of the 1st White Russian Front was sent out to consider – and agree to – Stalin's suggestion. He remained firm. Three times he returned and said "*nyet*". Finally Rokossovsky's plan was accepted. Events would prove that it was the right decision. When, on 23 May 1944, the group broke up after the three-hour conference, the definitive "Bagration" plan had been fixed: The Red Army was to launch six major offensives in six different sectors of the front, one after the other. This almost simultaneous offensive at six widely-separated places was to split the German defense, splinter its forces and prevent it from employing all available forces en masse at one point to defend against the Soviet attacking thrusts.

In addition to the four Soviet fronts, the Byelorussian partisans, the strategic air forces and the Dniepr Fleet were also to take part in the attack. On 31 May the Soviet High Command issued its directives in which it laid down all fronts, points of main effort, missions, attack times and objectives. Simultaneously every front was sent significant reinforcements. The 1st Baltic Front was reinforced by the 1st Tank Corps; the 3rd White Russian Front was assigned the 11th Guards Army and the 2nd Guards Tank Corps; the 81st Rifle Corps was incorporated into the 2nd White Russian Front. As well the Soviet High Command moved its own reserve, the 5th Guards Tank Army, into the 3rd White Russian Front's sector.

However the lion's share of the reinforcements were received by General Rokossovsky's 1st White Russian Front. It was sent the 28th Army, the 9th Tank Corps, the 1st Guards Tank Corps, the 1st Mechanized Corps and the 4th Guards Cavalry Corps solely for its right wing near Rogachev. As well it was assigned the 8th Guards Army, the 2nd Tank Army and the 2nd Guards Cavalry Corps for the southern Parichi assault group. The now superfluous 2nd Guards Army and 51st Army in the Crimea were sent toward White Russia as the High Command's reserve. All the fronts were sent tank and self-propelled gun regiments and brigades by the high command, as well as artillery, rocket and engineer units. The fronts' air armies were also reinforced by 11 air corps and 5 air divisions.

The Soviet High Command named Marshals A.M. Vasilevski and G.K. Zhukov as well as Aviation Chief Marshall A.A. Novikov and Aviation Marshall F.J. Falaleyev as its representatives for the coordination of operations at the front. During the night of 20 June 1944 there were explosions in every sector of the 700-kilometer-wide attack front and in the German-occupied hinterland. 240,000 partisans struck in White Russia. There were 10,500 explosions between the Dniepr and the Beresina. Rail lines, radio stations, airfields and bridges were crippled or blown up.

The wheels ground to a halt. The entire command apparatus of the General Officer in Charge of Transport Center, General Staff *Oberst* Hermann Teske, was paralysed. When the *Oberst* took off in a Fieseler Storch to inspect the destroyed communications channels on the morning of 21 June 1944, he was filled with a terrible foreboding: If the Russians come now the chaos will be complete. How, the *Oberst* asked himself, was he to evacuate the wounded still in the front-line hospitals? How was he supposed to transport to the front food and ammunition, to say nothing of the replacements that would be necessary in the event of a Russian offensive?

Immediately after this partisan prelude, on the morning of 20 June 1944, the 104th Soviet Tank Brigade set out toward the west, to the front. The tankers waited for an announced speech. This one was different. It was held in a tank by female radio operator Vera Proschina. She said:

"Today my dream is fulfilled! To kill the Hitlerites from a tank, to avenge the pain of my people, my own sorrow. The fascists have killed my mother and father. I will therefore destroy them mercilessly. I will show what a Russian girl is capable of. Death to the accursed conquerors!"

The radio operator stood in her tank: tall, with long, flowing hair, a modern Joan of Arc. What she had said hammered into the men, ate its way into their brains and filled them with a wild, all-destructive impetus.

"Tanks, forward!" The voice of the brigade commander rang through the steel giants. Rumbling and roaring, their exhausts spitting flame, the steel phalanx set itself in motion and rolled toward the front.

On that 20 June 1944 Hitler and his planning staff still did not believe that a Russian offensive was going to strike Army Group Center. Even when reports of demolitions and major troop movements reached the OKW (Armed Forces High Command) and OKH (Army High Command), those there were of the view that it could only be a diversionary attack. The army's operations section was convinced that the Russians were going to strike Army Group North Ukraine from their assembly area between Kovel and Ternopol.

Indeed, following the end of fighting in the area southwest of Kovel in the winter and early spring (until the end of April 1944), the enemy's dispositions suggested the formation of a point of main effort in the sector facing Army Group North Ukraine. However this was an elaborate ruse on the part of the Soviets, who had simulated a tremendous buildup in the area by moving in many long, empty trains.

So, on the basis of a proposal by *Feldmarschall* Model, the Commander-in-Chief of Army Group North Ukraine, strong armored units were pulled out of Army Group center's front and transferred south in preparation for a large-scale attack intended to clear up the situation in the Kovel area. A total of eight panzer and two panzer-grenadier divisions in Army Group North Ukraine's sector were supposed to prevent the enemy from driving through Lvov and Warsaw to Königsberg, a move which would have enveloped Army Group Center – and Army Group North – from the rear and severed their lines of communication and supply.

But the German military was wrong. In fact Marshall Stalin did not believe the Red Army to be capable of such a far-reaching operation. As a result of the German command's false assessment of the situation, Army Group Center was stripped of almost all its tanks and a third of its army units. *Feldmarschall* Busch, Commander-in-Chief of Army Group Center, thereupon declared that these measures had rendered him incapable of countering an enemy buildup opposite his front through the timely insertion of his mobile forces.

On 31 May 1944 the OKH responded through its Chief-of-Staff, *Generaloberst* Zeitzler, stating that this was only a temporary measure. Since, with the exception of the Kovel area, there was no indication of the formation of a point of main effort by the enemy, the army group agreed to this "temporary" measure. In its June 4th, 1944 assessment of the enemy, however, Army Group North pointed out that:

"The local massing of forces opposite our Eastern Front could be increased at any time by the insertion of substantial enemy reserves. It must be assumed that the enemy will continue the mode of operation practiced during the winter and carry out attacks in numerous places on the Eastern Front with a changing point of main effort, for the purpose of tying up the German forces."

In its assessment of 19 June 1944, the army group emphasized the delivery of strong enemy reserves to the front opposite Ninth Army, which had been found by aerial reconnaissance. Furthermore, enemy concentrations had been spotted in the area of the highway and southeast of Vitebsk. The Soviet 33rd Guards Army was identified near Ryasna, the 11th Guards Army at the highway and the 5th Guards Rifle Corps on the Sukhodrovka front. Finally it was reported that the 5th Guards Tank Army was located in the Smolensk area.

All of this suggested that the enemy was not just planning to carry out a holding attack against Army Group Center, but that there, and only there, the Germans had to reckon with "The considerably farther-reaching operational objectives of the Russian command." Added to this was the fact that the Russian Air Force opposite Army Group Center had abruptly been strengthened to 4,500 aircraft. All of this led to the conclusion that the Red Army's summer offensive would consist of powerful attacks on Bobruisk, Mogilev, Orsha and Vitebsk, with the objective of reducing Army Group Center's salient which projected far to the east.

This situation was in opposition to the OKH's assessment of the enemy situation. At a conference of army group and army chiefs in the OKH on 14 June 1944, the Chief of the Operations section, *Oberst* Heusinger, gave the impression that the main attack could still be expected against Army Group North Ukraine. The assaults against Army Groups South Ukraine and Center would be nothing more than secondary and holding attacks, not the main operation. Then, on 20 June, at an NSFO meeting in Sonthofen, *Feldmarschall* Keitel explained to the assembled command officers:

"The Soviets will not attack then, until the western allies have achieved a strategic breakthrough in Normandy with their invasion forces. And the focal point of the Soviet attack will lay farther to the south in Galicia."

So as the Soviets prepared to launch their offensive, Army Group Center, with a total of 38 divisions, sat in its thinly-manned front, an extended, 1,100-kilometer-long salient. Six divisions had already been condemned to death in cities which Hitler had categorically declared "fortified places":

In Vitebsk – three divisions. In Orsha – one division. In Mogilev – one division. In Bobruisk – one division.

The Red Army's great surprise onslaught against Army Group Center in White Russia began on 22 June 1944, the third anniversary of the start of Operation "Barbarossa". The commanders of the Red Army were confident that the assault on the German salient between Bobruisk and Vitebsk in the bloody triangle between the Dniepr and Beresina Rivers would result in a decisive German defeat. A total of 185 Russian divisions with 2.5 million soldiers went to the attack toward the west in a 700-kilometer-wide sector. Rolling with them was a steel spearhead of 6,100 tanks and assault guns.

45,000 guns opened the offensive with a barrage lasting up to 14 hours. 7,000 aircraft – including the feared Il 2 "Butcher", long- range bombers, night bombers, fighters and dive bombers – took part in the battle. Never before had the Russian theatre – already rich in superlatives – seen such a massing of weapons and men.

Facing this tremendous assembly of forces were about 500,000 German soldiers, of whom 400,000 were in defensive positions. At this decisive point Army Group Center lacked tanks and assault guns – they were now in northern Ukraine. Missing were the heavy weapons, which alone would have been in a position to stop the Russian steamroller. The disaster took its course. Whole divisions went under in the marshy region between the Dniepr and the Beresina and in the "fortified places". With them went the supply trains, civilians friendly toward the Germans and the wounded in field hospitals.

350,000 German soldiers disappeared in the marshlands between the Beresina and the Dniepr. They fell in the artillery fire, under the bombs and guns of the aircraft, they died under the tracks of the tanks and in the whirlwinds of death created by the multiple rocket launchers. They suffocated in the swamps, were killed by partisans or perished in the vast, impenetrable forests into which – wounded, exhausted, at the end of their strength – they had crawled. The Beresina, a deathtrap for a major army in the past, became in the bloody history of the Second World War an insurmountable barrier once more, before which accumulated the columns of the doomed. Some did get through, however, men filled with an unconquerable will to make it in spite of everything and on whose side luck stood.

The collapse of Army Group Center began on 22 June 1944 between Bobruisk and Vitebsk and ended two weeks later in Minsk. By then twenty-eight divisions with 350,000 men had perished on the battlefields. The Russian command now had the opportunity to roll up the center of the German front right to the Vistula and drive through to the East Prussian frontier. Such a move would have cut off the German forces in the Baltic States and opened the door to the Balkans. The fact that this disaster did not penetrate the consciousness of the German population, that the extent and consequences of this tremendous sacrifice in blood remained largely unknown, can be ascribed to the turbulent events surrounding the invasion in the West and the 20th of July 1944. It was only thanks to these two circumstances that the German supreme command was largely able to keep secret the destruction of German fighting strength in the East.

The version of events spread by Himmler through the party organs, that "treachery and sabotage" were responsible for the defeat in the east, was pulled completely out of thin air. In his address to the meeting of Gauleiters in Posen on 3 August 1944 he explained:

"Regarding the collapse of Army Group Center, we must be clear that something enormous has taken place. For it is not explicable by normal means alone that an army group with 28 divisions has been scattered to the four winds like sand and straw. Inside the troops had become absolutely unsettled, on the one hand through the absent or defeatist hand of command, the army and corps command, and on the other through the ever more common habit or bad habit of being taken prisoner and playing with Herr Seydlitz and the Russian generals."

The truth is, however, that the blame for this tragedy lies with the German Supreme Command alone, in particular with Hitler himself. The numerous false assessments of the enemy situation, the resulting erroneous decisions, and Hitler's tendency to hold onto captured territory – even at the loss of all his forces – helped turn the decision in favor of the far superior Soviets. Timely regroupings were forbidden by Hitler, those withdrawals that were begun were categorically forbidden by him. The result was the sacrifice of hundreds of thousands of German soldiers.

The Russian Distribution of Forces Before "Bagration", June 1944

The German Armed Forces faced four Soviet fronts along the 1,100-kilometer front between Lake Nescherdo and Verba: the 1st Baltic and the 1st, 2nd and 3rd White Russian Fronts. The 1st Baltic Front occupied an approximately 160-kilometer-wide sector between Lake Nescherdo and the area north of Vitebsk. The 3rd White Russian Front's sector extended from the area north of Vitebsk in a southerly direction to Bayevo and had a length of approximately 130 kilometers. Occupying the 160-kilometer-wide sector between Bayevo and Selets-Kholopyev was the 2nd White Russian Front.

From Selets-Kholopyev to Mosyr was the right wing of the 1st White Russian Front; the front's center and left wing lay between Mosyr and Verba.

The 1st White Russian Front was thus entrusted with a sector of 650 kilometers. Its main forces however were on the two wings, one aimed at Bobruisk, the other at Kovel-Lublin. In the center of this huge sector there was only the 61st Army, occupying a sector 350 kilometers wide which extended from the mouth of the Ptich to Ratno, in poorly-accessible Polesye on the south bank of the Pripyat.

The Hermann Göring Division Moves East

The Hermann Göring Parachute-Panzer Division was situated south of Florence when, on 15 June 1944, it received orders to disengage from the enemy and assemble in the Budrio area, north of Bologna. The drive to the assembly area was made more difficult in that a number of bridges over the Po River had been destroyed and all the others were under continuous fighter-bomber attack. On account of the constant threat from the air, crossings had to be made at night by means of ferries and pontoon bridges.

The division entrained in Verona and neighboring stations, the process being completed quickly. The division command required a total of 72 trains for this purpose. The route the trains would follow led through the Brenner Pass, Innsbruck, Regensburg, Eger, Beslau and Litzmannstadt to Warsaw.

The first train left on 25 July 1944. The division command was aware of the reason for this hastily-conducted transport. On the Eastern Front, Army Group Center had been attacked by Russian forces beginning 22 June. The objective of the Soviet offensive, called "Bagration", was to break through the German defenses with a concentration of forces never before seen, then outflank and encircle them. At the time of the Soviet planning conference the destruction of all of Army Group Center was not included in the plan, as it wasn't considered possible. The depth of the planned breakthrough was likewise not nearly as great as that which developed not a month later.

During a halt at a station near Warsaw, the transport leader of the train carrying the division's administration units received a map along with orders and suggestions for the subsequent journey "through the partisan region." Also included in the package were details of the unit's destination, detraining procedures and information about its planned employment. There were also special instructions for the behavior of the Wehrmacht in Warsaw. This included a description of the situation there, which revealed among other things that more than 50 German soldiers were disappearing without a trace in the greater Warsaw area each day and that the theft of weapons and munitions had become the order of the day. Attacks had been made on barracks, German posts and installations, and even on soldiers in the streets. All units were therefore directed to observe special security measures.

"I informed the transport unit chiefs of the orders. These in turn informed their men when the journey continued." The detraining station was the Warsaw-West freight depot; the first train arrived there at 2200 hours. It was pitch black. Enemy aircraft attacked the station with bombs just as the unloading began. When the attack was over Soviet long-range batteries opened fire on the station, for partisans had already informed the Red Army of the arrival of the division's units. The detraining continued as dawn broke.

The same day the division issued its Order No. 2 of 1944:

Hermann Göring Parachute-Panzer Division   Division Command Post 25.7.1944 – Ia – Br. B. Nr. 1372/44 geh. DIVISION ORDER NO. 2 / 44 For the arrival in the division's assembly area

(1) Enemy tank forces are advancing from the Lublin area and east toward Warsaw-Jadowo. For the time being the bridgehead east of Warsaw will be guarded by own weak security forces. Advance by enemy forces across the Vistula and in northwesterly direction is possible.

(2) Combat elements of HG Parachute-Panzer Division will assemble in the Rembertow area, supply elements in Warsaw (exclusively) – Modlin area, for probable action east of the Vistula in southeasterly direction.

(3) Unloading is to be carried out without delay after arrival of transport trains at the detraining station (in general Warsaw-West or Praga suburb), the troops are to move away from the unloading track, disperse and camouflage themselves (air cover). Each transport officer will report his arrival without delay personally or by phone to the division's detraining officer at Warsaw-West Station, giving his trip number and unit.

(4) After the completion of unloading the unit is to depart for the quartering

area. Unit quartering areas as per map. The route: Warsaw-East Station to the division command post has been marked with signs. After arriving at the detraining station an advance detachment is to be sent ahead to scout the quartering area; it is to make its initial report to the division command post. Required data shall include personnel strength, number of vehicles and weapons, as well as supply situation (fuel, rations, munitions).

(5) Security Measures: Each unit arriving in the quartering area is to organize itself – on receipt of detailed instructions from its parent unit or independently – to guarantee immediate defensive readiness against surprise enemy attack (attack on ground, bandit activity, paratroops). (Hedgehog!) All roads and approach routes from east and south are to be guarded. All available heavy weapons are to be deployed. The situation in the air requires careful camouflage (as in Italy). Vehicles are to be dug in and foxholes dug for all men immediately. All available anti-aircraft weapons (including machine-guns) are to be deployed. Preparations to be made for a rapid assembly for departure in a southerly or easterly direction. The unit must be ready to depart and fully combat-ready within two hours at the latest.

(6) Field elements to be committed exclusively on orders of the division. Requests by other divisions are to be refused and referred to division. Arrival in the quartering area is to be reported to parent unit or division immediately by NCO runner. The runner will then remain with Division HQ to deliver orders.

(7) Note attached memorandum. Units are to be briefed accordingly. For the division commander: "The First General Staff Officer." The unloading and movement to the quartering area proceeded as planned for all transport groups. The transport leader drove to division headquarters, which was located in a barracks camp about 10 kilometers east of Warsaw.

The transports arrived from late in the evening on the 26th until early morning on the 28th of July. The division headquarters detrained at the Warsaw-East station, as did elements of the HG Parachute Flak Regiment. Other detraining stations were Warsaw-West, Piastow and Pruszkow. By 30 July the following division units had arrived in the greater Warsaw area:

The 1st Parachute-Panzer-Grenadier Regiment

Elements of the 2nd Parachute-Panzer-Grenadier Regiment

I Battalion, Parachute-Panzer Regiment

III Battalion, Parachute-Panzer Artillery Regiment

The Parachute-Panzer Armored Reconnaissance Battalion

The Parachute-Panzer Assault Battalion

The Parachute-Panzer Pioneer Battalion

The Parachute-Panzer Signals Battalion

The Parachute-Panzer Assault Gun Battalion

The last units followed on 31 July. These were:

III Battalion, 2nd Parachute-Panzer-Grenadier Regiment

II Battalion, Parachute-Panzer Regiment

The battalions were quartered in Wlochy and Ulrychow on the western outskirts of Warsaw, where they waited for operational orders. Orders for the deployment of the division near Wolomin, east of Warsaw, reached the division units by 1 August. Toward midday they were channeled through Warsaw and readied for battle east of the city.

After this date the passage through Warsaw was no longer possible on account of the uprising by the Polish Underground Army under General Bor-Komorowski. The Polish Home Army had been preparing for this uprising for a long time, a fact which did not escape the attention of the Germans. Following the collapse of Army Group Center, Poland's government in exile decided to give the order to strike, counting on help from the Red Army, which was advancing rapidly toward Warsaw.

Battles in the Siedlce-Warsaw Area

On 29 July 1944 the Wehrmacht communiqué announced:

"East of the great bend of the Vistula powerful enemy forces are driving toward the river. An attempt to cross the river was thwarted. Bitter fighting continues southeast of Warsaw and near Siedlce."

The Wehrmacht communiqués of the next three days spoke of fresh defensive battles by the Army and Waffen-SS against attacks by the numerically-superior forces of the Red Army. In the course of these Soviet offensive efforts three tank corps, including the 3rd, received orders to capture the crossings over the Bug and Narew Rivers north of Warsaw. In carrying out these orders, on the 30th and 31st the Soviet armored wedges advanced on a front of 16 kilometers through Okuniew and Wolomin toward Radzymin. Several kilometers north of this city they stopped, ignoring the Polish Home Army and its situation. In the mistaken belief that the Red Army would now veer toward Warsaw to liberate the Polish capital, General Bor-Komorowski unleashed the uprising.

One reason for the halt by the Soviet forces was that their supplies had not kept pace with the advance and they now lacked fuel for their motorized units. Another was that this independent action by the Polish Home Front was an affront to Stalin. He had exerted strong pressure on the Polish government in exile in London. The latter, rightly fearing for its existence, had installed Bor-Komorowski in place of the Commander-in-Chief of Polish forces, who was loyal to Moscow. Of this Stalin said:

"I have come to the conclusion that the action in Warsaw represents an ill-considered, dreadful adventure, which will cost the population great sacrifices. In view of the developing situation the Soviet High Command has come to the decision that it must distance itself from the Warsaw adventure."

On 3 August 1944 Marshall Stalin held a conference, to which he invited not only the Polish exile Minister-President Mikolajczyk, but also his adversary, the Russian-oriented Lublin Committee. At the conference Stalin categorically demanded Polish renunciation of its 1935 constitution. When the Polish government in exile refused to do so, Stalin bluntly declared:

"Sooner or later the truth about the criminal band which engineered the Warsaw adventure to gain power for itself will become known to all. This element has exploited the trust of the citizens of Warsaw and has delivered up many people to German cannon, tanks and aircraft." (See: Secret and Personal Discussions by J.V. Stalin with Churchill and Roosevelt on 22.8.1944, in: *Churchill: Speeches, Letters, Telegrams*.)

One reason for this truly dishonorable attitude on Stalin's part was the fact that Sikorski and the Polish government in exile had asked the International Red Cross to investigate the case of the Polish officers found murdered in Katyn Forest; it was determined that Soviets were responsible for the many thousands of dead at Katyn.

Once again a quote from Stalin:

"We cannot abide and cannot come to terms with terrorists encouraged by the Polish emigrants killing our men in Poland and waging a criminal war against the Soviet troops who are liberating Poland. In these people we see the allies of our common enemy, and their radio communication with Mr. Mikolajczyk, which we have discovered on agents arrested on Polish soil, not only reveals their dastardly plan, but casts a shadow over Mr. Mikolajczyk and his people as well."

This ultimately led to the creation of a new Polish government, made up of the Lublin Committee sponsored by the Soviet Union, and to the division of Poland, in whose defence England and France had escalated the Second World War.

And what did Churchill have to say?

"This fight will not end properly if Poland does not receive full sovereignty, independence and freedom on the basis of friendship with Russia. – I thought we had agreed on this at Yalta."

However the revenge of the Soviet Union had a long arm.

The Encirclement of the Soviet 3rd Tank Corps

As early as 31 July 1944, Headquarters, Ninth Army had already recognized that it might be possible to encircle and destroy the 3rd Soviet Tank Corps. The result was a battle in the Radzymin-Wolomin-Okuniew area that lasted from 31 July to 10 August, which went down in military history as the Battle of Warsaw.

Command of the German forces in this battle lay in the hands of the proven *General der Panzertruppen* Dietrich von Saucken, commander of XXXIX Panzer Corps, which had been upgraded to a *Panzerkampfgruppe*. General von Saucken had the following units with which to counter the enemy forces advancing on a 16-kilometer front:

(a) The Hermann Göring Parachute-Panzer Division north of the Warsaw-Wolomin rail line.

(b) The 19th Panzer Division north of the Warsaw-Radzymin road.

(c) The armored battle group of the 4th Panzer Division on both sides of the road from Wyschkow to Radzymin, led by the 4th Armored Reconnaissance Battalion.

(d) The "Wiking" SS-Division, which followed the attack by 4th Panzer Division, echeloned to the left rear.

It was not possible to commit all of the HG Parachute-Panzer Divison's forces en masse. Several elements were still aboard trains en route to Poland. Other division units, among them III Battalion, 1st Parachute-Panzer-Grenadier Regiment and II Battalion, HG Parachute-Panzer Regiment with 20 Panzer IVs, were still tied up in Wola, at the eastern edge of Warsaw.

On 1 August the division commander ordered the division to go around Warsaw and use the Vistula bridge near Modlin. When the Ninth Army learned of this it sent the following order to the HG Parachute-Panzer Division:

"I forbid the movement of detrained elements through Modlin. These elements are to assemble and fight their way in a body through Warsaw over Reichsstraße VIII and the new bridge (Poniatowski Bridge) to Praga. Signed von Vormann."

The drive through Warsaw did not happen, however. The Ninth Army found other employment for the division. As in Warsaw, the situation in the Warka-Magnuszew area had become more threatening, with the result that on 3 August the army found itself compelled to divert all elements of the division not fighting near Wolomin southward into the Warka bridgehead. The following elements of the division remained in action near Wolomin and Okuniew:

The 1st and 2nd Parachute-Panzer-Grenadier Regiments (the latter less its III Battalion), I Battalion, Parachute-Panzer Regiment, III Battalion, Parachute-Panzer Artillery Regiment, elements of the Parachute-Panzer Flak Regiment, the Armored Reconnaissance Battalion, the Parachute-Panzer Assault Battalion, the Parachute- Panzer Pioneer Battalion and elements of the Parachute-Panzer Signals Battalion.

As per the corps order, on 2 August these units set out from north of the Warsaw-Wolomin rail line to the northeast and reached the western outskirts of Wolomin the next day. The previous day the 19th and 4th Panzer Divisions had met north of Radzymin. The Wehrmacht communique of 3 August reported the fall of Radzymin. The most forward of the three Soviet tank corps had been encircled. Two further tank formations suffered the same fate that day. One was wiped out between Radzymin and Wolomin by the 19th Panzer Division with help from elements of the 4th Panzer Division. The second was attacked south of Wolomin by the HG Parachute-Panzer Division and, in cooperation with other elements of the 4th Panzer Division, was encircled and destroyed. The Wehrmacht communique of 4 August announced:

"Northeast of Warsaw Soviet forces were cut off from their lines of communication to the rear by counterattacks by our panzers and squeezed into a narrow area. 76 enemy tanks were destroyed."

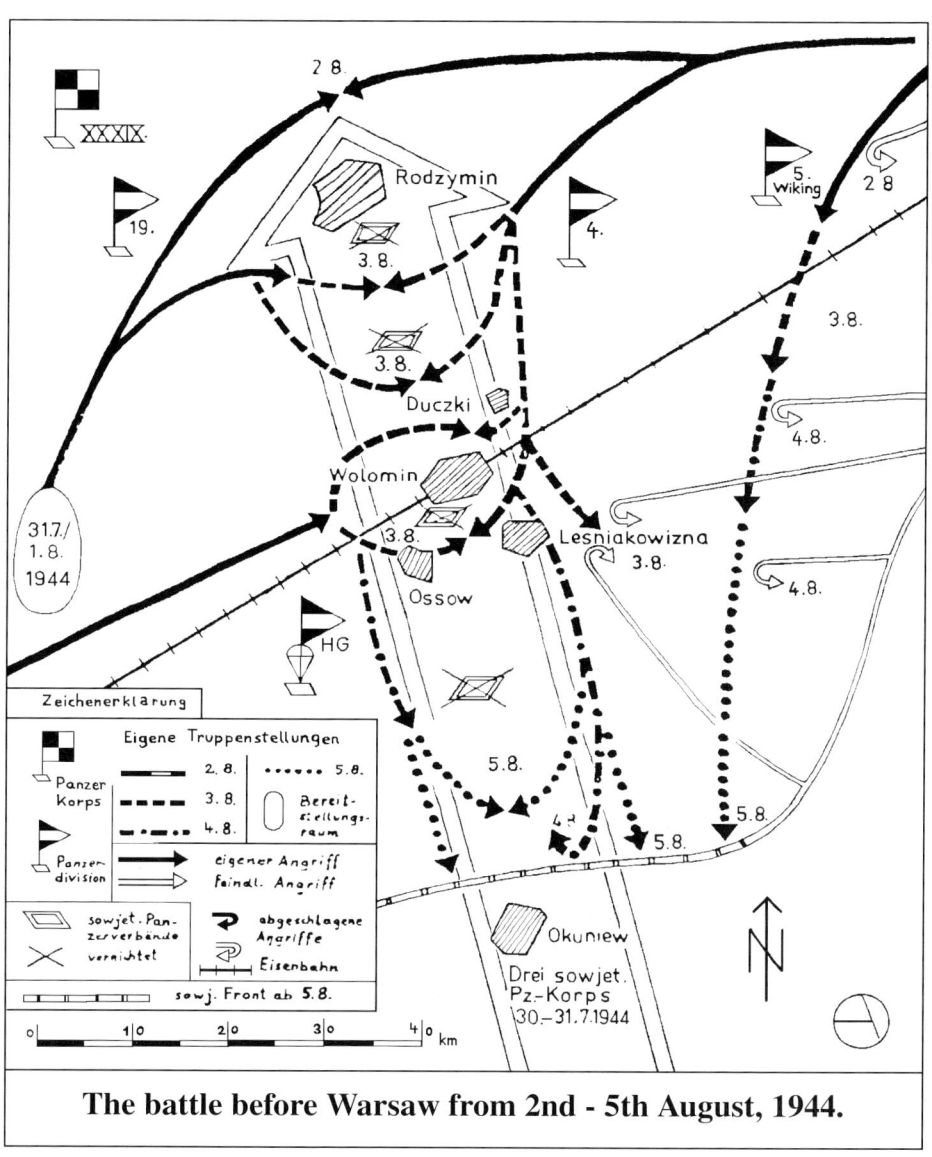

The battle before Warsaw from 2nd - 5th August, 1944.

A further, very strong armored formation in the shape of the Soviet 3rd Tank Corps drove south through Wolomin in the direction of Okuniew. In the following days this corps was stopped and cut off south of Wolomin by the Hermann Göring Parachute-Panzer Division and elements of the 4th Panzer Division. The main pressure was exerted on the southern part of the resulting pocket by the HG Parachute-Panzer Division.

Heavy fighting developed on 4 and 5 August in the course of these actions. The Russian units were able to repulse an attack toward Okuniew by the 4th Panzer Division and hold their positions. During the fighting from August 2nd to the 5th the *Wiking* SS-Panzer Division screened the combat zone to the east and prevented units of the Red Army from coming to the aid of their three threatened tank corps. The Wehrmacht communiques of 5th and 6th August described the ongoing battle and on the 6th declared:

"East of Warsaw the 3rd Soviet Tank Corps, which has been cut off since 1 August, was destroyed after several days of hard fighting. The bolsheviks suffered heavy losses. They lost 192 tanks and 45 guns."

Following the destruction of this last Soviet forces in this area the enemy pressure in the Wolomin-Okuniew area abated. The German forces were able to establish a continuous front in this area, running in a straight line north of Okuniew in an east-west direction. The elements of the HG Parachute-Panzer Division deployed in the battle zone near Warsaw were now also moved into the Warka bridgehead. The 4th Panzer Division was also withdrawn; however, it soon set out for the Courland, where the situation had meanwhile become more critical.

Battle for the Warka-Magnuszew Bridgehead

Beginning on 28 July 1944, even before the Ninth Army could meet the threat developing east of the Vistula, strong Soviet forces pushed to the Vistula in several places simultaneously. Initially the Germans were able to thwart every crossing attempt by the Soviets. Those forces that did reach the other side were driven back across the river by quick and resolute counterattacks. On 31 July, however, the enemy succeeded in gaining a foothold on the west bank of the Vistula, establishing bridgeheads at two places between Warsaw and Lublin. The first was located on both sides of Pulawy, while the second developed near the small village of Magnuszew, about 15 kilometers east of Warka.

The Ninth Army tried to eliminate both bridgeheads. Attacks by close-support aircraft on subsequent crossing attempts achieved great success on 1 August. No fewer than 29 ferries loaded with troops were destroyed. The Hermann Göring Parachute-Panzer Division first saw action in this area during the night of 3 August. It engaged the onrushing enemy forces southeast of Warka. Further elements were transferred into this area as they became available. The first unit arrived on 4 August and moved into position beside the 19th Panzer Division in the defensive barrier. The Warka bridgehead and half of the bridgehead near Pulawy lay in the area of VIII Army Corps, on the right wing of the Ninth Army, part of Army Group Center. The 17th

Infantry Division was engaged in defensive fighting near Pulawy, while the 19th Panzer Division, the HG Parachute-Panzer Division and the 1132nd Grenadier Brigade were in Warka. The 45th Volksgrenadier Division was supposed to arrive later.

The HG Division initially came under the command of VIII Army Corps. However when XXXVI Panzer Corps under *Generalleutnant Freiherr* von Lüttwitz assumed responsibility for the Warka sector, the division was placed under its command. The division's operations staff moved into an isolated forester's house in the forest east of Glowaczew. The Ib section occupied a barracks installation east of Jedlinko.

The enemy forces consisted of the Soviet 8th Army and the 57th Guards Army. Opposite the HG Parachute-Panzer Division were the 35th and 47th Guards Infantry Divisions and the 1st Soviet Tank Brigade. The Red Army employed everything at its disposal – not just to maintain the bridgeheads, but also to expand them and pour in more and more troops. A counterattack by II Battalion, HG Parachute-Panzer Regiment on 6 August drove back this powerful enemy back some distance to the east.

On 8 August, after all the elements of the division had assembled in the battle zone, it and the 19th Panzer Division launched a counterattack near Grabow-Pilica. The 19th Panzer Division's 74th Panzer-Grenadier Regiment drove deep into the enemy positions. The attack, which was continued the next day, was a success, with the enemy losing a large number of his tanks. German bombers and close-support aircraft kept up their attacks on Soviet river-crossing traffic. However the hoped-for destruction of the Warka bridgehead did not materialize. The Red Army had already moved strong forces across the Vistula, where they dug in. Only a powerful artillery bombardment could have dislodged them. However the artillery and air support available to the attackers was insufficient. They were especially short of artillery.

In the days that followed, the Soviets continued to reinforce their two bridgeheads. From there they launched strong attacks, in particular against the Hermann Göring Parachute-Panzer Division. Army Group Center was not in a position to free up any further forces for this battle zone other than those already committed. The dreadful losses which Army Group Center had suffered in the Russian "Bagration" summer offensive were having an especially aggravating effect there.

The Wehrmacht High Command reported on the battles in the bridgeheads no less than seven times between the 14th and 23rd of August. On the 23rd the Wehrmacht communique read:

"Renewed Soviet attempts to break through were thwarted southeast of Warka. A single panzer division (the 19th) destroyed 52 Soviet tanks in the fighting."

From the 21st to the 24th August the 19th Panzer Division had to be withdrawn from the battle because it was completely exhausted. It was pulled back into the area west of Warsaw as army reserve. The 19th Panzer Division and its commander, *Generalleutnant* Källner, were praised in the supplementary report to the quoted Wehrmacht communique. The enemy quickly took advantage of the weakening of this front. Fierce attacks were directed against the two remaining divisions. The Red Army achieved several deep penetrations which led to a further expansion of the bridgehead. Warka fell. The Wehrmacht communique of 27 August reported:

"In the Vistula bridgehead counterattacks partly repulsed enemy attempts to break through."

The Red Army subsequently ceased its attacks. This led the Ninth Army to withdraw the HG Parachute-Panzer Division as well. On 19 September its units transferred into the area between Warsaw and Modlin, but still east of the Vistula. There it took over the sector held by the Royal Hungarian 1st Cavalry Division under *Generalmajor* Ibranji. Its neighbor was once again the proven 19th Panzer Division. The new sector lay within the area of IV SS-Panzer Corps under *General der Waffen-SS* Gille. Also under Gille's command were the 3rd SS-Panzer-Division *Totenkopf* and the 5th SS-Panzer Division *Wiking*.

The front ran along the east bank of the Vistula from east of Warsaw to the Narew. The Red Army resumed its attacks on 10 September; once again its objective was to cross the Vistula. The Soviets attacked daily but were repelled each time and losses in tanks were heavy. All attempts by them to cross the Vistula were thwarted. In the neighboring sector to the south the Soviets succeeded in entering the Warsaw suburb of Praga, located on the east bank of the Vistula. Bitter house-to-house fighting broke out. Positioned on the corps' left wing up to the Narew, the HG Parachute-Panzer Division had to hold the front line on the east bank. The division headquarters was located in Lomna, southeast of Modlin, while the division quartermaster was situated in Neuhof (Nowy Dwor), several kilometers east of Modlin. In the battles of 21 and 22 September, immediately after arriving in this area, the division successfully repulsed powerful enemy, attacks. This success was mentioned in the Wehrmacht communique of 24 September.

During the two weeks of this action every Soviet attempt to force the German front back to the Vistula was defeated. It was then that initial preparations for the expansion of the division to the Hermann Göring Parachute-Panzer Corps began. This resulted in considerable hindrances and difficulties, not just for the command staff, but for the troops as well. Division headquarters had to reorganize itself into a corps headquarters, releasing expert advisors to both new divisions, while providing the best possible command to the units engaged in battle. The units themselves were weakened, in that they had to release personnel for the new battalions.

The process of enlarging the division to a corps was not achieved by adding complete, new units; to a large degree it was accomplished by dividing existing units. The new corps came into being on 1 October, although initial work had begun several days earlier.

IX. THE FORMATION OF THE HERMANN GÖRING PARACHUTE-PANZER CORPS

Corps Headquarters:

Commanding General: Generalmajor Schmalz

Corps Units:

HG Corps Assault Battalion

HG Anti-tank Battalion

HG Corps Signals Battalion

HG Corps Pioneer Battalion

HG Parachute-Flak Regiment with 4 battalions

I HG Supply Battalion

II HG Maintenance Battalion

HG Administration Battalion

HG Corps First-aid Battalion

HG Corps Field Post Office

1st HG Parachute-Panzer Division:

Division Commander: Oberst (later Generalmajor) von Necker, from Feb. 1945: Oberst (later Generalmajor) Lemke

Division Headquarters

HG Parachute-Panzer regiment with two battalions:

1st HG Parachute-Panzer-Grenadier Regiment (two battalions)

2nd HG Parachute-Panzer-Grenadier Regiment (two battalions)

1st HG Parachute-Panzer-Fusilier Battalion

1st HG Armored Reconnaissance Battalion

1st HG Parachute-Panzer Pioneer Battalion

1st HG Parachute-Panzer Artillery Regiment (three battalions)

1st HG Parachute-Panzer Signals Battalion

1st HG Replacement Training Battalion

1st HG First-aid Battalion

1st HG Field Post Office

2nd HG Parachute-Panzer-Grenadier Division:

Division Commander: Oberst (later Generalmajor) Walther

Division Headquarters

HG Parachute Assault Gun Battalion

3rd HG Parachute-Panzer-Grenadier Regiment (three battalions)

4th HG Parachute-Panzer-Grenadier Regiment (three battalions)

2nd HG Parachute-Panzer Fusilier Battalion

2nd HG Armored Reconnaissance Battalion

2nd HG Parachute-Panzer Artillery Regiment (three battalions)

2nd HG Parachute-Panzer Signals Battalion

  2nd HG Replacement Training Battalion

  2nd HG First-aid Battalion

  2nd HG Field Post Office

Other Units and Posts:

  Führer Flak Battalion (only in initial period)

  "Reichsmarschall" Escort Battalion

  HG Parachute-Panzer Replacement and Training Brigade with the 1st and 2nd Regiments (until March 1945)

  Brigade Commander: Oberst Meyer

  2nd HG Parachute-Panzer Replacement and Training Brigade with the 3rd and 4th Regiments (from March 1945)

  Brigade Commander: Oberst Breuer

  HG Replacement and Training Regiment in Holland

HG Parachute-Panzer Corps Home Headquarters, Berlin-Reinickendorf Hospitals for Minor Cases (Rest Homes) in Oberau and Reit im Winkel. Formation of the corps took longer than anticipated on account of shortages in personnel, weapons and vehicles. Planned authorized strengths were never reached.

Personnel Strength

Soldiers who served in the HG Parachute-Panzer ca. 60,000. Corps Survivors after 1945 ca. 15,000. In East Germany and Austria ca. 5,000. In West Germany ca. 10,000. Number of survivors in West Germany who have died ca. 3,000. Number of remaining survivors included in the ca. 4,000. Parachute-Panzer Veterans Association (Source: General Schmidt)

In spite of intensive investigations into the fates of those listed as missing in the past 41 years, the HG Parachute-Panzer Corps still lists as unexplained: 8,095 Number belonging to HG Parachute-Panzer Replacement and Training Brigade in the period January – March ca. 2,000 1945.

The relatively large number of unexplained fates is due to the fact that the units of the Hermann Göring Parachute-Panzer Corps lost 90% of their missing on the Eastern Front.

The Battle for East Prussia

On 5 October 1944 the Red Army opened its offensive against Army Group North in East Prussia. Its objective was to reach the Baltic and sever the lines of communication to the German forces still in the Courland. The 6th of October saw the alerting of the new, but still far from operationally-ready, Hermann Göring Parachute-Panzer Corps and its departure into the area of the Russian Warka bridgehead. The corps was moved by train – travel by motor vehicle was out of the question due to a lack of fuel – in the direction of Radom. Even before the last transports arrived there, they passed the first

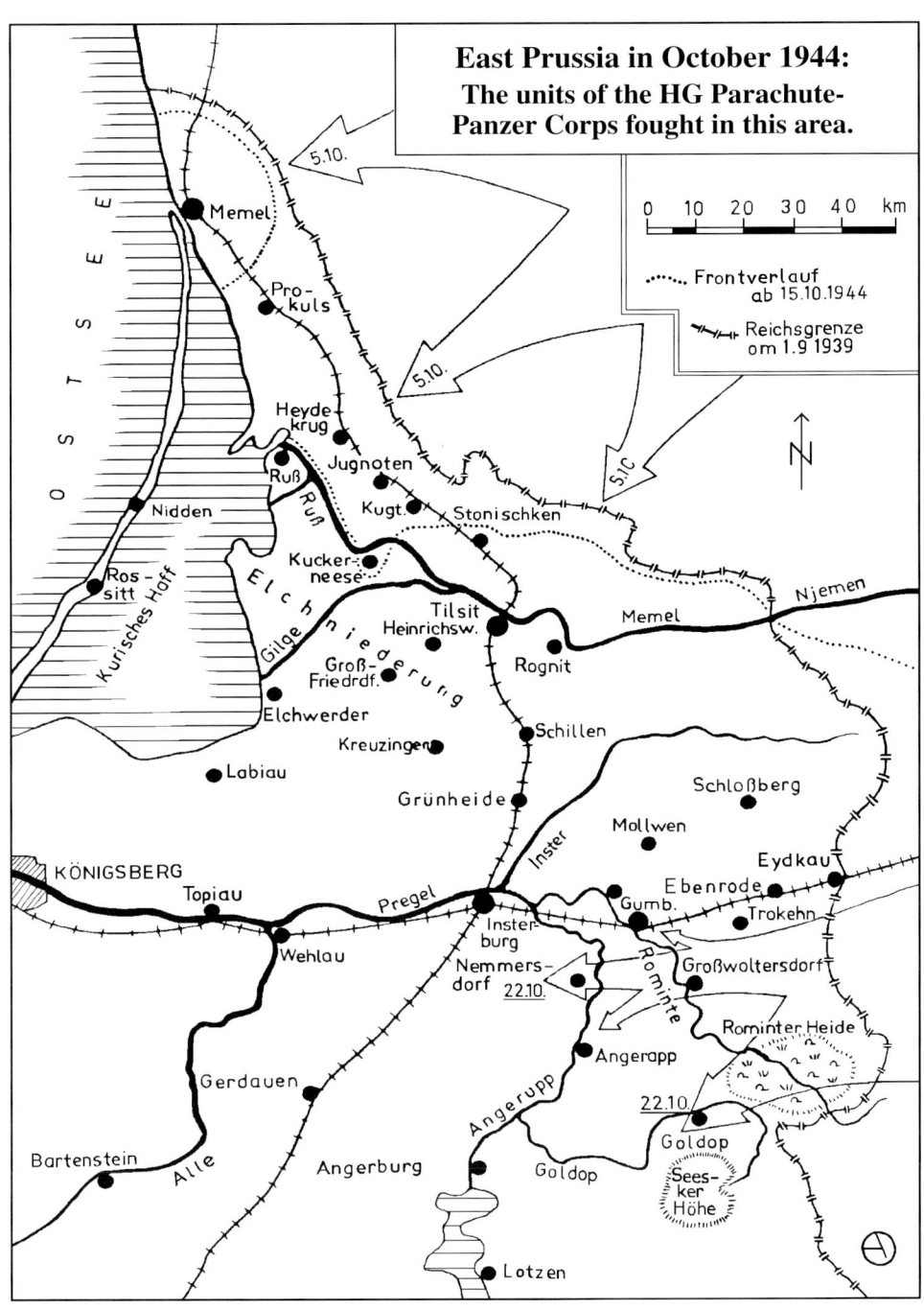

trains heading back on the opposite track. In Radom the last transports were also maneuvered onto the opposite track before heading back the way they had come. What did it all mean?

To the German Supreme Command, Army Group North's situation seemed more important than holding the Russians in the Warka bridgehead. Therefore while the corps was still en route to Warka, the OKW authorized the release of the units of the HG Parachute-Panzer Corps, which were still in the midst of reorganization, from Army Group Center to Army Group North.

The Soviet Offensive and German Countermeasures

In mid-October the Red Army launched an offensive toward Königsberg along both sides of the Vilkavishkis – Ebenrode road. Within the area of the Fourth Army under *General* Hoßbach the units of the HG Parachute-Panzer Corps fought bitter defensive battles against Soviet armored spearheads advancing between Angerapp and Nemmersdorf. The Red Army committed terrible acts of bestiality against the civilian population in the Nemmersdorf area.

The HG Parachute-Panzer Corps and its parachute-panzer regiment played a major role in not only preventing the planned Soviet breakthrough to East Prussia, but actually driving the attacking Soviet forces back beyond the Rominten Heath. War correspondent Boecker witnessed the Soviet attack as an observer with the tanks of the HG Panzer Regiment. He described the action in his report from the front on 8 December 1944.

"Never before have Soviet units been committed in such numbers and of this quality. Under the pitiless eyes of the STAVKA in the Kremlin, the Soviet assault is now to be directed at Königsberg. According to Stalin's order of the day, The Red Army is to take East Prussia within ten days.

The attack began early on the morning of 16 October 1944. In spite of a determined defence and heavy losses the attack could not at first be stopped. The Red Army succeeded in tearing open a gap in our front between Wirballen and Raschen. The first enemy tanks had already felt their way forward as far as Eydtkau. When the enemy then inserted a new Guards army on the right wing of the attack in order to force the breakthrough with fresh forces, on 19 October the young volunteers of the 'Hermann Göring' Parachute-Panzer Regiment, under the command of Knight's Cross wearer Major Roßmann, attacked from north to south into the enemy's flank.

Advancing rapidly, the Panther battalion under the command of Hptm. Trenz, wearer of the German Cross in Gold, rolled over the massed resistance of the enemy and toward evening on the 19th ran into a Soviet Guards tank corps which included a Moscovite division. According to statements from prisoners, this elite unit had been earmarked to spearhead the operation into the heart of East Prussia.

In the following battles, which exceeded anything expected of the Panthers, the enemy armored spearhead was completely smashed and the Soviet drive toward the west stopped. This success allowed a firm blocking line to be established 20 kilometers farther west, on which the strength of the Soviet attack was shattered. Many German soldiers distinguished themselves in this battle, among them Hptm. Werner Stuchlik from Görlitz, Hptm. Joachim Renz from Bergen auf Rügen and Oblt. Wilhelm Kuhlwilm from Hörde, near Dortmund. As well there was Oblt. Rupert Kraus from Munich, Oblt. Gerhard Tschierschwitz from Berlin, Oblt. Wallhäußer, Uffz. Werner Grunold from Berlin, Gefr. Albert Plapper from Blankenburg and Gefreiter Konrad Steets from Munich, all of whom rose above themselves and whose accomplishments were acknowledged by the awarding of the Knight's Cross.

Hptm. Joachim Renz, who was killed leading a counterattack on the fifth day of the battle, and his Panther battalion destroyed 93 enemy tanks, 45 anti-tank guns, numerous other weapons and a regiment of enemy infantry in those days. These five days saw the battalion in uninterrupted defensive fighting. With Joachim Renz always in the lead, it drove into the enemy from the flank, overran an enemy anti-tank front, and together with a leaderless infantry battalion formed a new main line of resistance, which held. By night the battalion assumed an all-round defensive posture. It attacked and defended to the last man.

Hptm. Joachim Renz, commander of I Battalion, HG Parachute- Panzer Regiment never received the Knight's Cross awarded him on 6 December 1944. He was killed in the defensive battle on 23 October 1944. Of the battalion's units, 2nd Company, led by Oblt. Gerhard Tschierschwitz, played a special role. Driving at the head of his company, Tschierschwitz rolled into the enemy's flank and took the village of Wirballen, whereupon he decided to attack and destroy the enemy from behind. Without infantry support, he fought his way forward from farm to farm. Then he received orders to push on and establish contact with an endangered infantry division. Before carrying out this order, Tschierschwitz attacked enemy tank assembly areas he had just located in Jägershagen. Employing direct fire, he destroyed an enemy command post before carrying out his mission.

In their subsequent charge across the entire width of the battlefield, Tschierschwitz and his company killed 300 Soviet soldiers and destroyed 16 tanks, 16 anti-tank guns, 6 artillery pieces and 13 machine-guns. Oblt. Rupert Kraus was also a member of 2nd Company, HG Parachute-Panzer Regiment. He and his handful of Panthers also succeeded in tearing open the flank of the Soviet spearhead. He arrived in the village of Kassuben almost simultaneously with the enemy; there he encountered a group of 14 tanks and together with his comrades destroyed them all.

When, the next morning, the enemy attacked there with fresh forces, Kraus' remaining tanks once more threw themselves at the foe. In the ensuing battle the enemy once again lost the bulk of his tanks. When the enemy partially outflanked the company, threatening it from the rear, Kraus was ordered to withdraw. However he did not carry out the order, which would have meant salvation for him but which posed a threat to the other units of his division. He held the position for another three hours. When the firing was at its heaviest he made his way to the platoon most threatened by the outflanking. He took two other Panthers and led them in a frontal attack against the enemy, losing one tank in the process. The enemy was completely smashed.

During the next two days two Panthers which had been put out of action with battle damage returned to the company, reinforcing it somewhat. They held a front six kilometers wide. On 22 October the company destroyed about 40 enemy tanks, 30 anti-tank guns and a battalion of Russian infantry. By now his company was down to a handful of Panthers. At his point of Soviet penetration Kraus was able to completely master the situation against a superior force.

The commander of 1st Company, 1st HG Parachute Anti-tank Battalion, Oblt. Karl-Heinz Wallhäser, and his company saw action at the focal point of the battle for East Prussia.

On 9 August he enabled his comrades of the panzer-grenadiers to establish a position by repelling several enemy advances and pursuing the enemy some distance into no-man's-land, destroying several enemy tanks in the process. Near Studziansk he launched a daring counterattack, advancing into a village behind several retreating enemy tanks. During the ensuing battle in the village his tank destroyers knocked out six tanks and destroyed several anti-tank gun emplacements. Although his gunner was put out of action, Wallhäuser was able to destroy two tanks and a heavy anti-tank gun position himself. Several companies of enemy infantry were destroyed with high-explosive shells and machine-gun fire. All further enemy attacks were stopped by the handful of tank destroyers.

On 26 October units of the Red Army broke into the main battlefield with far-superior forces, including about 50 tanks. Engaging the enemy with his tank destroyers, Oblt. Wallhäuser drove the attackers back to their departure positions in heavy fighting and reinforced his counterattack by collecting all the stragglers he came upon. When the neighboring unit was forced to retreat as a result of great pressure from the enemy's heavy weapons, he assessed the tactical situation correctly and carried out a surprise flanking thrust, in the process destroying a number of heavy weapons. On the way into the enemy position he succeeded in putting out of action about 300 Red Army soldiers.

This success prevented the Soviets from achieving their planned breakthrough on the road to Gumbinnen. Oberleutnant Wallhäuser's actions had created the conditions necessary for the establishment of a new main line of resistance and in the process had made an important contribution to the parrying of the Soviet attempt to break through to Königsberg. It was the panzer-grenadiers who bore the brunt of the defence at the side of these armored formations. One such man was Hptm. Werner Stuchlik, commander of II Battalion, 2nd HG Parachute-Panzer-Grenadier Regiment. His actions are highlighted here as being typical of all the panzer-grenadiers who fought like him.

When the numerically far-superior enemy achieved a penetration on the left wing of his grenadier battalion, Hptm. Stuchlik scraped together the members of his headquarters, a pioneer squad and three assault guns. With this

30-man-strong battle group he drove one kilometer into the mass of the onrushing enemy and spread confusion in the spearhead. The assault guns knocked out enemy tanks, then formed a hedgehog far beyond our lines with 15 men, which was held for three hours! Not until he received an order to withdraw did Stuchlik pull back to his own main line of resistance, taking all the wounded with him. Following a heavy bombardment the enemy, advancing along the road to Trakehnen, broke into the main line of resistance where Unteroffizier Werner Grunold, leader of the company headquarters squad of 3rd Company, 2nd HG Parachute-Panzer-Grenadier Regiment, was positioned. When the commander of 3rd Company was put out of action and no more officers were available, he assumed command of the company. Grunold scraped together 15 men, took three MG 42s and stormed forward from the left flank against the leading wave of enemy infantry. The furious fire from his three machine-guns split up the attack formation. About 300 Soviets who had broken into our main line of resistance were cut off from the following troops, after which they were wiped out by Grunold's force.

He then took command of the neighboring company, which was also leaderless, led it forward into the main line of resistance and manned all the machine-guns. Several anti-tank guns were also on hand and these he moved forward into position. When the enemy then attacked with seven tanks and fresh troops, Grunold ordered the machine-gunners to lay down flanking fire on the infantry. He himself crawled forward with his Panzerfaust and, firing from a range of 30 meters, hit and knocked out the leading tank. The remainder turned away. Grunhold fetched a group of his comrades from their trench and put the onrushing Red Army troops to flight, supported effectively by his machine-guns.

The same day Gefreiter Konrad Steets, battalion runner with II Battalion, 2nd HG Parachute-Panzer-Grenadier Regiment, was awarded the Knight's Cross. As battalion runner he had demonstrated his courage and ability on numerous occasions. He had long worn both Iron Crosses. In September he and a few comrades had attacked and cleared out a Russian advance strongpoint in the Warka bridgehead. In doing so he created the conditions necessary for an attack on the Vistula line, which was carried out the following day.

On 19 October he was unable to deliver a dispatch on account of heavy anti-tank fire. The obstacle, two anti-tank guns in good positions, had to be eliminated first. Steets and several comrades crept up to the anti-tank position and destroyed it with explosive charges. Steets' action allowed his company to reach its objective without further losses.

"On 24 October, while delivering a dispatch alone, he discovered an enemy battalion preparing to launch an attack at the boundary with the neighboring company. He worked his way forward into a well-concealed position. Positioning his machine-gun there, he allowed the enemy to pass halfway and then began firing into the mass of enemy troops from a range of less than 200 meters. With its high rate of fire, far more than 1,000 rounds per minute, the MG 42 cut broad swaths of destruction in the attacking wave. 100 dead were left lying in front of the German machine-gun. The attack was stopped dead in its tracks.

Enemy mortars and artillery opened fire on the position, which they believed contained a large number of troops. Steets took cover and dragged his machine-gun with him. When the enemy fire died down he returned to his hole. Once again he opened fire on the onrushing enemy. An eleven-man assault detachment heading straight for him was wiped out from very close range. Firing from the hip, Steets mowed down eight of the attackers and took the three survivors back to battalion as prisoners. Konrad Steets, only 18 years old, a volunteer in the HG Parachute-Panzer Corps, was awarded the Knight's Cross. In the opinion of his CO he was 'the best and most willing soldier' in his battalion. Konrad Steets was killed on 6 November, three weeks before he was to receive the Knight's Cross.

Gefreiter Albert Plapper, squad leader in 4th Company, 2nd HG Parachute-Panzer-Grenadier Regiment, was also eighteen when he underwent his great test of fire. Recognizing a serious threat to the sector – a machine-gun crew having been put out of action – he took over the weapon and brought the Russian attack in that area to a halt. The next enemy attack included tanks. Plapper stopped these with the Panzerschreck. Then, with his machine-gun at his hip, he and five other men attacked the enemy's open flank. They were nevertheless unable to halt the attackers. A breakthrough seemed imminent, especially when five T 34s, which were soon joined by several others, arrived to blast open a path for the infantry.

Using his Panzerschreck Plapper knocked out five enemy tanks while the machine-guns pinned down the infantry, and once again brought the attack to a halt. The danger of an enemy breakthrough against the 2nd HG Parachute-Panzer-Grenadier Regiment had been averted.

All of the mentioned battles were played out in the Trakehnen area, where the units of the Hermann Göring Parachute-Panzer Corps succeeded in halting the Red Army's breakthrough south of Gumbinnen. For several days the fate of East Prussia hung in the balance there, before the soldiers of the Reichsmarschall tipped the scales in their favor.

In addition to the Knight's Cross wearers mentioned here, the decoration was also won by Oblt. Wilhelm Kuhlwilm, a company commander in the 3rd HG Parachute-Panzer-Grenadier Regiment, on 30 November 1944. In spite of the desperate situation he led his company to victory against the vastly superior enemy."

The bravery displayed by nine of its members in the fighting in East Prussia added new glory to the banner of the HG Parachute-Panzer Corps. It does not need mentioning that the many thousands of other men of the corps, of whom these nine are representative, gave their best and many paid with their lives. The HG Parachute-Panzer Corps fought there to the point of self-sacrifice and was named many times in the Wehrmacht communique.

Let us now turn to another unit which saw action in the Gumbinnen area: 13th Battery, III Battalion, HG Parachute Flak Regiment under its commander Oblt. Barth. The battery, which was still in the formation process, had just received three new 88mm anti-aircraft guns. When it was sent from

Tilsit in the direction of Gumbinnen on 19 October 1944 the guns had neither been bore-sighted nor undergone a required technical inspection.

The 13th Battery, HG Parachute Flak Regiment at Gumbinnen

"When, in the afternoon hours of 20 October 1944, the enemy's approach to Gumbinnen became ever more threatening, the commander of the 13th Battery proposed to Gumbinnen's field commander, Oberst von Nardowski, that they deploy two of the unit's guns, which were not yet fully operational, together with a battle group formed from III Battalion's train to defend the town. At 1730 hours on 20 October 1944 the resulting Barth Flak Combat Team took up position at the northern exit from Ohldorf, south of Gumbinnen. Initially there was no contact with the enemy.

On 21 October the enemy changed his style and direction of attack. As a result of observations by the leader of the flak combat team, and with the approval of the Gumbinnen field commander, at 1600 hours the improvised flak combat team moved to a new position at a rail crossing two kilometers south of the Auenhof Estate, in order to temporarily close the large gap in the front there. The enemy had to be stopped there at all costs. Each member of the combat team was fully determined to achieve this goal. The enemy had to be prevented from taking Gumbinnen. The remnants of the 1st Parachute Company, about twenty men under the command of Lt. Berg, had earlier fallen back to a position north of the rail line. These troops were provided with Panzerfaust anti-tank weapons by the flak combat team leader and inserted into the newly-formed anti-tank barrier at the railway embankment, which linked up with the Angerapp barrier. Patrols were dispatched immediately, and these repulsed Russian patrols on the way from Bergerbrück to Nordbuden. Consequently the road from Bergerbrück to the Angerapp bridge remained under German control. As well a 30-strong group of soldiers belonging to the 11th Parachute Company, which had also been scattered, was able to hold the bridge until contact had been established there, after which the 11th Company was also incorporated into the flak combat team.

At dawn on 22 October enemy pressure increased, with heavy artillery and rocket fire, as well as tank fire, on the railway embankment, the main road to Gumbinnen, and identified nests of German resistance. At 0400 hours that day Oblt. Barth collected members of the Volkssturm, soldiers on leave, men separated from their units and police forces from the road in Zweilinden to reinforce this weak line. At 0900 hours he reported to Oberstleutnant Bertram that the combat team's strength was two 88mm flak, two parachute companies, 60 soldiers on leave and stragglers, 30 Volkssturm men under Major Ruhnke, and Schloßberg and his men. All units received a steady flow of reinforcements. Oberstleutnant Bertram placed the flak combat team under his command and immediately dispatched two 75mm anti-tank guns to join it.

At 0930 hours the enemy attacked with tanks and escorting infantry. This force was engaged by all units and repulsed. The enemy tanks then attacked

in strength in an attempt to break the German resistance, overrun the railway embankment, and break through to the main road. At 0934 hours the leading enemy tank, which had already crossed the railway embankment, came into the field of fire of Gun A. The first shot from 300 meters was a direct hit which destroyed the enemy tank. The remaining enemy tanks remained behind a hill at a distance of 500 meters for about 90 minutes and fired on Zweilinden's busy crossroads. Then they abruptly rolled forward and at 1025 hours Gun A opened fire again, this time from a range of 600 meters. The T 34 was hit and caught fire; the surviving members of the crew bailed out."
"One of the paratroopers crept up to the third T 34 and put it out of action with his Panzerfaust.

Meanwhile the fourth T 34 had moved up to the railway embankment. It sat there, out of reach of the defenders' weapons, directly in front of the German positions; from time to time it fired on the positions with its main gun and machine-guns. Finally an anti-tank gun was moved forward and the Russian tank withdrew. While trying to escape at high speed it was destroyed – once again it was Gun A – just before reaching the back slope. The flak combat team, reinforced by a handful of soldiers, held the Auenhof-Bergerbrück rail crossing on 21 and 22 October 1944, destroyed four T 34s, and kept open the Gumbinnen- Insterburg rail line and road. The flak combat team suffered no losses."

A Brief Account of the Assault Gun Battalion, Later the HG Parachute Tank Destroyer Battalion

In August 1944 the 10th and 11th Companies of the HG Assault Gun Battalion saw action in the Studzianka area. Under the command of Oblt. Wallhäuser, they were able to destroy six enemy tanks and an anti-tank gun in the period of 9th to 11th of August. In the course of these actions *Fähnrich* Schawalla, who was serving as a platoon leader, was badly wounded. He died of his wounds two days later.

On 12 August a Soviet armored thrust toward Studzianka was repulsed, in the course of which 10th Company destroyed its 25th enemy tank. Pulled back to Lipa on 13 August, the companies saw action in a prepared position for the infantry there from the 15th to the 19th. 19 August also saw an attack on Helenowek, during which an anti-tank position was overrun, five anti-tank guns destroyed, and five light artillery pieces put out of action in cooperation with the division's combat school. Obgefr. Schuler and Uffz. Siegle were wounded in the attack. Siegle died of his wounds on 24 August.

The attack on Lipa, which began on 20 August, was continued on the 21st. One enemy tank was destroyed. The unit was then pulled out of the line on the 22nd; Lt. Sebold joined the company the same day. Several enemy tanks were destroyed in the course of the actions at the cemetery in the Glowazow-Lezenice area. Oblt. Theophile and Lt. Ringel led 10th Company's two platoons. The handful of tank destroyers remained in this area until 19 September 1944, when they were withdrawn and transferred into the Radom area. From there they were initially sent in the direction of the Warka bridgehead, only to be shipped back to the Praga area near Warsaw as soon as they arrived in Radom. Hptm. Bellinger was slightly wounded there, as was Fw. Kanert.

On 7 October 1944, the 10th Company entrained in preparation for transfer to East Prussia. It was unloaded in the Insterburg area and on 11 October began an overland drive from Tilsit to Kukernese. There 10th Company, HG Assault Gun Battalion formed the basis of the new 1st Company, HG Parachute Tank-Destroyer Battalion. The company was issued 16 Panzerjäger IV tank destroyers and was placed under the corps' direct command in the role of a mobile fire-brigade. The company's first action was the reopening of the major Heydekrug-Memel crossroads.

In the following weeks the company carried out heavy attacks against the enemy. On Friday, 13 October, it launched an attack toward Pleine-Plakischken together with the HG Assault Battalion. The attack gained seven kilometers of ground before bogging down. At 1300 hours Fw. Kanert's tank destroyer was knocked out by a Latvian anti-tank gun from a range of 200 meters. Loader Vogeler and Kanert himself were slightly wounded. During the Russian attempt to break through to Gumbinnen the Jagdpanzer IVs, which had meanwhile been transferred to Gumbinnen and Groß-Waltersdorf, were deployed around Groß-Waltersdorf and Brückenthal to defend the towns against Russian infantry and tanks. These positions were held until 20 October.

On 20 and 21 October the company was once again called upon to defend against a Soviet armored attack, this time near Luschen and Groß-Trakehnen. "Spieß" Eckert destroyed five T 34s in the course of this action. On 22 October the Russians fired on Rodebach with a few salvoes from several captured German rocket launchers. Houses blew up, the whole village was set on fire. Afterward the Soviets attacked with tanks. Lt. Sebold's vehicle was knocked out by a T 34 in the fighting. No less than nine waves of Russian infantry charged the tank destroyers' positions; all were beaten back. Two T 34s were destroyed and with the help of two self-propelled guns the danger was averted.

Trakehnen was lost on 24 October. Two days later Russian tank attacks against Hochfließ and the flank of the defending 5th Panzer Division were repulsed. Three tanks, three anti-tank guns and two light artillery pieces were destroyed. Relative calm reigned until the end of December. The company was withdrawn from the front on 28 October. It then occupied blocking positions near Plicken, after which it built and occupied further blocking positions in front of Gumbinnen. There the company was visited by battalion commander *Rittmeister* Nichelski and his adjutant, Lt. Lindau. *Stabsarzt* Graf von Keyserling also visited the exposed company to check on the health of its personnel. The situation was to remain relatively quiet until the beginning of the Soviet offensive on 12 January 1945.

The entire Hermann Göring Parachute-Panzer Corps was stationed in the area southeast of Gumbinnen from November 1944 until 12 January 1945. A number of units were temporarily placed under the corps' command: the

Großdeutschland Panzer-Grenadier Division, the 21st and 61st Infantry Divisions, and the 349th and 549th Volksgrenadier Divisions, this in addition to the corps units and two divisions. Fighting was limited to local battles for individual positions. The Red Army had also been weakened by the battles in East Prussia. It had pulled back its shock armies to rest and bring them back up to strength for the next major assault.

The Fourth Army, to which the HG Corps was attached, likewise reorganized its forces in anticipation of a new Soviet attack. The 1st HG Parachute-Panzer Division was pulled out of the front as the corps' operational reserve. In mid-January, on orders from the OKH, the division was taken from the HG Corps and, following the assignment of I Battalion, HG Parachute Flak Regiment and a proportionate number of corps supply units, was moved to Radom. The German defenders were waiting for the Russian offensive which, following the Soviet breakout from their two bridgeheads on and beyond the Vistula, was to lead directly to the Reich capital.

1st Company, HG Panzer Regiment from October to December 1944

The completion of training on the new Panzer V, or Panther, which 1st Company received on 10 October 1944, placed an extremely potent weapon in the hands of *Oberleutnant* Kraus. On 19 October the company detrained in East Prussia and drove straight from the loading ramps to carry out an armored thrust against enemy troop concentrations north of Kassuben. This first action served as a demonstration of the new tank's outstanding maneuverability and firepower. During a night combat that evening the company smashed the enemy forces in the village of Kassuben and the next morning drove them back. Following several engagements in a defensive role, during the night of 22 October the company once again hammered an enemy armored force, this time near Rohdap. By 22 October only seven of the fourteen new Panthers were still in action near Trakehnen. By now I Battalion, HG Parachute-Panzer Regiment had destroyed approximately 100 enemy tanks. Of these 40 were credited to the Kraus company's account. *Oberleutnant* Kraus was subsequently awarded the Knight's Cross. On 24 October *Hauptmann* Renz was killed in action near Golzfelde, north of Trakehnen.

On 2 November *Major* Rossmann was mentioned in the Wehrmacht communiqué. He commanded the HG Parachute-Panzer Regiment and was always to be found where the fighting was heaviest, leading his panzers from the front and ready to exploit any opportunity presented him in the course of the battle.

The period from 27 October to 5 November was used by the Germans to construct bunkers and positions. On 12 December, 1st Company took up positions in several empty farms in Bismarckhöhe. Hptm. Kraus assumed command of the battalion there, while Lt. Weidling became commander of 1st Company. From the Bismarck Tower, located just behind the main line of resistance not far from Gumbinnen, the defenders had an excellent view of the East Prussian countryside to the Russian lines and beyond. The farms had been abandoned by the owners when the Soviet advance neared Gumbinnen.

The last Christmas of the war was celebrated in beautiful winter weather on 24 December 1944. The enemy undertook no hostile acts that evening. Even during the next few days there wasn't so much as harassing fire on the rear positions. A military welfare film truck brought the film "We're Making Music". In his description of this sector, Hans-Joachim Grau wrote:

"When we stepped out into the open air at midnight to wish each other a happy new year, flares suddenly climbed into the night along the not too distant front. The number grew, all the colors mixing together. Then we saw strings of pearls from the machine-guns and the 37mm flak joined in. It was now 1945, and in the days that followed reports of an imminent attack became more frequent. The expected date of the attack was between the 10th and 15th of January. An alert was sounded during the night of 11 January 1945. We loaded the tanks, but all remained quiet and after two hours the alert was cancelled. There was another alert the next night, which also turned out to be a false alarm. However, towards morning, at about 0200, the Red Army's new offensive began with a mighty barrage. The entire front seemed to be in motion. The sky was a blood-red color, and farms burned in the battle zone.

Finally the order came: "Panzers forward!" We left the small village in a long column. On the way we learned that we were to attack the following morning. We had to hold on to Insterburg, the most important traffic junction, and we were supposed to help repulse a Russian advance aimed at the city. Driving single file, with about 50 meters between tanks, we advanced toward the front. As the last vehicle in 3rd Platoon we brought up the rear. Our tank bore the number 133. Driving in front of us was Fw. Pius in tank 132 and in front of him was Ofw. Fritz Ruppert, our platoon leader, whose tank bore the number 131. Behind us followed the train vehicles.

We could hear nothing but the rattling of tracks and the droning of the motors. Radio communications had been forbidden. While under way we were attacked by 'highway crows', the Russian night bombers; apparently they had spotted the bright exhaust flames from our Panthers; but apart from an order to increase the interval between tanks nothing happened. A halt was ordered just short of Insterburg. There we learned that we were to be put aboard a train, even though we could clearly hear the thunder of guns from the front. We took shelter in a wooded area to one side of the road; the flatcars onto which we were to load our tanks had not yet arrived. The heavy snow had resulted in telltale tracks on the road and these had to be gotten rid of. It began to snow again. The icy east wind blew fat flakes before it, but luckily we were unaware of it in the forest. Fires were started in the small iron stoves which most of the tank crews had.

Not until evening did we entrain. We rolled through the city, which was empty of people, to Insterburg Station and there drove up a head-ramp onto the special cars. After being shunted several times the train pulled out at midnight. When I opened the hatch cover at dawn – we had to remain in the tanks, because no passenger cars were available – I saw the Elbing road sign glide past. Soon afterward we recognized the Marienburg. After frequent stops we crossed the Vistula near Dirschau. From then on our journey took us south through Graudenz and Bromberg to Posen. We later learned that we were one of the last transports to get out of East Prussia, which by now was almost completely cut off.

We reached the village of Ostrowo on 21 January 1945. Our eleven Panthers drove down the ramps and soon sat on the delivery roadway. There we learned of the Red Army's breakthrough along the entire line. There appeared to be nothing left of a solid front. Together with other units, we were given orders to advance through Kalisch and Sieradz to Litzmannstadt to keep open the Saucken Corps' avenue of retreat to the west. Beyond there was a wandering pocket, which was commanded by General Nehring. That was the only information available to us.

We rolled through Ostrowo in the direction of Kalisch but soon halted and went into position, as Russian tanks were said to be already in Kalisch. Not until the early afternoon of the following day did we resume our advance in a northeasterly direction. The objective was Kalisch. Ahead of us gunfire. We reached the outskirts of Kalisch as darkness was falling. The city was on fire in several places. We made our first contact with the enemy. An order to 'attack the bridge over the Prosna' led to a duel with T 34s, which we destroyed without loss to ourselves. The Russians had pulled back hours before and the tanks were obviously the rearguard.

After a bitterly-cold night we mounted up again in brilliant winter weather, rolled across the Prosna past the T 34s and T 43s destroyed the day before, and drove east toward Sieradz. Behind, beside and in front of us were numerous other Wehrmacht elements; grenadiers, anti-tank guns, self-propelled anti-aircraft guns and artillery, some from our division others from the Army. At Pionice the Prosna bridge had to be stormed once again; near Kalmen an enemy attack was repulsed. From then on the refugee columns we encountered were mixed with wounded and soldiers separated from their units heading toward the rear, often without weapons. We also met battered vehicles and the remains of units.

Contact with General Nehring's wandering pocket seemed to have been achieved and we were now in its midst. As darkness was falling we carried out an attack on Levkow. Once again we were able to destroy a number of T 34s and T 43s without loss. From then on we withdrew back through the corridor. This time 3rd Platoon drove point, with Ofw. Ruppert in the lead, then us and Pius Werner in tank 132. When the vague outlines of buildings appeared before us and we spotted a road which opened into our avenue, we all knew we had arrived. Then there was crash from ahead and to the left. There was a spurt of bluish flame as a shell struck Ofw. Ruppert's tank. We halted and fired three amour-piercing shells in the direction from which the shot had come and heard the sound of tracks moving away from us.

Oberfeldwebel Ruppert and Heinz Roßmann emerged from the knocked-out tank wounded and bleeding heavily. The three remaining members of the crew were unhurt. Ten infantrymen who had become separated from their unit came out of the building on the left. They were distributed on the rear deck of the nearest tank and looked after. The disabled Panther was blown up.

That morning, the 26th of January 1945, we took shelter in a farmhouse. The train and the field kitchen also found their way there, so that once again there was hot food. We refuelled our tanks, added to our stocks of ammunition and then set out to drive to Kobylin. We now faced the most difficult part of our mission: the breakout from the pocket. Armored cars and armored personnel carriers joined us at a crossroads just in front of Guhrau to lead the breakout wedge. Guhrau, that lovely Silesian city, was abandoned. We found quarters there. The tank commanders were summoned by the company commander. From him we learned that a Russian artillery regiment had installed itself not far ahead, in the village of Osten. In spite of this we had to capture a bridge or a fording place there if the breakout was to succeed.

'Attack begins at 2330 hours. We are to capture the village and the river crossing.' That morning officer cadets from an SS military school joined us. They were to come along as mounted infantry, clear the village of Osten of the enemy, and provide protection for us. An *Untersturmführer* and eight men rode on our tank. We rolled toward the village with throttled-back engines, driving in vee formation with a 30-meter lateral interval between tanks. The attack began half an hour past midnight with a salvo of high-explosive shells from all our tanks. Two more rapid salvoes were fired. Then we formed a line and turned onto the village road. On reaching the village the Waffen-SS men jumped off and cleared the houses of the enemy.

The Russians seemed completely surprised; in most cases only half-dressed, they ran to their parked vehicles or tried to move guns or machine-guns into position. There was a big concentration of vehicles parked in a large square in the center of the village. We fired several high-explosive shells into it. The vehicles caught fire and one exploded in flames. Our bow and turret machine-guns fired at the figures visible in the glare of the flames.

We saw an anti-tank gun being rolled into position off to the left and accelerated, rolling over the gun's trail. More trucks were burning, shot up by the other tanks. The Russians began to run. Driving down the sloping terrain toward the Bartsch, we reached the bridge, which was blocked by blown-up vehicles. Another tank joined us. A squad of Waffen-SS men followed and we formed a small hedgehog position. We learned by radio that there was still fighting going on in the village. At dawn we found the ford not far from the bridge. Tracks indicated that the Russians had taken this route.

The Russian 1525th Army Artillery Regiment had met its end in Osten. It took all day to channel all the units and tanks through the ford. It was already dark when the last, a row of armored personnel carriers with grenadiers, appeared. Only then did our panzers roll through as the last to cross. The next day saw the continuation of the march toward the west, to the Oder. Enemy-occupied Lübchen had to be taken by storm. Lt. Weidling, commander of 1st Company, was killed there. We also brought back the bodies of several other old comrades. We were supposed to reach the Oder that day. It was said that breaking through to our own lines from there would be child's play. On the other side were units of the *Großdeutschland* Division.

Leutnant Schmalohr had taken command of the six remaining Panthers. Soon afterward we came under fire. Pius' tank was hit. He returned fire and backed up a few meters. The tank had been hit twice, but luckily neither penetrated. We loaded an amour-piercing round and drove forward cautiously. Even before we reached the spot where Pius' tank had been sitting earlier, I saw a flash and immediately afterward felt a jolt as we were hit. But nothing happened. Then we, too, pulled back some distance. Meanwhile an armored personnel carrier with grenadiers arrived. The grenadiers got out and worked their way forward to the edge of the forest to the left and right of the road. When they returned the *Feldwebel* in charge reported that there was a Stalin tank 150 meters beyond the curve, against which we could do little from in front. Soon afterward the enemy tank withdrew.

The battalion's remaining tanks also arrived. In one of them was the former CO of 1st Company, now the battalion commander, *Hauptmann* Kraus.

We passed through a wood, driving through the undergrowth with our guns in the six o'clock position (pointing toward the rear). When we left the wood I had to drive on a certain distance in order to be able to traverse the turret with its long gun barrel to the front. I was just about to instruct the driver to back up again, when, standing in the turret, I saw a flash to the right in front of us. A fraction of a second later there was a crash as the shell struck the right side of our tank. A flash of flame struck me in the face. I screamed: "Get out!" But I could not get free. The rim of the shell casing bag had bent and was pinning my leg. The tank stank of smoke. Inside our gunner Jacob screamed; he was suffocating. The smoke that was choking us was from our own smoke candles. With a desperate jerk I got my leg free. I let myself roll onto the rear of the tank and then jumped off. Behind me came Jacob, gasping and coughing; the loader, Gerd Pfaffner, was shot in the buttocks while bailing out of the tank. The driver and radio operator escaped unhurt.

We lay on our bellies and stuck our burnt faces into the icy snow. Our tank was ablaze and all around us all hell was loose. The Ivans were firing everything they had. "Crawl away from here!" I ordered, for our ammunition might go up at any moment. None of us will ever forget that 30 January 1945. I ran to the command tank and reported to Hptm. Kraus. Another of our tanks was also in flames. We ran back in the direction from which the grenadiers were advancing. A Major with a knotty stick and pistol urged his men on: "Forward! Or shall the Ivans reach Berlin?"

Soon afterward we reached the forward dressing station. There we received medical attention and subsequently were taken to the other side of the Oder by ambulance along with other wounded. We were driven to Glogau and from there to the command hospital in Halle, from where I soon made my way back to the company. With this last action near Köben the wandering pocket had reestablished contact with our own troops. Of our eleven Panthers only two reached the other bank of the Oder."

In Königsbrück 1st Company, HG Parachute-Panzer Regiment was issued ten new Panther tanks and received replacement personnel. In mid-March it was transported by rail to Ottmachau and then took part in the defensive battle on the Neisse River.

"Our CO at that time, *Leutnant* Stedtfeld, was wounded there. He was replaced by *Oberleutnant* Sieger. On 10 April we were stationed near Schweidnitz and thus were among the units were supposed to relieve Breslau. But things turned out differently! After being transported by rail from Schweidnitz, in mid-April we rolled down the ramp at Görlitz and after a several-kilometer drive took up position in the village of Markersdorf. Two days later we moved to the front. Oblt. Sieger was killed. He was brought back and buried in Markersdorf cemetery.

The tanks of 1st Company which were still serviceable fought on in the Dresden area and near Bautzen, until finally the last tank was blown up during the night of 9 May 1945."

1st Company, 4th HG Parachute-Panzer-Grenadier Regiment in Action

In early November 1944 the 1st Company of the 4th HG Parachute- Panzer-Grenadier Regiment was located outside Großwaltersdorf. The company belonged to the regiment's I Battalion, which was commanded by *Hauptmann* Stahel. The regimental commander at that time was *Major* Stauch. After the conclusion of the frontier battles in East Prussia in late October the front in the Gumbinnen-Goldap area stabilized. Wehrmacht communiques reported "limited patrol activity". What this meant to the individual grenadier was described by Arnold Knüfermann.

"At the beginning of November my company and I were located outside Großwaltersdorf, which was in Russian hands. In the middle of the village stood a tall chimney which was visible from far and wide. From there a Soviet artillery observer observed the countryside deep into our division area.

One morning, before it became light, an eighty-eight went into position nearby, targeted the chimney, and brought it down with a single shot. Then it disappeared again before the Russians could make out its position. At the end of November the only Russian movements were a few patrols, all of which were repulsed; it was at that point that our parachute corps' assault battalion arrived. It was to carry out an offensive patrol and bring back prisoners, interrogation of whom was supposed to provide information as to enemy troop strengths and the Russian units facing us. The heavily-armed patrol moved out after a brief, intense preparatory barrage. In the midst of their own 'fireworks display' the comrades blasted a path through the mines and pressed forward to a bunker, which was likewise blown up. The patrol returned without a single prisoner, however. The bunker crew had been blown up with the bunker.

Two members of our company, *Unteroffizier* Schlögel and *Gefreiter* Bißwanger, were now given the job of bringing in a prisoner. The pair first observed how the Soviets conducted their patrols, then they tailed a suitable patrol and jumped the Russian walking at the end of the squad column. The Russian fought desperately and was killed in a pistol duel. Uffz. Schlögel died with him.

At the beginning of December the HG Parachute-Panzer Division was pulled out of the neighboring sector; as part of this reorganization our battalion also moved to new positions near Grünthal. The battalion established its command post in Hochfließ. The battalion's border on the left was the road to Grünthal. Patrols were regularly sent out from there. The objective of all our efforts was the bringing in of prisoners. Before Uffz. Gröbe's patrol departed, Gröbe made himself as familiar as possible with the terrain. The patrol took advantage of the noise from an artillery barrage to blast a lane through the mines. In this way it was able to penetrate a Russian trench unobserved. The enemy troops in the trench were overpowered. Once again none of the Russians survived, as a result of which Gröbe decided to advance further along the trench. At the same time, however, a Russian counterattack began, and Gröbe and his men were forced to withdraw after a brief exchange of gunfire.

Gröbe went into position in front of the mine field with his machine-gun and covered the retreat of his comrades, who were being pursued by the Russians. In doing so he was fatally wounded. Gröbe's body lay in no-man's-land. It was impossible to recover him and he lay there in the ice and snow and was soon covered by a snowdrift. A few days later a Russian patrol advanced through the same lane through the mines, which hadn't been mined again, and broke into our trench. An officer cadet and *Gefreiter* Bertram led an immediate counterattack which put the Russians to flight. Bertram sustained severe wounds. A badly-wounded Russian was brought back, but he died soon afterward, before he could be questioned. The Russian patrol activity ceased. A little later *Unteroffizier* Probst and *Gefreiter* Fleischer undertook a patrol operation at another location. At a salient in the front the pair had discovered a lane through the Russian mine field which was used by the enemy patrols.

One night at 0200 hours these two went through the lane by moonlight into the enemy trench, dragged a Russian from the sentry post there and brought him back. The prisoner turned out to be a Siberian, however, and was days before an interpreter could be found. It turned out that the man knew little about anything beyond his regiment and his company commander. *Unteroffizier* Heinz Probst was a rock amid the waves in that place. He went on more than a dozen patrols, intercepted Russian patrols, and also proved adept at defending against Russian armored attacks. He took them on with the Panzerfaust and Ofenrohr (bazooka) and destroyed seven enemy tanks. On 26 March 1945 he received the Knight's Cross. Formed from detachments from the 1st HG Parachute-Panzer-Grenadier Regiment in October 1944, the battalion had proved itself well in these battles. A large number of veteran soldiers formed the core of the battalion and the young volunteers sought to emulate their experienced comrades. The new regiment's armament was uniformly good. The grenadier companies were equipped with light and heavy infantry weapons. Submachine-guns and light machine-guns, Panzerfaust and Ofenrohr anti-tank weapons, and two additional heavy machine-guns for each company made up the basic equipment.

Each company included nine snipers. 1st Company's best marksman was *Gefreiter* Meyer, who raised his kill total to 180 confirmed. Meyer, a hunter by profession, was known for his uncanny accuracy. Some of his duels with Russian snipers lasted more than a day, until one of the two left himself open, resulting in his death. This contest of tricks and cunning was also a part of trench warfare on the Eastern Front. In addition to heavy mortars, the battalion's heavy company had an infantry gun platoon and a platoon of 20mm cannon on ground mounts. There was also a pioneer platoon. As they celebrated Christmas, each man knew that it would soon start up again and that Russian units would once again rage against their positions. On Christmas Eve Heinz Probst, who had meanwhile been promoted to *Feldwebel*, received extra presents as special recognition. Those that were edible were shared with his comrades."

X. THE HERMANN GÖRING PARACHUTE-PANZER REPLACEMENT AND TRAINING BRIGADE
(September1944 until March 1945)

Formation Sites – Formation and Mission

The following account of the formation and history of the HG Parachute-Panzer Replacement and Training Brigade was provided by retired *Major* Wolfgang Bach, former commander of the unit's II Battalion.

"With the expansion of the HG Parachute-Panzer Division to corps size on 24 September 1944, orders were simultaneously issued for the formation of a Hermann Göring Parachute-Panzer Replacement and Training Brigade. It is quite probable (there is no precise information to this effect) that the regimental headquarters of the Parachute-Panzer Replacement and Training Regiment in Utrecht, Holland initiated the first organizational measures.

Rippin (Rypin), West Prussia was selected as the brigade's base at the end of September. Rippin was part of a troop training camp which was under the command of an headquarters stationed in Strasburg, West Prussia. The personnel for the units to be formed in Rippin and the surrounding area came in most part from the HG Parachute-Panzer Replacement and Training Regiment stationed in Holland (Utrecht, Hilversum, Bussum, etc.). The brigade's commanding officer was *Oberst* (from 26 Aug. 1944 *Generalmajor*) Fritz Fullriede.

Another unit which detached personnel to the new brigade was the HG Parachute-Panzer Field Replacement and Training Battalion under *Major* Ilius, based in Wolanow, near Warsaw. This battalion was also entrusted with the formation of the brigade in West Prussia. This newly-created major unit of the HG Parachute-Panzer Corps was subordinate to the Commanding General in Charge of Training and Replacement Units of the Parachute Army, *General der Fallschirmtruppen* Conrath, while organizationally it belonged to *Luftgaukommando* III.

The OKL (General Staff HQ 2, Dept. II D) included the new brigade in its budget on 25 January 1945 and thereby laid the foundations for a unit which, in terms of organization and strength, differed considerably from the units already in combat."

Personnel:

"The Hermann Göring Parachute-Panzer Field Replacement and Training Battalion (*Major* Ilius), consisting of battalion headquarters and four training companies; sent from the Wolanow area to West Prussia in September 1944, it represented the first 'rib' of the new brigade. The personnel sent to the brigade in the following weeks and months represented a cross-section of every level of training and ability, determined of course by the front-line experience of the individuals. The soldiers had one thing in common: they had all volunteered to serve in the divisions of the Reichsmarschall. To better illustrate their origins, they may be divided into three groups:

I. Instructors with front-line experience, some disabled: Officers, NCOs and men.

II. Instructors without front-line experience: Officers, NCOs and men.

III. Recruits: Regular volunteers, volunteers for the 12-year period of service and officer cadets, some with limited pre-military training in the Reich Labor Service (RAD), flak units in Germany and pre-military training camps of various organizations.

"Members ranged from 16-year-old volunteers to veterans of the First World War. Younger men between the ages of 16 and 24, those born between 1920 and 1928, predominated. With the exception of disabled front-line soldiers of all ranks, the men of the new unit were suitable for any type of wartime service and were athletically trained and capable. The bulk of the soldiers were transferred to Rippin with their units, though some were sent individually. This applied to officers in particular. The arrival point was the Rippin railway station, where the Brigade HQ, Dept. II a/b and a message center were set up. The new arrivals were subsequently sent either to the 1st Regiment in Rippin (Camp A) or to the 2nd Regiment in Reselerwalde (Skrwilno). The following formations arrived there – as complete units but with greatly varying strengths – from October 1944 until January 1945:

I Battalion, HG Parachute-Panzer Replacement and Training Regiment (Oblt. Kranenburg), with HQ and two companies, from Utrecht.

– elements of the HG Parachute Flak Replacement and Training Battalion.
– elements of the HG Parachute Artillery Replacement and Training Battalion.
– elements of the 21st Luftwaffe Field Division.
– elements of 25th Airbase Garrison Headquarters/VIII (Silesia).
– 10622nd Special Purpose Heavy Flak Battery.
– elements of the 5th Luftwaffe Special Purpose Light Infantry Battalion.
– elements of the 608th Grenadier Security Regiment.
– elements of the HG Special Purpose Grenadier Battalion (Hptm. Mack).
– elements of the 16th Heavy Machine-gun Company (Hptm. Kurth).
– a platoon of paratroops, who had been forced to cease training as Rammjäger (close-range anti-bomber pilots) on 16 Dec. 1944).
– other small units, whose designations have become lost. (See also: Otte, Alfred: *Die Ausbildungstruppenteile HG*)."

Quarters:

"The HG Brigade had been assigned the Rippin Troop Training Camp as its quartering area. The extent of the area occupied by the brigade units was approximately 700 square kilometers; the area's dimensions were 35 kilometers east-west and 20 kilometers north-south. The country town of Rippin formed the approximate center- point of this area in the Dobriner Region. It was there that the brigade headquarters had taken up quarters. There were two barracks camps at the eastern outskirts of Rippin, Camps A and B. Both featured standard training camp accommodations with washrooms, heating, kitchens and so on.

Capacity of the two camps was estimated at 2,500-3,000 men. A Camp C was under construction but was never used to house troops. On account of their proximity to Rippin Station, both camps served as reception points for all new arrivals. These quarters were therefore periodically overfilled for one or two days. The question of living quarters was completely different in the villages and farms. Since there were no large schools, inns, apartment houses, etc. available, the brigade had to resort to using barns, storage buildings, granaries, cow sheds and the like. The new brigade's mission was: the training of recruits and converts of all ranks to provide qualified replacements for the grenadier, pioneer, flak and artillery units of the HG Parachute- Panzer Corps. There was also a requirement to train small numbers of personnel for specialized roles, snipers and tank-killing squads, for example.

In October the corps ordered preparations to be made to detach small groups to one of the parachute schools for jump training. As far as is known, nothing was done. In general a period of six weeks was allocated for the basic training."

All that remains to be covered is the brigade's organization and command structure. For this we once again turn to retired *Major* Bach, whose assistance in preparing this history of the brigade is much appreciated. His research activity over a long period of time is an expression of his comradely ties to his unit and to the men who were his comrades and superiors in the difficult war years. Jasper's words are applicable to such men:

"He who was a true comrade, unwavering in danger, proven through courage and objectivity, may preserve something impalpable in his world consciousness."

Organization of the Brigade

1. Schematic Overview:

The formation of the HG Parachute-Panzer Replacement and Training Brigade at the beginning of November 1944 was based for the following unit organization:

Brigade Headquarters

Command staff and Headquarters Departments

Brigade Headquarters Company Brigade Signals Company

Brigade First-aid Company Brigade Infantry Gun Company

Training and Conversion Battalion

1st HG Parachute-Panzer Replacement and Training Regiment HQ

Headquarters Company

　　　　1st Supply Company
　　　　I-III Battalions, 1st HG Parachute-Panzer Replacement and Training Regiment
　　　　HG Parachute-Panzer Pioneer Replacement and Training Unit
2nd HG Parachute-Panzer Replacement & Training Regiment HQ
　　　　Headquarters Company
　　　　2nd Supply Company
　　　　I (mixed) Battalion, Parachute Flak Replacement and Training Unit
　　　　II Battalion, HG Parachute Artillery Replacement and Training Unit

2. Brigade Headquarters
　　　　Operations Staff and Headquarters Departments
　　　　Headquarters savings bank and other buildings in Rippin and surrounding area
　　　　Military Post Office Number L 54 708 A

Headquarters Personnel
　　　　Brigade Commander Oberst Meyer (Change of commanders: on 10 Nov. 1944 Major Ilius, who had taken ill, was replaced by the former CO of the HG Parachute Flak Regiment, Oberst Meyer.)
　　　　Brigade Adjutant
　　　　Headquarters Company Chief , Legal Officer – Leutnant Güldner
　　　　Graves Registration Officer

I a	position unoccupied until 25 Jan. 1945, afterward Major Rebholz
O 1	position unoccupied until 13 Feb. 1945, afterward Hptm. Bach
I b	Hauptmann Zummach
I c	Hauptmann König
O 3	Leutnant Mostert
Brig.-Int. u. Lt.d.Abt. IVa	St.Int. Standke
IV b	Stabsarzt Dr. Renken
II a/b	Stabsarzt Dr. Hermann
Brigade Signals Officer	Oberleutnant Blumenhagen
NSFO	Oberst Lux, Oblt. Marzian

3. The Brigade Units
　　　　Brigade Headquarters Company Formation Holland (?)
　　　　Military Post Office Number – L 54 708 A
　　　　Quarters – Piekielko Farm (about 1 km west of Rippin)
Personnel:

Company Chief,	Lt. Güldner, Lt. Seek (?)
Brigade Guard Platoon,	Fähnrich Kaufmann, Ofw. Erke

Trials Echelon,	Fw. Witt
Motor Pool Readiness,	Ofw. Sandmann
Riding Stable,	Stfw. Zaradnitschek
Senior NCO,	Hfw. Wengenmayr

Brigade Signals Company:

The parent unit, the 1st reinforced Telephone Company (mot.) with construction platoon etc., was supposed to be enlarged to a signals battalion. Oblt. Blumenhagen, brigade signals leader, was made responsible for the formation of the Brigade Signals Battalion. No reliable information is available concerning the operational use and fate of the unit.

Brigade First-aid Unit (Company)

Commander,	Stabsarzt Dr. Renken
Adjutant,	Stabsarzt Dr. Hermann
Dentist,	Stabsarzt Dr. Thierfelder
1st Regiment Medical Officer,	Oberarzt Dr. Thomas
2nd Regiment Medical Officer,	Stabsarzt Dr. Lutterbeck

More detailed information on the first-aid unit, which was very well-equipped in personnel and equipment, is not available.

Brigade Infantry Gun Company (IGK)

Formation November 1944

Field Post Office Number – L 54 708 (15)

Quarters: Camp B in Rippin

Command Personnel:

Company Commander	Lt. Drews (?)
	Oblt. Zillmann
1st (hvy. inf. gun) Platoon Leader and Deputy Company Commander	Fw. Speidel
2nd (lt. inf. gun) Platoon Leader	?
Senior NCO,	Hfw. Noack

Personnel:

Recruits (age class 1928), NCOs and men with and without infantry gun training, Wehrmacht officials (conversion training).

Weapons:

2 heavy infantry guns, 33 (150mm), 4 light infantry guns (75mm).

HG Training and Conversion Battalion (the title Brigade Instruction and Conversion Battalion also existed)

Formation: November 1944

Military Post Office Number –   ?

Quarters: Camp A (Rippin)

Command Personnel:
  Commander, Hauptmann Friebe
  Adjutant, Leutnant Thamm
  O 1 Oblt. Feuerherdt
Officer Candidate Course (from 15 Jan. 1945: 1./A.-u.U.-Btl. HG)
  Military Post Office Number – L 54 708 F
  Quarters: Camp A (Rippin)
Command Personnel:
  Course Director/Company Commander, Oblt. Krauß
  1st Platoon Leader, Lt. Pfaff
  2nd Platoon Leader, Senior NCO
Instructional Personnel: Instructors with front-line experience.
  Personnel Replacements, OA age classes 1927 and 1928
NCO Candidate Course (from 15 Jan. 1945: 2./A.-u.U.-Btl. HG)
  Military Post Office Number – ?
  Quarters: Camp A (Rippin)
Command Personnel:
  Course-Director/Company Commander, Lt. Giesemann
  1st Platoon Leader, Lt. Krüger
  2nd Platoon Leader, Senior NCO
Instructional Personnel: Instructors with front-line experience
Personnel Replacements: Experienced front-line soldiers, detached from corps Conversion Course (from 15 Jan. 1945: 3./A.-u.U.-Btl. HG)
  Military Post Office Number – ?
  Quarters: Camp A (Rippin)
Command Personnel:
  Course Director/Company Commander, Lt. Freytag
  1st Platoon Leader, Fw. Lichtwark
  2nd Platoon Leader, Senior NCO
Instructional Personnel: Instructors with front-line experience
Personnel Replacements: NCOs and men from ground units and flying personnel, most with front-line experience.
Other:
Under this general designation fall all the detachments which were placed under the command of the Brigade HQ for long or short periods, but which did not participate in the defensive fighting in West Prussia.

4. 1st HG Parachute-Panzer Replacement and Training Regiment Head-quarters

  Formation, November 1944

Military Post Office Number – L 54 708 B
Quarters: Camp A (Rippin)

Command Personnel:
Regimental Commander (acting) Hauptmann Findeis
Adjutant, Oblt. Kutscher
O 1 Lt. Weiß, Lt. Munderloh
IV a ?
IV b Oberarzt Dr. Thomas
1st Trials Company, Hauptmann Ernst
HQ Platoon, Senior NCO

Units: I-III Battalions and Pioneer Battalion
Training regiment for panzer-grenadiers and Luftwaffe pioneers.

I Battalion, 1st HG Parachute-Panzer Replacement and Training Regiment Headquarters
Formation, November 1944
Military Post Office Number – L 54 708 C
Quarters: Zeising (Czyzewo)

Command Personnel:
Commander, Hauptmann Fuchs, from 15 Jan. 1945 Hptm. Vollmer
Adjutant, Oblt. Erb
O 1 Lt. Mölter
IV a HQ Platoon Senior NCO

Units: 1st-4th Companies

1st Company, 1st HG Parachute-Panzer Replacement and Training Regiment Formation November 1944
Military Post Office Number – L 54 708 C (1)
Quarters: Burgsee (Ugozcz)

Command Personnel:
Company Commander, Oblt. May, Lt. Brodhäcker
1st - 4th Platoon Leaders: Fw. Jacquay, Ofw. Wassermann, Stfw. Kurth, Uffz. Werner
Senior NCO, Schenk

Personnel Replacements recruits from age class 1927 and one platoon of paratroops forced to break off their training as Rammjäger on the Me 262 B-1 at the start of the Ardennes offensive.

2nd Company, 1st HG Parachute-Panzer Replacement and Training Regiment
Formation Military Post Office Number – L 54 708 C (2)
Quarters: Dalgenfeld (Dlugie)

Command Personnel:
	Company Commander,	Oblt. Hahn
	2nd Platoon Leader,	Lt. Weiss (07)

Senior NCO Cadre Personnel from HG Replacement and Training Regiment in Holland, Home HQ Berlin-Reinickendorf, from hospitals.
	Personnel Replacements recruits age class 1927

3rd Company, 1st HG Parachute-Panzer Replacement and Training Regiment
	Formation:	?
	Military Post Office Number – L 54 708 C (3)
	Quarters:	Gulbini

Command Personnel:
	Company Commander,	Lt. Selzer
	1st - 4th Platoon Leaders,	Senior NCO

4th Company, 1st HG Parachute-Panzer Replacement and Training Regiment
	Formation	?
	Military Post Office Number – L 54 708 C (4)
	Quarters:	Bören (Borzymin)

Command Personnel:
	Company Commander,	Oblt. Arnheiter
	1st Platoon Leader,	Fw. Diel
	Senior NCO,	Ofw. Franke

II Battalion, 1st HG Parachute-Panzer Replacement and Training Regiment Headquarters
	Formation:	Oct. 1944 (Holland), Nov. 1944 (Rippin)
	Military Post Office Number – L 61 957 A
	Quarters:	Camp A in Rippin

Command Personnel:
	Commanding Officer,	Hauptmann Bach
	Adjutant,	Leutnant Nüsse
	O 1,	Leutnant Dr. Hüfner
	IV a,	Oberzahlmeister Decius
	HQ Platoon
	W and S Platoon	Senior NCO

Units: 5th-8th Companies:
	5th Company, 1st HG Parachute-Panzer Replacement and Training Regiment
	Formation,	?

Military Post Office Number – L 61 957 B
Quarters: Camp A (Rippin)

Command Personnel:
Company Commander, Lt. Schneider
1st - 4th Platoon Leaders, Senior NCO, Hfw. Baum

Among others, 5th Company trained snipers, therefore the title "Sniper Company".

6th Company, 1st HG Parachute-Panzer Replacement and Training Regiment

Formation: Aug. 1944 in Wolanow and Oct. 1944 in Rippin
Military Post Office Number – L 61 957 C
Quarters: Camp A (Rippin)

Command Personnel:
Company Commander, Leutnant Ellwanger
1st Platoon Leader and
Deputy Company Commander, Leutnant Kunkel
2nd Platoon Leader, Leutnant Friedel (?)
3rd Platoon Leader, Stabsfw. Ladewig
4th Platoon Leader, Ofw. Schäfer, Lt. Krämer
5th Platoon Leader, Ofw. Kaufmann
Senior NCO, Hfw. Vothknecht

Cadre Personnel predominantly instructors with front-line experience Personnel Replacements. 1st, 2nd and 3rd Platoons recruits, 4th and 5th Platoons OA recruits.

7th Company, 1st HG Parachute-Panzer Replacement and Training Regiment

Formation: Sept. 1944 in Holland (Bussum and Hilversum)
Military Post Office Number – L 61 957 E
Quarters: Sedlau (Sadlowo), approx. 7 km northwest of Rippin

Command Personnel:
Company Commander, Leutnant Alf
1st Platoon Leader, Ofw. Löfgen
2nd Platoon Leader, Ofw. Rölleke
3rd Platoon Leader, Ofw. Neu
4th Platoon Leader, Fw. Schellitzki
5th Platoon Leader, Fw. Kentrup
Senior NCO, Hfw. Jungbluth

Cadre Personnel approx. 35 instructors with front-line experience
Personnel Replacements recruits (age classes 1927 and 1928), following

conclusion of training in mid-December 1944 transferred to corps in East Prussia.

8th Company, 1st HG Parachute-Panzer Replacement and Training Regiment

    Formation: Oct. 1944 in Holland Nov. 1944 in Rippin

    Military Post Office Number – L 61 957 D

    Quarters: Sasse (Zasady) approx. 12 km northwest of Rippin

Command Personnel:

Company Commander,	Oblt. Stürchen
1st - 4th Platoon Leaders,	Fw. Lensing, Fw. Richter, Fw. Fussen, Fw. Breidenbach,
Senior NCO,	Hfw. Niederweis

Cadre Personnel instructors with front-line experience.

Personnel Replacements recruits

III Battalion, 1st HG Parachute-Panzer Replacement and Training Regiment (Mack). Renamed "Mack Battalion" in December 1944

    Formation: November 1944 in Neumark an der Drewenz, West Prussia

    Military Post Office Number   ?

    Quarters: Neumark, Brattian, Radem (Radomno)

Command Personnel:

Commanding, Officer	Hauptmann Mack
Adjutant,	Oblt. Oetterer
O 1	Leutnant Hanweg
IV a	Zahlmeister Peppelreiter

Units: 9th Grenadier Company, Hptm. Mönkmeye, 10th Grenadier Company, Lt. Wolf

Swearing In 10 Dec. 1944 in Neumark Transfer. Transferred by rail to the HG Parachute-Panzer Corps in the Insterburg-Gumbinnen area (East Prussia) in January 1945. After being wounded once again (destruction of his leg prosthesis) Hptm. Mack reported on crutches to "Home Headquarters" in Reinickendorf (Berlin). Nothing more is known of the fate of the Mack Battalion.

III Battalion, 1st HG Parachute-Panzer Replacement and Training Regiment (Drotbohm)

    Headquarters Formation: mid-December 1944

    Military Post Office Number – L 54 708 E

    Quarters: Camp B (Rippin)

Command Personnel:

Commanding Officer,	Hauptmann Osterloff
	Hauptmann Drotbohm

Adjutant,	Leutnant Bender
O 1	Leutnant Roth (?)
IV a	?
HQ Platoon	Senior NCO

Units: 9th-12th Companies Transfer of III Battalion ("Drotbohm Recruit Battalion") back to Germany for the formation of 2nd Parachute-Panzer Replacement and Training Brigade (Oberst Breuer)

17/18 Jan. 1945	Departure from Rippin
27-29 Jan. 1945	Assembly at HG message center Jeschkowo west of Graudenz
30 Jan. 1945	Transfer by rail to Velten near Berlin, later to Wittstock airbase on the Dosse River.

9th Company, 1st HG Parachute-Panzer Replacement and Training Regiment

Formation:	?
Military Post Office Number – L 54 708 E (9) or E (2)	
Quarters:	Camp B (Rippin)

Command Personnel:

Company Commander,	Oblt. Schulz
1st-4th Platoon Leaders	?
Senior NCO	?

Personnel Replacements recruits age classes 1927 and 1928, arrival Rippin 1 January 1945.

10th Company, 1st HG Parachute-Panzer Replacement and Training Regiment

Formation:	?
Military Post Office Number – L 54 708 E (10) or E (3)	
Quarters:	Camp B (Rippin)

Command Personnel:

Company Commander,	Oblt. Zillmann (?)
1st-4th Platoon Leaders,	Fw. Lang, Fw. Kentrup
Senior NCO	?

Personnel Replacements: Recruits (age classes 1927 and 1928) arrival Rippin Christmas Night 1944 and 1 January 1945.

11th Company, 1st HG Parachute-Panzer Replacement and Training Regiment

Formation	?
Military Post Office Number – L 54 708 E (11) or E (4)	
Quarters:	Camp B (Rippin)

Command Personnel:
    Company Commander,   Oblt. Fasshauer
    1st-4th Platoon Leaders,   Ofw. Neu (?)

Personnel Replacements: Recruits (age classes 1927 and 1928). Arrival Rippin early January 1945. Courses for heavy mortar squads: 80mm Gr.W. 34/42, 120mm Gr.W. 42 and 81mm Gr.W.(it.).

12th Company, 1st HG Parachute-Panzer Replacement and Training Regiment
    Formation   ?
    Military Post Office Number – L 54 708 E (12) or E (5)
    Quarters: Camp B (Rippin)

Command Personnel:
    Company Commander,   Hauptmann Schäfers
    1st-4th Platoon Leaders   ?
    Senior NCO   ?

Personnel Replacements: Recruits (age classes 1927 and 1928). Arrival January 1945.

HG Parachute-Panzer Pioneer Replacement and Training Battalion
    Headquarters
    Formation: October 1944 in Rippin
    Military Post Office Number – L 54 708 E (?)
    Quarters: Camp A (Rippin)

Command Personnel:
    Battalion Commander (acting)   Oblt. Breig
    Adjutant,   Lt. Scheibe
    O 1   ?
    IV a   ?
    HQ Platoon   ?
    Senior NCO   ?

Units: 1st-3rd Parachute-Panzer Pioneer Replacement and Training Companies. Training battalion for Luftwaffe combat engineers.

1st-3rd Parachute-Panzer Pioneer Replacement and Training Companies.
    Military Post Office Number – L 54 708 A, B, C
    Quarters: Farms and schools in the villages of Szafarnia, Plonne, Ratsfelde and Tomkowo (all west of Rippin).

Command Personnel:
    Company Commander,   Leutnant Fuest (Cologne),
                                        Leutnant Piplack
    Platoon Leader,   Fw. Baggele

Cadre Personnel: Instructors with combat experience
Personnel Replacements: Recruits (age class 1927)
Water Practice Site Drewenz, NW Gollub-Dobrzyn
Pioneer Equipment Inflatable boats, explosives and propellants, barricading devices, etc.

5. 2nd HG Parachute Artillery Replacement and Training Regiment

Headquarters
    Formation: Oct./Nov. 1944
    Military Post Office Number – L 54 708 E
    Quarters: Rippin Savings Bank, from Dec. 1944 the Reselerwalde Estate (Skrwilno)

Command Personnel:

Commanding Officer,	Major Beinhofer, Major Graf
Adjutant,	Oblt. Schütte
O 1	?
IV a	?
IV b ,	Stabsarzt Dr. Lutterbeck
2nd Supply Company,	Lt. Kausch
HQ Platoon	?
Senior NCO	?

Units: I (mixed) Battalion, HG Parachute-Flak Replacement and Training Unit, and II Battalion, HG Parachute-Artillery Replacement and Training Unit.

The 2nd Regiment has wrongly also been identified as a grenadier regiment, although it was an artillery unit from the time of its formation. The later use of both battalions in an infantry role is responsible for this error.

I (mixed) Battalion, HG Parachute-Flak Replacement and Training Unit
Headquarters:
    Formation: November 1944
    Military Post Office Number – L 54 708 E
    Quarters: Reselerwalde (Skrwilno)

Command Personnel:

Commanding Officer,	Hauptmann Francois
Adjutant,	Leutnant Ruschitzka
O 1	?
IV a	?
HQ Platoon	?
Senior NCO	?

Units: 2 heavy and 2 light flak batteries (88mm and 20mm) Training battalion for heavy and light flak batteries

1st (heavy) Battery, HG Parachute-Flak Replacement and Training Unit
- Formation: November 1944
- Military Post Office Number – L 54 708 G 1
- Quarters: Reselerwalde

Command Personnel:
- Battery Commander, Hauptmann Schrader
- Reconnaissance, Ranging and Battery Officers
- Senior NCO

Personnel Replacements: Recruits, convalescents.
- Armament: 4 - 88mm Flak 18/36/37

2nd (heavy) Battery, HG Parachute-Flak Replacement and Training Unit
- Military Post Office Number – L 54 708 G (2)
- Quarters: Reselerwalde

Command Personnel:
- Battery Commander, Leutnant Müller
- Reconnaissance, Ranging and Battery Officers
- Senior NCO, Hfw. Meiring
- Armament: 2 - 88mm Flak 18/36/37

4th (light) Battery, HG Parachute-Flak Replacement and Training Unit
- Formation: November 1944
- Military Post Office Number – L 54 708 G (4)
- Quarters: Reselerwalde

Command Personnel:
- Battery Commander, Hauptmann Vollmer, Hauptmann Weigert
- Reconnaissance Officer
- Platoon Leader, Leutnant Heydecke(r)
- Senior NCO, Hfw. Dückers
- Armament: 6 - 20mm Flak 36

5th (light) Battery, HG Parachute-Flak Replacement and Training Unit
- Military Post Office Number – L 54 708 G (5)
- Quarters: Reselerwalde

Command Personnel:
- Battery Commander, Hauptmann Odenwald (?)
- Reconnaissance Officer, Leutnant Müller (?)
- Platoon Leader, Owm. Schade
- Senior NCO
- Armament ?

The 4th and 5th Batteries were training batteries for light flak. It seems likely that the 5th Battery did not get beyond the formation planning stage.

II Battalion, HG Parachute-Artillery Replacement and Training Unit. There are no longer any doubts concerning the artillery unit's existence. Unfortunately, information concerning its organization, quarters, armament, etc, remains very sketchy. According to available information the artillery unit was formed in December 1944 in Okalewo and organised as follows: Headquarters

1 light battery with l.F.H. 18 light field howitzers (105mm) and,

1 heavy battery with s.F.H. 18 heavy field howitzers (150mm).

During the fighting withdrawal in January 1945 artillery combat teams were deployed in the brigade's sectors. One such team with two heavy field howitzers reached Graudenz in February 1945.

At veterans gatherings units are repeatedly mentioned which were allegedly based at Rippin and belonged to the brigade, but of which no trace can be found, such as:

13th Mortar Company

    Military Post Office Number – L 54 708 G

14th Grenadier Company

15th Grenadier Company (Leutnant Piplack (?))

    Military Post Office Number – L 54 708 E (3)

16th (heavy) Machine-gun Company (Hauptmann Kurth)

    Military Post Office Number – L 54 708 E

The results of research into these units have so far been unsatisfactory. The following version of events seems most likely:

The four companies – 13th, 14th, 15th and 16th – which consisted only of cadre personnel coming from Holland or Berlin, were split up in the course of new formations in Rippin between November 1944 and January 1945 or were sent to the corps in East Prussia.

Experience has shown that compiling an accurate list of command personnel in a wartime situation is an extremely difficult task. This brigade history is no different. Lacking authentic sources I have, with exceptions, designated the holders of positions as chiefs or commanders and have not differentiated between company and battalion commanders.

Equipment and Armament

The motor vehicle complement for this new formation was also limited. There were only a few command, courier, supply and other vehicles, including a large proportion of captured and civilian vehicles. The numbers of heavy weapons were equally limited. In most cases only artillery and anti-aircraft guns were available to the instructors. Equipment of the type possessed by a front-line combat unit was not available.

A multiplicity of weapons types was used for the basic training of panzergrenadiers. There were almost equal numbers of German and foreign small arms, a situation obviously less than desirable for optimal training. Clothing was also of less than a uniform standard, however the greatest shortage faced by the new unit was winter clothing. The signals units were also badly off, for the signals battalions had no equipment. Radio and wire communications existed only in the brigade signals company and even there were very limited. Retired *Major* Bach said of this situation:

"Armament and equipment unmistakably bore the mark of Cain in the sixth year of the war. This fundamental material shortage could not be made good even through imaginative improvisation. The solid notion of adequate armament and equipment was turned upside down there. Nevertheless much was done by the departments of the brigade headquarters – employing every means humanly possible – to assure that the unit was supplied with what was needed. Following the replacement of the seriously-ill *Major* Ilius on 10 November 1944, *Oberst* Friedrich Meyer, commander of the HG Flak Regiment, took over the 'training offensive'. He demanded the maximum possible emphasis on all areas of training within the framework of basic training. In addition, winter combat training was practiced in the field day and night under extreme winter conditions and was assigned the highest priority.

The company commanders were unanimous that we should give our best, so that we could never be criticized for having conducted this important training in a lax or half-hearted manner. At that time this mixed unit, whose origins were extremely varied, needed instructors who possessed knowledge, confidence and strength of character. Unfortunately such persons were not available in sufficient numbers." This concludes *Major* Bach's account. Unfortunately space does not allow us to reproduce his valuable assessment in its entirety.

XI. DECISION IN THE EAST

The Lull Before the Storm

Beginning in November 1944 individual companies were moved up to the Vistula to dig entrenchments. The affected units were sent by special train into the Schütten (Szczutowo) area. Once there the train halted on an open stretch of track and from there the troops marched on foot to the system of positions being expanded, whose location and arrangement had been measured and marked by army pioneers. The primary objective there was to excavate an anti-tank ditch four meters wide and three meter deep. A secondary aim was the expansion of field positions. These installations ran east of Reichsstraße 78 between Rippin and Sichelberg (Sierpc) and included both Schüttauer Lakes. Farther south it linked up with the system of positions on the Skrwa River.

Only a few members of the brigade received Christmas leave. The enemy was on the Vistula and the Narew. The shortest distance from Rippin to the 2nd White Russian Front, which was massing north of Warsaw, was 120 kilometers. A series of standing patrols was mounted on Christmas Eve on orders of the Second Army. No further measures were taken, which obviously meant that a surprise breakthrough toward Rippin by the Red Army was not expected. During the period between Christmas and New Years the brigade's headquarters department heads arrived from the headquarters of the HG Parachute-Panzer Replacement and Training Regiment in Utrecht and the headquarters of the Commanding General of Training and Replacement Troops of the Parachute Army based in Berlin-Reinickendorf. There now began what was commonly known as an "office offensive": a huge mountain of paperwork, which diverted the company commanders from their vitally important mission – directing training. This paper war was deactivated by diplomatic means over a dinner of hare.

At the end of December there appeared a group of highly-decorated officer and NCO airmen – about 40 in number – under the command of a Luftwaffe *Oberst*. They were supposed to assume command of the panzer-grenadiers. Luckily this turned out to be only partly true. Hitler's New Years message, which was read out to the troops, was well received, for he spoke of the rebuilding of the Army:

"Division upon division is being formed. We have created Volksartillerie corps, rocket and assault gun brigades and panzer units."

This was not enough to banish the worries of the brigade command however. The decision would soon come. The enemy was preparing to launch an assault across the borders of the Reich. What and who was to stop him? In spite of the nagging doubts, for all the soldiers, especially the commanders, chiefs and leaders of units, there was no way in sight **But that of duty and loyalty in all military service obligations.** This way had become very uncomfortable, but it had proved itself countless times."

Many new recruits were still coming to Rippin in January 1945. It was completely incomprehensible to the officers of the brigade that at the beginning of 1945 posts in Germany were sending young volunteers to the training units in West Prussia without pay books, without identity disks, and above all without winter clothing. The first fatalities occurred in January 1945. Several soldiers died in quick succession in the field hospital which the brigade first-aid company had set up in Rippin's city hospital. One of the brigade's soldiers was shot by Polish partisans while standing night watch. The dead were buried at the military cemetery in Rippin.

On 13 January the men of the brigade learned from the Wehrmacht communique that the Red Army had launched its long awaited winter offensive on the Vistula front. The communique of 14 January provided more detailed information. On 15 January 1945 the brigade was assigned a three-day field exercise. While preparations were being made for this an order arrived from Second Army which placed the brigade on alert readiness for action at the front and simultaneously placed it under the command of XXIII Army Corps as corps reserve. Although well-founded, the objections of the brigade commander achieved nothing. *Oberst* Meyer was forced to change the practice alert into a real one, however he informed only his two regimental commanders, *Major* Graf and *Hauptmann* Findeis of the change.

The first unit sent to the front was the Parachute-Panzer Pioneer Replacement and Training Battalion, which was ordered by XXIII Army Corps into a readiness position east of Rippin during the night of 15 January 1945. Several other units also had to come to march readiness on the evening of 15 January. The departure of the 1st Regiment under *Hauptmann* Findeis was postponed several times. Both Camps A and B were at alert readiness.

The units assigned to take part in the "brigade exercise" left their quarters in Rippin at midnight on 15 January and dawn on the 16th. They headed out over snow and ice-covered roads toward the area of operations. Shrouded in a light ice fog, the long column moved southeast over the snow-covered, and in places icy, Reichsstraße 78. Prevailing temperatures ranged between 15 and 20 degrees below zero. En route the regimental command ordered the march to continue as far as Sichelberg.

At noon on the 16th brigade headquarters – which was still on the move – was ordered to occupy the prepared field positions along the Skrwa River, west and north of Sichelberg, and to come to defensive readiness. These positions were referred to as a blocking position by *Oberst* Meyer and as a line of security by the division command of the 83rd Infantry Division. Their purpose was to delay the enemy's advance. The brigade's general order was:

"The Second Army's front must be brought to a standstill."

Everyone in the position sensed that something tremendous was coming, but what it was no one knew. The prevailing opinion was that the Soviets would simply overrun them with their armored and motorized units. The only clue as to what was taking place was provided by the Wehrmacht communique of 15 January 1945, which stated that:

"After a several-hour-long bombardment the Red Army has broken out of its Vistula bridgeheads near Pulawy and Warka-Magnuszew, out of the Vistula-Bug triangle north of Warsaw, and out of the Narew bridgeheads on both sides of Ostenburg. Bitter fighting has broken out along the entire front."

The Defensive Battles

The Brigade's 1st (Findeis) and 2nd (Graf) Regiments formed an approximately 35-kilometer-long defensive line in the Skrwa sector; it more closely resembled a line of outposts than an actual defensive line. The defense line extended from a point south of Zochowo up the Skrwa River across Reichsstraßen 123 and 78, east of Schüttauer Lake and then east of Reselerwalde to Rippin in the north. The focal points lay on the three major roads, RS 123 from Warsaw through Sichelberg to Thorn, RS 78 from Sichelberg through Rippin to Strasburg, and the IA-II-B Road from Zuromin through Rippin to Dobrzyn Gollub.

The defenders there had to fight for time, had to halt the enemy advance; at the very least it had to be delayed. It seemed that the Russian steamroller couldn't be stopped, at least that's what the sparse reports from the front suggested. The brigade's battle order in the defense line between 16 and 20 January 1945 was as follows:

Right:	1st Regiment (Findeis) with reinforced II Battalion,
	1st Regiment (Hptm. Bach) elements of I Battalion,
	1st Regiment (Hptm. Vollmer)
Left:	2nd Regiment (Graf) with Heavy Panzer-Grenadier Battalion (artillery) (Major Francois) with four batteries
	Training and Conversion Battalion (Friebe)

The sector boundaries were moved several times by 20 January. These changes were the result of orders from the 83rd Infantry Division, to which the brigade was attached from 19 January 1945. The 83rd Infantry Division had taken over the entire Sichelberg sector on orders from XXIII Army Corps. The units of this division were still on their way to the front. They detrained in Sichelberg and marched immediately into the positions. The division commander, *Generalleutnant* Heun, had received the Knight's Cross on 9 December 1944.

The promised SS-Police Grenadier Battalion, which was supposed to take over the sector held by 7th Company, 1st Regiment under Lt. Alf in order to allow the recruit company to continue training, could not be delivered. On the evening of 19 January 1945 *Oberst* Meyer had himself brought up to date on the situation in his command post. He accepted the tactical concepts of his battalion commanders and held out the prospect of further reinforcements. Although it was still secret, he revealed to his commanders that when the Skrwa position was abandoned the brigade was to pull back to the Drewenz position, 45 kilometers away. The main direction of the enemy's advance was thus Graudenz, not Thorn.

Oberst Meyer informed the officers that his adjutant, Lt. Güldner, had spoken with Reichsmarschall Göring the day before in order to point out the catastrophic munitions situation. Hermann Göring spontaneously announced the arrival of a 26-car munitions train at the Hohensalza railway station west of the Vistula. It later turned out that all the primers were missing from this shipment.

Taking advantage of the good roads in the area, the Red Army moved quickly toward the Meyer Brigade's sector. Its objectives were Thorn in the west and Danzig in the east. Sichelberg, which lay before the brigade's right sector, fell into Russian hands. An enemy armored unit, which was followed by motorized infantry in American-supplied transports, neared the left sector on the Mielau – Zuromin – Rippin road.

Increasingly active partisan groups caused considerable problems for the rear-echelon services. Late in the evening of 19 January the 83rd Infantry Division received orders to disengage from the enemy in the Sichelberg sector, withdraw to Strasburg and establish a blocking position there. Sichelberg was lost in the course of these movements. Following the withdrawal of the 83rd Infantry Division *Oberst* Meyer realized to what extent his two regiments would be inferior to the attacking Russian units. His decision to have the units carry out a fighting withdrawal was the only correct one in this situation. *Oberst* Meyer endeavoured in vain to obtain permission from the "Staff Office Reichsmarschall" for the transfer to Berlin-Velten of all recruits who had arrived after 1 January 1945 and who lacked any sort of training whatsoever. The staff office insisted – probably due to orders from the highest level – that all of the brigade's available units see action at the front.

However *Oberst* Meyer was not prepared to carry out this senseless order. Acting on his own responsibility, he sent the approximately 100 untrained recruits back to Berlin-Velten under the command of the severely-disabled *Hauptmann* Drotbohm. Drotbohm and his charges arrived in Berlin, where they were organized and sent by a circuitous route to Wittstock air base on the Dosse River. There they began their basic training. Drotbohm and the recruits now belonged to the newly-formed 2nd Parachute-Panzer Replacement and Training Brigade. *Oberst* Meyer did his soldierly duty in this difficult time in January 1945, turning an absurd order into a sensible one. In doing so he placed his own head on the block in order to avoid senseless bloodshed.

On 20 January 1945 the first Russian armored spearhead – T 34/85 tanks with mounted or closely following infantry – broke through in the brigade's sector, taking advantage of the hard-frozen meadows and swamps. The brigade had no anti-tank weapons with which to face this mass of armor. The individual combat elements were forced to withdraw to avoid being outflanked and encircled. During the night of 20 January the Russians pushed forward into the sector held by II Battalion under *Hauptmann* Bach, advancing down both sides of RS 123. Beginning at dawn on 20 January, armored battle groups of the Red Army broke into the Bach Battalion's forward positions after a brief preparatory bombardment. The combat outposts pulled back as they had been instructed. The 1st Cannon-howitzer Battery, which gave the grenadiers covering fire as they withdrew, was spotted by the enemy and itself came under heavy fire.

The Russian spearhead halted 800 meters northeast of the bridge over the Skrwa, suspecting strong German anti-tank defenses there. During the developing firefight it was the brigade's snipers, most of whom were former foresters equipped with rifles with telescopic sights, who enjoyed the greatest success. In spite of their limited stocks of ammunition, the brigade's mortars succeeded in smashing several enemy assembly areas. Nevertheless on 20 January the enemy broke into the German line in several places, and that afternoon, following heavy fighting, broke through the brigade's defensive line in the Skrwa sector. The Soviets outflanked sections of the line and reached the brigade's rear, where they took a large number of prisoners. The Skrwa bridge lay under continuous rocket and machine-gun fire. When the Soviet armored spearhead then advanced with reinforced infantry forces (riding in trucks and on foot) on both sides of RS 123, Hptm. Bach was forced to order the brigade to fight its way back to the second line of resistance. The 5th Company under Oblt. Schneider, as well as the 6th (Ellwanger), 7th (Alf) and 8th (Stürchen) Companies, together with the attached soldiers of the Police Battalion, withdrew step by step.

Hauptmann Bach found the regimental headquarters and 7th Company in Schaltensee. A short time later a second company arrived and the units there were ordered to march in the direction of Thorn. The 60-kilometer march from the Schaltensee estate to Thorn began early on the morning of 22 January. When the retreating companies reached the second defense line they found that it existed in name only. The battalion had to act independently without losing any time. Hptm. Bach ordered his units to abandon this "line or resistance", assemble in Schaltensee and await further orders there. The initial reaction of the brigade headquarters was:

"Bach has opened a giant hole. XXIII Army Corps will not hesitate to have him court-martialled."

Nevertheless, when the companies came out of the abandoned Skrwa sector there was relief that the young soldiers had not been sacrificed trying to fulfil a senseless mission, even though they left behind most of their heavy equipment, including heavy machine-gun sleighs and complete mortars. Retired *Major* Bach said of this:

"Given a single platoon of tank destroyers, assault guns or a flak combat team and appropriate artillery support we would have been in a position to upset the Russians' plans west of Sichelberg. Under the existing circumstances our battalion could also have been destroyed in these operations near Sichelberg. The enemy was strong enough to do so."

On the evening of 20 January the brigade received orders to make a fighting withdrawal toward the Drewenz position and to establish itself in a defensive posture in this prepared river position. The 2nd Regiment (Graf) succeeded in maintaining cohesion within and between the withdrawing combat elements. The opposite was the case with 1st Regiment, which became fragmented on the evening of 20 January 1945. The brigade's withdrawal, which was orientated toward the west, was part of a general withdrawal by all German units in West Prussia. As a result of a lack of prepared reception positions it became an ever more rapid retreat, which continued far beyond the planned retreat sectors. 1st Regiment lost contact with its II Battalion and late in the evening on 20 January reported the battalion as lost.

This was not the case however, for, as previously related, on 21 January 1945 II Battalion's 3rd Grenadier Company marched toward the Schalensee Estate assembly point. The roads leading to the estate were blocked by snowdrifts, nevertheless the battalion reached Schalensee Estate as darkness was falling on 21 January. There Hptm. Bach learned that his 7th Company (Alf) had continued onward after a brief rest without orders from the regiment. The 1st Regiment also left the village just before the arrival of the battalion headquarters, not even leaving behind a rearguard detachment. As a result, II Battalion, 1st Regiment found itself in the snow-covered Polish village without orders and in the dark as to the situation. During the night of 22 January the battalion operations officer succeeded in establishing contact with brigade headquarters in Rippin by public telephone. The brigade order, which arrived after several delays, read:

"II Battalion, 1st Regiment hold position, establish all-round defensive position, be ready to march at any time."

Late on the morning of 22 January 1st Regiment's medical officer, *Oberarzt* Dr. Thomas, arrived in Schalensee with medical personnel, equipment and ambulances. The brigade medical officer, Dr. Renken, had informed him of the situation, which was a good thing, because a number of soldiers urgently required medical attention. *Hauptmann* Bach was surprised to learn that his regiment had reported that the battalion had been "Smashed at the Skrwa and the survivors taken prisoner by the Russians." Bach remarked, "As far as we're concerned they've been on the other side for a long time."

Following the medical officer, Hfw. Vothknecht had also made his way to Schalensee. He brought with him a truck loaded with food and provisions. As soon as the reappearance of the battalion had been reported Lt. Nüsse and *Oberzahlmeister* Decius began distributing the food. Lt. Nüsse, the battalion adjutant, had just returned from leave and had "borrowed" the truck and food. On 20 January *Oberst* Meyer had received orders to pull back toward the prepared defensive position on the Drewenz and had withdrawn toward Rippin to occupy an intermediate position near the city. The Russians followed hesitantly. Their leading tanks were placed under fire in a defile on the Okalewo – Rippin road by the brigade's artillery commander, *Hauptmann* Oberländer. As a result the enemy pressure abated and the withdrawal proceeded in an orderly fashion.

Several battered enemy tanks lay disabled in the defile, proof of the effectiveness of the artillery fire. Tank-killing squads awaited the enemy tanks in well-camouflaged positions on the outskirts of Rippin. They knocked out a series of attacking T 34s and destroyed more in close-quarters fighting. At this point misfortune struck the defenders; a number of Panzerfaust anti-tank weapons failed to function. The enemy tanks rolled over the foxholes and crushed the grenadiers. The Graf Regiment and its attached troops defended the main approaches to Rippin in the south and east and blocked them until the afternoon of 22 January. Following the loss of its infantry guns the brigade was instructed to seek artillery support from a foreign unit. However the backbone of the anti-tank defence was formed by three flak teams with 88mm and 20mm guns.

The enemy forces before Rippin grew stronger by the hour. Soviet tanks bombarded the regiment's positions at the city limits with everything they had. The order to withdraw came much too late. In an irony of fate, the supply goods in the two large dumps in Rippin had to be set on fire on account of a lack of transport space. On 23 January the brigade received orders from XXVII Army Corps, to which it had been subordinated the same day, to withdraw past the Drewenz positions, reach the line Briesen-Hohenkirch-Goßlershausen about 20 kilometers distant, and establish a defensive position there. The fall of Strasburg had a direct effect on 2nd Regiment, whose two battalions (Friebe and Francois) were en route to Hohenkirch via Hermannsruhe and Seeheim. This regimental unit was repeatedly attacked from Strasburg by Russian infantry and armored patrols. The resulting combats delayed the arrival of the units in the planned defensive sector at Hohenkirch.

In spite of these delays the brigade succeeded in directing both regiments into the Briesen-Hohenkirch-Goßlershausen line during the night of 24 January, establishing a main line of resistance along the village and the rail line which ran past it. The brigade command post was located in Kieslingswalde's school and dairy. It was learned that *Major* Graf, commander of the 2nd Regiment, and his adjutant, Lt. Boy, had been killed on the outskirts of Hohenkirch while scouting the new area of operations. Graf's driver, who was badly wounded, was able to save himself and report what had happened. An infiltrated enemy anti-tank gun had fired on the command car, taking the occupants by surprise. Both bodies were recovered by troops participating in a counterattack which was launched immediately.

The 2nd Regiment's new list of command personnel was:

Commanding Officer:	Hptm. Francois
Adjutant:	Lt. Ruschitzka
Operations Officer:	Oblt. Müller
IV b:	Stabsarzt Dr. Lutterbeck
2nd Supply Company:	Lt. Kausch
Special Duties Officer:	Fähnrich Richlin, Fähnrich Vock

Hauptmann Weigert assumed command of the Heavy Panzer-Grenadier Battalion.

On 25 January 1945 the brigade was sent the HG Special Purpose Parachute Pioneer Battalion under Hptm. Borgis. This represented a welcome reinforcement. While en route to East Prussia, the battalion was unexpectedly unloaded in Goßlershausen, placed under the command of the brigade and deployed on the 2nd Regiment's left wing. Attacking on a narrow front, on 24 January Russian assault units, led by a strong force of tanks, advanced toward the SSE-NNW road and attacked Hohenkirch. Half of the village was lost. XXVII Army Corps launched a vigorous counterattack which drove the enemy out of the village again.

Elements of the 2nd Regiment played a role in this success. The platoon commanded by *Leutnant* Giesemann, part of 2nd Company, HG Replacement and Training Battalion, suffered very heavy casualties in the street fighting in Hohenkirch. Only three members of the platoon came back! With the arrival of darkness Soviet units attacked from the east on a broad front. Shouting loudly, the enemy infantry charged up the snow-covered slope toward the battalion's positions, only to be repulsed by machine-gun fire. By noon the situation had become precarious as the machine-guns were almost out of ammunition. The regimental order to evacuate the position at the Kieslingswalde railway embankment saved the hard-pressed battalion from having to make a difficult decision. In spite of their considerable numerical inferiority in relation to the enemy, the brigade's soldiers fought with determination and bravery in their holes in the snow in the Hohenkirch defense sector. Had it not been for the selfless actions of each individual the brigade would have been wiped out there.

The recapture of Hohenkirch bought time for the columns of German refugees fleeing Lopatken-Kieslingswalde. The inhabitants of both villages were able to reach the free west. This bitter struggle had had a purpose after all. After deep penetrations in both neighboring sectors – near Briesen and north of Goßlershausen – and under growing pressure from the enemy, the brigade decided to withdraw on a broad front toward the northwest. Its destination was Graudenz, 30 kilometers distant. A delaying defence, the slowing down of the Russian pursuit, was the measure that had to be adopted. Both regiments withdrew while maintaining as wide a battle front as possible. The Red Army was always on the brigade's heels. The delaying defence was conducted from a series of defensive lines – near Deutschwalde, Gorinnen and the southern edge of Jammi forest, to name only the most important. This fight to gain time was conducted with great determination in the area southeast of Graudenz.

Understandably the overall condition of the unit worsened from day to day. The cold persisted, and the icy east wind easily pierced the soldiers' thin coats. For the young soldiers this daily routine became sheer torture; but they were volunteers and refused to give up. Their obvious bravery and willingness were indescribable and simply unimaginable to the youth of today. The battles of retreat from 26 January to 2 February in the approaches to the fortress of Graudenz were the worst experienced by these men. The defenders always managed to reach the next defense line, in some cases through deep snow and unfamiliar terrain. Everyone hoped for at least a brief rest in Graudenz. Some of their uniforms were torn, melted snow was used to wash out footwear. The troops had not washed or shaved for two weeks; the unit's strength had shrunk and it was exhausted. Wolfgang Bach:

"When our battalion received the order to give up the line of resistance at the southern edge of Jammi Forest and to move to the outer defense ring around Graudenz, east of Groß-Rudnicker Lake, I sensed a great relief. Within the brigade our two regiments had fulfilled their often very difficult missions with circumspection and bravery during the fighting withdrawal to Graudenz. This was much appreciated by the senior commanders. The praise expressed by *Generaloberst* Weiß, Commander-in-Chief of the Second Army, was lavish and entirely justified. During the night of 28 January advance detachments of the brigade reached the outer Graudenz positions on RS 384. The bulk of the combat troops arrived there between 29 and 30 January 1945."

II Battalion, 1st Regiment was the last of the brigade's units to pass through the outer defensive ring of Fortress Graudenz near Piasken, 7 kilometers southeast of Graudenz, before sunrise on the night of 2 February. Seen objectively, the brigade, which had been used exclusively as a rearguard, had had little chance of survival. Nevertheless it came through and discharged its responsibilities with admirable courage.

The Graudenz Bridgehead – The General Situation

Following the brigade's entry into Graudenz all the soldiers of this exhausted unit hoped that the brigade would now be brought up to strength and that they themselves would once again be brought into line and given a chance to rest. The most urgent need at the moment was new heavy weapons. The soldiers were surprised by the abundance of various Wehrmacht units in Graudenz. As well as garrison troops there were soldiers from every branch of the three Wehrmacht branches. Graudenz was a "military marshalling yard."

The two main Vistula bridges, the 1,100-meter railroad bridge and the 16-tonne military bridge, as well as the two spans over the frozen river at Groß Wolz and Schöneich-Deutsch Westphalen, were well-guarded crossings for the supplying of the units and as avenues of retreat. At the time the brigade moved into Graudenz there were also long columns of refugees heading for the city on the main and secondary roads, a common sight in West Prussia at that time. Their march discipline was good, and they always cleared the road for military units to pass. These treks of misery made clear to every last soldier just what was at stake there. After seeing the endless columns it was impossible for any soldier to think that his actions served no purpose.

Brigade Commander *Oberst* Meyer described the situation:

"For the young recruits, inadequately clothed and equipped, the road to Graudenz was paved with bitter experiences: hardship, deprivation, exhaustion and death. The weather, with frost, ice and snow, was pitiless. While in action many soldiers had to endure freezing conditions, because the lighting of warming fires was not permitted at night for security reasons and shelters did not exist. On several occasions the Russians broke into our defensive positions with tank support under cover of darkness. In most cases they were destroyed in close combat with Panzerfaust anti-tank weapons, concentrated charges, and so on. It was only the circumspection and combat experience of the officers and NCOs that allowed these young men to hold together in battle and reach the relative safety of Fortress Graudenz without excessive casualties."

On 27 January 1945 the Graudenz bridgehead position was declared a "fortified place". *Generalleutnant* Heun, commander of the 83rd Infantry Division, assumed command of all forces there, relieving the former commandant, *Generalmajor* Fricke. The 83rd Division's command post was set up in the Courbière fortress. The arrival in Graudenz of *Hauptmann* Eggemann and his I Battalion, 4th Parachute Artillery Regiment significantly increased the brigade's fighting potential. The brigade command assumed that the troops would be given several days to rest in Graudenz. This was a false assumption, however, for immediately after reaching the city suburbs the brigade received orders from the 83rd Infantry Division, under whose command the brigade had been placed effective 27 January, to immediately occupy several sectors in the outer defense ring. Contrary to the orders of the fortress commander, the brigade command had company size units withdrawn from the line in turns to rest and refit, on the one hand so that they could be issued winter clothing and on the other to allow them to undergo medical examination. In the course of these examinations brigade medical officer *Stabsarzt* Dr. Renken and regimental medical officers *Oberarzt* Dr. Thomas and *Stabsarzt* Dr. Lutterbeck found many serious cases of frostbite as well as minor wounds, injuries and illnesses. Many of the sick and wounded had to be sent to hospital to avoid serious consequences later. As a result the number of fighters decreased steadily.

The brigade's administrative officer, *Stabsintendant* Standke, had a particularly important role to perform, for he was in charge of the supply companies of both regiments; these were commanded by *Hauptmann* Ernst and *Leutnant* Kausch. It was also at this time that the wounded *Major* Rebholz rejoined the unit, which made him Brigade Ia. The last of the brigade's units to march into Graudenz was the Bach Battalion. It formed up in front of the infantry barracks on Rhedener Straße opposite the city park. *Oberst* Meyer addressed the assembled battalion, expressing his special appreciation for the unit's efforts. He humorously characterized the battalion as a "vagabond hedgehog" which had skillfully adapted to the constantly changing situation in the West Prussian desert of snow. He requested the battalion commander, *Hauptmann* Bach, to submit proposals for promotions and decorations. In closing he remarked:

"Through its courageous actions our brigade has become a front-line unit and no longer has anything in common with the former band of replacements."

German Defensive Measures

At the beginning of February 1945 the situation on the right bank of the Vistula in the south and southeast sections of the outer defense ring of Graudenz had so deteriorated that the brigade command was forced to put every available soldier into the line. Russian advance units had earlier moved against Graudenz on 24 and 27 January, but they had been beaten off by the

83rd Infantry Division with bloody losses. This defensive success was achieved by the division's two regiments, the 257th (*Oberst* Staedtke) and the 277th (*Oberstleutnant* Zornig). Soon afterward, however, these forward positions were lost to the Russians.

The brigade was deployed in the south sector of the fortress defenses. The sector extended from the right bank of the Vistula northwest of Rondsen, past the Hartenstein factory, to the north shore of Großrudnicker Lake, and from there through Conradsfelde to Liebenwalde. Manning the sector were the following units:

1st Regiment (Hptm. Findeis)

    I Battalion (Vollmer) with;

    1st Company (May), 2nd Company (Hahn), 3rd Company (Selzer)

    II Battalion (Hptm. Bach) with;

    5th Company (Schneider), 6th Company (Ellwanger), 8th Company (Stürchen)

    Infantry Gun Company (Zillmann, Speidel)

    Assigned weapons:

        several sGrW. 34 heavy mortars (80mm)

        two 20mm anti-aircraft guns

        two 75mm anti-tank guns

2nd Regiment (Francois)

    Heavy Panzer-Grenadier Battalion (Weigert)

    1st Company (Schrader), 2nd Company (Müller), 3rd Company (Wittig), 4th Company (?)

    Training and Conversion Battalion (Friebe) with;

    1st Company (Kraus), 2nd Company (Giesemann), 3rd Company (Feuerherdt), Alert Company (Van Damm)

    21st Parachute Pioneer Battalion (Borgis) with;

    1st Company (Wiechert), 2nd Company (Pfister), 3rd Company (Reimer)

Attached fortress units, elements of the 4th Parachute Artillery Regiment and other units reinforced this defensive line.

The brigade command post was located in the Villa Ventzki near the Schulz sawmill.

On 2 February powerful enemy forces attempted to break through from the south, southeast and east toward the Vistula bridges. A Soviet tank brigade was the first to assault the outer defense ring. The following assault battalions were shot to pieces. The enemy tanks that did manage to break through were destroyed by anti-aircraft and anti-tank guns, artillery, and tank-killing squads. Watching over the main line of resistance were forward combat outposts and outguards, whose responsibility it was to provide early warning of approaching enemy forces.

No one in the brigade believed that the fortress was supposed to be held to the bitter end, especially since Thorn had been given up (2 February 1945); but it had to be held initially in order to keep open the supply lines and avenues of retreat which led from the left bank of the Vistula to Danzig. *Generaloberst* Weiß, Commander-in-Chief of the Second Army, which was commanding there, had assured *Oberst* Meyer at the end of January that his brigade would be evacuated from this fortress area. Part of the defense front began to move following several deep penetrations by the Red Army against the south, southeast and east sectors between the 4th and 10th of February, which could not be cleared up in the long run. In the brigade's sector the Rondsen Estate, the Mischke railway station, Conradsfelde, Gatsch and Poln were all lost. The villages of Polnisch-Wangerau and Deutsch-Wangerau also fell to the enemy.

On 6 February 1945 the 2nd Regiment attacked the enemy forces that had broken into the defensive positions in an attempt to drive them back and regain the old defensive line. The pincer-style attack was a success. The troops reached a line from the southeast edge of the wooded area near Point 73 to the western outskirts of Polnisch and Deutsch-Wangerau. There the assault came to a halt due to a shortage of ammunition among the few artillery units. The next morning the Soviet batteries opened up with a terrific barrage and blasted the men of the brigade's 2nd Regiment out of the positions they had just won. The main line of resistance had to be withdrawn to the original jumping-off positions, however the positions at the southeast edge of the airfield were to remain in German hands until the complete encirclement of Graudenz in spite of repeated Soviet attacks.

Already on the night of 4 February Soviet motorized units and infantry had crossed the reinforced ice bridge at Schöneicher Herrenkämpe and reached the west bank of the Vistula. The same day, units of the 83rd Infantry Division picked up a group of German soldiers on the left bank of the Vistula northeast of Schwetz. Mostly Luftwaffe troops, they had broken out of Fortress Thorn.

On 8 February a chance hit set off the demolition charges installed on the 1,100-meter road and rail bridge. The officer in command of the fortress pioneers, *Major* Heckmann, had repeatedly urged the pioneer leader of the Second Army to disconnect the double ignition system installed on the bridge, but in vain. The result was the destruction of this vital bridge over the Vistula River. The Soviet ring around the city became tighter and tighter. The brigade command took charge of all Luftwaffe personnel flowing into the fortress and by 10 February was able to create three fully-equipped grenadier companies for each of 1st Regiment's two Battalions.

Both battalions were placed under the direct command of the Findeis Regimental Headquarters. As a result of this reorganization they were now called grenadier battalions or grenadier regiments. Both *Hauptmann* Bach and *Major* Rebholz were supposed to attend a general staff training course scheduled to begin 1 June (!) Wolfgang Bach was therefore forced to give up his battalion, becoming O1 in brigade headquarters. *Major* Rebholz became Brigade Ia. On the evening of 14 February the 1st Parachute-Panzer-

Grenadier Regiment (*Major* Findeis) was forced to evacuate its positions at the north edge of the Graudenz city forest and move into the south sector on the left bank of the Vistula in order to take over a new sector in the western bridgehead.

The regiment crossed the 16-tonne military bridge into the western bridgehead. Its mission was to halt the northward Russian advance toward Danzig on both sides of RS 380. Powerful forces of the Red Army attacked the western bridgehead from the southwest without pause. Their aim was to block the 16- tonne bridge, the last passable entrance to Graudenz. Two potent units of the Red Army approached from the southwest (Kulm/Schwetz) and from the west (from the Gruppe Training Grounds) with strong tank support. The regiment was placed under the command of the 257th Grenadier Regiment (of the 83rd Infantry Division) and thus became separated from the brigade.

On arriving in the western bridgehead on 14 February, the 1st Regiment received orders to join the 257th Grenadier Regiment (*Oberst* Staedtke) in an attack in the direction of Schwetz. This attack was effectively supported by I Battalion, 4th Parachute Artillery Regiment under *Hauptmann* Eggemann and it brought noticeable relief to the bridgehead position. The gap in the southern sector of the eastern bridgehead caused by the withdrawal of the regiment was closed by the Training and Conversion Battalion under *Hauptmann* Friebe in the course of 15 February. In spite of the order to evacuate, many inhabitants of Graudenz were still living in the cellars of their houses in mid-February. It was in mid-February that the supply column of the Second Army delivered the last shipment of supplies and ammunition into the city. When it left, the column took out all the wounded as well as the remaining women and children.

The battle for the city entered a decisive phase when, to the surprise of everyone, the 83rd Infantry Division left the fortress of Graudenz via the military bridge during the night of 17 February 1945 in order to initiate a march north to Danzig from the left bank of the Vistula. Furthermore the brigade was forced to detach the following units to the 83rd Infantry Division:

The 1st Parachute-Panzer-Grenadier Regiment (Findeis), two Luftwaffe pioneer companies, and I Battalion, 4th Parachute Artillery Regiment (Eggemann). In their place the 257th Grenadier Regiment (Staedtke) remained in the western bridgehead and was placed under the command of Fricke's fortress headquarters. The 257th Grenadier Regiment now had to defend the considerably reduced western bridgehead alone. *Hauptmann* Findeis and *Hauptmann* Eggemann prepared for their departure to the north. *Oberst* Meyer:

"In spite of the ominous fact that the Russians on the west bank of the Vistula were steadily increasing their attacks on the western bridgehead, compressing it more and more, the 83rd Infantry Division was withdrawn from the Graudenz area of operations. It headed north across the river over the wooden bridge during the night of 17 February. At the same time the brigade received orders to remain in the fortress and as well to release the

Findeis Regiment and I Battalion, 4th Parachute Artillery Regiment to the 83rd Infantry Division. The brigade saw this order as a disheartening weakening of its fighting strength. In spite of energetic protests a reversal of the decision could not be achieved."

The Red Army spotted the departure of the 83rd Infantry Division in time to lay down a heavy bombardment on the departure roads; in so doing it ignited a terrible inferno in which many soldiers and weapons were consumed. This entire process was not only inexplicable, it was also a death sentence for the brigade. To *Oberst* Meyer the decision showed how much store he could place in the word of a *Generaloberst*: none!

The 16-tonne bridge was destroyed by the infernal barrage fire. Soldiers in the western bridgehead who wanted to reach the city had to cross the destroyed bridge hand over hand, for there was drifting ice in the river. The Wehrmacht communiqué of 17 February 1945 reported:

"The continued Soviet assault on a broad front in West Prussia between Landeck and Graudenz led to penetrations into the difficult terrain of the Tucheler Heath and west of Graudenz. These are in the process of being sealed off."

The following is a list of the command personnel of 1st Regiment on the day of its departure:

Commanding Officer:	Hauptmann Findeis
Adjutant:	Lt. Weiß, Lt. Dr. Hüfner
O 1:	Lt. Nüsse, Lt. Munderloh
IV a:	Oberzahlmeister Decius
IV b:	Oberarzt Dr. Thomas
1st Supply Company:	Hptm. Ernst
Special Duties Officer:	Fähnrich Richlin
1st Grenadier Company:	Lt. Ellwanger, Lt. Hammerschmidt
2nd Grenadier Company:	Oblt. Stürcken, Lt. Thamm
3rd Grenadier Company:	Oblt. Faßhauer, Lt. Rammwitz
4th Pioneer Company:	Lt. Scheibe (?)
5th Pioneer Company:	Ofw. (?)

The Findeis Regiment repeatedly distinguished itself while serving with the 83rd Infantry Division. The regiment fought with daring and bravery in the battles on the left bank of the Vistula, such as in the repulsing of an enemy attack in the Neuenburg area and during the defensive battle at the Klempiner Berg, the last hill position before Danzig.

On 9 May 1945 what was left of the regiment, about 40 survivors, surrendered in Hela. I Battalion, 4th Parachute Artillery Regiment under *Hauptmann* Eggemann met a similar fate. The two HG units were separated on 11 March, when I Battalion, 4th Parachute Artillery Regiment was attached to the 7th Infantry Division.

The Russians launched a general offensive in West Prussia on the morning of 7 May. On the afternoon of 8 May 1945 *Hauptmann* Eggemann and the rest of his battalion caught the last ship out and arrived in Kiel on the 9th.

The Final Battle in Fortress Graudenz

With the return of the 257th Grenadier Regiment to Fortress Graudenz on 16 February, the encirclement of the troops left in the fortress on the right bank of the Vistula was complete. *Oberst* Meyer:

"It was clear to me that after this weakening the bridgehead on the west bank of the Vistula could no longer be held. The fortress commandant, Generalmajor Fricke, was therefore compelled to give up this hard-pressed bridgehead position during the night of 21 February and withdraw the 257th Grenadier Regiment and attached units back across the wooden bridge. This succeeded with minimal losses, thanks to the fighting spirit of the defenders."

From that hour all the soldiers in Fortress Graudenz were doomed. The Red Army now launched a mass attack from the south, southeast and east. Artillery fire from guns of every caliber supported the attack. A rocket regiment drove into position and blanketed the city with rocket projectiles. The Russians broke into the city in various places but the defenders counterattacked and drove them out again. Soviet tanks accompanying the infantry were destroyed by eighty-eight fire. The enemy suffered particularly heavy losses when they attacked across the open terrain of the airfield in the direction of the city. The attack collapsed. The brigade headquarters eventually had to move from the pioneer barracks on Gontzenbacher Straße to the Courbiére Fortress about 1,000 meters away.

On 21 February the fortress headquarters received a number of German soldiers who had been captured by the Russians and pressed into service as emissaries. They brought Russian surrender demands, which were ignored. At this time the fortress garrison consisted of the following units and detachments:

Fortress Headquarters Graudenz:
- Fortress Commandant: Generalmajor Fricke
- 34th Fortress Regiment: ?
- 828th Fortress Infantry Regt.: ?
- 65 Fortress Pioneer Battalion: Major Heckmann (elements)
- Fortress First-aid Unit: Oberfeldarzt Dr. Feldhahn, Oberarzt Dr. Pohl
- Fortress Veterinary Unit: Oberstveterinär Dr. Göhrs
- 257th Grenadier Regiment: Oberstleutnant Staedtke
- 75th Grenadier Replacement and Training Regiment: ?
- I Battalion, 257th Grenadier Regt: Hptm. Findeisen
- 3rd Grenadier Replacement and Training Battalion: ?
- 376th Grenadier Replacement and Training Battalion: ?

12th Pioneer Replacement and Training Battalion: Major Dr. Krebs
209th Regional Defence Pioneer Battalion: ?
II Battalion, 69th Army Artillery Regiment: Oberst Becker (also fortress artillery commander) Hptm. Overländer (HG)
Special Purpose Construction Battalion: ?
HG Parachute-Panzer Replacement and Training Brigade: Oberst Meyer
    HG Brigade Signals Company: Hptm. Schröder, Oblt. Marzian
    HG Brigade First-aid Unit: Stabsarzt Dr. Renken, Stabsarzt Dr. Lutterbeck
    HG Brigade Supply Unit: Stabsintendant Standke
    HG Infantry Gun Company (IGK): Oblt. Zillmann Fw. Speidel
    2nd HG Parachute-Panzer Replacement and Training Regiment: Hptm./Major Francois
    HG Heavy Parachute-Panzer-Grenadier Battalion: Hptm. Weigert, Oblt. Feuerherdt
    HG Training and Conversion Battalion: Hptm. Friebe
    HG 21st Special Purpose Parachute Pioneer Battalion: Hptm. Borgis

Also in the fortress was the 69th Marine Rifle Battalion (a navy probation unit) and a rearguard detachment of ground personnel from Graudenz airfield. There was also a Graudenz police unit, whose strength is unknown, as well as the *Volkssturm* with I Graudenz Battalion under *Hauptmann* Stüblewitz and II Graudenz Battalion under an unidentified commander. Following the removal of I Battalion, 4th Parachute Artillery Regiment the only artillery in the fortress was one heavy field howitzer (150mm), two heavy infantry guns (150mm), four light infantry guns (75mm), several Flak 88s, and a number of 20mm light flak.

The attack by the Soviet 37th and 209th Infantry Divisions, the former a Guards unit, was supported by the better part of an artillery division. 20,000 shock troops were allocated to the capture of Graudenz. Supporting them were armored combat groups and at least 100 guns. Opposing this force were 7,000 to 8,000 German soldiers.

The Battle of Graudenz was an extremely hard fight. There was bitter fighting for the tobacco factory and the slaughterhouse. The latter changed hands several times. Finally the Russians reached the railway station, part of the city's core. The defenders were forced to withdraw from one strongpoint to the next. In addition to "regular" troops, the Red Army also employed political officers in the struggle for the fortress. One such was Major Kopelev. They also included the front-line representatives of the Committee for a Free Germany, among them Army *Major* Bechler. A group which caused the defenders considerably more trouble was the Polish population left in Graudenz, who felt obliged to help shorten the battle for the fortress by secretly supporting the Russian troops. Obviously there were also personal advantages for those who participated.

The initiative had gone over completely to the attackers. The destruction or surrender of the defenders was only a matter of time. *Oberst* Meyer described the fighting in the so-called city limits settlement:

"There was particularly heavy fighting for the tobacco factory and the slaughterhouse, both of which still housed considerable stocks. The slaughterhouse changed hands several times. In spite of all our heroic defensive efforts the Russians reached the railway station, which was part of the city core. From then on the fighting was house to house, which was especially hard on our young soldiers because they were not used to it."

The forward positions were abandoned during the night. The situation around Graudenz was untenable, as evidenced by the Second Army's withdrawal on a broad front in the direction of Danzig. Inside the fortress stocks of artillery and small arms ammunition dwindled rapidly. The field hospital set up in the city filled extraordinarily quickly, as it was impossible to evacuate the wounded who could be moved. The hostility of the Polish population grew from hour to hour. An especially aggravating problem was the fact that the stockpile of supplies in the fortress, which was supposed to last 30,000 men six months, had begun to dwindle at the end of December. The remaining supplies would last the estimated 7,000 defenders no more than several weeks.

"There was no front any more," reported *Oberst* Meyer. "The battle for the houses was conducted mercilessly. There were heavy losses on both sides in close quarters fighting, man against man."

On 23 February the commander of the HG Training and Conversion Battalion, Hptm. Friebe, celebrated in his command post in the cellar of a brewery; it was his birthday and he had been awarded the German Cross in Gold. The artillery salvoes falling nearby prevented the development of any sort of euphoric mood. On account of their dwindling manpower, the defenders now had to conduct a fighting withdrawal to the Trinke position, the inner ring. This ran from the Trinkestraße across Mühlenstraße to the brewery and from there to the office of the District President and the corner of Kuntersteiner and Schweriner Streets. This resulted in a considerable shortening of the front, allowing the defenders to more adequately man their positions.

The inner defensive position had been augmented to the maximum extent possible by the pioneers and included field positions, roadblocks, and mines, as well as spanish horsemen and other obstacles. The approximately seven-meter-wide stream offered good protection against tanks. The area of intermediate terrain from the station to the Trinke position – about 1,000 meters wide – was fought over all day. The 2nd Regiment under Francois and the Friebe, Weigert, and Borgis Battalions were engaged in house-to-house fighting there. The 2nd Regiment, now called Battle Group Francois, occupied the Trinke position strongpoint-style. The defenders there fought with great determination, for they knew that if this position fell it would mean the loss of the last prepared defensive system.

The men in the Trinke position withstood the overpowering pressure exerted by the enemy for a week. The Russians broke through in several places at the end of February and the beginning of March; the position would have to be abandoned. Seen militarily, the abandoning of the inner ring was the end of the battle for Fortress Graudenz. The continuation of the battle in the houses in the center of the city, where men continued to hold out in the cellars, and the extremely precarious situation of the wounded should have meant an immediate end to hostilities. But the fortress commandant had orders to hold to the last man. *Generalmajor* Fricke discussed questions of international law and the Hague Rules of Land Warfare with the adjutant of the HG Brigade, *Leutnant* Güldner, an experienced jurist. *Generalmajor* Fricke especially wanted to know if it was legal to use captured soldiers as emissaries. After all, *Major* Bechler had acted as a representative of the Russians. Güldner informed him that the practice was illegal and noted that the Russians tended to subordinate all international rules and laws to their own interests.

Taking cover in houses and behind roadblocks and mine belts, the defenders fought on in the city. The smallest breach had to be closed immediately, for there was nowhere left to withdraw to and a successful penetration would put the enemy in the rear of the defenders. Particularly bitterly contested were the Victoria School, Adolf Hitler Square, the Winklerplatz, the post office, the Schloßberg and the penitentiary, the courthouse and the brewery, as well as the Kunterstein Barracks and several other points. German and Russian units faced each other on different floors of the multi-story buildings. Every room and stairway was fought for. *Oberst* Meyer described this period:

"The houses were joined by air-raid tunnels, and the Russians were able to penetrate our positions with the help of Poles familiar with the town. They approached our people from behind and killed them. In this way they rolled up block after block from south to north. Hand grenades and Panzerfaust anti-tank weapons were used in the close quarters fighting. The number of victims claimed by these battles in the center of Graudenz will never be known. The defensive ring around the Courbiére Fortress became ever tighter. Finally the Russians reached the red brick barracks in which the field hospital had been set up. It was filled with wounded. The hospital was surrendered without fighting, together with all the wounded who could not walk, doctors, and care personnel. It was a voluntary and heroic decision on the part of the doctors and care personnel not to abandon the wounded. The wounded who could still walk made their way back to their units. The fortress casemates were likewise filled with wounded. These formed the main dressing station."

In charge of the surgical department in the Courbiére Fortress was *Stabsarzt* Dr. Lutterbeck. The entire city was shrouded in smoke. In this period of defeat there was a man at work whose selfless readiness to help and bravery did not fit the contemporary notion of a political leader. District Leader (*Kreisleiter*) Lamperle, himself partially disabled, crawled through the cellars and tunnels to aid and comfort the civilian population. Lamperle was decorated with the Iron Cross, Second Class by the fortress commandant, *Generalmajor* Fricke, in recognition of his selfless actions in the spirit of true devotion to duty. The supplement to the Wehrmacht communiqué of 2 March 1945 cast a special light on current conditions in the city:

"In an heroic eleven-day battle, the courageous garrison of Fortress Graudenz, surrounded since 17 February, has, under its capable and determined commandant, Generalmajor Fricke, beaten off every enemy attack. The defenders have inflicted very heavy losses on the enemy and in doing so have at the same time tied down strong Bolshevik forces."

Major Bechler, one of the leading members of the pro-Soviet League of German Officers and a front-line representative of the National Committee for a Free Germany stated in his report titled:

"Concerning My Activity in the Graudenz Pocket from 20 February to 6 March 1945":

"In spite of our activities the German troops continued fighting, whereby the 'Hermann Göring' Brigade, which was partly made up of young replacements (including a full battalion of officer candidates), undoubtedly formed the heart and soul of the resistance."

The headquarters staff of the HG Brigade were certain of one thing: there would be no surrender! Therefore all that was left was an attempt to break out. Two plans were discussed. One was a breakout to the west across the still passable ice surface of the Vistula, the other a breakout to the northeast and a subsequent attempt to reach the front, now in East Prussia. Both plans entailed great risks. The plan to break out met with the full agreement of all Army and Luftwaffe commanders; however, after further consideration several commanders declared that their soldiers were no longer physically capable of conducting a breakout.

At the beginning of March *Oberst* Meyer reported to the fortress commandant. He learned from *Generalmajor* Fricke that the latter was firmly determined to defend the fortress as per the Führer's order. Meyer was unable to change Fricke's mind. *Oberst* Meyer:

"In this desperate situation the fortress commandant was unable to agree to my proposal to send a request for freedom of action by radio to Second Army. There were increasing demands, especially from members of the HG, to escape the uncertain fate of captivity by breaking out of the fortress."

This last decision sealed the fate of the soldiers and civilians in Graudenz. It affected about 4,500 soldiers still fighting and 1,500 wounded, as well as several tens of thousands of civilians, sick, and injured.

"We were still unable to obtain freedom of action. We could not and did not intend to give ourselves up as criminals." (Wolfgang Bach)

Brigade headquarters decided to make its own plans without the knowledge or approval of the fortress headquarters and to consult with the unit commanders on a case by case basis. In the end the brigade staff pursued two breakout plans, to be carried out only on the surrender of Graudenz. The first plan anticipated a breakout to the northeast by the 1st Battle Group under *Major* Francois. Only volunteers would participate. Responsibility for the preparation and carrying out of the breakout was handed to Headquarters, 2nd Regiment under *Major* Francois.

The brigade headquarters with all headquarters departments and detachments would make preparations for the breakout by the 2nd Group. Both plans required a high degree of willingness to accept responsibility, for in the end decisions would have to be made which fell outside the military norm. Various exits, some through the underground casemates of the fortress works which contained a labyrinth of passages, proved to be unacceptable. The last radio message to be received from Second Army conveyed promotions and decorations. *Hauptmann* Friebe and *Hauptmann* Bach were both promoted to *Major*. Bach was awarded the German Cross in Gold, which was pinned on his tunic by *Oberst* Meyer. Since there was no original available, Meyer presented Bach his own German Cross in Gold.

Wolfgang Bach said of the decoration:

"I wore this decoration as an acknowledgement of the accomplishments of my soldiers in II Battalion during the battles of retreat in West Prussia in January and February 1945."

Once again an excerpt from the writings of *Oberst* Meyer:

"Enemy bombers were always over the city, dropping bombs of every calibre. The inner structures and courtyards and the fortress streets lay under continuous strafing and artillery fire. The Russians were determined to employ all the force necessary to bring about the surrender of the fortress. Whole sections of the city were reduced to rubble by the hail of bombs and shells. On the German side the battle for the ruined houses was conducted with a desperation bordering on fanaticism. The final assault which would overwhelm us was not far off."

During the night of 4 March the units which had withdrawn quickly into the fortress front were shattered at the foot of the fortress. In rapid succession the resistance of the individual groups was extinguished. *Major* Rebholz and *Oberst* Meyer were ordered to report to the fortress commandant. *Generalmajor* Fricke accused them of preparing a secret breakout.

"He called us traitors and threatened us with court- martial." (*Oberst* Meyer) The following entry appears in the OKW war diary on 6 March 1945:

"Army Group Vistula: the offensive against Graudenz has begun. The garrison is squeezed into a small area in the Courbiére Fortress. The end of resistance is near."

The first soldiers to have escaped the inferno assembled in the Courbiére-North safety position. The brigade staff waited there, ready to act. On 4 March it was learned that the Findeisen Army Battalion (I Battalion, 257th Grenadier Regiment) had surrendered. Findeisen had neglected to inform the unit on his left, the Friebe Battalion, of his decision. For the remaining soldiers the consequences were catastrophic, for the battalion's surrender created a 200-meter-wide gap which could not be closed. Friebe's battalion, which had been reduced to 60 men, of whom only 50 were capable of fighting, received orders from 2nd Regiment to launch a counterattack to recover the abandoned street sector.

Following a brief conference with his officers, *Major* Friebe decided to end the senseless battle which must end with the complete destruction of his battalion. His last radio message to the regiment read:

"Götz von Berlichingen!"

Afterward the radio station was blown up and all fighting ceased. Soviet Major Kopelev had promised an honorable surrender without looting, however the opposite proved to be the case. The battle raged on and finally reached the foot of the hill on which the Courbiére Fortress stood. In the end the point was reached where a continuation of the defensive battle was senseless and would only have resulted in a final slaughter. During the night of 5 March *Generalmajor* Fricke finally gave what was left of the brigade freedom of action. Preparations for the breakout were made in all haste. For the fortress itself the orders were for a cease-fire, not surrender. *Generalmajor* Fricke wanted to try and negotiate an end to hostilities in order to avoid excesses by the Red Army.

The Francois staff was ordered to "Fall in at the north gate in preparation for breakout!" The command staff ordered: "Assemble in the Courbiére-North safety position, taking along the soldiers who do not wish to or are unable to take part in the breakout."

Resistance in Fortress Graudenz was extinguished on the afternoon of 5 March. On 7 March the war diary of the OKH reported:

"Resistance has ended in Graudenz. The enemy reports the capture of 5,000 men and one general."

On the evening of 5 March Oblt. Marzian, the brigade's NSFO officer, sent a final radio message. He sent the message to Second Army for transmission to Germany:

"The last remains of the fortress garrison in and around Courbiére Fortress donate 428,299 Reichsmarks to the Winter Relief Campaign. Group fighting with unparalleled devotion to the end for Führer, Volk, and Fatherland."

On 6 March 1945 the white flag waved over the Courbiére Fortress. The first Russian soldiers appeared at about 0530 hours, followed at about 0800 by two Russian generals, who walked into the city through the upper gate of the fortress grounds. The destruction of the Hermann Göring Parachute-Panzer Replacement and Training Brigade was complete.

XII. THE HERMANN GÖRING PARACHUTE-PANZER CORPS

The Frontier Battle in East Prussia

During the battles of October 1944 the HG Parachute-Panzer Corps belonged to the Ninth Army under *General der Panzertruppe* Freiherr von Lüttwitz. As previously described, it fought at the Vistula north of Warsaw, near Modlin. In a move which took everyone by surprise, on 6 and 7 October 1944 the corps was transferred back into the sector of the front containing the Warka bridgehead, where, while still a division, it had fought as part of VIII Corps in August and September 1944.

Officially in formation since 1 October 1944, the units for the corps were slow in arriving. The last assigned battalion did not arrive until Christmas 1944. This meant that the fighting strength of the HG Parachute-Panzer Corps was roughly only that of a division, especially since the cadre division had earlier suffered heavy losses. All of the corps' combat elements had to be thrown straight into the battle as they arrived, seeing action in the areas north of the Ruß River between the cities of Ruß and Kukernese.

When on 7 October it became obvious that the Russian offensive was not going to be stopped, permission was given for the evacuation of the Memelland. The sudden and deep advance by Russian armored units cut off many refugee columns. Russian tanks ruthlessly overran and plundered the columns of refugees. Soviet soldiers raped the women and girls and murdered without regard to age or sex. They didn't even hesitate to kill the many French prisoners of war who tried to protect the farm women for whom they had previously worked. Thus the only thing at stake in the heavy fighting for Ruß was to win time and keep open the way to the Reich for those fleeing the Russians.

The Red Army made its ultimate breakthrough on 19 October. The German defenders were only able to hold two bridgeheads, one north of Tilsit and the other north of Ragnit, until 22 October (the city of Ruß held out until 28 October). Memel was held as a bridgehead until 28 January 1945. The units of the HG Parachute-Panzer Corps also saw heavy fighting in the area around Ruß. After the front had firmed up somewhat it was withdrawn in order to see action elsewhere in East Prussia.

In mid-October there were increasing signs that a major Russian offensive was imminent. The Fourth Army, which had been sent the units of the HG Parachute-Panzer Corps, assumed battle positions on 15 and 16 October. The Red Army's opening barrage began at 0400 hours on the morning of 16 October 1944. Soon afterward the 3rd White Russian Front attacked between Memel and Sudauen with five armies consisting of 40 rifle divisions and numerous armored units. The attack received massive air support, with attacks on the German rear areas, including Gumbinnen. The border battle in

East Prussia had begun. The divisions of XXVI Army Corps under *General der Infanterie* Großmann and those of XXVII Army Corps under *General der Infanterie* Prieß found themselves fighting a defensive battle against a numerically-superior enemy.

The Soviet divisions achieved a deep penetration which could not be sealed off. The German front was able to hold together between Memel and the Rominten Heath, however it had to be withdrawn step by step in the face of the tremendous pressure being exerted by the Russians. The main direction of the Soviet thrust was along both sides of the Vilkavishkis – Gumbinnen road. A few days later, on 19 October, newly introduced Soviet armored units of the 11th Guards Army crashed through the German lines on both sides of Großwaltersdorf and reached the area west of the village of Nemmersdorf. There two armored spearheads veered toward Goldap and Gumbinnen.

In this hour of greatest peril the Fourth Army received desperately needed reinforcements from the Third Panzer Army in the form of the HG Parachute-Panzer Corps and the *Führer-Begleitbrigade Großdeutschland*, a panzer brigade only recently formed by that corps. During the night of 18 October the parachute-panzer corps was pulled out of the line; it was sent to what had just then been recognized as the focal point of the battle in East Prussia. The HG 1st Parachute-Panzer Division, which was under the command of *Oberst* Necker, was deployed in Ebenrode-Trakehnen with its front facing south. The command post was set up at the Trakehnen stud farm. Russian troops had established themselves in the numerous buildings and positions of this world-famous stud farm. It took heavy attacks by Stuka dive-bombers to drive them out. In the process many of the institution's installations were destroyed. In the course of the battle the division command post was moved to Jonasthal.

The corps' 2nd Parachute-Panzer-Grenadier Division turned off the Gumbinnen-Ebenrode road to Großwaltersdorf, while the corps units – including the HG Flak Regiment and the assault battalion under *Hauptmann* Lehmann – went into action from Gumbinnen in a generally southerly direction. The flak regiment destroyed a large number of Soviet tanks with its 88mm guns. Later part of the troops fighting their way toward the south turned and advanced through Brauersdorf and – farther to the south – the Plickener Mountains toward Nemmersdorf. The Army's 5th Panzer Division, which had been committed with the corps, continued to drive south in order to link up with the *Führer-Begleitbrigade* which, coming from Goldap, was advancing along the Rominte toward Großwaltersdorf from the south. The objective of this pincer attack launched by XXVII Army Corps was to seal off the Soviet armored spearheads and cut off the enemy's avenue of retreat.

On 21 October, after a forty-eight-hour battle, the German units linked up between Daken and Tellrode. The attack's preliminary objective had been reached. The commanding general of XXVII Corps, *General der Infanterie* Prieß, was killed in the bitter fighting on 21 October. Some of the Soviet units were destroyed. On 22 October the rest were forced to retreat back across the Rominte. Nevertheless Goldap fell into enemy hands for the first time on 22 October, but was retaken in an attack by 5th Panzer Division, which was joined by the 5th Infantry Division.

From the 22nd to the 28th of October the Soviet units renewed their attack from the line they had won between Memel and Goldap. Though weaker in numbers, the German defensive forces were able to repel all attacks and prevent the Red Army from achieving any noteworthy success. Units of the HG Parachute-Panzer Corps took part in all these actions. The last Wehrmacht communiqué from those days, dated 31 October 1944, reported that the enemy offensive had been halted in a four-day battle:

"The attack by more than 35 rifle divisions and numerous armored units was thwarted by the grim will to resist and determined counterattacks of our divisions, as well as the exemplary actions of the German Volkssturm. Soviet materiel losses were high. In the period from 16 to 28 October 1,066 tanks, 330 guns and 48 aircraft were destroyed or captured there. In the same period aviation units and the flak artillery of an air fleet under the command of Generaloberst von Greim shot down 264 Soviet aircraft in the air over East Prussia and destroyed 189 tanks."

The first battle for East Prussia had ended. The Commander-in-Chief of Army Group Center, *Generaloberst* Reinhardt, provided a military assessment of the actions of the units under his command in his daily report of 29 October. The report stated:

"As the enemy has limited himself to several local attacks since yesterday, the first phase of the battle in East Prussia may be considered over. After a nearly fourteen-day struggle, the units under the command of General der Infanterie Hoßbach, those of XXXXI Panzer Corps, General der Artillerie Weidling, of XXVII Army Corps, General der Infanterie Prieß, of the Hermann Göring Parachute-Panzer Corps, Generalmajor Schmalz, and of XXVI Army Corps, Generalleutnant Becker, have parried the onslaught by 5 armies with 37 to 40 divisions and numerous armored units with about 1,500 tanks. The enemy's losses were extraordinarily high. Thus the enemy's attempt to break through to East Prussia with a crushing superiority in men and materiel has foundered on the grim will to resist of our divisions and the daring and determined counterattacks of the panzer units."

The HG Parachute-Panzer Corps destroyed 114 enemy tanks during the fighting in the East-Prussian border region. The horrible fate of the civilian population of Nemmersdorf after the entry of Soviet troops, the murder and rape, was described in full detail in the book *Die Wehrmachtuntersuchungsstelle* by Zaya. Soviet soldiers committed unspeakable atrocities there without a single person in the whole world, not even in Germany, reporting a single word about the horrible fate suffered by women, elderly people and children, to say nothing of the laying of charges. In the new German creative use of the language these massacres fall under the heading of "acts of liberation by the Red Army."

But back to the unit. Having witnessed the bestial murder of civilians with their own eyes, the will to resist of the soldiers stiffened, resulting in a fanatical struggle to save the people trapped between the fronts. From that day on the German soldier in East Prussia knew exactly what he was fighting for. His strength and his will to resist had been raised to undreamt of levels in this drastic fashion.

Positional Warfare in the Winter of 1944-45

In this winter of decision the HG Parachute-Panzer Corps lay in the Schloßberg-Gumbinnen-Goldap defense line. The unit tried to make the line as strong and as winter-proof as possible. The headquarters established themselves in the massive cellars of the large farms, of which only ruins were left standing. The troops themselves took shelter in the houses just behind the front, from where they could reach their positions in a few minutes if the alarm was sounded.

In the course of the first weeks and months the HG Parachute- Panzer Corps received replacement personnel to bring the many decimated units up to strength. Other units arrived as well, to be placed under the corps' command or incorporated into it. One such unit was the 16th Parachute Regiment under the command of *Oberstleutnant* Gerhard Schirmer, which became the corps' 3rd Panzer-Grenadier Regiment. I Battalion, 29th Flak Regiment and the *Führer* Flak Battalion were incorporated into the HG Parachute Flak Regiment as complete units. The corps' operations staff occupied quarters in the village of Austinhof, located 14 kilometers southwest of Gumbinnen. The supply group took up quarters in Gerwen, 9 kilometers northwest of Gumbinnen. In November it moved to Großgauden, situated between Insterburg and Gumbinnen.

A continuous trench system was created between the villages of Ebenrode, Trakehnen, Weidendorf, and Großwaltersdorf, which was continuously manned by corps troops. In this area the Russian positions were often only about 50 meters from the German. The enemy positions were kept under observation each day from the area east of Peterstal-Schwarzenau, primarily by the soldiers of the HG 2nd Armored Reconnaissance Battalion. This was the district of the snipers. On both sides of the front the best shots lay in wait to kill the enemy with well-aimed shots. The war there became a contest of cunning and tricks. A single minor mistake, a raising of the head, meant instant death. Military activities were limited to reconnaissance and combat patrols, with the objective of keeping a watch on the other side. The Soviets rained leaflets on the German positions; they urged the defenders to surrender and offered assurances of life, good treatment, and a return home after the war. The effort failed to achieve the desired effect, however; the Reichsmarschall's soldiers had seen how things really were in Nemmersdorf.

The last Christmas of the war was celebrated within the realm of what was possible. Each soldier received a large Christmas cake as a special gift from the corps, whose bakery company had produced 45,000 such cakes. All the indications were that the enemy's next attack would not be long in coming. Hundreds of reconnaissance reports had allowed Fourth Army to form an accurate picture of the enemy's strength and armament. This revealed that the Red Army possessed a tenfold superiority in infantry. Where tanks were

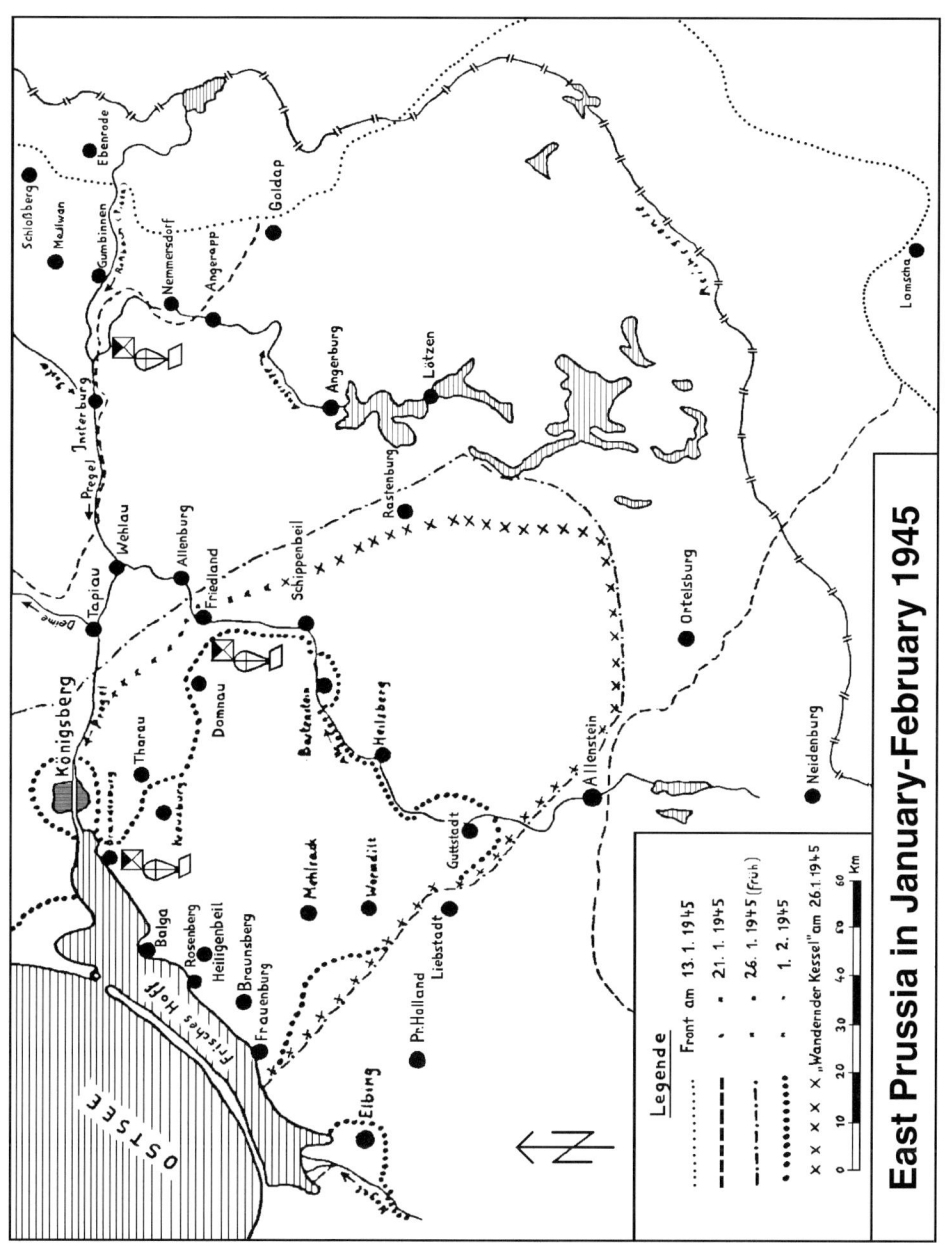

concerned the ratio was one to seven, artillery one to twenty. Each German division in the main line of resistance had to occupy and defend a sector of about twenty kilometers.

On 15 January 1945 Army Group Center's limited reserves were decisively weakened when the HG 1st Parachute-Panzer Division and the Panzer Corps *Großdeutschland* – less the corps' panzer-grenadier division – were withdrawn from the East Prussian theater and sent to Litzmannstadt to Army Group A. This meant the loss of the HG Parachute-Panzer Corps' strongest unit. As a result of these measures a successful defence of East Prussia was no longer possible. During the positional warfare in East Prussia the following units were under the command of the HG Parachute-Panzer Corps for lengthy periods:

    349th Volksgrenadier Division
    549th Volksgrenadier Division
    61st Infantry Division
    HG 1st Parachute-Panzer Division
    HG 2nd Parachute-Panzer-Grenadier Division
    21st Infantry Division

To the left and right of the parachute-panzer-corps were XXVI Army Corps and XXXXI Panzer Corps. In the course of several reorganizations the 349th and 549th *Volksgrenadier* Divisions were taken from the HG Parachute-Panzer Corps and placed under the command of XXVI Army Corps. The HG 1st Parachute-Panzer Division was also removed, as has been mentioned. As a result of these changes, just prior to the Soviet attack the corps had under its command the following units:

    61st Infantry Division
    HG 2nd Parachute-Panzer-Grenadier Division
    21st Infantry Division

Beginning 11 January the entire northern sector of the Eastern Front was placed on the highest degree of alert readiness. On 12 January the following report was issued to all units:

"This morning the Soviets launched their anticipated offensive from the Vistula bridgeheads at Baranow, Magnuszew-Warka and Pulawy."

The first assault was directed against Army Group A, commanded by *Generaloberst* Harpe, in the Polish battle zone. That day things still remained quiet for Army Group Center, and thus for the HG Parachute-Panzer Corps. During the night of 13 January the corps moved into battle positions. A few hours later, at 0700, several thousand Russian guns opened fire on the German positions in East Prussia. The units of the 3rd White Russian Front under General Chernyakovskiy struck at the boundary between the Third Panzer Army and the Fourth Army in an effort to exploit this weak spot. The divisions of XXVI Army Corps held firm against this first assault between Schloßberg and Ebenrode. The 61st Infantry Division, now part of Fourth Army, was sucked into the maelstrom. The battle lasted three days before XXVI Army Corps was forced to withdraw in the face of the enemy's superiority. Schloßberg was lost on 18 January.

At the same time the Red Army command had expanded its attacks in the south into the area north of Goldap and thus into the area held by the HG Parachute-Panzer Corps. The HG 2nd Parachute-Panzer-Grenadier Division, corps units, and the attached 21st Infantry Division, as well as the 61st Infantry Division, which was already in the thick of things on the left wing, managed to hold the entire corps sector in spite of strenuous efforts by the Russians. The day-long Russian assaults had been unable to break through this front and had also failed to achieve any deep penetrations.

In order to reinforce this hard-pressed sector the Fourth Army transferred the 50th Infantry Division from the less-threatened sector south of Goldap to the HG Parachute-Panzer Corps. In this way contact was maintained between the left wing of Fourth Army and the Third Panzer Army's southern wing, which was being bent farther back each day. What was missing there was the HG Parachute-Panzer Division and the Panzer Corps GD. Both large units arrived too late in their new battle zone. They were thus unable to close the gap there and were also absent from the fighting in East Prussia. Hitler's calculation, on which this transfer rested, had burst like a soap bubble.

Schloßberg, Mallwen, Gumbinnen, Insterburg, and Nemmersdorf were lost one after another in the bitter fighting that raged from 13 to 21 January. As the enemy pressure grew ever greater the HG Parachute-Panzer Corps was also forced to withdraw to avoid losing contact with the neighboring units. The enemy reached his objective on 23 January 1945. Soviet forces stood before Elbing, having split Second Army and isolated East Prussia.

A defence of East Prussia was hopeless with the forces available; because of the pocket situation no new forces could be sent. The Commander-in-Chief of Fourth Army, *General der Infanterie* Hoßbach, therefore decided – with the approval of the Commander-in-Chief of Army Group Center, *Generaloberst* Reinhardt – to regroup his army, including the attached XX Army Corps, fight his way west as a moving pocket, and regain contact with the Second Army, whose front line extended from Elbing to north of Marienwerder and further upstream along the Vistula at that time.

Hoßbach chose to move the pocket in East Prussia for two reasons: first he hoped to avoid a second Stalingrad for the approximately 400,000 soldiers in the pocket, and second it was his intention to take the East Prussian civilian population with him to the west. Numerous civilian columns were moving about East Prussia trying to escape the Soviets. Sadly this plan was frustrated in its early stages. Nevertheless, plans were prepared for the Fourth Army and consequently the HG Parachute-Panzer Corps. After completing its regrouping, with the bulk of its forces on the west side of the pocket, on 26 January 1945 the Fourth Army began its breakout to the west led by XXVI Army Corps' 28th Light Infantry Division as well as the 131st and 170th Infantry Divisions of VI Army Corps. The battle lasted three days and took the enemy completely by surprise; the target areas of Schlobitten, Preußisch-Holland, and west of Liebstadt were all reached. There the totally unexpected happened, however. The *Gauleiter* of East Prussia, Koch, sent a radio message to Hitler stating that the Fourth Army was fleeing East Prussia. The message ended with the bombastic words: "I will continue to defend East Prussia with the Volkssturm." (It should be noted that *Gauleiter* Koch later fled in a *Kriegsmarine* motor torpedo boat, taking with him his staff and his personal belongings.)

In any case Hitler saw treason. He ordered the immediate removal of *General* Hoßbach and the appointment of *General* Friedrich Wilhelm Müller as new army commander-in-chief. The breakout was prevented by an order of the Führer. During this time the HG Parachute-Panzer Corps had to fight off heavy enemy attacks. On 28 January 1945 the Wehrmacht communiqué reported:

"Forty-seven tanks were destroyed in the heavy fighting, 40 of these by the 'Hermann Göring' Panzer Corps."

On 25 January 1945 Army Group Center was renamed Army Group North. *Generaloberst* Reinhardt was relieved and replaced by *Generaloberst* Dr. Lothar Rendulic. In the course of the reorganization of the army group, on 30 January 1945 the HG Parachute-Panzer Corps, among others, was removed from Fourth Army and placed under the command of the Third Panzer Army. When, on 8 February 1945, Headquarters, Third Panzer Army transferred to Pomerania, the HG Parachute-Panzer Corps and all its attached divisions once again came under the command of the Fourth Army.

Hitler forbade further operations toward the west. On 30 January Fourth Army was once again forced to go over to the defensive. Attacks were now launched against the pocket from all sides. Losses in men and materiel could no longer be replaced from the Reich. South of the Pregel the HG Parachute-Panzer Corps was forced back by divisions of the 2nd White Russian Front. Further territory was lost in the remaining sectors of the pocket as well.

At the beginning of February 1945 the Fourth Army stood with its back to the sea in a line Frisches Haff – Braunsberg – west of Wormditt – east of Liegstadt – south of Guttstadt – Heilsberg – Bartenstein – Schippenbeil – west of Friedland – north of Domnau – south of Tharau – Brandenburg. All in all in the seven shattered corps the army had under its command 24 divisions, all exhausted and some of them badly battered. There was no hope of replacing losses. Facing these German units in the same area were about 100 enemy divisions, as well as numerous tank brigades and regiments which had recently been brought up to strength. These units of the Red Army were commanded by the 2nd and 3rd White Russian Fronts.

The fighting was extremely intense. The Wehrmacht communique of 10 February reported from this battle zone:

"More than 100 Soviet tanks were destroyed in bitter fighting, including 80 in the area of the HG Parachute-Panzer Corps alone."

The Fourth Army's mission was to gain time and hold the defended area as long as possible. It was imperative to save the refugees still in the pocket, numbering in the hundreds of thousands, and ensure their escape across the still-frozen bay and the Frische Nehrung. The fate of the Fourth Army and thus the HG Parachute-Panzer Corps had been sealed.

In the Heiligenbeil Pocket

When the Heiligenbeil pocket was closed the 150,000 men of the Fourth Army (Gen.d.Inf. Müller), of which 120,000 were combat troops, were surrounded by seven Soviet armies. These were the 5th, 28th and 2nd Guards Armies and the 31st, 50th, 3rd and 48th Armies. Since the end of February the German Fourth Army had been receiving only ammunition and fuel by sea. Personnel replacements were not sent. Soon the transport of materiel, too, was no longer possible. Fuel and ammunition became scarce in the pocket, whose center-point was the city of Heiligenbeil. The airfield there was used to fly in supplies and fly out wounded until it fell into enemy hands. There were seven hospitals in the city itself. About 4,000 wounded could be reckoned on for each day of heavy fighting. The number of dead was only slightly lower.

Enemy activity on the ground decreased from the beginning of March, however the Soviet Air Force kept up its attacks on the mass of people in the pocket. Soldiers and civilians alike were attacked by enemy fighter-bombers, fighters, and bombers. Until 13 March the defensive line ran north-south from the bay through Waldburg, Kobbelbude, and Konradswalde to Lindenau, Frauenburg, and the bay. The HG Parachute-Panzer Corps was deployed on the northern wing of this front. In addition to the divisions' own units, corps headquarters had under its command, from left to right, the GD Panzer-Grenadier Division, the 562nd *Volksgrenadier* Division and the HG 2nd Parachute-Panzer Grenadier Division. On the right was the 50th Infantry Division.

The next major attack by the Red Army took place on 13 March. In the HG 2nd Parachute-Panzer-Grenadier Division's sector between Konradswalde and Wesselshofen lay a section of the Elbing – Königsberg highway, which was cut in several places by the front line. Again and again these points were the scenes of determined attacks and equally determined defensive efforts by the HG units. The HG Parachute-Panzer Assault Battalion particularly distinguished itself there. The Soviet command had apparently selected the defense sector of the HG Parachute-Panzer Corps as the focal point of its offensive.

The fighting strength of the corps' units sank from day to day and could not be made good. The fuel situation was just as catastrophic as that of munitions and food. The battles which began on 13 March were of a dramatic nature. The HG Parachute-Panzer Corps' extended northern sector had to be pulled back hastily. The villages of Brandenburg, Konradswalde, Lank and others fell into Russian hands. A battalion of the Parachute-Panzer Flak Regiment destroyed 24 enemy tanks in one day of fighting, but hundreds of others rolled past, crushing beneath their tracks everything that got in their way. The fighting abated somewhat on 19 March, only to break out with renewed vigour on the 21st. Two days later all the towns south of the line Bladiau – Heiligenbeil – Leisuhnen had fallen into enemy hands.

On 24 March strong Soviet armored forces broke into Heiligenbeil. The final battles in the city were concentrated around the Gneisenau Barracks of

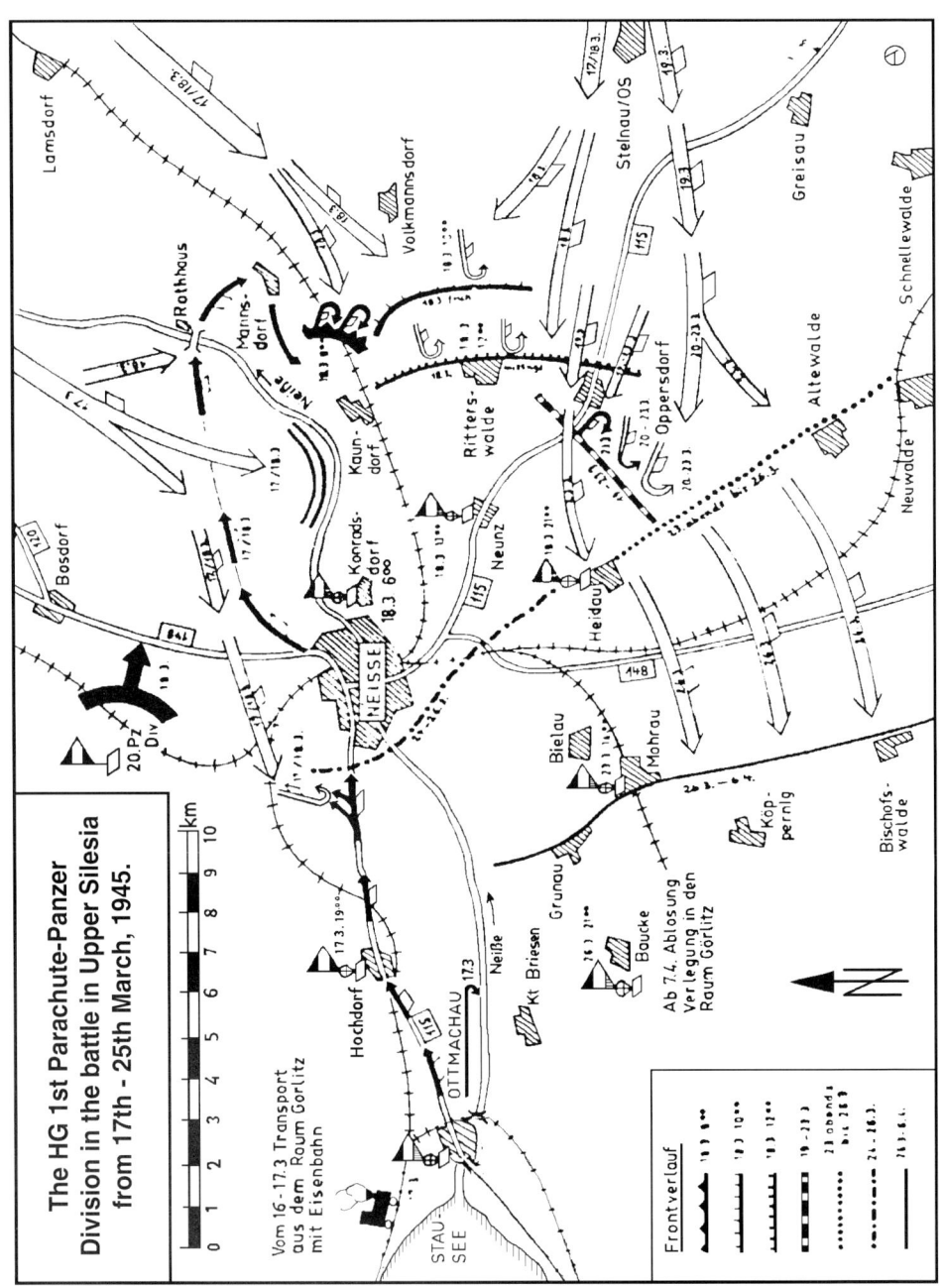

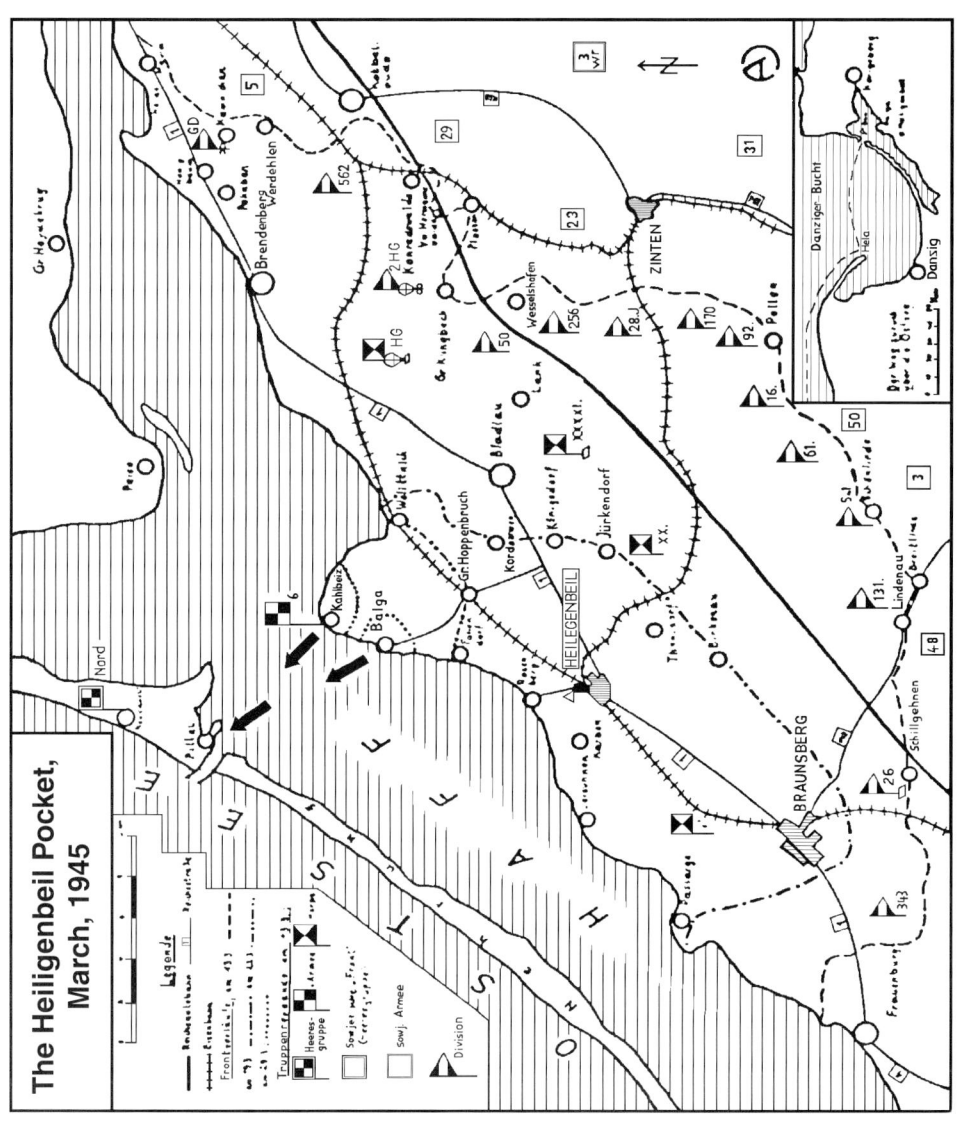

the 9th Machine-gun Battalion and the airfield lying in the direction of Rosenberg. These were also defended by units of the HG Parachute-Panzer Corps. Many military experts consider the fighting in the Heiligenbeil pocket to have been among the bloodiest of the entire Second World War.

On 25 March the corps still had under its command weak forces of the GD Panzer-Grenadier Division and the HG 2nd Parachute-Panzer-Grenadier Division. The 562nd Infantry Division had been totally wiped out. On the right was the 28th Light Infantry Division. The units previously there, the 50th Infantry Division and the 256th Volksgrenadier Division, no longer existed. The 25th of March witnessed a major effort by the Soviets. The defensive front was shortened further. The defenders were left with little more than the Balga Peninsula.

On 28 March some of the troops were surrounded in Balga and early on the morning of the next day the remainder were surrounded at the northern tip of the peninsula. The Wehrmacht communique of 29 March had already reported:

"At the Kahlholzer Horn the German rearguard troops have disengaged from the enemy and have crossed over to the Frische Nehrung."

The battle had thus come to an end – the East Prussian Stalingrad had become a reality. What was left of the HG Parachute-Panzer Corps crossed during the night of 30 March; the wounded had been moved to Pillau during the previous nights, where they were put aboard *Kriegsmarine* ships and transported back to Germany. Of the approximately 24,000 soldiers who served with the corps headquarters of the HG Parachute-Panzer Corps and the HG 2nd Parachute-Panzer-Grenadier Division since the beginning of the winter offensive, about 6,000 escaped alive from the Heiligenbeil pocket. These survivors assembled in Berlin-Reinickendorf and in the Velten barracks camp near Berlin. Several battalions were formed there by incorporating new replacements, which – as soon as they were ready to march – were sent toward the new battle zone in Saxony. The parachute-panzer corps was assembled between Hoyerswerda and Schwepnitz and readied for a new deployment.

The HG 1st Parachute-Panzer Division had meanwhile also arrived in the area of Saxony and thus finally rejoined its own corps. If the division had remained with the corps it would have represented a significant strengthening of the same, but would not have been able to change the unit's fate. From mid-April 1945 the HG Parachute-Panzer Corps was once again to see action in a body in Saxony. We now turn to the HG Corps' panzer division, but first the portrait of a soldier.

Oberst Bern von Baer: Portrait of a Soldier

When *Oberstleutnant* Bern von Baer and his battle group of the 16th Panzer Division advanced east from the Yelnichki area and drove 20 kilometers deep into enemy territory, he prevented the encirclement of an entire army corps and silenced the voices which had predicted that he would fail. Attacking by night, he succeeded in driving the enemy from the villages of

Alexandrovka and Chirkovichi and, after advancing a further 20 kilometers, established contact with the most forward elements of the encircled XXXV Army Corps west of Shazili.

Bern von Baer and his battle group were named in an Army Group Center order of the day. On 13 January 1944 he received the Knight's Cross for this feat. In early 1944 von Baer was transferred to the HG Parachute-Panzer Division, which had just been formed and transferred back into the Toscana to rest and refit. As the division's First General Staff Officer he played a role in the successes near Anzio-Nettuno and was one of the initiators of the defensive battles near Valmontone.

When the Red Army launched its great offensive on 12 and 13 January 1945, *Oberstleutnant* Bern von Baer handed over the corps headquarters' operations section to the Ia, in order to personally investigate the situation in the areas of operations, assemble scattered units with his small escort party, and deploy them where the front was weak. On 28 February 1945 von Baer became the 761st soldier to be awarded the Knight's Cross with Oak Leaves, in recognition of this action. *Reichsmarschall* Göring sent him a teletype message and congratulated him on winning the Oak Leaves. "But at the same time," said Göring, "I express my special thanks and fullest appreciation together with my best wishes for plenty of soldier's luck."

Having escaped the Heiligenbeil pocket across the bay, spit, and sea, after a period of rest and refitting in Berlin, von Baer led the corps headquarters through Silesia to Saxony into the new area of operations. On 1 April 1945 he set up the corps command post in Schwepnitz. In its last major action of the war, at the end of April the corps beat back a Polish division which was attempting to advance near Königsberg.

On 8 May the order to lay down its weapons reached the corps in the Dresden area. *Oberst* Bern von Baer was taken prisoner by the Red Army. He escaped from the Soviets in mid-May and in an adventurous flight escaped to the west. He rejoined his family in Reit im Winkl.

Now to the HG Parachute-Panzer Division and its employment outside the corps.

The Hermann Göring 1st Parachute-Panzer Division in the Final Battles

As recounted in the description of the evolution of the corps, the HG 1st Parachute-Panzer Division was taken into the corps and sent to Poland. On 12 January 1945 it was stationed in the Gumbinnen area as corps reserve. When the Soviet winter offensive began the division was attached to the *Großdeutschland* Panzer Corps under *General der Panzertruppe* Dietrich von Saucken. It entrained in Insterburg, in the process of which the correct tactical loading order was not followed. Instead of the combat elements, the first transport train carried the division headquarters with the commanding officer, *Generalmajor* von Necker, and the Ia with the divisional units. The entraining process was directed by General Staff *Hauptman* Fischer (of the Luftwaffe).

Disembarkation took place due northwest of Litzmannstadt on 17 January. Intense enemy aerial activity, in particular by Il 2 close-support aircraft, scarcely hindered the unloading; however a number of the selected detraining stations were already in enemy hands. Elements of the panzer regiment were forced to detrain on the open track. The division command post was set up near Kalino on 18 January. The division's mission was: "Attack in the direction of Petrikau in order to free units surrounded there, in particular the badly battered remnants of XXIV Panzer Corps under General Nehring."

The first engagements with opposing armored forces took place near Lancellenstadt while the division scouted the assembly area. The situation was uncertain. On account of the incorrect transport sequence the corps command first ordered the division to organize its units. By the evening of 19 January the division command post had been moved to Ruda Pabianizka. The division was fully assembled by the evening of 21 January. As part of the fighting withdrawal that had been ordered, that evening it arrived in the Moka area, about 3 kilometers northeast of Schieratz. Enemy cavalry units were already operating in the rear of the division. The bodies of about sixty, mostly older, Luftwaffe soldiers were found on a field road. The dead lay in a row; all had been killed by a single bullet to the back of the neck.

The next day near Schieratz the main body of the division made contact with cut-off elements of the unit under the command of *Oberst* Bertram, the commander of the 1st Parachute- Panzer-Grenadier Regiment. The fighting withdrawal continued and heavy enemy attacks were repulsed on 23 January. However the situation on both flanks made it necessary to withdraw farther toward the west. That evening the division command post was set up in Takomysle, 10 kilometers southeast of Kalisch.

The fighting withdrawal continued from the 24th to the 27th of January.

Oberfähnrich Hartelt in Action

The battles of January 1945 were conducted in the form of a moving pocket. The objective of the HG Division's panzer regiment was to delay the onrushing enemy in order to gain the time needed by the other units, in particular infantry divisions, for their retreat. Themselves constantly in danger of being surrounded and destroyed, each company and crew fought with the courage of desperation. When Hartelt's company commander was badly wounded on 23 January, Hartelt, just twenty years old, took command. His company's panzers were always employed as a rear guard or in the point position. Hartelt destroyed one enemy tank after another. On 25 January he was awarded the Iron Cross, First Class. His company became the regiment's spearhead.

On the morning of 24 January Hartelt was summoned by the commander of I Battalion, *Hauptmann* Renz. When Hartelt reported, Renz said to him:

"Hartelt, you are to form the division's rear guard. You and your five remaining tanks must hold up the pursuing enemy for at least four hours." *Hauptmann* Renz had just returned from *Oberst* von Heydebreck's command post. The latter had outlined the mission and then dismissed him with best wishes.

On the evening of 24 January the men of Hartelt's company could see the enemy artillery fire, joined now and then by the firing of a *katushka* battery. An unbroken stream of rocket salvoes roared toward them. Luckily for the tank crews they fell among the German positions about 2,000 meters away. *Hauptmann* Renz alerted the battalion. The tanks moved out. The five Panthers of Hartelt's company remained behind. They moved into position among the squat houses at the eastern edge of the village and took cover behind a hedge. The *Oberfähnrich* walked over to his Panther, climbed through the hatch and put on his throat microphone and headset.

"Everything in order, Becker?" – "Nothing special going on, *Herr Oberfähnrich*" replied the latter.

Hartelt then called the individual tanks. One after another they reported ready for action. Then the voice of *Oberfeldwebel* Amrein rang out:

"Track noises from the southeast, approaching rapidly." – "How many, Amrein?" asked Hartelt.

"Five at most, *Herr Oberfähnrich*." – "Thank you, I'm coming straight away." The command tank's driver set the vehicle in motion. Turning hard, he drove onto the road leading east, rolled along it about 100 meters and then rattled through the ditch and across a field in the direction of the tip of a wood, where Hartelt knew Amrein had positioned his Panther.

Peering through his binoculars, Hartelt strained to make out something in the darkness, but all he could see was the wall of flashes from the Russian artillery fire. When he reached Amrein's tank, the latter reported that the track noises had ceased. Hartelt stopped him halfway through his report, for the sound of roaring tank engines and rattling tracks had suddenly become audible. Hartelt called the four remaining panzers and told them to hold their positions. Then he cautiously moved forward toward the north, in the direction of the track noises. The two Panthers rolled through a depression whose upper rim was overgrown with dense brush. The heavy coating of snow had transformed the bushes into a dense jungle.

After advancing 300 meters Hartelt had his driver turn hard right. Slowly the Panther climbed up the flank of the depression. On reaching the top it pushed aside the wall of snow and bushes. At that moment Hartelt saw the enemy tanks. They were rolling toward the village one close behind the other.

"Battle readiness!" ordered Hartelt. He viewed the situation through the bullet-proof glass of the turret cupola. "We'll take the leading one, Percher. Range 500, one o'clock! – Fire when ready!"

A red lance of flame shot from the long barrel. The shell flitted across to the enemy tank, which had exposed its vulnerable flank to the Panther. The shot struck the rear of the T 34; in seconds the tank became a blazing torch. Loader Zittau rammed the next armor-piercing round into the breech. The turret traversed a few degrees left. Gunner Percher had the next T 34 in his sight. Another shot, a second hit. Disabled by the hit, the enemy tank sat immobilized. By now the remaining two T 34s had grasped the situation.

They opened fire on the company commander's Panther.

"To the left! Full gas!" Hartelt ordered his driver. The Panther jerked around and literally leapt forward. The enemy shells raced past, missing the rear of the tank by less than two meters. Something crashed hard against the side of the turret; a ricochet from a shell striking at a sharp angle. There was a flash from where Amrein's Panther was positioned. The third T 34 was immobilized with a shattered track. The next shot set it afire. Now there was only one left. It had been hit in the tracks but continued firing. The T 34 was destroyed by two shots from both sides.

Wolfgang Hartelt now ordered his meager force to attack. The five Panthers rolled toward the enemy in a broad wedge. Three times they ran into strong Russian patrols, which were scattered with high-explosive shells and machine-gun fire. *Oberfähnrich* Hartelt had his Panther move laterally to simulate an entire battalion, a move that obviously succeeded. The Soviet troops fell back at an increasingly rapid pace. Four hours had passed when Hartelt ordered his tanks to head back to the supply train in the village behind them. There the Panthers were refuelled and rearmed before continuing on their way. Hartelt assembled his crews around him.

"We must now establish contact with the division as quickly as possible so that the Ivans don't cut us off. The tank noises we've heard in the past hours from the south and north are moving west, which means that we are in the process of being outflanked. As we have no maps, we'll have to follow the tracks of the others. Sooner or later we'll find the division. So: in a line, forward!"

Oberfähnrich Hartelt led the way. In the twilight of morning the trees were visible as dark silhouettes. Five panzers rolled through no-man's-land alone. Hartelt stood in his open turret hatch and saw before him the tracks of the German tanks that had rolled through here before them. When a settlement appeared before the tanks, Hartelt suddenly had the feeling that there was danger there. But there was no way to bypass the village – the local terrain conditions, with woods and a depression, made this impossible.

Hartelt had two Panthers spread out to the left and right to guard the advance. The remaining tanks rolled toward the village in single file. They left the cover of the forest and approached to within 800 meters of the village before the dug-in enemy opened fire from the cover of houses, sheds, and hedges. The fireworks were caused by enemy tanks and anti-tank guns.

The five Panthers split up and spread out in all directions. One of them drove straight toward a haystack and crushed an anti-tank gun positioned there. The rest reached safe cover without being damaged seriously. The Russian tanks left the village to go over to the attack. The first took a direct hit from a range of 800 meters and was left burning and disabled. Ammunition exploded in its interior. The other Panthers joined the firefight. The village was in flames. The Panthers dodged from cover to cover, halting only to fire. Although the battle was only ten minutes old, seven enemy tanks lay burning or immobilized on the open plain in front of the village. All five Panthers were now involved in the engagement. Thanks to their superior speed they were repeatedly able to evade the charging enemy and open fire once again.

After 45 minutes of combat twenty disabled Soviet tanks lay in a wide semi-circle around the village. Some were burning, others had shed their tracks, while others displayed gaping holes. Only five or six enemy tanks were still firing. Hartelt ordered his small force to attack.

"Everyone take one," he called over the tank-to-tank frequency. The Panthers opened fire on the last surviving enemy tanks. Only one escaped. The Russian tank battalion, which had been moved forward during the night to prevent the Hermann Göring Division from withdrawing, was totally destroyed.

In the afternoon of 25 January 1945 all five Panthers reached the division. Each tank had only a few rounds of ammunition left. Hartelt was sent by *Hauptmann* Renz straight to the regimental commander. When he arrived, *Oberst* von Heydebreck greeted him with the following news:

"Hartelt, two hours ago we intercepted a Russian enemy situation report. It spoke of a tank battle with our rear guard. That rear guard was you. Congratulations to you and your men on the destruction of 25 enemy tanks. How many of these did you destroy yourself?"

"Seven, *Herr Oberst*," reported Hartelt.

"That now gives you 17 enemy tanks to your credit. As well you saved the division from heavy enemy attacks and enabled us to establish a new defensive line. I intend to recommend you for the Knight's Cross."

The defensive battle went on. Hartelt led his company with great success. Let us here move forward and review his actions before returning to the general events. On the morning of 20 March 1945 Hartelt and his company were ordered to hold a certain sector. The Soviets attacked with T 34s and super-heavy Josef Stalin I tanks. Hartelt threw his Panthers against the enemy armor. In the first duel with a Josef Stalin Hartelt's Panther was hit and disabled. Hartelt was still able to destroy an enemy tank before another Josef Stalin shot up his fuel tank.

Hartelt gave the order to bale out. A hard blow in the side caused him to fall back. He was pulled out of the burning Panther by his crew at the last second. Seriously injured, he was taken west within the moving pocket. Finally the division fought its way out and Hartelt was able to enter hospital. Wolfgang Hartelt received the Knight's Cross on 27 March 1945.

Battles of Retreat – The Attack on Steinau

On 27 January 1945 the troops of the HG Parachute-Panzer Division crossed the old Reich frontier near Waffendorf. The situation firmed up somewhat. Contact was reestablished to the left and right, but the enemy still exerted great pressure.

On 30 January the division was pulled back across the Oder. In the morning twilight the division crossed the Bartsch near Zapplau over a damaged bridge. An enemy artillery regiment, which was approaching the bridge with the same intent, was surprised by the panzer regiment and completely wiped out. Forty-five guns of greater than 100mm calibre were blown up by the pioneers. The Oder was crossed the following morning near Oberbeltsch. After the successful crossing the pontoons of the temporary bridge were destroyed. On 30 and 31 January the division command post was located in Alexanderhof, 6 kilometers north of Köben.

On 1 February it was learned that the enemy had crossed the Oder near Steinau and had surrounded the Steinau NCO School. The division headquarters set up quarters on the estate of the Crown Prince, the Gut Dornbusch. There plans and preparations were made for an attack on Steinau to relieve the NCO school. There was a heated disagreement between the Division Ia, General Staff *Major* W. Ebel, and the Crown Prince's Master of the Royal Household, who was incensed that the officers were ruining the inlaid floor with their hobnailed boots.

The attack on Steinau on 2 February 1945 made very slow progress. The command post was moved to Eisemost in order to be nearer to the troops. The attack continued on the 3rd, and elements of the NCO school which had risked a breakout were picked up by the division. The fighting for Mlitsch the next day was heavy. A thaw had set in, softening the roads. On 5 and 6 February there was bitter fighting in the "Little Lübener Heath". The fighting continued on 7 February.

The division launched the decisive attack toward the east on the morning of 8 February. At the same time heavy enemy artillery fire began. Twenty minutes later the Red Army counterattacked and achieved deep penetrations. The German tanks were ineffective in the wooded terrain. In the evening the main line of resistance was withdrawn and during the night the division was surrounded, together with the 16th Panzer and the "*Brandenburg*" Divisions. The surrounded German divisions launched a desperate attack and on 9 February smashed open a narrow corridor to the west. The same day saw *Generalmajor* Necker relieved. *Oberst* Lemke assumed command of the division, a position he was to hold until the end of the war. The breakout to the west was made south of Primkenau. Attacking by night, the German forces broke through the enemy blocking positions and continued their westward move during the night of 10 February.

They advanced west through the Kotzenau forest region and as the fate of the entire division was at stake, an officer-led patrol under the command of *Major* Ebel scouted the possibilities of crossing the enemy-held Kotzenau – Primkenau road. It was found that the Soviets had positioned anti-tank guns there.

Coincident with a feint attack toward the east, the tanks and assault guns were committed at the place selected for the breakout. The enemy forces positioned there were shot to pieces, the anti-tank guns overrun. The breakout between Weißig and Wolfendorf had been a success; pursuit by the enemy was hesitant. Toward noon the sounds of an armored engagement rang out from the north; Russian armor was attacking along the Primkenau – Sprottau road. The division's armored elements veered north and reached the road near Petersdorf. There they joined in the defence and in doing so helped protect the division's march columns which were flowing out of the Primkenau Forest.

A corps order incorporated the division into the defensive forces east of Sprottau. The defensive assignment lasted through 12 February and the division command post was moved there. The 12th of February saw bitter defensive fighting around Sprottau. The defenders threw *Volkssturm* and anti- aircraft auxiliary units into the battle. During the night there was a withdrawal into the Sagan area. The next day the defenders held their position east of the city. Not until the enemy increased his pressure in the direction of Sagan on 14 February and began bombing and shelling the city, was the main line of resistance moved closer to Sagan.

The subsequent gradual retreat on 20 February was supposed to be made in the direction of the Lausitzer Neiße. A bridgehead was to be established on the east bank of the river. While the bulk of the division occupied this new main line of resistance on the evening of 20 February, the rear guard, commanded by the Ia, *Major* Ebel, formed up on a broad front east of Zibelle. There it had to carry out several fast-moving counterattacks against the hard-pressing enemy. It received outstanding support from the flak battalion under *Hauptmann* Brinkmann, who had twelve Flak 88s at his disposal. His stocks of ammunition were enormous, and by utilizing the eighty-eight's great range, maintaining a very high rate of fire, and concentrating his fire, the battalion was able to support the rear guard's efforts most effectively. According to documents of the Division Ic, two enemy divisions were stopped by the rear guard.

The rearguard actions east of Zibelle continued on 22 February. Not until darkness fell was the rear guard withdrawn, as per orders, toward the Lausitzer Neiße and the Muskau bridgehead. The defensive battle in the Muskau bridgehead from 25 February to 3 March and the battles at the Lausitzer Neiße, which lasted until 10 March, gave the division a chance to move in replacement vehicles, armored cars, and light artillery. It even proved possible to supplement the number of Panzer IV tanks. The division also received a number of *Wespe* self-propelled 105mm howitzers. Ammunition stocks were adequate, but deliveries of fuel were a cause for concern.

As before, the anti-aircraft guns were provided with adequate stocks of ammunition. They increasingly came to be used in a ground role as artillery weapons. An attack against the bridgehead by a Soviet division on 12 March was repulsed. The next day saw a repetition of the attack, this time by two rifle divisions of the Red Army. The overall situation in Silesia had become critical, therefore the order to withdraw on 13 March did not come as a surprise. Movement of units was to be made by train, in order to conserve fuel.

The Battles from 13 March to 11 April 1945

At this point we will insert an account of the division's actions between 13 March and 11 April 1944. It is a detailed description of events contained in the personal diary of the Division Ia, *Major* W. Ebel. The account also includes material from the writings of former members of the division and several accounts of the fighting in Silesia by Alfred Otte, the official historian of the Hermann Göring Parachute-Panzer Corps.

But first the order of the day issued by Headquarters, Panzer Corps *Großdeutschland* on 13 March 1945:

"ORDER OF THE DAY – ORDER OF THE DAY – Soldiers of the Hermann Göring 1st Parachute-Panzer Division! On 10 and 11 March 1945 you achieved a great defensive success in the Muskau bridgehead. The forces of a bolshevik rifle division, augmented by tanks, were smashed to pieces on your firm will to defend and on your steadfastness and bravery. In these two days ObGefr. Willi Ritsege and Gefr. Fritz Blien of 5th Company, HG 1st Parachute-Panzer-Grenadier Regiment alone scored 29 sniper kills. Seven enemy tanks, including two Josef Stalins, were destroyed using close-range weapons. As far as I am concerned this is the best proof of your will to fight and win. I wish to express my greatest appreciation to your leader, Oberst Lemke, to his entire command, and to all of you for your exemplary actions.

Heil to our Führer!
signed Jauer."

The Hermann Göring Parachute-Panzer Division from 13 March to 11 April 1945

On 13 March the division received orders confirming that it was to be relieved. Beginning the evening of that same day, the units were pulled out of the line and sent by rail into the Görlitz area. The division was to be assembled there at the disposal of the army group. On 15 March division headquarters established its command post in Biesnitz, west of Görlitz, however only a few hours after its arrival orders were received stating that the division was to be employed elsewhere. The division command was ordered to make the appropriate preparations. The unit's advance personnel were soon on their way to Gnadenfrei via Lauban, Hirschberg, Landeshut, and Reichenau. There they learned from Headquarters, VIII Army Corps, to which the division was to be attached, that further orders were to be received from the local commander at Ottmachau as the situation there had become very critical.

At that point the front between Ratibor and Oppeln roughly followed the course of the Oder, veered westward at ninety degrees north of Oppeln, and then northward again southwest of Grottkau. In February the Soviets had been able to establish bridgeheads south of Cosel and near Krappnitz, situated between Cosel and Oppeln. These were defended tenaciously and had been enlarged somewhat. In mid-March German reconnaissance revealed that the Soviets were preparing a new operation against the Oppeln salient. In order to counter this, Army Group Center (*Generaloberst* Schörner) needed to reinforce the local sector, which lay within the area of the Seventeenth Army, by adding further units. Among the units which were to be sent there was the HG Parachute-Panzer Division. It was to be deployed in the sector of

XXXX Panzer Corps (*General* Henrici).

Individual elements of the division, which had been relieved in the Muskau bridgehead or which had not been deployed there, had already reached the assigned assembly area near Görlitz when the order to transfer to Ottmachau arrived. Since the necessary transport space was already standing by when the transfer order arrived, loading began immediately. The first units to entrain were those elements on hand in Görlitz. These included the main body of the panzer regiment, elements of the artillery, divisional units, and supply troops. Due to the limited time available loading did not take place in a tactically correct sequence, which was later to prove a great disadvantage. The first elements of the division to entrain arrived in Ottmachau during the course of 17 March and were moved up into the designated assembly area west of Neisse. The division command post was initially set up in Ottmachau's railway station and from 19.00 hours in Hochkirch, seven kilometers west of Neisse.

In the meantime it had become evident that the Russians had begun a pincer operation with armored and infantry forces. They thrust south from the Grottkau area, or toward Neisse, with one pincer, while the other drove south from the bridgehead south of Cosel toward Leobschütz – Hotzenplotz – Neustadt.

On the evening of 17 March the division commander, *Oberst* (as of April 1945 *Generalmajor*) Lemke, arrived at the division command post, bringing with him the corps order to attack the next morning. According to the order the division was to attack eastward from the area six kilometers east of Neisse and three kilometers south of the Neisse bridge near Rothhaus; its objective was to capture the Volkmannsdorf-Mannsdorf sector. The 20th Panzer Division, which was also on its way to the assembly area, was to attack simultaneously north of the Neisse. Enemy advances into the assembly area during the night of 18 March caused considerable disruptions in the assembly of the division. In places the march road had to be retaken from the enemy. On the other hand all was quiet in the assembly area between Konradsdorf and Kaundorf.

The execution of the attack depended exclusively on the timely arrival of supplies. The units' existing stocks of munitions and fuel were insufficient; fortunately the necessary supplies arrived during the night. The situation on the other side had meanwhile developed as follows: north of the Neisse a powerful group of enemy forces had succeeded in taking the commanding heights of the north bank and had pushed weak forces ahead as far as the area northwest of Neisse. Enemy armored forces were thought to be waiting behind this group. However the greater threat was developing around Steinau, fifteen kilometers southeast of Neisse, where aerial reconnaissance had detected a powerful concentration of armored forces. This threat could only be met through the possession of the sector assigned to the division as its attack objective. On account of the nature of the local terrain an enemy armored attack from the Steinau area toward Neisse could only be made through Oppersdorf-Neunz. Such an attack could be countered effectively from the flank from the Volkmannsdorf-Mannsdorf sector.

On the morning of 18 March the division command post was moved to Konradsdorf, two kilometers east of Neisse, or just behind the division's attack forces. The attack was begun with the limited forces then available. The main body of the division arrived too late; moreover it went into action in a tactically incorrect sequence. As a result of heavy enemy fire from the north bank the attack soon bogged down, even though frontally it met only weak resistance; however, the division lacked the means with which to eliminate the enemy's flanking fire. The attack by the 20th Panzer Division had proved ineffective. The division therefore went over to the defensive. In the course of regrouping it was assigned the following sector: left boundary roughly from south end of Kaundorf to south end Kl. Briesen, right boundary roughly from south end of Oppersdorf to south end of Köppernig.

With the arrival of further elements of the division the right boundary was extended further, so that it now ran roughly from the Schnellewalde in a westerly direction. During the course of the day the unit was reorganized in an approximate line Kaundorf – Ritterswalde – Oppersdorf. The division command post was moved to Neunz at noon. Throughout the day the units of the division fought off attacks on the still uncompleted front.

On the next day, 19 March, unremitting heavy attacks – with tank forces in the Oppersdorf area – led to local penetrations. These could not be cleared up, and during the night of 20 March the front had to be withdrawn a short distance. In the evening the division command post was moved to Heidau. The enemy mounted repeated strong attacks from 20 to 22 March, all of which were repulsed.

From a report on a visit to the units by the Commander-in-Chief of Luftflotte 6, *Generaloberst* Ritter von Greim, we learn that *Generaloberst* Schörner "criticised the middle command of the HG Parachute-Panzer Division" during an Army Group Center internal conference in Jermer-Josefstadt on 19 March.

Following a situation briefing, on 21 March *Generaloberst* Ritter von Greim visited the HG Parachute-Panzer Regiment commanded by *Oberstleutnant* Roßmann. The trip report stated:

"HG Parachute-Panzer Regiment attacking toward Schnellewalde; Commander-in-Chief Luftflotte 6 at forward regimental command post."

"During the course of the day's fighting nine tanks destroyed by the regiment. A police battalion in the main line of resistance was stormed by a Russian assault squad of 25 men. Regiment has destroyed 23 anti-tank guns and 17 tanks since 17 March. Regiment is bitter over treatment by Army. 'They want to take away our cuff bands!' Commander-in-Chief received following situation report:

"The Army erred in its calculations of the division's authorized strength. In truth the division was sent to the attack near Neisse while most of it was still on the march. Attacked without artillery or flak. Even the tanks had little fuel, no armor-piercing shells apart from 4 rounds per gun. Infantry was without transport. The Reichsmarschall receives daily reports on the course of the battle. Commander-in-Chief has requested copies in order to make corrections if necessary. The troops make an excellent impression."

Enemy regroupings were observed on 22 March, which pointed toward a massed attack in the Oppersdorf area the next day. In fact the expected enemy attack in the Oppersdorf area began at about nine o'clock the next morning. Some division units situated there were driven back. Afterward elements of the panzer regiment counterattacked. These encountered superior enemy armored forces which repulsed the attack. Twelve German tanks (Panzer IV) were lost within a short space of time. The enemy attack could not be stopped until just before the division command post in Heidau. The front was pulled back to a line running east of Heidau – east of Altenwalde – east of Neuwalde. As well the division command post was withdrawn to Mohrau at 1400 hours.

From the beginning of the battle the attack by the strong Russian armored forces from the bridgehead south of Cosel to the west through Leobschütz-Hotzenplatz toward Neustadt, approximately on the boundary line between Seventeenth Army and First Panzer Army, placed Seventeenth Army in a very dangerous situation. On the one hand there existed the threat that the five German divisions deployed along the Oder in the Oppeln salient might be encircled, but on the other hand there was also the danger that a breakthrough by the Russians might result in an advance into the protectorate, which could have shaken the structure of the German southern wing which had been guarded so laboriously.

This threat was averted just in time, as it was possible to deploy a hastily-assembled blocking unit, Blocking Unit "C", there. It was led by the senior pioneer leader *Oberst* Capelle, thus the designation Blocking Group "C". Under energetic leadership, hastily scraped-together units, including the division's armored reconnaissance battalion, were able to establish a defensive front at the last minute, destroying 12 tanks in the process. This allowed the units threatened with encirclement to escape. The defensive front ran along the Neisse- -Heidau – Altenwalde – Neuwalde – Ludwigsdorf road to the wooded heights south of Ziegenhals. On 23 March the units of the HG Division which had been moved back took over the northern part of this line. The city of Neisse, which had been declared a fortress, was lost during the night of 23/24 March.

On 26 March, under heavy enemy pressure and in conjunction with events at the front held by the neighboring units, the position occupied on 23 March had to be withdrawn to a line roughly from Grunau to Mohrau to Bischofswalde. At 2100 hours the division command post was moved to Baucke. This position was held by the division until 6 April. The Russians had achieved their goal of reducing the Oppeln salient and capturing further territory. On the other hand they had not succeeded in encircling the units between Oppeln and Cosel: the 20th SS Panzer-Grenadier Division, the 168th Infantry Division, the 344th Infantry Division, the 18th SS Panzer-Grenadier Division, and the 371st Infantry Division. These units were able to escape encirclement, but at the cost of considerable losses.

As grave as the loss of territory may have been, much more serious were the again heavy losses in men and military equipment which at this point, with the war having entered its final phase, could not be replaced. The civilian population, whose columns often became mixed up in troop movements and caught up in the fighting as they tried to flee the advancing Soviet armies, suffered terribly from the horrors of the war. Among the regrettable losses suffered by the division in this heavy fighting in the battle in Upper Silesia was the commander of the HG 1st Parachute-Panzer-Grenadier Regiment, *Oberst* Bertram. He was one of the unit's veterans and had made the entire journey from the days of the State Police. His posts during peacetime had included regimental adjutant of the General Göring Regiment. After the war began he commanded the HG Escort Regiment and most recently had been commander of the 1st Regiment since 1944. He was one of the division's bravest soldiers. When, on 28 March 1945, the division received a teletype stating that he had been awarded the Knight's Cross, the division commander, *Oberst* Lemke, made his way to *Oberst* Bertram and gave him his own Knight's Cross. Only a few hours later Bertram was fatally wounded by a shell fragment.

The situation quieted down somewhat in the first days of April; the division was pulled out of the line and assembled in the Schweidnitz area at the disposal of the army group. The advance personnel departed on 7 April. The division's units followed at short intervals and moved into the Schweidnitz area. There they received a badly needed rest. Contrary to expectations it was to be of short duration. The fighting in Poland and Lower Silesia and finally near Neisse had taxed the troops almost beyond human imagination; they had practically not been out of their clothes since their departure from East Prussia. They had been given no opportunity to rest, instead they had been moved from one hot spot to another. All the unit commanders did everything possible to make the units battle ready again as quickly as possible. Replacements were taken in, weapons and equipment supplemented, and – as strange as it may sound – battle training was resumed at once. Conducted in parallel was officer and NCO training, the objective of which was to familiarize replacement officers and NCOs with the tactics of modern warfare and the bitter experiences of the past months.

The heavy losses of recent months made necessary the disbandment of some companies and battalions, in order to bring the remaining units up to relatively acceptable combat strengths. At this time the division command post was located in Cammerau, four kilometers west of Schweidnitz. With the arrival of beautiful spring weather and the charming surroundings the soldiers soon regained their energy. In this period the division was familiarized with its possible future missions. Potential approach routes and battle sites were scouted in every direction. For example, an observation post was set up on the 718-meter-high Zobten, from where one could see as far as Breslau, where a battle for possession of the city was raging even then.

On 11 April Luftflotte 6 received the following teletype message:

"To Luftflotte 6:

(1) 'Hermann Göring' Parachute-Panzer Corps with both divisions will once again be grouped within the area of the 17th Army. All orders received by the 'Hermann Göring' Parachute-Panzer Division, which is already under

the command of the Seventeenth Army, concerning resting and refitting and operations remain in effect.

(2) The following are to be transported into the Hirschberg area and placed under the command of 17th Army: Headquarters, 'Hermann Göring' Parachute-Panzer Corps and 'Hermann Göring' Parachute-Panzer-Grenadier Division. With the arrival of the corps headquarters both 'Hermann Göring' divisions are to be grouped under its command. The corps is initially to assemble in the Schweidnitz – Bolkenhain – Hirschberg – Schmiedeberg – Landeshut area with the same missions as the 'Hermann Göring' Parachute-Panzer Division already in position there and is to refit the elements not suitable for operations. Orders for rest and refitting are to be issued separately.

(3) Corps advance personnel are to report to 17th Army.

(4) Effective immediately the 18th SS Panzer-Grenadier Division, initially without the regiment-size battle group still with the 1st Panzer Army, is placed under the command of the 17th Army. The combat-ready elements of this division can be withdrawn from their present cantonment area by the 17th Army and deployed in the front. Elements of the division which are currently under strength are to be sent to the rear sectors allocated to the division and brought up to strength by Seventeenth Army. The battalions still in training in the Prague area are to be moved out after a training period of 3 weeks.

(5) The 17th Army is to report on progress of the arrival and rejuvenation of the elements of the 'Hermann Göring' and the 18th SS Panzer-Grenadier Division on their way to the army in its daily report.

> Headquarters Army Group Center
> Röm. I a Nr. 2155/45 geh.
> signed von Natzmer, Generalleutnant"

Unfortunately for the remnants of the Parachute-Panzer Corps and the 2nd HG Parachute-Panzer-Grenadier Division which had escaped from the Heiligenbeil pocket, which were to be reunited with the HG 1st Parachute-Panzer Division in the area between Schweidnitz and the Riesengebirge, the rejuvenation phase referred to in this teletype message did not come to pass. The enemy plan gave the Parachute-Panzer Corps no peace. Those elements transported from East Prussia did not even reach the planned resting and refitting area, instead they were halted in the area north of Görlitz-Dresden and immediately thrown into the battle again. Only the joint command with the HG 1st Parachute-Panzer Division and their subsequent combined operations were to become a reality.

The panzer division's rest period in the area around Schweidnitz also came to a premature end. On 11 April the division received orders to come to march readiness within three hours and stand ready to depart for the Görlitz area. The wheeled elements made the journey overland; the tracked elements and artillery were moved by train. On its arrival the division stood ready to fight to the end.

On 12 April, as per orders, the division's advance detachment reported to the headquarters of the *Großdeutschland* Panzer Corps. When the Ia arrived there, orders were waiting for him to make his way to XXXVIII Panzer Corps, as the division had been placed under its command. The corps command post was located in Görlitz. There the HG Parachute-Panzer Division received orders to assemble in the area south and west of Görlitz and to make preparations to go into action in an easterly or northerly direction from its quartering areas.

By 14 April the division had arrived in the assigned area. That day the division command post was located in Groß-Biesnitz. At 0500 hours on the morning of 16 April the Soviets launched their offensive along the entire front on both sides of Görlitz. The division was placed on alert; then at 1100 hours *Generalfeldmarschall* Ferdinand Schörner appeared at the command post and informed the division commander that the enemy had broken through the front after successfully crossing the Neisse. He gave the division orders to move out at 1300, attack the enemy in the flank, and retake the main line of resistance along the Neisse. "The 20th Panzer Division and the 'Brandenburg' Division will attack on your left. You are to conduct the attack with all energy."

The attack began at 1300 hours; however the enemy had established a defensive flank to the south with strong forces, especially tanks, which put up determined resistance. On this day the units of the division destroyed a total of 65 enemy tanks. In spite of the continuation of the attack by night the division was unable to penetrate any deeper. Enemy resistance stiffened, and the attacking forces were forced to reorganize during the night. The HG 1st Panzer-Grenadier Regiment was temporarily placed under the command of the 20th Panzer Division. On 17 April, following the nocturnal reorganization and resumption of the battle, the division was forced to go over to the defensive; on the 18th it had to face heavy enemy armored assaults.

On the following day the attack by the 20th Panzer Division with the 1st HG Panzer-Grenadier Regiment also came to a halt. The Germans went over to the defensive along the entire front. There was a major engagement near Kodersdorf on 19 April. The following is a direct report by General Staff *Major* Ebel:

"A large enemy tank unit, which had previously been reported to us by air and land reconnaissance, suddenly emerged from the edge of a wood about 2 kilometers east of Kodersdorf. Our panzer regiment's mobile reserve, under its outstanding commander *Oberstleutnant* Roßmann, went into position with its 17 Panthers close to the stream beside which Kodersdorf lay. The enemy tank unit (we later discovered that it was the 1st Polish Tank Corps which had been formed by the Red Army) deployed into peacetime formation and rolled toward Kodersdorf. Not a shot was fired. Only when the leading tank had approached to within 50 meters did *Oberstleutnant* Roßmann open fire. The effect was devastating, every shot was on target. Forty- three enemy tanks were destroyed in 20 minutes, the rest showed the white flag. Twelve undamaged enemy tanks fell into our hands, including four of the Josef Stalin type. A few hours later, following the addition of the Balkenkreuz, they were put to use by us."

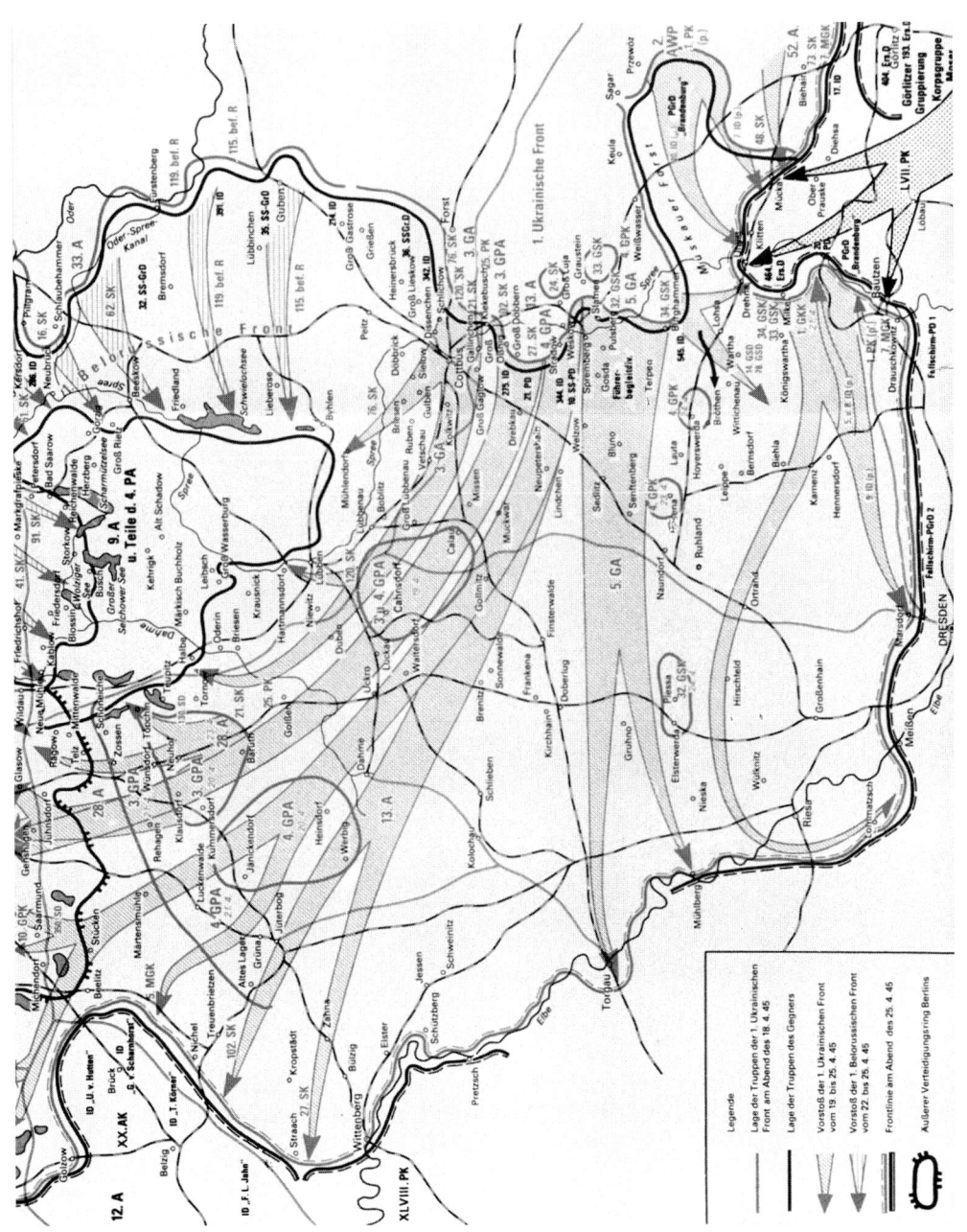

The advance by the 1st Ukrainian Front from 18th - 25th April, 1945.

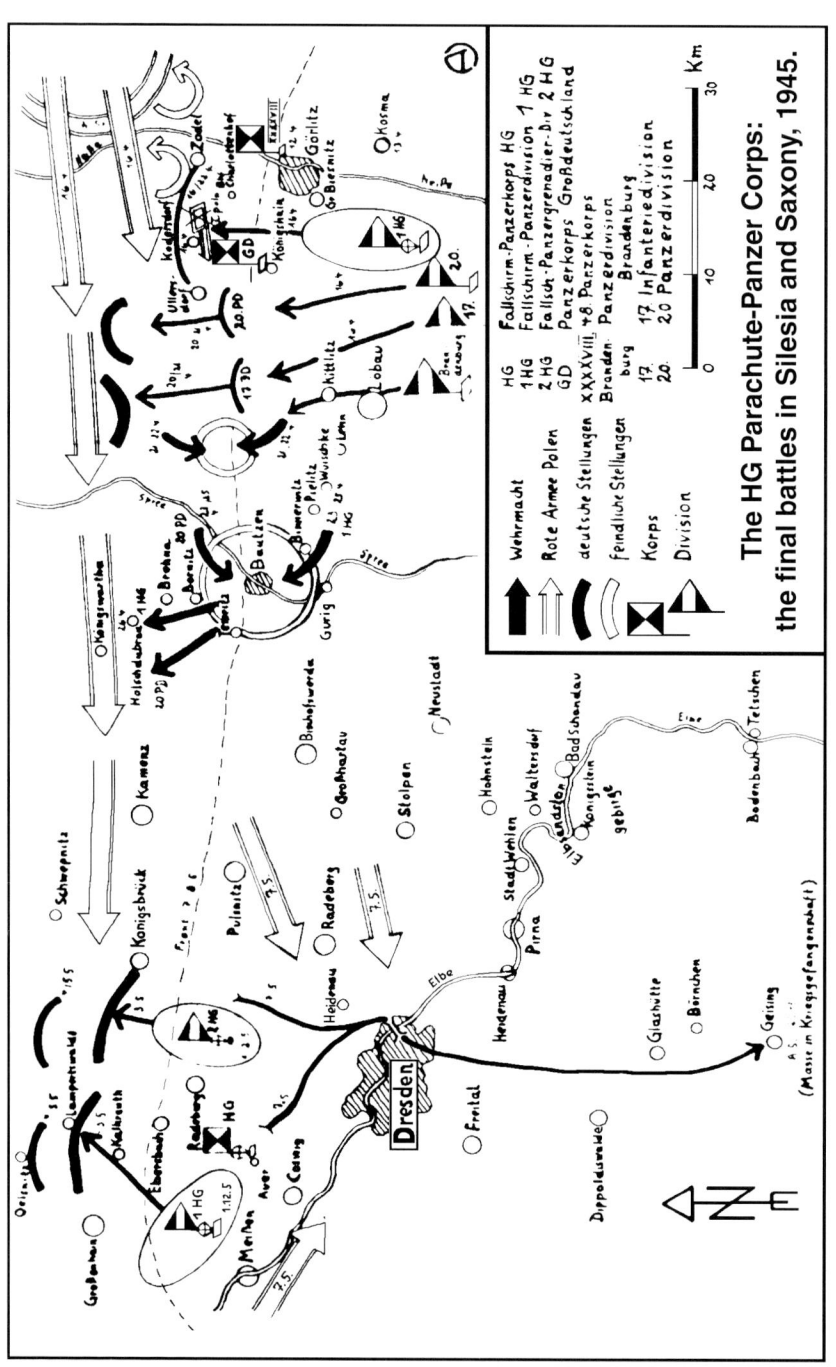

The HG Parachute-Panzer Corps: the final battles in Silesia and Saxony, 1945.

The remnants of the HG Parachute-Panzer Corps were evacuated from the Heiligenbeil Pocket by sea. After a brief period of rest and refitting they were supposed to be reunited with the corps' own panzer division as a unified corps. Rejuvenation of the units took place north of Berlin instead of in the Hirschberg/Riesengebirge area. Not all units could be rested and some were sent directly into the new area of operations.

"The HG Parachute-Panzer Corps Is Coming!"

In mid-April the corps headquarters and corps units of the HG Parachute-Panzer Corps and the HG 2nd Parachute-Panzer-Grenadier Division, the latter having been hastily brought up to strength and equipped in a makeshift fashion, arrived in the corps' new area of operations, Hoyerswerda-Bautzen. Soon afterward the HG Parachute-Panzer Division, whose defensive actions were described in the previous chapter, was once again placed under the command of its own corps after months of difficult operations outside the framework of the corps.

Following its defeat near Kodersdorf, the Red Army conducted no further serious offensive actions against the corps. It did, however, harass the German front with continuous attacks designed to tie up German forces. On 22 April the panzer division was pulled out of its positions and moved nearer the corps. On 22 April the division set up its command post in the Löbau area, near the corps. Direct communications were established with corps and discussions were held concerning a joint attack on Bautzen, which was occupied by the Russians.

The attack began on 23 April. It led through Wuischke, Pielitz, and Binnewitz directly into the city. Bautzen was taken in the first assault. The attacking battle groups pressed on to the northwest. During the night the attack forces regrouped for a continuation of the attack toward the north; on the afternoon of 24 April the division command post was moved to Temritz, three kilometers northwest of Bautzen. The attack was resumed on 25 April and continued the following day only to bog down in the wooded terrain north of Holschdubrau. The enemy had dug in there with strong forces and had assembled anti-tank and tank forces with which to launch a counterattack. The division command post was meanwhile located at Brohna, about 9 kilometers north of Bautzen.

The 27th and 28th saw defensive fighting against these enemy attacks. The division was relieved on 29 April and left the Bautzen area during the night, headed west. Finally, on 30 April, the last physical separation from the corps was overcome. The panzer division's advance detachment under *Major* Ebel reported to the corps command post near Großhartau and received instructions for the division to follow to Auerhaus, 10 kilometers east of Meißen. The division arrived there on the evening of 30 April. The reunification had been completed, even though the battle would last only a few more days. On 1 and 2 May, as the individual units arrived, the division was readied in the assembly areas for the upcoming attack.

The attack, whose long-range objective was Berlin, began early on the morning of 3 May. Initial progress was good and the attack spearheads reached the Königsberg-Großenhain road south of Lampertswalde. The entire Hermann Göring Parachute-Panzer Corps participated in the attack near Königsberg. An advancing Soviet armored spearhead, which included the 1st Polish Tank Division, was destroyed in heavy fighting. During the attack *Oberstleutnant* Roßmann and several of his officers drove into enemy-occupied Großenhain. They were able to escape unnoticed, however, and returned to their regiment unscathed.

At midday on 5 May the attack bogged down in the Oelsnitz area. The corps went over to the defensive and during the night pulled back some distance to reorganize its units. The advance toward Berlin came to an end on 5 May 1945. The corps took up position north of Dresden and the following day repulsed all attacks by the enemy. This position was evacuated on 7 May. The enemy pushed northwest along the Elbe and launched a direct attack on Dresden from the east. The danger thus existed that the units still north of Dresden might be cut off, making their planned move into the Erz Mountains impossible.

The division command post, located in Heide-Mühle in the Dresden Heath, was evacuated at 1400 hours on that day. This premature evacuation (it had initially not been planned until evening) had been ordered by radio, because enemy forces had broken through to Dresden from the east. The Elbe bridges had to be kept open at all costs. The Division Ia and the commander of the pioneer battalion rushed to the Loschwitz Bridge, which had been chosen as the division's crossing point, with a hastily assembled group of armored vehicles. The local commander had already ordered the bridge to be blown. The pioneers prevented the demolition, although they had to use threats of force to do so.

All of the elements of the panzer-grenadier regiment were also ordered to the bridge to form a bridgehead there and prevent the loss of the span at all costs. Russian tanks reached the Albertplatz in Dresden at 1600 hours and attempted to advance on the city's fixed bridges. These were then destroyed by German forces; however, the bridgehead on the east bank near Loschwitz was reinforced by the arriving units. Beginning at 1700 hours the division and elements of other units moved in an orderly fashion across the bridge to the south and southeast. The initial objective was Glashütte and the area to the south.

As one of the corps units, on 8 May 1945 the panzer division, mixed up with many refugee columns, marched through Heidenau-Glashütte into its assigned areas. The division commander was ordered to corps headquarters and there received orders to occupy a position on the crest of the Erz Mountains. At 1900 hours the HG Parachute-Panzer Division received a radio message from corps:

"Suspension of hostilities as of 20.00 hours. Unconditional surrender! Cease all movements."

The units blew up their weapons and ammunition. They had been instructed to head south immediately, through Czechoslovakia, and to the west in order to reach the Americans and escape the revenge of the Soviet soldiers. The Soviet armored spearhead under Marshall Konev, which had set out from Berlin in the direction of Prague, closed the pocket in which the greater part of the HG Parachute-Panzer Corps found itself. Only a few units succeeded in fighting their way through the Czechs, who had revolted, to seek captivity in the hands of the Americans. The bulk of the Hermann Göring Parachute-Panzer Corps was forced to begin the long march into Soviet captivity.

The Second World War was over. It had cost huge sacrifices, and following show trials many of the Reichmarschall's soldiers were sentenced to 25 years forced labor in Russia because they had belonged to an elite unit. The majority did not return to Germany until the end of 1949.

Generalfeldmarschall Model (right) in conversation with Generalmajor Schmalz.

Men of the Panzer Regiment HG; from left: Hauptfeldwebel Buchholz, Oberleutnant Dickel, Oberleutnant Franz Schuster, Oberleutnant Tschierschwitz, Oberleutnant von Rieben.

Officers of the Panzer Regiment HG; 2nd from left Major Roßmann.

In Italy and on the Eastern Front, Oberleutnant Wolfgang Bach proved to be a commander whose first thought was for the welfare of his men. He was awarded the German Cross in Gold.

Oberst Oehring, commander of the Parachute-Panzer Artillery Regiment HG.

Oberleutnant Knoblauch photographed in front of his command post near Giren, East Prussia, December 1944.

Knocked-out Soviet T-34/85 during the two day battle near Gumbinnen in November 1944.

Leutnant Tschierschwitz in the turret hatch of a Panzer V Panther.

This Panther has become bogged down.

A group of Knight's Cross wearers at the command post of the Parachute Panzer Corps HG; from left to right beginning with the back row: Oberst von Necker, Generalmajor Schmalz, Söth, Grün, von Baer, Roßmann, Kluge, Kulp, Rebholz, Ostermaier, Schlund.

Knight's Cross wearers of the Panzer Regiment HG. From the left: Stuchlik, Tschierschwitz, Kraus, Wallhäußer, Grunold, Steets, Plapper. On the extreme right is Oberfeldwebel Bowitz, German Cross in Gold.

Knight's Cross wearers of the Panzer Regiment HG with their commanding general. In the center are Generalmajor Schmalz and Oberst Necker.

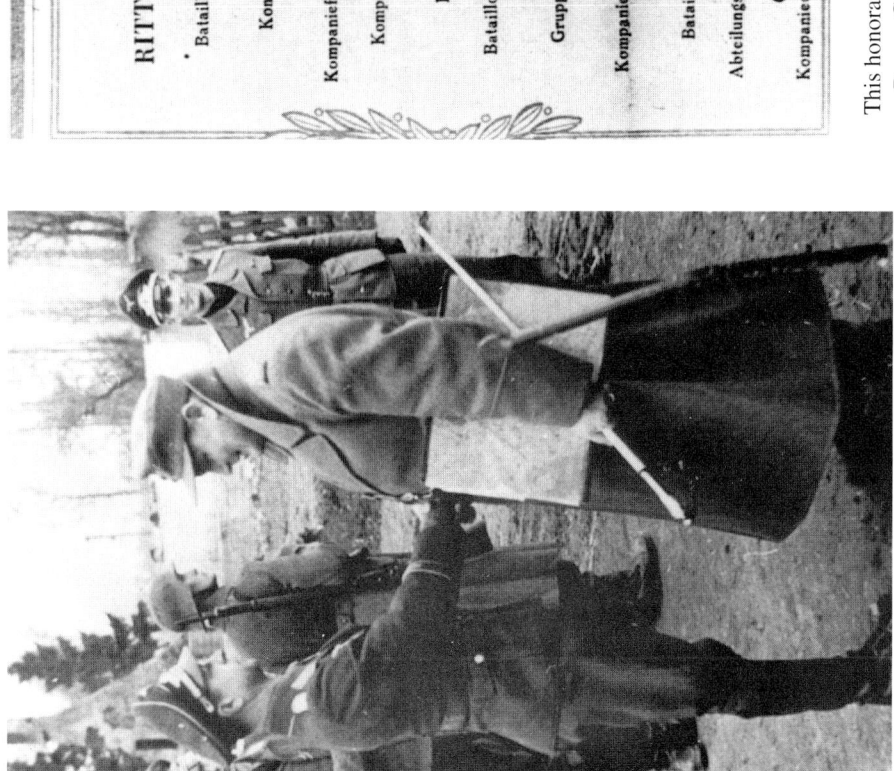

This honorary page titled "Eleven Knight's Cross Wearers and a Panzer Corps" appeared in the Luftwaffe's official gazette.

Oberst Erich Walther, commanding officer of the 2nd Parachute Panzer-Grenadier Division "HG" greets the Commander-in-Chief of the Luftwaffe.

Panoramic view of Bautzen. From left: the leaning Reichenturm, the Michaelis Church, the Petri Cathedral and the tower of the Town Hall.

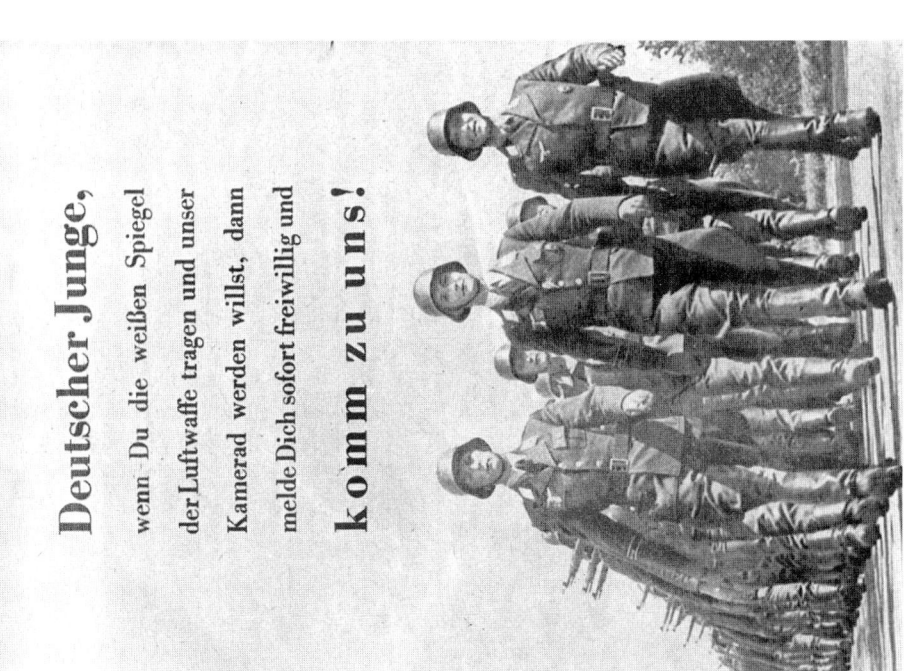

Two samples of recruiting material for the HG division.

Postwar (de-Nazified) Luftwaffe Close Combat Clasp. In its original version, a very rare decoration.

Two examples of the "HG" cuff title.

APPENDIX I
Evolution of the Hermann Göring Parachute-Panzer Corps

23 February 1933	Formation of the Wecke Special Purpose Police Battalion in Berlin-Kreuzberg
June 1933	Expansion to Wecke Special Purpose Police Group
17 July 1933	Redesignated Wecke Special Purpose State Police Group on the formation of the State Police
12 January 1934	Redesignated General Göring State Police Group
23 September 1935	Taken into the Luftwaffe as the General Göring Regiment
1 March 1942	General Göring Regiment expanded to become the Reinforced General Göring Motorised Regiment
21 July 1942	Expanded to Hermann Göring Brigade in France
17 October 1942	Formation of the Hermann Göring Division in Southern France
21 May 1943	Following the destruction of the Hermann Göring Division in North Africa: – New formation as Hermann Göring (Motorised-Tropical) Division – simultaneous formation of the Hermann Göring Special Purpose Brigade – in Southern France and Italy (Naples area)
15 July 1943	Reformed as Hermann Göring Panzer Division in Sicily
6 January 1944	Redesignated Hermann Göring Parachute-Panzer Division
24 September 1944	Formation of the Hermann Göring Parachute-Panzer Corps near Modlin with: – corps headquarters and division strength corps units – HG 1st Parachute-Panzer Division – HG 2nd Parachute-Panzer Grenadier Division – HG Parachute-Panzer Replacement and Training Brigade (Rippin, East Prussia)
14 March 1945	Formation of the HG 2nd Parachute-Panzer Replacement and Training Brigade in Velten and Joachimsthal/Mark Brandenburg, replacing the HG Parachute-Panzer Replacement and Training Brigade, which had been lost in the fortress of Graudenz.
9 May 1945	Surrender of German Armed Forces and thus the disbandment of all remaining units in Saxony, Berlin, on the Oder Front, in Bavaria, Holland and in the Rhineland. Most survivors became prisoners of war, the majority in Soviet hands.

APPENDIX II

The Commanders

Unit	Appointed	Rank, Name
Wecke Special Purpose Police Battalion	23 February 1933	Major der Schutzpolizei Wecke
Wecke Special Purpose Police Group	June 1933	Oberstleutnant der Schutzpolizei Wecke
Wecke State Police Group	17 July 1933	Oberst der Landespolizei Wecke
General Göring State Police Group	12 January 1934	Oberst der Landespolizei Wecke
General Göring State Police Group	6 June 1934	Oberstleutnant der Landespolizei Jakoby
General Göring Regiment	23 September 1935	Oberstleutnant Jakoby
General Göring Regiment	22 August 1936	General Staff Major/Oberstleutnant/Oberst Axthelm
General Göring Regiment	1 June 1940	Oberst Conrath
Reinforced Hermann Göring (Motorized) Regiment	1 March 1942	Oberst Conrath
Hermann Göring Brigade	21 July 1942	Generalmajor Conrath
Hermann Göring Division	17 October 1942	Generalmajor Conrath
Division elements in Africa	January 1943	Oberst/Generalmajor Schmid
Hermann Göring (Motorized-Tropical) Division	21 May 1943	Generalmajor Conrath
Hermann Göring Special Purpose Brigade	21 May 1943	Oberst Schmalz
Hermann Göring Panzer Division	15 July 1943	Generalmajor/Generalleutnant Conrath
Hermann Göring Parachute-Panzer Division	6 January 1944	Generalleutnant Conrath
Hermann Göring Parachute-Panzer Division	16 April 1944	Generalmajor Schmalz
Hermann Göring Parachute-Panzer Corps Commanding General	24 September 1944	Generalmajor/Generalleutnant Schmalz
HG 1st Parachute-Panzer Division	24 September 1944	Oberst/Generalmajor von Necker
HG 1st Parachute-Panzer Division	9 February 1945	Oberst/Generalmajor Lemke
HG 2nd Parachute-Panzer-Grenadier Division	24 September 1944	Oberst/Generalmajor Walther
HG Parachute-Panzer Replacement and Training Brigade	24 September 1944	Oberst Meyer
HG 2nd Parachute-Panzer Replacement and Training Brigade	14 March 1945	Oberst Breuer

APPENDIX III
WINNERS OF THE GERMAN CROSS IN GOLD

Altengarten, Manfred:	Uffz. and gun commander in the HG Armoured Recon. Battalion	30. 8. 1943
Augenstein, Wolfgang:	Lt. and company commander in the Armoured Pioneer Battalion	7. 2. 1944
Bach, Wolfgang:	Hptm. and Battalion CO in II Battalion, 1st Parachute-Panzer Replacement and Training Regiment	26. 2. 1945
Baitz, Heinrich:	Fw. and platoon leader in Panzer-Grenadier Regiment	20. 3. 1944
Bertram, Erik:	Major and CO of a Flak Battalion	2. 4. 1942
Bowitz, Fritz:	Fw. and tank commander 4th Company, Parachute-Panzer Regt.	10. 1944
Brandenburg, Otto:	Hptm. and Battalion CO HG Armoured Recon. Battalion	30. 8. 1943
Brandenstein, Bernhard Freiherr von:	Lt. and company commander in the HG Parachute-Panzer Division	- - - - -
Braun, Ernst:	Lt. and platoon leader in the Parachute-Panzer Regiment	- - - - -
Burchardt, Herbert:	Oblt. and CO of an armoured parachute reconnaissance battalion	1. 1. 1945
Dentzer, Gerhard:	Oblt. and battery chief in 7th Battery, Führer Flak Battalion	14. 3. 1943
Dickel, Franz-Wilhelm:	Oblt. and battery chief in the General Göring Regiment	10. 11. 1941
Dietrich, Karl:	Owm. and gun commander in Assault Gun Battery	1. 10. 1941
Dreher, Alfred:	Oblt. and CO 7th Company, HG Panzer Regiment	6. 3. 1944
Ebel, Werner:	General Staff Major, Ia 1st Parachute-Panzer Division	15. 4. 1945
Engel, Heinrich:	Hptm. and adjutant in the Armoured Artillery Regiment	10. 1. 1944
Findeis, Guenther:	Hptm. and Regimental CO 1st Replacement and Training Regiment	4. 1945
Fleischer, Erwin:	ObGefr. and company runner in 1st Company, 1st Parachute-Panzer Replacement and Training Regiment	5. 3. 1945
Frey, Walter:	Hptm. and adjutant, I Bn., Parachute-Panzer Regiment	1. 1. 1945
Friebe, Helmut:	Hptm. and CO Training and Conversion Battalion	23. 2. 1945

Fuchs, Kurt:	Hptm. and battalion CO in 1st Parachute-Panzer Division	– – – – –
Funck, Helmut:	Major and commander of elements of the 1st and 2nd Grenadier Regiments	1. 10. 1943
Geicke, Werner:	Hptm. and CO IV Battalion, General Göring Regiment	29. 1. 1942
Gerhardt, Rolf:	Oblt. and company commander in the HG Armoured Reconnaissance Battalion	30. 8. 1943
Glueher, Helmut:	Fw. and platoon leader in the Armoured Reconnaissance Bn.	30. 8. 1943
Graf, Rudolf:	Major and battalion commander in the Parachute Flak Regiment	1. 1. 1945
Gruene, Franz-Josef:	Hptm. and CO I Battalion, 1st Grenadier Regiment	1. 10. 1945
Hahm, Konstantin:	Hptm. and battle group leader in the panzer regiment	10. 1. 1944
Hansen, Werner:	Ofw. and platoon leader in the HG Armoured Reconnaissance Battalion	1. 10. 1944
Hein, Horst von:	Oblt. and battery chief in the HG Armoured Artillery Regiment	10. 1. 1944
Herrmann, Heinz:	Lt. and company commander in the Parachute-Panzer-Grenadier Regiment	1. 1. 1945
Hinrichs, Hans:	Oberfähnrich and Staff Officer in the 2nd Parachute-Panzer-Grenadier Regt.	1. 1. 1945
Hoberg, Fritz-Walter:	Major and battalion commander in the Parachute Armoured Artillery Regiment	1. 1. 1945
Hullmann, Werner:	Major and CO I Battalion, General Göring Regiment	19. 2. 1942
Ilius, Georg:	Major and battalion commander	– – – 1944
Jahnhorst, Pius:	Oblt. in the 2nd Parachute-Panzer-Grenadier Division	– – – – –
Kaiser, Otto:	Oblt. and battery commander in the Armoured Artillery Regiment	7. 2. 1944
Kempa, Werner:	Lt. and platoon leader in the HG Light Infantry Regiment	25. 1. 1943
Kluehe, Helmut:	Fw. and platoon leader in the HG Parachute-Panzer Division	– – – – –
Koenig, Heinz:	Oberfähnrich and platoon leader in the HG Parachute Assault Gun Battalion	– – – – –
Koeppe, Erich:	Oblt. in the 2nd Parachute-Panzer-Grenadier Regiment	– – – – –
Krause, Heinz:	Oblt. in the 1st Parachute-Panzer Replacement and Training Brigade	– – – – –
Leitenberger, Helmut:	Lt. and platoon leader in 3rd Company, HG Parachute-Panzer Regiment	– – – – –

Locher, Ottmar:	Fw. and pioneer platoon leader in the HG Armoured Reconnaissance Battalion	1. 1. 1945
Luebke, Martin:	Hptm. and battalion commander HG Armoured Reconnaissance Battalion	1. 10. 1944
Mees, Heinz:	Hptm. and company commander in the HG Parachute-Panzer Division	– – – – –
Meyer, Friedrich:	Oberst and CO Parachute Flak Regt.	1. 1. 1945
Muehlbacher, Fritz:	Hptm. and CO I Battalion, 2nd Parachute-Panzer-Grenadier Regt.	1. 1. 1945
Nagorny, Gerhard:	Hptm. and CO II Battalion, 1st Grenadier Regiment	1. 10. 1943
Naumann, Heinz:	Fahnenjunker-Oberfeldwebel in I Battalion, 3rd Parachute-Panzer Grenadier Regiment	5. 5. 1945
Neidt, Karl:	Oblt. and company commander in the HG Personnel Replacement Battalion	1. 1. 1945
Nowak, Georg:	Fähnrich and staff officerin the Parachute-Panzer-Grenadier Regiment	1. 1. 1945
Nussmaeker, Otto:	Gefr. in the HG Armoured Reconnaissance Battalion	30. 8. 1943
Oering, Hans:	Oberstleutnant and CO Armoured Artillery Regiment	10. 1. 1944
Ohme, Guenter:	Oblt. and flak combat team leader in the HG Anti-tank Battalion	7. 1. 1944
Paulus, Peter:	Hptm. and company commander in the HG Armoured Reconnaissance Battalion	10. 1. 1944
Pfeiffer, Reinhard:	Hptm. and CO II Battalion, 2nd Grenadier Regiment	1. 10. 1943
Piplak, Kurt:	Lt. and platoon leader in the Parachute-Panzer-Grenadier Regt.	1. 1. 1945
Podewils-Duernitz, Erdmann, Graf von:	Oblt. and chief, 1st Battery, 1st Parachute-Panzer Artillery Regt.	1. 1. 1945
Post, Heinrich:	Fw. in Parachute-Panzer-Gren. Regt.	– – – – –
Quednow, Fritz:	Oblt. and company commander in the Luftwaffe Light Infantry Regiment	26. 7. 1943
Renz, Joachim:	Oblt. and CO 3rd Company, HG Panzer Regiment	6. 3. 1944
Rinteln, Clemens:	Hptm. and battalion commander in the Parachute-Flak Regiment	1. 1. 1945
Ritterbecks, Hubert:	Hptm. and battalion commander in the Parachute-Panzer Regiment	1. 1. 1945
Ross, Werner:	Oblt. and battery chief in the Parachute-Panzer Artillery Regt.	1. 1. 1945
Rossmann, Karl:	Hptm. and CO I Battalion, HG Panzer Regiment	5. 6. 1944

Schaper, Karl-Heinz:	Lt. and company commander in the Parachute-Panzer Division	– – – – –
Schomburg, Heinrich:	Major and CO HG Reconnaissance Battalion	1. 1.1945
Schwarz, Heinrich:	Hptm. and company commander in II Battalion, 2nd Parachute-Panzer-Grenadier Regiment	26. 7. 1944
Stocker, Heinz:	Lt. and platoon leader in the HG Armoured Reconnaissance Battalion	30. 8. 1943
Strassburger, Albert:	Ofw. and tank commander in the HG Panzer Regiment	20. 3. 1944
Stronk, Wolfram:	Oblt. and flak combat team leader in 6th Company, HG Panzer Regt.	10. 1. 1944
Stuchlik, Werner:	Oblt. and reconnaissance officer in the 2nd Parachute-Panzer-Grenadier Regt.	10. 1. 1944
Teitge, Fritz:	Uffz. and squad leader in the HG Armoured Reconnaissance Battalion	30. 8. 1943
Thamm, Hans:	Lt. in the 1st Parachute-Panzer Replacement and Training Brigade	– – – – –
Thor, Hans:	Oblt. and company commander in the HG Armoured Reconnaissance Battalion	6. 3. 1944
Thrun, Siegfried:	Gefr. and squad leader in the HG Armoured Reconnaissance Battalion	30. 8. 1943
Uexkuell, Eduard, Graf von:	Oblt. and CI 2nd Company General Göring Regiment	8. 12. 1941
Volkmar, Hans:	Hptm. and adjutant in the Panzer-Grenadier Regiment	10. 1. 1944
Wallburg, Rolf:	Uffz. and gun commander in the HG Armoured Reconnaissance Battalion	30. 8. 1943
Werner, Heinz:	Lt. and battalion adjutant in the Panzer-Grenadier Regiment	10. 1. 1944
Werner, Wilhelm:	General Staff Major, Panzer Division Ia	1. 10. 1944
Wille, Erich:	Oblt. in the 2nd Parachute-Panzer-Grenadier Division	– – – – –
Wolf, Josef:	Oblt. and CO 1st Armoured Pioneer Battalion	1. 10. 1944

APPENDIX IV
WINNERS OF THE KNIGHT'S CROSS

OAK LEAVES WITH SWORDS

Walther, Erich: Oberst and CO of the HG 2nd Parachute-Panzer-Grenadier Division, 131st recipient, on 1February 1945.

Former members of IV (Parachute Infantry) Battalion, General Göring Regiment:

Kroh, Hans: Oberst and CO of the 2nd Parachute Division, 96th recipient, on 12 September 1944.

Schulz, Karl-Lothar: Oberst and CO of the 1st Parachute Division, 112th recipient, on 18 November 1944.

OAK LEAVES

Conrath, Paul: Generalmajor and CO of the HG Panzer Division, 276th recipient, on 21 August 1943.

Schmalz, Wilhelm: Oberst and Brigade Commander in the HG Panzer Division, 358th recipient, on 23 December 1943.

Fitz, Josef: Major and CO I Battalion, 1st Parachute-Panzer-Grenadier Regiment, 511th recipient, on 24 June 1944.

Schirmer, Gerhard: Oberstleutnant and CO of the 3rd Parachute-Panzer-Grenadier Regiment, 657th recipient, on 18 November 1944.

Rossmann, Karl: Major and CO of the HG Parachute-Panzer Regiment, 725th recipient, on 1 February 1945.

Baer, Bern von: General Staff Oberstleutnant and HG Parachute-Panzer Corps Chief of Staff, 761st recipient, on 28 Feb. 1945.

Ostermeier, Hans: Major and CO of the HG 3rd Parachute-Panzer-Grenadier Regiment, 834th recipient, on 15 April 1945.

Former members of IV Battalion (Parachute Infantry) General Göring Regiment:

Walther, Erich: Oberst and CO of the 4th Parachute Regiment, 411th recipient, on 2 March 1944.

Kroh, Hans: Oberstleutnant and CO of the 2nd Parachute Regiment, 443rd recipient, on 6 April 1944.

Schulz, Karl-Lothar: Oberst and CO of the 1st Parachute Regiment, 459th recipient, on 20 April 1944.

Gericke, Walter: Oberst and CO of the 11th Parachute Regiment, 585th recipient, on 17 September 1944.

Gröschke, Kurt:		Oberstleutnant and CO of the 15th Parachute Regiment, 693rd recipient, on 9 January 1945
Becker, Karl-Heinz:		Oberst and CO of the 5th Parachute Regiment, 780th recipient, on 12 March 1945.

KNIGHT'S CROSS

Conrath, Paul:	Oberst	4 September 1941
Graf, Rudolf:	Oberleutnant	6 October 1941
Roßmann, Karl:	Oberleutnant	12 November 1941
Itzen, Dirk:	Leutnant	23 November 1941
Schäfer, Heinrich:	Oberfeldwebel	8 August 1944
Kiefer, Eduard:	Hauptmann	18 May 1943
Schmid, Josef:	Generalmajor	21 May 1943
Schreiber, Kurt:	Hauptmann	21 June 1943
Scheid, Johannes:	Oberfeldwebel	21 June 1943
Kluge, Waldemar:	Major	2 August 1943
Rebholz, Robert:	Hauptmann	2 August 1943
Quednow, Fritz:	Hauptmann	5 April 1944
Knaf, Walter:	Leutnant	5 April 1944
Witte, Heinrich:	Obergefreiter	18 May 1944
Hahm, Konstantin:	Major	9 June 1944
von Necker, Hans-Horst:	Oberst	24 June 1944
von Heydebreck, George-Henning	Oberst	25 June 1944
Kulp, Karl:	Feldwebel	5 September 1944
Bellinger, Hans-Joachim:	Hauptmann	30 September 1944
Thor, Hans:	Hauptmann	30 September 1944
Schmidt, Fritz-Wilhelm:	Hauptmann	6 October 1944
Lehmann, Hans-Georg:	Oberleutnant	10 October 1944
Sandrock, Hans:	Major	18 October 1944
Stronk, Wolfram:	Hauptmann	18 October 1944
Birnbaum, Fritz:	Oberfähnrich	19 October 1944
Francois, Edmund:	Hauptmann	20 October 1944
Kalow, Siegfried:	Unteroffizier	29 October 1944
Schuster, Franz:	Oberleutnant	31 October 1944
Stuchlik, Werner:	Hauptmann	20 November 1944
Kuhlwilm, Wilhelm:	Oberleutnant	30 November 1944
Kraus, Rupert:	Oberleutnant	30 November 1944
Wallhäuser, Karl-Heinz:	Leutnant	30 November 1944
Grunhold, Werner:	Unteroffizier	30 November 1944
Plapper, Albert:	Gefreiter	30 November 1944

Steets, Konrad:	Gefreiter	30 November 1944
Renz, Joachim:	Hauptmann	6 December 1944
Tschierschwitz, Gerhard:	Oberleutnant	6 December 1944
Briegel, Hans:	Major	14 January 1945
von Majer, Hans:	Leutnant	15 January 1945
Köppen, Eckhardt:	Feldwebel	15 January 1945
Wimmer, Johann:	Hauptmann	28 January 1945
Köspel, Herbert:	Unteroffizier	7 February 1945
Kampmann:	Hauptmann	7 February 1945
Koenig, Heinz:	Leutnant	8 February 1945
Hansen, Hans-Christian:	Hauptmann	11 February 1945
Schweim, Heinz-Herbert:	General Staff Major	18 February 1945
Schirner, Lothar:	Gefreiter	19 February 1945
Hartelt, Wolfgang:	Oberfähnrich	23 February 1945
Herbst, Erhard:	Oberfeldwebel	February 1945
Rademann, Emil:	Gefreiter	23 February 1945
Krappmann, Heinrich:	Obergefreiter	28 February 1945
Klein, Armin:	Oberleutnant	12 March 1945
Lippe, Hans:	Leutnant	26 March 1945
Probst, Heinz:	Unteroffizier	26 March 1945
Bertram, Eric:	Oberst	26 March 1945
Schulze-Ostwald:	Hauptmann	5 April 1945
Leitenberger, Helmut:	Leutnant	17 April 1945
Zander, Wolfgang:	Feldwebel	28 April 1945
Rommeis, Gerhard:	Hauptmann	April 1945
Meyer, Friedrich:	Oberst	9 May 1945
Behre, Friedrich:	Leutnant	9 May 1945

Former members of the General Göring Regiment who received the Knight's Cross:

Axthelm, Walter von:	Generalmajor and Commanding General of I Flak Corps, on 4 September 1941.
Becker, Karl-Heinz:	Oberleutnant and company commander in the 1st Parachute Regiment, on 9 July 1941.
Bräuer, Bruno;	Oberst and CO of the 1st Parachute Regiment, on 24 May 1940.
Genz, Alfred:	Oberleutnant and company commander in the 1st Airborne Assault Regiment, on 14 June 1941.
Gericke, Walter:	Hauptmann and CO of IV Battalion, 1st Airborne Assault Regiment, on 14 June 1941.

Grösche, Kurt:	Major and CO of II Battalion, 1st Parachute Regiment, on 9 June 1944.
Hermann, Harry:	Oberleutnant and CO of 5th Company, 1st Parachute Regiment, on 9 July 1941.
Koch, Walter:	Hauptmann and CO of the Koch Assault Battalion, on 10 May 1940.
Kroh, Hans:	Major and CO of I Battalion, 2nd Parachute Regiment, on 21 August 1941.
Schulz, Karl-Lothar:	Hauptmann and CO of III Battalion, 1st Parachute Regiment, on 24 May 1940.
Schwarzmann, Alfred:	Oberleutnant and platoon leader in 8th Company, 1st Parachute Regiment, on 29 May 1940.
Walther, Erich:	Major and CO of I Battalion, 1st Parachute Regiment, on 24 May 1940.

Wearers of the Knight's Cross decorated prior to transfer to one of the Hermann Göring units:

Bär, Bern von:	General Staff Oberstleutnant and Ia of the 16th Panzer Division, on 13 January 1944.
Fitz, Josef:	Hauptmann and CO of I Battalion, 74th Panzer-Grenadier Regiment, on 11 December 1942.
Lemke, Max:	Major and CO of the 17th Armoured Reconnaissance Battalion, on 18 October 1941.
Ostermeier, Hans:	Hauptmann and leader of a battle group of the "Feldherrnhalle" Panzer-Grenadier Division, on 23 August 1944.
Schmalz, Wilhelm:	Major and CO of I Battalion, 11th Rifle Regiment, on 28 November 1940.
Söth, Wilhelm:	Hauptmann and CO of II Battalion, 56th Artillery Regiment, on 28 November 1940.
Grün, Werner:	Hauptmann and CO of I Battalion, 5th Panzer Regiment, on 8 February 1943.

Officers of the Fallschirmkorps Hermann Göring in a POW camp in Concordia, Kansas.

The Honor Grove in the Armor School in Munster. Left: Commemorative Stone of the Fallschirm-Panzer Division Hermann Göring, on the right, one for the Fallschirm-Panzer-Grenadier Division 2 Hermann Göring.

Oberst Meyer-Schewe, after his return from captivity, awarded the Knight's Cross on 8. 5. 1945

Thilo von Werthern

Friedrich Meyer-Schewe

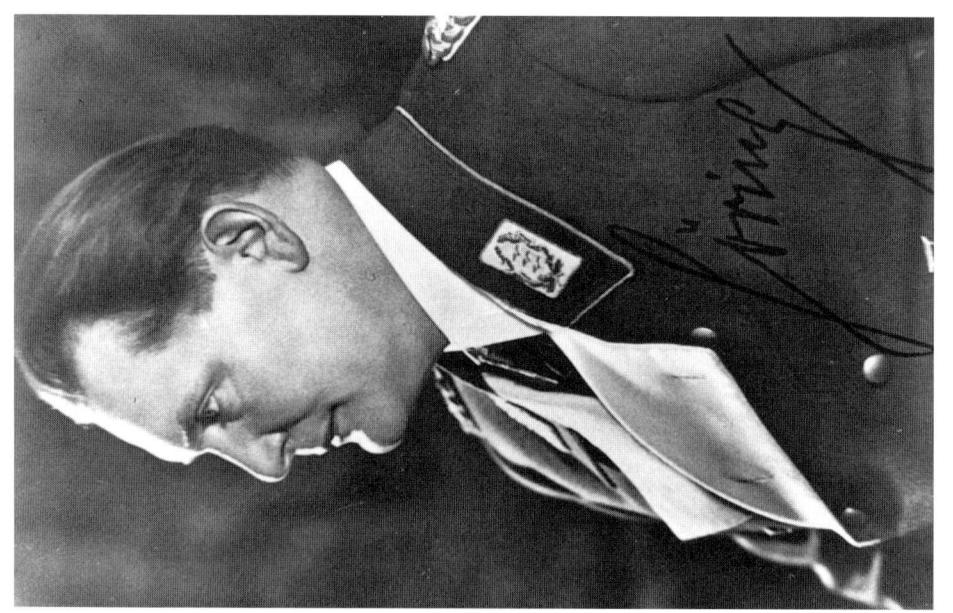

Hermann Göring

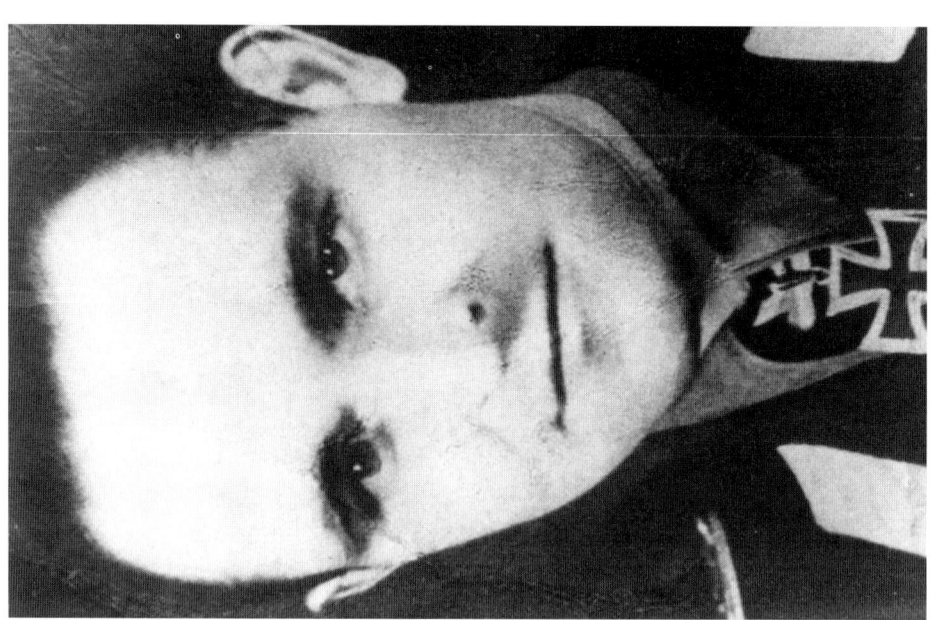

Edmund François

Albert Plapper

Wolfgang Hartelt

Walther von Axthelm

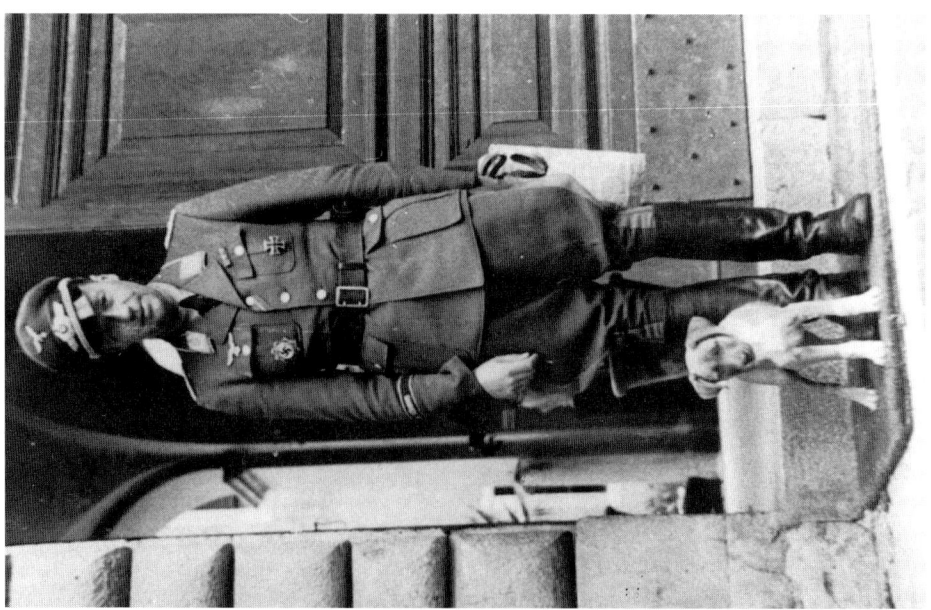
Oberstleutnant von Bergengruen
(German Cross in Gold)

Erich Walther

Fritz Birnbaum

Emil Rademann

Hans-Georg Lehmann

Left to right: Kraus, Roßmann and Tschierschwitz.

Max Lemke

Gerhard Tschierschwitz

Oberstleutnant Hullmann
(German Cross in Gold)

Walter Koch

Karl-Heinz Wallhäußer

Hermann Göring with his wife Emmy and daughter Edda.

Konstantin Hahn

Hans-Christian Hansen

GenMaj. Conrath with Major von Bergengruen.

Hanns-Horst von Necker

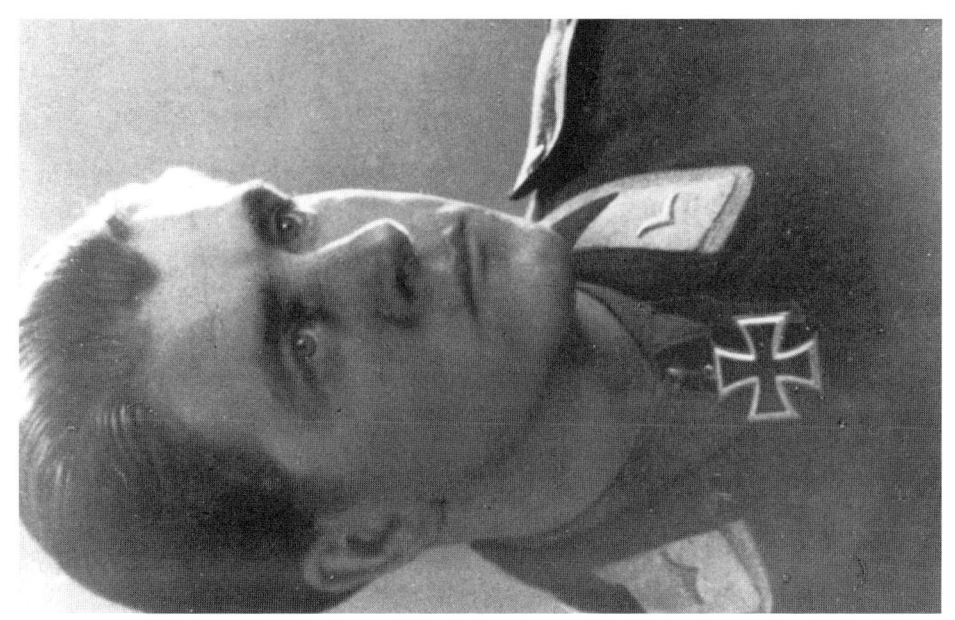

Herbert Köpsell

GFM Model and Bern von Baer

Gerd Schmock

Hauptmann Paulus

Gerhard Tschierschwitz and his wife.

Karl Roßmann (left) and Gerhard Tschierschwitz.

Werner Stuchlik

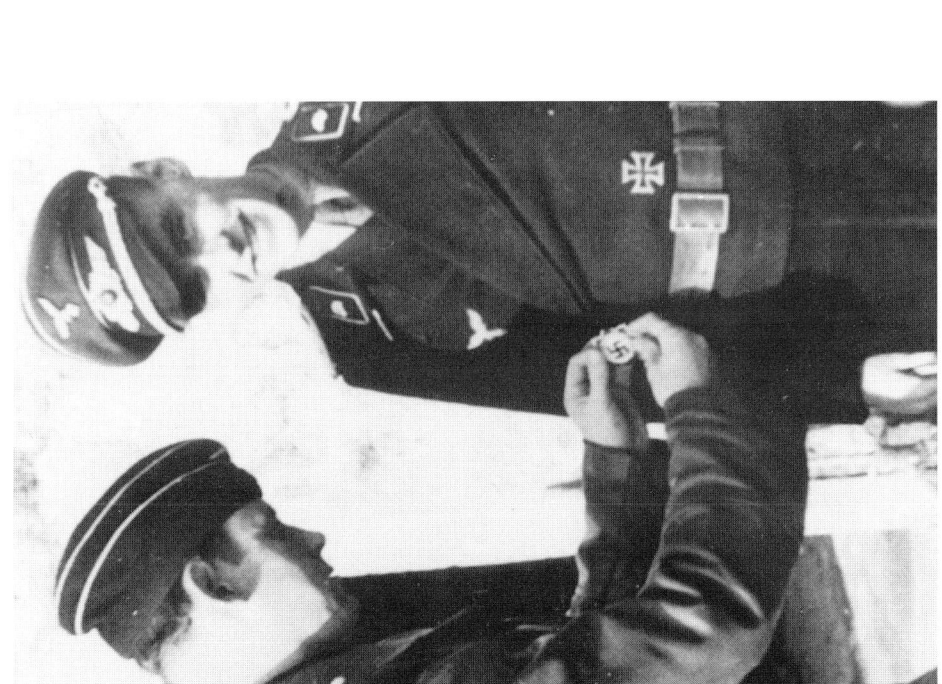

Wolfram Stronk receives the German Cross in Gold.

Kurt Mörgel

Oberleutnant Heinz Göring

Gerd Mischke

Paul Conrath

Hans Briegel

Paul Conrath (left)

Wolfram Stronk

Left to right: von Rieben, Roßmann and Tschierschwitz.

Roßmann congratulates Stuchlik and Kraus.

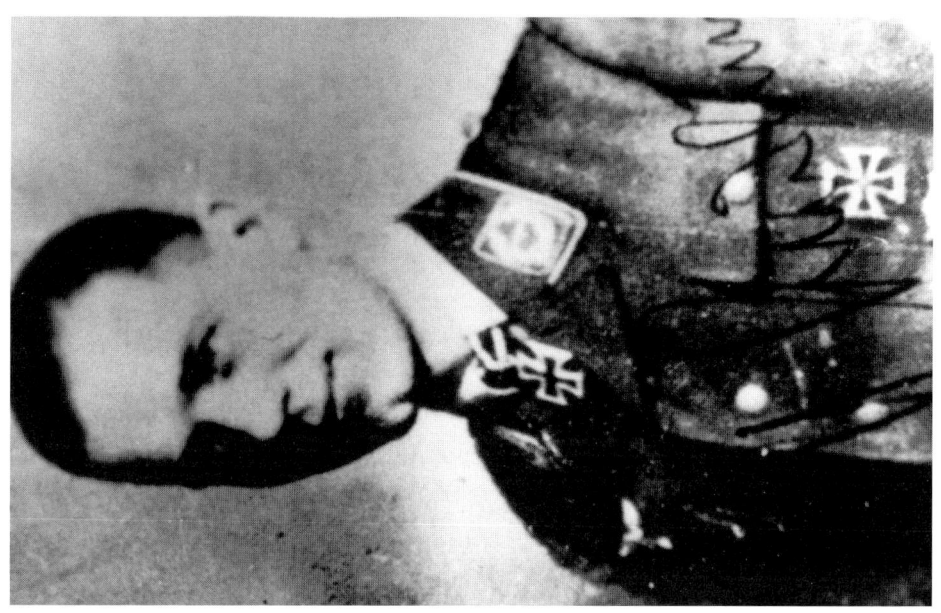

Heinz-Herbert Schweim

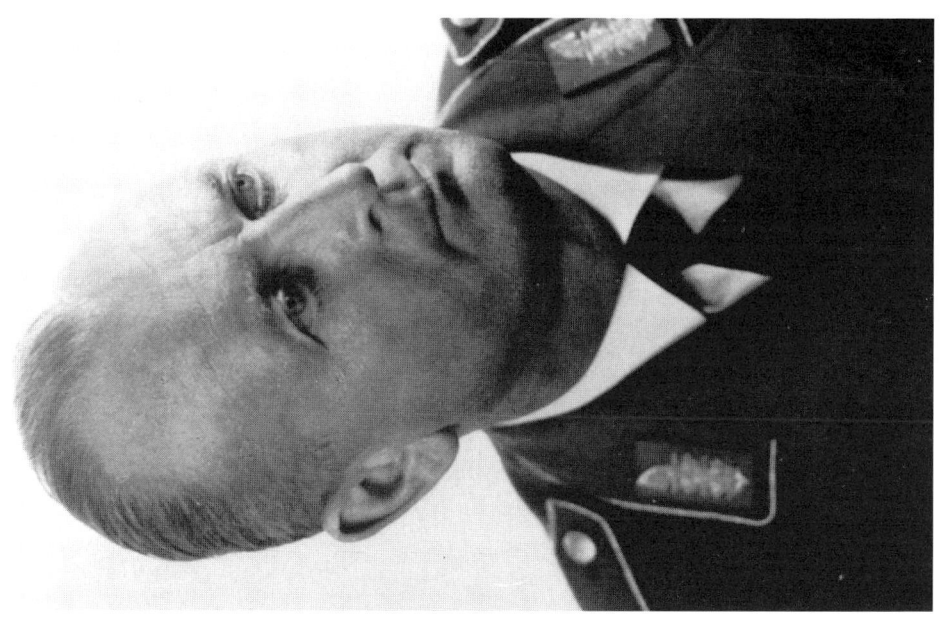

Bern von Baer

Werner Stuchlik (left) and Gottfried Weber (as Maj.Gen. and commander 0f the 12 Luftwaffe Field Division. Weber was the 490th recipient of the Oak Leaves on 9. 6. 1944).

Erhard Milch

Josef (Beppo) Schmid

Dr. Karl Roßmann

VORLÄUFIGES BESITZZEUGNIS

DER FÜHRER
UND OBERSTE BEFEHLSHABER
DER WEHRMACHT
HAT

DEM   Major Karl Roßmann

DAS EICHENLAUB
ZUM RITTERKREUZ
DES EISERNEN KREUZES

AM   1. Februar 1945   VERLIEHEN.

Berlin   , DEN 14. Februar   1945
Der Chef der Luftwaffenpersonalamts
m.W.d.G.b.

General der Flieger

Interim certificate for the awarding of the Knight's Cross with Oak Leaves to Major Karl Roßmann.

Hauptmann Stronk

Johann Wimmer

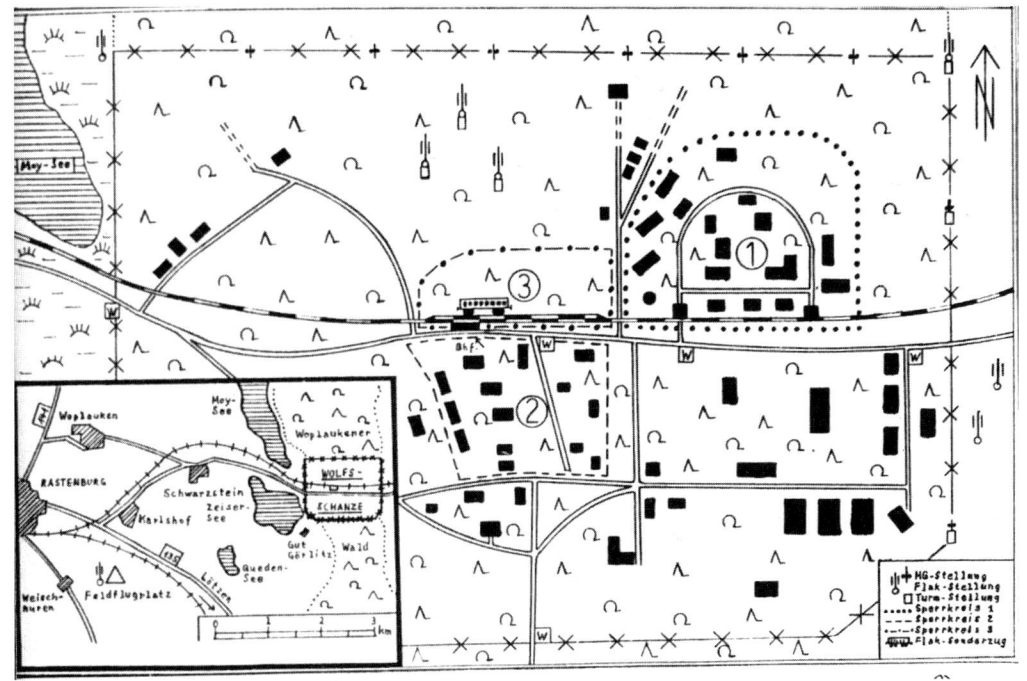

Wolfsschanze Führer Headquarters

Layout of the "Wolfsschanze" Führer Headquarters near Rastenburg in East Prussia. The three restricted areas were secured by fences and guarded heavily by sentries. Access was by special pass only. Hitler and the Reich Ministers, as well as the Armed Forces Headquarters, had their bunkers within Restricted Area I. Restricted Area II contained the quarters of the guard personnel, and in Restricted Area III were the railway installations with the station and special trains.

The RGG in 1936

Rgt. General Göring Einheit	Offz.	Uffz.	Mannech.	Bes.	Summe.	l.MG	s.MG	Flak	Scheinw.	Pferde.
Rgt.St./St.Kp.	6	13	54	3	76					6
Musikkorps		28	10		38					
Reiterzug	1	12	51		64					62
13. Krdsch.Kp. mit Pz.Kw.Zg.	6	49	174		229	12		3		
14. Pi.Kp.	5	72	112		189	9				
15. Wach-Kp.	5	37	157		199					
St.u.Rgt.Einh./RGG	23	211	558	3	795	21		3		68
St./I.Jäg.Btl./RGG	3	16	19	4	42					2
N. Zg.	1	4	39		44					
Pi. Zg.	2	25	53		80	3				
1. Jäg.Kp.	4	50	129		183	9				1
2. Jäg.Kp.	4	50	129		183	9				1
3. Jäg.Kp.	4	50	129		183	9				1
4. MG.Kp.	4	46	110		160		12			1
I. Jäg.Btl./RGG	22	241	608	4	875	30	12			6
St./II.Jäg.Btl./RGG	3	16	19	4	42					2
N.Zg.	1	4	39		44					
Pi.Zg.	2	25	53		80	3				
5. Jäg.Kp.	4	50	129		183	9				3
6. Jäg.Kp.	4	50	129		183	9				1
7. Jäg.Kp.	4	50	129		183	9				1
8. MG.Kp.	4	46	110		160		12			1
II. Jäg.Btl./RGG	22	241	608	4	875	30	12			6
St.und N.Zg. III.Flak-Abt./RGG	8	15	43	8	74					
9. Battr. (3.7 cm)	5	24	99		128			6		
10. Battr. (2 cm)	4	32	135		171			12		
11. Battr. (2 cm)	4	32	135		171			12		
12. Battr.(Scheinw.)	4	23	97		124				6	
III. Flak-Abt./RGG	25	126	509	8	668			30	6	
Stärke RGG 1.10.36	92	819	2283	19	3213	82	24	33	6	80
Dazu ab 1.4.37 16. Wach-Kp.	5	37	157		199					
Stärke RGG 1.4.37	97	856	2440	19	3412	82	24	33	6	80

The RGG in 1937

Rgt. General Göring Einheit	Offz.	Uffz.	Mannschft.	Beamte	Angestellt.	Lohnempf.	Summe.
Rgt. St./ St. Kp.	9	37	68	3	25	6	148
Musikkorps	1	46	14				61
St. Battr.	9	50	118	9	11	44	241
1. Battr. (8.8 cm)	4	35	132			3	174
2. Battr. (8.8 cm)	4	34	132			3	174
3. Battr. (8.8 cm)	4	34	132			3	174
4. Battr. (3.7 cm)	5	32	168			3	208
I. schw. Flak-Abt.	26	187	682	9	11	56	971
St. Battr.	8	42	79	9	11	44	193
5. Battr. (2 cm)	6	37	181			3	227
6. Battr. (2 cm)	6	37	181			3	227
7. Battr. (2 cm)	6	37	181			3	227
II. le Flak-Abt.	26	153	622	9	11	53	874
St. Kp.	6	61	55	6	17	117	262
Reiter-Zug	1	13	51				65
8. Krdschtz. Kp.	6	59	180			3	248
9. Wach-Kp.	5	37	157				199
10. Wach. Kp.	5	37	157				199
III. Wach-Btl.	23	207	600	6	17	120	973
St. Kp.	7	53	84	7	8	29	188
11. Fsch. Schtz. Kp.	4	56	164			2	226
12. Fsch. Schtz. Kp.	4	56	164			2	226
13. Fsch. Schtz. Kp.	4	56	164			2	226
14. Fsch. MG. Kp.	4	52	163			2	221
15. Fsch. Pi. Kp.	5	37	157			2	201
IV. Fsch. Schtz. Btl.	28	310	896	7	8	39	1288
Stärke RGG 1. 10. 37	113	940	2882	34	72	274	4315

Militärpersonen : 3969   Zivilpersonen : 346

The RGG in 1938

Rgt. General Göring Einheit	Offz.	Uffz.	Mann-schaf-ten	Be-am-te	An-ge-st.	Lohn-empf.	Summe.	MG	Flak	SW	Kfz.	Anh.	Krä-der	Krd. mit Beiw.	Pfer-de.
Rgt.St./St.Battr.	9	37	68	3	25	6	148				30		16	7	
Musikkorps	1		46	14			61								
St. Battr.	9	50	118	9	11	44	241				28	1	10	2	
1. Battr. (8.8 cm)	4	35	132			3	174		6		22	10	10	3	
2. Battr. (8.8 cm)	4	35	132			3	174		6		22	10	10	3	
3. Battr. (8.8 cm)	4	35	132			3	174		6		22	10	10	3	
4. Battr. (2 cm) m. Z.	6	37	181			3	227		12	4	41	18	19	4	
5. Battr. (2 cm) m. Z.	6	37	181			3	227		12	4	41	18	19	4	
I. schw. Flak-Abt.	33	229	876	9	11	59	1217		72	8	176	67	78	19	
St. Battr.	8	42	79	9	11	44	193				19	1	8	2	
6. Battr. (3,7cm) m. Z.	5	32	168			3	208		9	4	35	15	16	4	
7. Battr. (2 cm) Sf.	6	37	181			3	227		12	4	41	5	19	4	
8. Battr. (2 cm) Sf.	6	37	181			3	227		12	4	41	5	19	4	
9. Battr. (2 cm) m. Z.	6	37	181			3	227		12	4	41	18	19	4	
II. le Flak-Abt.	31	185	790	9	11	56	1082		45	16	177	44	81	18	
St. Battr.	8	41	77	8	11	44	189				20	1	5	2	
11. Scheinw. Battr.	5	38	191			3	237			9	47	29	16	6	
12. Scheinw. Battr.	5	38	191			3	237			9	47	29	16	6	
13. Scheinw. Battr.	5	38	191			3	237			9	47	29	16	6	
III. Scheinw. Abt.	23	155	650	8	11	53	900			27	161	88	53	20	
St. Battr.	8	42	79	9	11	44	193				19	1	8	2	
15. Battr. (3,7cm) m.Z.	5	32	168			3	208		9	4	35	15	16	4	
16. Battr. (2 cm) m. Z.	6	37	181			3	227		12	4	41	18	19	4	
17. Battr. (2 cm) m. Z.	6	37	181			3	227		12	4	41	18	19	4	
IV. le Flak-Abt.	25	148	609	9	11	53	855		33	12	136	52	62	14	
St. Kp.	6	61	55	6	17	117	262	14			45		21	9	
Reiter-Schwadron	2	33	135			6	176	9			4		1	1	152
1. Wach-Kp	5	37	157				199	13							
2. Wach-Kp.	5	37	157				199	12							
3. Wach-Kp.	5	37	157				199	12							
Wach-Btl. RGG	23	205	661	6	17	123	1035	59			49		22	10	152
Starke RGG 1. 11. 38	145	1005	3668	44	86	350	5298	59	110	63	729	251	312	88	152

Militär-personen : 4862
Zivil-personen : 436

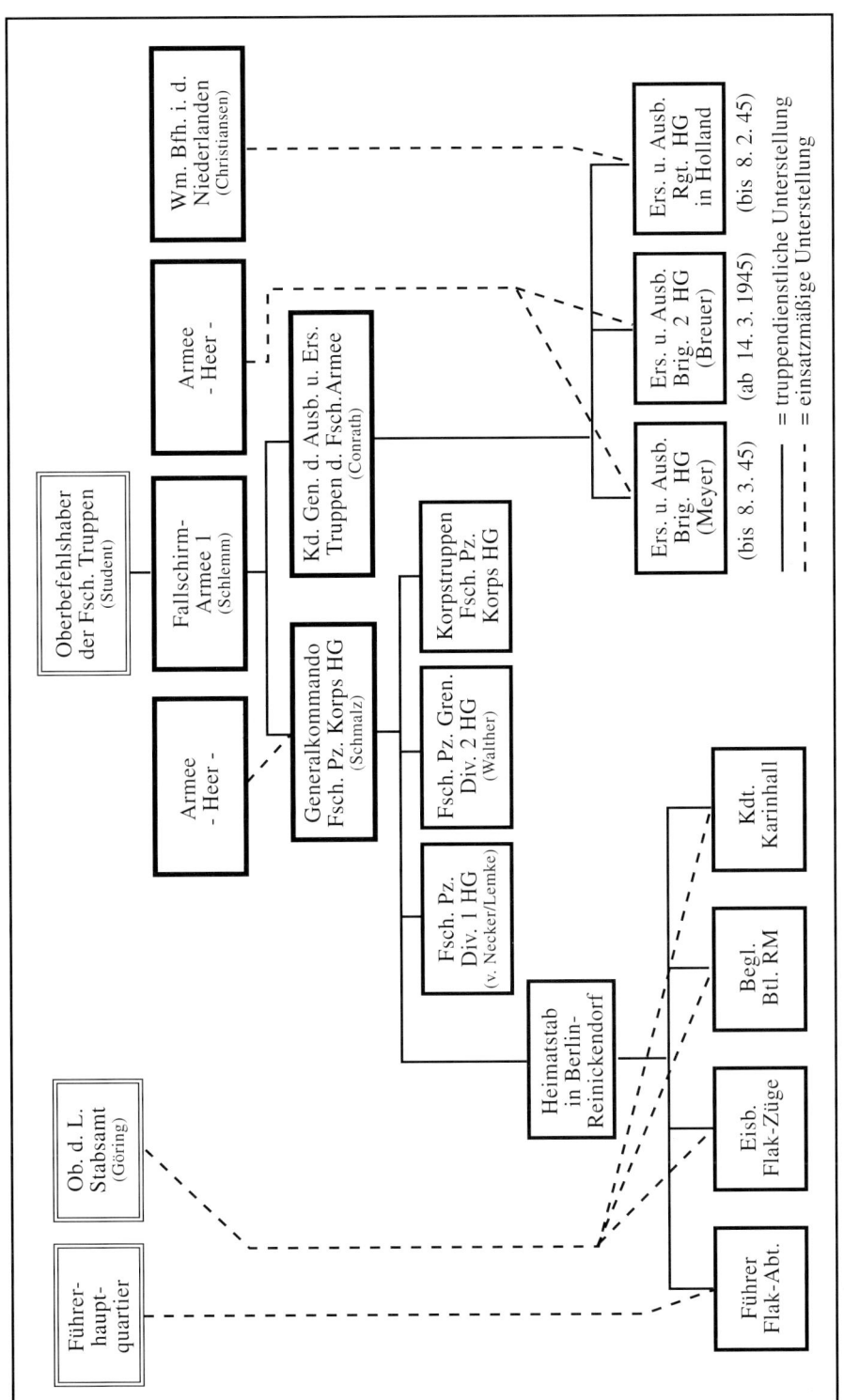

The Parachute-Panzer Corps: Chart Depicting All Units, 18th April, 1945

Armament of the HG Parachute-Panzer Division on 1 June, 1944

Type of Weapons	Authorized	Actual
Carbine and Rifle 98	15,134	15,385
Submachine-guns	2,185	1,871
Light machine-guns	1,354	906
Heavy machine-guns	86	73
Machine-guns in tanks	208	160
Mortars	70	51
Heavy Anti-tank Rifle 41	241	7
20 mm Flak 38	91	70
20 mm Quadruple Flak	42	42
37 mm Flak 37	12	8
88 mm Flak 36 and 37	36	35
Light Infantry Guns	28	16
Heavy infantry Guns	14	14
Light Field Howitzer 18	24	21
Heavy Field Howitzer 18	16	16
100 mm Cannon 18	8	7
Hummel Heavy Field Howitzers	6	–
75 mm Pak 40 Anti-tank Guns	58	35
150 mm Nebelwerfers Rocket Launchers	9	12
Heavy Rocket Launcher 41	12	9
37 mm Anti-tank Guns (motorized and in armoured personnel carriers)	4	4
20 mm Tank Cannon in Armoured Cars	60	8
75 mm Cannon 37 (self-propelled)	30	14
Bazookas	60	144
Flamethrowers	80	69

The Armoured Vehicles of the HG Panzer Regiments

	Panzer III	Panzer IV	Panzer V	Assault Gun	Tank Destroyer
Special motor vehicle (SdKfz.) number	141/1	161/2	171 A	142	162/2
Combat weight	23 t	25 t	45.5 t	21.8 t	25 t
Crew	5 men	5 men	5 men	4 men	4 men
Armour:					
Front	50 mm	80 mm	50 mm	50 mm	80 mm
Side and rear	30 mm	30 mm	40 mm	30 mm	30 mm
Deck	10 mm	16 mm	16 mm	–	–
Engine output	300 PS	300 PS	600 PS	300 PS	300 PS
Speed (road)	40 km/h	40 km/h	46 km/h	40 km/h	40 km/h
Range (road)	165 km	210 km	200 km	120 km	160 km
Length (minus gun)	5.48 m	5.93 m	6.88 m	5.40 m	6.15 m
Width	2.95 m	2.88 m	3.42 m	2.95 m	2.92 m
Height	2.44 m	2.68 m	3.10 m	1.96 m	1.94 m
Tank gun (KwK)	7.5 cm*	7.5 cm	7.5 cm	7.5 cm	7.5 cm
Ammunition supply	87 rnds.	87 rnds.	79 rnds.	50 rnds.	76 rnds.

* also with 50 mm gun

Vehicle status of the HG Parachute-Panzer Division HG on 1 June, 1944

(only elements of the division deployed in Italy)

Vehicle	Authorized Strength	Actual Strength	Operational	Under Repair	Shortfall
Armoured Vehicles:					
Assault Guns	31	16	8	8	15
Panzer III	19	13	2	11	6
Panzer IV	98	56	18	38	42
Armoured Personnel Carriers	366	306	280	26	60
Self-propelled anti-tank guns	28	16	7	9	12
Motor Vehicles:					
Motorcycles	864	716	645	71	148
Automobiles	1,100	868	662	206	232
Trucks	2,700	1,318	1,027	291	1,382
Tonnage (t)	6,919	3,924	2,918	1,006	2,995
Prime movers	322	148	125	23	174

The authorized numbers include the vehicles of the Panzer Regiment's I Battalion, which is in Holland reequiping on the Panzer V "Panther", while the actual numbers do not.

The Guns of the HG Flak Regiment

	20 mm Flak	37 mm Flak	88 mm Flak	105 mm Flak
Initial velocity of shell	835 m/s	820 m/s	830 m/s	900 m/s
Range	4,800 m	6,500 m	14,860 m	18,000 m
Ceiling	3,700 m	4,800 m	11,000 m	13,000 m
Weight in firing position	450 kg	450 kg	5,000 kg	7,000 kg
Weight in driving position	770 kg	1,950 kg	7,200 kg	–

Fallschirmtruppe Commanders, March 1945

Lfd. Nr.	Unit	Rank	Name
1	Oberfehlshaber d. Fsch.Tr.	Generaloberst	Student (Kurt)
2	Komm.Gen.d.Fsch.A.u.E.Tr.	Gen.d.Fsch.Tr.	Conrath (Paul)
3	Fallschirm-A.O.K.	Gen.d.Fsch.Tr.	Schlemm (Alfred)
4	Komm.Gen. I. Fsch.Korps.	Gen.d.Fsch.Tr.	Heidrich (Richard)
5	Komm.Gen. II. Fsch.Tr.	Gen.d.Fsch.Tr.	Meindl (Eugen)
6	Komm.Gen.Fsch.Pz.Korps HG	Generalleutnant	Schmalz (Wilhelm)
7	1. Fsch.Jg.Div.	Gen.Maj.	Schulz (Karl-Lothar)
8	2. Fsch.Jg.Div.	Gen.Lt.	Lackner (Walter)
9	3. Fsch.Jg.Div.	Gen.Lt.	Schimpf (Richard)
10	4. Fsch.Jg.Div.	Gen.Maj.	Trettner (Heinz)
11	5. Fsch.Jg.Div.	Gen.Maj.	Heilmann (Ludwig)
12	6. Fsch.Jg.Div.	Gen.Lt.	Plocher (Hermann)
13	7. Fsch.Jg.Div.	Gen.Lt.	Erdmann (Wolfgang)
14	8. Fsch.Jg.Div.	Gen.Maj.	Wadehn (Walter)
15	9. Fsch.Jg.Div.	Gen.Lt.	Wilke
16	10. Fsch.Jg.Div.	– – – –	
17	11. Fsch.Jg.Div.	– – – –	
18	Fsch.Jg.A.u.E.Div.	Gen.Maj.	Barentin (Walter)
19	Fsch.Pz.Div. 1 HG	Gen.Maj.	v. Necker (Hanns Horst)
20	Fsch.Pz.Gren.Div. 2 HG	Oberst	Walther (Erich)
21	Fsch.Pz.E.u.A.Brig. HG	Oberst	Meyer (Friedrich)
22	Fsch.Pz.E.u.A.Brig. 2 HG	Oberst	Breuer

Organization of the Fallschirmtruppe in March 1945

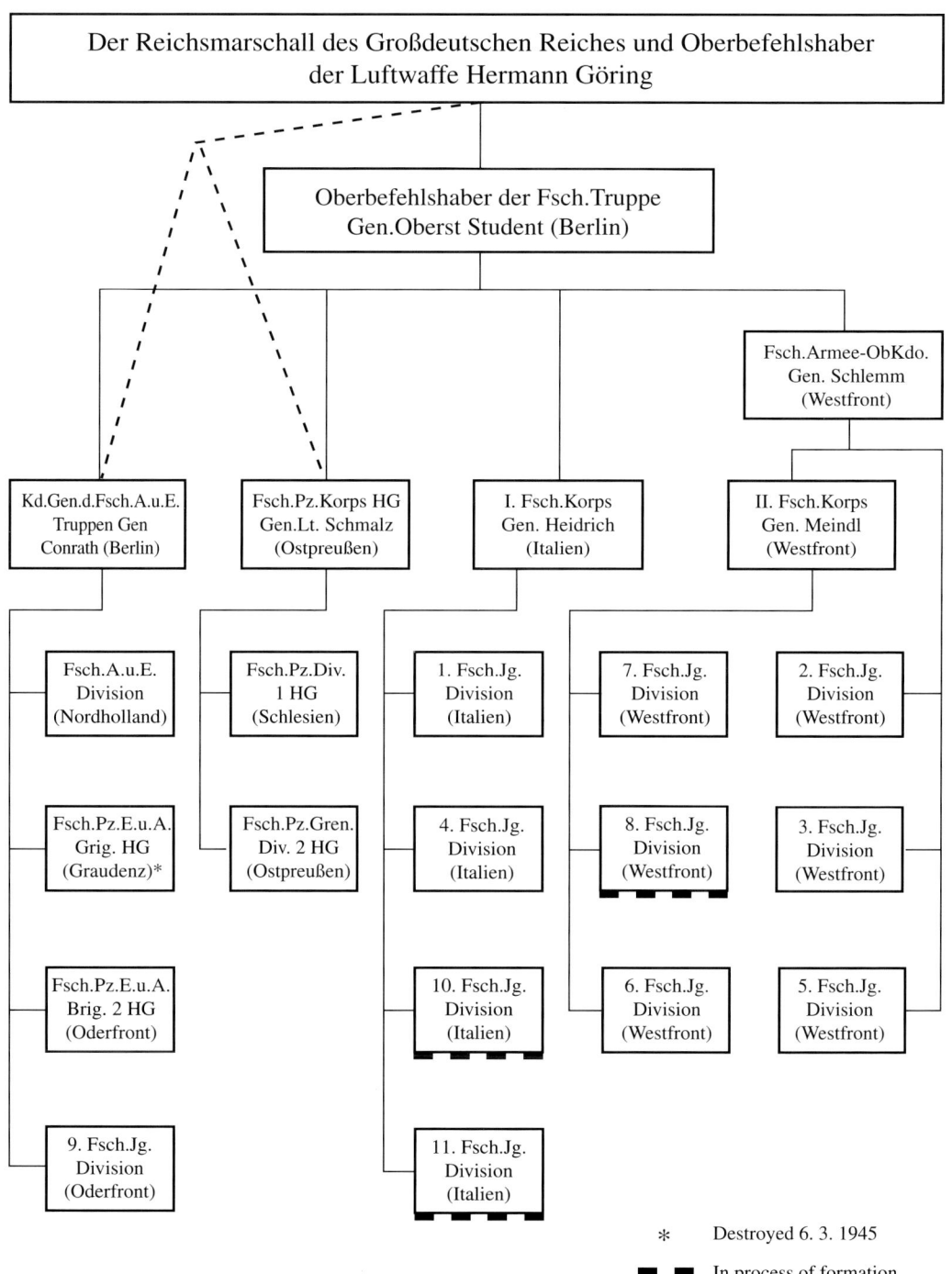

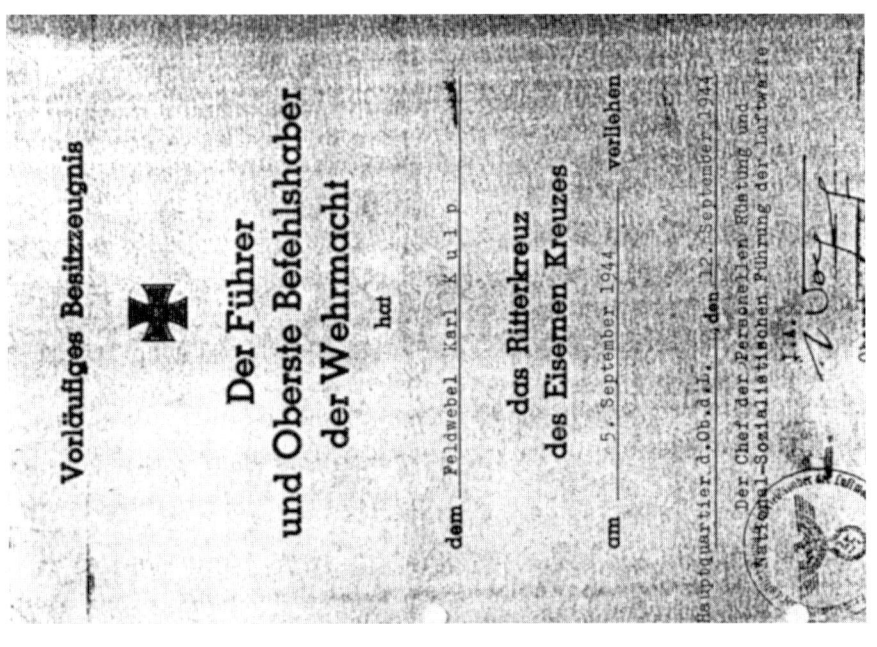

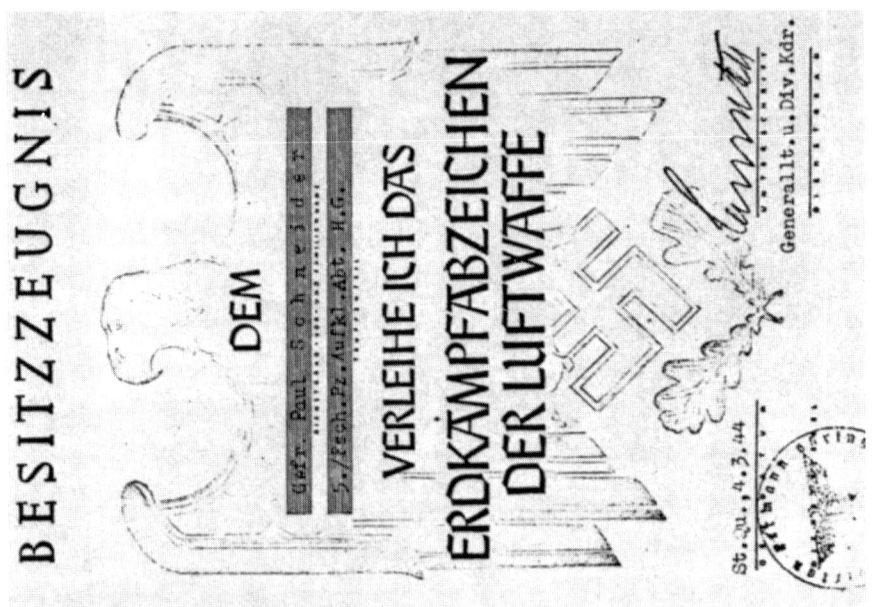

Interim certificate for the awarding of the Knight's Cross to Feldwebel Karl Kulp.

Deutsche Luftwaffe

Erlaß des Führers an Generalfeldmarschall Göring

Der Führer und Oberste Befehlshaber der Wehrmacht hat an den Oberbefehlshaber der Luftwaffe, Generalfeldmarschall Göring, folgenden Erlaß gerichtet:

An den Oberbefehlshaber der Luftwaffe

Die Luftwaffe hat am 15. und 16. März 1939 bei der Besetzung Böhmens und Mährens durch ihren kühnen Einsatz trotz ungünstigster Wetterverhältnisse höchste Einsatzbereitschaft und persönlichen Mut bewiesen. Ich spreche Offizier und Mann für ihre Leistung und Haltung meine besondere Anerkennung aus.

gez. Adolf Hitler

Tagesbefehl des Oberbefehlshabers der Luftwaffe

Der Reichsminister der Luftfahrt und Oberbefehlshaber der Luftwaffe, Generalfeldmarschall Göring, hat folgenden Tagesbefehl an die Luftwaffe erlassen:

Kameraden! Berlin, 21. März 1939

Durch eure gewissenhafte Ausbildung und schlagfertige Einsatzbereitschaft habt ihr dazu beigetragen, daß der Führer am 16. März zur Überraschung der ganzen Welt auf der Prager Burg erscheinen und am nächsten Tage unter dem Jubel der deutschen Bevölkerung in Brünn einziehen konnte.

Nach der Ostmark und dem Sudetenland sind nun auch die alten deutschen Länder Böhmen und Mähren Teile des Großdeutschen Reiches geworden. Unser Volk hat einen Zeitabschnitt gewaltigsten geschichtlichen Ausmaßes erlebt. Der Kampf wurde gewonnen, als der Führer seine und des Volkes Kraft für die Lebensinteressen des Volkes einsetzte.

Wir danken dem Schicksal, daß dieses Ziel auf friedlichem Wege erreicht werden konnte. Garant für die Erhaltung des Friedens in den entscheidenden Tagen der vorigen Woche war die starke deutsche Wehrmacht.

Als Oberbefehlshaber der Luftwaffe sage ich meiner Fliegertruppe, Flakartillerie und Luftnachrichtentruppe Dank für die in den letzten Monaten geleistete Arbeit zur Sicherung unseres Reiches und spreche meine besondere Anerkennung für euren tatkräftigen Einsatz und eure vorbildliche Haltung beim Einmarsch in das Protektorat Böhmen und Mähren aus. Dieser Dank und diese Anerkennung gilt aber auch denen, die in treuer Pflichterfüllung von der Heimat aus ihren Teil zur Hebung der Einsatzbereitschaft der Luftwaffe und zur Sicherung des deutschen Lebensraumes beigetragen haben.

Seid froh und stolz, daß ihr diese geschichtlichen Tage miterleben durftet.

Unter schwierigsten Verhältnissen habt ihr euch des Vertrauens, das der Führer in euch gesetzt hat, würdig gezeigt. Wetter und Wege haben das äußerste von euch verlangt. Der Führer hat mir seine Anerkennung hierfür ausgesprochen.

Unsere deutschen Brüder in Böhmen und Mähren und das ganze tschechische Volk haben die imponierende Stärke unserer stolzen Luftwaffe in den letzten Tagen gesehen, sie sollen durch die Kraft unserer Waffe für ewig beschirmt sein.

In steter Einsatzbereitschaft werden wir wie bisher zum Schutz von Volk und Vaterland unsere Pflicht erfüllen. Unser Führer und Oberster Befehlshaber Adolf Hitler Sieg-Heil.

gez. Hermann Göring

The Führer's decree to Generalfeldmarschall Göring, and Göring's order of the day to the forces of the Luftwaffe, issued after the successful occupation of Bohemia and Moravia in March 1939.

Der Oberbefehlshaber
der Heeresgruppe 3

Prag, den 15. April 1939

Soldaten der Heeresgruppe 3!

In dem Zeitpunkt, an dem ich die vollziehende Gewalt in Böhmen an den Herrn Reichsprotektor übergebe und damit zum Ausdruck bringe, daß die Befriedung des Landes durchgeführt und gesichert ist, danke ich Euch für Eure Leistungen und Eure Haltung. Beides kann ich nicht besser würdigen, als durch die Worte:

„Ihr könnt stolz darauf sein, dabei gewesen zu sein!"

Wieder einmal haben wir dem Willen unseres Obersten Befehls= habers Geltung verschafft, jederzeit bereit, seinem neuen Rufe zu folgen.

Es lebe unser Führer Adolf Hitler!

General der Infanterie.

Verteiler:

Bis zu den Einheiten der am Einmarsch in Böhmen beteiligten Verbände der Heeresgruppe 3.

Message from the Commander-in-Chief of Army Group 3 to his soldiers, commending them for their efforts in the occupation of Bohemia and Moravia.

IV./Rgt.General Göring   Abt.Gef.St., den 9.10.1939
     - Kdr. -

Abteilungsbefehl Nr. 20.

    Durch Verfügung des Reichsministers der Luftfahrt und Oberbefehlshaber der Luftwaffe zum Regiments-Kommandeur des Flak-Regiments 102 im Flakkorps I ernannt, lege ich mit dem heutigen Tage bewegten Herzens das Kommando über die IV./Rgt.General Göring, an dessen Spitze ich arbeitsfrohe und stolze Tage verleben durfte, nieder.

    Ich weiß, daß es für mich eine Auszeichnung bedeutet, aber trotzdem begebe ich mich schweren Herzens auf die Reise. Es gab nichts, das mir höher stand als meine IV.Abteilung, die ich mit Euch aufgestellt habe und an der ich mit ganzem Herzen hänge.

    Frohe und ernste Zeiten sind an uns gemeinsam vorübergezogen, wir haben sie gemeinsam geteilt. Mancher Offizier, Unteroffizier und Kanonier ist meinem Herzen nähergetreten und mir guter Kamerad geworden.

    Meine Gedanken werden oft und gern bei der IV.Abteilung weilen. Meine besten Wünsche begleiten jeden Angehörigen meiner alten Abteilung auf seinen ferneren Lebenswegen. Ein schriftlicher oder mündlicher Gruß aus den Reihen meiner alten, lieben Abteilung wird in späteren Tagen stets eine große Freude für mich sein.

    Es liegt mir in dieser Stunde des Abschieds am Herzen allen Offizieren und Beamten, allen Unteroffizieren und Mannschaften der Abteilung meine volle Anerkennung für die vorbildliche Leistung, meinen Dank für das bewiesene Streben und die bewährte alte militärische Gesinnung auszusprechen. Ich scheide mit dem Wunsch, daß der Geist der IV.Abteilung, der Geist voller selbstloser Hingabe an den Dienst, treuester Pflichterfüllung und enger Kameradschaft erhalten bleibt und wünsche Ihnen allen viel Erfolg und für die Zukunft das Beste.

Verteiler A.

                                                            Oberstleutnant und Kommandeur.

Battalion order issued by IV Battalion, General Göring Regiment on 9 October, 1939.

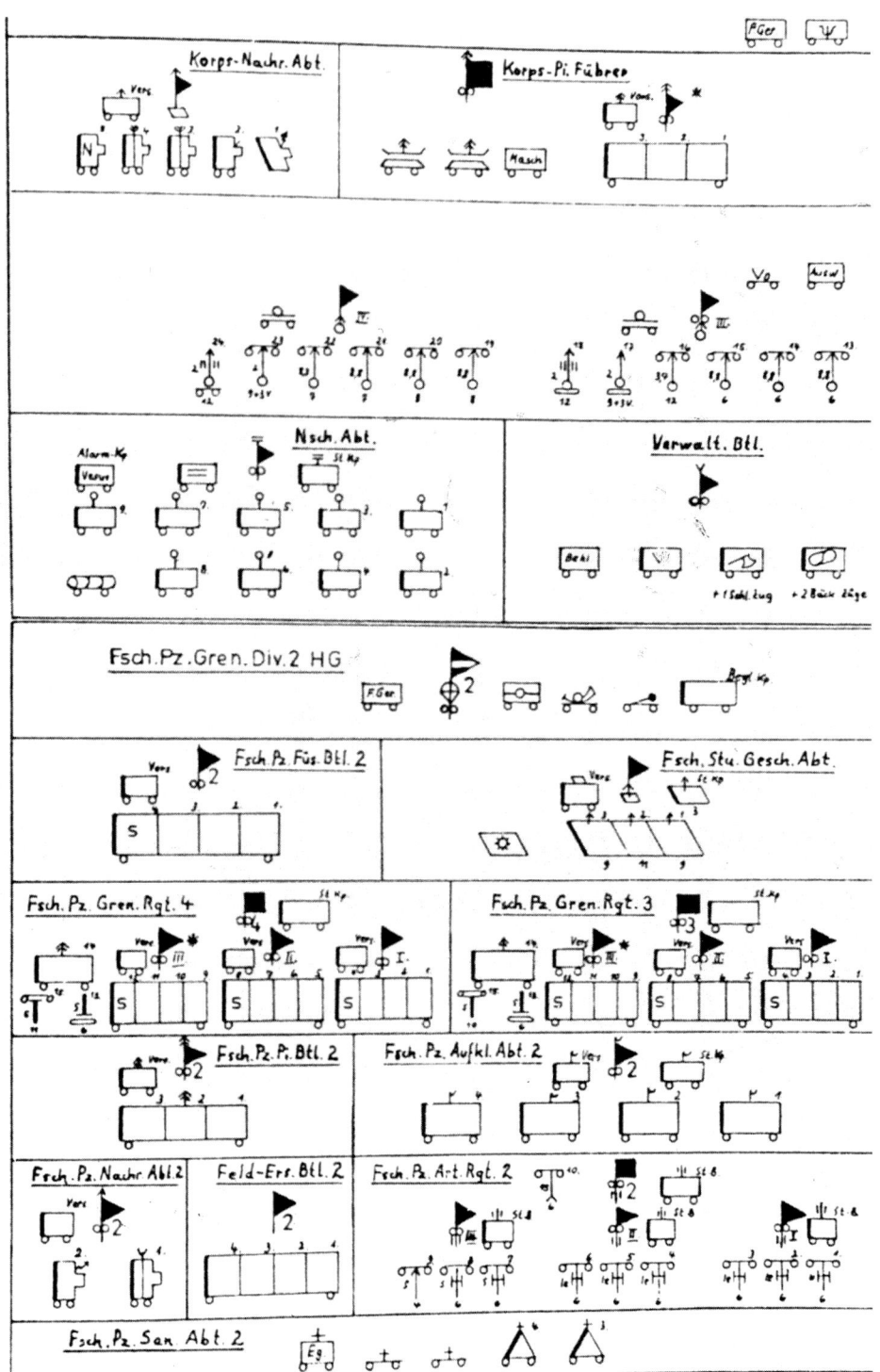

ORDER OF BATTLE
JAN 1 1945

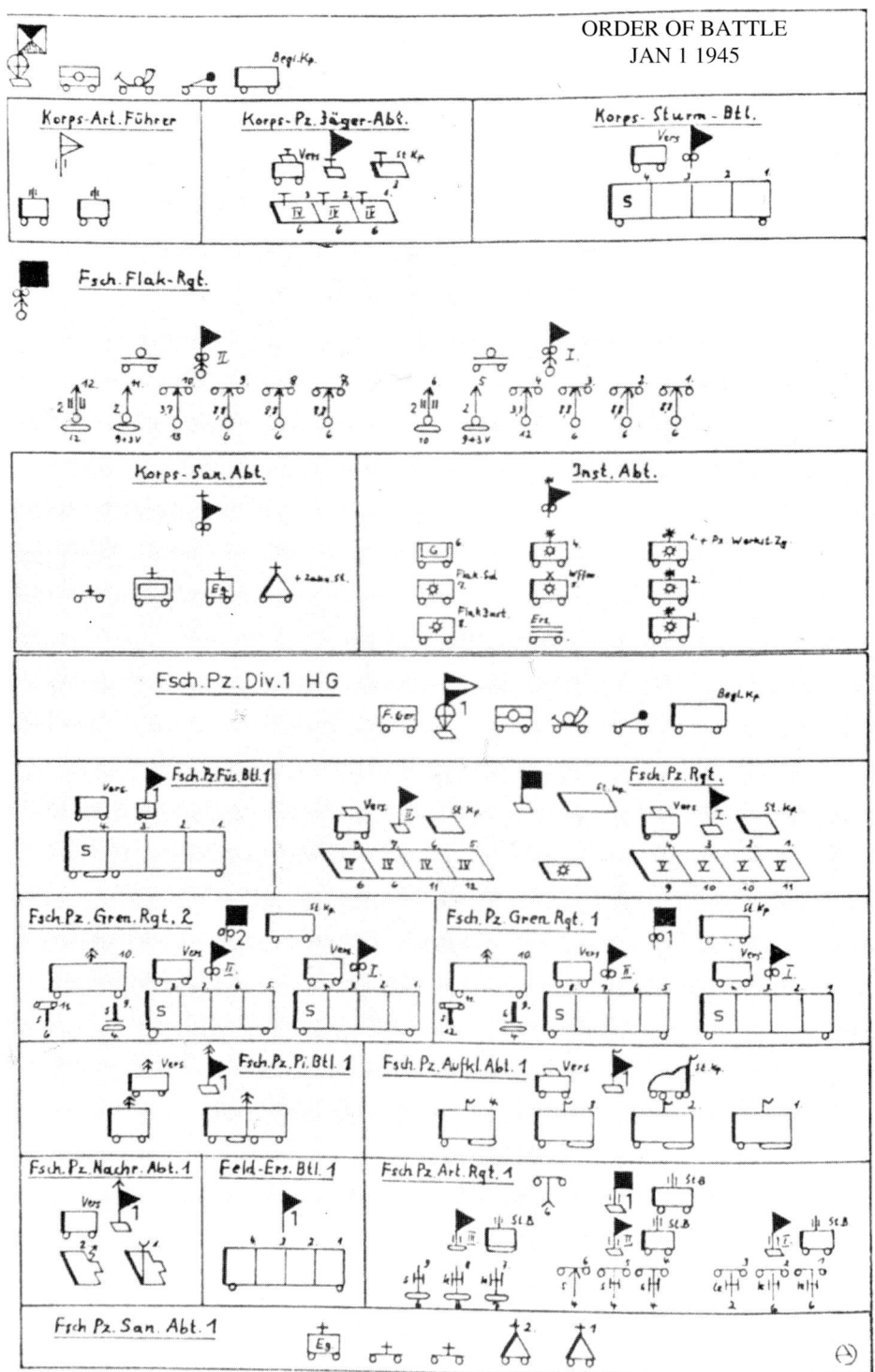

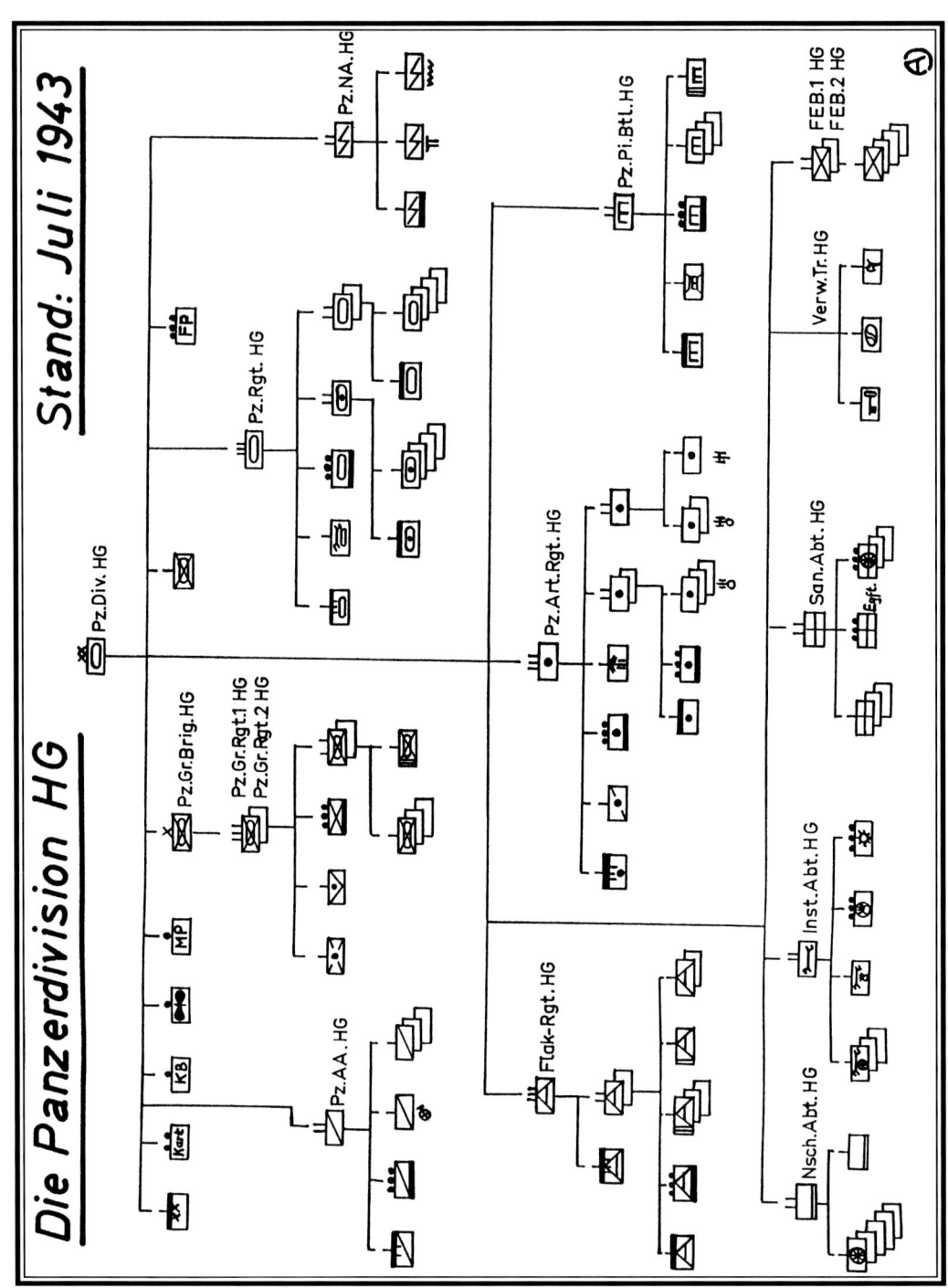

State of the Hermann Göring Panzer Division, July 1943.

TO A GRENADIER OF THE HERMANN GÖRING DIVISION

Welcome!. You are in action again. For the third time in the southern front. First Sicily, then from Salerno to Volturno and now in the cliffs and shot-up mountain nests of central Italy.. We captured the old Hermann Göring men in Tunisia. They are now at home with us, taking it easy ...

You are in action again and are probably amazed at how much talk there is of becoming a POW. Suddenly they tell you that we Anglo-Americans mistreat prisoners of war. The reason for this is as follows: should you find yourself in a hopeless situation, they wish to prevent you from surrendering. Instead they offer you a hero's death.

No, dont allow yourself to be taken prisoner, even though the war is lost for Germany, even though the heroic deaths of German soldiers can now have only one purpose: to prolong the war for a few months. Or are perhaps "secret weapons" supposed to come to your rescue.

You are a soldier. Ask yourself quite honestly whether it still makes any sense to sacrifice yourself. You have the strength to see the facts as they are, the duty to see the hard truth: the right to draw the conclusion from it.

AN EINEN GRENADIER DER HERMANN GÖRING DIVISION

Willkommen! Du bist wieder im Einsatz. Zum dritten Mal hier an der Südfront. Zuerst Sizilien, dann von Salerno zum Volturno und jetzt in den Felsen und zerschossenen Burgnestern Mittelitaliens. Wir kennen uns schon gut. Die alten Hermann Göringer haben wir schon in Tunesien einkassiert. Die sitzen jetzt bei uns zu Hause und lassen sich's gut gehen...

Du bist wieder im Einsatz und wunderst Dich wohl, warum jetzt soviel von Kriegsgefangenschaft die Rede ist. Plötzlich erzählt man Dir, dass wir Anglo-Amerikaner Kriegsgefangene misshandeln. Der Grund dafür liegt auf der Hand: Falls Du in eine hoffnungslose Lage gerätst, will man verhindern, dass Du Dich gefangengibst. Statt dessen bietet man Dir den Heldentod.

Nein, gefangen darfst Du Dich nicht nehmen lassen, trotzdem der Krieg fuer Deutschland verloren ist, trotzdem der Heldentod deutscher Soldaten nur mehr einen Zweck haben kann: den Krieg für ein paar Monate zu verlängern. Oder sollen vielleicht "geheime Waffen" die Lage aendern? Das Do-Geraet, die Pressluftbombe, der Raketenwerfer, der 6-motorige Bomber und wie sie alle heissen, sind keine geheimen Waffen mehr.

Du bist Soldat. Frage Dich ganz ehrlich, ob es jetzt noch einen Sinn hat, sich zu opfern. Du hast die Kraft, den Tatsachen ins Auge zu sehen, die Pflicht, die harte Wahrheit zu erkennen: das Recht, aus ihr den Schluss zu ziehen.

A welcoming message from the other side for the soldiers of the Hermann Göring Division.

10th (Assault Gun) Company, HG Parachute-Panzer Regiment
Certificate

It is certified that Uffz. Kanert participated in combat on the following days:

1. 15.7.43 — Destruction of enemy parachute troops near Lentini.
2. 17.7.43 — Close-quarters defense against enemy attacks toward the Simento.
3. 29.2.44 — Advance south of Cisterna.
4. 28.7.44 — Success defence against an armoured assault near Siennica.
5. 29.7.44 — Tank battle near Pogorzel.
6. 30.7.44 — Defence against armoured attack near Mieszylesie.
7. 1.8.44 — Attack on Struga.
8. 19.8.44 — Attack on Helenowski.
9. 13.10.44 — Attack on Pleine.
10. 22.10.44 — Defence near Bissnen and Rodebach.

---

10. (Sturmgeschütz-) Kp./Fsch.Pz.Rgt. H.G.

Bescheinigung

Dem Uffz. Kanert werden folgende Erdkampftage bescheinigt:

1. 15.7.43 — Vernichtung feindlicher Fallschirmjäger bei Lentini
2. 17.7.43 — Abwehr feindlicher Angriffe gegen den Simeto im Nahkampf
3. 29.2.44 — Vorstoß südlich Cisterna
4. 28.7.44 — Erfolgreiche Abwehr eines Panzervorstoßes bei Siennica
5. 29.7.44 — Panzerkampf bei Pogorzel
6. 30.7.44 — Abwehr eines Panzerangriffes bei Mieszylesie
7. 1.8.44 — Angriff auf Struga
8. 19.8.44 — Angriff auf Helenowek
9. 13.10.44 — Angriff auf Pleine
10. 22.10.44 — Abwehr bei Bissnen und Rodebach

(Dienststempel)

gez. Wallhäußer
Oberleutnant u. Kompanieführer

Certificate of days involved in surface fighting for Uffz. Kanert.

Deutscher Soldat: Wir versprechen Dir weder Utopien noch das Schlaraffenland, falls Du in Kriegsgefangenschaft gelangst. Aber auf die folgenden Tatsachen kannst Du mit Bestimmtheit rechnen:

1. "FAIRE" BEHANDLUNG wie es sich einem tapferen Gegner gebuehrt. Der Rang des Gefangenen wird anerkannt. Deine eigenen Kameraden sind Deine unmittelbaren Vorgesetzten.
2. GUTE VERPFLEGUNG. Viele Deiner Kameraden sind erstaunt, wie gut die Nahrung bei uns ist. Wir haben mit Recht die bestgenährte Armee der Welt. (Mancher Landser zieht das deutsche Kommissbrot unserem Weissbrot vor, aber über unseren Kaffee und die Zubereitung unserer Speisen hat sich noch niemand beklagt.)
3. ERSTKLASSIGE SPITALSPFLEGE für Verwundete und Kranke. Gemaess der Genfer Konvention erhalten Gefangene dieselbe Spitalspflege wie unsere eigenen Truppen.
4. SCHREIBGELEGENHEIT. Du kannst im Monat drei Briefe und vier Karten nach Hause schreiben. Die Postverbindung ist schnell und zuverlässig. Du kannst Briefe und auch Pakete erhalten.
5. BESOLDUNG. Gemäss der Genfer Konvention behält der Kriegsgefangene das Anrecht auf seine Entlohnung bei. Für etwaige freiwillige Arbeitsleistungen erhältst Du aber selbstverständlich Bezahlung. Für das Geld, das Du erhältst, kannst Du verschiedentliche Waren und Luxusartikel kaufen.
6. WEITERBILDUNG. Sollte der Krieg noch länger dauern, dann kommst Du wahrscheinlich noch dazu, Dich an den verschiedentlichen Bildungs- und Lehrkursen, die von Kriegsgefangenen selbst organisiert werden, zu beteiligen.

Und selbstverständlich kommst Du nach Kriegsende nach Hause.

Leaflet for German soldiers

German soldier: We promise you neither Utopia nor the land of milk and honey should you become a prisoner of war. But you can definitely count on the following facts:
1. "FAIR" TREATMENT as warranted by a brave opponent. The ranks of prisoners will be recognized. Your own comrades are your immediate superiors.
2. GOOD FOOD. Many of your comrades are astonished at how well-fed we are. We truly have the best-fed army in the world. (Many soldiers prefer the German army bread to our white bread, but no one has yet complained about our coffee, and the way we prepare our food.)
3. FIRST-CLASS HOSPITAL TREATMENT for the wounded and sick. As per the Geneva Convention, prisoners receive the same hospital care as out own troops.
4. THE OPPORTUNITY TO WRITE LETTERS. You can send home three letters and four cards per month. The postal service is fast and reliable. You may receive letters as well as parcels.
5. PAY. As per the Geneva Convention the prisoner of war retains his right to pay. Obviously you will receive pay for any sort of voluntary work. With the money you receive you can buy various goods and luxury items.
6. TRAINING. Should the war go on for a longer period of time, then you can probably participate in the various training and instructional courses organized by the prisoners themselves.

And of course you can go home after the end of the war.

SOURCES

Abel, W.:	*Die Kämpfe der FschPzDiv. 1 HG in Polen, Schlesien und Sachsen vom Januar bis Mai 1945.*
Barth:	*Kampfbericht einer Flakbatterie*
Clark, Mark:	*My Road from Algiers to Vienna.*
Deckert:	*Die 1./FschPzRgt. HG im Einsatz.*
Friedrichsmeyer, Günther:	*Gefangennahme in Afrika*
Grau, Hans-Joachim:	*Vom Ostpreußen nach Schlesien: die 1./FschPzRgt. HG im Einsatz.*
Greiner, Heinz:	*Battle of Rome – Inferno on the Po.*
Hermann, Ernst:	*Kritische Tage in Januar 1944.*
Knöfermann, Arnold:	*...nur geringe Spähtrupptätigkeit*
Lübberstedt, Hein:	*Flak im Zweikampf mit Panzern* (in manuscript).
Kesselring, Albert:	*Soldat bis zum letzten Tag*
Kurowski, Franz:	*Generalfeldmarschall Albert Kesselring*
Otte, Alfred:	*Die Fallschirmpanzerdivision HG an der Weichsel.*
"	*Das Unternehmen Otto.*
Ringel, Werner:	*Kampf um Castelforte*
Schmalz, Wilhelm:	*Einsatz der Fallschirmpanzerdivision HG in Italien vom 26.5. bis zum 5 Juni 1944•.*
"	*Die Kämpfe der Brigade Schmalz vom 10.7. bis 15.7. im Raum Syrakus-Augusta-Catania* (in manuscript).